Donald C. Weiskopf

American River College

RECREATION AND LEISURE

Improving the Quality of Life

Second Edition

Allyn and Bacon, Inc.
Boston   London   Sydney   Toronto

Library of Congress Cataloging in Publication Data

Weiskopf, Donald C., 1929–
    Recreation and leisure

    Includes index.
    1. Recreation.   2. Leisure   3. Quality of life.
I. Title.
GV14.W43   1982   7901.01'35   81-22921
ISBN 0-205-07712-9   AACR2

Cover photographs courtesy U.S. Forest Service, Bicycle
Manufacturers' Association of America, and H. A. Schader.

Series Editor: Hiram Howard

Printed in the United States of America.

10 9 8 7 6 5 4 3 2 1   87 86 85 84 83 82

To the late Professor Charles K. Brightbill, whose pioneer efforts as a leader, teacher, and philosopher have left a lasting mark on the field of recreation and leisure, under whom I had the privilege to learn and study, and whose attitude toward life has so much influenced my own.

Contents

Preface

Recreation and Leisure: Improving the Quality of Life provides an introduction and in-depth overview of the exciting and ever growing field of organized recreation and leisure services. The leisure boom has resulted in explosive growth in a multitude of leisure–time activities. Americans are spending more than $240 billion annually on leisure and recreation, and, as a result, leisure–time activities have become the United States' number one industry. This huge expenditure is a good indication of how zealously Americans today pursue "the good life" beyond their work and home.

Since the release of the first edition, entitled *A Guide to Recreation and Leisure*, the leisure services industry has experienced considerable growth and development. A larger scope of leisure services and recreation resources, increased leisure awareness and the availability of more free time, and greater expenditures for recreation have combined to produce a society more oriented to leisure. Numerous social forces and problems continue to influence the development of the leisure and recreation field. A study of the impact of these forces, coupled with a comprehensive and authoritative description of the rapidly expanding array of organized recreation services, is the basis for this new edition.

If the recreation and leisure services field is to realize its vast potential, professional leaders must meet new and stronger standards than those of their predecessors. The professional needs of the future and the complexities of a changing society will demand a level of expertise far greater than that which has served the profession in the past. Professional leadership, job skills and competencies, and the quality of educational programs and experiences provided will have to be stronger and more effective if the field is to succeed in its quest for true professionalism.

While the first edition of *Recreation and Leisure* has enjoyed widespread use, a stronger effort was needed to produce a more dynamic, substantive, and diversified account of the leisure services industry. In this new and comprehensive edition the basic concepts and professional competencies required of an introductory course are presented. The author believes his sixteen years of experience teaching the introductory class, combined with many years of experience as a practitioner, have given him some valuable insights on course content.

How does this edition of *Recreation and Leisure* differ from the first? First, this text provides a more comprehensive picture of the overall recreation and leisure services system and a fuller understanding of recreation behavior and resources. Second, it offers the most up–to–date coverage of the significant changes and social forces that affect the industry, the recreation and park movement, and the leisure behavior of people. In addition, the photographs throughout the book not only provide an appealing picture of the field but illustrate many of the recreation and leisure concepts, experiences, and resources discussed in the chapters.

The book has been designed as a text in college and university courses and as a basic guide for professional recreators on all levels of organized recreation service. The book should also be an excellent reference and source guide for community and civic leaders, agencies, and organizations of all types, including members of boards and commissions, volunteer leaders, club leaders, and planning committees.

Parts I, II, and III provide an understanding of recreation and leisure as an important part of American life. A comprehensive study of today's organized recreation services, which involve sponsorship by a diverse array of governmental, voluntary, private, and commercial agencies and organizations, is presented. The economic, social, and psychological and physiological aspects of recreation and play are covered in an indepth and appealing fashion. The history and background of the recreation movement receive thorough study, with particular emphasis on the rapid development of recreation and leisure as a growing profession. Chapters 7 and 8 discuss the role of the professional and the preparation and training necessary to meet new and stronger professional standards. Recreation professionals should have a basic knowledge of all kinds of recreation behavior, resources, and programs—from urban areas to the wilderness.

The functions and services of governmental agencies on all levels, from the local unit up, including the growing emphasis on urban parks and recreation programs and resources, receive careful and up–to–date treatment. The chapter on international recreation provides a stimulating and creative approach to organized recreation and leisure services on a worldwide basis.

Part IV, "Organized Recreation in Other Sectors," describes three of the most promising sectors in the recreation and leisure industry: private and commercial recreation, industrial recreation, and voluntary youth–serving agencies. "Recreation in the Community" deals primarily with the home, school, and church. The chapter on "Recreation for Special Groups" provides considerable impact in its response to the growing sensitivity and concern for the special populations in our society.

Part VI, "Leadership, Program Planning, and Organization," offers a practical and challenging study of those organizational practices and program leadership methods that have proven their worth in communities and areas throughout the United States. The major program areas and activities are presented, followed by planning and organizational data that can produce exciting and stimulating programs.

An absorbing and practical approach to the problems and major issues confronting the field is offered in chapter 21, followed by an update and challenging coverage of the major trends which have a profound effect on the leisure and recreation movement. The author concludes by presenting some very significant challenges for the future.

Perhaps the most important challenge for those in the recreation and leisure services industry is the task of educating people to accept and use leisure. The wise use of leisure time is the challenge of our era. People must acquire leisure literacy if they are to use leisure time constructively. Unfortunately, society and particularly education, until only recently, have done little to prepare people for a life of meaningful leisure. The great majority of the American people does not know how to use leisure in a creative, positive way.

While free time continues to increase for most people, many are not emotionally and psychologically ready for it. Using leisure time more actively and creatively, therefore, can be a very effective solution to their problems. More than ever, we need to develop an ethic of leisure to guide the use of our free time.

DCW

Acknowledgments

Sincere thanks must go to the outstanding professional recreators and educators who shared their experiences, provided materials, and appeared in photographs. The author would like to acknowledge and express his appreciation to a number of agencies, organizations, and individuals who provided information, data, and photographs relative to their programs and activities.

Special recognition should go to the Chicago Historical Society; Jane Addams Hull House, Chicago; Decatur, Illinois, Park District; United States Forest Service in the Department of Agriculture; National Park Service in the Department of Interior; National Recreation and Park Association; State of California Department of Parks and Recreation; Metro–Dade County Park and Recreation Department, Miami, Florida; Naperville Park District, Illinois; U.S. Army Corps of Engineers; Oregon State Highway Division; Chicago Park District; Seattle Department of Parks and Recreation; Camden County Parks Department, New Jersey; South Dakota Tourism Division; Huntington Beach City Recreation and Parks Department; Wolf Trap Farm Park for the Performing Arts; Tennessee Valley Authority; South Carolina Division of Tourism; Montgomery, Alabama, Parks and Recreation Department; Marriott's Great America, Santa Clara, California; American Motorcycle Association; Scouting USA; Big Brothers/Big Sisters of America; National Bowling Council; German National Tourist Office, Los Angeles; Bicycle Manufacturers' Association of America; Bowling Proprietors' Association of America; Association of Handicapped Artists, Inc., Buffalo, New York; Government of British Columbia; MGM Grand Hotel, Reno, Nevada; New Games Foundation; North American Recreation; National Playing Fields Association, London; Canadian Parks and Recreation Association; National Industrial Recreation Association; *U.S. News and World Report;* President's Council on Fitness and Sports; Michigan Special Olympics Committee; C. S. Mott Foundation and Flint, Michigan, Community Schools.

The author received information from many educators, administrators and staff members of park and recreation departments and agencies on all levels of government and in every area in the United States and from many nations of the world. They include the following people: Miss Susan Lee, daughter of the late Joseph Lee, the "father of the playground movement;" Joseph Davidson, former deputy commissioner, New York City Department of Parks and Recreation; Professor Lester Rhoads, Kingsborough Community College, Brooklyn, New York; Homer Dowdy, Mott Foundation, Flint, Michigan; Larry Lenox, Milwaukee Public Schools; the late George Hjelte, Los Angeles City Recreation and Park Department; Rafael Maldonado, Gateway National Recreation Area, New York; Eric Reickel, Oakland County Parks and Recreation Commission, Michigan; David O. Laidlaw, Huron–Clinton Metropolitan Authority, Detroit, Michigan; Robert Crawford, Philadelphia Department of Recreation; Lou Quint, Jr., Old Crow Canyon Racquetball Club, San Ramon, California; Professor Emeritus Allen Sapora, University of Illinois; Janet Pomeroy, San Francisco Center for the Handicapped; Eric Ovlen, Lockheed Employees' Recreation Association, Sunnyvale, California; William D. Cunningham and Nelson Melendez and the World Leisure and Recreation Association; Drummond Abernethy, London; Richard M. Brown, Texins Association, Dallas, Texas; Solon Wisham and Kenneth Harris, City of Sacramento Department of Community Services; Dean Wallin, Central Michigan University; Dr. Robert Hodge and Frank Vaydik, Kansas City, Missouri, Park and Recreation Department; Gloria Rogers, St. Louis County Department of Parks and Recreation; Bluford W.

Muir, U.S. Forest Service; Fred R. Bell, National Park Service; Steve Johansen, Oregon State Parks and Recreation Division; Brent Arnold, Xerox Corporation International Center for Training, Leesburg, Virginia; Major Ashley and Irene Sabin, U.S. Army; Vince Alit, Syncrude Canada, Ltd.; Donald Henkel, National Recreation and Park Association; James Negley, American River College, Sacramento; Barbara Godfrey, H. A. Schaden, and Steve Bogart, Sacramento; Ron Pineda and John Spencer, MWR Division, Mather AFB, California; and Kinji Kawamara, Tokyo, Japan.

Among the many distinguished authors and writers who made important contributions to this text are Richard Kraus, Clayne R. Jensen, Geoffrey Godbey, Sidney Lutzin, Edward Storey, Joseph E. Curtis, Thomas Stein, H. Douglas Sessoms, the late Charles K. Brightbill, John Neulinger, Tony Mobley, Reynold Carlson, Janet MacLean, and Theodore Deppe. Acknowledgment should be given to professors Robert Cipriano, Edward Heath, William Theobald, and Larry Williams who reviewed the new and old manuscripts and made many important recommendations and evaluative observations.

Sincere appreciation must go to the author's wife, Annegrete, and daughter, Christine, who devoted many hours of their time to typing and handling many of the details necessary in the development of this manuscript. The author is also grateful to his wife and daughters, Christine and Lisa, whose leisure participation, like his, had to be restricted while this manuscript was being prepared.

Finally, editors Hiram Howard, Valerie Ruud, and Jeffrey Seglin, and the staff of Allyn and Bacon should be specially acknowledged for their excellent editorial and production assistance and constructive ideas. Valerie's page layouts are particularly outstanding.

I
The Nature and Significance
of Recreation and Leisure

Figure 1–1 Leisure living. The United States are riding the crest of a leisure boom. Here, a young couple play a round of golf at beautiful Hilton Head Island in South Carolina. (Courtesy South Carolina Division of Tourism.)

1
The Growth of Leisure Time

Today, Americans have more leisure than any other people have ever had in the history of the world. People are working less and experiencing more leisure. Furthermore, the amount of leisure available to most individuals is increasing as a result of our automated existence and the common feeling that one should enjoy the fruits of one's labors. Never before have the people of any country had at their disposal so much leisure and such varied outlets for its use.

Despite inflation, taxes, gasoline shortages, and the energy crisis, Americans have not lost their enthusiasm for a good time. They now spend twice as much time at leisure as they do on their jobs. Increasingly, vacationing Americans are taking to the woods, mountains, deserts, and seashores with their families, discovering and rediscovering the nation's scenic wonders.

Recreation and leisure time are no longer luxuries for most Americans. They are built into their lifestyle. Forecasters predict that by the year 2000 most working people will spend only four days a week at their jobs, and leisure time will increase correspondingly.

LEISURE—WHAT IS IT?

There are many interpretations of the word *leisure*. Leisure has been referred to as an activity, an attitude, and as a state of mind. This has confused our attempts to understand what leisure is. Etymologically, the English word *leisure* seems to be derived from the Latin *licere*, meaning "to be free." From *licere* come the French *loisir*, meaning "to be permitted," and such English words as *license* (meaning freedom to deviate from

rule, practice, etc.). These words are all related, suggesting free choice and the absence of compulsion. The ancient Greek word for leisure, *schole*, meant "serious activity without the pressure of necessity." The English word *school* is derived from the Greek word for leisure, thus implying a close connection between leisure and education.

Freedom seems to be the essence of leisure—freedom of time and attitude. Clayne Jensen explained that "In terms of time, leisure is that period of life not spent in making a living or in self–maintenance. As an attitude it is related to free will, lack of compulsion and freedom of choice."[1] Free time and leisure, of course, are not necessarily identical. While people may have more free time, they may not have more leisure.

The most common definition and interpretation of leisure is that it represents the free time that people have after they take care of their necessities and after their work has been performed. Leisure time has been defined as ". . . that period of time at the complete disposal of an individual, after he has completed his work and fulfilled his other obligations. Leisure hours are a period of freedom, when man is able to enhance his value as a human being and as a productive member of his society."[2]

Indeed, leisure scholars are in agreement that the freedom of choice lies uniquely at the heart of leisure. Jean Mundy and Linda Odum supported this view by saying that "During leisure, the individual has the freedom to choose meaningful avenues of human experience that are at that moment compatible with his or her inner feelings and needs. It allows one to be freely, uniquely, and beautifully one's real self."[3]

According to Sebastian de Grazia, "Free time cannot be identified directly with leisure, since leisure implies such things as a state of being, a mental attitude involving contemplation and serenity."[4] As de Grazia points out, anyone can have free time but not every person can have leisure.

This is what prompted Jay B. Nash to explain that "It is possible to be free from the pressures of daily life and still not have leisure. This occurs when one has no interest in leisure and no ability to make worthy use of his free time."[5]

Charles Brightbill believed that much of the confused thinking about leisure results from a failure to recognize the difference between real leisure and enforced leisure. Real leisure is never imposed upon the individual. Rather, it is a state of doing, of being free from everyday necessity, the time to rest, reflect, meditate, or enjoy a creative or recreative experience. "Enforced leisure, however, is not the leisure which people seek or want," said Brightbill. "It is the time one has on his hands when he is unemployed, ill, or made to retire from his work when he wants to continue."[6]

From the many explanations of leisure, the author prefers the following: Leisure is freedom of time to choose activity which is voluntary, satisfying, and restorative.

A leading French sociologist, Joffre Dumazedier, defines leisure as nonwork activity that people engage in during their free time. "Leisure is activity—apart from the obligations of work, family, and society—to which the individual turns at will, for either relaxation, diversion, or broadening his knowledge and his spontaneous social participation, the free exercise of his creative capacity."[7]

Perhaps the biggest misunderstanding of leisure is the idea that it implies nonwork, non-activity, doing nothing, or idleness. Leisure time cannot be equated with idleness. Leisure is a positive attitude while idleness is a negative one. Leisure is a quality rather than a behavior, and it is not what one does but how one does it.

The essence of the leisure experience is what happens to the individual as a result of it. As Charles Brightbill has stated so effectively, "Tell me what you do when you're free to do as you wish and I will tell you what kind of person you are."[8]

THE QUALITY OF LIFE

Even more difficult to define than leisure is the quality of life for people. It has different elements and components for each individual. At a national conference on "Leisure and the Quality of Life" in La Costa, California in 1970, however, a survey of leading behavioral and social science authorities resulted in considerable agreement concerning the various elements making up the quality of life.[9]

The highest ranked items were self–respect (self–confidence), achievement (sense of accomplishment, meaningful activity), health (physical well–being, feeling good), affection (love, caring, understanding), freedom, involvement, challenge (stimulation, competition), and security (peace of mind, stability). Comfort, status, and novelty were rated in lesser but still prominent positions.

Leisure can improve the quality of life. "The ultimate way of improving the quality of life is striving for a leisure society," said John Neulinger. "Irrespective of what one's definition of leisure is, be it one of free time, of activities, or a state of mind, the nature of that leisure will affect the person's quality of life which will in turn affect one's leisure."[10]

The task of measuring the quality of life though is not a simple one, nor is the attempt to improve it. However, as Neulinger points out, the situation is not hopeless. "There is considerable agreement among individuals, within societies, and even between societies, in what constitutes the good life, at least in some fundamental aspects. Leisure is the guideline needed for any decision relating to the quality of life."[11]

A LEISURE–ORIENTED SOCIETY

Indeed, we live in an age of urbanization, mechanization, automation, computers, nuclear energy, spaceships, and jet–propelled transportation. Although these changes have been nothing short of fantastic, the end is not in sight. We stand at the threshold of a leisure–oriented society, a nuclear age with unlimited possibilities for the enrichment of human life. The potential of recreation and leisure–time services for satisfying, creative, and enriched living is limitless.

For those Americans whose lifestyles were shaped from the social movements of the 60s, careers have grown less important and leisure more important. According to recent survey findings, when work and leisure are compared as sources of satisfaction, only one in five Americans (21 percent) states that work means more to them than leisure.[12]

In 1850, the average workweek in industry and farming was approximately seventy hours. In 1950, it had dwindled to forty hours. Today, an estimated ten million persons work thirty–seven hours, thirty–five hours, or even less, with predictions of a thirty–two–hour workweek by the end of the decade.

On the basis of a forty–hour workweek, the average industrial worker spends more than

Figure 1–2 The leisure to escape. Americans are escaping at a rapidly accelerating rate and heading for the outdoors as if the year were one long weekend. Here, a young family enjoys the camping facilities at George Washington National Forest in Virginia. (Courtesy U.S. Forest Service.)

two thousand hours a year on the job and has approximately three thousand hours off the job. However, it should be noted that this free time is reduced by "moonlighting," commuting to and from work, working at "do-it–yourself" jobs, doing household chores, and shopping.

Americans, then, are involved in an economic and social revolution. The past half century has brought technological changes at such an accelerated pace that our lives have been revolutionized. New industrial machinery, incredible mobility, television, and miracle drugs are just a few of the new and exciting influences that have changed the lives of Americans.

The implications of such a revolution are so vast that every aspect of our lives will be affected. Many Americans will be experiencing shorter working hours and a greater amount of free time. Predictions for the future indicate a work year of eleven-hundred hours with four–day weeks and at least thirteen weeks of vacation.

Leisure has increased particularly among older people. A longer life span—and early retirement with social security and pension—have combined to give them considerably more leisure time. Yet there are those who believe a leisure–oriented society is still many years away. For it to happen, they feel that greater numbers of people must learn how and where to use increasing amounts of leisure time.

Perhaps of even greater urgency is the need for balance—a balance between work and meaningful leisure and recreation. Work without pleasure can make life a continual struggle. Millions of people in countries throughout the world have discovered that the right combination between recreation and work gives more fulfillment to life.

THE THREAT OF LEISURE

A major problem for society will be the task of creating a civilization that does not degenerate under leisure. We have already learned that leisure can be either an asset or a liability. What we do with it will determine our fate. Leisure that cannot be used constructively can be just as dangerous as no leisure at all.

"We have in our society at the present time almost no concept of preparing people for a life of meaningful, significant leisure," said Edwin Staley. "We have been culturally conditioned to getting personal satisfaction from a 'job well done.' We do not even know whether people can accept leisure as a resource for a satisfying way of life."[13]

The tragedy is that we are doing little to prepare ourselves or the younger generation for a life of "meaningful, significant leisure." There is an urgent need for people to learn how to relax, to contemplate their existence.

We must learn to choose between what is helpful and what is hurtful. To be able to choose, an individual must have a trained intellect and possess a wide range of skills. Intelligent and constructive choices cannot be made unless the individual has the broad knowledge and emotional make-up to want to use leisure constructively. The ability to make wise choices, perhaps, is the key to our existence.

Alexander Reid Martin, the noted psychiatrist, states that, "A great number of people become extremely uneasy when they have free time. Many continue to work to avoid it. Others consciously desire free time, but are always too busy. A great majority of our people are not emotionally and psychologically ready for free time."[14]

Many people have very little free time because of the hectic pace of their lives. As a result of many interests, pressures, and individual needs, they have voluntarily scheduled their free time. Getting more leisure and using it more actively and creatively can be the most effective solution to their problems.

When individuals join an organization, such as a club, church, or fraternity, they obligate themselves to devote a portion of their time on behalf of the organization. They obligate much of their time and set up time-consuming routines. As a result, they lead a highly organized life. According to Dan Corbin and William Tait, "They are al-

ways hurrying to a meeting, cannot sit still, complain that there are too few hours in the day, and feel guilty if they take a coffee break."[15]

Unobligated time is often referred to as free time. "Free time is the small units of time between scheduled activities," said Corbin and Tait. "By tight scheduling, we can collect these units into a sizeable parcel."[16]

> To reap the richest harvest from leisure, one must be conditioned and made ready for it.
>
> **Charles K. Brightbill and Tony Mobley**

EDUCATION FOR LEISURE TIME

Unfortunately, for many citizens, the gift of free time will come more as a detriment than

Figure 1–3 A family bike ride. This family is among the 100 million cyclists in the United States. Nearly half of the U.S. population are bicyclists! (Courtesy Bicycle Manufacturers' Association.)

as a blessing. Too many of us are unprepared for it. This is because leisure carries no guarantee of Utopian happiness. True, it may bring opportunities for the enjoyment of art, music, and science; for the development of health, strength, and satisfaction. Conversely, a great amount of leisure may bring boredom, idleness, escape through drugs, overindulgence, deterioration, or corruption.

> **The wise use of leisure time is the challenge of our time.**

In order to have a strong society, leisure hours must be spent in a constructive rather than a destructive manner. Individuals must be given help in developing those areas where deficiencies exist in their personal development. For example, the person who spends long hours every day at a desk doing mental work should be given the opportunity to spend some time engaging in physical activity.

The development of the "seven cardinal principles of education" in 1918 was a landmark in education. One of the principles is "the worthy use of leisure time."[17] Yet, this country has never developed a philosophy of play or recreation. Many people are not prepared to enjoy their increased free time because they did not develop many leisure skills when they were growing up. If leisure time is to be spent in free choice activities, the individual should know what free choice activities are available. Therefore, education should strive to provide tastes which would enable people to use their leisure more intelligently.

In a democratic society the use of leisure will always remain the prerogative of the individual. However, with the great increase in leisure time, society should be entrusted with some obligations and responsibilities for making adequate provisions for its use.

The role of community leaders—recreators, teachers, social workers, and others—in helping people to develop the various qualities and competencies of good living will be a vital one. Society can do much to provide the skills, understanding, appreciations, attitudes, and values that will motivate its people to spend their leisure hours in a profitable manner.

The major purpose of leisure education, as in any form of education, is to bring about certain desirable changes in students. These changes involve attitudes, knowledge, skills, and behavior. If we can teach people to use their leisure without feeling guilty, we will be contributing to positive, mentally healthy attitudes.

Education for leisure at a young age is the best solution to a growing problem. Fortunately, leisure education increasingly is being added to the high school curriculum. While the merits of the traditional physical education curriculum cannot be denied, Pasqual Cavataio and many more educators

Figure 1–4 Leisure skills. The schools have a vital responsibility for not only teaching leisure skills such as those in badminton, but the interests and appreciation to go with them.

believe we must educate and involve the student not only on an activity level, but on a personal and social awareness level.[18] Students should develop an awareness of the importance of leisure in society and a recognition of the significant values that it may contribute to their lives.

"Education for leisure is not to impose a particular definition of leisure on everyone," wrote John Neulinger. "Rather, it means to promote the conditions, within the person and within the environment, that will bring about a certain state of mind. It is a state where one is active . . . where things are done with enthusiasm, with joy, without haste or hurry, without undue pressure."[19]

> **Education falls short if it equips us only for work.**
>
> **Luther H. Gulick**

YEARS OF YOUR LIFE

John McHale heavily dramatized the "Years Spent in Various Life Activities." Interestingly, twenty–seven of those seventy years are spent in leisure time. This is a very provocative and good selling point when trying to justify to students or a lay group of people why leisure and recreation is so important as a human need. "Think about our educational system and the amount of time that is spent on educating for leisure," challenged Edwin J. Staley, "compared to educating for work at which we are only to spend about 7½ or 8 years."[20]

Years spent in various life activities

Years	Life Activities
27	Leisure Time, including childhood play
24	Sleeping
7.33	Working
4.33	Formal Education
2.33	Eating
5	Miscellaneous
70	

DEVELOPING A LEISURE ETHIC

There is a need to develop an ethic of leisure as a guide for the use of free time. People must acquire leisure literacy if they are to use leisure time constructively. Bertrand Russell stated that "The final test of a civilization is the ability to use leisure intelligently."[21]

People's attitudes toward leisure must undergo profound changes. Their ability to use it as a potent force must experience significant improvement. New forms of leisure must be encouraged—to stretch the mind, develop an individual's potential, and make life more significant.

"The leisure problem is fundamental," said Julian Huxley. "Having to decide what we shall do with our leisure is inevitably forcing us to reexamine the purpose of human existence and to ask what fulfillment really means."[22]

The leisure ethic is a set of attitudes, a value system, a way of helping individuals make decisions about leisure and seeing the outcomes of those decisions. Establishing a leisure ethic should be a major priority in the educational process. "To reap the richest harvest from leisure, one must be conditioned and made ready for it," wrote Staley.[23]

LEISURE AND THE SCHOOLS

It is becoming increasingly clear to a growing number of people that the school can be a vital instrument in converting leisure into an asset of major significance. Although the education field has always advocated the optimum use of leisure time as one of its cardinal principles, schools have failed to devote sufficient emphasis on its execution and application. "In a nation where leisure constitutes more than half of the waking hours of its citizens," wrote Howard Danford, "there can be no possible justification for the failure of the schools to prepare young people for the creative use of their leisure time."[24]

Now, it appears that there is a growing trend by all areas and departments of education to prepare students for a better education for leisure than they have ever been provided before. Schools, in greater numbers, are assuming responsibility for helping students acquire life–long interests, appreciations, and skills in art, music, reading, outdoor education, sports and games, and many other worthwhile activities. These leisure pursuits may continue throughout their lifetimes.

Few people actually know how to play. They lack skills, interests, and other motivating factors. In short, they do not feel that recreation and play has an important place in their lives. Generally, most people prefer to participate in those activities that are satisfying and enjoyable. The interest and enjoyment of the students largely will be determined by the manner in which teachers present their subjects.

The school, being our primary institution of education, has a vital responsibility for leisure preparation. Brightbill and Mobley emphasized that "No education can be considered complete which does not educate the individual for leisure and provide him with a sense of responsibility for the good of all society."[25]

Leisure is a time when choices must be made. But to be able to choose, we must have the intelligence, along with a sense of values, appreciations, interests, and skills. Furthermore, people must be disciplined in making choices not only for their own good but for the good of society as a whole.

Figure 1–5   Schools and colleges should help students prepare not only for a work–centered existence, but also for a leisure–centered life. Above, William J. Tait, leisure educator and author, discusses leisure living with college students.

Schools of the future will have to help generate appreciations, develop interests, nurture values, and sharpen skills that go far beyond those needed in the world of work to those called for in living a full life. In addition to learning skills, students need to be inspired and stimulated, their sense of values developed.

THE CHALLENGE OF LEISURE

The future challenges society to come up with an individual prepared for and capable of full living. "In a leisure–centered society, more than ever before we are going to have to be in love with life," wrote Brightbill and Mobley. "In the end, there is only one measure of life and that is living! Life is to be lived, and much of it in the future will be lived in leisure."[26]

For many Americans, work fails to provide opportunities for optimum growth and development. Therefore, leisure must assume a more important role than mere freedom from work. To be enjoyable to the individual, as well as constructive to society, leisure must provide some satisfaction to people's basic needs. It must serve a rehabilitative or therapeutic function.

The time for challenge is here! New forms of leisure should be used to stretch our minds, serve society, and provide creative contributions to develop our personal potential. People should have opportunities to express themselves through cultural activities, such as painting a picture or enjoying a good book. To experience satisfaction and enjoyment, though, they should have developed the necessary skills, interests, and appreciations.

Values are perhaps at the heart of human behavior, including leisure behavior. "Everything we do is reflected in our scale of values," explained Brightbill and Mobley. "It is not that leisure education and society require new values, but rather different ones, or at least a different priority listing. Our decisions and behavior are based on our values."[27]

Values are acquired through the influences of the home, school, church; through friends, peers, and leaders outside the home; and through total society. "Values and beliefs are acquired, not inherited," wrote Brightbill and Mobley. "They must be learned through teaching, influence, or experience. They cannot be imposed."[28]

Indeed, leisure has the capacity to help people realize their full potential, and to live lives of quality. Leisure, as well as providing fun, joy, and pleasure, can help a person, as Maslow suggests, "to become the best that he is able to become—a self–actualized person."[29]

Who should carry the message of the new leisure ethic? Definitely recreation professionals have a major role to play but then

Figure 1–6 Take time to hear the surf. It is sundown along the smooth sandy beach at Oswald West State Park in Oregon, as a couple take the opportunity to relax, to contemplate their existence. (Courtesy Oregon State Highway Division.)

everyone in the community has a responsibility of communicating a positive image of leisure. "Indeed, education for leisure must not be restricted to a classroom situation or the recreation experiences," said John Neulinger. "It must reach out to everyone, at every opportunity."[30]

If individuals have a responsibility to prepare themselves for leisure, a heavy obligation automatically falls on parents. "The home is the first school and recreation center; the parent the first teacher and recreation leader," wrote Brightbill and Mobley. "The

quality of family life, including leisure as an increasingly large part, is crucial to our social survival."[31]

Coping with future leisure time should be a challenge, not a problem, as to what choice the individual would like to pursue. "If it were only a matter of teaching a person a hobby or a skill, the task would be easy," stated Norman Cousins. "But we have to build a new kind of man. We have to provide him with a better understanding of his own human needs, and the potential of leisure to satisfy those needs."[32]

QUESTIONS FOR DISCUSSION

1. Describe your interpretation of leisure. What is leisure?
2. Compare and contrast the definitions of leisure presented in this text.
3. Discuss the challenge of leisure. How can leisure be an important asset to every individual?
4. Why do people fail to use their leisure time in a positive, constructive manner? What suggestions do you have for these people?
5. Why is there considerable disagreement as to whether or not leisure is increasing in our society?
6. Do you think leisure is increasing in our society? What evidence can you cite that would support your belief?
7. What does "education for leisure" really mean? What is the major purpose of leisure education?
8. What effect does education have on the way people spend their free time?
9. Have our educational institutions prepared us for the increasing amount of leisure time we now face and will face in the future?
10. What should be the parent's role in leisure education? What role does the school have?
11. Why is developing a leisure ethic essential for an individual?
12. Getting more free or unobligated time is regarded as a very important factor in developing a leisure lifestyle. List some ways in which an individual can get more free time and cut down on obligations.

REFERENCES

1. Clayne R. Jensen, *Leisure and Recreation: Introduction and Overview* (Philadelphia: Lea & Febiger, 1977), p. 5.
2. Editorial Advisory Board, "Charter for Leisure," *Leisure Today*, 1972, p. 15.
3. Jean Mundy and Linda Odum, *Leisure Education: Theory and Practice* (New York: John Wiley & Sons, 1979), p. 4.
4. Sebastian de Grazia, *Of Time, Work and Leisure* (New York: Doubleday–Anchor, 1962), p. 5.
5. Jay B. Nash, *Philosophy of Recreation and Leisure* (Dubuque, Iowa: W. C. Brown Company, 1964), p. 161.
6. Harold Meyer, Charles K. Brightbill, and H. Douglas Sessoms, *Community Recreation—A*

Guide to Its Organization (Englewood Cliffs, N.J.: Prentice-Hall, Inc., 1969), p. 30.

7. Joffre Dumazedier, *Toward a Society of Leisure* (New York: Free Press, 1967), pp. 16–17.

8. Charles K. Brightbill, *Education for Leisure–Centered Living* (Harrisburg, Pa.: Stackpole Company, 1966), p. 43.

9. Edwin J. Staley, "Leisure and the Quality of Life," *California Parks and Recreation*, April/May 1972, p. 7.

10. John Neulinger, *To Leisure: An Introduction* (Boston: Allyn and Bacon, Inc., 1981), p. 65.

11. Ibid., p. 66.

12. Special Report on Work, *Psychology Today*, May, 1978, p. 4.

13. Edwin J. Staley, "Leisure and the Struggle for Significance," *Leisure Today, Journal of Physical Education and Recreation (JOPER)*, March 1976, p. 3.

14. Alexander Reid Martin, "Leisure and Our Inner Resources," *Parks and Recreation Magazine*, March 1975, p. 10.

15. H. Dan Corbin and William J. Tait, *Education for Leisure* (Englewood Cliffs, New Jersey: Prentice-Hall, Inc., 1973), pp. 4–5.

16. Ibid.

17. Jay B. Nash, *Recreation: Pertinent Readings* (Dubuque, Iowa: William C. Brown Co., 1965), p. 7.

18. Pasqual Cavataio, *California Parks & Recreation*, June 1975, p. 18

19. John Neulinger, *Leisure Today, JOPER*, March 1976, p. 4.

20. Edwin J. Staley, "Human Needs: Mandate for Professional Preparation," *Proceedings of 1975 Dallas-SPRE Institute*, National Recreation and Park Association, October 1975, p. 3.

21. Ibid., p. 4.

22. Ibid., p. 4.

23. Ibid., p. 5.

24. Howard G. Danford and Max Shirley, *Creative Leadership in Recreation*, 2nd ed. (Boston: Allyn and Bacon, Inc., 1970), p. 23.

25. Charles K. Brightbill and Tony A. Mobley, *Educating for Leisure–Centered Living*, 2nd ed. (New York: John Wiley and Sons, 1977), p. 110.

26. Ibid., p. 76.

27. Ibid., p. 71.

28. Ibid., p. 72.

29. Edwin Staley, "Leisure and the Quality of Life," Prepared for Special Edition, "Outlook," *Pasadena Star-News*, January 1, 1972, p. 19.

30. John Neulinger, quoted by Edwin Kiester, Jr. in "They'll Help Organize Your Leisure Time," *Parade Magazine*, February 25, 1979, p. 28.

31. Brightbill and Mobley, *Educating for Leisure–Centered Living*, pp. 108–109.

32. Staley, "Leisure and the Quality of Life," p. 16.

Figure 2–1 Recreation is a life necessity. It refreshes the mind as well as the body. Here, two young college students participate in a tennis game of doubles during their leisure time away from classes. (Courtesy Flint, Michigan, Community Schools.)

2
Philosophical Concepts of Leisure, Recreation, and Play

There are many philosophical concepts which affect experiences in leisure, recreation, and play. In our society, leisure and recreation are often used synonymously. Likewise, play and recreation tend to overlap. They are not identical processes. Therefore, it is essential that some understanding be reached about what these words mean. As was discussed in chapter 1, the term "leisure" has been conceptualized in three basic contexts: "time, activities, or a state of mind." Similarly, the conceptualizations of recreation often vary.

How does leisure relate to the concepts of recreation and play? Leisure affords an opportunity for both recreation and play. "The bulk of our leisure in modern society is filled with a variety of recreational pastimes," wrote Richard Kraus, "although it may also be used for such activities as continuing education, religion, or voluntary community service."[1]

Leisure should not be confused with recreation. How can you be at leisure when you are out trying to return a tennis serve or beat a short hit to first base in a softball game? This may be recreation, but it is not leisure. We speak of a leisurely walk around the neighborhood. We run leisurely to catch the bus.

Play represents not so much an activity as a form of behavior, such as competition, exploration, teasing, or make-believe. Play can occur during work or leisure, whereas recreation, in general, occurs only during leisure. A more modern conception, however, is that recreation can be work, as a growing number of jobs in the leisure services industry will support. Kraus suggested

that "Recreation is seen as a form of human activity and experience that, although often playful in manner, is not always so, as in the case of such recreational pursuits as traveling, going to museums, reading, and other cultural and intellectual activities."[2]

Recreation is generally regarded as goal–oriented and constructive activity, while play covers a wide range of possibilities, from the most highly creative and self–enhancing behavior to activity which is negative and self–destructive.

Professional recreators, increasingly, are beginning to redefine recreation and leisure in terms of human growth and development. Seymour M. Gold wrote: "In the emerging view, it is not activities, facilities, or programs that are central, it is what happens to people."[3]

CONCEPTS OF LEISURE

There are numerous concepts which deal with leisure in a contemporary society. While the phenomenon of leisure continues to experience continual change, the explanations and concepts by the major theorists have produced many consistencies and commonalities. A review of them will provide the reader with differing orientations, from which a personal philosophy can be developed.

Explanations of leisure have fallen into four general categories:

1. *Leisure as contemplation*—high intellectual and cultural involvement; a state of mind or being. This concept tends to de-

scribe leisure in terms of the pace at which people do things, performing their work or recreation in a leisurely manner.

2. *Leisure as activity*—usually qualified as "nonwork" activity. This definition of leisure has been broadened to include self–fulfillment values. Many park and recreation professionals label the experience recreation instead of leisure.

3. *Leisure as free time, discretionary time, choosing time.* This time can be used in a variety of ways and may or may not be linked to the work we do as paid employment. The word *leisure* has turned into the phrase *free time*, and the two are now almost interchangeable. The most common approach to leisure is to regard it as nonobligated or discretionary time. The *Dictionary of Sociology* defines leisure as "the free time after the practical necessities of life have been attended to . . ."[4]

4. *Leisure from a holistic viewpoint*, which integrates the other three and includes aspects of activity, attitude, and setting. The holistic perspective is an integrating view that seeks to fuse work and nonwork and establish the relationship and relevance of leisure in terms of other human behavior. It is not seen simply as activity but includes time and attitude toward time along with certain nonwork activities. This view incorporates all possible interpretations of leisure into one definition.[5]

The holistic approach involves the study of all aspects of a person's experience as well as all varieties of people. The holistic approach enables the recreator to have a broader perspective of the persons whom he or she is serving. Christopher Edginton, David Compton, and Carole Hanson pointed out that "By conceptualizing the needs of an individual while considering all of the aspects of his or her existence, the professional is able to better understand and meet the needs of the individual."[6]

Max Kaplan wrote: "Far more than simply free time or a listing of recreational activities, leisure must be viewed as a *central element in culture*, with deep and intricate ties to the larger questions of work, family, and politics."[7]

The sharp contrast between work and leisure has become blurred in recent years, according to Kraus. Once viewed by proponents of the Protestant work ethic as solely *the means to restore people for work*, leisure is now often thought of as the richer, more significant aspect of existence, while the interest and significance of work have declined.

Kraus wrote: "The earlier views of leisure either as an end in itself (the classical view, which sees leisure as a celebration of life) or as the means to an end (leisure as recreation for renewed work, or as a form of social control or therapy) are now being fused in a holistic concept of leisure."[8]

In their definition of leisure, Norman Miller and Duane Robinson's implication is that "free time becomes leisure only when it is spent in the deliberate pursuit of significant and worthwhile experiences."[9] However, Kraus suggested that: "If one accepts the premise that only free time spent in desirable or self–enriching ways is really leisure, a philosophical question arises. Is there some universally acceptable set of values that can be used to determine what is a desirable use of free time?"[10]

Many people engage in activities that society as a whole regards as harmful or antisocial, such as the use of illegal narcotics, criminal gambling activity, or adulterous sexual involvement. "Clearly, the task of determining which activities are desirable becomes extremely difficult if one relies only on the judgment of participants," wrote Kraus. "It is equally difficult if one attempts to use as criteria the rules established by society."[11]

Thus, it becomes extremely difficult to classify leisure solely as time spent in the pursuit of desirable and socially constructive values. Perhaps it would be more realistic to state that leisure represents *all* free time and provides the basis for freedom of choice.

CLASSICAL VIEW OF LEISURE

Aristotle regarded leisure as "a state of being in which activity is performed for its own sake."[12] In contrast to work or purposeful action, it involved instead such pursuits as art, political debate, philosophical discussion, and learning in general. The Athenians saw work as ignoble. To them work was boring and monotonous. Thomas Kando wrote that "Greek civilization defined work as a function (namely the absence of leisure) whereas we do the exact opposite, defining leisure as non-work."[13]

The Athenians saw leisure as the highest value of life, and work as the lowest. "Since the upper classes were not required to work, they were free to engage in intellectual, cultural, and artistic activity. Leisure represented an ideal state of freedom, and the opportunity for spiritual and intellectual enlightenment."[14]

As to how meaningful is the classical view of leisure today, Kraus, in citing a drawback, explained that "It is linked to the idea of an aristocratic class structure based on the availability of slave labor. In modern society, leisure cannot be a privilege reserved for the few. Instead, it is widely available to all. It must exist side by side with work that is respected in our society, and it should have a meaningful relationship to work."[15]

De Grazia rejects the modern concept of recreation. "Recreation is purposeful and intended to restore one for further work," he said. "Therefore, it cannot be considered part of leisure. The tendency of modern Americans to fill their free time with chores, hobbies, trivial pursuits, and various community-service projects means that they have no real leisure."[16]

LEISURE AND WORK

Must work exist for leisure to exist? Leisure is traditionally seen as free time from work, but how can one conceive of leisure without work? According to the Protestant ethic, both leisure and recreative activity could be justified only if they helped to restore one for work. If one did not work, one was not entitled to leisure and by definition did not have any.

Figure 2–2 Restoring one for work. Recreation has the capability of restoring people for renewed work through relaxing and satisfying leisure activity. Below, employees of the Lockheed Corporation of Sunnyvale enjoy a golf outing near Monterey, California. The concept of "restoring one for work" is limiting in scope, however, since the ill, handicapped, and aging do not work and they need recreation too. (Courtesy Lockheed Corporation.)

"If this premise is accepted," wrote Kraus, "one might then ask, 'Who does not work?' The answer would include several classes of people—the very rich, young children, retired persons, unemployed people, people in prisons, and the ill and handicapped. But what about the very poor person who cannot find work—or the severely handicapped individual who will probably never be able to work?"[17]

SEMI–LEISURE

Activities in which there is a degree of such obligation of purpose is regarded as "semi–leisure", said Joffre Dumazedier. Semi–leisure occurs when the world of work and of primary obligations partially overlaps with the world of leisure.[18] Some uses of free time that are not clearly work nor paid for as work may contribute to success at work, such as reading books and articles, attending evening classes, and joining a club for its value in making business contacts or sales promotion.

Sebastian de Grazia points out that none of these semi–leisure activities should be regarded as true leisure. "A more generous view of leisure than de Grazia's would suggest that many of these activities such as going to church, making love, reading the newspaper, or visiting relatives, might indeed be construed both as uses of free time and as leisure activity."[19]

"The most important element in making such a determination," observed Kraus, "would be whether the individual in question has a reasonable degree of free choice, and whether he perceives the time as leisure."[20]

RECREATION—WHAT IS IT?

No one experience or activity can be labeled recreation. What is recreation for one, may be work or even drudgery for another. Reynold Carlson, Janet MacLean, Theodore Deppe, and James Peterson suggested that "What is recreation for the same individual may be less than satisfying on a different day, with different individuals, or under different circumstances."[21]

Traditionally, recreation has been viewed as activity carried on within one's free time, primarily for relaxation and self–renewal for further work. Only in recent years has recreation been viewed as a valuable aspect of personal growth, a significant social institution, and an important community asset. Indeed, recreation is a life necessity.

> Recreation is any enjoyable leisure experience in which the participant voluntarily engages and from which he receives immediate satisfaction.
> **Reynold Carlson, Theodore Deppe, and Janet MacLean**

Although recreation is widely regarded as activity rather than idleness or rest, some authorities suggest that we should not think of recreation as activity at all. David Gray and Seymour Greben suggest instead that recreation should be seen "as a peak experience in self–satisfaction that comes from successful participation in any sort of personal enterprise." They suggest that "Recreation is an emotional condition within an individual human being that flows from a feeling of mastery, achievement, exhilaration, acceptance, success, personal worth, and pleasure. It reinforces a positive self–image. Recreation is a response to aesthetic experience, achievement. It is independent of activity, leisure, or social acceptance."[22]

> Recreation may be thought of as activity voluntarily engaged in during leisure and primarily motivated by the satisfaction or pleasure derived therefrom.
> **Charles K. Brightbill and Harold Meyer**

Some authorities regard recreation as a social institution in its own right. As Elliott Avedon explains recreation, "it has a formal relationship pattern sanctioned by society, a form and structure that arises and persists because of a definite felt need of the members of society, as in the case of education and the hospital system."[23]

> **Recreation is the natural expression of human interests and needs seeking satisfaction during leisure.**
> **Gerald B. Fitzgerald**

DEFINITIONS OF RECREATION

The term "recreation" comes from the Latin word *recreatio*, meaning that which refreshes or restores. Max Kaplan wrote: "In its traditional sense, recreation has been viewed as a period of light and restful activity, voluntarily chosen, which restores one for heavy, obligatory activity, or work."[24]

The view that recreation should be light and relaxing is much too limiting. The feeling that recreation is primarily intended to restore one for work can also be questioned since retired people who have no work need recreation to make their lives meaningful.

Recreation is a worthwhile activity in which the participant engages voluntarily during leisure time and receives pleasure and satisfaction. A modern point of view was expressed by Sebastian de Grazia: "Recreation is activity that rests men from work, often by giving them a change, and restores them for work. When adults play—as they do, of course, with persons, things, and symbols—they play for recreation. Like the Romans, our own conception of leisure is mainly recreative."[25]

However, this concept of recreation lacks acceptability today because as work becomes less demanding, people are becoming more involved physically and mentally in their recreation than in their work.

In his text, *Recreation and Leisure in Modern Society*, Kraus defined recreation as "activities or experiences carried on within leisure, usually chosen voluntarily by the participant—either because of satisfaction, pleasure, or creative enrichment derived, or

because he perceived certain personal or social values to be gained from them."[26]

Modern definitions of recreation fall into one of the following three categories:

1. An activity carried on under certain conditions or with certain motivations.
2. A process or state of being—something that happens within the person while engaging in certain kinds of activity with a given set of expectations.
3. A social institution, a body of knowledge, or a professional field.

Most definitions have regarded recreation as a form of activity or experience. Martin and Esther Neumeyer, for example, defined recreation as "any activity pursued during leisure, either individual or collective, that is free and pleasureful,' having its own immediate appeal, not impelled by a delayed reward beyond itself or by any immediate necessity."[27]

John Hutchinson referred to the element of social acceptability when he defined recreation as "a worthwhile, socially accepted leisure experience that provides immediate and inherent satisfaction to the individual who voluntarily participates in an activity."[28]

Today, recreation provides employment for large numbers of people in the "recreation and parks industry," or the rapidly expanding "leisure economy." Thus, recreation becomes more than a concept or a form of activity. Instead, it refers to all the governmental agencies and social insitutions that have been formed to meet the leisure and recreation needs of our society.

In recent years, the public has accepted recreation, along with leisure, as the terms most applicable to the broad field of leisure services and experiences, including such institutional forms as community agencies, professional organizations, and occupational involvement.

Community recreation is commonly thought of as those recreation activities that society provides through various social institutions such as the municipal recreation department, the school, the home, and the church.

Figure 2–3 The people's lap sit is one of many New Games where participation rather than competition is stressed. Here, 2416 students, faculty, and residents of Central Michigan University combine efforts to set a new world's record at Mt. Pleasant. Cooperation and human interaction are two of the elements in the New Games concept.

CHARACTERISTICS OF RECREATION

The term recreation implies certain basic characteristics:

- The choice of activity or involvement is voluntary.
- Recreation occurs during leisure time.

- Recreation is the time when one is free from the demand of work of self–maintenance.
- Recreation provides enjoyment, fun, and personal satisfaction.
- Recreation usually provides a refreshing change–of–pace.
- Recreation is widely regarded as activity as contrasted with sheer idleness or complete rest.
- Recreation is broad in concept. It includes

an extremely wide range of activities.
- Recreation is prompted by internal motivation and the desire to achieve personal satisfaction, rather than by extrinsic goals or rewards.
- Recreation is heavily dependent on a state of mind or attitude; it is not so much what one does as the reason for doing it, and the way the individual feels about the activity, that makes it recreation.
- Although the primary motivation for recreational participation is personal enjoyment, it usually results in intellectual, physical, and social growth.
- When recreation is provided as part of a community service program, it must meet appropriate standards of morality and provide healthy and constructive experience.

OBJECTIVES OF RECREATION

The field of recreation has many worthwhile objectives such as the following:

1. Satisfying basic human needs
2. Promoting total health
3. Lessening the strains and tensions of modern life
4. Encouraging abundant personal and family life
5. Developing good citizenship and a democratic society

One of the best statements of objectives was discussed by the Commission on "Goals for American Recreation."[29] The objectives are six in number:

1. Personal fulfillment, the need for each person to become all that he or she is capable of becoming
2. Democratic human relations
3. Leisure skills and interests
4. Health and fitness
5. Creative expression and aesthetic appreciation
6. Environment for living in a leisure society

NEEDS OF PEOPLE

The joy that comes from engaging in recreation activities should be experienced by everyone. These activities must fit people's needs, interests, and desires.

A doctoral study by Norvel Clark at New York University in 1962 investigated the needs and interests of junior high school students in the Bedford–Stuyvesant area of Brooklyn, New York. The purpose of the study was to develop a recreation activity program based on the identified needs and interests. According to Charles A. Bucher, "The study revealed the rank order of needs of children as evaluated by experts in the field of education, recreation, social group work, and community education."

The needs were as follows:

1. The need to achieve
2. The need for economic security
3. The need to belong
4. The need for love and affection
5. The need for self–respect through participation
6. The need for variety as relief from boredom and ignorance
7. The need to feel free from intense feelings of guilt
8. The need to be free from fear[30]

An opportunity to have challenging work is what people really want and need in life if they are to enjoy a sense of belonging. According to Jay B. Nash, "Leisure alone is not enough to satisfy; neither is work unless it has significance. Recreation and work, together, make for fullness. To people who do not work, leisure is meaningless. To people who are overworked, leisure may become just as meaningless."[31]

THE VALUES OF RECREATION

The relationship of recreation to personality is very important. Since each individual's personality is unique and distinct, each has his or her own ideals, attitudes, habits, interests, and desires. However, the various elements of personality are not all present in equal degree or arranged exactly alike among all people. Since the various personal elements fit well together, the person with a well–integrated personality knows how to enjoy and make the most of new experiences.

William Menninger of the famed Menninger Clinic in Topeka, Kansas, has stated that "The happy and healthy person today is the one who has recreation pursuits. Good mental health is directly related to the capacity and willingness of an individual to play."[32]

Personal Values in Recreation

Recreation can make three major contributions with respect to the growth and development of its participants:

Psychological aspects of recreation Recreation has been recognized as an important tool in the prevention of mental illness and in the rehabilitation of mentally ill patients. Recreation can offer important outlets for frustrations, as petty worries and unnecessary concerns may be forgotten as the individual focuses attention and interest on active as well as passive forms of recreational activity.

Recreation is recognized by leading psychiatrists as essential to the mental health of all individuals. Menninger strongly subscribes to the view that the value of recreational experience is an essential part of happy and well–balanced living. He stresses the great importance of hobbies, sports and games, and group involvement in maintaining emotional health.

Physical aspects of recreation Recreation in the form of sports, games, and moderately strenuous outdoor pastimes can make an important contribution to the physical well–being of all Americans. Emphasis should be on activities involving moderately physical exercise that can be carried on through adulthood. If they are enjoyable, people will perform them willingly. There is

a significant need for providing physical activities suitable for the later years. Until recently, this has not been sufficiently recognized and exploited.

Social aspects of recreation Recreation can provide the opportunity for group experiences that meet fundamental human needs. According to the distinguished social work authority, Gisela Konopka, "Next to the biological necessities, man's deepest longings are to love and to be important—important to someone." Dr. Konopka points out that this important need can be met through a healthy group life.[33]

Through recreation, an individual can develop respect and understanding for others and a recognition of one's own place in society. Even personal faults may be overcome through recreational activities.

For a growing number of people, recreation has been responsible in part for the development of character traits such as initiative, self–reliance, restraint, courage, perseverance, ingenuity, honesty, love of fair play, and consideration for others. No wonder, the various character–building organizations use recreation as a major tool for the attainment of their aims and objectives.

In the view of Thomas Kando, intellectual pursuits should not really be thought of as forms of recreation. He writes that "recreation . . . frequently refers to sports and outdoor activities and almost never refers to activities that are intellectually strenuous."[34] Kraus, however, believes Kando's point of view is unfortunately narrow, both in its theoretical base and its practical implications. "There is no reason why intellectual, artistic, or other culturally significant activities should not be considered legitimate forms of recreational participation. Clearly, such pursuits belong within the domain of recreation."[35]

RELATIONSHIP OF RECREATION TO OTHER AREAS

There is a close and significant interrelationship between recreation and related areas such as work, education, religion, health, and social welfare.

Education The goals of recreation and education are similar; both are working toward the enrichment of life for individuals.

Work The general view is that activity is not recreation when its nature is money–making or prestige. However, there are many instances today of recreation professionals who find themselves involved in recreation activity as a part of their job. Activity specialists and travel/tour guides are prime examples.

Physical education Recreation and physical education are complementary, not identical. Emphasis in physical education is on physical fitness and the development of attitudes, interests, and skills. Recreation experiences contribute to the satisfaction of such human needs as creative self–expression, personal fulfillment, and living in a leisure society.

Group work Group work and recreation are not synonymous. However, participation in group recreation activity may be one method of achieving desired goals.

Adult education The goals, organization, and methods of the adult education profession closely resemble those of recreation. Generally, adult education pertains to activities used for vocational progress, while recreation relates to skills and appreciations. Classes in sewing and woodcrafts are good examples of recreational activities offered by adult education programs.

THE MEANING OF PLAY

The term *play* is generally regarded as an activity carried on within leisure for purposes of pleasure, satisfaction, and self–expression. It is often carried on in a spirit of competition, exploration, fun, or make–believe.

The word play is derived from the Anglo-

Figure 2–4 Personal benefits of leisure. Recreation is person–centered, in that the focus is on what the activity does to the individual and how he or she feels about it. Here, this fisherman is obviously delighted with the steelhead he caught on the Copper River in British Columbia. (Courtesy Tourism British Columbia.)

Saxon *plega*, meaning a game or sport, fight, or battle. It consists of enjoyable activities that individuals engage in for their own sakes, in a free and spontaneous way.

Although the words *recreation* and *play* have often been used interchangeably or synonymously, most textbooks have distinguished between these two terms in various ways. Both describe play as spontaneous, physical activity, while recreation is re-creative, organized, and relaxing activity. Generally, most textbook authors accept recreation as the broad term that includes play. Play is generally carried on by children, while recreation is an adult's concern. However, adults may engage in both play and recreation, as may children.

Allen Sapora and Elmer Mitchell defined play as "Self–expression for its own sake."[36] This view was also supported by Kaplan, who suggested that the term play is used in one of two senses:

1. a light, informal, make–believe action, such as the play of children;
2. a more formal, stylized, intense and even serious presentation of some aspect of life on a "stage."[37]

De Grazia wrote that "Play is what children do, frolic and sport. Adults play too, though their games are less muscular and more intricate. Men may play games in recreation; indeed except for men who work, play is a form of recreation. When adults play, as they do, of course, they play for recreation."[38]

However, for play to be thought of as just frolic and sport, or as light, informal, make–believe activity is an oversimplification. Today, play is recognized as an important means of learning, a vital element in the development of children and youth. As Kraus suggested, "Both play and recreation may be examined in their relationship to work. While, by definition, recreation cannot exist within work, play (both in terms of the spirit of participation and the manner in which one approaches a task) certainly is part of work for many individuals."[39]

THE PLAY ELEMENT IN CULTURE

In his famous work, *Homo Ludens*, Johan Huizinga, the Dutch social historian, advanced another influential theory of play. In Huizinga's view, play pervades all of life. "Having certain characteristics, play is a voluntary activity, marked by freedom and never imposed by physical necessity or moral duty," said Huizinga. "Play is controlled by special sets of rules, demands absolute order, and is marked by uncertainty and tension. It has its own ethical value in that its rules must be obeyed."[40]

According to Huizinga, play reveals itself chiefly in two kinds of activity—contests for something and representations of something. He regarded play as an important civilizing influence in human society.[41]

As Huizinga pointed out, "Even war itself developed historically as a kind of game. Many sports, for example, once represented military skills. Hunting, horsemanship, archery, fencing, and shooting are recreational activities once essential to warfare."[42]

In modern society, there has been a tendency for play to be regarded as nonserious, even frivolous, as Kraus suggests. However, play may be carried on for stakes that are as important as life or death. The most obvious examples of this are high risk sports such as hang gliding or extremely violent spectator sports.[43]

Figure 2–5 People of all ages benefit from play. Play is regarded as a critical aspect of human growth and development.

THEORIES OF PLAY AND RECREATION

Why do people play? This question has been asked for centuries, and down through the years, educators and scholars have attempted to answer it with a variety of theories. In re–examining play and its theories, M.J. Ellis said: "Theories are important because they are simplifying explanations of previous experiences and data that seem to have the capacity to predict what will come about. A theory has no worth beyond its value to promote insights into and predictions of outcomes. A theory, then, is an ordered way of moving from previous experience into the future."[44]

There have been many theories that attempted to explain the development of the modern concept of recreation and play. Their inadequacy can be attributed in part to the fact that many of these theories were partial and incomplete. Many were based upon the play of children, rather than the recreation of people of all ages. Although these theories present a number of differences, there are also points of agreement. None of the theories limit the forms that play and recreation take.

Classical Theories

The classical theories are the best known play theories and are regularly discussed in introductory texts. Surplus energy, instinct, recapitulation, preparation, and relaxation are theories that originated before the beginning of the twentieth century. In general, classical theories have been concerned with those elements in the nature of humanity that led people to play, and with the purposes that play served.

Surplus energy theory   According to this theory, play is the expression of "animal spirits." The individual, charged with muscular energy, cannot keep still. Play is caused by the existence of energy that is surplus to the needs of survival. Although energy can be stored, storage is limited. Therefore, excess energy must be expended.

According to Herbert Spencer, play among children represents the dramatization of adult activities. Physical activities such as chasing, wrestling, and taking one another prisoner, involve 'predatory instincts.'

The fallacy of this theory is revealed by the fact that children play when fatigued or near the point of fatigue. Thus, a surplus is not

Figure 2–6 Expending excess energy. A spirited, fast–moving game of basketball can provide the means for children to let out some of their surplus energy.

Figure 2–7 High adventure. This woman finds climbing a healthy form of physical and emotionally stimulating activity, a release from her daily job in the office. The peak she is climbing is high above the Pacific Coast Trail in the North Cascades of Washington's Okanogan National Forest. (Courtesy U.S. Forest Service.)

necessary for play. Many people engage in recreational activity even though their physical or mental energy has largely been depleted. We cannot, then, explain their motivations by the surplus energy theory.

Instinct theory Play is caused by the inheritance of unlearned capacities to emit playful acts. The determinants of our behavior are inherited in the same way we inherit the genetic code that determines our structure.

This theory can be criticized because it ignores the obvious capacity of people to learn new responses that we classify as play.

According to the instinct theory, play can prepare an individual for adult life. Karl Groos' studies on the play of animals and humans suggested that certain basic instincts were inherent and served as a motivation for play behavior.

Groos suggested that play helped animals in the struggle for survival by enabling them to practice and **perfect** the skills they would need in adult life. According to Groos, play assumed the role of a single, generalized instinct. In practice, it took four major forms: (1) fighting play, (2) love play, (3) imitative or dramatic play, and (4) social play.[45]

Recapitulation theory Play is caused by the player recapitulating the history of the development of the species during its development. However, the theory has been criticized because there is no linear progression in our play development that seems to mirror the development of a species.

Play is the result of biologic inheritance, based on the idea that children were a link in the evolutionary chain from animal to human being, experiencing the history of the human race in their play activities throughout childhood and adolescence. Research with twins has tended to prove that environment has somewhat more influence than does heredity on play choices and actions.[46]

Relaxation theory According to this theory, play relieves the stresses and strains of the individual. Play is viewed as being pleasurable and sought for its own sake; it is a release from work, compulsion, and the struggle to live.

Applying more to the play and recreation of adults, the relaxation theory is similar to the surplus energy view that play is an outlet for pent–up emotions.

According to George Patrick, humankind needs healthy forms of physical and emotional activity to compensate for these added strains and tensions and for the inability to use traditional activities as outlets for emotion. Thus, play is seen as having the critical function of providing relaxation in modern life.[47]

Recent Theories of Play

Many additional explanations of play were introduced after the turn of the century, theories such as generalization, compensation, catharsis, psychoanalytic development, and learning. These theories had a different character than the classic theories,

being more concerned with the content of the play behavior and the play of an individual.

According to M. J. Ellis, "The explanations of generalization and compensation are in the process of being tested and they have some appeal since work still features as a powerful influence in the lives of schoolchildren and adults."[48]

Compensation theory Play is caused by players using their play to satisfy psychic needs not satisfied in or generated by their work. In play or leisure the player will avoid behaviors that are unsatisfying in the work setting. The player selects leisure experiences that meet psychic needs. Leisure preferences are selected in order to compensate for the inability to satisfy basic human needs in other life involvements.

The theory has been criticized because it seems to exclude the play of pre–school children. Furthermore, it assumes that work is damaging.

Generalization theory According to this theory, play is caused by the player using experiences that have been rewarding at work. The player transfers to play or leisure those types of behavior that are rewarded in another setting. This theory can be criticized because it seems to exclude the play of preschool children and because it assumes that at least some aspects of work are rewarding.

Catharsis theory This theory suggests that play is caused in part by the need to express disorganizing emotions in a harmless way by transferring them to a socially sanctioned activity. Play is viewed as a safety valve for pent–up emotions such as anger.

Although it has some validity, the theory fails to explain the nature of recreation for relaxation that characterizes many forms of play.

Play represents the release valve which keeps an individual from "blowing his or her top." William Menninger praised the benefits of recreation as healthful sublimation of frustration or aggression.

The catharsis theory suggests a vital necessity for active play to help children and youth burn up excess energy and provide a socially acceptable channel for aggressive or hostile emotions and drives.

However, this theory offers a narrow view of play, dealing with active and competitive activities, ignoring motivations for sport other than the need to express hostility.

Psychoanalytic theories   Play is caused in part by the players repeating in a playful form some strongly unpleasant experiences, thereby reducing their seriousness and allowing their assimilation.

As yet, however, there is no very clear–cut contribution to the play behavior of people not driven to play by an unpleasant experience. "To the extent that the client is 'normal' and is not beyond the pleasure principle," said Ellis, "then the psychoanalytic view of play behavior does not seem helpful—particularly since it does not look forward to predict future behavior."[49]

Developmentalism theory   Play is caused by the way in which a child's mind develops. Thus, play is caused by the growth of the child's intellect and is conditioned by it. As a result of play, the intellect increases in complexity. Ideally, this concept should be integrated with a more precise theory of motivation and learning.

Learning theory   Play is caused by the normal processes that produce learning. The individual acts in such a way to maximize the likelihood of pleasant outcomes and vice versa. Thus, children play because they learn to play.

As children accumulate experiences, they become more complex and eventually approximate adult behavior.

Recreation theory   Play is viewed as the natural change–over from work in that it refreshes, replenishes, and restores energy. Play is quite as essential as rest. Moritz Lazarus suggested that "Rather than serving to burn up excess energy, play provides a way of conserving or restoring it. When one is exhausted through toil, play recharges one's energy for renewed work."[50]

Self–expression theory   Two leading educators, Elmer Mitchell and Bernard Mason, saw play primarily as a result of the drive for self-expression. In "The Theory of Play," they wrote that a human being was perceived as "an active, dynamic creature, with a need to find outlets for his energies, to use his abilities, and to express his personality."[51]

The specific types of activity that people engage in were influenced by such factors as physiological and anatomical structure, physical fitness level, environment, and family and social background.

Figure 2–8   A desire for play is enthusiastically expressed by these elderly residents of a convalescent home. Among other personal benefits, this popular casino event satisfied a desire for self–expression, accomplishment, and competitive fun.

In gaining widespread acceptance by educators and recreation professionals alike, this theory incorporated a variety of motivations and psychological theories that had gained influence in the early part of the twentieth century.

The theory tries to identify factors that influence play behavior, such as: (1) the physical or anatomic structure of the individual; (2) one's degree of fitness at any given moment; and (3) psychological inclinations or predispositions.

Various "universal" wishes of the human being were influential in shaping play attitudes and habits; including the wish for:

1. New experience
2. Participation in a group enterprise
3. Security
4. Response and recognition from others
5. The aesthetic

Familiarity or spillover theory Individuals tend to choose leisure outlets that are familiar to them and thus provide less risk and more chance for success.

Balance theory People choose those kinds of recreational experiences that will lend balance to their lives. The balance can be physical, psychological, or social. Those who live alone may seek social interaction in recreation, whereas individuals who do demanding intellectual work may desire physical activity to sustain balance.

Modern Theories of Play

There are two modern theories of play: play competence and play arousal. Both theories are concerned with the existence of surplus behaviors and try to explain why the child, adult, or animal continues to behave when apparently all needs have been satisfied.[52]

Arousal–seeking theory Play is a class of behaviors concerned with increasing the level of arousal of the organism. Play is caused by the need to generate either inter-actions with the environment or interactions with the individual that elevate arousal. "There comes a time when they cease to be arousing," wrote Ellis. "Then, the need for continued stimulation causes the person, or animal, to search for and generate other interactions that are stimulating. As the process proceeds, the person becomes more complex and so do the necessary interactions.[53] The recreation professional, therefore, is involved in facilitating the delivery of opportunities for people to optimize their arousal levels.

Increasingly, play is considered to be a form of arousal–seeking behavior. Instead of being used to reduce drives or tension, or to create a state of calm or relaxation, the purpose of play is frequently to stimulate the individual, to provide excitement and challenge.

The stimulus–arousal theory of play suggests that a key motivation for play is the need to seek novelty, excitement, physical challenge, and risk. Rather than be content with the safe and familiar, many individuals seek the excitement of the unknown or dangerous.

Competence motivation theory Play is caused by a need to produce effects in the environment. Such effects demonstrate competence and produce feelings of effectiveness. Ellis believes that competence motivation is merely a subclass of arousal–seeking behaviors, but at this time, the theory does not add anything to the arousal–seeking model.[54]

The competence–effectance theory is based on the observation that a great deal of play consists of exploration. A primary purpose of such play is to demonstrate competence and to master the environment.

Integrating the Theories

Only three of the above theories can be integrated: developmentalism, play as learned response, and the arousal–seeking model.

The arousal–seeking model provides us

with a motive for the continuance of surplus energy. The organism has a need for optimal arousal, and arousal–elevating behaviors are not necessarily surplus or trivial.

In the case of the child, a further restraint is imposed on the interactions that can produce appropriate arousal—the cognitive complexity of the child. Early in life, a child has fewer experiences and knowledge, and simple interactions are arousing.

In summary, theories of play are too important to us to be ignored. "We need to develop an approach to theory as professionals," stated Ellis, "so that we are constantly testing and evaluating the fundamental theoretical bases of the profession—one class of which concerns play. Play theories are legion and many are logically or empirically inadequate. It is important to evaluate them critically, to actively reject theories that are of no use to us, and accept those that are useful in our everyday practice."[55]

QUESTIONS FOR DISCUSSION

1. What does recreation mean to you? Give your interpretation of recreation.
2. Compare the definitions of recreation and leisure presented in the first two chapters. Establish an understanding of the differences between the terms *leisure* and *recreation*.
3. In what ways are the concepts of recreation and leisure similar? In what ways are they dissimilar?
4. Which explanation of recreation best describes the term? Develop your own definitions of recreation and leisure.
5. More and more people are supporting the concept that "Recreation is a life necessity." Do you agree? Why?
6. What is your philosophy toward recreation?
7. What factors may influence a person's choice of recreation or a leisure experience?
8. How important is the attitude of the individual toward the activity?
9. What does the term *play* mean? Why do people play?
10. Select one theory of play and recreation and explain why you believe it is valid, logical, and useful.
11. Why is recreation such a fundamental human need?
12. Discuss: "No one is ever too big or too old to play."

REFERENCES

1. Richard Kraus, *Recreation and Leisure in Modern Society*, 2nd ed. (Santa Monica, Calif.: Goodyear Publishing Company, 1978), p. 44.
2. Ibid., p. 45.
3. Seymour M. Gold, "Urban Leisure Environments to Come," *Parks & Recreation Magazine*, May 1979. p. 53.
4. Martin Neumeyer and Esther Neumeyer, *Leisure and Recreation* (New York: Ronald Company, 1958), p. 19.
5. James F. Murphy, *Recreation and Leisure Service* (Dubuque, Iowa: Wm. C. Brown Company Publishers, 1975), p. 8.
6. Christopher Edginton, David Compton, and Carole Hanson, *Recreation and Leisure Programming* (Philadelphia: Saunders College, 1980), p. 113.
7. Max Kaplan, *Leisure: Theory and Policy* (New York: John Wiley and Sons, 1975), pp. 18–19.
8. Kraus, *Recreation and Leisure*, 2nd ed. p. 44.
9. Norman Miller and Duane Robinson, *The Leisure Age* (Belmont, Calif.: Wadsworth Publishing Company, 1963), p. 6.

10. Kraus, *Recreation and Leisure*, 2nd ed. p. 43.
11. Ibid.
12. Charles A. Bucher, *Foundations of Physical Education* (St. Louis: C. V. Mosby Company, 1972), p. 245.
13. Thomas Kando, *Leisure and Popular Culture in Transition* (St. Louis: C. V. Mosby Company, 1975), p. 23.
14. Kraus, *Recreation and Leisure*, 2nd ed., p. 38.
15. Ibid.
16. Sebastian de Grazia, *Of Time, Work and Leisure* (New York: Doubleday–Anchor, 1962), p. 5.
17. Kraus, *Recreation and Leisure*, 2nd ed., p. 43.
18. Joffre Dumazedier, *Toward a Society of Leisure* (New York: Free Press, 1967), p. 250.
19. Kraus, *Recreation and Leisure*, 2nd ed., p. 42.
20. Ibid.
21. Reynold Carlson, Janet MacLean, Theodore Deppe, and James Peterson, *Recreation and Leisure—The Changing Scene* (Belmont, Calif.: Wadsworth Company, Inc., 1979), p. 12.
22. David Gray and Seymour Greben, "Future Perspectives," *Parks and Recreation Magazine*, July 1974, p. 49.
23. Elliott M. Avedon, *Therapeutic Recreation Service* (Englewood Cliffs, N.J.: Prentice-Hall, 1974), p. 47.
24. Max Kaplan, *Leisure in America: A Social Inquiry* (New York: John Wiley, 1960), p. 19.
25. De Grazia, *Of Time, Work and Leisure*, p. 233.
26. Kraus, *Recreation and Leisure*, 2nd ed., p. 37.
27. Neumeyer and Neumeyer, *Leisure and Recreation*, p. 22.
28. John Hutchinson, *Principles of Recreation* (New York: Ronald Press, 1951), p. 2.
29. The Commission on Goals for American Recreation: "Goals for American Recreation," Washington, D.C., 1964.
30. Charles A. Bucher, *Foundations of Physical Education* (St. Louis: C. V. Mosby Co., 1972), p. 245.
31. Jay B. Nash, *Philosophy of Recreation and Leisure* (Dubuque, Iowa: William C. Brown Co., 1970), p. 106.
32. Bucher, *Foundations*, p. 244.
33. Gisela Konopka, *Social Group Work, A Helping Process* (Englewood Cliffs, N.J.: Prentice-Hall, Inc., 1963), pp. 39–40.
34. Kando, *Leisure and Popular Culture*, p. 28.
35. Kraus, *Recreation and Leisure*, 2nd ed., p. 36.
36. Allen Sapora and Elmer Mitchell, *The Theory of Play and Recreation* (New York: Ronald Press, 1961), pp. 114–15.
37. Max Kaplan, *Leisure in America*, p. 20.
38. De Grazia, *Of Time, Work and Leisure*, p. 233.
39. Richard Kraus, *Recreation and Leisure in Modern Society*, (New York: Appleton–Century–Crofts, 1971), p. 265.
40. Johan Huizinga, *Homo Ludens, A Study of the Play Element in Culture* (Boston: Beacon Press, 1960), p. 5.
41. Ibid.
42. Ibid.
43. Kraus, *Recreation and Leisure*, 2nd ed., p. 29.
44. M. J. Ellis, "Play and Its Theories Re–Examined," *Parks and Recreation Magazine*, August 1971, p. 51.
45. Kraus, *Recreation and Leisure*, 2nd ed., p. 21.
46. Ibid., p. 22.
47. Ibid., p. 23.
48. Ellis, *Play and Its Theories Re–Examined*, p. 53.
49. Ibid.
50. Kraus, *Recreation and Leisure*, 2nd ed., p. 20.
51. Kraus, *Recreation and Leisure in Modern Society*, 1st ed., p. 266.
52. Ellis, *Play and Its Theories Re–Examined*, p. 55.
53. Ibid.
54. Ibid.
55. Ibid., p. 90.

Figure 3–1 A recreation boom has resulted in explosive growth in a multitude of leisure time activities, such as amusement and theme parks. People literally flip for the Tidal Wave roller coaster at Marriott's Great America in Santa Clara, California.

3
The Economics of Leisure

Recreation and the leisure services field has emerged as one of the world's fastest growing industries that has great economic significance. Figures compiled by the Economic Unit of *U.S. News and World Report* show that Americans spent more than $244 billion on leisure and recreation in 1981, up from $105 billion in 1972.[1] The outlays accounted for about $1 out of every $8 of consumers' personal spending. The steady increase in the amount of money poured out for leisure extends to all sorts of markets, from camping gear, baseball tickets, and recreational vehicles to cruises, seats for the opera, and tennis rackets.

These direct purchases of services and goods when filtered through our complex economic system, cause a *total* effect that is much greater than the amount of the direct expenditure.

Money spent on travel, sports, equipment, campers, boats, summer houses, and a host of related items reaches into almost every aspect of the nation's economy.

Americans of all ages are caught up in a recreation boom which has resulted in explosive growth in vacationing, sports, and other recreation. They are developing a leisure mentality. According to the *U.S. News & World Report*, "It's a phenomenon sparked by longer paid vacations, more three-day weekends and rising family incomes that give people extra cash for their spare-time pursuits."[2]

Most Americans have more leisure time than ever before, and this important economic trend will continue in the years ahead. More and more opportunities for people to recreate have been provided by such factors as labor-saving devices, the shorter workweek, automation, greater mobility, increased family income, better working conditions, longer vacations, and a higher standard of living for more people.

Indeed, leisure spending provides a huge impact on business. The total far exceeds annual outlay for national defense, or for home building. Yet, inflation and the energy crisis are forcing Americans to make basic changes in the way they spend their money. With the discretionary dollar getting tighter, they are tightening the strings on the family budget. Many are turning to leisure activities which do not require large sums of money.

The *U.S. News and World Report* reported: "Pushed hard by double digit inflation, fuel shortages, higher gasoline prices and heavy loads of debt, consumers have cut back on the four-year buying spree that helped carry the nation through one of its longest recorded periods of economic expansion."[3]

RECREATION AS AN ECONOMIC FACTOR

Millions of people are employed in the numerous industries that produce equipment, materials, and services designed to meet our leisure needs.

Leisure-time activities provide direct employment, both full-time and part-time, to several hundred thousand people in the United States, and indirect employment to a considerably larger number. Included are all the producers and distributors of recreation products and services, planners, designers, builders, and maintenance and

Figure 3–2 Outdoor enthusiasts launch their boats at Dodge State Park in Michigan. (Courtesy Michigan Department of Conservation.)

custodial workers of all types. Also included are the recreation and park professionals and paraprofessionals—executives, supervisory staffs, specialists, leaders, seasonal or part–time workers, as well as educators.

Leisure expenditures affect community growth, land values, and governmental income. Recreation, parks, and leisure services make communities more desirable places for homeowners, industrialists, and business investors and create wider markets for capital and consumer goods, for services, and for jobs. Land and property values are generally increased by park areas and recreation facilities. This is particularly true if the areas are properly maintained and operated.

"The increase in property values, of course, is not automatic," points out Douglas Sessoms. "If a recreation center, for example, is improperly located, unattractive, causes traffic and parking problems, is noisy, or is a nuisance in any way, then chances are that it will decrease rather than increase property and land values."[4]

Figure 3–3 Influence of recreation on land values. Nowhere is the influence of recreation on land values more pronounced than along shorelines where plenty of water is accessible for swimming, bathing, boating, and fishing.

Recreation is also given credit by the insurance industry for the reduction in accident and health expenses by helping to keep people alert and healthy. Similarly, if more money were spent for wholesome and constructive recreation from childhood through adulthood, law enforcement officials believe there would be less need to spend public money to control juvenile delinquency and crime.

A sizeable portion of recreation and leisure funds is spent on goods and services for outdoor recreation, such as skiing, boating, hunting, fishing, camping, mountain climbing, sightseeing, outdoor photography, and many other outdoor activities.

Clayne R. Jensen cites the following example: A recreationist buys a boat from a boat distributor, and that purchase represents a direct expenditure of $1,000. To know the impact of that purchase, one must recognize that the boat was made by a manufacturer. The manufacturer purchased certain parts and products from other manufacturers, who in turn purchased certain raw materials that had to be originally taken from the earth. When finally completed, the boat represents $1,000 worth of materials and services.[5]

Jensen pointed out, however, that "It is difficult to accurately determine the economic values of leisure time activities. There are few exact figures with which to deal and the scope of the leisure time market is extensive. Further, there is no clear-cut definition of what should and should not be included under the label of leisure time activities."[6]

UNDERSTANDING ECONOMICS

The use or consumption of goods and services is the final purpose of all economic processes. There is little need to produce goods unless they are consumed. Unless there is production, there is no supply. If there is no consumption, there is no demand. Therefore, the economy of a society depends upon production and consumption, supply and demand.

Income

Few aspects of life in the United States are more impressive than the tremendous amount of goods and services produced by the American people. The total annual market value of goods and services is referred to as the *gross national product* (GNP).

If goods and services are to be consumed, people must want them and have the money to purchase them. They must also have the time to use them—hours available beyond the time needed to produce the goods. This is the leisure time, the consumption time, the time which becomes increasingly significant, economically, in a leisure–centered society.[7]

The GNP is the broadest measure of productivity and the economy's direction. The government's index of economic indicators is a compilation of "leading indicators," statistics of current business activity that point to how the economy will behave in the near future.

Americans have more buying power today than ever before. In 1930 the GNP was approximately $105 billion. By 1970 it had increased to $970 billion, and it now exceeds $1200 billion per year.

Greater expenditure in all phases of life has been the result of this additional income per individual and per family. Although one cannot accurately predict all of the influences that will result from additional income, in all probability, people will spend more on hobbies, sports, entertainment, and other recreational activities that provide increased enjoyment.

"How Americans spend their leisure and how they spend their money during leisure have profound economic consequences," wrote Reynold Carlson, Janet MacLean, Theodore Deppe and James Peterson. "As much as one–fourth of the national income is based on recreation, and in many states it is the major source of income."[8]

Money and Recreation

Money has been a basic part of modern culture. It is simply a means for measuring the value of goods and services and permitting the flexible interchange of those goods and services from human to human, a process called "buying, selling, hiring, and paying for."

Joseph E. Curtis pointed out that "Our financial system functions on credit, commonly referred to as the "enjoy now—pay later" theory. Used wisely, a calculated credit enables people to enjoy the benefits of soundly planned recreation facilities and construction projects such as parks and swimming pools while we pay for them, rather than requiring the long wait until they are fully paid for."[9] "What is disturbing, however, about credit and debt is the frightening dynamics of the thing, the way it mushrooms and grows almost without control."[10]

Inflation has been gnawing away at the dollar's value for fifteen to twenty years, eroding its purchasing power. "The answer to inflation is not artificial controls, ceilings, or gimmicks," said Curtis. "The answer is productivity—the manufacture of more and better goods and services at lower unit costs than before."[11]

How Money Was Spent On Recreation in 1978

Out of every $100 (after taxes), $6.68 was spent on recreation. The breakdown on the typical American's recreation budget was as follows:[12]

Books, maps	.40
Newspapers, magazines	.73
Toys, Sporting goods	1.92
Radio, TV records, musical instruments	1.55
Spectator amusements	.54
Other	1.54
Total	6.68

Recreation Expenditures

During the past decade, there has been a tremendous upsurge in leisure spending, and from all indications, leisure will be the dynamic element in the domestic economy in the decade ahead.

More money is being spent on recreation and leisure services and equipment than ever before. Manufacturers of everything from boats to backpacking equipment are finding huge profits in the leisure–time market. Expenditures for fun and amusement are rising faster than consumer spending as a whole. Despite worries about inflation, a recession, and the energy crisis, the leisure industry continues to expand in many directions, as people seek the "good life."

GROWTH OF PARTICIPANT SPORTS

The competitive spirit of the American people and the popularity of sports have increased sports participation dramatically over the years. The growth of participant sports indicates a significant change in American habits and values—a turning away from passive pleasure.

The average young sports enthusiast tries a wide range of activities and has fun at several. Many young people are looking for something that is not intensely competitive that gives them a sense of fulfillment. People of all ages, not just the young, are heading outdoors. Even more of the elderly are playing golf, shuffleboard, and sometimes tennis.

More than one hundred million Americans participate in swimming. Forty million people now play tennis in the United States, twice as many as ten years ago. Some thirty–five million are jogging or running. There are approximately one hundred million bicyclers. Sixty million fish, twenty million hunt, ten million ride, twelve million snow ski, another fourteen million water ski, twenty–two million Americans now roller skate, while twenty–seven million skate on ice.[13]

PHYSICAL FITNESS

Never before have so many Americans spent so much time, energy, and money to get into shape and stay there. Tens of millions of men and women have made physical fitness a part of their lives, regularly setting aside time for tennis, swimming, bicycling, jogging, and the like. Nearly all segments of American society are participating in the physical fitness boom. According to a recent Gallup poll, 47 percent of all Americans say they engage in some type of physical exercise. One of the most important trends in the fitness boom is the marked increase in women sports participants.

The sport of running is booming, with an estimated twenty million Americans who run for reasons as varied as the runners themselves. Considering all the running books and magazines, shoes, clothing, and films, the running industry is bringing in an estimated $400 million a year.

Jogging may be a popular American pastime, but walking ranks as the favorite form

Figure 3–4 Fitness has become a booming business. Millions of women and men have membership privileges at health spas and fitness centers, or they have home–exercise equipment of their own.

of exercise among Americans aged twenty and older. Calisthenics is the second most popular type of exercise, followed by swimming and bicycling. Indeed, catering to fitness has become a booming business. The National Sporting Goods Association reported sales in 1980 of more than $15 billion.

"Fitness is not just a passion: it is big business," wrote Marc Leepson. "Americans spent more than $12 billion on sport and exercise equipment. . . . They bought fifty million pairs of athletic shoes, a billion–dollar outlay."[14]

Sporting Events

Despite a significant increase in the televising of football, baseball, and tennis, major sporting events were attended in 1978 by more people than ever, at least 255 million spectators. Horse racing continues to be king of the spectator sports, drawing nearly forty–five million watchers. Big–league baseball was second, with nearly forty–one million spectators in 1978. Collegiate football attendance came next, with thirty–three million ticket holders.

ITEMS IN THE LEISURE BUDGET

Sporting Goods and Equipment

Manufacturers of sporting goods and related clothing and equipment estimated sales at $15 billion in 1978. Some 4.5 million Americans, for example, spend an average of about $500 each for skiing equipment. Millions of joggers tend to lay out as much as $100 each for proper attire for their growing sport. More than forty–one million tennis enthusiasts were equipped for the courts during the year. The sharp growth in racquetball, squash, and other racquet sports has produced volume sales in the millions of dollars. An estimated thirteen million people tried water–skiing, spending about $100 million in the process. Millions of additional dollars bought equipment for golfing, bowling, horseback riding, ice–skating, canoeing, snowmobiling, backpacking, and gardening. The divisions experiencing the greatest success are those related to active sports participation, physical fitness, and health.

Bicycling

With 100 million riders, bicycling has become the second most popular activity nationwide in terms of participants. People ranging in age from five to seventy-five years accounted for sales totaling more than $1 billion. Nearly half of the U.S. population are bicyclists!

Side effects of the latest bicycle boom: construction of thousands of miles of bicycle paths where motorized vehicles are banned. Behind much of the growing popularity of bicycling is an expanding network of motor-free trails, with more than fifty thousand miles now completed. The boom in bicycling has resulted in sales climbing steadily from about a half billion dollars in 1975 to $750 billion.

Golf

Golf continues to attract a great number of participants, who on an average play fifteen rounds or more of the game each year. According to the National Golf Foundation, Americans play an estimated 300 million rounds of golf annually on 12,300 courses. When green fees, club memberships, cost of clubs and other expenses are added together, the sport becomes a $4 billion-a-year activity!

Racquet Sports

In addition to the great popularity of tennis, racquetball, squash, paddle tennis, and other sports requiring a racquet have experienced phenomenal growth the past decade. The increasing number of racquetball clubs account for the sharp increase in equipment, goods, and services for these popular sports.

Skiing

Skiing is another sport requiring significant spending, as cross-country skiing continues to grow in popularity. More than seven million participants spend over $2.5 billion a year for equipment, lodging, travel, lift tickets, and entertainment at ski resorts. The Ski Retailers Council estimates that more than 4.5 million skiers spend at least $400 each on

Figure 3–5 The bowling market is made up today of more than 64 million Americans, with approximately 40 million older than eighteen years of age. (Courtesy Bowling Proprietors' Association of America, Inc.)

their outfits, which include skis, boots, bindings, gloves, and apparel.

Travel and Vacation Businesses

Tourist travel and the vacation business is the largest item in leisure expenditures. Non–business foreign and domestic travel amounts to more than $65 billion a year, including such areas as transportation, food, lodging, sightseeing, entertainment, supplies, and guide services.

For growing numbers of Americans, a vacation at sea is becoming an ideal escape from workday pressures. The Caribbean remains the most popular touring zone, but there are a growing number of trips in other directions. By the thousands daily, for example, tourists are flocking to Hawaii—the tropical Eden many could only dream of before.

Americans continue to vacation in foreign countries, even though their dollars in many places will buy less than in the past. The Commerce Department's Travel Service estimates that 23.5 million Americans visited foreign countries in 1978, 800,000 more than in 1977. The Air Transport Association of America reported a 10 percent jump in foreign air travel. Ship lines are booking cruises faster than ever.

People in record numbers are taking pleasure boat cruises. Caribbean cruises, for example, are being booked to capacity. Package tours have been very successful. American Express reported its nationwide bookings for Mexico, Central America, and South America doubled in 1978.

Theme Parks

Theme parks represent an entertainment phenomenon that is a combination of old–time amusement park and small–scale world's fair. Since Disneyland opened in Anaheim, California in 1955, they have proliferated greatly. Many operators of theme parks have added new attractions. Despite inflation and recession, long lines continue to be the rule. Discount promotions are nu-

Figure 3–6 Skiing continues to grow in popularity. In addition to those who enjoy the slopes, the winter–time sport is attracting millions of cross–country participants. (Courtesy South Dakota Division of Tourism.)

merous, as the economy minded public shop for bargains. Some parks are open daily all year, while others close or remain open only on weekends during slow seasons.

Theme parks almost always attract record crowds. Walt Disney World in Orlando, Florida, the largest theme park, attracted more than fourteen million visitors during 1979, while Anaheim's Disneyland, the oldest theme park, drew nearly eleven million.

Home Entertainment

Home entertainment is on the upswing, too. With 90 percent of all United States

Table 3–1 Most Popular Indoor Recreation Activities[15]

	Participants Millions	Share of Population
Watching TV, nineteen hours per week	156	97%
Reading	145	90%
Entertaining guests at home. Social gatherings. Going out to eat.	112	70%
Movies (One per month)	103	64%
Exhibits, museums, musical events, plays	51	32%
Attending indoor sports events	48	30%
Indoor activities, swimming, bowling, court games, pool, billiards, etc.	19	12%

Total Population Which Used Recreation Activities—161 million

households now equipped with television, an estimated thirteen million homes were wired for cable–television reception, paying a total of $1 billion annually in fees. Viewers watch television more than two hours per day.

Sales of stereo gear, radios, television sets, home computers and other consumer electronic products were valued at well over $12 billion. Book sales, table board games such as backgammon and chess, are also on the upswing.

Second Homes

The housing market has profited from the vacation mania. Nearly two million American families now own second homes. Sales of recreational housing have now surpassed $1.5 billion annually. These vacation homes are of many kinds, including A–frames, condominium apartments, townhouses, factory–made "pre–fab" units, and standard, year–round models.

Camping

To accommodate more than fifty million American campers each year, new and improved equipment has increased the financial investment in camping. More than $2.5

billion a year is spent on recreation vehicles, trailers, tent trailers, four–wheel–drive vehicles, snowmobiles, and motor homes. More than six million trailers and motor homes are in use in the United States.

Approximately eight million children a year experience outdoor living at some eleven thousand camps, and many other camps are attracting an increasing number of adults and senior citizens.

Snowmobiles

Snowmobiles account for a significant share of the recreational vehicle market. There are now more than seventeen million participants of this cold–weather sport. More than four million snowmobiles are now in use. This all–purpose snow vehicle can carry two people at speeds up to fifty miles an hour. Snowmobilers spend an estimated $2.6 billion yearly on the sport and have created some one hundred and ten thousand jobs in the United States and Canada.[16]

FAVORITE OUTDOOR RECREATION ACTIVITIES

The number of persons who are taking part in these twenty–four activities five or more times a year, as estimated by the U.S. Department of the Interior.[17]

Activity	Number of Persons
Walking or jogging	96.7 million
Picnicking	84.0 million
Pool swimming, sunning	83.5 million
Bicycling	66.1 million
Fishing	61.9 million
Nature walking	61.9 million
Beach swimming, sunning	59.5 million
Tennis	40.0 million
Boating	34.3 million
Riding off–road vehicles	33.8 million
Hiking or backpacking	28.1 million
Developed–site camping	21.0 million
Sledding	20.8 million
Golfing	18.9 million
Ice Skating	15.7 million
Primitive–site camping	15.0 million
Horseback riding	13.5 million
Water–skiing	13.1 million
Canoeing or Kayaking	9.0 million
Snowmobiling	7.8 million
Sailing	7.8 million
Downhill skiing	7.3 million
Cross–country skiing	2.0 million

Water Sports

Judging from sales of boats and boating equipment, the desire to get on the water is almost as strong as that to get on the road or ski across the snow. In 1978, Americans bought more than 700,000 boats and 485,000 outboard motors with a total value of about $2.5 billion. All in all, boating adds up to a $5.6 billion–a–year business, including sales of used craft, accessories, safety devices, club memberships, launching fees, and insurance.

Waterskiing, another aquatic pastime, is attracting enthusiastic devotees in growing numbers. According to the American Water Ski Association more than fourteen million people tried the sport at least once in 1978, spending around $125 million.

Diving is proving a lure for people who like the water. More than one million scuba divers spent $500 each, on the average, for equipment ranging from suits and depth gauges to air tanks and waterproof watches. Snorkeling has about three million participants who spend about $35 each for fins, a mask, and a snorkel.

Flying

Flying for pleasure, long considered a sport for the rich, is now becoming very popular with the general public. Pool ownership makes it possible for a person to buy a share, e.g. one–tenth of an airplane, which entitles the individual to use it a certain number of hours per month or per year. Other challenging aspects of flying for pleasure are glider flying, hang gliding, parachuting, and skydiving.

Skydiving

For those who like sports with high risks, skydiving is gaining wider appeal. Those who participate in this activity range from experienced parachutists who own jumping gear valued at up to $1,000, to rank amateurs who spend $40 for lessons and from $15 to $30 a day in fees to dive from an airplane.

THE HOBBY INDUSTRY

The leisure surge is spawning new hobbies and reviving old ones. American hobbyists spend nearly $2 billion a year on equipment and supplies—an increase of about 65 percent over a decade ago. According to the Hobby Industry Association of America, the money will be spent mostly on collectors' hobbies (including stamps), crafts (including ceramics, macrame, needlepoint), model railroads, model planes, scale models and miniatures, model cars, scientific kits, hobby tools, and wooden model kits.

An increasingly popular hobby that often requires weeks or months of hard labor is the restoration of old cars, furniture, and houses. Nostalgia for the past, ethnic pride, and fear of additives have impelled many into gourmet cooking as a hobby.

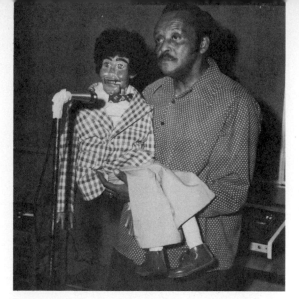

Figure 3–7 Entertainment specialists are being used increasingly in the growing leisure services industry—in clubs, social events, residence homes, and community centers. This ventriloquist began his puppet act as a satisfying leisure time hobby, but the popularity of his performance prompted him to become a professional entertainer.

Photography Boom

Photography now appeals to a much wider range of people. Amateur photographers are shelling out billions for equipment and film. In 1978, amateur photographers alone spent an estimated $5 billion on their hobby. Purchases by professionals added billions more. The accent continues to be on equipment that minimizes the skills required to take good pictures. The most expensive cameras are becoming as easy to use as cheaper models. More cameras will be sold with zoom lenses as standard equipment. Big developments are on the horizon, too, for movie cameras. Enrollment in photo classes has climbed, and darkrooms are being installed in more and more homes.

The videotape recorder can give a tremendous boost to home photography. To make movies for home television, the hobbyist simply links up a small television camera to a videotape recorder and television

Figure 3–8 Musical shows, from Broadway to the west coast are setting attendance records. Here, Donn Arden's "Hello, Hollywood, Hello" is a multi–million dollar production which has drawn rave reviews at the MGM Grand Hotel, Reno. (Courtesy MGM Grand Hotel, Reno.)

set. Videotapes then can be made for instant replay of, say, the children's birthday parties.

Boom in the Arts

Throughout the United States the arts are exploding into community life, and millions are getting involved. A Louis Harris survey concluded that serious participation in the arts now exceeds American's participation in sports. The arts are now a year–round activity. Outdoor summer festivals are popping up all over the land, with national attendance estimated to have doubled in the last ten years. Off season or not, customers are flocking to outdoor theaters and concert stages from coast to coast.

"We are reaching entirely new kinds of audiences with these performances," said one official of Wolf Trap Farm Park for the Performing Arts near Washington, D.C. Attendance is expected to reach 750,000 this year. Nationwide, summer arts attendance is estimated to have doubled over a ten–year period.

Movies and Theaters

Moviegoers paid nearly $3 billion for tickets in 1978, up 17 percent from the record level in 1977. Broadway theaters, meanwhile, broke attendance records in 1978 with well over ten million patrons. Opera and ballet also are thriving across the United States. In New York, the Metropolitan Opera ran at 94 percent of capacity during the 1978–79 season. Nationwide, a Harris Survey found that sixty–two million Americans attended at least one live theater performance, twenty–four million attended a dance performance, and seventy–eight million visited some kind of museum yearly.

Traditional American Music

What do the blues, barbershop harmony, country music, Dixieland jazz, bluegrass, and folk music have in common? Mick Martin explained: "For one thing, they are all traditional American music forms. And secondly, there are numerous active organizations across the country dedicated to their preservation and promotion."[18]

In addition to a love for music, the societies were formed because of a genuine need to keep these music forms alive and available. "We've learned that you cannot rely on the mass media to give us this music," said Jeff Hughes, president of the Sacramento Blues Society. "All you can find around you in the media is mainstream, mass–culture popular music. But that ignores a great body of authentic American music that is the foundation for popular music."[19]

Opera Music

Opera in the United States—once the plaything of a privileged few—has blossomed into a box–office smash. More than ten million admissions were sold to opera performances during the 1978 season, compared to four million for 1970. There are now 913 opera companies in the United States, compared with 77 before World War II.

A major reason for the growth is that Americans are beginning to identify more with a once alien mode of music. In the process, United States composers, singers, and producers are rising to greater prominence in a field formerly dominated by Europeans.

Social Dancing

Disco and various other types of social dancing became one of the biggest entertainment phenomena of the 1970s. The disco mania brought with it dressy clothes and created a special disco sound and a new market for records. Today, young and old people alike are showing up in big numbers at ballrooms and nightclub floors. Indeed, good grooming and touch dancing are back. Whether it is dancing or exercising to music, people of all ages are finding it very exhilarating and satisfying. Dancers are doing their own thing, from the disco beat and the hustle, to Latin dances, conventional rock, and the swing and boogie dancing of years gone by.

Gambling

The start of legalized gambling in New Jersey could foster a nationwide boom across the United States. "Long operating in the shadows of American society, the gambling business is now making a bid for respectability. Estimates are that Americans bet $500 billion a year, 90 percent of it illegally."[20]

"The key issue," said Richard Kraus, "is whether as a nation we can permit such huge amounts of money to be spent on forms of play that in many cases are seriously harmful to personal or family well–being."[21]

According to James Tuite, "The state's need for fresh tax revenue will continue to push the world of sports toward legalized gambling. It started with horse racing and lotteries, and ultimately, football and basketball betting cards are likely to emerge in some states."[22]

Legal gambling, including all forms of pari–mutuel betting, state sponsored lotteries, and reported turnover in licensed casinos, represents a $20 billion per year industry. In addition, illegal gambling involves about $50 billion a year, with a sizeable portion falling into the hands of organized crime.

While many people will challenge whether gambling should be regarded as recreation, Kraus notes that "There is little question that the majority of its participants regard it as an enjoyable and acceptable form of leisure activity."[23]

ECONOMIC CRISIS

Recreation and park agencies are currently faced with some economic problems that affect government on all levels. The sustained inflation, recession, unemployment, the energy crisis, and serious social problems have added to the cost of operations on all levels of government.

The financial problem is particularly serious in the cities. The costs of municipal government have risen steadily in cities throughout the nation. As businesses and industries have left the central cities and relocated in new suburban shopping areas or urban industrial plazas both the tax base and overall revenues have tended to decline as the financial burden of the cities has grown.

Many local park and recreation systems are in serious financial condition. Public recreation and park services, in general, appear to be absorbing disproportionate budget cuts, moving toward fee–based programs for those who can pay, and having difficulty in getting sufficient political support. Diana Dunn wrote that: "For many economic reasons, the ability of the public sector to provide new recreational facilities in the future appears likely to be limited."[24]

The federal government has been forced to cut back some of its programs and services related to recreation and parks. The National Park Service, for example, was forced to accept severe budgetary restrictions.

Budgetary cutbacks have been imposed on park, recreation, and conservation departments, youth bureaus, and programs serving the aged or physically handicapped.

The Consumer Price Index is designed to measure the cost of living for a typical American city dweller. In June 1980, it stood at 247.6, which means goods and services that cost $100 in 1967 now cost $247.60. The 1967 dollar was worth only 40.4¢ in 1980. The Consumer Price Index is only one of several price indexes, and it has tended to show the highest inflation.

QUESTIONS FOR DISCUSSION

1. What contribution does recreation make to the American economy?
2. Why do you feel the term *leisure boom* has been used to describe the ever growing leisure industry?

3. Discuss some of the new and exciting recreation and leisure services which have contributed to the ever growing leisure–time market.
4. Discuss the impact of the tight economy and "economic crisis" on the recreation and leisure industry.
5. What does the GNP (Gross National Product) indicate?
6. Identify some major trends in the recreation and leisure services industry which have had an important influence on the economy.
7. To what do you attribute the great popularity and growth of participant sports?
8. Discuss some of the many activities which have contributed to the "Fitness Boom."
9. The travel and vacation business is the largest item in leisure expenditures. Identify some of the popular areas in this segment of the leisure industry.
10. Identify some of the major economic problems which governmental agencies in parks and recreation are finding difficult to cope with.

REFERENCES

1. ————, "Recreation: A $244 Billion Market," *U. S. News & World Report*, August 10, 1981, p. 61.
2. ————, "People are shelling out more than ever for a good time," *U. S. News & World Report*, February 21, 1977, page 40.
3. ————, "Consumer Buying: The Party is Over," *U. S. News & World Report*, August 6, 1979, p. 42.
4. H. Douglas Sessoms, Harold Meyer, and Charles Brightbill, *Leisure Services, The Organized Recreation and Park System* (Englewood Cliffs, N. J.: Prentice–Hall, Inc., 1975), pp. 188–89.
5. Clayne R. Jensen, *Outdoor Recreation in America* (Minneapolis: Burgess Publishing Company, 1970), p. 215.
6. Clayne R. Jensen, *Leisure and Recreation: Introduction and Overview* (Philadelphia: Lea & Febiger, 1977), p. 219.
7. Harold Meyer, Charles Brightbill, and Douglas Sessoms, *Community Recreation—A Guide to its Organization* (Englewood Cliffs, N. J.: Prentice–Hall, Inc., 1969), pp. 50–51.
8. Reynold Carlson, Janet MacLean, Theodore Deppe and James Peterson, *Recreation and Leisure—The Changing Scene*, 3rd ed. (Belmont, Calif.: Wadsworth Company, 1979), p. 55.
9. Joseph E. Curtis, *Recreation—Theory and Practice* (St. Louis: C. V. Mosby Company, 1979), pp. 234–35.
10. Ibid., p. 235.
11. Ibid.
12. ————, "Consumer Buying: The Party is Over," *U. S. News and World Report*, p. 43.
13. ————, "Americans Play, Even With Economy in Spin," *U. S. News & World Report*, Sept. 8, 1980.
14. Marc Leepson, "The Fitness Boom: Part of our New American Life Style," *Sacramento Bee*, April 25, 1978.
15. ————, "Leisure Boom—Biggest Ever," *U. S. News & World Report*, April 17, 1972.
16. Ron Koehler, "Snowmobiles refuse to disappear," *Sacramento Bee*, January 1, 1981, E8.
17. ————, "Leisure Where No Recession is in Sight," *U. S. News & World Report*, January 15, 1979, p. 44.
18. Mick Martin, "Preserving American Music," *Sacramento Union*, July 22, 1980, p. B1.
19. Ibid.
20. ————, "Gambling Spree Across the Nation," *U. S. News & World Report*, May 29, 1978, p. 35.
21. Richard Kraus, *Recreation and Leisure in Modern Society*, 2nd ed. (Santa Monica, Calif.: Goodyear Publishing Company, 1978), p. 113.
22. James Tuite, "A Growing Acceptance of Sports Betting," *San Francisco Chronicle*, December 26, 1978.
23. Kraus, *Recreation and Leisure*, 2nd ed., p. 113.
24. Diana Dunn, *Open Space and Recreation Opportunity in America's Inner Cities* (National Technical Information Services, Springfield, Virginia, July 1974).

Figure 4–1 Americans today have more leisure time and less work. Many are using this increased free time for recreation and various leisure pursuits. Above, a family is taking a stroll along a nature trail in Bankhead National Forest, Alabama. (Courtesy U.S. Forest Service.)

4
Social Forces that Influence Leisure

As the recreation and leisure movement moves into the 1980s, those in the United States have the task of dealing with the various social forces and problems that influence their leisure. These forces greatly affect the people—how and where they live, as well as their leisure behavior. The influences include their work, greater leisure time, higher income, education, changes in the family, energy shortages, communication, and mental stress. The impact of these forces determine to a large degree the leisure and recreation experiences of those in our society.

The evolution of recreation as a social institution did not occur by itself. Rather, mass leisure and the rapidly growing recreation movement were shaped and influenced by a complex of conditions, developments, and determinants that have been a part of the total picture of our progressive, modern nation.

To comprehend the social forces that have influenced the development of the leisure and recreation field, one must understand the rapid advances of American civilization, particularly people's perennial struggle for enlightenment. While it is true that American technology has contributed much to create our leisure opportunities, it should also be observed that the changes in the behavior patterns of people, institutions, and communities have also been instrumental in giving "rise to recreation as a major design in contemporary society."[1]

Ever since the scientific and industrial revolutions began, the recreation movement has been faced with many challenges caused by the numerous and rapid changes in our lives. A galaxy of great social changes has buffeted society during recent history resulting in the conditioning of the kind and number of leisure uses, the universal demand for recreation and its relative importance in people's lives.[2]

Since change takes place at such an accelerated rate in today's society, people must be flexible and have the ability to adjust. The sociologist in the study of social change focuses on factors that influence change and resistance to change. Leisure behavior is significantly affected by improvements in technology and new social ideas. The impact of the television upon leisure behavior, for example, can be considered in terms of the attitudes of society toward leisure.

Individuals and groups are not always in favor of new ideas and technological changes. In fact, they may demonstrate a resistance to change. According to Christopher Edginton, David Compton and Carole Hanson, "Resistance to change occurs because of two reasons: 1. people are uncertain as to the effect that the change will have upon their lifestyle; and 2. habit conditions the individual to follow a predetermined behavioral response."[3]

"The recreation and leisure professional not only must be cognizant of the changing environment," said Edginton, "but also must act as an agent or facilitator of social change among those he or she serves."[4]

CULTURE LAG IN SOCIETY

Sociologists point out that there is a "culture lag" in society. This is the gap between technology and the way people live. An editorial in *Parks & Recreation Magazine* stated: "Technology has taught us how to save time, but it has not taught us how to use time. This is the challenge to the recreator!"[5]

The editorial continued: "Even though we have materially reduced the workweek, extended earned vacation time, and achieved earlier retirement, the fact is becoming apparent that this is not, as many have assumed, producing equivalent leisure for most Americans. The truth is that the production worker is opting for more overtime work and a second 'moonlight' job in the 'free time' he has achieved. He prefers the increased income he can earn to buy the conveniences produced by technology. His image of a higher quality of life may be related more closely to possession of more hardware rather than more leisure. As a result, the trend is no longer toward the massive growth of leisure many had envisioned. Leisure is now growing at a very gradual rate."[6]

The problem is how leisure eventually will be distributed. Who is going to get it? Will it be distributed on the basis of class, to the upper or lower social and economic classes of society? Will it accrue on the basis of age, with the greatest leisure reserved for the older members of our society? Or will other elements emerge which will be society's answer?

"Despite technological advances, we are not creating all of the real leisure we had anticipated," said Stanley Parker and Kenneth Roberts. "Nothing has happened to effectively reduce the dehumanization of the assembly line and similar production techniques, despite improved technology. And even the figures on productivity—the key to further reduction of work time—are not very promising. The American worker's rate of productivity lags far behind that of workers in other western industrial nations."[7] Society in the United States appears, at this time in our history, to be attempting to find itself.

WORK AND LEISURE

Our attitudes and behavior toward work are changing, but so are the conditions of our lives. The rising levels of income, greater leisure time, the energy shortage, the development of private pension plans, the in-

Figure 4–2 Increased income is still a strong incentive for workers to buy luxuries like this beautiful sailboat. More people than ever are seeking a life style of leisure and seem willing and able to pay for it. (Courtesy Tennessee Valley Authority.)

troduction of social security, and other factors are changing the way that Americans look to the present and the future. Former Secretary of Labor J. D. Hodgson wrote: "In the past century, reduction of the average work week by about 13 hours has netted the American worker 675 hours of free time annually. Added to increased vacation time and more paid holidays, this amounts to a total gain in time free of work of nearly 800 hours annually, or roughly one month out of twelve."[8]

Despite the growth of leisure activities, Americans still find themselves firmly anchored to work. With the United States' labor force at an all–time high, more people are working than ever before. However, hours worked per person are going down, as they have been for years.

According to 1978 data reported in the *Wall Street Journal*, office workers in Newark, New Jersey average only 36 hours per week while their counterparts in New York City put

Figure 4–3   Combining work with a leisure life style. These executives find that their weekly tennis outings give them considerable satisfaction, and help them perform better on the job.

in 36.4 hours. The statistics show a trend toward a shorter workweek.[9]

The worker in the United States has more holidays with pay and more paid vacations. But countering that is the fact that many people are moonlighting. Somewhere between 5 and 7 percent of the population holds more than one job. More than 60 percent of all American women between the ages of eighteen and sixty–four work outside their homes.

In the face of high inflation and an uncertain economy, working Americans of all backgrounds and occupations are becoming less satisfied with their jobs. Consequently, keeping workers happy on the job is a major concern to employers. What is crucial is to find ways to motivate workers who have been turned off by routine and who demand more say in what happens on the job.

Perhaps the question a person must ask is not just whether he or she likes the job, but whether he or she is happy with his or her total role in life, whether work and leisure combined give reasonable satisfaction.

According to the *U. S. News & World Report*, "Workers who do not like the kind of work they are doing accept it as the price to be paid for the enjoyment it buys for them away from the job, whether it is a forty–foot cabin cruiser, a CB radio or a vacation home at the beach or in the mountains."[10]

4/40: The Rearranged Workweek

The four–day, forty–hour workweek has shown growing appeal with workers. In their quest for more leisure, workers are becoming more receptive to the idea of squeezing the same number of hours into a reduced number of days. Workers currently under the 4/40 plan point out the savings they realize by elimination of the fifth work day. Transportation and parking cost is reduced, and working mothers need the services of sitters or the nursery one day less.

The initial testing of the ten–hour day, four–day week has drawn mixed reactions. Proponents of the plan argue it will reduce absenteeism, save energy, reduce pollution, and give employees more time with their families. Opponents contend that the plan will increase moonlighting by employees working on days off, thereby reducing job opportunities for the unemployed. They further argue that it would lead to employee fatigue, bringing decreased productivity and more on–the–job accidents.

A Gallup poll survey in 1980 indicated that Americans would like more flexible working hours and a four–day workweek. The four–day workweek, though, lends itself only to certain industries and at least for the immediate future is expected to affect only a small percentage of the U.S. labor force in the next decade. Labor union leaders have voiced opposition to the four–day, forty–hour workweek and favor plans that would reduce the total number of hours worked.

Flexible Working Hours

Many United States companies have initiated a program called "flextime," and it appears to be catching on. With flextime, companies set certain "core hours" in which employees are required to be on the job. Basically, employees can vary their starting and stopping times so long as they put in the required total number of hours. Early risers can begin at seven o'clock and quit at three o'clock in time for tennis, shopping, or to pick up a youngster at school. Others may, if they wish, stroll in at ten o'clock.

Flextime gives people much more freedom to organize their lives, reduces pressure on transportation systems, and improves productivity. The program is especially suc-

cessful with working mothers who like to get home early. Some people work extra hours early in the week, then take off early on Friday, giving them a long weekend. Many companies have reported higher employee morale, and a lower absenteeism rate.

CREATIVE AND CHALLENGING WORK

The importance of work has dwindled for many of the less skilled workers in our society except as a source of income. This is particularly true of the workers on the production line whose ego involvement in work has diminished markedly. Instead, emphasis has been shifted toward leisure activities to find identity, self–satisfaction, and enrichment in their lives. In discussing what he called "the moral equivalent of work," Jay Nash stated that "Work must be viewed in the light of accomplishment and mastery, as craftsmanship work has always been, not as a curse on the brow of man. Through accomplishment, by work and craftsmanship, man's ego, small enough at best, gets a chance to expand. His work is partly himself." Leisure and work, together, make for fullness in living. In Nash's words, "Work, creative, challenging, and meaningful—is one of man's significant wants and needs."[11]

Retirement from Work

More older workers are choosing to delay retirement as a result of longer life expectancy, and inflation and legislation prohibiting discrimination against older workers. A vast majority of American workers believe nobody should be forced to retire because of age and, for the first time, most of them want to keep working instead of retiring, according to poll taker Louis Harris. The reason is not hard to find. They not only think such work contributes to their own mental and physical and material well being but they also feel that they can contribute to the mainstream of American society.

Future of Work

Work in the United States is changing, along with its economy. The nation is developing a high–technology, service–oriented economy in which the best job opportunities will demand special skills. The American work life will be longer and today's movement toward earlier retirement will play a still greater role in the work force.

Labor experts predict a workweek of thirty–two hours within the next decade or two. The failure of the workweek to be reduced can be attributed to the fact that people have taken much of their additional free time in vacations and three–day weekends. The unions have been slow to push for the shorter workweek, although the United Auto Workers are now calling for a cut in working hours.

EFFECT OF INCREASED LEISURE

The shift in the ratio of working hours to leisure hours has had a significant effect on the average worker. "For one thing, it has made him more conscious of the opportunities that his leisure hours present him," said Hodgson. "Such sports activities as golf, tennis, and boating have suddenly come within the economic reach of the average worker who now happily has the time to enjoy them."[12]

With more leisure hours available and more money in the pocket, the American worker has become culture conscious. We see this in the big cities where places like New York and Washington's Lincoln and Kennedy Centers for the Performing Arts and Minneapolis' Tyrone Guthrie Theater regularly play to sold–out houses. But we see it even more dramatically in smaller towns and cities throughout the nation where the community theater movement has mushroomed; local light–opera companies feature talent recruited from the ranks of office and factory workers; and art supply stores find themselves selling easels, paints, and brushes to amateur artists who spend their leisure hours fulfilling their urge "to do something creative."[13]

The potential for increased leisure is expected to continue. Further reductions in working time are likely to be small, with attention centering on the reshuffling of time free of work in order to provide larger blocks of leisure.

AUTOMATION

Automation will continue to present unique problems for our society, challenging our values and the ways we express them. Unemployment, retraining, re–deployment of personnel, increased leisure time, and the guaranteed minimum wage are just some of the present problems posed by the automation wave.

> Automation will require a substantial alteration of our philosophy concerning: the value and necessity of work, the function and value of leisure in American Society, the kind of work suitable for human beings, the causes and cure of unemployment, the economics of abundance, and a host of other concerns. . . .
> Automation is frequently confused with mechanization but the two are not the same. When machines do man's work that is mechanization but when they do man's work and control their own operation, that is automation.[14]

Increasingly, automation is freeing workers from tedious routine tasks. In turn, it has shortened working hours necessary to maintain a high standard of living, and has made goods available on an unprecedented large scale. On the other hand, as a result of automation, the number of employees in manufacturing has decreased although production has increased. In New York City alone, automatic elevators have displaced thousands of operators.

If the process of automation continues, its ultimate effect will be to severely limit the work available to most people. Will we then be capable of developing a society that does not depend on work to give it meaning?

Norbert Wiener, an eminent scientist in this field, has said, "Automation is bound to devalue the human brain. Will man have a sense of place in society? Man certainly needs to feel needed and wanted. He needs to achieve something. What will happen when automation produces a situation in which, for the first time in history, people will be spending more of their lives in leisure than in work?"[15]

TECHNOLOGY

A new generation of achievements in United States technology is emerging from the laboratories which will reshape life in the years ahead. Light–wave communications to talking computers and new energy sources are among many discoveries which will result in profound shifts in the way people will live, work, and even play.

The computer revolution is gaining momentum in the home as well as the office and factory, including machines that can read, write, talk, understand the spoken word, and do complex mechanical chores requiring humanlike intelligence. The list of games that have been programmed for home computers continually lengthens. Included are bridge, chess, battleship, blackjack, and backgammon. One program displays a monopoly board on the screen, with pieces that move and dice that roll randomly.

Thousands of corporations and individuals are expending time and money into the search for new ways to generate, save, and use energy. Many planners believe that thermonuclear fusion and solar energy will eventually become the United States' primary power sources as petroleum and other fossil–fuel supplies dwindle.

The *U. S. News & World Report* stated: "The impact of technology's bounty on the quality of play among children: seemingly endless hours of television watching, along with an abundance of electronic toys that require

only a push of the button, are seen as engendering a passivity that is stunting the emotional and intellectual growth of many of today's young."[16]

"Some of these youngsters could be in a real mess when the workweek shortens or they have to retire," said Lynn Barnett of the University of Illinois. "They will be empty shells."[17]

FAMILY AND HOME LIFE

Indeed, the impact of societal changes has altered the roles of members of American families. All aspects of recreation, the reasons, forms, and times, have changed markedly. Thomas Yukic expressed the belief that "The stereotype of the stable, close–knit family is rapidly becoming outmoded since sons and daughters marry earlier, gain freedom sooner, and in most instances break away from the family unit."[18] In addition, the modern mother is no longer confined strictly to a domestic role. The American woman has become an active force in the community.

Still, the family is the most important structure in our society. It is the core strength of our society. Yet, in the last two or three decades, nearly every new force in our society has been instrumental in weakening family ties.

The *U. S. News & World Report* said that: "As households change or break up, children are increasingly under the care of a single parent, a working mother, a day nursery—or the television set. And, in a growing shift from the past, more than 450,000 youngsters are living with their divorced or separated fathers. An estimated 34 percent of all wives with preschool children are working at outside jobs. Day care nurseries are proliferating to look after their youngsters."[19]

Where once the typical American family was composed of father, mother, children, and grandparents living and working together in an agrarian setting, today the shape and living situation of the family are very diverse, reflecting society's gradual acceptance of varied lifestyles.

More than 30 percent of school–age children are living with parents who have been divorced at least once. Because of rising rates of divorce, desertion, and illegitimacy, one–sixth of all United States children under eighteen live in one–parent families. At the same time, a majority of American mothers of school children now hold jobs outside the home, delegating child care increasingly to schools, nurseries, and baby–sitters—many of them government–supported.

Why the rise in family breakups? Most sociologists dealing with the family blame social change. Society is more tolerant now of people splitting up, and a divorce is easier to get in most states. In addition, there are more general stresses on people's lives and higher expectations of happiness.

One family counselor cites a recent study showing that the average family spends only about thirty minutes each week in serious discussion of family problems and issues. Also weighing heavily on today's middle–class families are the enormous economic costs of child rearing. Many new parents seem unprepared to cope with the basic needs of children in the infant and preschool years, a crucial time when the bulk of a child's emotional and intellectual potential is formed.

Despite the pressures from economic and social forces, however, experts argue that most families will adjust. Mary Jo Bane of the Harvard Graduate School of Education says: "American families are here to stay."[20]

The American family is under enormous pressures, but the family as an institution is neither dead nor breaking down. That is the conclusion of the Carnegie Council on Children, which was formed in 1972 to study the effects of American society on its families and children.[21] In the words of the Council, "Families are not now, nor were they ever, the self–sufficient building blocks of society, exclusively responsible, praiseworthy and blamable for their own destiny. They are deeply influenced by broad social and economic forces over which they have little control."[22]

A difficult decade lies ahead for the nation's households. Among the trends that will continue to persist include movement of mothers from home to job, a high divorce level, and a low birth rate. The size of the average family will dwindle, as many couples choose not to have children or to have only one or two. Among the reasons: the high cost of raising youngsters in an inflationary era and the growing importance of careers to women.

In spite of the high divorce figures in the United States today, 85 percent of the survey respondents indicate their expectations of happiness in marriage are being fulfilled. Seven out of every ten married readers say they share enough interests and activities with their spouse and 63 percent say they talk often enough with their spouse.[23]

Recreation Impact on the Family

Recreation can help to strengthen family relationships by enriching the environment and content of family life. There are so many ways in which wholesome recreation can

Figure 4–4 Day care centers and private nurseries are increasing, as more mothers take outside jobs. Many are assuming leadership roles such as this activity leader.

help the family unit. Indeed, the family that does interesting things together will be more likely to stay together.

The little things that families do together are often remembered as the most fun, such as:

—a hike in the woods
—an evening around the fire
—making a garden
—building a birdhouse

Basic principles not taught in the home will probably not be taught at all. Truth, honesty, responsibility, respect, and integrity should be learned in home situations.

LIVING ALONE: THE SINGLES PHENOMENON

Millions of unmarried Americans are creating a new lifestyle that is affecting every part of the country. The "singles phenome-

Figure 4–5 Taking a young child to the park was commonplace years ago. What's happened to that? Cooperation, love, and happiness come about in activities done as a family.

non" is affecting housing, social contacts, and recreation on a scale the United States has never seen before. The number of Americans living alone or with unmarried roommates has risen more than 40 percent over the last six years. Singles, including those raising children, now make up one out of every three households in the United States. According to the U. S. Census Bureau, the number of adults younger than thirty–five who live alone has more than doubled since 1970, despite an uncertain economy. This is far greater than the expansion of this age group in the population.[24]

Robert Reinhold wrote: "The trend toward single living is a reflection of several other shifts in American family and social life in recent years: the tendency to postpone or even forego marriage, the growing career ambitions of women, the easing of salary and credit discrimination against women, the mounting divorce rate, a general independence of young people from their parents and a wide new tolerance for unconventional living arrangements generally."[25]

In interviews, fifty young people all over the country almost invariably cited freedom and independence as the chief reasons for living alone. "You can come and go as you please, you don't worry about treading on another person's feet," said Heather Keiser, 25, a Philadelphia receptionist.[26]

One of the most popular centers for singles on the west coast is Marina del Rey in Los Angeles, where 9,500 apartment dwellers live on 400 acres of the Pacific waterfront. Marina City Club is the largest group of sixteen–story towers. Among the amenities are three private restaurants, a wine–tasting room, 341 private boat slips, swimming pools, and courts for tennis, paddle tennis, and handball.

POPULATION

The population profile of the United States is undergoing far–reaching changes. The nation's growth is diminishing; marriages are down and divorces are up. The birthrate is declining sharply, as young couples put off having children. More and more unmarried people are living with members of the opposite sex.

There has been a dramatic decline in birthrates in the United States. The U.S. Census experts once thought we might have about 100 million more people by the year 2000 than they now project. The expectation now is that we may have under 266 million people in 2000.

Unfortunately, the population boom continues around the world, and it is growing most rapidly in those areas of Asia and Latin America where people are already hungriest. An estimated 7.5 billion people will fight for existence in the year 2000. People are beginning to ask: "Can our earth ever support its 3.6 billion people at anywhere near U.S. standards?"

A key factor in the decade ahead is the continued aging of the unusually large group of Americans born from the late 1940s to the early 1960s. Since 1970, the median age of the United States population has risen in 1.5 years to 29.4 and is expected to continue climbing to an all–time high of 38 over the next fifty–three years.

A dramatic increase in population is expected in the oldest age bracket, people seventy–five or older. Conversely, the number of Americans younger than twenty will fall below 30 percent of the population for the first time in history. As a result, it appears that low birthrates in the last twenty years will assure graduates in the coming decade of a welcome in the job market.

The growth rates of population nationally and worldwide will play a vital role in determining the future recreation patterns of people. Michael and Holly Chubb wrote: "No social problem appears to have a greater potential for radically changing the lifestyles of the majority of the earth's people than population growth."[27]

Overpopulation is a growing threat to many of the earth's major biologic systems on which all life depends. The nations of the world, increasingly, will be competing for depleting resources as they cope with the problems of emigration from overpopulated countries.

Many recreation resources are already showing the effects of overuse, particularly those in or around urban areas. By the year 2000, more than 50 percent of the world's population will be crowded into urban areas. Therefore, as Chubb and Chubb pointed out, new and more efficient administrative and management techniques will need to be adopted to accommodate the expanding population growth of our cities.[28]

URBANIZATION

Little more than a decade ago, United States cities were torn by riots that erupted, yet today the outlook for many of the nation's big urban centers, ironically, is bright. A

Figure 4–6 Revitalizing the nation's cities. The development of urban parks and recreation areas has contributed to a brighter outlook for large urban centers. Above, the new thirty–five–acre New World Center Bicentennial Park is on the threshold of Miami's business district. (Courtesy Miami Metro Department of Tourism.)

back–to–the–city trend among middle–class families is reviving more run–down urban neighborhoods. Luring the newcomers are tantalizing home values and the chance to live close to work and to cultural facilities. Of course, the energy shortage has been an important factor in a greater movement of middle–class whites back to the city.

While the flight to the suburbs has not ended, cities, for the first time in many years, are being viewed as a realistic alternative for family life. The activity will likely quicken in coming years because higher fuel costs will make suburban living more expensive.

According to *U.S. News & World Report:* "All this does not mean that the great advantages enjoyed by many suburbs over cities will disappear overnight, but more observers now agree that a slow but sure equalizing process is under way in many metropolitan areas."[29]

Cities are struggling to move from their old role as dense manufacturing centers toward a new image as meccas for services, retail trade, and entertainment. According to economist Thomas Muller of the Urban Institute: "The cities that will do best are those that have something vital going on: Wholesaling, merchandising, banking, tourism. Success also will depend on whether a city can lure and keep enough upper–income people."[30]

More than four hundred thousand homes will be rehabilitated in cities and in close–in suburbs during the decade of the 1980s. Leading this back–to–the–city movement will be singles, young couples with few or no children, and older couples who have raised their children. Most of these people will be higher–income professionals working in government, finance, and other white–collar jobs.

Urban ills, such as poor housing, school problems, recreation problems, and numerous other social problems, have arisen from the movement to the city. Probably the most urgent problem facing today's cities involves the disadvantaged, who have been victimized because of their race, nationality, socioeconomic status, or a combination of these factors.

SUBURBIA

Intensive urbanization in America has given rise to suburbanization. Suburbia is often referred to as a place, an area that lies just outside the central city boundaries. "This is incorrect," wrote Reinhart Knudsen. "Suburbia is actually an attitude of mind. Suburbia stood for certain ideas about the 'good life' that profoundly changed the face of America after World War II."[31]

People believed there was a better way to live than in crowded cities, so they sought open space and country living without being farmers. But now the open space is filling up, density is increasing, streets and sidewalks make suburbia look more and more like a city after all. Suburbia was made possible by the automobile and cheap gasoline. Now gasoline is expensive and auto use limited.

"The biggest single factor for moving to the suburbs," said *Time* magazine, "is people's desire to have a home of their own. Next in order of importance came the search for a better atmosphere for their children, a goal that is not always realized."[32]

Suburbanites introduced the age of informality, backyard entertaining, barbeque pits, and jeans. Now many of the new homes have formal dining rooms. Suburbanites avidly pursue varied interests outside of their careers. They go heavily into sports, outdoor activities, camping, boating, rafting, and airplane flying. But many of these activities are now being crimped by preservationists on one side, and the remorseless tide of development on the other.

"Most suburbanites still adhere staunchly to the values and reasons for their great migration," said Knudsen. "They visualized a better life and strove to attain it. Now, the question is—can they preserve it?"[33]

INFLATION

Inflation has become the number one worry for most people. In countless ways, it is changing the lifestyles of American consumers and investors. For tens of millions of working Americans inflation is running away with the buying power of their paychecks. Higher prices are outstripping them of earnings. Consumers have plunged deeply into debt. Inflation is also significantly running up business costs. People are wondering where to put their money with the hope of salvaging its purchasing power in months ahead.

More wives are going back to work to help balance the family budget. Many older people are postponing retirement out of fear that company pensions and Social Security benefits no longer will cover mounting property taxes, medical costs, and everyday necessities.

Higher property values and inflated city and county budgets have sent property taxes sky-high in many localities and set off a nationwide tax revolt.

Is there any way to lick inflation? According to Herbert Stein, professor of economics, University of Virginia, "We can stop inflation over time, basically, if you halt or drastically reduce the rate of growth of the money supply. We don't know how long it will take, and a great concern is that it would involve a serious recession as a byproduct."[34]

According to George P. Schultz, "There are certain fundamentals that you have to do: monetary discipline, budget discipline, and productivity. If we have them, we will lick inflation."[35]

Economists predict that "The increase in prices that people pay, soaring this year (1980) at a rate of more than 13 percent, will drift down to 5 percent by 1990. Despite inflation, people's real purchasing power—the amount of goods and services that their incomes will buy after taxes are paid—will go up by almost a third in the decade ahead."[36]

UNEMPLOYMENT/WELFARE

Unemployment undermines nearly every aspect of family life materially and psychologically. Many observers agree that continuing high unemployment is the single most important factor in the decline of the family.

Welfare has become a problem of great magnitude. The nation spent about $14.2 billion on welfare in 1970, more than twice the outlay of what was spent five years earlier. Yet the 13.5 million Americans or 6.3 percent of the population who received that aid are only half the estimated number of the needy and eligible. "Increased by the recession and the growing activism of welfare rights groups, the rolls continue to grow in every part of the country," wrote *Time* magazine. "After thirty-five years of legislation and programs, the world's wealthiest nation seems caught in a paradoxical trap: the more the U.S. spends on its poor, the greater the need seems to be to spend more still."[37]

Unemployment is expected to lessen, however, due to a sharp decline in the number of teenagers, resulting from the smaller rate of births in the 1960s and 1970s. Although job opportunities may grow faster than the labor force, unemployment will not necessarily decline during the 1980s. The reason, according to the *U.S. News & World Report*, is that "Many new workers will not be properly trained for the available jobs. Officials are particularly concerned about hundreds of thousands of economically disadvantaged young people who are not literate enough to qualify for entry-level white-collar jobs."[38]

WAR ON POVERTY

The rise in prosperity has not spread to all sections of the American public. With an estimated thirty-two million—or about 17 percent of the population—living in poverty, society is faced with the prospect of a "poverty war" for a generation.

Approximately one out of every six persons over 65 in the United States has an income below the government-defined "poverty index." However, the number took a dramatic drop in 1972, due largely to the 20 percent increase in Social Security payments. The Social Security Administration in 1973 defined poverty as an income of $1,980 for a single elderly person and $2,520 for a couple annually. In addition to these 3.1 million elderly Americans who are considered impoverished, an estimated two million would be in that category if they did not live with families whose incomes are over the poverty threshold.

THE IMPACT OF TELEVISION

The most significant influence on the use of leisure today, unquestionably, has been television. "No single invention has had such subtle and powerful influence on public tastes, appetites, desires, and recreational pursuits," wrote Joseph E. Curtis. "In addition to occupying a vast amount of people's free time, television programs have taught golf, tennis, swimming, fly–casting and an infinite number and variety of diversions from around the world."[39]

Unfortunately, most people watch far too much television, not that what they view is terribly harmful in itself but much of the programming is empty, escapist—just something to pass the time. Critics, and there are many, point out that the overuse of television, particularly by children, has crippled their creativity and curiosity. Others believe television programs have hurt family life with too much emphasis on sex and violence.

Wilson Riles, state superintendent of public instruction in California, believes "Television violence has definite and lasting effects on children. The continued exposure of our children and young people to excessive violence on television is contributing to the development of attitudes that pose serious consequences for their future."

Most parents are attempting to control their children's television viewing. Among the types of control most commonly used by parents of older children: deciding what programs children view, requiring them to do their homework before watching, deciding how many hours they can watch television, and setting a television curfew.

Despite all the bad things, there are also many admirable aspects of television. If the television industry would pay more attention to the ideal of excellence in programming, the situation could improve.

TRANSPORTATION/MOBILITY

One of the most distinctive features about American life has been its mobility. Comfortable and rapid means of transportation are available to the people, whether traveling long or short distances.

However, Americans in the future will be leaving their cars in the garage more often when they take off for long trips. The *U.S. News & World Report* stated that: "Transportation experts predict a gradual shift to airplanes for intercity travel. Buses and trains will prove more popular, too, especially for short journeys. Behind the switch: climbing fuel prices and the limited comfort of today's smaller cars."[40]

Bus firms are expected to get more riders for trips in the 200–to–300–mile range. To attract more middle and high–income riders, buses will be better looking, have a nicer interior and bigger windows. Terminals will be much improved—cleaner and safer. To a lesser extent than planes and buses, the nation's trains also stand to benefit from the gasoline shortage.

Despite an increase in plane, bus, and rail travel, the car—and the extensive interstate highway network—will still play a prominent role. A nation with 110 million cars is not about to give up a mobile way of life established over seventy–five years. "The American people will give up almost anything before their automobile," said former Transportation Secretary Brock Adams.[41]

Cars of the future will become smaller, lighter, and considerably more expensive. Some smaller models will be able to get more than fifty miles per gallon. Big cars will be too expensive to operate for everybody's use. Future autos will be safer and more sophisticated. "The real challenge to automakers," said Adams, "is to build a car that gets fifty miles per gallon, meets all pollution–control standards but without pricing cars out of the reach of ordinary Americans."[42]

Figure 4–7 Parks closer to the people. With an eye on their gasoline gauges and wallets, more and more Americans are flocking to parks in or near big population centers, especially on weekends, and staying away from distant ones.

ENVIRONMENTAL DETERIORATION

The environmental movement, an important political force during the 1970s, is faltering. Thwarted by inflation, recession, and the energy shortage, environmentalism has been losing ground. According to Janet Welsh Brown, executive director of the Environmental Defense Fund, "Steady pressure in the name of energy development and inflation control will continue in the 1980s to roll back some standards protecting the environment."[43]

As a result, the golden age of environmentalism of the last two decades appears to be receding. The administration's drive to cut government costs, curb inflation, and produce more energy has relaxed enforcement of federal anti–pollution standards.

Many environmentalists are redirecting their efforts from the nation's wilderness areas to the urban environment. Future legislative efforts will be aimed at the urban environment, such as congestion and pollution.

One bright outlook for environmentalism is the continued federal protection of scenic and wild areas. In 1978, President Carter issued an executive order to protect nearly 100 million acres of wilderness land.

Indeed, the 1980s will present a stern test for environmental leaders. Survey polls indicate that the American public still cares deeply about the environment, but warns former Interior Secretary Cecil B. Andrus: "We must understand that no one can sign a blank check for open–ended environmental costs."[44]

VIOLENCE AND VANDALISM

Crime is at an all–time high in America. Vandalism has been increasing at an alarming rate throughout the country. Deliberate breakage, littering, and even arson have forced many recreation and park agencies to either close or severely restrict the use of some parks and facilities. A major contributing factor to violence and vandalism has been the widespread use of drugs and alcohol among young people.

Crime, violence, and vandalism significantly restrict recreation opportunities, and must be vigorously dealt with by those responsible for law enforcement and recreation and park agencies. The protection of users and the prevention of crime and vandalism represent a serious problem which requires constant neighborhood vigil and surveillance. The solution, of course, goes much deeper.

Due to the willful and often pointless destruction, defacement, or defilement of property, the total cost of vandalism in the United States is more than a billion dollars a year. Broken bottles, smashed toilet fixtures and lights, strewn rubbish, and clogged toilets add significantly to the operations and maintenance costs of facilities and areas.

Criminologists report, however, that "The rate of serious crime in America is expected to subside in the 1980s. The reason: A decline in the number of teenagers and young adults. Those under twenty-five accounted for 56 percent of all arrests in 1977."[45]

MENTAL ILLNESS AND STRESS

The increase in the frequency of mental disease is the result of a modern society which subjects its members to social strain, personal problems, and mental stresses. Some of the most prevalent influences in our way of living are a hurried pace of living; anxieties and stresses caused by such situations as unemployment and economic insecurity; a decline of acceptable family and neighborhood living; and a high rate of delinquency, vice, and suicide.

Between 10 and 15 percent of the population have serious mental illness today. Emotional tensions and anxieties contribute directly to the increasing incidence of serious illnesses. As people try to cope with new lifestyles, they often end up smoking, eating poorly, turning to alcohol or drugs, and failing to exercise properly.

Working people in growing numbers are asking whether their drive for success is taking too great a toll on themselves and their families. About three-fourths of the people who consult psychiatrists are suffering from problems that can be traced to a lack of job satisfaction or an inability to relax. Dr. Tobias Brocher, a psychiatrist for the Menninger Foundation, says it is not work overload that causes most job tensions. He believes that "many of the frustrations, especially for young executives, result because the job is not fulfilling or challenging enough."[46]

Physicians and psychologists believe many people grow ill because their lives have too little stress. Some of the most satisfying work that people do is that which is performed under stress. For example, Bob Wiener, a public relations executive in New York City, commented that "I'm in a field in which stress is an inherent part of the job. I find it quite stimulating."[47]

I'm convinced that stress need not be bad for people. If we weren't stressed—and distressed—by the challenges of our world, then nothing would get done. A lot of people, particularly executives, thrive on stress. Take it away and their jobs become boring. But these people have developed strategies that allow them to deal with stress and slough it off before it takes over their lives.[48]

Self-help groups provide support to their members. Hobbies can establish networks to provide contact with others who have similar interests. The tremendous interest in citizens-band radio is fostered by the feeling that people alone in their cars can reach out across the cosmos and get close to somebody. Everyone needs to have a bridge to others that they know will be there when it is needed.

Indeed, the disturbing trend toward increased mental stress has substantiated a need for recreation and leisure living. Recreation, more than ever before, is being recognized as a strong asset to individuals, groups, and the community in maintaining favorable mental health conditions.

QUESTIONS FOR DISCUSSION

1. Discuss some of the social forces that have influenced the development of the leisure and recreation field.
2. List some specific social forces and changes which have resulted in more free time for most Americans.
3. Discuss the "culture lag" in society and its many implications on the growth of leisure and work in America.
4. With increasing companies on a four–day workweek, what will be the effects of the four–day week on society, particularly the leisure lifestyles of American workers?
5. Discuss the relationship between work and leisure. Do you look for Americans to remain anchored to work? How soon will the thirty–two hour workweek be realized?
6. Discuss two of the new trends in work: the 4/40 workweek and flextime.
7. How has the dehumanization of labor in a technological society affected the need and demand for re–creative leisure time opportunities?
8. What effect will increased leisure have on our society?
9. The roles of members of the American family have been altered by the impact of societal changes. How will these changes affect the leisure interests and lifestyles of the family?
10. What impact has recreation had on the family?
11. How important an influence is the family on leisure attitudes?
12. Discuss the movement of people nationwide to and from the city, relative to "back to the city" or "moving to the suburbs."

REFERENCES

1. Thomas S. Yukic, *Fundamentals of Recreation* (New York: Harper & Row, 1970), p. 40.
2. Ibid., p. 41.
3. Christopher Edginton, David Compton, and Carole Hanson, *Recreation and Leisure Programming* (Philadelphia: Saunders College, 1980), p. 119.
4. Ibid.
5. Editorial, *Parks & Recreation Magazine*, May 1976, p. 19.
6. Ibid.
7. Ibid.
8. J. D. Hodgson, "Leisure and the American Worker," *Leisure Today*, 1972, pp. 5–6.
9. Jonathan Woman, "The Future of Work," *Sacramento Union*, August 13, 1978, p. B4.
10. *U.S. News & World Report*, p. 61.
11. Jay B. Nash, "The Moral Equivalent of Work," *The Physical Educator*, May 1965, p. 51.
12. Hodgson, "Leisure and the American Worker," pp. 5–6.
13. Ibid.
14. David Gray, "The Changing Pattern of American Life," *Parks and Recreation Magazine*, March 1966, pp. 212–19.
15. Ibid.
16. ——, "How Americans Pursue Happiness," *U.S. News & World Report*, May 23, 1977, p. 61.
17. Ibid.
18. Yukic, *Fundamentals of Recreation*, p. 55.
19. ——, "The American Family," *U.S. News & World Report*, October 27, 1975, p. 30.
20. ——, "Two Reports on the American Family," *Family Weekly*, January 1, 1978, p. 4.
21. Ibid.
22. Ibid.
23. Ibid.
24. ——, "What's Happening to the American Family," *Better Homes and Gardens Magazine*, August 1978.
25. Robert Reinhold, "Living Alone: A Growing Phenomenon," *The Sunday Denver Post*, June 19, 1977, pp. 12–13.
26. Ibid.
27. Michael and Holly R. Chubb, *One Third of*

    Our Time? (New York: John Wiley & Sons, Inc., 1981), p. 696.

28. Ibid., p. 699.
29. ———, "Comeback for Cities, Woes for Suburbs", *U.S. News & World Report*, March 24, 1980, p. 53.
30. ———, "As the Cities Seek A New Role," *U.S. News & World Report*, October 15, 1979, p. 67.
31. Reinhart Knudsen, "So What is Suburbia, Anyway," *Sacramento Union*, December 18, 1980, p. 8.
32. ———, "Suburbia: The New American Plurality," *Time*, March 15, 1971, pp. 14–20.
33. Reinhart Knudsen, "So What is Suburbia, Anyway," p. 8.
34. ———, "Is there Any Way to Lick Inflation" *U.S. News & World Report*, March 10, 1980, p. 25.
35. Ibid.
36. ———, "Monetary Discipline will Halt Inflation," *U.S. News & World Report*, March 10, 1980, p. 26.
37. ———, "Welfare: Trying to End the Nightmare," *Time*, February 8, 1971, pp. 14–15.
38. ———, "Tomorrow's New Jobs," *U.S. News & World Report*, January 21, 1980, p. 66.
39. Joseph E. Curtis, *Recreation—Theory and Practice* (St. Louis: The C. V. Mosby Company, 1979), p. 13.
40. ———, "Changes in the Way You Will Travel," *U.S. News & World Report*, July 2, 1979, p. 48.
41. Ibid.
42. Ibid.
43. ———, "Hard Times Come to Environmentalists," *U.S. News & World Report*, March 10, 1980, p. 49.
44. Ibid., p. 50.
45. ———, "Challenges of the '80's," *U.S. News & World Report*, October 15, 1979, p. 49.
46. ———, "Cracking Under Stress," *U.S. News & World Report*, May 10, 1976, p. 59.
47. Ibid.
48. Roy W. Menninger, "Coping with Life's Strains," *U.S. News & World Report*, May 1, 1978, p. 80.

Figure 5–1 Play contributes to child development. A flexible and encouraging home play environment is very beneficial and can enhance a child's creativity. Here, a youngster finds a tree in the family yard convenient to climb on, yet the tree does not sufficiently meet his play needs. (Courtesy Health Insurance Institute.)

5
Sociological, Psychological, and Physiological Aspects of Leisure and Play

Recreation and leisure activities and experiences have a significant potential for aiding people toward social satisfaction, as well as psychological stability and physiological well being. Indeed, the recreation and parks field can provide society with very important services which can have a profound influence on the quality of one's life.

"Leisure is part of the person's life experience," wrote John Neulinger. "It is subject to all the forces, personal or environmental, impinging on the individual and, in turn, it leaves its mark on the individual's lifestyle."[1]

According to many noted psychologists, play and recreation are decisive factors in the psychological development and maturing of human beings. Recreation in the form of sports, games, dance, and outdoor activities makes a valuable contribution to the physical well-being of people of all ages. Play has come to be regarded as an important experience through which children can develop emotionally, psychologically, and socially. Through play, important patterns of behavior can be formed that will prove beneficial throughout their lifetime.

Studies dealing with the sociological investigation of play examine the relationship between patterns of leisure activity and such variables as social class, age, sex, residence, occupational status. Numerous factors directly influence leisure behavior. By understanding these factors and their relationship to individual behavior, the professional recreator can plan more effectively and efficiently for the delivery of services.

The behavioral sciences are comprised of three disciplines—psychology, anthropology, and sociology. Psychology is regarded as the study of the behavior of human beings, and animals, while anthropology is the study of the characteristics, customs, etc. of human kind. Sociology is the study of human society and social behavior. Sociologists seek to understand society, social systems, norms of behavior, customs, roles, and patterns of change in order to better understand the social behavior of human beings.

Physiology is the science dealing with the functions and vital processes of living organisms. Physiological fitness implies the capacity for skillful performance and rapid recovery. Clayne R. Jensen wrote that "As physical fitness increases, depression, anxiety and self-centeredness decrease and self-satisfaction and social adjustment increase."[2]

SOCIOLOGY OF LEISURE

Leisure is both a social phenomenon and a form of social interaction which is influenced by such variables as socioeconomic class, occupational prestige, lifestyle, disability, economic capability, and ethnic or racial affiliation.

Leisure is a modern sociological problem, evolving out of various historical and social conditions. Furthermore, it is a very controversial problem that is expected to become even more crucial in the future.

Social Class as a Leisure Determinant

Early studies of social class and leisure found that Americans differed significantly in their recreational interests, according to social class. The term *class* generally refers to the horizontal stratification of a population by such factors as family background, occupation, income, community status, group affiliation (race, religion, or nationality), and education.[3]

Lloyd Warner, a leading sociologist, wrote: "By class is meant two or more orders of people who are believed to be, and are, accordingly ranked by the members of the community, in socially superior and inferior positions. A class system also provides that children are born into the same status as their parents. A class society distributes rights and privileges, duties and obligations, unequally among its inferior and superior grades. A system of classes, unlike a system of castes, provides by its own values for movement up and down the social ladder . . . in technical terms, social mobility."[4]

In 1934, George Lundberg, Mirra Komarovsky, and Mary Alice McInerney reported that 90 percent or more of the leisure of all classes except students, was divided among seven activities: eating, visiting with friends, reading, public entertainment, sports, listening to the radio, and motoring. Each group examined had characteristically different patterns of behavior. This study was unique in being a pioneer attempt to study the relationship of leisure to key sociological variables.[5]

R. Clyde White conducted a systematic study of the relationship between social–class differences and the uses of leisure. Using a sampling of families that was representative of income, education, racial composition, occupation, and age distribution, he grouped them into four social classes: upper–middle, lower–middle, upper–lower, and lower–lower. White found that the home was the most frequently used leisure setting, followed closely by commercial amusements. The study found that the lower social classes made greater use of community–provided facilities than the middle classes.[6]

White stated that "The tendency to choose leisure activities on the grounds of membership in a particular social class begins in the adolescence and becomes more pronounced in maturity. As people get older and settle into the ways of the class to which they belong, they choose leisure activities which are congenial to their class."[7]

Increasingly, however, sociologists are suggesting that "the traditional concept of social class is no longer useful in predicting leisure interests and attitudes. Max Kaplan explained this viewpoint by suggesting that "The concept of 'class' was becoming less useful in the social sciences: inexpensive travel and the mass media." He believes "Widespread affluence has brought many forms of leisure within the reach of almost everyone. In leisure activity, more than in any other area of American life, 'social class' had become an outmoded concept."[8]

Sociologist Nels Anderson, similarly, wrote that class lines have become less strictly drawn. He said that "All classes attend the same ballgames, the same prize fights, the same night clubs, even the same opera. The difference is in money outlay, how much is spent for the fishing outfit, the automobile, the television set, the seat at the opera or the table at the night club."[9]

Yet, Kraus pointed out that "It would be sheer nonsense to suggest that the pastimes of all levels of society are basically the same, that it is only a matter where we sit at the opera. There continues to be two important distinctions in the choice of leisure activity that are closely related to social class, cultural taste and opportunity."[10]

Leisure Values and Attitudes

People in the highest prestige classes participated in the greatest variety of leisure activities, according to a 1969 study by Rabel Burdge. In his investigations, Burdge found that such outdoor recreation activities as water–skiing, snow skiing, and sailing were significantly associated with the highest prestige level. Other outdoor recreation activities like fishing, hunting, and bicycling involved subjects on the second–highest prestige level. Members on the lowest prestige level most frequently attended such spectator sports events as stockcar races, boxing, and wrestling matches.[11]

Burdge observed that one of the ways "people prepare for entrance into a higher social class is to imitate the leisure behavior of that group."[12]

FAMILY LEISURE PATTERNS

Although other influences increasingly are affecting leisure behavior, the family is still a major source of the development of leisure attitudes of its members. Indeed, the quality of the family is crucial to our social survival. While much has been written and said about "the decline of family leisure," actually, most families today are experiencing a great variety of new leisure activities. "Quite possibly, today's family produces more of its own recreation than did the family of fifty or hundred years ago," wrote Clark Vincent.[13]

The home remains the most vital and dynamic force in the development of a child. According to Geoffrey Godbey and Stanley Parker, "The family provides a setting in which the attitudes of children are developed toward all major institutions, including recreation and leisure. Within the family acceptable and unacceptable ways of behaving are learned: when and how to play, with whom, what to do and what not to do."[14]

The greatest problem in integrating leisure and family styles exists when family members differ in their expectations. The difficulty lies in helping families integrate leisure styles into their family styles.

Activities, such as game playing, casual conversation, and hiking, require each person to recognize the needs of the others. Dialogue becomes necessary for successful participants and reinforces the ability of the family members to adjust to one another in other situations as well.

The threat to the companionship family comes from too much concentration in individual pursuits or activities with non–family persons. The father, the mother, and the children seek and find leisure interests, good and bad, outside the home.

Figure 5–2 Integrating leisure and family styles can contribute to the quality of family life. The use of joint activities such as this chess game is particularly critical to a couple during early marriage.

The quality of family life, including leisure as an increasingly large part, is crucial to our social survival. Sociologists, psychiatrists, and other scholars are warning that a return to stability in national life cannot be achieved without a strong family base. More and more, critics are zeroing in on the home, not society at large, as the source of troublesome youngsters.

Collective Behavior

Collective behavior can be described as the mass actions that occur within a society. This type of behavior is usually very spontaneous and rapidly changing. Fads, demonstrations, and social movements are forms of collective behavior. Christopher Edginton pointed out that "Recreation and leisure services and products are subject to fads; this week, skateboarding may be in and hula hoops out."[15]

Mass culture and mass leisure are two forms of collective behavior that are relevant.

Mass culture is the culture of the majority, numerically, often based on the mass media and the concepts and products these media disseminate. Mass leisure commonly refers to the leisure activities typically engaged in by the mass of society, the activities most often sought and desired by the largest number of individuals.

According to Edginton, Compton, and Hansen: "The two most common differences between groups within society are: 1) the variations of groups through social stratification, and 2) the variations in lifestyle and opportunities for development among societal groups from different ethnic, racial, and social backgrounds."[16]

The social stratification of groups involves the classification of individuals according to status levels, roles, and social classes. There is considerable debate among sociologists over the validity of the social class system within society. American society is an open class society in which individuals occupy different levels according to ability and merit. An individual has the opportunity to be ranked in the social system based on his or her knowledge, skills, and ability.

SOCIOLOGY OF SPORT

Research in the sociology of sport is broadening and deepening. According to John W. Loy, Jr., and Gerald S. Kenyon, "There is a growing spirit of scientific inquiry regarding the role and cultural significance of sport throughout the major nations of the world."[17] The social sciences are particularly concerned with the customs, traditions, value systems, and economic aspects of sports, and its place in the cultural hierarchy.

Considering the tremendous preoccupation with sport in the United States, and the corruption of values that exists on the various levels of sport, there is an urgent need to better understand its place in the complex fabric of our society. According to Kenyon and Loy, "The framing of intelligent questions and the design and execution of sound research in the sociology of sport will contribute greatly to our dealing effectively with these issues and problems in modern society."[18]

Influence of Racial and Ethnic Identity

Racial and ethnic affiliation has had a significant influence upon leisure attitudes, opportunity, and participation. The words "disadvantaged" and "black", are often linked as though synonymous in books and publications on recreation and leisure in the urban setting.[19]

In their 1927 study of children in elementary, junior and senior high schools, Harvey C. Lehman and Paul A. Witty, concluded that "black children tended to participate much more actively in social forms of play than white children."[20]

In his landmark study of the American black, Gunnar Myrdal, the Swedish sociologist, in "The American Dilemma," investigated the inadequate provisions of recreation programs and services for blacks in American communities.[21]

Since the 1960s, there has been a considerable reduction of interracial tension and prejudice in the United States, and it should be noted that American blacks are more fully accepted on all levels of social and economic life than in the past. Kraus stated, however, that "it would be self–deluding to suggest that social exclusion and differences in the quality of recreation and leisure no longer exist."[22]

SOCIOLOGY OF PLAY

In examining play experiences, Roger Caillois, the French sociologist, classified games characteristic of various cultures and identified their apparent functions and values. His analysis provides a rich historical perspective on play activity, showing how many play artifacts and activities are the cultural residue of past "magical" beliefs and rites.

Caillois established four major types of play and game activity:[23]

Agon refers to activities that are competitive and in which the equality of the participants' chances of winning is artificially created. Most modern games and sports, including many card and table games involving skill, are examples of agon.

Alea includes those games or contests over whose outcomes the contestant has no control; winning is the result of fate rather than the skill of the player. Examples of alea include games of dice, roulette, and lotteries.

Mimicry is based on the acceptance of illusions or imaginary universes. It includes a class of games in which the common element is that the subject makes believe that he or she is someone other than her or himself.

Ilinx consists of play activities based on the pursuit of vertigo or dizziness. Historically, ilinx was found in primitive religious dances or other rituals. Today it may be seen in children's games that lead to dizziness by whirling rapidly, and in the use of swings and seesaws.

ANTHROPOLOGY OF PLAY

In their studies of play in primitive societies, modern anthropologists have seen it as a revealing and significant aspect of daily life. According to Edward Norbeck, "Human play should not be regarded simply as childish behavior, or as a form of trivial or light-hearted amusement. Play is found among many living creatures and throughout the entire class of mammals.[24]

Human play typically occurs at times of religious celebration, shifts in work, and changes in social status. Play behavior is commonly found at rites of birth, coming of age, marriage, and death and burial—indeed, all the important social events of humankind tend to be incorporated into social observances that include a rich element of play. Play is both a biological and a socio-cultural phenomenon.

"Play is universal human behavior," said Norbeck. "It is therefore presumably vital to human existence. Societies regard and han-

dle play differently."[25] Food is frequently a part of ceremonies of a religious character, at harvest celebrations, seasonal feasts, or the return of successful hunters or fishermen.

The ceremonies of American Indians are frequently used in one form for tourist exhibitions and in another quite different form as part of traditional religious practice. According to Felix Keesing, traditional play practices are most likely to persist when they have a continuing functional relation to social structure, child rearing, religion, or other behaviors linked to important social needs and values.[26]

PSYCHOLOGY OF LEISURE

Increasingly, psychologists are studying the motivations, values, attitudes, and perceptions of leisure involvement. John Neulinger and Rick Crandall suggest that this new research emphasis can be attributed to the fact that "We are no longer satisfied to name the activities that people engage in; we now want to know what they mean to participants."[27] As the humanistic and holistic approach to leisure becomes more accepted, psychological analysis of play activities will contribute to our understanding in this field.

According to Neulinger and Crandall, "A psychological definition of leisure . . . emphasizing self–development and fulfillment through freely chosen, meaningful activities, makes leisure particularly relevant and valuable for those sections of our society that are presently underprivileged in one way or another."[28]

Social psychologists predict that a key aspect of play behavior—the dynamics of group participation—will become an increasingly important subject for investigation.

PSYCHOLOGY OF PLAY

Play has become widely recognized as a significant aspect of human development and behavior. The young child learns more and develops better through play than through any other form of activity. Opportunity for varied play under healthful outward conditions is beyond doubt the chief need of children.

According to Lawrence Frank: "Play is the way the child learns what no one can teach him. It is the way he explores and orients himself to the actual world of space and time, of things, animals, structures, and people. Through play he learns to live in our symbolic world of meaning and values, of progressive striving for deferred goals, at the same time exploring and experimenting and learning in his own individual way. Through play the child practices and rehearses endlessly the complicated and subtle patterns of human living and communication."[29]

Men and women who participate in sports are more emotionally well-adjusted than those who do not. Involvement in sports tend to go hand in hand with psychological well-being and a well-adjusted personality. One of the reasons, apparently, is that sports provide stimulating and diverting interaction with other people.

John E. Gibson wrote: "People who engage in sports involving a high level of physical activity have different attitudes and lifestyles than those whose leisure involves low physical activity. The physically active tended to have better self-concepts (higher self-esteem), and to have a greater social orientation toward life."[30]

Yet, during the early decades of the twentieth century, play was regarded by many authorities as an experience of dubious worth. An article appearing in a 1914–15 edition of *Infant Care* stated that "The dangerousness of play is related to that of the ever-present sensual pleasures which must constantly be guarded against."[31]

Gradually, though, in the years that followed on up to modern society, authorities came to regard play as natural and desirable. Ruth Strang, a leading expert on child guidance, in 1951 wrote, "The play life of a child is an index of his social maturity, and reveals his personality more clearly than any other activity."[32]

FORMS OF BEHAVIORAL INVOLVEMENT

Recreation has a wide range of possible behaviors and satisfactions. Recreation behaviors, like the types of activity, can also be grouped according to the physical or psychological character of the participation.

James Murphy and John Williams suggest a wide range of behaviors, such as follows:

Socializing Behaviors Activities such as dancing, dating, going to parties, or visiting friends, in which people relate to each other with a minimal consciousness of social role.

Associative Behaviors Activities in which people group together around common interests, such as car clubs, stamp–gem collecting, or similar hobbies.

Competitive Behaviors Activities including the whole range of sports and games, and competition in the performing arts, or in outdoor activities.

Risk-taking Behavior Recreation pursuits which clearly involve considerable risk. In sport parachuting, the jumper assumes a life or death risk with each jump.

Exploratory Behaviors Recreation experiences involving exploration refer to such activities as travel and sightseeing, hiking, and scuba diving.

Vicarious Experience Modern recreation consists of such experiences as reading, watching television or motion pictures, viewing the art works of others, listening to music, or attending spectator sports events.

Sensory Stimulation Behaviors which center about the stimulation of the senses as a primary concern, such as the enjoyment of sexual activity, drinking, drug use, and visual experiences like light shows and rock concerts.

Physical Expression Many activities such as running or jumping, swimming, dancing, and yoga, may involve physical expression without emphasizing competition against others.[33]

ROLE OF PLAY IN PERSONALITY DEVELOPMENT

No one can teach what a child learns while playing. By exploring and experimenting, the child learns to live in our symbolic world of meaning and values, continually striving for goals and trying to meet basic needs.

Children can develop inner strengths and learn self–control through play. As they move from the toddler age to about five or six, children shift from solitary activities to side–by–side play. Finally, they become involved in integrated, cooperative play projects.

The role of play has been examined at each stage of life. The first form of play during infancy is identified as "sense–pleasure" play, in which the baby discovers and relishes moving, exploring his or her own body, and experiencing such environmental stimuli as sounds, flavors, and tactile sensations. Later, children begin to explore "skill–play," exercising their capacity for action. Early in the toddler period, young children take part in "dramatic play," acting out functional relationships and roles of everyday life.

Bruno Bettelheim wrote that as simple a game as "peek–a–boo" symbolically means to the children that even if they are temporarily out of her sight, their mother will not abandon them but will look for and find them. Thus, they gain confidence and learn that they need not always be under her careful protection.[34]

Another form of children's play that involves fear and risk is the game of "hide–and–seek" involving dark hiding places. It symbolizes the child's leaving a secure home and being able to return to it safely.

Play may become a form of information seeking, of testing an environment, or of

Figure 5–3 Socially satisfying group activity can provide an opportunity for involvement with others, a sense of acceptance and security within the group, which can contribute to psychological well–being.

seeking novelty, surprise, laughter, or release. Jean Jordaan, and others, wrote: "As such activity occurs, the participant is continually and actively involved in the process of interaction with the environment. As he investigates the environment, he seeks to control or master it, gaining, if successful, a feeling of personal competence and mastery. This motivation for play is now regarded as the 'competence–effectance' drive."[35]

The relationship of play and recreation to the social and emotional growth of teenagers has undergone much research by psychologists. They have found that the adolescent's self–image is closely related to participation in extracurricular activities. High school students with a high degree of self–esteem tend to take part actively in sports, musical groups, publications, and social activities. Those with a low degree of self–esteem were less involved in their involvement and participation.

OPTIMAL AROUSAL AND INCONGRUITY

Play is motivated by the optimal arousal both in childhood and adulthood. In describing his arousal–seeking theory of play, M. J. Ellis emphasized the need for optimal arousal as a key motivator of play. He maintained that the optimal level of arousal (stimulation or level of interest) ranges from person to person. "When interacting with the environment, a child constantly learns new things," explained Ellis, "The accumulative effect of such learning increases the complexity of interactions."[36]

Instead of calling it arousal–seeking, J. Mc. V. Hunt referred to the motivated behavior as seeking "incongruity." "When the environment provides too many inputs and stimuli for the child to handle, then the child withdraws from the environment. On the other hand, when the environmental inputs are overly similar to the coded and stored information and experience, the child becomes bored and seeks situations which offer more incongruity, uncertainty, novelty, and complexity."[37]

Iso–Ahola suggested that "A tendency to seek the optimal incongruity channels the child's play. Unfortunately, many children live in an environment that impedes their attempts to achieve the optimum amount of arousal or incongruity. This is particularly true for children in families with 'low' social class levels."[38]

In discussing his views of the implications of optimal arousal and incongruity, Ellis suggested that: "First, the child should be given opportunities for exploration and manipulation in the home. He should be able to experience novelty, incongruity, arousal, increasing complexity, and control. This can be achieved by providing arousing stimuli, e.g. playthings. For toys to be stimulating, they must be novel enough to induce exploration and sufficiently complex to puzzle the child and to prompt investigation. They should also be responsive so that manipulation is possible."[39]

"As children often look to adults for stimulation," said Iso–Ahola, "They should be allowed to play at the adults' feet, between legs, on the back, and in the lap. Unfortunately, many young couples are faced with a difficult problem, in that living in modern apartments is very restrictive physically, thereby limiting children's mobility, discouraging play, and impeding indulgence in arousal seeking."[40]

The theory of play as incongruity seeking has strong implications for the design of playgrounds. Typically, playgrounds offer standard equipment, such as swinging, slides, and various other devices. These facilities are fixed and cannot be modified or manipulated. Consequently, they provide little to be explored and investigated.[41]

What then is a good playground? According to Iso–Ahola, "It is one which changes and is open to continuous modification by children; it cannot be fixed or standard. Children have to be able to dig, build, and alter their playgrounds. There must be sand, dirt, earth, bricks, lumber, or other modifiable substance in the play environment."[42]

Ellis calls these places adventure and junk playgrounds. He believes that many playgrounds are repetitive and boring because they offer the same thing time after time.

Since play activities reflect the rudiments of adult leisure behavior, D. R. Yoesting and D. L. Burkhead wrote that it is important to understand how the need for optimal incongruity is met through the child's play. "What is optimally arousing for an individual as a child is likely to affect the optimum level of arousal when he is an adult," said Yoesting and Burkhead.[43]

The psychological consequences of play may be many. One of them is satisfaction resulting from feelings of competence and self–determination achieved in intrinsically motivated play. Play also contributes to children's cognitive development, particularly the effects of play on children's problem–solving ability and creativity.

Figure 5–4 Improving self–concept. A sense of achievement, a feeling of personal value, and recognition by others can do much for an individual's self–esteem. Here, two young boys receive kite flying instruction in the Outreach program of the New Orleans Recreation Department.

BASIC HUMAN NEEDS

Abraham H. Maslow, in his classic book, *Motivation and Personality*, arranged the basic human needs in sequence from the most basic to the higher needs. Maslow believed that the higher needs develop only when the basic needs are fulfilled.[44]

Maslow stressed the need for individuals to develop to their fullest degree of independence and creative potential. Maslow developed a convincing theory of human motivation, as part of which he identified a number of important human needs, arranging them in a hierarchy of priority. As each of the basic needs is met in turn, humans are able to move ahead to meet more advanced needs and drives.

Maslow stressed the need for individuals to be more spontaneous and creative, and to see meaningful values in a variety of expressive experiences, both work and play.

Maslow's theory included the following levels of need:[45]

Physiological The most basic of human needs are the physical drives, such as hunger, thirst, sleep, sexuality, and many others.

Safety needs self–protection needs on a secondary level—protection against danger, threats, or other forms of deprivation.

Social needs needs for group associations, acceptance by one's fellows, giving and receiving affection and friendship.

Love and belonging People whose physiological and safety needs are fulfilled rather consistently feel motivated to satisfy their needs for love and belonging.

Self–esteem Every individual has a need for self–esteem, which means a feeling of personal value, enhanced status, sense of achievement, self–respect, confidence, and recognition by others.

Self–actualization The need for self–actualization is the need to do what one is capable of doing to achieve self–fulfillment, and realizing one's maximum potential.

Knowledge and understanding The higher needs of people include their impulses to satisfy curiosity, to know, to explain, and to understand.

Aesthetic needs Beauty can be a purely internal experience, such as feeling the beauty of ideas of philosophical concepts that are meaningful to us.

ROLE OF PLAY IN PSYCHOANALYTICAL THEORY

During the early twentieth century, Sigmund Freud was the dominant figure in the development of psychoanalytical theory. Kraus pointed out that many of Freud's fundamental concepts of personality development, as well as his exposition of psychological mechanisms, have profound implications for the understanding of play.[46]

Freud believed that the child brings into the world a somewhat unorganized mentality, called the *id*, which is dominated by powerful drives for self–preservation, the alleviation of hunger, and sexual expression (called *libido*)—all linked to the continuation of the species. As the child grows older, Freud suggested a portion of the *id* becomes transformed into the *ego*, which tries to govern the *id* when it behaves in socially disapproved ways. When sharp conflicts arise between the two, neurosis occurs.

A third element, the *superego*, represents a modified or exaggerated part of the *ego*. It personifies all the prohibitions and strict rules of conduct imposed on the child by authority figures and may be perceived as a powerful conscience and sense of duty.

As a child moves from instinct–dominated infancy to socially adjusted adulthood, many conflicts and frustrations are dealt with or worked out through play. Play is constantly used to reenact unpleasant experiences or frightening events, in order to gain control over them and dispel their effects.

In the continuing attempt to resolve conflicts between the drives of the *id* and the controls exerted on them by the *ego* and the *superego*, a number of psychological mechanisms are employed. Freud described these as sublimation, regression, compensation, repression, and identification. Each may be directly related to play involvement.

A number of Freud's other theories had a significant impact on the concepts of play and recreation. His "pleasure principle" suggests that the human being's basic desire is instinct gratification. Freud also asserted that human beings are dominated by a "repetition compulsion," the effort to repeat and master unpleasant events through play.

ROLE OF PLAY IN THE LEARNING PROCESS

For many years, psychologists felt that children's play was little more than an expression of excess energy and good spirits. The importance of their activities was questioned. The primary function of play was to "let off steam" so that the child could return to the more important business of study and learning. Recently, however, studies of how intelligence develops in children have revealed that play is the way in which children develop intelligence.

According to Richard Dattner, "Play is a child's way of learning. . . . Control of children's play is one way in which a society prepares the child to participate eventually in the world of adults. Train up a child in the

Figure 5–5 Play is a child's way of learning. Children are shown involved in deeply absorbing play as they enjoy their nature experiences in Sequoia National Forest, California. (Courtesy U.S. Forest Service.)

way he should go, and when he is old, he will not depart from it."[47]

Play has contributed significantly to the learning process. A number of psychologists who investigated child behavior during the early decades of the twentieth century concluded that play was essential to develop a child's initiative, resourcefulness, and originality.

During the so–called progressive education period in the United States, considerable use was made of playlike projects and approaches to learning. In recent years, the contributions of play as an aspect of learning have been supported by research in several different areas.

Richard Louv wrote that: "Children deprived of play that allows them to use their initiative and creativity are often the very ones who later become dropouts, drug users, suicide victims, criminals—or compulsive risk takers."[48]

Play in Cognitive Development

Jean Piaget said there are two processes basic to all mental development—assimilation and accommodation. Assimilation is the process of taking in, as in the case of receiving information in the form of visual or au-

ditory stimuli. Accommodation is the process of adjusting to external circumstances and stimuli. Within Piaget's theory, play is especially related to assimilation, the process of mentally digesting new and different situations and experiences.[49]

Accommodation, which is complementary to assimilation, occurs when variations in the environment demand a modification in man's pattern of behavior. "Accommodation occurs when a previously learned response fails to work in a new situation, and the organism modified its response."[50] Assimilation and accommodation are the two processes by which the child gradually develops intelligence from the primarily instructural reponses of infancy to the eventual achievement of adult logical thinking. This development takes place in stages, each with its own characteristic forms of play.[51]

Piaget regarded play primarily as repetition of an activity already mastered, rather than as an attempt to investigate or explore it further and develop a capability for dealing with it more effectively. Piaget's analysis of play however, has been criticized as being severely limited. Although Piaget regarded play and imitation as distinctly separate phenomena, most systematic observers of children's behavior regard imitative activity as a basic element of play.[52]

Relationship of Play and Mental Health

There is a strong relationship between play, recreation, and leisure values on the one hand, and emotional well–being on the other. Karl Menninger, for example, pioneered the use of play and recreation in the treatment of the mentally ill. He believed that a well–rounded play life is essential to maintaining a healthy emotional balance. Under

When children become interested in the natural and man–made world their curiosity is best satisfied by first–hand experience

Richard Dattner

Menninger's direction, a study found that the well adjusted patients pursued nearly twice as many hobbies as the patients who were seriously ill. In his work with psychiatric patients, Menninger consistently found them deficient in the capacity for play, and unable to develop balanced recreation interests and skills.[53]

Alexander Reid Martin, in his studies on the problem of leisure in relation to mental health today, found that "the Protestant work ethic and the overemphasis on work values in our society have made it extremely difficult for many people to use their leisure in self-fulfilling and satisfying ways. He noted that "Within his professional practice, he has found many highly successful individuals who can justify themselves only through work, and who feel intensely guilty about play."[54]

Martin suggests there is a real need for individuals to become autonomous and to develop a set of inner values and resources that will help them use their leisure in confident and enjoyable ways. "What is critically needed," Martin said, "is a fuller understanding of the meaning of leisure in our society, and a stronger effort to build those inner resources that will see play and recreation as worthy forms of personal expression."[55]

PSYCHOLOGY OF SPORT

Interest in the field of sports psychology is growing rapidly. Likewise, play and recreation are becoming increasingly important subjects for scientific investigation. Robert Singer believes "The myths, superstitions, and half-truths that have provided the basis for much instruction and coaching in sport will soon be replaced by a body of valid information gathered through rigorous experimental and observational methods."[56]

The American Psychological Association has identified a number of specialty areas as branches of psychology. The areas most relevant to sport psychology are: developmental, personality, learning and training, social, and psychometrics.

Figure 5–6 The secret to lifetime enjoyment of a sport is finding an activity satisfying. A participant must possess the skills to play the game well enough to want to continue playing it. Here, Paula Sperber Carter demonstrates her bowling technique. (Courtesy National Bowling Council.)

Psychological Benefits of Lifetime Sports

In addition to the recreational activities of childhood, young people should be taught how to play the lifetime sports, the kind they can play and enjoy as long as they live. To be prepared physically and psychologically for the future, children need to learn the basic skills of such sports as golf, tennis, bowling, water sports, and winter sports.

Sports that carry over into one's lifetime can offer many psychological benefits which will help meet the stresses of our present way of living. Children must not only be taught the benefits of play, but also how to play. Too many adults are reluctant to start bowling, skiing, or golfing because they don't want to experience the embarrassment of learning.

And if they fail to learn when they are young, they very likely will lose all interest in participating later in life when they really need to be active.

The value of regular activity in maintaining physical fitness is rarely questioned, but activity is equally important in the matter of psychological fitness. In psychiatric hospitals, participation in sports has aided recovery and contributed significantly to the individual's rehabilitation.

More and more psychiatrists feel that sports participation can contribute to the prevention of mental illness. They believe the person who participates regularly in sports is better adjusted. In addition to having a better self–image the person will have increased potential to cope with crisis situations. Having stronger faith in her or himself and those about her or him, the person will have the emotional control so necessary to enjoy a fuller life.

If young people are not given the opportunity to play in a wholesome atmosphere, they will likely seek the same experiences in less constructive and desirable pursuits. Finding the activity satisfying is the secret to a lifetime enjoyment of participation in a sport. The individual must possess the skills to play the game well enough to want to continue playing it.

PREVENTIVE ASPECTS OF PLAY

The extensive research and study relative to the problems tormenting many young people today lead to an unavoidable conclusion. Psychologists and psychiatrists should focus less of their time and energy upon therapy and a great deal more upon prevention. Arthur Weider, Director of Behavioral Research of the Outdoor Game Council USA and a supervising psychologist at Roosevelt Hospital in New York City, wrote: "I am convinced that children today would be better off if they played more. Not only would they enjoy their childhood more, but, in my opinion, they would be better able to cope with the complexities of modern life."[57]

What does Dr. Weider mean by prevention? "In the case of children," he said, "I think of play activities. Play is to children what living and working is to adults. Who does not remember with fond nostalgia the free–play activities of their youth—racing around the block or hiding behind a tree in an exciting game of hide–and–seek; playing softball in the school yard, a game of jacks, or just playing one of those solitary outdoor games like not stepping on sidewalk cracks? I am convinced that our children today would be better off if they played more of these games."[58]

According to Weider, free play is good prevention against the psychological problems tormenting many young people today. "When a child is allowed to play without adult supervision," said Weider, "he is allowed to express his personality; he can release the feelings and attitudes that have been pushing to get out in the open. Free–play affords the child the opportunity to 'play out' his feeling and resolve frustrations just as the individual adult 'talks out' his difficulties."[59]

Weider pointed out numerous spin–off values of free–play:

1. Free–play encourages the development of self–reliance.
2. Free–play inspires respect for the individual.
3. Free–play offers abundant opportunity and experience for social interaction and adjustment.
4. Free–play is a training ground for coping with competition.[60]

PHYSIOLOGICAL ASPECTS OF PLAY

Physical activity and exercise can have a strong and positive physiological effect on people. The Greek philosopher Aristotle stated: "The body is the temple of the soul, and to reach harmony of the body, mind, and spirit, the body must be physically fit."[61]

If a person is physically fit, the body system will function more efficiently. He or she

Figure 5–7 Jogging is one of the most popular forms of exercise in the United States. Joggers find scenic parks like this one very pleasant to do their running. To make running more challenging, individual goals should be set or it can get boring.

will have sufficient strength to engage in vigorous physical activity. The body needs regular exercise to function properly. Hippocrates, the father of medicine, said, "That which is used develops and that which is not used wastes away."[62]

The goals of exercise and sports participation, besides the obvious pleasures derived, are health and a longer life. The key to any exercise program is intensity, duration, and frequency of exercise.

Aerobics training improves heart and lung function. To produce energy for exercise, muscles need oxygen. The way to get oxygen to muscles efficiently is to have a heart that pumps efficiently and lungs that can efficiently extract oxygen from the air we breathe.

THE FITNESS BOOM

One of the dramatic changes in American lifestyles to take place during the last two decades is the increase in the numbers of Americans who regularly exercise.

According to George Gallup: "Although one American in two gets virtually no exercise at all, that leaves more than 100 million who claim to participate regularly in some form of exercise or sport activity. Tens of millions have made fitness such an integral part of their lives that it has been called "our new national religion." Today, 47 percent of Americans say they participate in some form of physical exercise daily—twice the percentage recorded in 1961 when the figure was 24 percent."[63]

The form of exercise that has undoubtedly received the most attention during this period of the "exercise boom" is jogging. Most joggers are traveling at least one mile during their routine. So popular has exercising become that there now are an estimated five thousand health clubs and spas around the country, with several million members.

Improving Cardiovascular Fitness

To prevent heart attacks, exercise should have as its primary purpose the enhancement of cardiovascular fitness. A decade or two ago, the definition for fitness included such qualities as flexibility, strength, power, endurance. Now the emphasis is on endurance, or cardiovascular efficiency. It is not as important any more for people to be superstrong.

Any exercise that increases pulse rate for a long–enough time, at least twenty minutes, is what is needed. Swimming, jogging, jumping rope, and stationary bicycle riding all stimulate increased heart activity and oxygen consumption. In so doing, they are rated better for improving cardiovascular fitness than tennis, golf, hiking, baseball, or any activity in which the participant can halt or slow down.

Evidence keeps mounting that regular physical activity may be of significant benefit in the prevention of coronary heart disease, the United States' number one killer. In a recent study of San Francisco longshoremen, those whose jobs required heavy physical activity had 46 percent fewer deaths due to coronary disease than longshoremen with less physically demanding jobs.

Exercise—Its Effect on Heart Disease

Exercise, even if relatively mild, apparently helps the blood destroy dangerous clots, a discovery that may explain why people who work out have fewer cases of heart disease and fewer strokes. Doctors know that those who regularly jog or exercise have healthier hearts than the general population, but they were not sure what happens inside the body to protect the vital organ.

The latest study, done at Duke University Medical Center, found a dramatic increase in the release of proteins that attack blood clots when people are in good physical shape. The study measured the effects of ten weeks of mild physical exercise on sixty–nine healthy adults who had not been exercising regularly.[64]

The doctors found that after the ten weeks, the lining of the volunteers' blood vessels released greatly increased quantities of proteins called *plasminogen activators*. *Plasminogen* dissolves *fibrin*, a stringy protein that helps form blood clots. Blood clots in important blood vessels cause heart attacks and strokes.

How Often Should One Exercise?

At least three times a week. That is the minimum requirement for developing heart and lung fitness and also for showing significant changes in body weight and fat, according to Dr. Michael L. Pollack.[65] Most experts agree that at least three to four uninterrupted half–hour periods a week of hard physical activity, performed at three–quarters of our maximum heartbeat, are necessary.

Everyone should, of course, be in good shape before starting an exercise program, so it is a very good idea for an individual to have a doctor's checkup, especially if he or she is older than forty. One who exercises, must be consistent, exerting the body without interruption, for at least a half–hour three times a week.

The real secret of exercise is to habitualize it, to make it as automatic as eating lunch. The psychological goal of an exercise program is clear: reduce punishment and increase reward. Dr. Pollack explained: "Essentially, that means increasing the rate of exercise slowly so that at no point do you feel discomfort great enough to overcome the rewards of exercise as you perceive them. That is the key."[66]

Popular Forms of Exercise

Jogging and tennis have developed into two of the most popular exercise forms in this

Figure 5–8 Lifetime leisure activities are practiced by these young women, backpacking in the Ozarks. (Courtesy Department of Parks and Tourism, Arkansas.)

country. Tennis, of course, is more social, but jogging is more helpful in preventing heart attacks. Jogging is also good for mental health. Running can relieve anxiety, reduce emotional stress, and combat depression.

Swimming is excellent exercise, if the individual keeps moving for a half–hour without stopping. Running in place, dancing, bicycling, rowing and jumping rope also can provide the proper energy output because they not only are rhythmic but also involve the entire body. The thing about jogging is that some competitive goals should be set or it can get boring. And if one gets bored, he or she is likely to give up.

Weightlifting is great for conditioning and losing weight. Women need not worry about developing the dimensions of musclemen. They lack the male hormones, testosterone, which is responsible for those dimensions. Weightlifting will contour the bodies of women and give them a firmer waist and bust and better muscle tone.

Most Americans prefer exercise that is enjoyable—sailing, skiing, tennis, golf, and other so–called "leisure" or "lifetime" sports. Former astronaut Captain James A. Lovell stated that "I practice these sports whenever I can, and I involve my family in them at every opportunity."[67]

QUESTIONS FOR DISCUSSION

1. Discuss the role recreation plays in child development, its contribution to self–worth and positive personality in children.
2. Define the behavioral sciences and discuss their usefulness in understanding leisure behavior.
3. Discuss the following: The home remains the most vital and dynamic force in the development of a child. Theoretically, this is true, but where do the problems lie?
4. Many authorities are warning that a return to stability in national life cannot be achieved without a strong family base. Do you agree? Explain your answer.
5. An increasing number of people, professional recreators and social psychologists alike, are wanting to know what activities mean to participants and what the activity or experience does to people. Discuss the reasons for this growing concern.

6. Discuss the role of play in personality development and the learning process. Why do arousal stimuli and incongruity seeking have such strong implications for the design of playgrounds and a stimulating play environment?
7. What can be some harmful effects on children who are deprived of play opportunities?
8. Discuss some of Maslow's basic human needs, particularly his theory of self–actualization. Why is Maslow's theory of human motivation so relevant to recreation practitioners?
9. What are the psychological benefits of lifetime sports?
10. How does sport affect the political, social, economic, and educational structures of society?
11. According to Dr. Arthur Weider, "Children today would be better off if they played more." Do you agree or disagree with Dr. Weider? Why?
12. What are some of the values and benefits of regular exercise relative to fitness and good health?

REFERENCES

1. John Neulinger. *The Psychology of Leisure* (Springfield, Ill.: Charles C. Thomas Company, 1974), p. 92.
2. Clayne R. Jensen, *Leisure and Recreation* (Philadelphia: Lea & Febiger, 1977), p. 91.
3. Richard Kraus, *Recreation and Leisure in Modern Society*, 1st ed. (Santa Monica, California: Goodyear Publishing Company, 1978), p. 66.
4. W. Lloyd Warner and Paul S. Lunt, *The Social Life of a Modern Community* (New Haven, Conn.: Yale University Press, 1941), p. 82.
5. Kraus, *Recreation and Leisure*, 1st ed., p. 67.
6. R. Clyde White, "Social Class Differences in the Uses of Leisure," in Larrabee and Meyersohn, *Mass Leisure* (Glencoe, Ill: The Free Press, 1958), pp. 198–205.
7. Ibid., p. 204.
8. Max Kaplan, *Leisure in America: A Social Inquiry* (New York: Wiley, 1960), p. 92.
9. Nels Anderson, *Work and Leisure* (New York: Free Press, 1961), p. 34.
10. Kraus, *Recreation and Leisure*, 1st ed., p. 70.
11. Rubel J. Burdge, "Levels of Occupational Prestige and Leisure Activity," *Journal of Leisure Research*, Summer 1969, pp. 262–74.
12. Ibid.
13. Clark Vincent, "Mental Health and the Family," *Marriage and the Family*, February 1967.
14. Geoffrey Godbey and Stanley Parker, *Leisure Studies and Services: An Overview* (Philadelphia: W.B. Saunders Company, 1976), pp. 78–79.
15. Christopher Edginton, David Compton, and Carole Hansen, *Recreation and Leisure Programming* (Philadelphia: Saunders College, 1980), p. 118.
16. Ibid., p. 117.
17. John Loy and Gerald Kenyon, *Sport, Culture, and Society* (New York: Macmillan Company, 1969), p. 14.
18. Loy and Kenyon, *Sport, Culture, and Society*, pp. 76–77.
19. Kraus, *Recreation and Leisure*, 1st ed. p. 77.
20. Harvey Lehman and Paul Witty, *The Psychology of Play Activities* (New York: A.S. Barnes, 1927), p. 161.
21. Gunnar Myrdal, *The American Dilemma* (New York: Harper and Row, 1944, 1962), pp. 346–47.
22. Kraus, *Recreation and Leisure*, 1st ed., p. 79.
23. Roger Caillois, *Man, Play and Games* (London: Thames and Hudson, 1961), p. 21.
24. Edward Norbeck, "Man at Play" in *Play: A Natural History Magazine*, Special Supplement, December 1971, p. 53.
25. Ibid.
26. Felix Keesing, "Recreative Behavior and Culture Change," *Papers of the Fifth Congress of Anthropological and Ethnological Sciences*, 1956, pp. 130–31.
27. John Neulinger and Rick Crandall, "The Psychology of Leisure," *Journal of Leisure Research*, 3 August 1976, pp. 181–84.
28. Ibid.
29. Lawrence Frank, quoted in Ruth Hartley and

Robert Goldenson, *The Complete Book of Children's Play* (New York: Thomas Y. Crowell, 1963), p. 43.

30. John E. Gibson, "How do Sports Affect Your Life?" *Family Weekly*, October 26, 1975, p. 14.
31. Kraus, *Recreation and Leisure*, 1st ed., p. 47.
32. Ruth Strang, *An Introduction to Child Study* (New York: MacMillan, 1951), p. 495.
33. James Murphy, John Williams, William Niepoth, and Paul Brown, *Leisure Service Delivery System: A Modern Perspective* (Philadelphia: Lea and Febiger, 1973), pp. 73–76.
34. Bruno Bettelheim, "What Children Learn from Play," *Parents' Magazine*, July 1964, pp. 4, 9–10.
35. Jean Jordaan, Donald E. Super, Reuben Starishevsky, and Norman Matlin, *Career Development: Self–Concept Theory* (Princeton, N.J.: College Entrance Exam., 1963), p. 42.
36. M. J. Ellis, *Why People Play* (Englewood Cliffs, N.J.: Prentice–Hall, 1973), p. 118.
37. J. Mc. V. Hunt, as referred by Seppo E. Iso–Ahola, *The Social Psychology of Leisure and Recreation* (Dubuque, Iowa: Wm. C. Brown Company, 1980), p. 83.
38. Ibid., p. 83.
39. Ibid., p. 86.
40. Ibid., p. 103.
41. Ibid., p. 88
42. Ibid.
43. D. R. Yoesting and D. L. Burkhead, "Significance of Childhood Recreation Experience on Adult Leisure Behavior: An Exploratory Analysis," *Journal of Leisure Research*, 1973, pp. 25–36.
44. Abraham H. Maslow, *Motivation and Personality*, 2nd ed. (New York: Harper and Row, 1970).
45. Kenneth Jones, Louis Shainberg, and Curtis

Byer, *Dimensions, A Changing Concept of Health* (New York: Harper & Row, Publishers, 1979), p. 9.
46. Kraus, *Recreation and Leisure*, 1st ed., p. 57.
47. Richard Dattner, *Design for Play* (New York: Reinhold, 1969), p. 17.
48. Richard Louv, "Playgrounds: Kids Build 'Em Better," *Family Weekly*, December 2, 1979. P. 4.
49. Kraus, *Recreation and Leisure*, 2nd ed., p. 55.
50. Dattner, *Design for Play*, p. 24.
51. Ibid.
52. Kraus, *Recreation and Leisure*, 2nd ed., p. 55.
53. Karl Menninger, *Love Against Hate* (New York: Harcourt, Brace and World, 1942), p. 185.
54. Alexander Reid Martin, "Leisure and Our Inner Resources," *Parks and Recreation Magazine*, March 1975, p. 10a.
55. Ibid.
56. Robert N. Singer, "Sports Psychology," *Journal of Physical Education and Recreation*, September 1976, p. 24.
57. Arthur Weider, "The Way Our Children Play Can Save Their Mental Health," *Family Weekly*, July 4, 1971, p. 7.
58. Ibid.
59. Ibid.
60. Ibid.
61. Charles A. Bucher, *Physical Education for Life* (New York: McGraw–Hill Book Company, 1969), p. 42.
62. Ibid., p. 45.
63. George Gallup, "Exercising Doubles in Two Decades," *Sacramento Union*, October 6, 1977, p. A10.
64. Ibid.
65. Ibid.
66. Ibid.
67. Ibid.

II
An Overview and Understanding of the Recreation Profession

Figure 6–1 Early Central Park, the play space for the privileged in the winter of 1862, served people from all segments of the population. (Courtesy Harry T. Peters Collection, Museum of the City of New York.)

6
History of the Recreation Movement

Like other social movements of great significance, the history of municipal recreation in the United States and Canada cannot be interpreted fully in terms of a series of specific events characterized by distinct periods of development. Rather, "The recreation movement was the result of a combination of ideas, experiments, and developments," wrote George Butler, one of the United States' most distinguished historians on the study of play and recreation. "Some of them were closely related to each other in time, place, and influence, while others had little connection with preceding, current, or subsequent happenings."[1]

Any great social movement grows out of a pressing social need. The events of the closing years of the nineteenth century brought about the realization that there was a growing need for recreation. Although individual developments in recreation were made throughout the nineteenth century, they were relatively isolated in scope and intensity.

To generate a force of sufficient magnitude to meet the need for recreation, it remained for the pressures of a changing industrialized society to force individual leaders, municipalities, and private and public agencies to unify their efforts. Along with technological and industrial progress, the advance of science and medicine, more widespread education, and changing social attitudes were other social forces that played prominent roles in the growth of recreation in the United States and Canada.

The recreation and park movement in the United States and Canada, in general, has developed along two main themes:

1. *Municipal recreation* (often called community recreation), sometimes referred to "activity–oriented recreation" and urban park systems. Municipal recreation includes areas, facilities, and programs in a community.
2. *Natural resource oriented recreation*, frequently referred to as "outdoor recreation." The various forms of outdoor recreation depend largely upon such natural resources as camping, fishing, boating, and skiing.

ORIGIN OF THE PLAY MOVEMENT

Play and recreation activities are as old as recorded history, and the idea of parks can even be traced back to the ancient Egyptians and Babylonians. The Greeks wrote about the parks and gardens of Persia. The Romans had their numerous villas and hunting grounds, first located on the outskirts of towns or in the countryside, but later constructed in the city of Rome.

The first evidence of any form of recreational facility for the public in the United States was the establishment of the New England town commons, which dates back to the early part of the seventeenth century. These commons were town squares that were used for public meetings and socials. The Boston Common, established in 1634 and regarded by many historians as the first city park, was initially used by militiamen to hold drills and by boys to play.

In 1682 William Penn laid out Philadelphia according to a regular square with square ornamental plots. He included in his plan numerous small parks and ornamental plots.

Recreation in Colonial America, though, was not held in high esteem. Idleness was thought to be associated with evil, loose morals, and personal degeneration.

Between 1821 and 1830, outdoor gymnasiums were built for the first time in the schools of New York City and the New England states. In 1821, the Salem (Massachusetts) Latin School opened an outdoor gymnasium with equipment, but did not provide for a supervisor. The Round Hill School at Northampton, Massachusetts, opened one in 1825 equipped with German gymnasium equipment, and a supervisor was provided. Harvard and Yale were the first colleges to provide outdoor gymnasiums in 1826.[2]

Organized sports were in their infancy during the early half of the nineteenth century, as the schools' interest in physical activities began to mount. The early emphasis in gymnastics, tennis, foot races, and other active pursuits were steadily giving way to spectator amusements. Like swimming pools in the first years of the century, gymnasiums were few and far between. They were located in privately owned athletic clubs, the YMCA, and the high schools.

Although in colonial times public gardens, plazas, and public squares were set aside for the enjoyment of the people, it was not until 1853, when New York City acquired Central Park, that any city set aside land for strictly park purposes.

Creation of New York's Central Park involved a new recognition of the need for places within cities which would be available for the leisure use of all residents. The success of Central Park encouraged other cities to develop parks as sanctuaries from urban crowding and blight and as places for relaxation in a work oriented, industrializing society. For many years, however, parks were considered primarily for rest and relaxation and not for recreation activity.

In 1867 San Francisco acquired a 1,000 acre tract of sand dunes and marshland which John McLaren transformed into Golden Gate Park. Beautifully landscaped

with an exceptional variety of facilities for recreation, this magnificent urban park and Central Park have served as examples of large park areas which other cities throughout the nation have tried to emulate.

Sidney Lutzin and Edward H. Storey wrote: "As cities reached out into the suburbs, and metropolitan areas spread over the countryside, urbanites became increasingly conscious of the value of open space and of the need for action to secure and preserve it."[3]

The federal government played a major role early in the recreation and park movement to conserve large open space areas and other natural resources. The national park concept, which began with protection of the Yosemite Valley in 1864 and establishment of Yellowstone National Park in 1872, contributed to later growth of state, county, and municipal park systems. Acquisition of Yellowstone Park marked the beginning of the national park movement—to preserve the park for the enjoyment of future generations.

This period was characterized by the thoughtless exploitation of natural resources. "Forests, grasslands, wildlife, and water resources were laid waste with a prodigal hand," said Carlson, MacLean, Deppe, and Peterson. "Too late the cost of this careless policy was made apparent, and today America is still paying the cost of its early extravagance."[4]

The establishment of the American Forestry Association in 1875 helped unify the movement to save the forests. By the end of the nineteenth century, the first federal forest reserve was set aside in the West.

Educators were beginning to see the values in outdoor education and recreation. In 1861, Frederick William Gunn of the Connecticut Gunnery School for Boys took his entire student body on a two week camping trip, generally considered the first camping experience of its kind. About twenty years later, Ernest Balch organized the first private camp, and the YMCA started a camping program in its national organization.

The rise and development of voluntary

agencies characterized the nineteenth century, several of which took the responsibility of providing wholesome recreation opportunities and education for leisure. In 1851, the Young Men's Christian Association was introduced in Boston from England, and later, in 1866, the national YMCA was formed. By 1860, the first Boys Club was established in Hartford in an attempt to counteract the ills of the city. The first Young Women's Christian Association (YWCA) was organized in Boston in 1866.

In 1872, Brookline, Massachusetts, became the first city in the United States to set aside public lands for playgrounds, purchasing two lots for such purposes. During the same year, the Young Men's Christian Association built an outdoor gymnasium in Boston, which provided for games, athletics, and a running track.

The establishment of the "sandgardens" in Boston in 1885 and 1886 has come to be accepted by many historians as the origin of the "play movement." According to Martin and Esther Neumeyer, "The sandgarden was not a playground in the strict sense but was the beginning of a movement which eventuated in the establishment of playgrounds."[5]

The idea for the sandgardens originated with Dr. Marie E. Zakresewska when she was visiting in Germany. While summering in Berlin, she observed that children were playing with heaps of sand in the public parks. The first sandpiles in America were started in the yards of the Parmenter Street Chapel and the West End Nursery in Boston. There were no regular play supervisors provided during the first years, but in 1887, several women supervisors were hired.

In 1889, the Boston Park Department converted a ten-acre tract along the Charles River in a congested neighborhood into an open-air gymnasium for boys and men; two years later, one was opened for women and girls.

With the opening of the frontiers and the rise of cities in the nineteenth century, recreation took on many interesting forms, such as: folklore, social and square dancing, sleigh rides and skating, excursions to the beaches, travel to Europe, theaters, amusement parks, circuses, billiard rooms and pool halls, hunting and fishing, the bicycle, and growing interest in games, athletes, and sports.

The Industrial Revolution which began in the early 1800s mushroomed in the late years of the nineteenth century. Reynold Carlson, Janet MacLean, Theodore Deppe, and James Peterson wrote: "The rise of industry and the development of machine power brought drastic changes in the life of the people. As the machine replaced manpower work hours were decreased and new leisure became a right of all. The increase in industry resulted in a significant shift to urban living, with accompanying problems. With overcrowded conditions in the urban areas, the streets became the playgrounds. Organized efforts had to be made to set aside space for recreation opportunities."[6]

The experience in playground organization in Boston had a direct influence upon the organization of similar movements in other cities. A "model" playground was opened at Hull House in Chicago in 1892. The playground provided sandboxes as well as facilities for playing handball and indoor baseball. It was much larger than the earlier sandgardens and was able to accommodate older children. New York City provided for thirty-one playgrounds in 1898 under the direction of the State Board of Education. The city moved quickly to develop a network of playgrounds that would be paid for and administered completely by the city. All schools were required to have open-air playgrounds. The demand for city playgrounds was gradually supported by prominent civic leaders, businessmen, social and church workers, reformers, educators, and newspapermen. By the close of the century, fourteen American cities had made provision for supervised play facilities. "In each case, private initiative and financial support were prominent factors in getting the first playgrounds under way, and in bringing pressure upon city governments to accept responsibility for providing play areas."[7]

The founding of settlement houses was an

Figure 6–2 Chicago's Hull House, the first settlement house, had a major impact on the promotion of play activity in the United States. Jane Addams, founder of the Hull House, was very concerned with the need to provide varied forms of play in urban slums. In 1892, she was responsible for opening the first independent playground in Chicago in a vacant lot adjoining Hull House, and equipped it with swings, see–saws, slides, and sandboxes. (Courtesy University of Illinois Library at Chicago Circle Campus, Jane Addams Memorial Collection.)

attempt by social workers to meet the increasing problems resulting from urban living in the 1880s. The social settlement, which grew out of the humanitarian movement to aid the poor, made a great impact on the promotion of play activity in America. A well organized settlement provided recreation facilities for gymnasium and playground activities, swimming, club work, dramatics, dances, and various types of games and sports.

The first expression of the movement in the United States was in New York in 1887, fol-

lowed by the opening of the Hull House in Chicago by Jane Addams in 1889. Commonly called the community center, social settlements originally were located in slum areas but later became centers of education, recreation, and welfare activities in other areas of the community.

As the working people achieved a higher standard of living, increased leisure, and purchasing power, they also developed a new perspective for amusement and entertainment. Commercial amusements and various forms of play equipment also began to appear in the late nineteenth century. The circus reached its highest peak in the last quarter of the nineteenth century. Large shows played cities and towns, "pitching the big top wherever they could hope to draw a crowd. P. T. Barnum, William C. Coup, James A. Bailey, and the Ringling brothers were all instrumental in establishing the Greatest Show on Earth and attracting great popularity in the circus.

Adult roller skating, so popular in the 1880s, began to wane as bicycling became the most universal sport of any city and town. The 1890s, became known as the golden age of the wheel. Through the bicycle, an increasing number of Americans rediscovered the outdoors. People of all walks of life took to the wheel.

Toward the end of the 19th century, with transportation more easily available, amusement parks sprang up in the outlying districts of cities. By this time the penny arcade, the traveling medicine show, and the annual visit to the circus "big top" had become popular. Band concerts in the parks, huge holiday celebrations with fireworks on the Fourth of July, "taffy pulls" in the homes, and museums were now in small and large towns across the nation.[8]

During the closing years of the nineteenth century, blacks were still largely segregated from public recreation service. However, some voluntary organizations were attempting to bridge the gap. "During the early years of the recreation movement, the northern black was a recipient of some YMCA and settlement house recreation programs," wrote James Murphy, "although basically white children were the beneficiaries of organized recreation in the initial years of the movement.[9]

Meanwhile, municipal parks were being developed in areas throughout the country. The first metropolitan park system was established in Boston in 1892, while the first county system was in Essex County, New Jersey, in 1895. The New England Association of Park Superintendents, later known as the American Institute of Park Executives, was organized in 1898, bringing together park su-

perintendents to discuss and promote their professional concerns.

In 1904, Los Angeles was the first city in the United States to establish a municipal department with authority to organize, promote, conduct, and supervise recreation activities for people of all ages. The first record of anyone being employed in a leisure time occupation was in 1887, when several women were hired as supervisors for children's playgrounds in Boston.

In 1898, New York City opened thirty–one supervised playgrounds under the direction of the State Board of Education, and soon after, the city of New York developed a large network of playgrounds paid for and administered by the city government.

By the end of the nineteenth century, at least fourteen American cities had made provisions for supervised public recreation. By the turn of the century, the pattern for municipal park and recreation programs was well established.

A number of pioneers of the public recreation movement—men such as Joseph Lee, Henry Curtis, Clark Hetherington, and Luther Halsey Gulick—made major contributions in providing a fuller rationale for the need for public recreation. Many noted psychologists and educators provided their views and theories regarding the values of play in human growth and development.

SOCIAL REFORMS INFLUENCING THE RECREATION MOVEMENT

Toward the end of the nineteenth century, people began speaking out on the national scene deploring the breakdown in human relationships that the Industrial Revolution had created. Social investigators became deeply concerned by the suffering, poverty, and squalor of the masses who lived squeezed into the United States' large cities. Newspapers, books, and magazines all aroused the American public to support great social and civic reforms.

Social movements were beginning to stir. The YMCA, founded in Boston in 1851, grew rapidly and was soon offering basketball leagues, baseball, gymnastics, and other athletic events. Free public schools, perhaps the most notable achievement in American society, began to appear in growing numbers. New concepts in education and psychology made a more realistic approach to the needs of children. Churches took the initiative in developing recreation programs for children and families, which contributed much to social interaction.

Many of the conditions that gave rise to the recreation movement had their origins in the last half of the nineteenth century. Some of the conditions that influenced the shape of the movement included the following:

1. Effects of the Industrial Revolution
2. Modern science and technology
3. Changing work patterns
4. Urbanization
5. Increase in population
6. Rise in crime and delinquency
7. Depletion of natural resources
8. Increase in mental illness patients
9. Expansion of commercial recreation opportunities
10. Greater mobility of the population
11. Need for greater unification in recreation efforts

According to Thomas Yukic, the recreation movement in the United States was essentially a social one from its beginning. Social leaders pointed out such evils as dangerous streets, delinquency, unsanitary living conditions, child labor, congestion of cities, and lack of space for play and rest. A new psychology emerged during the movement that declared that "the child should be the center of the educational effort and that his play during leisure was acceptable and worthwhile."[10]

The idea of providing organized recreation programs as a social service originated with private settlement houses, not with governments. The private social welfare movement, led by Joseph Lee of Boston, was the first to understand the importance of play programs for children of immigrant tenement dwellers. The success of these private efforts resulted in pressures on municipal governments to provide similar services. As America changed from a rural to an urban society, increasing numbers of citizens were concentrated in dense residential and industrial districts.

THE EARLY TWENTIETH CENTURY

By the early 1900s, most large cities had parks much like Central Park and the role of urban governments as park land providers was well established. Public support for municipal parks continued to grow throughout the country.

With the exception of Boston, Chicago's South Park playground system influenced the development of playgrounds and recreation in the United States more than any other city. Indeed, the creation of small parks in Chicago made a tremendous impact on the growth of the recreation movement.

Voters of South Chicago approved a $5 million bond issue to acquire and develop neighborhood parks in 1903, and two years later neighborhood parks were opened. Soon, the concept of "parks to the people" was being accepted nationwide, as municipal governments began to assume increasing responsibility for neighborhood and community recreation programs.

The success of the planned parks was a great influence in extending the recreational use of parks in other cities. Reynold Carlson, Theodore Deppe, and Janet MacLean wrote: "With their carefully planned fieldhouses and their spacious outdoor areas, the playgrounds represented the first acceptance of public responsibility for indoor and outdoor recreation facilities, for varied interest programs, for recreation outlets for all ages, for year–round activities, and for leadership as well as facilities."[11]

In the early 1900s, small parks began to appear in many city neighborhoods. A trend began to emerge—city planning, esthetic influences, and a new concern for play habits of people. From 1900 to 1904, four cities—

Figure 6–3 Creation of small parks in Chicago's South Park District represented the first acceptance of public responsibility for play, sports, and social centers in congested industrial neighborhoods. The outdoor scene above was an adult lawn game at Washington Park soon after the neighborhood parks opened in 1905. (Courtesy Chicago Historical Society.)

Chicago, Los Angeles, Rochester, and Boston—developed recreation centers that could be open twelve months of the year to the public. In the South, however, blacks were still denied access to most public facilities and were restricted almost entirely from recreation participation.

As industry expanded into great corporations with thousands of employees, further economic and social changes became apparent. Work patterns became more specialized. The rapid growth in population was matched by a strong move toward urbanization. The result was a serious congestion of large cities, giving rise to slums, crime, epidemics, and other social ills.

By 1906, the movement for municipal public recreation had grown to such a level that playground promoters meeting in Washington, D.C., founded the Playground and Recreation Association of America (PRAA), later to become the National Recreation and Park Association. Luther Halsey Gulick became its president, while Henry Curtis was elected its first secretary. Formation of the association was considered by many historians as the single most important event in the American recreation movement. The drive for playgrounds was given new impetus and qualified national leadership. Richard F. Knapp wrote that "Leaders of the organization soon began to foster municipal responsibility for provision of public recreation for all people, a wider concept of recreation, and a sense of professionalism among workers in the field."[12]

Within a few years, two new leaders accepted the top positions in the PRAA and were to head it for decades. Joseph Lee, a Harvard–bred Boston philanthropist and social worker, was elected president, while social worker Howard Braucher became its executive secretary. Under the effective leadership of Lee and Braucher, the association, as well as the playground movement, prospered and moved closer to the so–called "community movement," which enjoyed its peak influence in the United States during World War I.

By 1914, attention was centered on neighborhood and community interests. Increasing emphasis on the importance of the community received widespread acceptance by the PRAA and the recreation movement. Encouraging an attitude of community and cooperation among the users of public recreation, Braucher felt citizens should be able to develop a stronger community spirit. According to Clarence Rainwater, the period from 1915–18 was known as the "neighborhood organization" stage. Through its field secretaries and annual conventions, the PRAA promoted community spirit and was most instrumental in developing municipal recreation on a neighborhood basis. The number of municipalities with recreation centers in schools soon increased to more than 150 cities.[13]

Forest and park conservation programs at all levels of government were given considerable impetus by creation of the United States Forest Service in 1905 and the National Park Service in 1916. Although nineteen colleges and universities had estabished schools of forestry by 1910, there was still no curriculum established for the primary purpose of training people for the management of outdoor recreation resources for recreation.

Professional training in recreation is said to have started in 1909 when a normal course in play was assembled and published by a committee of twenty–three pioneers in the recreation movement under the chairmanship of Clark W. Hetherington. Within a year after its organization in 1906, and at its first National Recreation Congress, the association appointed the committee on the normal course in play.

FATHER OF THE AMERICAN PLAYGROUND

Joseph Lee, known as the "father of the playground movement," was perhaps the most influential of the pioneers of the recreation movement. Born in 1862, Lee was a lawyer and a philanthropist who came from a wealthy New England family. His father instilled in young Lee a sense of social responsibility and a desire to serve humanity. His social work experience in the 1890s proved very useful in learning the importance of both governmental and private responsibility in social improvement. It also taught him the necessity for well–planned and organized campaigns of reform.

Shocked to see boys arrested for playing in the streets, Lee organized a playground for them in an open lot, which he supervised. In 1898, Lee was responsible for the creation of a model playground in Boston, which featured a play area for small children, a boys' section, a sports field, and individual gardens.

As his influence expanded, Lee was in great demand as a speaker and writer on playgrounds. He recognized the great creative power of individuals, and argued that the key element in a municipal recreation system was the one who headed it. He often lectured on the relationship of strong individuals to a healthy society. If he emphasized individualism, however, he also supported cooperation and the community of individuals. Before 1902, he wrote that "It is no longer what I can do for you, but what we can do for ourselves and our country." If people would just get together and work for the common good, all of the individuals too could benefit.[14]

Lee was the first to express, in *Play in Education* (1910), a modern interpretation of play and its meaning to society and youth. Play, Lee argued, was the serious activity in children's adjustment to life. He felt recreation had vital significance not only for children but also for everyone who wanted a meaningful life.

According to Lee, quality was more important than quantity, in both individual and community efforts. He believed in efficiency. The key to quality was through fixed goals, organization, and expertise. He emphasized education for the wise use of leisure as the means to help people achieve happy, creative lives.

Lee was president of the Playground Association of America from 1910 until his death in 1937 and was also a leading lecturer of the National Recreation School, a one–year course for carefully selected college graduates. The tremendous expansion of municipal recreation during this period was largely due to the work of the Association under his leadership.[15]

THE SECOND DECADE OF THE TWENTIETH CENTURY

During the early part of the new century, a social and civic center movement began in the public schools to meet the needs of an adult population through social, educational, cultural, and civic activities.

Although the school building was considered taboo for recreational use, a system of social centers was initiated in Rochester, New York, in 1907, under the leadership of a former minister and athlete, E. J. Ward.

The Rochester plan was a pioneer attempt to establish the public school center as a catalyst in American social life, to help develop community interest, and to spread democratic ways. Spurred on by Rochester's successful example, other cities began to use

Figure 6–4 Father of the American playground—Joseph Lee. As president of the Playground Association of America from 1910 to his death in 1937, Lee was instrumental in the tremendous expansion of municipal recreation during this period. (Courtesy Ms. Susan Lee.)

their schools as centers for music, drama, and other cultural interests. . . . As early as 1910, pioneers such as Clarence A. Perry adopted an educational philosophy which recognized that the school plant belonged to the people and it was proper for it to be used for social purposes.[16]

By the end of the first decade of the twentieth century, educators as well as recreation and park leaders were advocating the need for enlarging school building sites to accommodate playgrounds. Increasingly, playgrounds were being located near primary and intermediate schools and on neighborhood playfields and parks adjacent to junior and senior high schools.

An early application of the park–school concept was made in Glencoe, Illinois, in 1931. Increasing emphasis was being placed upon the importance of cooperation among school, park, recreation and municipal authorities in meeting community needs for indoor and outdoor recreation areas and facilities. The park–school idea continued to spread in the 1940s and 1950s. The use of schools as community centers increased during World War I.

Until the first public playgrounds and parks, there were no planned and supervised recreation activities. School grounds were fenced and closed after three o'clock on school days and all day on weekends and vacation days. Children and youth were forced to find their play in the public streets and in vacant lots, which were ill–suited to organized games.

The first playgrounds were dirt or sand fields, leveled, fenced, and equipped for childhood and youth sports, such as running and tag games, baseball, basketball, football, and soccer.

The Boy Scouts of America was organized in 1910, while the Girl Scouts and Camp Fire Girls were started in 1912. The organization of these agencies emphasized the growing concern for organized recreation for youth. The camping movement received much impetus between 1910 and 1914, as many youth camps and private camps were organized.

Schools, both high schools and colleges, were placing more emphasis on athletics. Intramural sports gained a foothold about 1914 and have made steady progress since.

When the United States entered World War I, the recreation needs of men serving their country were soon recognized as being of great importance. In 1917, the War Department requested the PRAA to assist communities near training camps in providing recreation activities for soldiers and sailors. The War Camp Community Service (WCCS) was organized to entertain in homes, and

musical, social, and athletic programs were developed for training camps. "Before the war ended," wrote Thomas Yukic, "WCCS had organized social and recreation resources of over 6500 communities near military camps and 50 war industry districts. As a result, a great range of local communities had, through this participation, become conscious for the first time of the power and functions of organized recreation."[17]

Service to underprivileged communities was beginning to receive stronger emphasis in organized recreation programs. A concept of recreation service for the entire community began to emerge as programs increased at playgrounds and recreation centers.

The problems and needs of black Americans were beginning to be recognized by a growing number of those in the field. In 1919, the Playground and Recreation Association of America hired Ernest T. Attwell, a black, to work for the Association. Although concerted efforts were made by Attwell and the Bureau of Colored Work to reach all citizens, still only token results were achieved in the black community. "Some Negroes found private and voluntary recreation facilities as good alternatives to public, tax–supported programs," said James Murphy.[18]

Perhaps the most significant contribution of education to the recreation movement during the decade was the inclusion of the "worthy use of leisure" as an important objective for education in the National Education Association's Seven Cardinal Principles of 1918.

THE DECADE AFTER WORLD WAR I

A period of prosperity followed the war and brought with it a marked increase in appreciation of the importance of recreation. Americans had more money to spend for leisure than at any previous time. Laboring classes were working shorter hours, and the population of cities was increasing. Indeed, the nation in the "Golden Twenties" had become a nation at play as well as at work. For the first time, play was beginning to be recognized as one of the major interests of life.

Automobiles, radios, motion pictures, tourist travel, large sports events, and many other opportunities came within the reach of many people. A phenomenal upsurge of interest in both private and public recreation facilities such as new parks, community houses, swimming pools, dance halls, picnic areas, golf courses, beaches, skating rinks, and bowling establishments swept the country.

"The automobile through these years progressively opened up broader and broader horizons in the field of recreation," wrote Foster Rhea Dulles and Preston W. Slossan. "It provided the easiest possible means of transportation from the country to the amusements of town or city, and from town or city to the sports and outdoor activities of the country. For countless millions the automobile was for the first time bringing the golf course, tennis court, or bathing beach within practical reach. It made holiday picnics in the country and weekend excursions to hunt or fish vastly easier. It greatly stimulated the whole outdoor movement, making camping possible for many people. It provided a means of holiday travel for a people always wanting to be on the move."[19]

An emphasis on legislation for recreation and parks also followed World War I. New laws were passed in many states giving cities the legal authority to provide organized park and recreation services. In addition to the school board or park group, recreation commissions were created with power to expand appropriations, employ workers, and provide year–round systems.

During the period from 1915 to 1925 more than twenty states passed enabling legislation permitting their political subdivisions to set up and operate broad recreation programs. A spurt in recreation spending followed such favorable legislation.

The forty–hour workweek became a reality, and public officials, educators, and recreation professionals began to give increased thought to extending recreation programs and facilities.

In 1921, the National Conference of State Parks was organized to further the state park movement, preceded by the formation of the National Park Service in 1916. By 1926, the number of cities possessing parks grew from 100 in 1892 to 1620 in 1926.

Many state park systems were established between 1920 and 1940. They were strongly encouraged by expanded federal conservation assistance programs of the New Deal period.

Commercial recreation boomed for a population with increased purchasing power. Spectator sports increased in popularity, and women began to join in sports activities without fear of embarrassment. Interest in the development of outdoor recreation prompted President Calvin Coolidge to call a National Conference of Outdoor Recreation in 1924.

By the quarter century mark, the concept of parks had changed, and as organized active recreation began to be accepted, there was a greater demand for facilities for active recreation, such as ball grounds and tennis courts. At this time, a distinct conflict arose. Many playground leaders were trained in physical education and had no training in landscape architecture or general park design. At the same time, according to Charles Doell and Gerald Fitzgerald, "The disciples of Olmstead frequently lacked the breadth of understanding to accept the new trend of recreation and to incorporate those demands into suitable designs."[20] As a result, active recreation facilities often marred previously well–designed parks, and barren–looking playgrounds were established in many neighborhoods.

THE GREAT DEPRESSION

After the period of heavy spending and inflation in the 1920s, a great depression followed which was unequaled in history. In the depression years, employment was very scarce. Unemployment reached as high as 28 percent of the working force of the nation. In 1931, revenues of municipal government declined.

To combat the mass unemployment, the Roosevelt Administration's New Deal started an extensive public works program that operated on the principle that any kind of work was better than none. Work projects were established including a project in the field of community public recreation. These relief programs served to stimulate mass recognition of recreation in the community. The federal public works and social programs of the 1930s placed substantial emphasis on park, recreation, and cultural efforts in the cities.

During the third year of the depression, the Federal Emergency Relief Administration (FERA) was established with the prime purpose of providing employment. The FERA took two approaches: (1) the construction of facilities; (2) the development of recreation programs and activities under trained leadership.

The FERA, the Works Projects Administration (WPA), and the Civilian Conservation Corps (CCC) all served to advance the status of recreation. They also aided in the rehabilitation of the country. Besides providing jobs, the projects were responsible for the construction and improvement of centers, parks, picnic areas, roads, trails, and similar facilities. In addition, the WPA provided one of the most intensive training programs for recreation workers ever attempted.

To supplement the work of these agencies, a demand arose for recreation leaders to supervise the new facilities and to provide direction to the programs. Thus, many recreation jobs were created in the newly constructed recreation centers. WPA leaders worked under the supervision of local tax–supported units such as recreation departments, park boards, planning boards, departments of education, recreation councils, and welfare boards.

Interestingly, an increased emphasis on recreation was one result of the depression. Carlson, MacLean, Deppe, and Peterson explained that: "The modified workweek, shortened in order to spread available work among more people, gave more leisure. Commercial recreation programs closed for lack of business, since people no longer could pay admission prices. A heavier demand was placed on facilities and programs of voluntary and municipal agencies, which were unable to handle the increased needs. This dilemma caused federal agencies to try to take up the slack, giving the recreation movement more impetus."[21]

There were numerous errors or shortcomings in the emergency programs in the 1930s, but there was no doubt of the beneficial contributions they provided the rapidly growing recreation and parks field.

To meet the increased demand for professionally trained personnel for administrative and leadership positions in the broad recreation field, recreation majors and curriculum in various forms were initiated in several colleges and universities. The first college conference on training recreation leaders was held in 1937 under the joint sponsorship of the University of Minnesota and the WPA Recreation Division.

New municipal and county departments were being established with combined park and recreation functions, and many of the separate park and recreation departments were being consolidated.

RECREATION AND WORLD WAR II

The nation was slowly recovering from the depression when the United States entered World War II in December 1941. The American people have never united and cooperated so strongly in war work as they did during World War II. Nearly total effort went into the operation of agencies and organizations which contributed directly to those in the armed forces.

As the United States went to war, so did recreation—the USO, American Red Cross, Army Special Services Division, the Welfare and Recreation section of the Bureau of Naval Personnel, and the Recreation Service of the Marine Corps. They promoted programs in training centers, close to the battle fronts, on ships, in hospitals and rest centers, in industrial centers, and in every area of the nation where people were working to produce

Figure 6–5 As spectator sports increased in popularity, many large athletic stadiums and facilities, such as beautiful Wrigley Field in Chicago, were built in the larger cities. (Courtesy Chicago Cubs National League Baseball Club.)

for war. Recreation contributed to every aspect of the war effort. It was recognized as a definite "morale builder," relieving tension and lessening the worries of the millions of citizens in the thousands of communities throughout the nation.

The Special Services Division in the Army had charge of providing facilities and programs for recreation and entertainment on the various military posts. Approximately twelve–thousand special service officers and several times that number of enlisted men and thousands of volunteers made possible the program.

The United Service Organizations, formed in 1941, consisted of six national agencies: Salvation Army, Catholic Community Services, YMCA, YWCA, Jewish Welfare Board, and the National Travelers Aid. Their prime role was to serve the leisure needs of the armed services in community settings and to provide recreation for industrial workers engaged in the war effort.

The American Red Cross provided recreation in leave areas overseas, on posts throughout the world, and for programs in hospitals, both overseas and at home. The program offered opportunities in all fields of recreation.

In 1941, industry accepted a responsibility for recreation as it organized the National Industrial Recreation Association.

Meanwhile, in American communities, many civilian programs had to be curtailed during World War II due to worker shortage and travel restrictions. However, local recreation and park departments offered new programs to support the war effort. These included salvage drives, victory gardens, learn–to–swim programs, and many teen–

Figure 6–6 Founder of the Los Angeles City recreation and parks department—George Hjelte. Among his many accomplishments, Hjelte was a major force in the acquisition, development, and operation of fourteen miles of public beaches along the Pacific coast. Retiring as general manager in 1962, he had devoted sixty years to the public recreation field. In 1974, he was recognized by the National Recreation and Park Association for contributions in the American park and recreation movement—as an administrator, author, and speaker; statesman, consultant, and true professional. (Courtesy City of Los Angeles Recreation and Parks Department.)

canteen programs to counteract the increase of juvenile delinquency. Youth–serving agencies made equipment and supplies for military recreation centers and sold war bonds. Many municipal recreation departments extended their facilities and services to local war plants, serving war–industry workers around the clock.

FOLLOWING WORLD WAR II

By the end of the war, the great numbers of servicemen and servicewomen who had been exposed to the variety of recreation programs and services had developed a new appreciation of this field of organized service. The many individuals who had been trained and gained experience in recreation programs were ready to assume professional jobs in civilian life.

Many communities established parks, pools, civic centers, and other recreation facilities as memorials to their war dead. Much of this activity was used to build much needed recreation facilities which supplemented existing community buildings or areas.

From 1950 to 1970, there was an unprecedented growth in the number of new departments of recreation and parks opening in cities, counties, and other municipal units. A trend by municipalities to combine the formerly separate departments of parks and recreation into one governmental agency developed during the late 1950s.

Tax–supported public recreation systems increased in number. The expansion of state participation in the recreation field was a striking postwar trend. The states increased their efforts in establishing programs to improve recreation facilities and services. New state recreation commissions and boards, state youth authorities, and state interagency recreation committees were established. The formation of special districts was a growing trend throughout the country.

The development of recreation programs in the hospitals was advanced significantly, particularly in Armed Forces hospitals, veterans' hospitals, state neuropsychiatric hospitals, and children's hospitals.

Public recreation had become an established part of American culture and an accepted reponsibility of all levels of government. According to Knapp, "Outdoor recreation was available in national, state, and local park systems. Expenditures for public recreation by local governments exceeded by several times the combined state and federal outlay."[22]

Increase of public interest in recreation and the rise of inflation resulted in sharply increased expenditures for recreation on all fronts. As a result, more money was being spent for commercial recreation, as well as community recreation. Youth centers gained popularity as enthusiastic parents, genuinely interested in the welfare of their children, provided increased support to these and other community endeavors.

During the first half of the twentieth century, "the National Recreation Association provided significant leadership in fostering the expansion of organized municipal recreation in the United States. The Association rendered important services, such as field assistance to local proponents of public recreation, a central clearinghouse for information, training programs as well as the formulation of standards to further the establishment of a new profession on a solid footing."[23]

THE 1950s TO THE PRESENT

A tremendous expansion of recreation and leisure activity occurred in the 1950s in all areas of the field including public recreation, voluntary agency recreation, employee recreation, Armed Forces recreation, commercial recreation, and recreation for the ill and handicapped.

The medical profession, psychiatrists and physical medicine specialists in particular, became interested in the potentials of recreation for helping in the treatment and rehabilitation of the ill and injured. During this period, the Council for the Advancement of Hospital Recreation was organized.

Growth of Leisure

Leisure pursuits were changing significantly. Leisure continued to increase for many segments of the population, such as the aged person, the school dropout, the unemployed, the unemployable, and the youth who refused to accept establishment work roles. A great many Americans found themselves with more discretionary time and money. Tremendous increases in international travel also occurred during this period.

Commercial Recreation Boom

The decade of the 1960s witnessed a tremendous expansion of commercial and outdoor recreation facilities. The boating and camping industries became billion dollar businesses. Creative amusement parks such as Disneyland were being established, and professional and collegiate sports enjoyed unprecedented success.

Environmental Concerns

In the late 1960s and the early 1970s, the American public developed a great concern for the quality of the environment. The nation became alarmingly aware of the vanishing forests, air pollution, water pollution, inner city decay, noise pollution, and the problems of population explosion. President Nixon's first official act in 1970 was to approve the National Environmental Policy Act of 1969, which declares that it is the policy of the federal government, in cooperation with other levels of government and public and private organization, "to create and maintain conditions under which man and nature can exist in productive harmony." With more people, increased leisure, and greater mobility, public lands were being used more extensively. A new challenge involved the struggle for open space, not merely its acquisition, but its maintenance protection.

A nationwide survey concluded in 1961 by the National Committee on Encroachment of Recreation Lands and Waters did much to alarm the nation of the scope of the encroachment threat.

The survey indicated that within a ten–year period, 2687 acres of recreation land were lost in 257 areas recording encroachment. The estimated land value in 44 of these areas alone was nearly $9 million. Millions of dollars of irreplaceable park lands and open spaces slipped away from public recreation use, into the path of highways, commercial and industrial enterprises, schools, community buildings, and housing developments.[24]

The National Park Service and the United States Forest Service both implemented new programs to improve and develop the national parks and recreation areas. The Outdoor Recreation Resources Review Commission established by Congress requested an estimate of needs for outdoor recreation space in the year 2000. Subsequently, in 1963, President John F. Kennedy created the Bureau of Outdoor Recreation in the Department of the Interior.

Urban Affairs

In the 1960s, the federal government substantially increased its involvement in urban affairs through such actions as:

- Establishment of the Department of Housing and Urban Development to coordinate and administer national urban programs.
- Creation of Model Cities and community action programs to address the needs of disadvantaged city residents and improve inner city living conditions.

- The Open Space Land Program to help shape urban growth and provide urban parks and recreation facilities.
- Expanded urban renewal programs to rejuvenate blighted areas.

With the sharp increase in the number of elderly citizens, stronger emphasis was given to programs and facilities involving the aged population. The White House Conference on the Aging in 1961 placed considerable emphasis on recreation for "senior citizens."

In 1965, the Administration on Aging was established as a part of the Social and Rehabilitation Services of the Department of Health, Education, and Welfare. Older Americans Act of 1965 provided for federal assistance to local agencies for the improvement of centers and programs for the aging, including recreation facilities and activities. In 1974, the Housing and Community Development Act was passed, enabling communities to make applications to the Department of Housing and Urban Development for grants in support of various kinds of community improvements.

The Land and Water Conservation Fund was initiated in 1964 to provide federal aid in outdoor recreation to states and local communities. This act provides matching grant–in–aid funds to the states and their political subdivisions to be used for planning, acquiring, and developing outdoor recreational areas.

The Job Corps and other community action programs, under provisions of the Economic Opportunity Act, prepared young people for work, similar to the Civilian Conservation Corps activity of the 1930s.

The creation of the Urban Affairs Department by the National Recreation and Park Association in 1967 and the employment of Ira J. Hutchison, Jr., has brought increased focus and recognition to the culturally deprived. Forums, seminars, and institutes have brought together national professional and lay leaders to identify areas of need and to establish guidelines and steps for serving the urban disadvantaged.

Figure 6–7 Environmental quality. The need to protect and preserve our natural resources began to receive governmental and public attention. The Wilderness Act of 1964 was designed to preserve areas in their natural form and provide a natural habitat for the diminishing wildlife population, like this scenic area in Gallatin National Forest in Montana. (Courtesy U.S. Forest Service.)

Professional Merger

In 1965, five different organizations within the broad field of recreation and parks merged into a single body known as the National Recreation and Park Association. Soon, other groups, such as the National Association of Recreation Therapists and the Armed Forces Section of the American Recreation Society, fully merged their interests with the newly formed organization. Today, the National Recreation and Park Association is an independent, nonprofit organization intended to promote the development of the park and recreation movement.

Other highly significant governmental ac-

tions included the establishment of a unified wilderness system in 1964; the 1966 Historic Preservation Act; and the creation of the Wild and Scenic Rivers Program in 1968 for the purpose of establishing within the United States certain rivers of national significance. The intent of the legislation is to preserve these rivers in their free–flowing conditions for the benefit and enjoyment of present and future generations.

The Water Resources Development Act of 1974 provided the legislation to undertake the initial phase of the engineering and design plan of seventeen multipurpose water resource projects at various locations in the nation. The projects developed by the Army

Corps of Engineers have demonstrated strong outdoor recreation potential.

The 1954 Supreme Court decisions affecting integration paved the way for desegregation of public recreation and amusement facilities. As a result, segregation in public recreation facilities, public housing, and interstate travel facilities was held to be unconstitutional. The blacks' demands for equality began to spread throughout the nation. The demonstrations in the early 1960s at lunch counters and outdoor theatres were followed shortly by much stronger demands and protest demonstrations.

Youth Fitness

New concern for the physical fitness of youth and adults received strong emphasis in the 1950s. The Kraus-Weber survey showed that American youth lagged far behind young Europeans in basic levels of physical fitness. Almost 58 percent of Americans were unable to pass a series of tests; only 8.7 percent of Europeans failed. Soon after, in 1956, President Eisenhower's newly created Council on Youth Fitness called for a national conference on youth fitness which produced significant results. Programs to improve fitness were developed in most states. Many public recreation departments expanded programs involving fitness classes, conditioning, jogging, and sports for people of all ages.

Special Populations

Increased emphasis was given to the provision of special services for the physically and mentally disabled, as the specialized field of therapeutic recreation services expanded steadily in this period. The federal government, in particular, sharply increased its aid to special education. In recreation, new services aided retarded children, youth, and adults.

Additional concern for mental fitness and the role of recreation in mental health included the Washington Conference on Recreation for the Mentally Ill in 1957 by the American Association of Health, Physical Education, and Recreation.

A "cultural explosion" involving the performing arts as leisure outlets resulted in a marked expansion of cultural centers, performing organizations, museums, and art centers. Evidence of the increased national impetus is the 1958 act of Congress that made possible the National Cultural Center for the Performing Arts.

The growing urban crisis, civil unrest, dissent, and alienation marked the late 1960s and the early 1970s. Many problems continued to plague the nation: the needs of disadvantaged citizens, particularly members of minority groups; growing black militancy; the wave of urban riots in the 1960s; relaxation of moral standards; drug abuse; violence and a growing disregard for law and order; distrust in government; the energy crisis, and the economy.

Youth Rebellion

Conflicting lifestyles and interests, particularly between generations, seemed to threaten the stability of the society. Young people wanted new kinds of experiences and personal relationships, as many of the traditional forms of recreation seemed no longer relevant. Although the youth rebellion subsided in the 1970s, it had made a significant mark on society.

Federal Funding

Communities experienced numerous changes in the 1960s and 1970s which have affected the role of public recreation. The impacts of federal contributions to local financing were broadened through enactment of General Revenue Sharing, Community Development Block Grants, the Comprehensive Employment and Training Act and other public works and employment programs. The change which had the strongest impact has been development of federal grant programs and the surrender of state and local controls under federal pressure. This has produced new guidelines, standards, social and po-

Figure 6–8 Gateway National Recreation Area in New York City provides an opportunity for urban dwellers to experience the relaxing benefits of a natural environment close to the sea. Gateway's Sandy Hook unit, above, provides long, wide beaches and quiet bayside coves—a haven for a wide variety of shore birds and other wildlife. Interpretive nature walks, like the one at left at the Staten Island unit, are conducted regularly at Gateway. (Courtesy New York City Department of Parks and Recreation.)

litical values, and a tendency towards uniformity of guidelines under federal supervision.

As Jesse Reynolds and Marion Hormachea pointed out: "Local and state governments, short of new sources of local revenue, have tended to be dependent on the federal government for funds and this has, in turn, resulted in greatly increased federal control, often politically oriented."[25]

Every level of government in the 1970s substantially increased expenditures for recreation resources and services. However, these increases have not kept pace with in-

flation in costs of land, construction, energy, and staffing. As a result, many of the open space and recreation problems identified in the 1962 Outdoor Recreation Resources Review Commission (ORRRC) Report and most of the urban problems of the 1960s still exist. The 1978 National Urban Recreation Study Report stated that: "These problems have been intensified by the fiscal crisis in many cities and by the energy crisis which calls for more close–to–home recreation opportunities."[26] In the 1970s, these concerns stimulated proposals for urban national parks, leading to the establishment of National

Recreation areas in New York City (Gateway), San Francisco (Golden Gate), and the Cleveland–Akron area (Cuyahoga Valley).

Urban Recreation

From 1973 on, proposals increased for national action in urban areas around the country, and many bills for new urban recreation areas were introduced in Congress. The National Urban Recreation Study Report suggested that: "These proposals pose a dilemma for Congress, and the Department of the Interior. On the one hand were recognized needs for acquisition, development, and management of existing and authorized parks; on the other were seemingly astronomical costs for land, facilities, and services in newly proposed national urban recreation areas."[27]

Leisure Services

Increasingly, the mission of the park and recreation movement had become clearer: to enhance the quality of life through the provision of opportunities for the meaningful use of leisure. New patterns of recreation behavior were established, including membership in local private recreation clubs, enrollment in adult education, and increased tourist and travel activity.

The Education Amendments Act of 1974 (Community Schools Act) focused attention on the use of public schools by establishing a program to provide educational, recreational, cultural, and other related community services through the use of the community education program as a center for such activities in cooperation with other community groups.

Professional Curricula

Curriculums in the professional preparation of recreation and park personnel expanded rapidly during the 1960s and 1970s. Two-year curriculums in community colleges and junior colleges have developed associate degree programs, which can lead to four-year undergraduate degrees and the master's and doctor's degrees. The number of colleges and universities offering undergraduate and graduate training in professional recreation leadership increased sharply as municipalities rapidly established local departments of recreation and parks.

Professional committees and conferences were organized to deal with the need for personnel standards and controls, including certification and registration planning. Janet MacLean wrote: "With the upgrading of professional preparation and the implementation of certification and registration procedures, the recreation and park profession is better able to ensure qualified leadership for the profession."[28]

International Recreation

International recreation received growing attention as a result of international conferences and travel abroad by recreation and park personnel for study and observation. In 1956, the International Recreation Association was formed, and its first congress was held in Philadelphia.

New Innovations

With the pressure of increasing social crisis in the cities, austerity budgets, and the changing roles of government, those responsible for recreation services have found it necessary to develop innovations and new approaches to program planning and to secure additional means of financial support. In meeting the needs of a new technological age and a society rapidly becoming leisure-oriented, all aspects of recreation program planning, including the underlying philosophy, have had to be revised.

RECREATION AND PARK DEVELOPMENT IN CANADA

While the history of recreation and park development in Canada paralleled in many ways that of the United States, there were certain differences. There are a number of major differences between the countries, with respect to geography and climate, ethnic makeup, and cultural tradition.

Leslie Bella, recreation educator in Canada, wrote of her country's "bilingualism and multiculturalism; curious constitutional bondage to Britain; Northern climate and native peoples; national parks, sparse population and resource–based industries; and acceptance of government involvement in many areas."[29]

According to Elsie McFarland, "Public recreation was slow to develop in Canada's larger cities, but with a dramatic growth in population and trend toward urbanization following World War II, there was a major

growth of local public recreation authorities. Canadian federal and provincial governments have shared responsibility with local governments for the financing and construction of numerous parks, centers, and other facilities, along with assisting in special programs and projects."[30]

As in the United States, supervised playgrounds in Canada were developed to meet the needs of poor families in urban slums with a high incidence of crime, disease, and drunkenness. Private citizens were instrumental in promoting the needs for playgrounds.

"There is ample evidence that the playground movement in Canada was part of the same movement that was spreading across

Figure 6–9 Federal and provincial governments in Canada increasingly are promoting recreation and leisure services. Ski areas in British Columbia are among the world's finest, as pictured by this beautiful winter scene at Cypress Provincial Park in West Vancouver. (Courtesy Tourism British Columbia.)

the United States," wrote McFarland. "Canadian leaders received much of their inspiration from United States' leaders and took an active part in United States' conferences."[31]

In cities located particularly in western provinces, citizens' organizations concerned with civic development, the schools, or promoting athletics or cultural activities, merged into community leagues. These leagues promoted the development of playgrounds, swimming pools, community centers, and similar recreation facilities.

Federal and provincial governments, increasingly began to take an interest in community recreation. Provincial grants were assigned to local recreation committees to aid them in sponsoring programs. The growing public concern about recreation led to plans for the preparation of professional leaders in this field. The Canadian Parks and Recreation Association, founded in 1945, has been very instrumental in promoting professional development in Canada.

In her 1970 report on leisure in Canada, McFarland wrote: "Much progress has been made in public recreation in Canada in recent years. Recreation was now recognized to the extent that universities were offering degree programs in it, and federal grants had given sufficient assistance to municipalities to permit them to offer competitive salaries to recreation professionals."[32]

A national conference on leisure at Montmorency, Quebec in 1969 resulted in several major recommendations which called for: (1) a clarification of values of leisure in Canadian society, to involve not only the providers of recreation, but also the consumers; (2) national goals and interdepartmental planning and legislation to insure environmental resource protection and appropriate development of facilities and open spaces in both urban and rural settings; (3) a strengthened program of education for leisure, as well as improvement of research efforts in this field; and (4) the development of strategies for effective programs of cooperation, involving major federal, provincial, and local agencies, as well as voluntary and nongovernmental organizations.[33]

The recommendation which seemed to characterize the feelings of those who participated in the Montmorency Conference was "the desire to develop coherent and intelligent leisure policies applicable to the Canadian context, rather than to continue to develop without planning or to be excessively influenced by patterns of professional development in other nations."[34]

QUESTIONS FOR DISCUSSION

1. The recreation movement is said to be the result of a combination of ideas, experiments, and developments. Discuss those which have had the greatest impact.
2. Identify some of the social forces that played prominent roles in the growth of recreation in the United States.
3. Establishment of the sandgardens is generally accepted as the origin of the play movement. How did the idea originate?
4. Why did the creation of small parks in Chicago in the early 1900s make such a tremendous impact on the growth of the recreation movement?
5. Many historians consider the formation of The Playground Association of America as the single most important event in the American recreation movement. Why was the PRAA (later NRPA) so instrumental in the development of parks and public recreation?
6. What were some of Joseph Lee's great qualities and why is he known as the "father of the playground movement?"

7. How did the economic depression of the 1930s in the United States contribute to the growth of recreation?
8. Describe the unprecedented growth of recreation and park systems from 1950 to 1970.
9. In the 1960s, the federal government's involvement in urban affairs increased substantially. What programs had the greatest impact on the recreation and parks movement?
10. Review the nation's growing concern for environmental quality and identify some major federal legislation which was designed to protect and preserve our natural resources.
11. What factors were responsible for the development of urban national parks and recreation areas and "Bringing Parks to the People?"
12. Discuss some of the dissimilarities of the recreation and park development in Canada with that of the recreation movement in the United States.

REFERENCES

1. George D. Butler, *Introduction to Community Recreation* (New York: McGraw–Hill Company, 1967).
2. Clarence E. Rainwater, *The Play Movement in the United States* (Chicago: University of Chicago Press, 1922), pp. 13–14.
3. Sidney Lutzin and Edward H. Storey, *Managing Municipal Leisure Services* (Washington, D.C.: International City Management Association, 1973), p. 18.
4. Reynold Carlson, Janet MacLean, Theodore Deppe, and James Peterson, *Recreation and Leisure, The Changing Scene*, 3rd ed. (Belmont, Calif.: Wadsworth Company, 1979), p. 42.
5. Martin H. and Esther S. Neumeyer, *Leisure and Recreation* (New York: A.S. Barnes and Company, 1936), p. 255.
6. Carlson, MacLean, Deppe, and Peterson, *Recreation and Leisure*, 3rd ed., pp. 42–43.
7. Richard Kraus, *Recreation and Leisure in Modern Society* (Englewood Cliffs, N.J.: Prentice–Hall, Inc., 1971), pp. 184–85.
8. Harold D. Meyer, Charles K. Brightbill, and H. Douglas Sessoms, *Community Recreation: A Guide to Its Organization* (Englewood Cliffs, N.J.: Prentice–Hall, Inc., 1969), p. 13.
9. John A. Nesbitt, Paul D. Brown, James F. Murphy, *Recreation and Leisure Service for the Disadvantaged* (Philadelphia: Lea & Febiger, 1970), p. 115.
10. Thomas S. Yukic, *Fundamentals of Recreation* (New York: Harper & Row, 1970), p. 26.
11. Reynold Carlson, Theodore Deppe, and Janet MacLean, *Recreation in American Life* (Belmont, Calif.: Wadsworth Publishing Company, 1972), p. 41.
12. Richard F. Knapp, "The Playground and Recreation Association of America in World War I," *Parks and Recreation Magazine*, January, 1972, p. 27.
13. Rainwater, *The Play Movement in the United States*, pp. 46–48.
14. Richard F. Knapp, "Play for America: The National Recreation Association, 1906–1950," *Parks and Recreation Magazine*, October 1972, pp. 21–23.
15. Jay B. Nash, *Recreation: Pertinent Reading* (Dubuque, Ia.: William C. Brown Co., 1965), p. 52.
16. Yukic, *Fundamentals of Recreation*, pp. 28.
17. Ibid., p. 29.
18. Nesbitt, Brown, and Murphy, *Recreation and Leisure Service for the Disadvantaged*, p. 121.
19. Foster Rhea Dulles, *A History of Recreation* (New York: Appleton–Century–Crofts Co., 1965), pp. 318–19.
20. Charles E. Doell and Gerald B. Fitzgerald, *A Brief History of Parks and Recreation in the United States* (Chicago: Athletic Institute, 1954), p. 12.
21. Carlson, MacLean, Deppe, and Peterson, 3rd ed., p. 47.
22. Richard F. Knapp, "Play for America: Part VIII—A Trial Balance," *Parks and Recreation Magazine*, January 1974, pp. 27–28.
23. Ibid., p. 55.

24. Meyer, Brightbill, and Sessoms, *Community Recreation*, pp. 25–26.
25. Jesse Reynolds and Marion Hormachea, *Public Recreation Administration* (Reston, Va.: Reston Publishing Company, 1976), p. 11.
26. *National Urban Recreation Study Report* (Washington, D.C.: Executive Report, U.S. Department of the Interior, 1978), p. 19.
27. Ibid.
28. Carlson, MacLean, Deppe, and Peterson, 3rd ed., p. 52.
29. Leslie Bella, *Recreation Canada*, 6, No. 33, 1975, p. 17.
30. Elsie M. McFarland, *The Development of Public Recreation in Canada* (Vanier City, Ontario: Canadian Parks/Recreation Association, 1970), p. 1.
31. Ibid., p. 37.
32. McFarland, *The Development of Recreation in Canada*, p. 77.
33. ———, "Leisure in Canada," *Report of Montmorency Conference on Leisure*, Montmorency, Quebec, 1969.
34. Ibid.

Figure 7–1 Recreational professionals are people in leadership, supervisory, and administrative capacities, who are employed in the recreation, parks, and leisure services field.

7
The Professional

One of the newest and most rapidly growing service fields in the United States and Canada is the recreation and leisure services industry. Serving an industry which exceeded $240 billion in expenditures in 1981, professionally trained workers in more than sixty different occupations are involved in the provision of leisure services.

There are many exciting and diverse opportunities for those who are interested in employment in the leisure industry. Leisure–time occupations refer to the various jobs that people engage in to provide opportunities for other people during leisure hours. The occupational specialities associated with them are many and varied. Recreation professionals have found that the rewards of working with youth and adults during their leisure time offers personal satisfaction and an enjoyable way of life.

In discussing employment in the leisure services field, Richard Kraus wrote in 1978 that "Between 200,000 and 250,000 individuals with a primary concern for the provision of recreation and park facilities and services are employed today in federal, state, municipal, and voluntary nonprofit agencies throughout the United States. In addition, several times that number are probably employed in private and commercial recreation related positions."[1]

Professionals in the field of recreation and leisure services are those serving in administrative, supervisory, and other leadership capacities. Such professionals have college degrees in recreation or related fields and are employed as administrators or supervisors.

Not everyone engaged in recreation and leisure services is considered a recreation professional. Indeed, leisure services involve a multitude of businesses and professional activities that employ millions of personnel. Travel, nightclubs, restaurants, professional sports, and many other services are very much a part of the exploding leisure market; their staff and leaders, however, are not regarded as recreation professionals.

In addition, there are many job opportunities in theme parks, resorts, tourism and travel, sports complexes, apartment recreation, private campgrounds, cruise ships, bowling establishments, golf, swimming, tennis and racquetball clubs, country clubs, the merchandising of leisure goods and services, design and planning, private retirement communities, and as leisure consultants.

There have been substantial increases in the salaries of people working in the recreation and parks field. Salaries for full–time recreation positions range from approximately $12,000 to more than $50,000 per year.

Financial columnist Sylvia Porter, as early as 1965, predicted a glowing future for the recreation and parks field when she stated: "The soaring profits–and–paycheck importance of 'fun' in the United States emerges with brilliant clarity. . . . Today's surge in travel, sports, vacation . . . has become a major creator of jobs—going far beyond the familiar categories of camp counselors, lifeguard, park ranger and the like. Recreation is becoming a big, booming, professional business!"[2]

A PROFESSION

A profession is regarded as a rather broad field, within which there are areas of specialization. According to Morris L. Cogan, "A profession is a vocation whose practice is founded upon an understanding of the theoretical structure of some department of learning or science, and upon the abilities accompanying such understanding."[3]

Each profession must have a body of common knowledge, a core content, to which is added material pertaining to the specialized branches. Medicine, for example, includes surgery, neurology, pediatrics, and other branches. Similarly, recreation has numerous branches, such as municipal, industrial, therapeutic, and correctional recreation.

Professionalism is more than just knowledge, education, and experience. It implies the willingness to accept predetermined goals, ethics, and standards of performance. In the recreation and leisure services field, standards are set by a number of professional organizations, in addition to the colleges and universities. Paul Douglass suggested that "A profession is a body of career practitioners who by specialized education and skills assume the responsibility and power needed to (1) certify the adequate preparation and personnel and (2) assure ethical performance in the course of duty within a field of service that is regarded as a public trust."[4]

There are several ingredients or components that are basic to the development of a profession, against which the progress of the recreation and park movement can be evaluated.

- General acceptance of the field
- Basic body of knowledge
- Professional education
- Research and literature
- Personnel standards
- Recruitment
- Professional organizations
- Registration, certification, and accreditation
- Code of ethics

An additional criterion was given by Charles Hartsoe, "A professional culture, based on professional organizations, shared values, and traditions."[5]

H. Douglas Sessoms suggested that "As a body, we need to accept that recreation and parks is not a profession but a field embracing many professional roles and service occupations. The leisure service delivery system is a field of work. It embraces many professions and occupations. All those who work in the field are not recreation/park professionals."[6]

A PROFESSIONAL IMAGE

A major goal among those in the parks and recreation field is the development of a favorable public image—an image of leadership, professional competency, and responsibility. Indeed, a powerful force in any democracy is public awareness and favorable opinion.

Actually, there is a definite lack of public understanding of the field of recreation, and the problem is primarily one of image. Most Americans are not yet fully aware that recreation is a distinct area of professional service.

The lack of public visability is a continuing problem facing the profession. Professor William Theobald of Purdue University referred

Figure 7–2 A favorable public image. The ability of recreation professionals to speak effectively in public is most essential in developing a good image. The public is becoming more aware of recreation as a profession—an image of effective leadership, professional competence, community responsibility, and service.

to it as "a lack of public understanding of what we are about." He explained that "If each of us, as well as our students or staff cannot verbalize what we do, how then can the public understand and support what we have devoted our lives to?"[7] The leisure services field itself must clarify its role, so that a single clear image emerges.

THE PROFESSIONAL RECREATOR

The title "recreation professional" is commonly used to describe those employed in the recreation and park field. "Recreation leader" is also a common term. There are also those who prefer "recreator."

Sidney Lutzin and Edward Storey suggested that "There is more to leadership than face–to–face contact. Recreation leadership implies organization, planning, development of sound programs, and guidance of individuals and groups into purposeful and constructive free–time activities. The professional is able to identify recreation needs, plan the programs and facilities to meet those needs, and then evaluate the effectiveness of the program."[8]

There are a number of competencies that a professional recreator should have. Among the most important are the abilities to speak and write effectively. In dealing with the public, the professional should use good judgment, tact, even restraint when encountering difficult situations, complaints, or criticism. Always conscious of the value of good public relations, he or she should be an able interpreter in describing department programs and activities to the public.

Recreation and park professionals should have a good knowledge of the behavioral and social sciences. The social needs of the future will demand a level of expertise comparable to that of sociologists and psychiatrists.

According to Charles E. Hartsoe, "The future of recreation as a new profession will be influenced by its ability to grasp, adapt, and innovate in a society characterized by constant change."[9]

PROFESSIONAL COMPETENCIES

Additional competencies of the professional person:

- Reads constantly
- Joins professional associations, pays dues, and attends meetings
- Seeks new ideas and trends in the field
- Accepts membership on professional committees and is an active participant
- Conducts himself or herself with dignity and in a way that commands respect
- Bases his or her behavior on high moral and ethical principles
- Works effectively with all organizations and individuals in the community
- Demands high standards of excellence
- Is receptive to suggestions and ideas from others
- *Enjoys life!*

Personal Characteristics

Successful recreation leaders have many personal characteristics in common. Thomas Yukic listed the following traits as most important:[10]

- Common sense
- Pleasing personality
- A sense of humor
- A sense of human worth
- Productive energy
- A desire to serve people
- Ability to get along with others
- Good physical and mental health

TYPES OF PROFESSIONAL RECREATION PERSONNEL

Traditionally, professional employment in the field of recreation and parks involved three levels of service: executive, supervisory, and leadership. Today, however, there appear to be five job levels at which recreation personnel are employed.

1. *Executive level*—recreation director, superintendent, general manager, or administrator; or in a combined department, director or superintendent of parks and recreation, assistant superintendent of recreation.
2. *Supervisory level*—recreation supervisor (general or specialist, concerned with a particular type of activity or with a special population group).
3. *Center director level*—recreation center director, playground director, facility manager, or assistant center director.
4. *Leadership level*—recreation leader (general or specialist, program or activity specialists, senior leaders, leaders, and assistant leaders).
5. *Trainee*—recreation intern, recreation aides or attendants, student recreation leader, or junior recreation assistant.

Administrative Positions

This position involves major responsibility for planning and administering a recreation and park program to meet the needs and interests of the area served. Most administrators today are responsible for both the program and the park operations.

Traditionally, administration is synonymous with management. Hersey and Blanchard defined management as "working with and through individuals to accomplish organizational goals."[11]

In addition to the administrator, there are also superintendents or directors of separate divisions, such as the superintendent of recreation or the director of park maintenance. These positions involve a high level of responsibility and are considered administrative.

Specific responsibilities of the administrator include:

1. Administering the work of the department in accordance with governing policies.
2. Recruiting, selecting, training, assigning, supervising, and evaluating the department staff.
3. Acquisition, planning, construction, improvement, and maintenance of areas and facilities.
4. Preparing budget, directing, controlling, and accounting for all expenditures, revenues, and fiscal operations.
5. Effective public relations.
6. Organizing, directing, and controlling all program activities.
7. Maintaining and preparing records, and reports.
8. Evaluating and performing research studies.
9. Motivating and inspiring personnel.

Comparable positions in park maintenance and facilities management call for administrative and supervisory responsibilities. The person responsible for the operation and maintenance of physical facilities is often given the title of park superintendent.

Figure 7–3 The recreation administrator directs the total operation of the department, usually administering both the park and the recreation program operations. Solon "Doc" Wisham, Director of the Sacramento City Community Services Department since 1969, has more than 475 full–time workers in his department and a budget of over $9.5 million to administer. His yearly salary is $47,000.

Qualifications The qualifications of an administrator usually include graduation from a recognized college or university with a bachelor's degree in recreation administration, park management, or a closely related field, plus successful experience over a period of years in recreation supervision and/or administration.

Supervisory Positions

Representing a secondary level of administration often referred to as "middle management," supervisors are responsible for the overall recreation or park operations, usually within a major category of program service.

In addition to management responsibilities, the supervisor has the basic responsibility of carrying out the functions of management at the face–to–face leadership level. According to Jesse Reynolds and Marion Hormachea, "The supervisor is responsible for translating administrative objectives, rules, regulations, other guidelines and assignments into effective and efficient programs of action."[12]

Recreation supervisor (general) A general recreation supervisor is responsible for all phases of the recreation program within an area and for the supervision of all personnel in the area. Under direction, the supervisor plans, organizes, and supervises a variety of programs and services. The supervisor's primary function is coordinating and directing the work of others, scheduling activities, and serving as liaison between the administrator and leaders in the field.

Specific responsibilities include:

1. Assisting the administrator and superintendent of recreation in administering programs.
2. Planning programs to meet the needs of the district.
3. Supervising, training, and evaluating assigned personnel.
4. Overseeing maintenance and use of facilities and areas.
5. Maintaining good public relations, publicity, and promotion.
6. Planning, research, and evaluation.
7. Assisting in budget preparation.
8. Maintaining records and preparing reports.
9. Selecting or supervising selection of new employees.
10. Determining the need for specialized personnel in the various programs.
11. Reviewing plans developed by subordinates.

Special supervisor A recreation supervisor who has more specialized responsibilities would be involved with a specific area of activity. A special supervisor's main functions might include being in charge of a large community center or other recreation complex or overseeing a major area of activity, such as athletics, aquatics, performing arts, or outdoor programs. Responsibility might also include programs involving special groups such as the handicapped, the aging, or youth.

Figure 7–4 Women in greater numbers are taking on administrative and supervisory areas of responsibility in the leisure services industry. Many governmental and private agencies and organizations are hiring women in key areas of responsibility.

Qualifications Normally, the qualifications for supervisors include graduation from a recognized college or university with a degree in recreation, or recreation and parks, or a closely related field, along with a specified period of professional experience in recreation.

Leadership Positions

Some departments have several grades of recreation leaders, such as Leader I, II, and III, who operate directly in face–to–face relationships with groups of participants. Many employ a senior leader in addition to the regular leaders. A senior leader often is required to supervise part–time personnel. Leadership jobs call for generalists as well as specialists.

Recreation leader A full–time, professional position, the recreation leader is responsible for planning, organizing, and supervising recreation programs. He or she may work in one or more facilities as a general leader, or in a particular area of activity, or may function as a specialist in a leader or teaching capacity.

Working directly with groups, the leader is responsible for the organization, direction, and supervision of recreational activities. In some situations, the leader is in full charge of the program, having been delegated various responsibilities by the supervisor. As a rule, however, the leader is responsible to the supervisor, who should always be kept informed.

The primary responsibilities of recreation leaders include:

1. Organizing and directing a variety of programs.
2. Maintaining inventories of supplies and equipment, and requisitioning new materials when necessary.
3. Carrying out an effective program of local publicity and community relations.
4. Recruiting and working with volunteers.
5. Being responsible for maintaining sound

Figure 7–5 The leader is a face–to–face group leader or program specialist, who provides direct leadership to individuals or groups of participants. The leader here is taking sign–ups at a Play Day event.

policies of safety, group control, and discipline among participants.
6. Keeping records of attendance and special events.
7. Assisting in the evaluation of department activities.

As a specialist, the recreation leader is responsible for a given area of activity and will promote the activity throughout the district. He or she may be responsible for a special tournament, show, or event.

Qualifications For full–time positions, civil service qualifications for recreation leader specify the completion of two years of college in recreation or a related field and six months of paid or voluntary experience as a group leader in an organized recreation program. Experience above the minimum required may be substituted for the college education on a year–for–year basis.

Part–time or summer leadership positions

are being filled by upper and lower division students, particularly those majoring in recreation. Increasingly, community colleges are providing personnel on this level of service through leadership training programs.

CAREERS IN RECREATION AND PARKS

Rapid growth in the recreation and park profession is creating many career opportunities for men and women graduates of college and university training programs. The need for professionally trained and educated personnel has grown proportionately with the increase in the number of organizations and agencies involved with recreation and leisure services.

The local government level, including city, county, and district recreation agencies, constitutes a major source of employment, from administrative positions down to specialist and leadership roles. State government positions are not as numerous as local positions, but they have increased significantly in relation to the growth and development of a broader range of recreation services. Similarly, the federal government offers a diversified scope of job positions that appeal to young men and women graduating from colleges and universities.

Increasingly, professional recreators are assuming attractive job positions with commercial recreation agencies. Their training and background have made them ideal candidates for management and supervisory roles at private clubs, commercial enterprises, industrial firms, apartment complexes, retirement communities, golf and country clubs, bowling alleys, ski resorts, camps, resort areas, housing development recreation areas, sports organizations, and the many residential communities currently being developed.

Through classification and standardization of job titles, public agencies have been able to establish a career ladder that provides opportunities for promotion. The top

administrative staff is usually directly appointed and not a part of the Civil Service system.

Associate degrees in recreation from two-year colleges are quite common today and have served a valuable role in meeting the face-to-face leadership needs of the field. The associate professional has filled a role that requires minimal administrative and supervisory responsibilities and is more involved in planning, organizing, and conducting various recreation activities in different program areas. Direct leaders have responsibilities such as organizing and directing athletic contests, managing recreation areas and facilities, directing aquatic programs, teaching dance, promoting and directing cultural arts productions, and leading children in playground activities.

Higher education is the key to advancement for persons holding associate degrees. Those who wish to reach higher levels of service can enter a part-time or full-time program to achieve a four-year degree in recreation. If an organization has a structured job classification system, it is difficult, often impossible, to move up without meeting the educational qualifications.

> **A job is what you do with your days. A career is what you do with your life.**

AREAS OF EMPLOYMENT

The following is a listing of types of positions or settings available in the recreation and leisure services industry:

- *Municipal park and recreation agencies* Administrator, superintendent/director, aquatics specialist, program supervisor, park supervisor, specialist in sports or performing arts, dance instructor, community center director, activity director, facility manager, playground leader, recreation aide, youth sports coach, public relations

Figure 7–6 National park ranger. This dog sled demonstration is conducted by a park ranger–naturalist at Mount McKinley National Park in Alaska. (Courtesy National Park Service Photo Library.)

officer, fitness specialist, senior citizens director/supervisor, handicapped program planner, recreation therapist, leisure education specialist, museum guide, stadium manager, volunteer agency supervisor.

- *State and federal agencies* Park director/superintendent, ranger, outdoor education specialist, outdoor planner, naturalist, researcher, environmental interpreter/naturalist, conservationist, forester, wildlife manager, recreation facility manager, extension agent, museum director, tour guide.
- *Commercial recreation* Resort manager; retirement community program director; sport ranch superintendent; director/manager/pro of program or facilities of golf courses, ski shops, singles condominiums, tennis complexes, or family housing complexes; carnival game operator; hotel manager; equipment sales and distributions; concessionaire; theme park manager; cruise ship activity director; fitness specialist; high–risk recreation facilitator; leisure counselor; leisure specialist; tour guide; travel agency consultant; travel planner.
- *Industrial recreation* Program director, facility manager, recreation specialist, pre–retirement counselor, fitness specialist, recreation therapist, resort or center director for union.
- *Outdoor recreation* Activity outfitter, camp director/manager, campground attendant, interpreter, researcher, outdoor educator, camp counselor, trail developer, forester, park ranger, naturalist, outdoor and waterway guide.

- *Therapeutic/Special groups recreation* Recreation therapist; activity therapy specialist/coordinator; worker/specialist in management, programs, or research in state hospitals, developmental centers for the retarded, centers for aging, rehabilitation centers, or organizations for the ill and handicapped; leisure counselor; senior citizen programmer.
- *Military* Director/superintendent, service club director, special activities supervisor, youth activities director.
- *Corrections* Recreation director/coordinator, recreation specialist, counselor.
- *Youth–Serving agencies* Director, program supervisor, facility manager, recreation specialist, activity leader, coach in YMCA, Boys' Clubs, Boy Scouts, Girl Scouts, 4–H, and other youth agencies.
- *Church/Religious organizations* Church recreation director/coordinator.
- *Colleges, universities, and schools* Educator/professor, faculty in recreation, park, and leisure services departments, campus recreation or intramural director, recreation sports specialist, college union program director, community education director/coordinator, leisure education specialist.

JOBS WITH THE GOVERNMENT

In most of the states and provinces, Civil Service systems provide the procedures by which recreation and park personnel are selected and hired. Operating on all levels of government, i.e. federal, state, and local, Civil Service represents a government–sponsored system of establishing job titles, descriptions, and hiring practices. Most of the jobs with the government are awarded through a merit system in which an applicant is rated by the results of a test or by a review of educational or work experience. After testing or review at a Civil Service Commission office, an applicant's name goes on a list with others qualified for the same kind of job.

When personnel officers have vacancies, they ask the commission for names of qualified individuals. The official normally chooses from the three candidates rated highest on the list.

Examinations are classified into two types: "competitive," which applies to the majority of full–time, professional positions; and "non–competitive," which test basic proficiency without comparison of scores of other examinees, for such positions as recreation specialist, lifeguard, and swimming, craft, or skiing instructor.

Federal Job Opportunities

The federal government currently employs more than four thousand persons nationwide and overseas in numerous occupational areas dealing with parks, recreation, and related fields. Qualified individuals can apply for employment through the "Federal Civil Service System."

Salary schedules for all federal employees are as follows:

GS–5	$10,507—13,657
GS–7	$13,014—16,920
GS–9	$15,920—20,699
GS–11	$19,263—25,041
GS–12	$23,087—30,017
GS–13	$27,453—35,688
GS–14	$32,442—42,171
GS–15	$38,160—47,500[13]

Among the various types of jobs available are: park technicians, technicians (other than park), recreation assistants, outdoor recreation planners, park management, recreation specialists, foresters, and landscape architects.

Although other federal agencies may occasionally have positions for park and recreation personnel, the following agencies account for the majority of the hiring:

Department of Agriculture
  U.S. Forest Service
  Soil Conservation Service
Department of the Interior
  Bureau of Land Management
  National Park Service
  U.S. Fish and Wildlife Service

Heritage Conservation and Recreation Service
Department of Defense
Corps of Engineers
Armed Forces Recreation
Veteran's Administration

The Peace Corps

The Peace Corps provides opportunities for skilled Americans to serve in developing nations overseas. More than 13,000 people have served or are serving as Peace Corps Volunteers in 46 nations overseas. While most of the volunteers work in educational and community development programs, there are positions available in more than 300 separate skill areas. Recreation leaders are needed to organize scouting and youth activities programs, begin boys' clubs, build recreation facilities, and develop programs in camping, crafts, and water safety. A college degree is not required.

Applicants must be at least eighteen years of age and American citizens. Married couples are eligible if they have no dependents under eighteen. For further information on opportunities for service, and instructions for application, write the Office of Public Affairs, Peace Corps, Washington, D.C. 20525.

OPPORTUNITIES IN MILITARY RECREATION

There are some very lucrative administrative jobs in military recreation. At Mather AFB in Sacramento, for example, the Director of Morale, Welfare, and Recreation has an annual salary of more than $40,000, while the Chief of the Recreation Services Branch receives $34,000. Overseas employment, retention rights, and a multitude of other benefits are available.

The Morale, Welfare, and Recreation Division of the Armed Forces (MWR) receives more than $600 million in appropriated fund support annually. Military resale activities such as exchanges, clubs, bowling centers, golf courses, sports, hobby shops, youth activities, and theaters take in more than $5 billion each year.

To administer and manage the complex MWR program, it takes approximately ten thousand military personnel (officers and enlisted personnel), twenty thousand full-time appropriated and non-appropriated fund civilian employees plus an additional twenty-five thousand part-time employees to provide for the needs and interests of the service members and their dependents.[14]

Types of Positions

The number of civilians employed to direct recreation activities vary from installation to installation. According to George Marchas and Frances B. O'Malley, "Some programs may employ twenty (20) to thirty (30) individuals, while others may employ only two (2)."[15]

Recreation specialists (GS–188) plan, organize, advise, assess, and administer a variety of recreation programs. Within the MWR Division, these usually include community, outdoor, and youth activities.

Qualifications

GS–5   Bachelors degree in recreation
GS–7   plus one year of specialized experience
GS–9   plus two years of specialized experience
GS–11   and above plus three years of specialized experience.

OR, in all the above grades, three (3) years of experience, equivalent to the knowledge gained through education, can be substituted for the bachelor's degree in recreation.

OR, any equivalent combination of education or experience.

Recreation aides and assistants (GS–189) use a practical knowledge of one or more recreational activities, combined with skills in the maintenance and use of recreational materials and equipment.

Sports specialists (GS–030) plan or carry out sports programs, evaluate program effectiveness, conduct clinics or seminars to train coaches, officials, or others, train and develop athletes, plan and carry out tournaments.

Funding

All positions used in providing recreation for military personnel through the MWR Division of the Armed Forces are funded by two means:

Appropriated Funds are provided by tax payers through the Congress of the United States and the Department of Defense, on a fiscal year basis.

Non-Appropriated Funds are generated by the individual bases by use of registration fees and user fees.

Avenues to Employment

Federal job announcements are not continuously open for applications, therefore individuals may not apply whenever they wish. However, applications will be accepted from students who expect to complete all requirements for a degree within nine months of the date the application is filled.

Recreation Specialist Register

Individuals interested in GS–5 to GS–7 level positions should apply to the U.S. Civil Service Register at the following address: Charleston Area Office, Office of Personnel Management, Federal Office Building, 334 Meeting Street, Charleston, South Carolina 29403.

Mid–Level Register

Graduate degree holders or those individuals with several years of professional experience may apply for mid–level positions at the GS–9/11/12 levels. They may contact the Office of Personnel Management, Regional Office for the area in which they wish to work.

Overseas Registers

Positions in Alaska, Hawaii, and Puerto Rico are filled by the area office in each location. Entry level positions, GS–5/7, in Europe go through the Area Office in Charleston. For overseas positions with the Army, individuals can contact: Recreation Services Branch, Overseas Recruitment Center, Department of the Army, Washington, D.C. 20315.

EMPLOYMENT IN STATE PARKS

State parks provide a nationwide system of areas and facilities for recreation and conservation of outstanding natural and historical resource. Approximately forty–five thousand individuals are currently employed by state park systems in either a year–round or seasonal basis. More than sixty–five hundred of these employees are in professional positions, including landscape architects, foresters, historians, naturalists, park planners, administrators, recreation coordinators, recreation consultants, public relations, and nurses.[16]

The employment setting might be at a state forest, heritage site, state park, beach, campsite, boating area, or a children's farm, with responsibilities ranging from regional to district to local facility levels.

"We need resource–managers," emphasized Russell Porter, Assistant Director, State of California Parks and Recreation Department. "We are becoming very conscious of that as our parks systems at every level grow in size."

Types of Jobs

State park system administrators plan, organize and direct all administrative, fiscal budget and technical activities of the state park system. Preparing budgets, administering programs, preparing reports, initiating plans, and public relations duties.

Possible titles: Director of state parks, superintendent, division chief.

Education: Usually requires a bachelor's degree in park administration, forestry, park and recreation administration, fish and game management, or related field.

Chief ranger directing and assisting in park operations, construction and maintenance; supervising of permanent and seasonal personnel; training personnel; registering park visitors; patrolling park.
Possible titles: District ranger; park ranger.
Education: Usually requires a bachelor's degree in park management, outdoor recreation management, forestry, or park related field.

Park rangers maintaining of grounds and facilities, registration of visitors, assigning camp spaces, providing information on facilities, rules, and regulations, and historical data. Upper grade park rangers may supervise, as well as patrol parks, enforce rules and regulations, and prepare reports.
Education: May require a two–year associate degree in a park related field to a bachelor's degree.

Summer Jobs with Federal and State Agencies

Each summer there are a limited number of opportunities for summer jobs with federal and state agencies. These positions vary from office jobs to park rangers and are located throughout the United States.

Most appointments available in the Forest Service are limited to students majoring in the fields of forestry or related sciences. Each national forest does its own selecting and hiring.

The National Park Service has a limited number of park ranger, park technician, and park aid positions available for applicants eighteen years of age or older. Applications should be sent to the superintendent of the park where the individual desires employment.

Various federal agencies have special work–study programs. Applicants who are appointed participate in specific training programs during vacations and attend col-

lege full–time during the academic periods.

Summer jobs are usually filled by February or March of each year. Anyone interested in summer employment should file an application by or even before January first of each year. The federal government publishes an announcement each year of "Summer Jobs." This information is available by writing: "Summer Jobs" Publication, Announcement Number 414, United States Civil Service Commission, Washington, D.C. 20415.[17]

EMPLOYMENT IN CORRECTIONAL INSTITUTIONS

Professional recreators have a very weak foothold within correctional systems. "The creation of recreation programs, in some instances, was to provide the 'favorite' guard with a more desirable working environment," wrote Wally Lynch and Vicky Annand. "Because this individual had athletic skills or interests, he/she became the logical choice to assume responsibilities for recreation services. The Civil Service system has relieved some of this favoritism, but it will take several years before untrained individuals are replaced by professional recreators."[18]

PRIVATE AND COMMERCIAL RECREATION SETTINGS

The private and commercial sector for parks, recreation, and leisure is spread through a number of employment settings. Professionals and paraprofessionals are employed by such recreation and leisure service enterprises as racquetball, swim and tennis clubs, sports clubs, health spas, waterfront or ski resorts, golf courses, private camps and clubs, amusement parks, tourist attractions, beach and boating resorts, travel agencies, housing and condominium complexes, and vacation excursions.

Facility management and operational skills are essential to those employed in clubs, apartment complexes, or other commercial enterprises and leisure service facilities. Leadership comes with management, and those who work in the private and commercial sector should have good management training.

Amusement parks in the United States employ approximately one hundred and twenty–five thousand people during the summer operating season, the large percent of them being high school and college students.

Most private and commercial enterprises advertise in various trade journals such as:

- Golf Business
- Tennis Industry
- Tennis Trade
- Resort Management
- Golf Industry
- Amusement Business
- Travel Trade
- Golf Journal

Tourist and travel offices are located in each state. They can provide names and addresses as well as suggestions for contacting resorts, camps, and amusement parks in their state.

The following is a list of career opportunities in travel and tourism:

- Travel agent
- Tour guide
- Tour operator
- Fairs and expositions
- Hotel and motel management
- Convention and visitors bureaus
- Theme parks
- Transportation (airlines, cruise lines, trains, buses, automobiles, etc.)

A Career In Club and Apartment Management

With private club and apartment complex membership increasing every day, the potential of club management is very appealing. Those who would like to pursue a career as a club manager should have a thorough understanding of the work they will be involved in.

Strong personal standards are a must. Among the important personal requirements are a good appearance, personal integrity,

Figure 7–7 Facility management, in addition to sound business practices, requires a strong desire by the staff to serve people. Above, Jim Nunes, manager of International Spa Fitness Center in Sacramento, offers a friendly greeting to one of his clients.

a strong moral sense, loyalty, and a sense of humor.

Individuals desiring a career in club management should gain part–time employment during the school year and during summer vacations. Many clubs offer intern programs for students which involve on–the–job training.

Types of jobs A director is often employed to handle the programs at one or more apartment complexes. More specialized positions are available at the larger developments. Apartment communities with a golf course, for example, may hire someone to serve only as a golf pro and shop manager.

Directors in apartment complexes have considerable involvement in resident contact, programming, bookkeeping, facility management, budget preparation, and newsletter writing.

Qualifications Generally, the specific requirements depend upon the type of job. A degree in recreation is helpful but not essential in obtaining a general position. Experience in sales, business, or housing has proven very beneficial to those employed in apartment complexes.[19]

A person who can relate well to the tenants and who can sell the programs will likely be a very successful director or leader. The director should have the ability and personality to follow through with effective public relations and good will.

According to Lynn Mikels and Elaine Potts, "The best way to prepare for employment at an apartment complex is to do field work experience under a complex recreation director."[20]

EMPLOYMENT IN THE INDUSTRIAL SECTOR

There is an urgent need for trained professional recreators in the industrial sector. Only a small percentage of companies have established full–time positions, with the large majority of companies using recreation personnel on a part–time basis only. People are often selected from worker and lower management ranks and groomed upward.

There is a definite growth in the employee recreation field as evidenced by the fact that the National Industrial Recreation Association (NIRA) has more than doubled its membership in the last few years (approximately two thousand). As organizations develop the need for an employee recreation administrator, NIRA has promoted the idea of hiring a recreation professional. An estimated one–thousand major industries currently employ one or more full–time recreational staff persons, representing approximately fifteen hundred jobs. Salaries for industrial recreation administrators in large firms range from $12,000 to $50,000.

While the number of individuals employed by industrial programs vary, the following list is typical of the positions found in industrial recreation:

- Manager/Director
- Recreation Specialist
- Aquatic Specialist
- Physical Fitness Specialist
- Social–Cultural Specialist

Enrollment in the NIRA Referral Service will provide an individual with a professional referral service and a subscription to *Recreation Management* magazine, the Association's official publication. For more information and application forms contact: National Industrial Recreation Association, 20 North Wacker Drive, Chicago, Illinois 60606.

RECRUITMENT

The success of any profession depends on the quality of the individuals who are attracted to the field. With the intense competition of other more established professions, it is extremely important that recruitment for recreation leadership begin early so as to enable the field to recruit youth who have the strongest leadership abilities.

The advantages and rewards of recreation as a career should be effectively interpreted by the counseling services of secondary schools. Ideally, those who enroll as a recreation major at a college or university have had some prior leadership experience as a leader or aide. Young people who enjoy working in sports, aquatics, playground programs, youth agencies, camps, and in other recreation activities are excellent prospects for the professional recreation field. Whether the on–the–job training experience is part–time, on a paid or volunteer basis, the importance of such experience will prove most beneficial later on. With such a background, the student is much better oriented and ready for job preparation.

AFFIRMATIVE ACTION IN HIRING PRACTICES

An area of concern to the recreation and park profession today is the need to provide greater opportunity for professional placement and advancement to various population groups, particularly women, racial or ethnic minorities, and people with handicaps.

The Code of Federal Regulations which enacts the provisions of Title VI of the 1964 Civil Rights Act in the United States stipulates that agencies or institutions receiving federal funding may not discriminate in the provi-

Figure 7–8 More opportunities for professional placement and advancement are becoming available to women and minorities. These two recreators supervise a special softball program for people with handicaps.

sion of service or in hiring practices on the basis of race, color, sex, or national origin.

Federal, state, and local departments and agencies are hiring women and minority applicants in greater numbers than in the past. In addition, there are more vocationally oriented educational opportunities available today to minorities.

PROFESSIONAL ASSOCIATIONS

There are a large number of national and statewide organizations that are contributing to the recreation movement. While space will not permit a description of all, there are a number of professional organizations that have promoted significantly the development of parks, recreation, and leisure services.

National Recreation and Park Association

The National Recreation and Park Association (NRPA) is a nonprofit educational and public interest organization which serves as the national voice for the park, recreation, and conservation movement in the United States.

The association was founded in Boston in 1898 as the New England Association for Park

Superintendents. In 1906, the Playground Association of America was founded at a meeting in Washington, D.C. Under the leadership of Laurance Rockefeller, the NRPA took its present form and name in 1965 through the merger of five professional and citizen organizations.

Currently, NRPA membership totals sixteen thousand members and includes park and recreation administrators, planners, and supervisors at all levels of government and in the private sector; recreation specialists working with the aged, ill, people with handicaps, and with people in institutions; those serving military personnel and their families; educators; students preparing for careers in the field; elected and appointed members of public policy boards and commissions; and citizens concerned with the social need for adequate park and recreation opportunities.

The association is governed by a sixty–five member national board of trustees of which thirty–four must be citizens or non–professionals. Regional offices, state affiliate organizations and regional councils give NRPA its broad–based national structure.

NRPA leads national efforts to provide opportunities, facilities and services for meaningful leisure experiences for all peoples including people with handicaps and the elderly. In its advocacy role, NRPA provides comprehensive documentation and testimony in major policy and legislative areas.

For further information, write: National Recreation and Park Association, 3101 Park Center Drive, Alexandria, Virginia 22303.

Canadian Parks/Recreation Association

With its national office in Ottawa, Ontario, this association is the major Canadian organization in this field. Having more than two thousand members, the Canadian Parks and Recreation Association (CPRA) receives strong support from the Canadian government.

Major objectives include:

1. To acquaint Canadians with the significance of leisure in a changing society.

2. To assist in the development, organization, and promotion of the parks and recreation service delivery system in Canada.
3. To involve the membership in the development of national policies of significance to the parks and recreation movement.

Among the major functions of CPRA are publishing a bimonthly magazine, *Recreation Canada;* sponsoring an annual conference; providing consultation and technical assistance to both government and non–government agencies in the leisure field; conducting open–space studies; and representing Canadian interests at international meetings.

For further information, write: Canadian Parks and Recreation Association, 333 River Road, Vanier City, Ontario, K1L 8B9.

American Association for Leisure and Recreation

The American Association for Leisure and Recreation (AALR) is a new association as an entity of its own, but has been in existence since 1934 when the recreation division within the American Association for Health, Physical Education, Recreation, and Dance was first established. Those active in this division come from colleges and universities and from recreation departments in the public schools.

The association has been involved with functions that include professional preparation, research, workshops and institutes, leisure counseling, and leisure education. The AALR is governed by a Board of Governors, consisting of the presidents of each of the seven associations, representatives from the six districts, and the executive committee.

For information, write: American Association for Leisure and Recreation, 1900 Association Drive, Reston, Virginia 22091.

National Industrial Recreation Association

The National Industrial Recreation Association (NIRA) is a nonprofit organization dedicated to the principle that employee recreation, as well as fitness and service programs are essential to effective personnel management. Its members are the directors and suppliers of such programs in business, industry, government, and the military.

NIRA promotes employee programs as a means of improving productivity by fostering good relations among employees and between employees and management. Members of NIRA direct and conduct recreational activities in sports, educational opportunities, travel fitness and health programs, hobby clubs, and community service projects.

In addition to a subscription to *Recreation Management*, members receive many services, including newsletters, product and service discounts for employee groups, program ideas and consultation, professional certification, international awards and national and regional tournaments.

For more information, write: National Industrial Recreation Association, 20 North Wacker Drive, Chicago, Illinois 60606.

American Camping Association

The American Camping Association is a nonprofit organization of persons interested in the values and importance of organized camping. The purposes are to establish standards and to maintain a standard of excellence in organized camping. Members include camp directors and owners, camp staff, educators, clergy, and others interested in camping and outdoor education programs.

The ACA serves as the voice of camp leaders throughout the nation, stimulating high professional standards among leaders and their agencies. In addition to publishing *Camping Magazine* each month, the ACA sponsors national and regional conferences for improving leadership and camping programs.

The Association can be contacted by writing: American Camping Association, Bradford Woods, Martinsville, Indiana 46151.

QUESTIONS FOR DISCUSSION

1. What is a profession?
2. List the ingredients or components that are important for any field to be considered a profession. Do you believe recreation is a profession?
3. In developing a more favorable public image, what must the parks and recreation field do?
4. What are the competencies of the "professional person?"
5. Describe the responsibilities and duties of the three major types of professional recreation leaders.
6. What are the personal qualities of a good recreation leader?
7. List the major career opportunities available to recreation graduates. Which area or option do you think you have a preference for at this time? Explain.
8. What are the primary purposes of a professional organization?
9. Discuss some ways in which the quality of preparation of recreation personnel can be improved.

REFERENCES

1. Richard Kraus, *Recreation and Leisure in Modern Society*, 2nd ed. (Santa Monica: Goodyear Publishing Company, 1978), p. 281.
2. Sylvia Porter, "The Business of Fun," *New York Post*, 14 May 1965.
3. Edward H. Storey, "Education for Leisure", *Position Statement of the Society of Park and Recreation Educators*, September 1972, p. 4.
4. Paul Douglass, "The Profession of Recreation on the Threshold of the Aesthetic Age" (Address at National Recreation Congress, Minneapolis, October 1965).
5. Charles E. Hartsoe, "Recreation—A Profession in Transition," *Parks and Recreation Magazine*, July 1973, p. 33.
6. H. Douglas Sessoms, "Programs and Professional Preparation in the 1980s," (Presented at the 1979 NRPA Congress of Parks and Recreation, New Orleans, La.)
7. ———, "President's Message," *News of Society of Parks and Recreation Educators*, NRPA, Arlington, VA., July 1981, p. 1.
8. Sidney G. Lutzin and Edward H. Storey, *Managing Municipal Leisure Services* (Washington, D.C.: International City Management Association, 1973), p. 243.
9. Charles E. Hartsoe, "Recreation—a Profession in Transition," p. 60.
10. Thomas S. Yukic, *Fundamentals of Recreation* (New York: Harper & Row, 1970), pp. 156–57.
11. Paul Hersey and Kenneth A. Blanchard, *Management of Organizational Behavior* (Englewood Cliffs, N.J.: Prentice–Hall, Inc., 1972), p. 3.
12. Jesse Reynolds and Marion Hormachea, *Public Recreation Administration* (Reston, Virginia: Reston Publishing Company, 1976), p. 209.
13. ———, "The Federal Civil Service Systems," *EMPLOY*, National Recreation and Park Association, November 1976.
14. ———, "Recreation Career Opportunities with the Armed Forces," *EMPLOY*, National Recreation and Park Association, April 1980, p. 1.
15. Ibid., p. 3.
16. Christine C. Badger, Editor, "State Park Employment," *EMPLOY*, National Recreation and Park Association, January 1977, p. 1–2.
17. ———, Parks and Recreation Summer Employment Information," *EMPLOY*, December 1977.
18. Morris W. Stewart, "Employment in Correctional Recreation," *EMPLOY*, National Recreation and Park Association, April 1978, p. 4.
19. ———, "Apartment Complex Recreation," *EMPLOY*, National Recreation and Park Association, January 1978, p. 5.
20. Ibid., pp. 3–4.

Figure 8–1 The quest for stronger professional standards begins on the front line of leadership. The quality of a program, in terms of human growth and development and what it does to people, in large measure is determined here. Professional preparation programs have no greater responsibility than to upgrade the qualifications and effectiveness of face–to–face leaders. Here, an efficient supervisor–program leader relationship is a big factor in the success of a youth sports program sponsored by the Alameda Recreation Department.

8
Professional Preparation

A dramatic and sharp growth in professional preparation in recreation and parks has occurred during the past fifteen years. Indeed, the growth of both curricula and numbers of majors indicates the changes and progress in professional preparation. From one curriculum in the late 1930s, there are today over 300 curricula.

Since 1978, however, enrollments in parks and recreation curricula have stabilized. "The forces that are affecting recreation and park education are the same as those that are affecting education in general," wrote H. Douglas Sessoms. "There is a declining number of students attending universities and colleges."[1]

The first specialized training in recreation and park administration took place during the 1920s, when the National Recreation Association sponsored a one–year graduate training institute. However, it was not until a decade later that colleges and universities entered this field of professional service.

Soon after World War II, a number of institutions initiated curricula for undergraduate and graduate recreation majors, usually as a part of the health and physical education department. In 1950, approximately fifty colleges were offering programs for recreation majors. Following a period of relative stability, recreation and park enrollments began to rise sharply in the 1960s.

The demand for more qualified and better prepared professionals has grown over the years. The diversification of the leisure services field has also resulted in greater specialization. College curricula now offer many specialties and emphases of training and education to meet the needs of the various sectors and program areas.

NEW STANDARDS

Professional leaders, supervisors, as well as administrators today must meet new and stronger standards than those of their predecessors. In large measure, the upgrading of leadership and management can be attributed to the efforts of professional organizations and their committees and to those institutions that have provided recreation curricula. Additional training in the form of workshops, institutes, courses, and in–service training has been responsible for raising the standards of the recreation field significantly.

The need for higher standards and professionalism was most effectively expressed by Donald Henkel, Director of Professional Services for the National Recreation Park Association (NRPA), when he stated that "Standards provide the basis for minimum and consistent level of competence. They turn noise into identifiable and nondistorted tone. Standards are no guarantee of excellence, but without them, I know of no way that excellence is even a possibility."[2]

PROFESSIONAL EDUCATION

The professional recreation curricula offered by two–year and four–year colleges and universities have assumed the major responsibility for preparing personnel for the growing number of job positions that demand recreation skills and background. Opportunities at all levels of service are available depending on the type and extent of educational preparation.

Janet MacLean wrote: "Our product—the students who move through our curriculums—must be prepared not only as managers and distributors of leisure services, but as dynamic social change agents, sensitive to not just the demands, but the needs of individuals and groups in a complex world."[3]

The three programs offering professional recreation education are as follows:

1. *Two years in a community or junior college* will prepare an individual for a position as a leader, technician, or specialist with career ladder opportunities to climb upward. Graduates can begin as recreation leaders, recreation center supervisors, and special facility technicians.

2. *Four years in a college or university* will provide preparatory training for a professional career as an administrator or supervisor, or numerous other jobs based on the type of curriculum. With experience, students completing a bachelor's program can qualify as program specialists, assistants to

directors in park and recreation departments, or directors in small communities.

3. *Postgraduate courses and degrees* will qualify the individual for higher levels of responsibility in top positions in one of the professional fields of specialization. Top administrative, educational, and research positions require advanced degrees on the master and doctoral level. Increasingly, many professional recreators are returning to the campus for advanced education and more specialized training.

The scope of recreation, parks, and leisure education programs at a given college will vary widely as to its role. Above all, colleges should select carefully the roles for which they assume responsibility.

Not all professional education in recreation and parks is in formal degree programs of colleges and universities. Numerous agencies provide in-service education programs, and professional organizations conduct periodic seminars, conferences, and training sessions for practitioners in the field.

UNDERGRADUATE PROFESSIONAL CURRICULUM

Undergraduate preparation should contribute a solid background for future growth and the minimum competencies for beginning professional service. Fifty percent of the course work is devoted to general education, the humanities, language arts, physical and social sciences; the remaining one-half is allocated to professional recreation education and its related areas.[4]

The undergraduate student should receive numerous laboratory and work experiences which will result in the learning of greater skills and a close familiarity with the professional field of recreation. In order to gain some specialization, he or she should take a sufficient number of elective hours.[5]

After conferences with the adviser, the student should be able to choose an effective integration of courses in allied disciplines, as well as in laboratory and in theoretical experiences.

Figure 8–2   The pursuit of excellence both in the academic classroom and in the professional field should be an unending challenge to educators and practitioners alike. Here, Drummond Abernethy, an international authority on leisure and play, speaks to recreation students at American River College, Sacramento.

Fieldwork offers the student–leader laboratory situations in which he or she is confronted with practical situations. Fieldwork should be a cooperative effort between the student, the institution, and the agency or department he or she is working for. Directed field experience is divided into two types: (1) observation and participation, (2) internship.

PROFESSIONAL STANDARDS

The progression of a student's educational experiences should follow a logical sequence. Upper level opportunities should build upon the foundation of understanding and skills acquired in general education and introductory professional requirements.

Approved by the National Council on Accreditation, the following standards delineate the professional foundation for all students in recreation, park resources, and leisure services.

The professional education core shall provide:

8.01 Knowledge of the history and development of the recreation, park resources, and leisure services profession.

8.02 Knowledge of the theory and philosophy of leisure and recreation.

8.03 Knowledge of human and natural resources and their relationship to the recreation experience.

8.04 Knowledge of the role and interrelationship of private, nonprofit and public recreation, park resources, and leisure service delivery systems.

8.05 Knowledge of the legislative process at the local, state, and federal levels and its impact upon leisure services.

8.06 Knowledge of the nature and diversity of leisure activities including the ability to analyze activity for participant requirements.

8.07 Knowledge of appropriate assessment techniques for the delivery of recreation, park resources, and leisure services.

8.08 Knowledge of the planning process as applied to program development including the specification of objectives, selection of activity content and facilitation techniques, identification strategies, designation of required resources, and the development of evaluation plans.

8.09 Knowledge of use of a variety of individual and group facilitation techniques.

8.10 Knowledge of the responsibility of the recreation, park resources, and leisure services profession to disadvantaged and special populations.

8.11 Knowledge of activity modification techniques, accessibility concepts and assistance techniques which would enable the participation of special populations.

8.12 Knowledge of principles and procedures related to planning, development, design, and maintenance of recreation, park resources, and leisure services areas and facilities.

8.13 Knowledge of management principles and procedures including:
8.13:01 Organization
8.13:02 Legal foundations of operations
8.13:03 Planning
8.13:04 Marketing and promotion
8.13:05 Finance
8.13:06 Public relations
8.13:07 Personnel practices and labor relations
8.13:08 Business practices
8.13:09 Decision making
8.13:10 Problem solving
8.13:11 Evaluation

8.14 Knowledge of the role and function of leisure education including philosophical concepts and programmatic applications.

8.15 Knowledge of contemporary professional issues and how they impact the delivery of leisure services.

8.16 Knowledge of the concept of a profession as related to the recreation, park resources, and leisure services fields.

8.17 Knowledge of the purpose, basic procedures, and the interpretation and application of research related to recreation, park resources, and leisure services.

8.18 Professional field experiences shall be required.

8.19 Knowledge of the advocacy role of the recreation, park resources, and leisure services professional in attaining public understanding of the value of recreation.[6]

Douglas Sessoms' description of a professional recreator emphasized the following competencies: "The professional recreator should know how to assess, diagnose, organize, implement, and monitor the recreation and park service delivery system regardless of the setting. He should be able to conceptualize, interpret, and evaluate the effectiveness of the system. Just as the physician determines the treatment plan for the patient and the engineer, the construction plan for the bridge, the recreator should determine the strategies for the implementation of recreation and park services."[7]

SPECIALIZATION

Indeed, the recreation and parks field has become quite extensive in scope. The field is so broad that it has become an impossibility to prepare students for all specialties.

Within each professional emphasis, there is a diversity of specializations, settings, and clientele which may require specialized competencies. For example, the therapeutic recreation specialist, in addition to general education, professional education, and recreation program services, will require an orientation to, and understanding of, handicapped conditions. The various levels of responsibility require additional specialized competencies.

While there has been a trend toward subspecialties, there is growing evidence which suggests a return to the generalist approach at the undergraduate level. Too much specialization, advocates of a general program believe, can fragment the profession and prevent the student from receiving a broad educational background. Proponents of specialization, however, believe the development of competencies are needed "for effective performance as beginning professionals within the subspecialties."[8]

INTERNSHIPS

Professional internships or trainee programs involve a special program of on–the–job supervision and training. Normally, internship at a four–year college or university is not less than nine months, nor more than twelve months' duration. Supervision is provided by college and agency supervisors.

During the internship period, conferences should be regularly held between the intern, the supervisor, and the administrator of the agency or department. This is essential to the success of the internship concept.

The attitude of the professional recreator, the person under whom the intern serves, is crucial to the success of the intern program. Joseph Curtis stated that "If he or she believes there is a genuine need for such fieldwork and maintains a close and conscientious contact with the intern throughout the training period, the intern experience holds every promise of being successful and rewarding."[9]

Curtis outlined several steps which recreation students can establish fieldwork or intern positions:

1. Select an area of concentration, e.g., public recreation, therapeutic, outdoor recreation, and notify faculty advisor of choice.
2. Choose two locations which offer a wide variety of work experiences.
3. Write formal business letters to the administrator of each of these choices, requesting permission to intern and including background material.
4. On acceptance, prepare for coming assignments by obtaining and studying all possible material relative to training site.[10]

For years, Ron Pineda, administrator of the Morale, Welfare and Recreation Division at Mather AFB, California, has successfully supervised many interns and field work students. "When you get an intern, you just can't

Figure 8–3 Parks and recreation as a career field is attracting an increasing number of female undergraduate and graduate students. Likewise, women are beginning to close the gap as educators in recreation and leisure studies.

send them into the corner and say, 'Answer the telephone for the rest of the day'," said Pineda. "You have to give them some responsibility! Give them a program that you know will fly anyway, but the difference is that it will fly higher if he does a good job."

CAREER OPTIONS

Within the college or university curriculum are numerous options available to students in the recreation and parks field. Sufficient diversification is provided to enable a student to enter any of several professional fields in recreation. The need for career options and specialization is the result of the extensive scope of the leisure services industry.

Recreation–Park Administration

This option places an emphasis on leisure service management, community recrea-

tion, public administration, business, planning, and the natural resources. Students are prepared for employment in recreation and park agencies at the various levels of government.

Therapeutic/Special Groups

The student is prepared for recreation service employment in such locations as hospitals (general and special), convalescent and nursing homes, special schools and training centers for the disabled, developmentally disabled, specialized programs offered by public recreation agencies, and homes for the aged.

Corrections

This option meets the general requirements for employment in correctional institutions at the local, state, and federal levels, such as prisons, reformatories, juvenile detention centers, and training facilities.

Outdoor Recreation

Emphasis is on management, conservation, interpretation, and utilization of forest, wilderness areas, waterways, fish and wildlife.

Private and Commercial Recreation

Professional recreators are needed to manage and supervise private clubs, commercial enterprises, employee recreation programs, athletic clubs, golf courses, marinas, and other recreational facilities.

The career option in private and commercial recreation has two alternatives: 1. to be a professional employee or manager for an established business. 2. to use the knowledge gained from recreation education and field experience to develop a personal business.

Armed Forces

Civilian and military employment opportunities are available for the direction and supervision of service clubs, libraries, sports, hobby shops, bowling alleys, and music for military personnel and their dependents.

Voluntary Youth Serving Agencies

Recreation leadership is the backbone of most youth–oriented groups such as the YMCA, Boy Scouts of America, Girl Scouts of America, Campfire Girls, and other activity–minded organizations. Group work agencies need professionally trained personnel for positions as executive directors, workers and leaders, specialists, field and regional secretaries, and research specialists.

Recreation Resource Management

Employment involves the planning, development, maintenance, and protection of resources, both natural and synthetic, used for leisure–time experiences. These jobs deal primarily with recreational areas, facilities, and natural resources.

Figure 8–4 The private and commercial sector demands a sound background in management and operational skills, such as those shown here by the manager of a local racquetball club.

Additional career options include environmental interpretation; and environmental planning management.

GRADUATE PROFESSIONAL PROGRAM

With the new demands for stronger standards for recreation personnel, graduate study has become essential. The larger agencies in many communities now require a master's degree for their top administrator. Generally, teachers, research specialists, and program planners are now required to have graduate degrees.

The objectives of a graduate program include the following:

Administrative techniques
Research and investigation
Specialization in an area

Figure 8–5 Preparation for employment in the recreation and leisure services field has been assumed largely by four–year and two–year colleges and universities. While community colleges train young men and women for jobs at the program and face–to–face level (left), the four–year schools are providing the field with personnel to fill administrative and high–level supervisory positions.

Observation and survey
Problem solving
Professional growth

The applicant for admission to a master's degree program should have had an undergraduate preparation in the field of graduate specialization, or should be required to make up deficiencies by proficiency examination or by courses specified by each institution. Acceptable standards of writing and speaking should be demonstrated by every advanced degree candidate.[11]

Graduate preparation should capitalize on the previous experiences of the candidate. Students should be given opportunities to plan, organize, and supervise programs. They need to become more familiar with basic evaluative and research techniques, as well as the ability to make oral and written presentations. They must gain an understanding in the following areas:

- Philosophy and principles of recreation
- Administration of recreation

- Research and evaluation
- Personnel management
- Public relations

GROWTH OF COMMUNITY COLLEGE PROGRAMS

The community college movement offering associate degrees in recreation leadership has made an important contribution to the professional preparation of leisure services personnel. This development can be attributed to two major factors: (a) the rapid expansion of two–year colleges; and (b) the need for direct leaders and program assistants.

The primary purpose of the two–year degree curriculum should be to prepare individuals both to live a more enriched life, to foster an awareness of the need and devotion for service, and to develop the background and skill competencies for recreation leadership. This role involves the preparation of the student for both early entry into the field and/or transfer to a four–year program to continue his or her education toward a bachelor's or master's degree.

The art of leadership, development of specialized skills, practical work experience, and general education requirements are four important elements which should be given high priority by two–year programs. The professional core curriculum is designed to develop within the student the skills and knowledge necessary to carry out the job functions. These courses give the student an opportunity to develop a philosophy of leisure service, and an understanding of leadership, management, and maintenance of programs and resources.

Early Entry Program

Graduates of the two–year curriculum can find employment in leadership roles where they can move into positions of more responsibility through experience and additional education.

Increasingly, community colleges are training people for paraprofessional entry–level jobs with leisure service agencies. With a growing number of career opportunities available to qualified associate professionals, the community college has responded to the need by providing vocational or career–oriented curricula. In achieving this end, the two–year curriculum contains the basic knowledge and training skills to prepare the student to function effectively in a face–to–face leadership capacity in a variety of recreational settings.

Many community colleges have seen the need to develop option programs or areas of emphasis involving some of the fastest growing sectors in the leisure services field, such as commercial and private recreation, therapeutic recreation services, and park technology.

Transfer Program

Two–year college graduates can continue their education at four–year schools for a bachelor's degree. The four–year institution offers full–fledged professional competencies, with extensive training provided to prepare students for the higher salaried supervisory and administrative positions.

While the major objective of the curriculum is to produce recreation leaders, the two–year program offers the basic professional courses in recreation which will be acceptable and transferable to four–year schools.

Community college students are prepared sufficiently in the area of recreation skills. In addition to the core courses in recreation, they have many general education requirements to meet, such as social and natural sciences, psychology, art, music, and language arts. Recreation centers, playgrounds, schools, and parks are a few of the places where the student may work in directed work experience on the leadership level.

While it is difficult to provide students with broad professional training, community college programs in recreation leadership have been able to impart the basic skills and knowledge needed for many specialized jobs.

National Guidelines Approved

In October 1978, in Miami, Florida, a major milestone was achieved when the Society of Park and Recreation Educators Board of Directors formally approved and adopted National Guidelines for Recreation and Park Education at two–year colleges. The guidelines were written to assist institutions of higher education in developing the highest quality programs possible.

The guidelines recommended the following roles for the two–year programs:

Role 1—Career based technician oriented program (including transfer). Preparation of recreation program leaders and park technicians in a variety of areas. Students should be prepared to assume employment at an entry level position or transfer to a four–year institution for greater depth of professional preparation.

Role 2—Continuing, in–service education. Upgrading and retraining practitioners in the field through workshops, seminars, and extra–mural courses.

Role 3—Leisure education. Greater emphasis on leisure education for all community college students.

Role 4—Community service. Provision of recreation services to the community, such as consultation, leadership, and supervision of programs, shared use of facilities, planning and direction of community sevices or related functions.[12]

Articulation

Two–year and four–year college relationships continue to be a major area of concern to those involved with recreation and park education. Unquestionably, the people most affected by articulation, or lack of it, are the students who transfer from two–year programs to four–year colleges and universities. They can either benefit from a smooth articulation process, or be the victims of a poor relationship between two–year and four–year programs.

Transferability should be a local or regional concern since there is a lack of uniformity in course quality and content. To avoid duplication, clarification of the specific requirements is necessary to ensure that each level of instruction fulfills its appropriate objectives.

JOB STUDIES OF SUPPLY AND DEMAND

Conducting a local and regional job study and analysis was a major recommendation of four regional workshops conducted by the Society of Park and Recreation Educators in 1978. A local labor power study can determine:

1. What jobs should the college train the students for.
2. The competencies required by students to function in that job.[13]

A job study project, for example, can identify and conduct research on the availability of jobs in the private and commercial sector. As a result, curricular patterns can be developed to reflect the diversity of this rapidly growing market.

ACCREDITATION

With the rapid growth of recreation curricula, there is an apparent need to determine their degree of effectiveness and to strengthen them. If they are to be improved, the accreditation of college and university programs is essential.

Accreditation is a process established by a professional organization to enable a college or university to be recognized as having met certain predetermined standards.

After years of development, an accreditation program for college and university recreation education curricula has become a reality. National Recreation and Park Association (NRPA), in cooperation with the American Association for Leisure and Recreation (AALR), currently accredits baccalaureate and master's degree programs in parks and recreation. The National Council on Accreditation is composed of nine members who meet twice a year to consider recommendations from teams of educators and practitioners who have visited schools requesting accreditation.

According to Dr. Janet MacLean, "Accreditation's main purpose is to improve the quality of professional preparation and to give assurance to the prospective student and potential employer that the professional preparation available at the school has met minimum standards."[14]

The process entails the following criteria:

- Establishment of standards
- Development of evaluative criteria or schedules
- Inspection by accrediting agency
- Enforcement of standards

With the successful initiation of accreditation at the baccalaureate level, the effort to accredit two–year programs is a logical development. The National Council on Accreditation asked the NRPA educator group, Society of Park and Recreation Educators, to develop two–year associate degree accreditation standards.

Standards for Two–Year Colleges

In October 1981, in Minneapolis, Minnesota, another significant step toward stronger programs was made when the Society of Park and Recreation Educators Board of Directors approved a document of standards and evaluative criteria for the accreditation of two–year college programs in recreation, parks and leisure studies. The standards were developed by SPRE's Two–year/Four–year Issues Committee for the purpose of recommending them for adoption by the Council on Accreditation.[15]

CLARIFYING A CAREER LADDER

The need to clarify a career ladder in the preparation of recreation and parks personnel has long been a major concern to educators and practitioners alike. As to the recommended competencies that should be taught, a significant advantage to the accreditation process is that there be a degree of commonality from one college or university to the next. Robert Cipriano wrote, "In view of the proliferation of recreation and park curricula throughout the country, a set of minimal criteria for course content in recreation education should be established."[16] More effective articulation between specific educational levels is also possible through this approach.

The following is a compilation of specific tasks that personnel should be able to perform at six distinct educational levels, including the junior or community college, senior college, and graduate school.[17]

Associate Professional

General skills to be performed in the areas of instructing and leading activities.

Junior or Community College The job tasks that may be assigned to personnel with two years college include:

1. Instruct and lead sports activities.
2. Plan activity programs.
3. Lead special events and programs.
4. Prepare and operate equipment and supplies for events.
5. Prepare periodic activity reports, with appropriate evaluations.
6. Evaluate the useability of equipment and supplies.
7. Instruct, lead and low–level supervision of specific activities (crafts, music, drama, table games, etc.).
8. Low–level supervision of volunteers and/or paraprofessionals.
9. Prepare specific program budgets.
10. Assist with publicity and public relations.

Professional Level

Three education programs are involved on the professional level of the curriculum continuum: baccalaureate, master's, and doctorate.

Senior College The professional emphasis should emphasize planning, conducting, and administering programs in a variety of settings and program fields. Students graduating with a bachelor's degree in recreation and park curricula should be able to perform the following tasks:

1. Plan activity programs.
2. Program evaluation.
3. Prepare observation reports of people.
4. Evaluate the useability of equipment and supplies.
5. Supervise activity leaders.
6. Train volunteers and pre–professional staff on an orientation, in–service basis.
7. Assist with public relations.
8. Direct large recreation center or resource facility.
9. Lead a special group (handicapped, aging, etc.).
10. Prepare budget materials and financial reports.
11. Develop agency newsletter.

Graduate School Tasks that may be assigned personnel with a master's degree are in the areas of direct supervision, including the following skills:

1. Plan, organize and develop programs.
2. Direct or operate a recreation or park program (community, institution, outdoor resource, etc.).
3. Supervise program and staff.
4. Supervise public relations.
5. Conduct evaluations (staff, facilities, etc.).
6. Prepare budget and annual reports.
7. Develop policies and practices consistent with philosophy of the department.
8. Articulate professional issues in the recreation and park field.
9. Plan, design, develop, and maintain recreation areas and facilities.
10. Plan, conduct, interpret, and report research.

STUDENT INVOLVEMENT

Faculty at both undergraduate and graduate levels are encouraged to seek student involvement in departmental affairs and curriculum planning. Student evaluation during and at the end of each course can be most helpful.

Students should be assisted by members of the faculty in establishing and maintaining a student club and developing its programs. However, students should be responsible for the affairs of the club.

A 1974 Student Section study conducted by the National Recreation and Park Association (NRPA) listed the following weaknesses felt by students about their own professional preparation:

1. The poor quality of most field work experiences.
2. Instructors without practical experience or enthusiasm.
3. Lack of exposure to and participation in professional organizations.
4. Need for a more demanding curriculum and more stringent entry requirements.

5. The absense of any real effort to develop professional attitudes.
6. Too many outdated and outmoded classes.[18]

LICENSING AND CERTIFICATION

These two terms generally refer to the process of evaluating the credentials of persons in occupational or professional fields and giving them legal permission to practice. They are another effort to upgrade the standards of the recreation and park profession.

The term *licensing* governs the scope of professional practice, defining the specific services that may be provided, the populations served, or other conditions. In contrast, the term *certification* governs the use of a professional title, protecting the field and the public against unauthorized or untrained practitioners. Frequently, it is used synonymously with recreation.[19]

Licensing and certification documents usually spell out education, experience, and performance qualifications for administrators, supervisors, leaders, technicians, and specialists. Testing procedures include written and oral exams, in addition to personal recommendations.

Private agencies have developed standards that involve certification of their personnel. Civil Service commissions, for years, have required comprehensive examinations for those applicants seeking positions in governmental agencies.

Although certification appears to be a logical means of enforcing professional standards among those employed in recreation and park positions, it has not been widely adopted. Many people in the recreation and parks field, however, predict that certification will soon become mandatory.

In expressing strong concern, Kraus stated that: "Nonetheless, it is widely accepted that the lack of an effective means to screen out unqualified personnel and to provide recognition for professional training is a major hindrance to the development of professionalism in recreation and parks."[20]

REGISTRATION

Registration is a process through which the park and recreation profession attempts to assure the general public and the employing agency of the competence of park and recreation professionals. It consists of a review of the credentials of applicants by state or national professional societies, which indicate that the applicants have or have not met certain qualifications. For example, the state of New York has a voluntary registration plan, with standards established by the New York Recreation and Park Society for nine levels of responsibility.

Different state societies have established various forms of registration standards and procedures to identify qualified personnel. However, Kraus explained that "since such plans have been more or less voluntary rather than compulsory, they depend on the cooperation of appropriate state and munic-ipal agencies to respect and enforce their requirements."[21]

The New York plan defines personnel standards for each job level, based on the duties and distinguishing features of the position, the knowledge and abilities required for the position, and the minimum education and experience required. California has a similar registration plan, with a board of recreation personnel that establishes standards for administrators, supervisors, and leaders, and provides incentive pay in many communities for registered personnel.

MacLean emphasized that "Registration means little without accreditation to insure that the degree designated for registration was achieved through a curriculum which at least met proposed standards. And neither registration or accreditation is meaningful unless employers support them in their hiring practices."[22]

The National Recreation and Park Asso-

Figure 8–6 Professional development and continuing education services have contributed significantly toward higher standards and upgrading of the field. Here, an outstanding panel of recreation practitioners and educators participate in the 1978 Society of Park and Recreation Educators Far West Regional Workshop in Sacramento.

ciation has recognized the difficulty of maintaining standards through fifty different state plans, and has developed and implemented a process of national registration. In 1974, the NRPA adopted *A Model Registration Plan for Park and Recreation Personnel*, and the national plan is now in operation.

IN–SERVICE TRAINING

The professional advancement of the practitioner and educator should never end. Experience on the job should be combined with a well–organized in–service education program. In–service programs can be conducted independently or jointly with other agencies. Increasingly, colleges and universities have been cooperating with agencies in providing opportunities for in–service training.

Techniques that are often used include: conferences, staff meetings, seminars, institutes, workshops, symposia, individual or committee projects, and home study or correspondence courses. Professional periodicals and bulletins, textbooks, films and slides, radio, and television are other sources of learning and training.

CONTINUING EDUCATION

A broad array of continuing education programs are sponsored and co–sponsored by the National Recreation and Park Association. In addition to the annual national congress which features 150–200 separate education programs, each NRPA region and special interest group sponsor a number of conferences and workshops.

COOPERATIVE EDUCATION

An increasing number of colleges and universities are participating in cooperative education programs with various governmental agencies, such as the United States Forest Service and the Bureau of Land Management. Under signed agreements, agency personnel have an opportunity to engage in academic study over a specified time period.

JOB PLACEMENT

Colleges and professional organizations have made significant progress in their efforts to improve the placement process through which qualified candidates are directed to job opportunities. Numerous organizations have prepared career information booklets or pamphlets to ensure that those entering the field are aware of job opportunities and are able to prepare for them effectively.

The National Recreation and Park Association publishes *Park and Recreation Opportunities*, a bulletin including detailed analysis of career fields in specialized groupings and comprehensive nationwide job listings, as part of its total placement service. *EMPLOY*, published monthly by NRPA, is designed to assist individuals to prepare for the job search.

PREPARING FOR THE JOB SEARCH

Securing employment requires considerable planning and thought on the part of the individual. Preparation, of course, begins with education, but in moving through the formal learning process, Christine Badger suggests that a person should also be prepared in the following ways:

- Investigate the field, i.e. what areas of employment are available, particularly the new areas.
- Prepare yourself financially. Allocate funds to support the job search.
- Get to know professionals in the field by attending conferences, visiting agencies, and becoming involved in professional groups.
- Be ready to present yourself to the employer with a resume that has been carefully prepared.

- In approaching an interview, research the position vacancy. Know as much about the agency and position as you can.
- Prepare for the interview, with such methods as test questions, pressure interview techniques, and personal appearance.[23]

RESEARCH

Recreation and leisure services as a field has, in the past, been rather weak in conducting research and investigative study. However, significant progress in the area of research was achieved during the 1970s which gives every indication that the 1980s will see continued improvement and achievements.

Carlson, Deppe, MacLean, and Peterson wrote that: "Through quality research and continuous evaluation, professional leaders must explore new horizons and plan creatively from factual data, if the recreation profession is to meet its mounting responsibilities."[24]

Unquestionably, the establishment of graduate programs in recreation and leisure studies in colleges and universities has generated an unprecedented number of research projects. In addition, the research symposium held in conjunction with the National Recreation and Park Association Congress has provided significant impetus, not only to graduate students and faculty but to practitioners in the field.

The *Journal of Leisure Research*, published by the NRPA beginning in 1969, has provided a good stimulus for quality investigation. The journal provides a medium for interdisciplinary exchange.

In addition to institutions of higher learning, many governmental agencies on the local, state, and federal levels have conducted recreation research, including industry, foundations, and various service organizations. Public recreation departments, on occasion, conduct studies in an attempt to secure information and data, and to solve some of their problems.

QUESTIONS FOR DISCUSSION

1. Discuss some new and stronger standards and competencies that would upgrade and strengthen the preparation of recreation and parks personnel.
2. Describe the growth and development of recreation curriculums in the United States. What program options do you believe are the most viable today?
3. What steps should recreation students take in establishing a fieldwork or intern position?
4. How can an individual prepare for the job search?
5. What major factors have contributed to the development of the community college movement?
6. What are the benefits of good articulation between community colleges and four year schools.
7. Why is accreditation of college and university professional development programs in recreation so essential?
8. Explain the term *certification*. Do you think that professional recreators should be certified? Explain your answer.
9. Discuss the type of opportunities for in–service education training that should be provided both the practitioner and educator.
10. Suggest how the field of recreation and leisure services can create more emphasis on research and make it more meaningful, from the standpoint of both the educator and practitioner.

REFERENCES

1. H. Douglas Sessoms, "Education in the Eighties: Forecast—Change", *Parks and Recreation Magazine*, May 1981, p. 49.
2. Donald Henkel (Keynote Address, SPRE Far West Regional Workshop, Sacramento, Calif.), April 4, 1978.
3. Janet R. MacLean, "Charge for 1974: Active Involvement," *Communique*, National Recreation and Park Association, September/October 1973, p. 15.
4. Report of a national conference, "Professional Preparation in Recreation Education," Washington, D.C.: American Association for Health, Physical Education and Recreation, 1962, pp. 89–90.
5. Ibid.
6. "Standards and Evaluative Criteria for Recreation Leisure Services and Resources Curricula," Established by the National Council on Accreditation, National Recreation and Park Association, Revised October, 1981, p. 8.
7. H. Douglas Sessoms, "Programs and Professional Preparation in the 1980's", *News of SPRE*, National Recreation and Park Association, Vol. III, No. 2, March 1980, p. 9.
8. H. Douglas Sessoms. "Education in the Eighties: Forecast—Change," p. 50.
9. Joseph E. Curtis, *Recreation—Theory and Practice* (St. Louis: The C. V. Mosby Company, 1979), p. 271.
10. Ibid.
11. Standards and Evaluative Criteria, 1978, pp. 14–15.
12. "Guidelines for Recreation and Park Education at Two–Year Colleges," Developed by the Society of Park and Recreation Educators, Branch of the NRPA, Arlington, Virginia, 1979, p. 2.
13. Ibid., p. 3.
14. Janet R. MacLean, "Preparing for Accreditation," Proceedings of 1977 Las Vegas–SPRE Institute, National Recreation and Park Association, October 2, 1977, p. 21.
15. "Standards for Two–Year Colleges," Developed by the Society of Park and Recreation Educators, Arlington, October 1981, p. 1.
16. Robert E. Cipriano, "A Paradigm For Conceptualizing a Task Analysis Approach to Curriculum Development," Unpublished Report, Southern Connecticut State College, New Haven, Connecticut, 1980, pp. 1–2.
17. Ibid., pp. 4–5.
18. Don Jolley and Jennie Hicks, "Leisure Education: Who's Responsibility," *Management Strategy*, Summer 1977, Vol. 1, No. 2, p. 3.
19. Richard Kraus, *Recreation and Leisure in Modern Society* (Santa Monica: Goodyear Publishing Company, 1977), p. 293.
20. Ibid.
21. Ibid., p. 294.
22. MacLean, p. 24.
23. Christine C. Badger, "Preparing for the Job Search in Parks," *Recreation and Park Association*, July 1978, p. 1.
24. Reynold Carlson, Janet MacLean, Theodore Deppe, and James Peterson, *Recreation and Leisure*, 3rd ed. (Belmont, Calif.: Wadsworth Company, 1979), p. 266.

III
The Role of Government in Recreation and Parks

Figure 9–1 Close–to–home facilities and programs are among the urgent needs of people who live in urban areas, according to the 1978 National Urban Recreation Study. This group of children in Sacramento found the playground tire swing just the thing to release some pent–up energy. (Courtesy *Sacramento Bee.*)

9
Local/Urban Government

The provision of park and recreation opportunities in urban areas is primarily the responsibility of the local government. Localities generally have the power to zone and acquire land, and to provide public services, including recreation. Traditionally, management of urban recreation systems has been the responsibility of local governments, while the primary role of state and federal governments is to provide technical and financial assistance in support of local recreation.

Before the twentieth century, local government was relatively simple and concerned with few functions and services. Today, however, municipal government has taken on a new dimension, the result of a growing acceptance that government should contribute to the welfare of the people.

As the recreation movement grew in scope, and the facilities and services increased, there developed a need for specific legislation giving municipalities the power to appropriate funds for parks and recreation services.

Indeed, recreation is an important human service which can help meet other social objectives, including crime prevention, employment, and job creation. "Recreation and leisure services is one of the major front line services of local government," explained Solon "Doc" Wisham, director of parks and recreation in Sacramento. "We provide opportunities for citizens to improve the quality of their lives. Yet, we are not a life support or sustaining service, like police and fire. Therefore, we have more difficulty in competing against other services for the scarce dollar."

In the present age of inflation, government agencies are faced with continuing problems of rising costs. Most public recreation programs in urban cities are under-financed and under-staffed. The 1978 National Urban Recreation study revealed that: "Programs in many large cities are often limited in scope, poorly distributed, seasonal, and serve only small segments of the population. They usually fail to meet the diversified recreation needs of present urban residents."[1]

The decline indicates a relative shift in resources away from parks and recreation toward other higher priority local services such as police, fire, and education. To compensate, some cities are turning to other sources of local support such as user fees, donations, and cooperative funding arrangements. An alternative for many has been to reduce the scope and level of service delivered to the constituency.

Deficiencies in recreation programs are most evident in the low-income areas of inner cities. The serious program deficiencies already existing in most neighborhoods have been worsened by budget cuts. Staff cutbacks have reduced program opportunities and facility maintenance, often while use of facilities has increased.

Recreation and leisure time opportunities are also limited for handicapped persons, senior citizens, and the economically and socially-disadvantaged. While both public and private recreation sectors have become more involved in providing program services, programs for special population groups still meet only a small portion of the potential demand.

DEFINITIONS

According to George Butler, "The term 'local government' is considered applicable to any local unit of state government such as the county, city, village, borough, or township, or school, park, and recreation districts. The term 'municipal recreation' is intended to include services provided by park or school authorities as well as by other local governmental agencies."[2]

As commonly used, the term *urban* is a confusing one, applying to census defined places of between 2,500 and 7.5 million population.

THE NEED FOR MUNICIPAL RECREATION

The recreation and park services provided by a local municipality are determined primarily by the expressed will of the people and their readiness to pay for them from tax funds. In cities throughout America, the people have indicated that they consider recreation a needed function of local government.

However, the local municipality cannot meet all the recreation and leisure needs of all the people. The needs and interests of a community are too diverse and expensive for any one municipal agency to serve. Instead, the resources and services of all recreation agencies, organizations, and institutions are needed to serve the ever growing leisure–time needs of our society. For a nation which is rapidly becoming leisure–oriented, there is a growing demand for a great variety of recreation activities and park services.

In meeting the needs of the community, municipalities have the resources and ability to acquire, develop, and maintain a system of areas and facilities. They also have the financial capabilities through taxation, special assessments, and bonding powers to appropriate the funds needed to fulfill their responsibilities.

URBAN CRISIS: PUTTING PARKS WHERE THE PEOPLE ARE

The National Urban Recreation Study released in 1978 by the Department of the Interior noted that forty–five million Americans live in households without cars. The study cited the urgent need for federally supported facilities in densely populated urban centers.[3]

A major finding of the study indicated quite conclusively that people in urban areas want a well–balanced system of recreation opportunities which includes close–to–home neighborhood facilities and programs for all segments of the population.

Many urban residents have become very concerned about the loss of existing and potential recreation lands, facilities, and programs. Opportunities have actually declined in recent years because of aging facilities and fiscal restraints.

"By European standards, American cities are park poor—and getting worse," declared Jere Stuart French. "The growth in park acreage is nowhere near proportional to the growth in area of our cities, particularly the faster growing cities."[4]

Figure 9–2 Central Park, the great green belt in Manhattan, is one of the world's most famous parks. It is a green oasis between 59th and 110th streets. The magnificent park is a pleasure ground that provides a healthful atmosphere and a rural retreat as a positive contrast to city conditions. (Courtesy New York City Department of Parks and Recreation.)

TYPES OF SPONSORSHIP

Within the United States many groups and agencies strive to meet the recreation and leisure needs of a community. Essentially, the following four groups contribute the greatest portion of the community recreation program:

1. *Public agencies and institutions*, created and controlled by governmental bodies on local, state, and federal levels, and supported by taxes. The local municipality has a major responsibility of providing, maintaining, and operating a system of major areas and facilities, such as parks, playgrounds, recreation buildings, golf courses, athletic fields, community centers, playfields, water and winter sports facilities, and outdoor reservations. The recreation department should also provide leadership for a diversified program of sports, arts and crafts, drama, music, social recreation, outdoor recreation, special events, and other activities at the local facilities.
2. *Voluntary group work* agencies, consisting primarily of youth–serving organizations supported by membership fees and community funds. Even though the local government has taken over many of the recreation functions of the voluntary agencies, these agencies will continue to meet important leisure needs of the community. The voluntary agency, however, usually restricts its primary service to a limited membership group.
3. *Private groups* such as industry, clubs, churches, armed forces, and fraternal and social groups that are supported by membership fees. They include private tennis and racquetball clubs, golf clubs, yacht or sailing clubs, athletic or sport clubs, chess and bridge clubs, and many others. Private agencies will continue to support the overall community recreation effort. Many types of private agencies offer enjoyable recreation for their members in restricted recreation groups.
4. *Commercial recreation enterprises* which are organized to gain a profit from their services and are designed to meet a specific leisure activity need of the people. The varied array of privately owned, profit–making businesses, facilities, or enterprises include spectator activities, outdoor attractions and amusements, participative activities, mechanized sports, clubs, resorts, and housing developments and associations.

ORGANIZATION OF CITY GOVERNMENTS

The two types of incorporated cities in the United States are charter and general law cities. Gus Gerson wrote that "The citizens within the charter city have voted on a government operation unique to that city. The charter is like a small constitution that outlines the form of government. The charter city can have almost any form of government it desires as long as it is not in conflict with the state or federal constitution."[5]

A general law city is governed by the laws of the individual state. It does not have an individual charter. Gerson emphasized that many states allow some financial advantages to general law cities. He stated that "Throughout the United States the majority of states have provided for general law cities to be organized in the council/manager form of government."[6]

LEGAL AUTHORITY FOR RECREATION

To operate as a local governmental function, a municipal recreation department must receive legal authority from the state before a program can be organized. City and county types of government and the scope of their power are derived from the state constitution and statutes.

The legal bases for local government participation in the parks and recreation field and open space preservation are state enabling laws, local charters, and ordinances. They allow local governments to acquire land and buildings for park and recreation purposes by negotiated purchase, donation, bequest, or lease. Many cities may acquire land for park purposes by condemnation, which involves the right of eminent domain.

State enabling laws for recreation enable communities in the state to establish and conduct recreation programs under any type of administrative authority. Such an act means that the local community has the legal authorization of establishing the local recreation program most appropriate for its needs. Such acts also permit local governments to acquire land and spend public funds for land and buildings, and provide the authority to join with other local governments in cooperative efforts.

Many states have passed laws that have authorized county, district, or metropolitan park and recreation districts. Some state recreation and park enabling laws empower school districts, municipalities, counties, and other units of local government to join together to establish, operate, and maintain park and recreation systems.

LOCAL CHARTERS AND ORDINANCES

Operating under home–rule charters, cities and counties have the authority to establish and operate park and recreation systems under the power of such charters to promote the general welfare of citizens. Charter provisions related to recreation and parks usually provide for the creation of a park and recreation department, the appointment of an administrator, and an advisory board.

A local government that does not act under home–rule may create a park and recreation department and an administrative board by use of ordinances. Like charters, most ordinances will indicate the manner in which the park and recreation director and the administrative board are selected and will outline their duties. Ordinances provide the park and recreation agency with the permission to pass regulations and rules pertaining to the uses of parks and recreation

facilities. Typical rules provided in city ordinances indicate speed limits to be observed in parks, closing hours for facilities, and types of conduct allowed.

ORGANIZING A RECREATION DEPARTMENT

After identifying and clarifying its need for establishing a municipal recreation program, a community must determine the administrative authority that is best suited to administer its recreation program. In addition to the type of authority, it should also consider the best use of tax funds and offer the best possible services and program.

No one authority is best suited to administer the recreation program. In the past, recreation has been administered by: (1) the park department, (2) a separate recreation authority, (3) the school administration, and (4) a combined department of parks and recreation, which has gained strong popularity in recent years.

Since community conditions vary, a number of factors must be considered that will determine the type of administrative authority. First, the existing state statutes should be examined to determine how such legislation will affect the local government in establishing a new department. Since the ability to obtain funds is an important consideration, the organizing committee must determine under what agency the most adequate funds can be provided. In order to secure the most widespread community support, the committee should determine the public's attitude toward the various types of organizations. The logical authority to direct the recreation program is the agency that can develop policies, coordinate plans, and secure the close cooperation with other organizations in the community.

Many large cities maintain separate park and recreation departments, each with its own director and some degree of autonomy. A large park department usually has a general manager, superintendents for both parks and recreation and special assistants

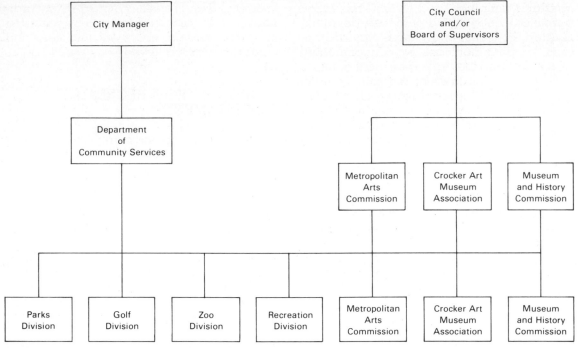

Figure 9–3 Organizational chart, City of Sacramento.

for each. However, small to medium–sized cities tend to maintain a combined department of parks and recreation with one director and a separate supervisor of parks as well as a supervisor of recreation.

In Philadelphia, recreation functions are filled by three tax–supported agencies: the Department of Recreation, the Board of Public Education, and the Fairmont Park Commission. The three agencies work closely together, participating in the joint planning of numerous capital construction projects.

In Kansas City, the three–member parks and recreation board operates under the legislative control of the mayor and council, but once appointed to office, is independent of the mayor who has appointed it. Once funds are appropriated to the board, no one including the city council can interfere with the board's expenditure of its funds.

In a small community, the director or administrator usually is responsible for both parks and recreation. Under the combined department system, the administrator is apt to be a person trained in recreation with an experienced park foreman to handle the park work.

Some metropolitan areas have formed park districts that have elected commissioners as the primary decision–making body. San Francisco combines a city and county recreation and park department which operates under a general manager. The general manager has both a superintendent of parks and a superintendent of recreation.

TYPES OF ADMINISTRATIVE AUTHORITY

Although there are various types of managing authorities, administering recreation as a separate function has been the most practiced approach in America. However, there is a continuing shift in management from separate departments to a combined

Figure 9–4 Opening of an urban neighborhood swimming pool. A new pool at Whittier Playground in Philadelphia was officially dedicated by Robert Crawford, former Director of the Philadelphia Recreation Department. (Courtesy Philadelphia Department of Recreation.)

park and recreation authority. The main types of administrative patterns are as follows:

1. *Administration of recreation as a separate function.* Those who advocate this approach feel that more prompt and efficient management occurs with a separate department directly under the mayor or city manager. By centralizing all resources in a separate recreation authority, greater concentration on the responsibility for recreation can be attained.

Establishing recreation under a board or commission is advocated by the majority of recreation professionals. The general feeling is that a board provides for more opportuni-

ties for greater citizen involvement, better continuity of policy and programs, and more effective use of public opinion.

Major disadvantages of separate departments are that they generally compete for budgetary appropriations, and the respective leaders are often unwilling or unable to coordinate the efforts of the two departments. Also, duplication of equipment and personnel often leads to a more expensive operation.

2. *Park administration of recreation.* In its early developments, recreation joined forces with park departments. However, those who argued against having park departments administer recreation programs stated that park administrators were more concerned

with administration of areas and equipment. They contended that park officials were more involved with maintaining beautiful lawns, trees, and plants than with getting more people to use the recreation areas. Fortunately, park directors today are more oriented toward recreation and people. They realize that, essentially, public parks have one primary function—to help people enjoy their leisure time.

3. *School administration of recreation.* School administrators are becoming more aware of the need in the community for recreation services. For many years, many professional recreation and park planners have strongly encouraged recreational use of school facilities and school use of recreation facilities. Since the school board and administrative officials have the respect from parents and the public, backers of this type of authority feel that the public would respond favorably to the schools' direction of recreation programs. Indeed, the schools have the facilities, such as buildings and playgrounds, to contribute significantly to an overall community recreation program.

Many school recreation programs emerged from the community center movement. Today, the "community school" theory has been effective in promoting recreational uses of the school plant. The "community school" is a modern concept of community education in which the school is considered an agency that makes maximum use of its facilities and other resources to serve both the educational and recreational needs of the community.

However, school districts are usually not in a position to operate an adequate total park and recreation system. A large portion of the public recreation demand is for golf courses, swimming areas, hiking trails, boat–launching facilities, and shaded picnic areas, which for the most part are outside the range of a school district's interest, jurisdiction, and financial capacity. Still, the school district can make a significant contribution to the park and recreation program and should cooperate to the fullest in the planning and use of local areas and facilities.

4. *Combined department of parks and*

recreation. In recent years, considerable attention has been given to the consolidation of parks and recreation into a single department. In fact, where new departments are now being established, nearly 100 percent are combined departments of parks and recreation.

The combined department of parks and recreation often results in a more effective integration of maintenance and program which benefits from greater centralization of control and direction. In addition, the combined agency results in financial savings, improved services, and better perspective with which to balance program needs.

5. *District or regional park department.* The establishment of district, county, or met-

Figure 9–5 Festival in the park. This popular event for square dance groups is sponsored annually by the Montgomery, Alabama, Parks and Recreation Department. Recreation and leisure services such as these are a major responsibility of municipal agencies. (Courtesy Montgomery Parks and Recreation Department.)

ropolitan park and recreation departments has been a recent trend in recreation administration. They are often formed under the terms of enabling state legislation to meet certain local needs not satisfied by existing governments. Special districts have been accepted by the state as regional complements to both local and state park systems. They are allowed to levy taxes and issue bonds with voter approval.

FUNCTIONS OF MUNICIPAL RECREATION AND PARK AGENCIES

Municipal recreation and park departments have three major responsibilities, which Richard Kraus categorized as:

1. Direct provision of Recreation Opportunities. Recreation and park agencies acquire, develop, and maintain facilities needed for recreational participation, and provide skilled leadership to meet the needs of various age groups and individuals.
2. Coordination of Other Programs. Municipal agencies provide in–service training and advisory services for other private, voluntary, or therapeutic agencies in the community, and help them coordinate their efforts to avoid duplication and overlap.
3. Cooperation with Other Government Agencies. They work closely with other governmental agencies to develop long–range planning, land acquisition, and when needed, joint programs of direct service.[7]

FINANCE

No agency or department can operate effectively without adequate financial support. While there are still many individuals who feel that recreation is a personal concern, most communities in the United States have accepted recreation as a vital governmental function. Finding a consistent and effective source of financing for recreation and park-

land acquisition and improvements still remains a problem in most American cities.

Money is needed to acquire areas and facilities, to provide qualified leaders, to purchase supplies and equipment, and to maintain the parks, playgrounds, community centers, and other facilities that are essential for a well–rounded program. A steady flow of funds, therefore, is required to finance a strong park and recreation system. Money may come from such sources as the general fund, special tax levies, bond issues, fees and charges, federal and state grants, donations, gifts, and concessions.

Many of the most serious problems facing park and recreation agencies today are the result of inadequate financial support. Park and recreation departments of economically hard–pressed cities now have fewer dollars to provide recreation services than they did five years ago. As a result, many local governments have had to seriously cut back on services, raise taxes, or operate with deficit financing. Cities, though, appear to be in better shape to absorb tax cutting initiative legislation than counties and special districts because cities have funding sources other than property taxes.

"General revenue sharing is the greatest thing that the federal government has ever done for local government," declared Solon Wisham, Sacramento's director of parks and recreation. "If we had no revenue sharing and anti–recession funds, community development revenue sharing, and others, we would have gone under a few years ago."

METHODS OF FINANCING RECREATION

Financing municipal recreation is normally divided into two categories of funds: current operating funds, which are the day–to–day spending to carry on the ongoing program of activities and services; and funds for capital outlay, which involve outlays for items that result in the acquisition or addition of fixed assets such as land, new building, and others.

Current Operating Funds

The following are considered to be the prime sources of current operating funds:

1. *Appropriations from the general fund.* A widely used method of securing money for recreation is for the recreation department to submit a budget to the appropriating body. Following approval by the reviewing boards, the money is drawn from the city's general fund. The general fund is created and maintained to finance the many functions of municipal government. Along with such departments as police, fire, and public works, the recreation department strives to obtain its fair share of the city's tax funds, which come primarily by property assessments.

The local general fund is still the largest single source of support for parks and recreation, although general fund support has been eroding as cities divert recreation dollars to what they determine as more pressing needs. The general fund now consists of community development revenue sharing and general revenue sharing, in addition to the various unrestricted fees and charges that cities take in, such as water and sewer fees.

2. *Special recreation tax.* Authorized in many states, a special tax levy for recreation involves a special revenue fund. Created through statutory provisions, this type of fund provides definite revenue for parks, recreation, and schools. The special tax is usually expressed in terms of a certain number of mills on each dollar of assessed valuation, or so many cents per hundred dollars of assessed valuation.

3. *Fees and charges.* Fees charged for certain services or use of facilities are another means of supporting municipal recreation. They are often charged where certain facilities or services have a high initial cost and have limitations as to the number of people they accommodate. Two of the most common examples of facilities for which fees are normally charged are swimming pools and golf courses.

To make up for budget cuts caused by tax

cutting initiative legislation such as Proposition 13, many park and recreation agencies, have increased user fees. Critics of user fees say that charging a fee amounts to double taxation, since they have already paid for the parks and are paying to operate them. Still, there are those who maintain that the user should not expect to be completely subsidized by tax money supplied by the non–user. The user should offset at least a part of the cost of operating and maintaining parks by paying fees for the privilege of use.

Funds for Capital Outlay

Some of the principal sources of funds for capital outlay are as follows:

1. *Bond issues.* In order for large and costly projects to be funded, such as the construction of community buildings, swimming pools, or golf courses, the issuance of bonds involves borrowing for capital acquisitions and major improvements. Voters must approve a bond issue authorizing the governing body to borrow money and pay it back over a specified period of years. Bonds are a supplement to taxation and should not be considered actual revenue, since they create a liability that must be paid from future taxes.

On a national basis, bond issues are on the downgrade, due primarily to the fact that they usually require a 66⅔ percent vote. A bond issue is a direct levy on a property tax. The revenue bond issue is questionable simply because there will be no direct levy on the tax rate. However, it has to be self–supportive, like water, sewer, or a garbage operation. Recreation and park operations usually are not self–supportive.

2. *Special assessments.* Special assessments are commonly used to finance permanent improvements, which are paid for in whole or in part by the property owners in the area who benefit from the services. In essence, the cost of services is placed on those who benefit and are willing to pay. An example of a special assessment is when a community charges for the cost of a particular recreation or park project against the spe-

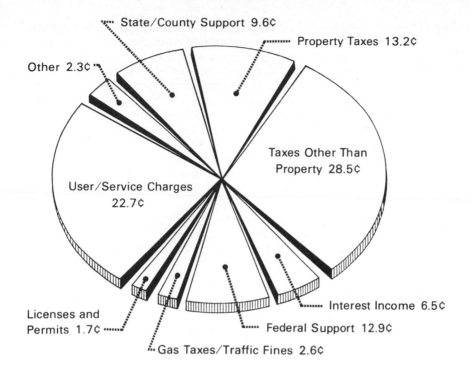

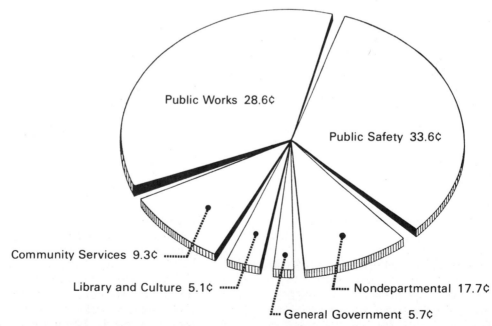

Figure 9–6   How the budget dollar is received (above) and spent (below), fiscal year 1980–81, City of Sacramento, California.

cific neighborhood which will receive much of its benefit.

Many cities have a park development tax, which is actually a fee on building permits. When a prospective sub–divider or home-owner comes in and wants to construct a building, a permit must be purchased which includes a park fee. For a three–bedroom house or more, for example, the park fee will cost about four–hundred dollars. This money will be used primarily for park purposes.

3. *Grant–in–aid assistance.* Many communities have received financial assistance from federal and state governments. Not all states have grant–in–aid programs, however. The six classes or general types of state grant–in–aid programs include specific activities, specific situations, funds to complement federal matching grants, acquisition, acquisition and development, and revenue sharing.

Many sources of revenue have been reduced or eliminated. Money is being placed where the people are—in an urban context. In addition to grants from the states, there will be more grants relating to operations.

4. *Donations and gifts.* Gifts from philanthropic organizations and civic–minded individuals have been a prime source of funds for capital outlay for many of the semi–public agencies. Valuable gifts have been presented to municipal park and recreation departments as well.

Based on the value of the dollar, the problem is getting assistance from a very wealthy philanthropist. "Recently, I had a land dedication worth $250,000," said Wisham, "which proves to me that donations and gifts are still available. You just have to be receptive, and you have to promote them. What you do is look for a tax advantage for donors."

PARK AND RECREATION PLANNING

The local planning agency or the park and recreation department normally has the responsibility for the development of a park and open space plan for the community. Most master plans are drawn up by the park and recreation agency in cooperation with the local planning commission.

In some cities and counties, the park and recreation department draws up the master plan and submits it to the planning department. The plan is then coordinated with other segments of the total community plan. It is often advisable for the local planning agency to prepare the master plan with assistance from the recreation department. Officials of the park and recreation agency can propose acquisition of particular sites and prepare designs for their development.

Generally, the procedure of planning can be separated into three major phases:

1. Collection of information and data on present recreation supply and demand, such as population and existing areas, facilities, and programs
2. Analysis of future recreation and park needs of the people
3. Formulation of proposals to meet present needs

Before the first phase of the planning process is undertaken, a list of basic principles should be developed.

Master Plan

A master plan is a guide:

- to the orderly development of existing areas;
- for the selection and development of new areas and facilities;
- for a comprehensive program to serve all age groups; and
- for immediate and long–range action with respect to program, areas, facilities, and finances.

A boulevard system connecting Kansas City's major parks would not have been possible without master planning done far in advance of funds becoming available. The master plan of 1965 includes the concept of a recreational site within a half mile of every residence in the city.

ZONING

Cluster or density–zoning ordinances have been enacted in some communities to preserve open spaces in new residential areas. Essentially, a cluster–zoning ordinance establishes an overall density for the area, usually in terms of acreage for each dwelling unit. However, it allows the developer to reduce the lot sizes and group the homes as long as the overall density is maintained.

An increasing number of local municipalities have found that cluster developments are a practical way to preserve adequate open space. According to Clayne Jensen, "One section of the tract may be developed at a high density with the remaining portions developed at a lower density, or all development may be centered in one section with the remaining open space preserved for park and recreation purposes."[8]

The more recent new communities of the United States have been built in response to burgeoning population expansion and to relieve the crushing strain on the over–burdened urban centers where two–thirds of American people are now concentrated.

"A cluster development may work very well in a lagoon or creek area, where there are flood plain conditions," said Wisham. "Financially, they can be a great strain—to leave that much open space."

New techniques of grouping single–family and apartment units around lakes, recreation areas, and garden–like courts and plazas are being developed in other areas of the country. In Alameda, California, a sizeable portion of the land was set aside by the developers for a planned community. Lakes, golf courses, swimming pools, parks, woods, tennis courts, and other recreation facilities were constructed on the land.

Cluster–zoning ordinances should clearly indicate whether open space is to be retained and maintained by private organizations or by the local government.

LAND ACQUISITION

An increasing challenge to all city and county officials is the acquisition of adequate park, recreation, and open–space acreage to meet the needs of a growing population. Indeed, land is being consumed for subdivisions at an alarming rate. Bigger shopping centers surrounded by large parking spaces are becoming commonplace. Additional land is needed for residential purposes, wider highways, and larger industrial establishments.

Due to a great uncertainty on operations costs, recent budgets have indicated a high emphasis on acquisition and a low emphasis on development. As a result, many cities are more or less "land–banking it."

Rising spectacularly is the price of land, particularly sites suitable for parks. Many public officials fear a crisis is developing. Land values generally are rising throughout the country at the rate of 10 percent annually, and the value of land for recreation purposes is increasing at an even higher rate. The most successful and widely used method of obtaining land is negotiation with the owner on price and then cash purchase. Some departments have been able to acquire much of their park land by donation.

Occasionally, it is necessary for local governments to exercise the right of eminent domain. A provision in the law allows governmental agencies to condemn privately owned land and acquire it for public use at the appraised market value. Normally used as a last resort, it does serve as a useful protective measure on behalf of public interest.

AREAS AND FACILITIES

To provide attractively developed recreation areas that meet the leisure needs of its citizens is a major concern of the modern city. Properly spaced and creatively developed land is essential if a well–balanced recreation program is to be achieved in the community.

If adequate recreation areas and facilities are to be provided, a city or county must perform several functions, including:

1. Acquire, develop, and maintain sufficient land for the needs of the community
2. Provide an organized program with supervision
3. Develop immediate and long–range plans and goals
4. Coordinate the use of areas and facilities
5. Curb the danger of encroachment

Each community must determine its own standards after considering such factors as population size, age, diversity, distribution, and ethnic character. In addition, planners should consider the type and number of other public facilities available in the area: geographic location as it relates to climate; and available finances.

According to the 1978 National Urban Recreation Study, the distribution and adequacy of recreation facilities varies considerably within and among cities. Still, urban residents in all study areas clearly desire a variety of both indoor and outdoor recreation facilities located close to home. They placed high priority on close to home recreation facilities. Neighborhood schools have great potential for satisfying the need for indoor recreation.

The larger, older cities have serious physical problems relating to the age and design of their recreation facilities. They are most severe in core city neighborhoods with dense populations and aging facilities.

Problems which have reduced the quality and quantity of recreation facilities in almost all the urban areas studied are:

- Substandard operation and maintenance
- Inadequate distribution and improper location
- Inaccessibility

- Understaffing
- Vandalism
- Rising energy costs and general inflation
- Poor or improper design
- Changing recreation demands as neighborhood populations shift
- Overcrowding and intensive use[9]

TYPES OF LOCAL PARKS

Generally, there are three basic types of in–city parks. They are miniparks, neighborhood parks, and community parks. In addition, it is desirable for each city or community to have access to large urban district and regional parks, as well as special resource areas and facilities, including reservations, forests and nature preserves, wilderness areas, streams and trails, and fish and wildlife areas.

Mini–Parks and Vest–Pocket Playgrounds

In the more densely populated sections of the city where ground is not available for the larger playgrounds, vest–pocket playgrounds have occupied areas ranging from one–fourth of an acre to a few acres. Serving all age groups, they are similar to the larger playgrounds, except that there are no ball fields or turf areas. They are often referred to as tot lots or kiddy playgrounds.

Neighborhood Parks

These areas provide active and passive recreation facilities for all age groups within walking distance of neighborhood residents. Ranging from four to eight acres in size, these parks generally provide playground, playfield, active sports, sometimes a pool and space for quiet activity. Many congested urban areas provide only one and one–half to two acres.

Regarded as the most important park unit on the urban scene, the neighborhood park usually consists of two acres of parkland for every one thousand people.

Figure 9–7 An outdoor oriented regional park. This developing park in rural Auburn, California, offers a variety of facilities, including a path for walking, jogging, and bicycling; a lake for fishing; ball fields; picnic sites; and nature trails. The path, or trail, around the lake continues to be popular among planners, in the tradition of those in Europe and America.

> **"Taking the kids to the park was common in my days as a child. What happened to this experience?"**
> Leo Buscaglia

Community Parks

Ranging in size from fifty to four hundred acres or more, community parks generally draw large crowds who use such special facilities as a golf course, playfield, swimming pool, playground, picnic and nature activities, as well as bicycling and hiking trails.

A community playfield is used for sports such as baseball, softball, soccer, football, and a variety of special events. Auxiliary features include a shelter building, rest rooms, picnic area, and parking. A standard of fifteen to twenty acres is desirable, ideally within one–half to one mile of each home.

Large Urban Parks

An urban park may occupy a huge center area of property such as the eight hundred acres which make up Central Park in New York. Lying within the perimeter of a large urban park are often smaller playfields or playgrounds, along with hills, forest groves, bridle paths, trails, lakes, picnic areas, and open space such as meadows. A minimum of one hundred acres is desirable, but three hundred or more acres are recommended.

District Parks

The preservation of natural resources is emphasized at district parks, with as much as 40 to 60 percent of the land left undeveloped. Ranging from four hundred to eight hundred acres in size, they feature such outdoor activities as biking, picnicking, and walking, as well as facilities for golf, picnicking, swimming, boating, and fishing. Generally, there are playfields which provide play space for various team sports.

Regional Parks

Regional parks are outdoor oriented and generally have a minimum size of one thousand acres or more. As much as 50 to 80 percent of the land remains undeveloped. Typical facilities for regional parks include hiking, bicycling, bridle and nature trails, picnic sites, nature center, and provisions for swimming, boating, fishing, and camping. Regional parks in colder regions of the country offer facilities for winter sports.

The Reservation

A large tract of land kept in its natural state, this type of facility offers activities such as bicycling, camping, horseback riding, nature study, and riflery. Often located at the edge of large cities or beyond, a reservation requires considerable acreage; a minimum of one thousand acres is considered adequate.

Special Areas and Facilities

These are areas set aside for one specific activity, each acquiring a substantial piece of acreage. Recommended sizes of special areas are:

Golf course—9–holes (50 acres); 18–holes (110 to 160 acres)
Athletic Field—6 to 8 acres
Sports stadium—25 to 50 acres
Beaches—from 2 to 3 acres on up
Swimming pool complex—(with buildings, parking, etc.) 3 to 10 acres.

Figure 9–8 Softball complex. This imaginative layout in Montgomery, Alabama, provides for five playing fields surrounding a central service building and separated by bleachers and landscaping. The $1.1 million complex provides play not only for local leagues, but enables Montgomery to host state, regional, and national tournaments. (Courtesy Montgomery Parks and Recreation Department.)

SOFTBALL COMPLEX LAGOON PARK
City of Montgomery, Alabama

GOODWYN ENGINEERING CO., INC.

TYPES OF AREAS AND FACILITIES

The following is a list of some of the main types of recreation areas and facilities:

Community Centers

Community centers take on a variety of forms. They may serve as a meeting place for all ages or may be confined to youth, elderly people, people with handicaps, or some other interest group. Community centers are designed to offer a wide variety of wholesome group and individual recreational opportunities. Most centers provide facilities such as general–purpose rooms, club and meeting rooms, game rooms, an auditorium, or gymnasium, arts and craft rooms, library or reading rooms, a kitchen, lounge, and office, service and storage rooms. Activities can range from formal classes to informal free–play; from the highly organized to the self–directed.

Playground

Playgrounds consist of play lots and play areas that can be found at neighborhood and community parks. Serving children from tots to teenagers, playgrounds vary in size from one–fourth of an acre to five acres or more. Ideally, they should be located within easy walking distance.

Playgrounds offer facilities such as: apparatus areas, multiple–use areas, areas for field games, shelters, tot–lot areas, areas for crafts and quiet games, and informal play space.

Recreation Center

There appears to be a demand for separate modest–sized but well–built recreation centers. Despite their cost, they have advantages over conventional school buildings. With at least five thousand square feet of space, a recreation center should contain a large multi–purpose room or floor, director's office, small meeting activity rooms, rest rooms, and an area for food service.

Other Types of Recreation Use Facilities

Libraries	Zoological Parks	Museums
Aquariums	Nature centers	Gardens
Arboretums	Conservatoriums	

PROGRAMS OF MUNICIPAL RECREATION DEPARTMENTS

The evergrowing array of municipal programs and activities are grouped into the following major categories: arts and crafts, performing arts, sports and games, aquatics, outdoor and nature oriented programs, special services, social programs, hobby groups, and various other playground and community center activities. In addition, municipal recreation and park departments regularly sponsor large scale special events such as festival programs, art and hobby shows, holiday celebrations, sports tournaments, and pageants.

While existing park and recreation programming efforts place greatest emphasis on competitive sports, public demands are growing for non–competitive sports programs, and for enlarged cultural and artistic programs. Access to existing programs is often limited in many areas due to overcrowding, limited staff, inadequate facilities, and the increased participation of women in active sports. Many recreation programs serve only limited segments of the urban population due to the inadequate distribution of programs or the total lack of programs in some areas.

THE ARTS

Most of National Endowment for the Arts grants go directly to cities or city organizations to expand public awareness of and participation in community art. The endowment's performing arts programs in music, dance, and theater have helped to fund free performances in many city parks. The Expansion Arts Program is the endowment's major source of funding for recreation–related community activities.

PROFILE OF A MUNICIPAL RECREATION AND PARK DEPARTMENT

Decatur, Illinois

The Decatur park system, which was organized in 1924 under the "Submerged Land Act," established the governing authority of the district as a board of five commissioners, each elected to a six-year term, all serving without pay.

The recreation department is regulated by the park district, but it is financed by a special tax levy. Its purpose is to design and supervise activities for children and adults of all ages. In addition to those activities carried on in the parks, the recreation department supervises activities in facilities provided by outside agencies as well, such as schools, YMCA, and YWCA.

Organizing and supervising activities for the park district is a year around job and the recreation department has handled it by designing separate summer and winter programs. In Decatur, EVERYBODY PLAYS!

To handle the large amount of activities under its jurisdiction, the recreation department has developed a summer staff of more than one-hundred leaders and supervisors which operates twenty-five playgrounds. In the summertime, the department supervises leagues for team athletic events for both children and adults. Special activities include supervision of the Municipal Day Camp for children six to thirteen, band concerts, senior citizens center, dramatics, crafts exhibits, play day, baton twirling, and many others.

The recreation department's winter program extends from October to May. Individual activities include crafts, Halloween parade, Christmas celebration, and recreation centers for the fifth grade and up. Adult recreation clubs have regular meetings throughout the winter, and the department coordinates social activities such as dances and parties.

Figure 9–9 The summer play day is an annual, all–day event in Decatur, Illinois. Children from Decatur's twenty–five playgrounds meet at one of the larger parks and participate in games and contests. Below, the children listen to entertainment by the Summer Staff Singers, made up of park leaders and supervisors who perform at special events, ice cream socials, and for service clubs. (Courtesy Decatur Recreation Department.)

Few cities have effective coordination of arts and recreation programs. Good program coordination and joint planning among recreation departments, art councils and private institutions is a key element in successful art recreation programs.

Cultural activities are often limited to highly visible events and to routine arts and crafts for young children and the elderly.

ENVIRONMENTAL EDUCATION

"Environmental education efforts remain a low priority at all governmental levels," according to the 1978 National Urban Recreation Study. "Particularly lacking in nearly all cities studied is a significant involvement by park and recreation agencies in initiating new environmental education programs or supporting existing ones."[10]

While most large cities report that they conduct environmental education activities, the field studies reveal that such programs were usually aimed at a small portion of potential user groups, and were largely conducted on a one–time basis.

Private groups are the strongest advocates of environmental education in the study areas and are usually the major suppliers. Despite general public acceptance of the need to increase our understanding of the environment, federal support of environmental education remains minimal.

MOBILE RECREATION

Mobile recreation units which operate daily during the summer in many large cities are designed to bring programs to the neighborhood playground that go beyond the scope of the typical daily schedule of activities. Among the sixteen mobile units operated by the Memphis Recreation Department are the skate mobile, puppet mobile, arts and crafts mobile, science and nature mobile, instant playground, golf mobile, zoo mobile, cultural arts mobile, and the movie mobile.

Many park and recreation agencies in large cities are using mobile recreation units to bring opportunities to areas deficient in recreation services. Mobile recreation vans on closed streets improve the delivery of neighborhood services in such cities as Boston, Cleveland, Detroit, Houston, and New York.

Mobile units have brought arts, crafts, games, theater, music, and even swimming to residents who would not otherwise have such opportunities.

A COORDINATED APPROACH TO COMMUNITY RECREATION

For the entire community to be effectively served, there is a strong need for the activities of community recreation agencies to be coordinated. Otherwise, the special interests of individual agencies are considered of greater importance than the overall good of the community. The end result is often duplication or overlapping of programs, services, and facilities. Competition for the leisure interests of the young people becomes a severe problem.

In spite of the wide range of programs and facilities offered, recreation and leisure opportunities are still inadequate in many American cities and towns.

Inflation, funding restrictions, and increased demands for public recreation in cities make it very important that public service agencies coordinate program efforts whenever possible. Interagency cooperation and coordination not only leads to improved effectiveness of such agencies in the city, but to more prudent use of tax dollars and to increased service.

Only through an integrated and coordinated approach can the best interests of an entire community be achieved. A well–rounded community recreation program is the result of all agencies and organizations working together for the best interests of the people.

A varied and comprehensive community recreation program demands a unified total effort involving public, private, semi–public, and commercial agencies. It also requires the coordinated efforts of the home, the church, the school, and other social and civic institutions that offer recreation activities. Each agency and organization must determine its role and function, and how it can best contribute to the total community effort.

COORDINATING COUNCILS

First organized with the prime purpose of preventing juvenile delinquency, the interests and functions of coordinating councils have expanded to cover all phases of community service. In large cities, coordinating councils are operated on a neighborhood basis; in small communities, these councils are usually organized on a community basis.

Community councils have proven very effective in improving life in the community. In approaching existing needs and problems, a council is often instituted to survey, plan, and initiate action to improve the existing conditions. Health, schools, government, welfare, and recreation are some of the needs to which community councils give their attention.

To be successful, the council should represent all groups in the community, such as youth–serving agencies, churches, government agencies, women's groups, service clubs, lodges, business organizations, health organizations, recreation clubs, and special interest groups. If a coordinated effort is to be achieved, both lay and professional leaders of representative agencies should participate on the council.

ADVISORY COUNCILS

An advisory council or board is a group of citizens, members, clients, or participants who serve an organization through an established, ongoing relationship in order to represent the interests of the organization's clientele. "An advisory council has no executive or legislative powers," said Godbey. "It may recommend courses of action, but it has no power to make decisions arising from these recommendations or to set action in motion to implement them."[11]

Advisory councils deal with specific issues, such as school recreation agency coordination, the operation of particular recreation facilities or programs, or the recreation needs and interests of some subgroup within the community, e.g. the elderly, people with physical handicaps, and others.

Some recreation agencies initially hold a mass meeting open to the public. Any interested person can attend. The first meeting begins with a discussion on why a recreation advisory council is needed. At the second meeting, the slate of officers is presented, nominations received from the floor, and officers and council members elected.

HEARINGS

A public or private hearing represents an opportunity for the members of a community or organization to be heard by government or "management" concerning issues that affect them.

According to Godbey, "Hearings fulfill a number of distinct and diverse roles in the decision–making of government and organizations. In many cases, a hearing represents merely tokenism. The granting of a public forum or hearing is frequently done only as a measure of appeasement. Often, policy decisions have already been made and will be implemented regardless of the outcome of the hearing."[12]

CITIZEN INVOLVEMENT

There is a new awareness throughout the country concerning the need for citizens' participation and leadership in the priority–setting and decision–making process of government agencies. According to the late Robert M. Artz, former staff member of NRPA, "The citizen is continuing to demand a much greater voice in the use of his or her tax dollars."[13]

Figure 9–10 Heavy citizen turn–out for budget session. Solon Wisham, Director of Recreation and Parks, addresses the Sacramento City Council during the 1978 Proposition 13 budget considerations for Recreation and Parks. Citizens, either individually or in groups, have the opportunity to influence basic decisions about agency operations. (Courtesy *Sacramento Bee*.)

Volunteer citizens, historically, have been instrumental in charting the course which has led to the general acceptance of public recreation as a basic function of government. Indeed, it is at the community level that the interests and needs of all the people can be best understood and served.

According to Sidney Lutzin and Edward Storey, "Citizen interest, knowledge, and action are the foundations of top quality public services. This is especially true in the public recreation and park setting. Recreation, like education, by its very nature is close to people. It requires a people–to–people relationship between policy makers and participants."[14]

PARK AND RECREATION BOARDS

One of the important and effective areas of citizen involvement is service on a recreation and park board or commission. State legislation provides for independent, semi–independent, or advisory boards and commissions with a large share of the responsibility for governing and developing recreation and park services.

The effectiveness of a board or commission depends upon one essential ingredient—the people who serve on it. Whether elected or appointed, policy making or advisory, the individuals themselves are the real key to success.

Types of Boards

Most boards, especially the independent and semi–independent ones, are composed of five or seven members. Advisory boards are sometimes much larger in size.

Basically boards and commissions fall into three main categories:[15]

1. **Separate and independent boards** with full responsibility for policy formulation and implementation. This type serves the legislative function and is a fully autonomous body. Independent financial support clearly differentiates this type of board from the two other main types. Decision–making is not passed on to another body.

2. **Semi–independent boards** with policy–making and administrative authority over the recreation and park function. Most park and recreation agencies operate under this type of board, which depends upon another jurisdiction such as the city council or county commission for ultimate decision–making.

3. Advisory boards with no final authority or responsibility for policy or administration. The advisory board has no power but may serve important functions in the interpretation of the program, facilities, and services as well as in making studies and serving as a sounding board.

Board–Executive Relationship

Together, the board and executive should operate under a partnership philosophy, i.e., they work together and are responsible to the community for the effective operation of the agency. Each has specific responsibilities as well as common or shared responsibilities.

The specific role of the executive is to manage the agency to the end that its objectives are realized. The board's chief responsibility is to determine policy and maintain the conditions under which the staff may render high quality sevices.

Policy planning and formulation are the responsibility of both the board and the executive, whereas policy determination is the responsibility of the board alone. Policy implementation is the responsibility of the executive and his or her professional staff.

Defining the role of the chief executive and the lines of responsibility and authority between the board and the executive is paramount to ensuring a sound working relationship.

QUESTIONS FOR DISCUSSION

1. Why are close–to–home facilities and programs so urgently needed today in heavily populated urban areas?
2. What four types of sponsorship strive to meet the recreation and leisure needs of a community?
3. List and briefly explain four common types of administrative patterns in recreation and parks.
4. List three methods used to finance recreation departments. What are the principal sources of funds for capital outlay?
5. What effects does a recreation–oriented community have on property values, attracting business and industry, and alleviating conditions that generate social problems?
6. Discuss the funding of public recreational services from the points of view of: (a) the taxpayer who participates in and sees the benefits of it; (b) a person who believes it a waste of taxpayer's money.
7. List the three basic types of in–city parks.
8. What is a master plan? How important is it in the development of a park system?
9. Explain local government's right of eminent domain.
10. Explain the purpose of cluster–zoning.
11. Describe the type of recreation program and park facilities you believe should exist in a city or community.
12. What are the three main types of boards?
13. How should citizens be involved in planning?
14. Discuss the political aspects of public recreational services as they apply to special interest groups within a politician's jurisdiction.

REFERENCES

1. Executive Report, National Urban Recreation Study, Heritage Conservation and Recreation Service, 1978, p. 50.
2. George D. Butler, *Introduction to Community Recreation* (New York: McGraw–Hill Company, 1967), p. 68.
3. National Urban Recreation Study, pp. 42–45.
4. Ibid., p. 33.
5. Gus Gerson, *Situational Administration for Public Recreation and Park Delivery Systems*, unpublished manuscript, California State University at Northridge, 1978, p. 1.
6. Ibid.
7. Richard Kraus, *Recreation and Leisure in Modern Society*, 2nd ed. (Santa Monica, California: Goodyear Publishing Company, Inc., 1978), p. 246.
8. Clayne Jensen, Outdoor Recreation in America (Minneapolis, Minn.: Burgess Publishing Company, 1970), pp. 150–51.
9. National Urban Recreation Study, p. 43.
10. National Urban Recreation Study, pp. 57–58.
11. Geoffrey Godbey, *Recreation, Park and Leisure Services* (Philadelphia: W. B. Saunders Company, 1978), p. 324.
12. Ibid., pp. 335–36.
13. Robert M. Artz, "School–Community Recreation and Park Cooperation," *Management Aids Bulletin* No. 82, Arlington, Virginia: National Recreation and Park Association, 1970.
14. Sidney Lutzin and Edward Storey, *Managing Municipal Leisure Services* (Washington, D.C.: International City Management Association, 1973), p. 60.
15. Lutzin and Storey, *Managing Municipal Leisure Services*, pp. 65–66.

Figure 10–1 Mobile units such as this show wagon have been a great asset to the Naperville Park District, which covers a large area of suburban Chicago. This evening drama show can be presented to many neighborhoods spread throughout the district. (Courtesy Naperville Park District.)

10
County and District Government

Counties traditionally have been the regional open space providers but, as they become more urbanized, pressures increase to broaden the scope of their recreation service. Since the early years of the twentieth century, a most significant change in the functions of county government has been the growth of new services more closely related to local government. County libraries, airports, hospitals, health services, utility systems, and park and recreation services are prime examples of the new functions of county government.

The future of the county as a form of governmental service appears to be tending toward facility oriented developments, more regional parks and facilities, and less program activities and services. They will continue to grow towards a regional concept of providing facilities.

During the last two decades, interest in county–wide park and recreation services has grown steadily, and it appears that county government in the United States is headed for a much greater role in our system of government. Indeed, a most promising trend is towards the urban county, which arose when counties began to provide new services not offered by state government.

James Arles cited several factors as being responsible for creating a stronger demand for county services:

1. Since much of the available land lies outside the city boundaries, the counties have the resources to plan area–wide park systems.
2. More outdoor recreation facilities closer to home are being demanded by urban residents.
3. County government offers a broad tax base which can finance major land acquisition and the development of specialized facilities.
4. Superior transportation today provides the mobility for urban people to use facilities and resources farther from home.
5. Federal and state grants–in–aid programs have had an accelerating effect on county governments.[1]

A county, metropolitan, or regional park system is known by one of a number of names. The most common are regional park systems, metropolitan park systems, park districts, county forest preserves, and regional park and planning commissions.

For a large portion of the country, county parks are a relatively new development. However, some counties in New York, Michigan, and California have enjoyed county–developed facilities for many years. The greatest deterrent to park and open space development by counties has been a lack of funds.

Today many counties throughout America are acquiring and developing sites for camping, boating, picnicking, and other activities. Like most rural park or outdoor recreation areas, these sites provide the space, facilities, and services to meet the vacationing and camping needs of both local residents and tourists.

HISTORICAL DEVELOPMENT OF COUNTY GOVERNMENT

County government has evolved largely since World War I when significant changes occurred in its functions and structure. The county is the main political subdivision of the state and all other political subdivisions are within the county boundaries. Rather than operating as an administrative arm of the state, county departments today operate more independently as units of local governments. Most state enabling laws permit counties, or districts, to function for recreation.

The first county park was established in Essex County, New Jersey, in 1895, with the expressed desire to develop a system of parks. During the 1920s, a significant increase in county park acquisitions took place.

By 1930 the number of county parks increased from 22 to 415, and the acreage expanded from 2,169 to 108,485. Today, we find 358 counties reporting the operation of a park and recreation system with a total of 4,149 park areas totaling 691,042 acres. Total county expenditures for parks and recreation gradually increased from its meager beginning of $410,000 in 1913 to $7.6 million in 1957, to $195 million in 1965.[2]

GROWTH OF COUNTY PARK AND RECREATION SYSTEMS

During the past two decades, there has been a substantial increase in county government's involvement in providing park and recreation services. Joseph Curtis wrote that "The strengths of both county and local governments are needed if the important goals of wholesome recreation for the public are to be attained."[3]

One very promising trend is the trend toward the urban county. Where metropolitan areas lie within a single county, it is possible for county government to become the main unit of local government.

"The Essex County park system was conceived and developed fundamentally to take the place of individual municipal park systems," said Sidney Lutzin and Edward Storey. "In effect, the Essex County Park Commission provided a total municipal park system for an entire metropolitan area."[4] According to Charles E. Doell and Louis F. Twardzik, "The Essex system was to provide for *all* the park needs of the entire county including its cities and towns."[5]

During the 1960s, there was a substantial increase in county government's involvement in providing park and recreation services. According to Norman Beckman, the reason for this is that county government has a priceless asset which many municipalities do not have: adequate area jurisdiction or space. In addition to "space," it has high political feasibility. It is directly accountable to an electorate that, under recent court decisions, will be reasonably representative. Finally, it has a broad tax base and well established working relations with the state and federal governments on the one hand and cities on the other.[6]

Figure 10–2 Recreation and park services have become a major responsibility of county government. More outdoor recreation facilities closer to home are being demanded by urban residents. This county park in Cambria along the coast of California provides ample play space for young and old alike.

CLASSIFICATION OF COUNTY PROPERTIES

Charles Doell and Louis Twardzik developed the following classification of county or regional properties:

1. The large reservation of native land containing one thousand or more acres may be zoned according to intensity of use, e.g. (a) native sanctuaries, (b) native areas for light intensity use, and (c) intense daytime use for swimming, boating, picnicking, etc.
2. Recreation areas or parks, developed largely for active daytime use but with a native environment predominant.
3. Special use parks, such as zoos, stadiums, museums, and cultural complexes.
4. Parkways or scenic highways, a parkway being a broad thoroughfare beautified with trees and turf.
5. Historical parks, encompassing items of historical significance.[7]

Definitions

Boulevard—A broad, "grand" avenue or thoroughfare, beautified by turf and trees.
Parkway—A roadway through a park beautified with trees and turf.
Scenic Highway—A parklike thoroughfare which passes through attractive native scenery.

RESPONSIBILITY OF THE COUNTY

Essentially, county responsibility for the provision of park and recreation services rests somewhat between that of the municipality and the state. Although most counties are more involved with meeting the needs for regional recreation areas and facilities, some county authorities also provide a local recreation service to people in the unincorporated areas.

A wide divergence of operational procedures and departmental objectives characterizes the administration of parks and recreation in the counties. In serving the recreation needs of the people, counties have taken different approaches in the provision of resources and programs.

Early in the 1960s, the County Supervisors Association of California adopted an overall recreation policy designed to serve as a guide for individual counties. The report as officially adopted listed, in part, the following recreation responsibilities for the counties of California:

1. Encourage the provision of neighborhood and community recreation facilities and activities through planning, consultation, and other services.
2. Assist and recommend the means of financing unsatisfied community and neighborhood recreation and park needs.
3. Provide day-use regional recreation facilities within the county.
4. Investigate the feasibility of utilizing the "user-pay" concept in meeting public demands for recreation.
5. Should not offer property tax inducements to private recreation suppliers.
6. Voluntary inter-county cooperative agreements are strongly recommended when day-use recreation demand crosses county boundaries.
7. Local agencies requesting recreation services for unsatisfied community and neighborhood recreation and park needs should first make such requests to the county.

In 1964, the National Association of Counties published its "National Policy for County Parks and Recreation." A condensed statement of this policy follows:

The special role of the county is to acquire, develop, and maintain parks and to administer public recreation programs that will serve the needs of communities broader than the local neighborhood or municipality, but less than statewide or national in scope.

In addition, the county should plan and coordinate local neighborhood and community facilities with the cooperation of the cities, townships, and other intra-county units, and should itself cooperate in state and federal planning and coordinative activities.[8]

While Los Angeles County, California and Dade County, Florida provide both recreation programs and facilities, Suffolk County, New York and Cook County, Illinois provide only park facilities and rely on individual jurisdictions to provide recreation programs.

Suburban residents want more close–to–home facilities and recreation programs. Since individual suburban jurisdictions are often too small to have the expertise or financial capability to provide these services, counties are increasingly being called upon to fill this gap.

The Milwaukee County Park System not only absorbed the park system of the city of Milwaukee but all other incorporated towns in the county. It has more of the characteristics of an urban system than of a regional system. In fact, the whole county is now virtually one metropolis served by one park department.

Many of the county parks in Los Angeles are no different from city parks and perform essentially the same functions. The systems tend to complement each other in providing recreational service.

CREATION OF A BOARD

County commissioners have the authority to prepare an ordinance creating a park and recreation board. In addition, the commissioners can appoint a recreation advisory council of twenty–five to thirty members with county–wide representation. As a general practice, the county planning commission serves as the executive committee for such an advisory council. The park and recreation board has the initial responsibility of hiring the most qualified personnel available to serve on the park and recreation staff.

THE COUNTY AND THE PRIVATE SECTOR

Some two–thirds of the nation's land is privately owned. Collectively, these lands have

an enormous potential for park and recreation development, at private expense, which has been only partially realized. Counties should seek opportunities to stimulate such development. County cooperation should include the provision of access roads, where feasible and where traffic volume will justify, to permit the park and recreation development of private lands.

Counties should cooperate with and support in every way possible the efforts of private businesses and of charitable, service, and civic organizations to acquire and appropriately manage recreation and park sites that serve public needs.

LAND ACQUISITION

Vigorous programs of land acquisition were essential to obtain and protect land while it was still available and before prices increased to such a prohibitive extent. Many counties have enacted laws requiring home developers to set aside recreation and park areas in the community. Since 1957, Anne Arundel County, Maryland, for example, has required all developers to allocate 5 percent of the land to be developed for park areas.[9]

A number of county governments are establishing permanently protected green belts to halt the tide of construction. To permit cluster zoning of homes with larger and more concentrated open spaces, zoning policies are being strengthened and more flexible building codes adopted.

The concept of parkways is a corollary of the park systems idea. "The latter concept implies not only the development of different types of open spaces," wrote Lutzin and Storey, "but the relating of these open spaces to one another so as to form a unified whole, and the relating of them to the people whom they are designed to serve."[10]

PERSONNEL

Like the programs offered by municipal agencies, the key to a successful county recreation program lies in the quality of its leadership. The serious concern that county agencies have for the administration of its park and recreation functions can be reflected by the employment of competent, qualified professional personnel.

Doell and Twardzik wrote that "The operation of a park recreation service at any and all levels of government is dependent on a systemized banding together of many talents and of people who possess those talents in such a way as to act as a unit. Briefly it is called personnel organization."[11]

FINANCE AND BUDGET

County park and recreation programs should be financed principally through general taxation. This may be supplemented by such sources as general obligation and

revenue bonding, donations of money, land and services from private individuals and groups, and fees.

County governments have strongly supported the concept that users of certain kinds of public park and recreation facilities and programs should pay for such use. Revenue from this source should be applied toward the acquisition, development, maintenance, and administration of parks and recreation programs.

Many county agencies are experiencing a shrinking budget. Of increasing concern to administrators is: "How will we continue to provide services with limitation on the amount of taxes that can be raised from the local tax base?" There will be less tax money, and a greater reliance on user fees and other sources of revenue. Significantly, the county no longer has the ability to levy community services taxes in special areas and districts.

Figure 10–3 Fishing piers at the Concord Park area in Knox County have been adapted to meet the growing need of the handicapped. The piers were built by the Tennessee Valley Authority and are operated by the Knox County Park Commission. (Courtesy Tennessee Valley Authority.)

PROFILES OF COUNTY DEPARTMENTS

Huron–Clinton Metropolitan Authority (Detroit, Michigan)

The Huron–Clinton Metropolitan Authority was created exclusively to develop large park units and to preserve for public use the scenic beauties and recreational resources along the two principal rivers, the Huron and the Clinton. The ten Huron–Clinton Metroparks serve a five county population of 4.5 million.

The Huron–Clinton Metropolitan Authority was sanctioned by the Michigan State Legislature in Act No. 147 of the Public Acts of 1939, and was approved in 1940 by the citizens of the five counties which constitute the metropolitan district. Since its inception it has created large public parks located on the best natural resources possible, considering population trends within the district and with a minimum disruption of existing land use.

The governing body for the authority is a seven member board of commissioners. Two are appointed by the governor of Michigan; each of the other five is elected by the board of supervisors of his or her county.

The authority is financed principally by a tax levy, limited to one-quarter of one mill, which is established by the board of commissioners on the regular county property tax in accordance with state equalized assessments.

Four staff officers—the director, deputy director, secretary, and controller—are appointed by the Board of Commissioners, to whom they are responsible for all phases of organizational work including planning, land acquisition, construction, procurement, maintenance, and operations of the Metropark system.

Most Huron–Clinton metroparks are fairly good size, at least 1,000 acres. They are a pleasing blend of the natural re-

Figure 10–4 Beach site. The orderly appearance of Maple Beach in Kensington Metropark is apparent in this aerial photograph. Sailboats are busy on Kent Lake, while bathers are in the water, on the beach, and relaxing on the grass panels. Kensington Metropark covers 4300 acres and was the first regional park developed (1948) by the Huron–Clinton Metropolitan Authority in suburban Detroit, Michigan. (Courtesy Huron–Clinton Metropolitan Authority.)

sources such as a lake, river, woods or wildlife area with facilities for picnicking, swimming, nature study, or other outdoor recreation. Most metroparks are within an hour's drive for most residents of the region.

Camden County (New Jersey)

Camden County is a highly urbanized area located within the country's most densely populated state. The city of Camden continues to experience major problems, like fiscal crises, crime, widespread unemployment, high taxes and fewer services. Yet, within the county, its residents find a welcome escape in the 2,000 acres of woodlands, fields, streams, ponds, and playgrounds known as the Camden County Parks. The sixteen parks in fourteen municipalities that comprise the Camden County Park system are visited annually by more than four–hundred–thousand people.

The Camden County Park Commission was established in 1926 by a county–wide referendum. The first funds made available to the Commission were a $25,000 grant from the Board of Freeholders in 1927. During the 1930s most of the parks and recreation facilities were actually created by the W.P.A. (Works Progress Administration). Cooper River Park was actually dredged out of a tidal marsh and constructed acre by acre.

A major acquisition, over 1,000 acres of land along the Egg Harbor River in Winslow Township was approved by the 1974 Board of Freeholders of Camden County. The one and a half million dollar purchase was half funded by State Green Acres money and the remainder by the county.

Oakland County (Michigan)

The history of the Oakland County Parks and Recreation System, which began in 1966, is a story of growth and improvement. In that year, the Oakland County Board of Supervisors made an initial loan of $100,000 to the Commission for organization, preliminary planning, and acquisitions. Voters in Oakland County

Figure 10–5   Annual Serendipity Sunday Celebration in Camden County Park lures in excess of 250,000 people to the banks of the Cooper River each August. It is one of the largest craft fairs on the East Coast, attracting people from all over Delaware Valley. (Courtesy Camden County Park Commission.)

approved a $250 thousand tax levy, and with funds from this tax, the Commission immediately began to acquire and preserve park lands on the fringes of suburban Detroit. These acquisitions were made and financed through the cooperation of state and federal agencies.

The Parks Commission is comprised of nine appointed members. They are responsible for the development of a park system that provides unique and specialized facilities and programs not normally provided by local agencies.

"When all the parks have been improved, it is our goal to have them self-supporting whenever possible, with the millage being used only for acquisition and capital improvements," said Eric Reickel, manager of the Parks and Recreation Commission.

Today, there are seven Oakland County park areas covering more than twenty-five hundred acres which offer a wide variety of recreational facilities to all citizens of Oakland County as well as the Detroit metropolitan area.

Sacramento County (California)

Rapid urbanization of the unincorporated areas of Sacramento after World War II created a need for recreational facilities that were not being supplied at a rate comparable to the urban growth. In 1956, a twelve-member committee on parks and recreation appointed by the County Board of Supervisors recommended that a county-wide plan be prepared for a system of regional park and recreation facilities, and in 1959, the County of Sacramento Parks and Recreation Department was established.

The department's major objectives were: (1) to institute an aggressive acquisition program to provide regional park and recreation facilities; (2) to acquire this land as close to the expanding urban core as was economically feasible;

and (3) to defer funding of developments, if necessary, in order to preserve funds for acquisition of the choicest possible recreation lands.

Since the department was established in 1959, the county has been successful in providing regional day-use recreation opportunities. In addition to the regional functions of the department, the county has been able to meet the need for neighborhood facilities within a given community.

The Sacramento Department of Parks and Recreation today has five major areas of concern:

1. the park maintenance division
2. the program services division
3. the planning and design division
4. the administrative section
5. American River Parkway

The American River Parkway has received extensive development as a recreational and natural open space green belt. The idea of protecting the American River for its recreational qualities, while still retaining its natural beauty, can be attributed to the vision and foresight of various local conservation and recreation groups. Among the recreation activities enjoyed along both shores of the American River are rowing, rafting, water skiing, fishing, hiking, bicycling, motorcycling, picnicking, and motor boating.

Since 1970, the Sacramento County Regional Park System has more than doubled in size with the acquisition of some thirty-seven hundred acres of new park land and improvements. Unfortunately, improving or even maintaining the enhancement of one of the community's finest amenities is in jeopardy. Most of the progress was achieved with $12.6 million of county general obligation bonds approved by the voters in 1972, but these funds were expended June 30, 1980.

More emphasis must be given to an efficient and economical operation. Administrators and other county officials will need to know what it will cost to maintain and operate facilities. They should know the people they are serving, and how to deliver the services and facilities they want, and are willing to pay for. In short, those responsible for management and the operation of recreation areas and facilities must start taking lessons from the business world on how they are to function.

Urban counties, in general, spend a much greater share of their parks and recreation budget on capital improvements than cities do. The primary role of urban counties is providing open space and regional park facilities. In Iowa, for example, nearly all of the ninety–nine counties have become involved in the purchase and development of park lands under the authority of the state law.

RECREATION ACTIVITIES AT COUNTY PARKS

County parks and recreation areas under their jurisdiction offer a wide range of leisure–time activities and experiences, most of them outdoor oriented.

Theme parks Storyland Park in Nassau County (New York) now consists of many small parks each drawn around a theme based on children's stories such as *Robinson Crusoe*, *Alice in Wonderland*, and others.

Hiking and riding Hiking and riding trails are plentiful in San Mateo County (California) which owns and operates 2,200 acres of park recreation lands. Memorial Park is open all year and offers camping, hiking, swimming, picnicking, and other outdoor activities.

Figure 10–6 Evening campfire programs. Accompanied by the guitar playing of two Sacramento County park rangers, this group of family campers enjoys singing and eating marshmallows around the campfire at Ancil Hoffman County Park.

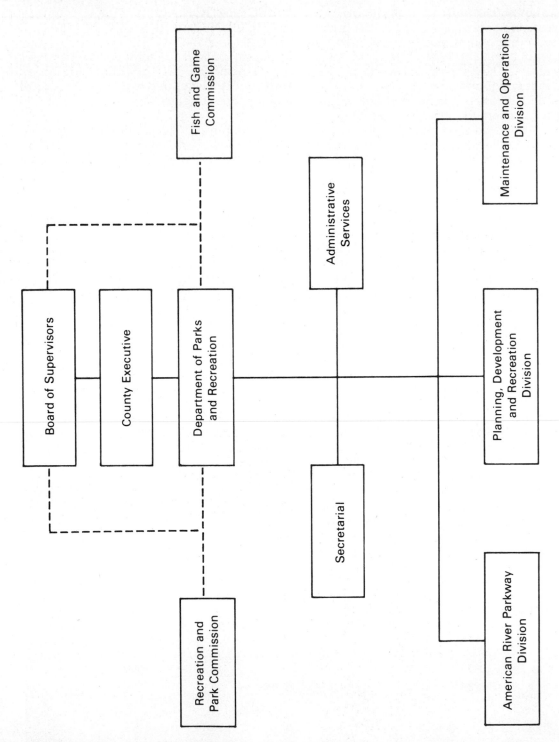

Figure 10–7 Organizational chart of a large county recreation and parks department. (Courtesy Sacramento County Park and Recreation Department.)

Water and ocean beaches The Metro–Dade County parks system is water–oriented since most people come to Florida primarily for sunny beaches, fishing, and year–round outdoor living. The more than eighteen million visitors each year like to swim, boat, camp, or take a nature walk.

The arts The Prince George County Recreation Department in Maryland operates a highly successful arts program in a suburban setting, owns and operates its own theater for use by dramatic, dance, and music groups, runs programs at twenty–three community centers with assistance from ninety local recreation councils.

Rafting and bicycling Numerous outdoor recreation activities are enjoyed in and along the shores of the American River in Sacramento, but rafting and bicycling have proven the most popular. White–water rafting farther up the American River has been a hit with the young and old alike. A system of bike–hike–horse trails extends twenty–three miles through the heart of the populated area of Sacramento.

REGIONAL PARK DISTRICTS

The regional park concept is still relatively new in the United States. Essentially, regional parks do not differ from county parks except they can involve more than one county and therefore cross political boundaries. Regional parks are funded by a regional park district that has the legal power to levy taxes for the establishment, development, and maintenance of outdoor recreation sites.

The establishment of regional park systems did not occur until approximately 1920. Permissive legislation had been passed in some states by which the organization of park districts was encouraged. "At one time, Chicago had in excess of twenty such districts which later were combined into one Chicago Park District."[12]

In Illinois, the various park district enabling laws, beginning with 1893 Pleasure Driveway and Park District Act and culminating in the 1951 Park District Code, gave to nonurban and metropolitan areas (exclusive of Chicago) the authority to develop parks independent of the corporate authorities or boundaries of individual municipalities.

The Cook County Forest Preserve District and the Act of 1913 under which it was established, grew out of efforts originally directed toward achieving an outer green belt park system for Chicago and its suburbs. Lutzin and Storey noted that "The primary emphasis as the system has developed has been on the preservation of natural forested areas in contrast to city parks—to preserve the areas both from and for people."[13]

The locations of the forest preserves are in such geographical shape as to form an almost continuous belt of forest preserve properties about Chicago. Doell and Twardzik wrote that "Its function in interrupting the continuous urbanization of land outside of the city of Chicago is looked upon as something of great merit."[14]

The East Bay Regional Park District (Oakland, California), created in 1934, is regarded as one of the most progressive park agencies in the country. With the aid of a $53 million bond issue approved in 1973 and a new master plan for the acquisition and development of new parklands, the district today possesses more than forty–one thousand acres in spectacular, scenic hills and mountains, bay beaches, lakes, streams, and meadows.

To assist its development program, the East Bay District has received over $7 million from HUD and the Land and Water Conservation Fund. Kraus wrote that: "Creative fund raising, outstanding public and community relations, solicitation of citizens' suggestions, involvement of all social, ethnic, and economic classes, and environmental education are keynotes of the development of the East Bay Regional Park District and of its planning for the decades ahead."[15]

SPECIAL DISTRICTS

The park or recreation district has performed an important service to those areas of the country where county government does not exist or is inadequate to meet the needs of the people. In many instances, the special district has provided park and recreation services in a most efficient manner.

Recreation districts, or a combination of recreation and park districts, often include all incorporated areas in the county. The creation of special districts is particularly prevalent in smaller counties, or when two or more districts operate in larger counties. Typically, a district board, similar to municipal recreation boards, is responsible for administering the recreation and park functions.

Depending on their specific purpose, special districts may be responsible for recreation programming or for park land open space acquisition and development, or both. The district is governed by an elected five-member policy-making board of directors.

Special taxing districts have made it possible for small communities to provide collectively for recreation and park services that individually they would be unable to give their residents. Communities located in adjacent counties have been successful in pooling their facilities, money, and leadership in the operation of a special district.

Illinois and California are two examples of states in which the district system has been well established by state law and local practice. If a special district includes two or more jurisdictions it would, in effect, be a region.

All states have provisions for the establishment of special districts for special purposes. They are usually autonomous, independent of other local governing entities, and are provided, in effect, with all the powers of any political subdivision of the state. The residents of the locality involved must initiate the request for the establishment of a special district. It is governed by an elected or appointed board, sometimes separate and sometimes as an additional function of a legislative body.

The forecast is for fewer special districts, many of them being consolidated or annexed. Special districts, particularly those in California, are greatly hampered and will be in the future, which leads many to believe

Figure 10–8 A community center contributes to a sense of community identity. This multipurpose center in the Sunrise Recreation and Park District in Citrus Heights, California, was built with block grant funds. Eugene Ahner, District Administrator, right, believes the complex has provided a substantial hub for community activities within the district.

that in order to survive, special districts will have to reorganize. State government will continue to pressure special districts to consolidate in order to cut expense. Consolidating voluntarily, of course, is preferred over mandated procedures.

In California, the revenue of special districts was slashed by more than 50 percent and state bailout funds were much less generous than were those for cities and counties. The general feeling is that aid to special districts is being constricted to encourage local officials to consolidate or eliminate many of them.

Many special districts are governed by county boards of supervisors. These are the most likely candidates for early consolidation or elimination in the post–Proposition 13 era. Or, they could become arms of county government with virtually no disruption. The most controversial districts are those that are both independently governed and tied to the property tax.

QUESTIONS FOR DISCUSSION

1. List the factors responsible for creating a stronger demand for county services.
2. Discuss the responsibilities of the county in providing regional and local park and recreation services.
3. Describe the characteristics of a regional park.
4. How are county recreation and park agencies commonly administered?
5. Discuss the financial dilemma confronting most counties today: How should they provide services with limitations on the amount of taxes that can be raised from the local tax base?
6. In setting up and operating a well–rounded county park system, what areas and facilities could be planned and developed?
7. What are some popular leisure activities and experiences offered at county parks and recreation areas?
8. Develop a profile of the county park and recreation agency in your area.
9. What role have special districts played in providing recreation and park services?
10. What is the forecast for special districts, their chances for survival?

REFERENCES

1. James Arles, "County Government," *Parks and Recreation Magazine*, August 1969, pp. 30–31.
2. Ibid.
3. Joseph Curtis, *Recreation, Theory and Practice* (St. Louis: C.V. Mosby Company, 1979), p. 26.
4. Sidney Lutzin and Edward Storey, *Managing Municipal Leisure Services* (Washington, D.C.: International City Management Association, 1973), p. 20.
5. Charles E. Doell and Louis F. Twardzik, *Elements of Park and Recreation Administration*, 3rd ed. (Minneapolis: Burgess Publishing Company, 1973), p. 92.
6. Norman Beckman, "Taking Account of Urban Counties," *American County Government*, 30, No. 68, October 1965.
7. Doell and Twardzik, *Elements of Park and Recreation Administration*, pp. 100–101.
8. "Policy for County Parks and Recreation," *Recreation*, June 1964, pp. 271–72.
9. *Richard Kraus, Recreation and Leisure in Modern Society* (Santa Monica, Calif: Goodyear Publishing Company, 1978), p. 244.
10. Lutzin and Storey, *Municipal Leisure Services*, p. 21.
11. Doell and Twardzik, *Elements of Park and Recreation Administration*, p. 145.
12. Ibid., p. 92.
13. Ibid., p. 21.
14. Ibid., pp. 94–95
15. Kraus, *Recreation and Leisure in Modern Society*, p. 244.

Figure 11–1 Developing environmental awareness and understanding is a major objective of state and other governmental agencies involved with outdoor recreation. An increasing number of people are coming to state parks for outdoor recreation and to learn more about their outdoor heritage. To meet these interests, nature interpretive programs such as this interpreter's tour have been developed at many state parks and recreation areas.

11
State Government

The most significant development of state government in recent years has been the multiplication of public services. Today, a multitude of state departments and agencies provide park and recreation areas and services. They are responsible for such areas as parks, forests, wayside picnic areas, winter sports facilities, game preserves, monuments, historical sites, museums, and waterways.

Indeed, the states have a critical role in giving local government the additional capabilities to provide needed recreation services and to protect open space. States, in the past, have left the provision of urban recreation to the cities and counties, but today, there is a pressing need to more adequately meet the recreational needs of those living in our urban centers who are not highly mobile. As a result, the development of urban parks is now a major concern of state park planners and administrators.

According to the United States Constitution, the states have a responsibility to authorize the establishment of local services. The Tenth Amendment to the Constitution gives the individual states authority to provide recreation services as the need for such services becomes evident.

All powers not delegated to the nation reside in the states. In addition, statewide services that are beyond the scope of the subdivisions of the state are often rendered by state agencies.

Through divisions, commissions, councils and many other political administrative units, the fifty state park systems are striving to meet the "onslaught by leisure," estimated at 400 million visits to state parks annually.

However, unless new funding sources are found, many departments will be facing some harsh realities in the future. These realities could force an end to the physical growth of the state park system.

BACKGROUND OF STATE PARKS

State park systems today have evolved from a late nineteenth–century tradition. "A state is responsible for the preservation of outstanding natural and historical resources," wrote Barry Tindall, "and a system of lands and waters for public recreation. California, with Yosemite State Park, in 1865 (now Yosemite National Park); Michigan's Mackinac Island State Park in 1895; and New York and New Jersey's Palisades Interstate Park in 1900, helped set a pattern and stimulate action for the future."[1]

According to Elvin R. Johnson, "The state park concept is believed to have started in California, although other states, such as New York and Michigan, founded early systems. In 1864, Abraham Lincoln signed an act of Congress whereby the world–famous Yosemite Valley and the Mariposa Grove of giant sequoia trees were granted to the state of California to be held for public use for all time. The Yosemite land grant formed the first state park in the nation. In 1902, the California Redwoods State Park, now known as Big Basin Redwoods State Park, was set aside as the first California State Park."[2]

Illinois is credited with establishing the first state agency for managing a state park system. In 1903, Illinois acquired Fort Mossac as a state park. In 1909, the state legislature appointed a commission to study the use of state lands for public parks.

As early as 1921 when the National Conference on State Parks was formed, Stephen T. Mather, founder and the first director of the National Park Service, believed that state and local support for the federal government to take over large and small scenic areas had to be redirected. Mather's well–defined concept of national parks stated that they be areas of some magnitude, distinguished by scenic attractions, natural wonders and beauty, and distinctly national in interest. He also felt that there were many scenic areas of importance to individual states that should be preserved. It was his feeling that in many instances, the states were in danger of having their natural landscapes vanish forever. In 1920, Mather's strong belief in the need for state parks resulted in the start of serious discussions on the possibilities of a conference to organize the states.

In 1921, Mather convened a meeting in Des Moines, Iowa that resulted in the organization of the National Conference on State Parks. Devoting itself to the improvement of state parks, it is known today as the National Society for Park Resources, a branch of the National Recreation and Park Association.

North Carolina was the first state to establish a separate recreation agency when it created a state recreation commission in 1945. Other states followed slowly, particularly when Land and Water Conservation Fund money became available in 1965.

In 1964, the National Conference on State Parks recommended the following classifications:

1. *Parks*—relatively spacious areas of outstanding scenic or wilderness character, oftentimes containing significant historical, archeological, ecological, geological, and other scientific values, preserved as nearly as possible in their original or natural conditions and providing opportunity for recreation which will not destroy or impair the features and values to be preserved.
2. *Monuments and historic sites*—areas, usually limited in size, established to preserve objects of historic and scientific interest and places commemorating important persons or historical events.
3. *Recreational areas*—areas selected and developed primarily to provide non–urban outdoor recreation opportunities to meet other than purely local needs and still having the best available scenic qualities.

The conference also classified but did not define: wayside rests and campgrounds, wilderness, nature preserves, beaches, parkways, scenic roads, trails, free flowing streams, forests, and underwater parks.

TYPES OF STATE PARK ADMINISTRATION

There are three common patterns of administration of parks used in the various states. Most of the states operate within one of the following types of structure:

1. Administration within a department that administers all natural resources.
2. Administration within a department that also administers forests.
3. Administration by a separate department.

In some states the state park agency is a separate department of state government as in Arizona, Georgia, Idaho, and Kentucky, where the park system is administered by the State Park Department. In several states, the park system is a division within a larger department. For instance, in Alabama, New York, Illinois, Iowa, and several other states, it is a division within the Department of Conservation. In Alaska, California, Hawaii, Indiana, Utah, Michigan, and other states, the park system is within the Department of Natural Resources. In Oregon, it is a division of the Highway Department.[3]

STATE RECREATION COMMISSIONS OR BOARDS

The basic responsibility of state commissions and boards is not to operate recreation

Figure 11–2 A scene of natural beauty. Some of America's great tourist attractions are the many beautiful beachlands along Oregon's 400–mile Pacific Ocean seashore. These impressive coastal seascapes are located at Ecola State Park on U.S. Highway 101. (Courtesy Oregon State Highway Department.)

programs themselves but to advise local communities, sponsor training institutes, organize conferences, and make surveys. Although they have performed ably as a separate function of state government, few states have established separate commissions or boards.

CLASSIFICATION OF AREAS

A prerequisite of the establishment of a good state park system is the classification of areas. The task of classifying areas is made easier when the agency has some criteria on which to base its selection.

According to Clayne Jensen: "State parks vary considerably in type, depending on the geographic features in the state and the philosophy and purpose on which the particular state park system is based. They are primarily intermediate type areas, usually being more remote than municipal areas but closer to the using population than national parks and forests. Typically, they contain considerable wild features along with synthetic improvements in the form of picnic and camp sites, boating accommodations, and various sports facilities."[4]

State park systems are generally grouped into several different classifications, each of which is managed to best preserve its values and serve its visitors:

State parks These are areas set aside to preserve a unique natural resource within various landscape provinces; major regions with outstanding scenic, natural, cultural, or ecological values.

Wildernesses These areas are left nearly untouched in order to retain their primeval character.

State reserves These areas preserve a specific and unique cultural or natural resource. They are set aside for that purpose alone. They have limited or no development and are basically for scientific and cultural research and investigative purposes. The most prominent area in California is the Point Lobos preserve that was set aside to preserve the unique groves of Monterey cypress and the unique relationship of the ocean and the land in that particular area.

Historical units Preserve places and objects of statewide historic significance, with improvements generally limited to access, parking, interpretation, and occasionally picnicking.

Several classes of units are devoted to recreation:

State recreation areas These are areas set aside not because of any landscape value but to provide for the recreational needs of the people. They are selected, developed, and operated to provide outdoor recreation opportunities.

Underwater recreation areas Selected for surface and subsurface water–oriented recreational opportunities that can be enjoyed without damaging basic resource values. These areas are unique because of their underwater topography, the existing flora, and the quality of the underwater environment.

Vehicular recreation areas Selected very carefully to ensure that no substantial natural values are lost because of their use by off–highway vehicles.

Beaches Set aside for the preservation and the utilization of the beaches; for swimming, boating, fishing, sunbathing, surfing, and the like.

Wayside campgrounds and wayside rests Small units, convenient to major highways, that are suitable for overnight stops and camping. These areas are also used by the highway department to provide for the daytime rest of travelers.

Any of the units might contain a:

Natural preserve An area of outstanding natural or scientific significance with rare or endangered plant species or unique geological or topographical features.

Cultural preserve Established to protect distinct areas containing outstanding cultural resources such as archeological sites, buildings, or significant zones.

PURPOSES OF STATE PARKS

State park systems have three main purposes: the preservation of significant features; provision of outdoor recreation; and education. In addition to managing the natural and cultural resources, state parks have a further responsibility of managing people.

Park ranger positions are not only being filled by people trained in resource management but those who are trained in the social sciences, in order to combine both resource management and people management.

"Unless we understand people, their motivations, and teach them to enjoy and appreciate the resources," said William Penn Mott, Jr., former Director of the California State Parks and Recreation Department, "we are convinced that people can destroy the very resources that they want to preserve."[5]

RESPONSIBILITY OF STATE PARKS

Generally, the role of state parks can be divided into five categories of responsibility:

Recreation—Providing lands of state or regional significance for outdoor recreation use.

Figure 11–3 Managing people is a very important responsibility of state park personnel. Here, Helen Smith of the California Department of Parks and Recreation conducts a tour of the Vikingsholm, a castle built in the Scandinavian tradition at Emerald Bay State Park, Lake Tahoe.

Protection—Protecting unique natural, historic, and recreation landscapes of state and regional significance.

Assistance—Assisting local government in meeting recreation demands and coordinating activities of agencies that supply public recreation facilities.

Planning—Evaluating natural, historic, and recreation resources.

Information—Supplying information on public recreation and providing interpretive and educational opportunities.

FUNCTIONS OF THE STATES

In providing recreation facilities and services, each of the fifty states has operated within the following eight functions:

1. *Promote outdoor natural resources and recreation opportunities.* Each state operates a comprehensive network of parks and other outdoor recreation areas to meet the needs of both its citizens and visiting tourists. Special emphasis has been the preservation of the state's cultural, historic, and natural heritage, as well as scenic landscape.

2. *Promote conservation and open space.* State agencies have the responsibility for promoting conservation and educational programs and supporting open–space and beautification efforts by local municipalities.

3. *Enabling legislation.* Enabling laws enacted by the states authorize local authorities to operate recreation and park facilities and programs.

4. *Assist local governments.* State agencies provide varied assistance to local authorities, such as technical guidance or consultation, subsidies for special programs for youth and the aging.

5. *Serve special populations.* State governmental agencies operate a variety of recreation programs that serve special populations, such as aging persons, those in penal or corrective centers, the mentally ill, and the retarded.

6. *Develop and enforce standards and regulations.* The states serve an important function in screening personnel by establishing standards and regulations for personnel. Employment procedures are established, and a growing number of states have set up certification and registration programs in the field.

7. *Promote professional advancement in recreation and parks.* State colleges and universities provide higher education in recreation and park administration. They sponsor conferences, workshops, and research in recreation.

8. *Promote leisure and recreation involvement as good economy.* A wide range of leisure activities have received strong promotional support by state agencies, such as tourism, vacationing, and a wide array of outdoor recreation activities.

ENABLING LEGISLATION

The legal authority for the operation of public programs is granted to the local communities by the states. Through its own enabling laws, each state designates the means by which counties and municipalities

Figure 11-4 Attractive boating facilities are located at High Cliff State Park in Wisconsin. Water resources at state parks provide numerous outdoor recreation experiences. (Courtesy Wisconsin Natural Resources Department.)

may operate recreation programs, whether by schools, parks, or separate recreation agencies. Local government authorities are permitted by the states to conduct recreation programs under the type of administrative organization considered most effective.

Today, each of the fifty states has legislative codes that empower local government to acquire land, develop recreation and park facilities, tax the people for recreation purposes, and provide direct program services.

Recreation professionals in a given state should be acquainted with the enabling legislation of that state in order to have knowledge of the legal circumstances under which the local programs are managed.

FINANCING STATE PARKS

States differ significantly in the ways in which they finance the development of parks. Some parks are gifts from private benefactors, while others occasionally will exchange land with the federal government or acquire federal property by transfer. However, states are finding it increasingly necessary to purchase their park lands,

financing the purchases through bond issues, taxes, and income from offshore oil.

Federal matching funds through the Land and Water Conservation Fund have provided states with considerable financial assistance. Cove Lake State Park in Campbell County, Tennessee, for example, is being redeveloped with the assistance of a $743,751 federal grant. The grant was matched with an equal amount of state money. Facilities to be redeveloped include the campground, picnic area, shelters, restrooms, and water supply. New facilities will include tennis and basketball courts, a fishing pier, and additional shelters and restrooms. Additional income comes from gate and seasonal fees, parking fees, fees for use of special facilities, and concession returns.

OUTDOOR RECREATION SERVICES

Traditionally, state parks have provided outdoor recreation opportunities for those who desire this type of leisure–time experience. Some state parks have been primarily historical and featured a diversity of unusual natural areas to be preserved; other parks have offered a variety of recreation activities and facilities.

State parks have a definite advantage in providing opportunities in outdoor recreation. There is considerably more flexibility of location when servicing the people of an entire state than there is in city and local parks. There are also many more potential sites available for selection by the state park system.

HISTORICAL SITES

A major dimension closely related to state park and recreation services is historical events and the people and sites associated with them. Considerable resources in many states are being devoted to this type of program. For instance, the park program of New Hampshire is being shifted from the acquisition of large, natural tracts to acquisition of unusual and historic sites.

STATE FORESTS

Most of the fifty states have a state forest system which is usually administered by a separate state forestry agency. In a few states, however, state forests are administered in combination with other state–owned lands. State forests, considerably more extensive in area than state parks, have always received good use for recreation purposes. Unlike state parks, state forests are usually open to hunting and fishing.

Camping areas for families and resident youth camps are available on state forest lands. Sites for summer homes are often leased in state forests. State forests also accommodate such popular outdoor activities as hiking, horseback riding, sailing, swimming, canoeing, boating, sightseeing, and skiing.

A "forestry" program for cities has been launched by the California Department of Forestry. The program is aimed at planting more trees in urban areas and improving management of existing urban vegetation.

The project is aimed at improving the quality of the urban environment by arresting the decline of urban forest resources.

PUBLIC EDUCATION

Education for leisure has now become recognized as an important function of the public schools. Modern education provides valuable skills, attitudes, and abilities in various recreation activities.

Professional preparation programs for recreation leaders are now offered by many state colleges and universities. An increasing number offer specialization in outdoor recreation. Nearly one hundred educational institutions in the United States now offer majors in recreation and forty offer graduate degrees in recreation.

WATER RESOURCES

Administrative responsibility for state water resources is often assigned to the department of natural resources. Water resources are most essential to outdoor recreation in the state. Lakes, streams, and coastal areas constitute major recreation attractions and the various resorts and camps need pure water for drinking, bathing, and other uses.

FISH AND WILDLIFE

A separate department or a major division within a department has been created by each of the fifty states to administer a program of fish and wildlife management. Essentially, the responsibilities of a state fish and wildlife agency are to propagate, manage, and distribute game animals, fur–bearing animals, game birds, and game fish. The department manages game land and fisheries and issues licenses for hunting, fishing, and trapping.

A variety of wildlife areas, such as reserves, sanctuaries, game farms, fish hatcheries, and special shooting grounds, are administered by state fish and wildlife departments. Most states provide broad programs for regulating and improving hunting and fishing. The departments work very closely with the Bureau of Sports, Fisheries and Wildlife at the federal level, and with several other federal and state agencies.

A major wildlife problem in many states is that private lands have been increasingly unavailable to the majority of sportsmen. Much of the good land and water areas is under private ownership, in the form of hunting and fishing clubs. Steps have been taken by state fish and game authorities, however, to open private lands to the public and to make them more productive to wildlife.

CAMPING

The most significant increase in state park usage has been in tent and trailer camping. State parks throughout the United States have been overwhelmed with demands for campsites. In fact, since World War II the use of state parks has expanded about eight times as fast as the population.

To help meet expenses and finance improvements, many state park systems have had to charge fees. Although fees should be kept to a minimum, many authorities believe at least 50 percent of the cost should be borne by the park users. Typical sources of funds are gate and parking fees, admission charges for the use of special facilities, and returns from concession operations.

RESORTS AND LODGES

An increasing number of states are providing resort and lodge facilities for both state residents and the traveling public. Lake Barkely Lodge and Resort Park in Kentucky is highly regarded for its functional beauty as well as its services, resources, and facilities.

TOURISM

Tourism and recreation have been one of the states' largest income–producing activities. Tourists spend substantial sums of money while traveling, for such items as food, drinks, and various other leisure or resort expenses. From the economic standpoint, this money is turned over many times on various levels of the local economy which provides substantial employment.

HIGHWAYS AND ROADS

The state highway departments are charged with the responsibility to construct roads into certain areas of recreational value. They also participate in maintaining such roads and often keep roads open to certain winter sports areas. Many recreation areas would receive much less use if they were not readily accessible by good roads.

Roadside parks and historic markers are often the responsibility of state highway departments. Roads inside state–owned recreation lands, such as state parks and state forests, are usually constructed under the authority of this department.

PARK INTERPRETATION PROGRAMS

State park systems today provide much needed "Park Interpretation Programs." In addition to the park situation, these programs attempt to teach visitors the basic facts about the natural environment and its management. Many innovative programs have been introduced in the state park systems that have helped people to re–evaluate their own role in the natural world.

Many states have developed interpretive services programs designed to provide visitors with a deeper understanding and appreciation of the natural or historical features in or near the area visited. Services of this type make the park experiences more meaningful and enjoyable. In addition to various

Figure 11–5 Interpretation programs. State park systems today provide much needed park interpretation programs. These programs attempt to teach visitors the basic facts about the natural environment and its management.

STATE ORGANIZATIONAL PLANS

California

The majority of the state of California's responsibility for outdoor recreation is centered in the Resources Agency, one of the major divisions of the state government. The three departments within the Resources Agency that have principal outdoor-recreation responsibilities are the Department of Parks and Recreation, the Department of Harbors and Watercraft, and the Department of Fish and Game.

Acting under the authority of the governor, the head of the Resources Agency is responsible to the governor for the ef-ficient operation of the various departments, boards, and commissions within the agency. Formulation of policy and long-range programs is also under the governor's jurisdiction. Within the agency, the administrators of the various departments are directly responsible to the administrator of the Resources Agency.

The state park and recreation commission has the responsibility for classifying units in the state park system. In California, the commission consists of nine people on a staggered term and appointed for four years. They determine the policy for the director to carry out the responsibilities of administering the park system for California.

Michigan

Michigan's state park system has long been recognized as one of the finest in America. Indeed, it has come a long way since 1895 when Mackinac Island State Park was created to take over military lands and buildings previously controlled by the federal government.

In Michigan, the principal state agency involved in the administration of outdoor recreation is the Department of Natural Resources. Other agencies involved on a more limited basis include the State Waterways Commission, the Huron–Clinton Metropolitan Authority, the State Highway Department, state universities and colleges, and the Department of Public Instruction.

The Department of Natural Resources is headed by a seven–member commission appointed by the governor with the consent of the senate. The commission annually appoints a director and a secretary. The various functions to the departments are organized into divisions, whose heads are directly responsible to the director.

Within the parks division, the development and operation of the State of Michigan Park System revolves around three major sections: 1. *Park design,* 2. *Policies, procedures, and special services,* and 3. *Programming.*

Oregon

The concept for a system of state parks in Oregon dates from 1921 when the legislature gave the Highway Commission (now the Oregon Department of Transportation Commission) authority to acquire land beyond rights–of–way for scenic preservation. By 1929 the commission had acquired 26 sites, totaling more than 6,000 acres.

Public request for various types of developed outdoor recreation facilities increased in the 1950s. To respond to this demand for recreation facilities, the division changed its program emphasis from land acquisition to construction of picnicking areas, campgrounds, and swimming beaches.

The Parks and Recreation Division is part of the Oregon Department of Transportation. For management purposes, the division is divided into eight sections: administrative services; design and engineering; operations and maintenance; program planning and rivers; recreation trails; historic preservation; property management; and public information.[6]

Traditionally, division responsibility has emphasized acquisition, development or rehabilitation, and management of park units having state or regionwide scenic, recreation, or historic values. In recent years, however, the division has assumed an equally important responsibility for managing special–purpose recreation programs such as scenic waterways, ocean shores, trails, historic preservation, and the Willamette Greenway.

During the 1979–81 biennum, state parks have relied on self–generated revenues, and on a general fund allocation as major sources of revenue, since the division no longer receives highway fund support. Federal grant programs such as the Land and Water Conservation Fund (LWCF) and the Historic Preservation Fund provide secondary assistance to capital improvement and rehabilitation projects.[7]

Since 1965, the LWCF has provided approximately $30 million in matching funds to Oregon. Approximately 30 percent of the regular LWCF and apportionment coming to Oregon have been used by state parks for capital projects, primarily land acquisition. The balance of these monies transfer to counties, cities, and park districts for local park acquisitions and developments.

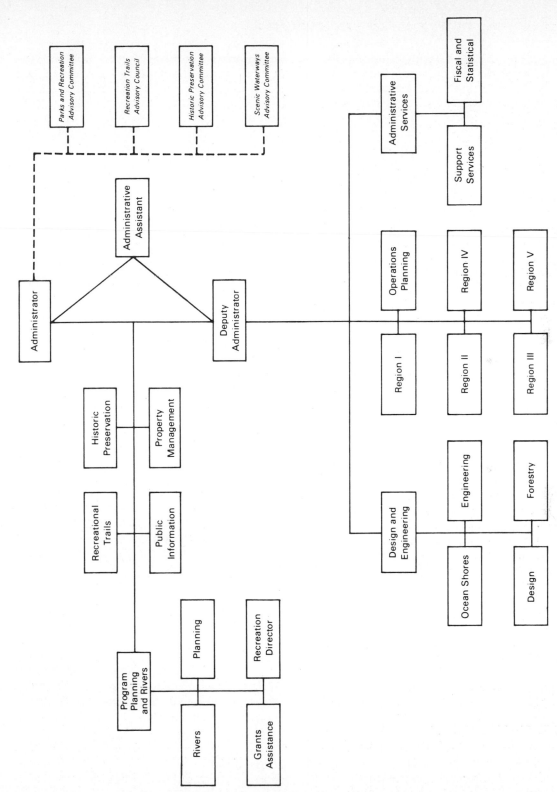

Figure 11-6 Organization chart, State of Oregon Parks and Recreation Branch.

publications and personally conducted programs, wayside exhibits, interpretive buildings, and self–guiding trails are offered.

Utilization of resources for environmental awareness programs is an area experiencing greatly increased attention among state park agencies. Environmental education programs with local school systems, vocational school programs, and inner–city youth work projects are another area which has provided another dimension to state parks.

NEW DEVELOPMENTS IN STATE PARKS

The most interesting developments taking place in state parks in the United States are related to a number of new recreational activities.

Snowmobiles and Other Winter Vehicles

While they have been an exciting and exhilarating activity, snowmobiles continue to create problems for park and recreation departments in the snow country of such popular outdoor areas as the Sierras, the Rockies, the Midwest, and New England. Hazardous areas and unfamiliarity with the snow country have presented numerous problems for those who use such recreational vehicles. However, tighter controls, safer and quieter machines, the creation of snowmobile trails and banning the vehicles from roads have combined to reduce significantly problems created by snowmobiles.

New Hampshire, like most states with large numbers of snowmobilers, requires snowmobile registration and bans the machines from roads.

Motor Bikes and Other Recreation Vehicles

A rapidly growing activity involves recreation vehicles such as sand or dune buggies, motorcycles, four–wheel jeeps, and various other motor bikes or cars. As a result,

an increasing number of state parks and recreation departments have set aside and planned special areas and facilities for this kind of recreation activity. In California, for example, the state parks department has set aside a 300–acre canyon area at Pt. Mugu recreation area near Los Angeles where recreation vehicles can be used.

Underwater Exploration

Underwater exploration by divers for photography, fishing, and exploring has become a very popular activity. In addition to setting aside and preserving underwater areas along the Pacific Coast, the State of Califor-

Figure 11–7 Underwater exploration. This underwater scene was photographed at Pennekamp Coral Reef State Park in Key Largo, Florida. (Courtesy Florida News Bureau, Department of Commerce.)

nia designed and built an underwater park on the land and then filled in the reservoir. The most exciting area is probably the La Jolla Canyon near San Diego, where the canyon comes almost to the shore and then continues into the ocean to great depths that provide exciting archeological study of underwater areas.

Bringing Parks to the People

A greater number of state parks are being built that are within a two–hour drive of major cities. While the unique and scenic state park far from the city is accessible only to the long weekender, increased effort is being made to provide nearby areas that are accessible to those who prefer a one–day outing.

CURRENT PROBLEMS

Because of changing economic conditions, equipment, and recreation trends, flexibility is required to meet the changing demands for public recreation.

As in the case of other levels of government, state agencies continue to face serious problems as a result of inadequate financial support. Many departments have had to cut back services, or drastically curtail park development.

Wisconsin's Bureau of Parks and Recreation has expressed concern for land acquisition. Their most serious problem is the inability to acquire key parcels of land at a rapid enough rate to consolidate state park projects and stay ahead of the subdivider.

With open space land becoming increasingly scarce, many state agencies have adhered to the philosophy of acquiring as much needed land as possible now. Increased service costs and inflation have hit state parks, requiring revisions and restructuring of fee schedules.

Arsonists are responsible each year for thousands of fires which occur in state parks and recreation areas. In 1978, for example, arsonists set more than six hundred and seventy–five fires on land protected by the California Department of Forestry. Why do they do it? "Every one we catch has a different reason," said Walt Bolster of the California Department of Forestry law enforcement division.

QUESTIONS FOR DISCUSSION

1. What changes in American life contributed to the tremendous rise in demand for outdoor recreational opportunities?
2. What are the three most common types of administration of parks used among the states?
3. What types or groupings of state park units make up a typical state park system?
4. What are the three main purposes of the state park system?
5. Discuss functions of the state park system.
6. How is the development of state parks financed?
7. Why is the responsibility of interpreting to the public the natural and cultural values of state parks of such importance and need?
8. What are some of the most interesting developments taking place today in state parks.
9. Discuss one of the most interesting trends among state parks today: "Bringing Parks to the People."
10. Identify some of the major problems that state park personnel are currently faced with.

REFERENCES

1. Barry S. Tindall, "Land for all Seasons," *Parks and Recreation Magazine*, December 1970, p. 25.
2. Elvin R. Johnson, *Park Resources for Recreation* (Columbus: Charles Merrill, 1972), p. 109.
3. Clayne R. Jensen, *Outdoor Recreation in America* (Minneapolis, Minn.: Burgess Publishing Company, 1970), p. 122.
4. Ibid., p. 121.
5. William Penn Mott, Jr., taken from a recorded speech, "The Role of the California State Park System," American River College, Sacramento, Calif., November 18, 1971.
6. *Oregon State Parks System Plan, 1981–1987*, Parks and Recreation Division, Department of Transportation, Salem, Oregon, p. 5.
7. Ibid., pp. 61–62.

Figure 12–1 Millions of Americans find enjoyment in their national parks and forests each year—refreshment of mind, body, and spirit. This family cooks an early morning meal at a wilderness trail rider camp in Montana's Flathead National Forest. (Courtesy U.S. Forest Service.)

12
Federal Government

Through the years, the government has expanded its involvement in recreation–related activities. Today nearly every major division of federal government contributes in some measure to outdoor recreation. In addition to landholding, the federal government participates in a broad spectrum of recreation and leisure services.

Originally, the recreational activities of the federal government centered around the use of federal land and water areas for recreation. Steadily, the government expanded its involvements in recreation–related activities, until today nearly every major division of federal government contributes in some measure to outdoor recreation.

Federal involvement in outdoor recreation and conservation programs is well–recognized, but the increasing impact of federal revenue sharing, community development, public employment, and public works programs on behalf of city recreation efforts is not as well–known. The ability of local governments to meet recreation needs is strongly affected by federal programs in social welfare, housing, transportation, environmental education, arts, and other recreation–related activities.

FEDERAL AGENCIES INVOLVED IN OUTDOOR RECREATION

The types of federal land–administering agencies are divided into two groups:

1. Those administering natural lands, such as the National Park Service, the Bureau of Land Management, the Bureau of In-

dian Affairs, and the Fish and Wildlife Service
2. Water–resource developing agencies that acquired lands for the purpose of developing dams and reservoirs, such as the Corps of Engineers, the Bureau of Reclamation, and the Tennessee Valley Authority

FUNCTIONS OF FEDERAL GOVERNMENT IN RECREATION

Essentially, federal government's function in recreation evolved as a secondary outcome of other programs. The federal government first became involved in outdoor recreation chiefly because of its position as custodian of public lands. The following represent the varied functions of federal government.

Direct Management of Outdoor Recreation Resources

Federal agencies such as the National Park Service and the Bureau of Land Management own and operate a huge network of parks, forests, lakes and reservoirs, seashores, and other facilities which are heavily used for outdoor recreation.

Assistance to Open–Space and Park Development Programs

The federal government, through funding authorized by such legislation as the 1965 Land and Water Fund Conservation Act, has provided hundreds of millions of dollars in matching grants to states and localities to promote open–space development. Housing and urban development projects have subsidized the development of many local parks, playgrounds, and centers.

Conservation and Resource Reclamation

In assisting programs related to conservation, wildlife, and anti–pollution controls, the federal government reclaims natural resources which have been destroyed, damaged, or threatened. The Department of the Interior is the federal government's principal conservation agency that is responsible for developing better ways to manage the nation's natural resources and improving the quality of life.

Advisory and Technical Services

State and local groups receive advisory assistance from federal agencies. Economically and socially disadvantaged populations have been assisted by numerous community programs sponsored by the Department of Housing and Urban Development, Department of Health, Education, and Welfare, (now Health and Human Services) and others.

Research and Education

Federal agencies have conducted a broad spectrum of research involving studies on tourist and travel opportunities, the use of and demand for leisure, wildlife problems, forest recreation, natural and historical resources, etc. The government has provided numerous training grants for professional preparation of recreation and park personnel.

Regulation and Standards

Federal Regulations affecting recreation and parks have included standards and controls for environmental quality, pollution control, timber production, and watershed protection.

Direct Programs of Recreation Service

The federal government operates a number of direct programs of recreation and leisure service in veterans' hopitals, military installations, and federal institutions, as well as national parks and forests and wildlife reserves.

DEPARTMENT OF THE INTERIOR

The Department of the Interior has responsibility for most of our nationally owned public lands and natural resources. This includes fostering the wisest use of the United States' land and water resources, protecting fish and wildlife, preserving the environmental and cultural values of national parks and historical places, and providing for the enjoyment of life through outdoor recreation.

The department assesses energy and mineral resources and works to assure that their development is in the best interests of all the people. The department also has a major responsibility for American Indian reservation communities and for people who live in island territories under United States administration.

The Department of the Interior has five basic organizational units, each headed by an assistant secretary:

Policy, Budget, and Administration
Fish and Wildlife and Parks
Land and Water Resources
Energy and Minerals
Indian Affairs

THE NATIONAL PARK SERVICE

From the establishment of Yellowstone, the first national park, in 1872, national parks have evolved through Congressional enactments into a system covering nearly three–hundred areas and more than thirty million acres of federally owned land. These National Park System areas attract more than 250 million visits a year.

Figure 12–2 The first national park. Established in 1872, Yellowstone set a worldwide precedent for people's esthetic appreciation of pristine beauty. This spectacular painting by Thomas Moran hangs in the U.S. Department of the Interior Museum, Washington, D.C. (Courtesy National Park Service.)

The National Park System consists of 297 areas, and 18 affiliated areas, of such natural, historical, or recreational distinction as to be of national significance. The system includes 37 national parks, 82 national monuments, 17 national recreation areas, and 10 national seashores.

The national parks were set aside in 1916 "to conserve the scenery and the natural and historic objects and the wildlife therein, and to provide for the enjoyment of the same in such manner and by such means as will leave them unimpaired for the enjoyment of future generations."[1]

The National Park Service developed rapidly under the aggressive leadership of its first director, Stephen T. Mather, a young industrialist and outdoorsman from California. A great organizer, Mather set the pattern for the park service as it is today—career service with outstanding *esprit de corps*, and an agency without partisan politics.

In 1933, all national parks and monuments, national military parks, national battlefield parks and sites, the national capital parks, national memorials, and certain national cemeteries were consolidated under the administration of the park service.

The National Park Service, in administering America's vast park system, officially acts as a national recreation consulting agency for federal, state, and local governments. This responsibility was given to the park service in the Park, Parkway, and Recreation

Area Study Act of 1936. The act provides that the National Park Service make comprehensive studies and develop plans to provide adequate public park, parkway, and recreational area facilities for the people of the United States.

As a bureau of the Department of the Interior, the National Park System is composed of three categories of areas: natural, historical, and recreational.

1. *Natural areas*—the great scenic wonderlands: unspoiled mountains, lakes, forests, desert canyons, and glaciers.
2. *Historical and archeological areas*—examples of ancient Indian cultures, as well as buildings, sites, and objects that have been witness to great events of American history.
3. *Recreational areas*—together with recreation areas administered by other agencies, provide healthful outdoor recreational opportunities for a population which today is increasingly urban.

What should a national park be? According to Robert Binneweis, superintendent of Yosemite Park, "National parks should reflect this nation's highest ideals and aspirations—that they should be showcases of our vast and varied scenic and cultural landscapes."

The legendary John Muir once said: "Yosemite Park is a place of rest. A refuge . . . in which one gains the advantage of both solitude and society . . . none can escape its charms. You will be willing to stay forever."[2]

Each national park has some distinctive feature that justifies its inclusion in the system. Mt. Rainier contains more than fifty square miles of glacial ice; while the park at Carlsbad protects one of the largest known natural caverns in the world. The Grand Canyon National Park features the timeless erosion and canyon construction of the Colorado River, which has excavated more than one vertical mile of the ancient rocks of the Kaibab Plateau. In the east, Acadia National Park in Maine protects a portion of the most rugged and rocky wave–pounded coastline of the Atlantic Ocean.[3]

Figure 12–3 Father of the national parks. Stephen T. Mather was the first director of the National Park Service, serving from May 16, 1917, to January 8, 1929. He believed that "only those areas of truly great scenic, scientific or historical value and of unquestioned significance should be added to the park system." (Courtesy National Park Service.)

The Preservation–Use Concept

The basic idea of the National Park Service is to preserve in their natural condition areas of national significance, in order that these areas will be available for the enjoyment of people in the future as well as the present. The preservation concept must be balanced with the use concept, since the primary justification for preservation is the use the areas serve for the people. However, the use must be controlled in such a manner that the areas are preserved in their natural condition for future use.

The park service, for example, has been trying since 1968 to resolve problems caused by overcrowded conditions at Yosemite Park. The National Park Service in 1979 approved a new general management plan for Yosemite Park which was designed to serve as the major management guideline for the park. Major changes are expected to reduce park and concession administrative functions from Yosemite Valley, reduce and eventually eliminate automobile use in the valley, develop an integrated public transportation system, and establish an expanded reservation system.

Although the National Park Service has been criticized by some preservationists for being too recreation–oriented, some recreationists and resource–user groups have objected to the strong preservation concept employed by the park service. Clayne Jensen explained the current philosophy, "The essence of the whole preservation–use idea seems to be 'Eat as much of the cake as we can, but be sure we still have it to eat in the future.' "[4]

Unfortunately, the vacation crowds that usually pack national parks thinned in 1979, apparently because of higher gasoline prices and shortages. Only parks close to urban areas, such as the Golden Gate National Recreation Area, where the number of visitors is up more than 60 percent, are the exception to the general pattern. People are going to fewer parks and staying longer, and usually at parks closer to home.

The Urban Park Dilemma

Some key questions have been raised about the basic mission of the National Park Service, particularly with respect to meeting urban recreation needs. An editorial in *Parks and Recreation Magazine* stated that "Some defenders of the National Park Service argue that there is an inherent conflict between urban recreation and the objectives for environmental and historic preservation that have typified the Park Service's primary mission since 1916. Other park service defenders are equally persuaded that the only way to strengthen, and perhaps to avoid the loss of a broad citizen constituency for the national park system, is to bring the system closer to where people live and work."[5]

The problem has been made even more severe by overcrowding, reduced staffs, budget cuts, and increasing vandalism and thefts in the national parks. "An obvious problem with all federal outdoor recreation programs," wrote Kraus, "is the need to provide sufficient budgetary support to meet the growing public demands for facilities and programs."[6]

In a dramatic departure from past policies, the National Park Service is now charged

Figure 12–4 Gateway National Recreation Area brings "parks to the people." Jamaica Bay, on the southeastern shore of Staten Island, offers one of the most successful bird sanctuaries on the east coast, a wildlife refuge with the Manhattan skyline in the background. (Courtesy Gateway National Recreation Area, National Park Service.)

with the management of three national recreation areas: Gateway in New York and New Jersey; Golden Gate in San Francisco, California; and Cuyahoga Valley between Cleveland and Akron, Ohio. This action was a federal response to the urban concern of the 1960s and early 1970s. Gateway, however, is among urban parks that may be turned over by the United States to state and local governments.

UNITED STATES FOREST SERVICE

Indeed, with the tremendous public demand for recreational use of the land, the Forest Service is currently very much in the recreation business. Recreational use of the national forests in 1977 was estimated at nearly 205 million visitor–days, representing a great increase over the forty–six million visitors in 1955.

Administered under the Department of Agriculture, national forests are based fundamentally upon the Act of March 3, 1891, which authorized the president to reserve, by proclamation, certain lands from the public domain and to designate such lands as forest reserves.

Created in 1905, the United States Forest Service "found itself attempting to manage recreation in order to minimize fire hazards, stream pollution, and hazards to the recreationists themselves. Once having become involved, the Forest Service personnel apparently adapted themselves to the situation. In so doing, they caused the official policy of the U.S. Forest Service to become one of encouraging recreational use of the forests."[7]

The Forest Service administers approximately 200 million acres of outdoor land within 154 national forests, nineteen national grassland areas, and various small land utilization projects. Douglas M. Knudson wrote that: "Most of the Forest Service lands, featuring mountains, trees, streams and lakes, are scenically attractive to American recreationists."[8]

The many types of resources are protected

Figure 12–5 Trail riders at White River National Forest head out toward Maroon Bells Wilderness Area in Colorado for a two–week pack trip. While preservation is still the major responsibility of federal outdoor agencies, both the Park Service and Forest Service are encouraging people to use these areas. (Courtesy U.S. Forest Service.)

and managed under a system of multiple use and sustained yield. "On a given square mile of national forest land there may be a ski area, or a campground on a stream or lake, or a dam providing flood control and hydroelectric power, or a controlled logging operation."[9]

As a bureau of the Department of Agriculture, the administration of the forest service begins with the secretary of agriculture, with the service staff headed by the chief forester and operated in Washington, D.C. Regional offices administer the forests from headquarters across the nation.

Each national forest has a forest supervisor as its head. In turn, this supervisor has a staff of specialists in timber and range management, protection, public relations, recreational activities, and engineering.

A long-time emphasis on outdoor recreation opportunities by the Forest Service has produced a network of campgrounds, picnic areas, and wilderness preserves. According to Knudson, "Logging activities have left many roads and trails, which provide excellent access for hikers, hunters, fishermen, and ORV riders, as well as those just out for a Sunday drive on the improved roads. The forests contain numerous ski resorts, the nation's longest hiking trail system, a large proportion of the big game and fisheries resources, as well as outstanding scenery."[10]

CORPS OF ENGINEERS

Since the Revolutionary War, the Corps of Engineers has served the United States in peace and war. The corps exercises primary federal responsibility for water resources development. Organized in 1775, the Corps of Engineers of the U.S. Department of the Army, is responsible for the improvement and maintenance of rivers and other waterways to facilitate navigation and flood control. In doing so, this agency affects recreation by constructing and operating reservoirs, protecting and improving beaches, and providing harbors and waterways used by recreation craft.

The recreation program at corps-built lakes and waterways has grown from an incidental amenity to a major program providing outdoor recreation opportunities for millions of Americans. In just twenty-five years, attendance at corps lakes and waterways has reached 420 million.

Approximately two-thirds of Corps multipurpose lakes built for flood control, water supply, hydroelectric power, navigation, fish and wildlife, recreation, and other uses are located within a fifty-mile radius of Standard Metropolitan Statistical Areas (urban areas containing at least one city of fifty-thousand inhabitants or more).

The agency operates about three hundred and ninety major reservoirs in states covering approximately eleven million acres. Like other federal agencies, the corps cooperates fully with local government and private interests in many aspects concerning the betterment of water resources.

To carry out its recreation-resource management practices, the corps employs professional personnel with many talents—biologists, foresters, engineers, rangers, landscape architects, and outdoor recreation planners.

BUREAU OF LAND MANAGEMENT

Operating under the Department of the Interior, the Bureau of Land Management (BLM) is another agency that is concerned with maintaining and strengthening the quality of our natural resources. Created in 1946, the bureau has jurisdiction over federally owned public lands that have not been incorporated into specific national forests, parks, or other recreation areas.

BLM holdings were long neglected and ignored as recreation assets until passage of the Classification and Multiple Use Act of 1964. Thereupon, the BLM role in recreation began to enlarge. By 1974 approximately 196 million acres, primarily in Alaska and the eleven western states, were classified as usable or suitable for recreation. Recreational use of the national resource lands increased

Figure 12–6 Recreational facilities on Corps of Engineers' owned lands attract millions of visitors each year. As the demand for water–oriented recreation opportunities grows, the Corps' twin tasks of recreation and resource management assume a growing importance. Located on the Calaveras River near Stockton, California, the New Hogan Dam and Reservoir Project is a sixteen million dollar earthfill dam, completed in 1964. (Courtesy U.S. Army Corps of Engineers, Sacramento District.)

from nine million visitor–days in 1964 to fifty–five million in 1974, and currently surpasses seventy–five million. This land includes a total of about one–fifth of the United States, or approximately 470 million acres located chiefly in Alaska and the western states.

Resource lands under BLM authority feature some of America's most spectacular desert, mountain, and canyon scenery. Raft trips, hiking, off–road vehicle activity, and picnicking are among the many recreational pursuits enjoyed on BLM areas.

BLM, the nation's largest land manager, is a major producer of revenue, accounting for approximately $4 billion annually. Although its recreation efforts are not in the same scope as those of the National Park Service and the National Forest Service, the bureau is growing in importance, and its facilities and services should help to relieve the pressures on the more prominent areas. Properties of the

Bureau of Land Management are being used increasingly for camp and picnic sites, trailer areas, swimming beaches, and boat launching ramps.

BUREAU OF RECLAMATION

Another agency in the Department of Interior is the Bureau of Reclamation which has a primary responsibility for water resource development, primarily for irrigation and power in the seventeen western states.

Since its establishment in 1902, the Bureau of Reclamation has created 264 synthetic reservoirs and other bodies of water, bringing opportunities for people to rest and relax in a great outdoor environment. Today, recreation–resource management is a vital part of reclamation's multipurpose water development program.

The majority of recreation areas in reclamation lands are operated by local, county, or state agencies. Some are managed by federal agencies such as the Forest Service or the National Park Service, and few are managed directly by reclamation.

For many years, the bureau has permitted boating, fishing, picnicking, swimming, hiking, and other recreation activities on its reservoir areas. Rather than develop and administer the recreation resources of its areas, however, the bureau's policy has been to transfer them to other appropriate federal, state, or local governmental agencies.

Millions of people spend their weekends and vacations at reclamation reservoirs. The West is dotted with these synthetic lakes—Lake Mead in Nevada, Millerton Lake in California, and Lake Granby in Colorado, to name only a few. Reclamation water areas in the seventeen western states attract more than sixty million visitors each year.

THE FISH AND WILDLIFE SERVICE

The U.S. Fish and Wildlife Service consists of two separate bureaus: the Bureau of Sports Fisheries and Wildlife and the Bureau of Commercial Fisheries. Within the Department of the Interior, the Fish and Wildlife Service has the responsibility for the protection of fish and wildlife on federal properties throughout the United States. It administers laws for the protection and propagation of birds, mammals, reptiles, and amphibians; enforces federal game laws; and cooperates with state fish and game agencies.

The Bureau of Sports Fisheries and Wildlife uses public land only for wildlife refuge areas, fish hatcheries, and waterfowl production areas. Much of its work is advisory and involves research on fish, game animals, and game birds.

In 1962, Congress declared recreation to be an appropriate "secondary purpose" of the National Wildlife Refuge System, followed by the passage of the Endangered Species Preservation Act in 1966. Both acts have been very beneficial to the wildlife conservation program of the Bureau of Sports Fisheries and Wildlife.

Many of its 300 national wildlife refuges covering more than 28 million acres afford not only havens for game but facilities for boating, camping, picnicking, and nature study.

LAND AND WATER CONSERVATION FUND

Enacted into law by Congress in 1965, this fund was created to provide urgently needed public outdoor recreation areas and facilities to states and local governments, and other federal agencies in their outdoor recreation and open–space programs. In order to be eligible for funding assistance, each state is required to prepare a comprehensive outdoor recreation plan, analyzing the needs of the various cities.

Funding is derived mainly from admission and user fees at federal recreation areas, net proceeds from the sale of surplus federal property, and the federal tax on motorboat fuels. Of the total amount, 40 percent is made available to federal agencies and 60 percent to states and territories as grants–in–aid on a 50 percent matching basis for planning, acquisition, or development projects. Emphasis is on acquisition rather than development, and on sites for direct recreation use rather than historic sites or museums.

The Land and Water Conservation Fund (LWCF) was established to provide: (1) a funding source for federal land managing agencies to acquire lands for their systems, and (2) grants–in–aid to states, and through them to localities, for the acquisition and development of outdoor recreation areas.

The fund has been very useful for the acquisition of land by the federal government and for land acquisition and facility development by state and local governments. However, the federal share of the fund has been spent largely in rural areas. Only 16 percent has been used in central cities which contain 30 percent of the national population.

The fund's future role was seriously aggravated when the Reagan Administration froze remaining 1981 LWFC appropriations totaling $250 million and requested Congress to rescind the funds. The 1982 fiscal budget revisions called for $45 million for "emergency federal land acquisitions" and no funding whatever for state and local assistance.

HERITAGE CONSERVATION AND RECREATION SERVICE

Created in 1978 by the U.S. Department of the Interior, the Heritage Conservation and Recreation Service (HCRS) took the place of the Bureau of Outdoor Recreation (BOR) which was established in 1962. HCRS was designed to coordinate a broad range of conservation and recreation activities by citizens in the public and private sectors. The service formed the nucleus of the National Heritage Program, a process of identifying, evaluating, and protecting our cultural and natural resources, and served as the focal point for assuring adequate recreation opportunities.

On February 8, 1981, Interior Secretary James Watt signed orders to abolish the HCRS and transfer a majority of its functions to the National Park Service. Watt took the action to "achieve economies in the utilization of funds, personnel, and equipment and to improve services by effecting the transfer and consolidation of the major functions of HCRS into the National Park Service."[11]

Severe budget cuts and the demise of HCRS were interpreted by many as "the Reagan Administration's abandonment of a strong federal coordination and assistance role in recreation and parks."[12] Watt's action was regarded as a severe setback for parks and recreation in the United States, particularly if the National Park Service fails to receive the direction or funds necessary to continue the coordination functions.

A NATIONAL OUTDOOR RECREATION PLAN

After many years of study, the Bureau of Outdoor Recreation in 1973 submitted to the president the first Nationwide Outdoor Rec-

reation Plan. The comprehensive plan, which included input and suggestions from all levels of government, private citizens, and educational agencies, focused on the following primary national systems and legislative acts:

1. *Wild and natural rivers* In an effort to save and restore certain rivers and streams, the National Wild and Scenic Rivers Act of 1968 began a system whereby seven rivers (five more were added in 1976) were designated for immediate protection and others were marked for study and possible future protection.
2. *National Trails System* In 1968, Congress passed the National Trails System Act which provided for two categories of trails—national scenic trails and national recreation trails. By 1973, forty–two national recreation trails had been established.
3. *Wilderness* Wilderness protection was the basis of the Wilderness Act of 1964. The act designated fifty–four units with more than nine million acres and required the departments of Agriculture and Interior to study and report on other lands to include in the system. By 1977, approximately fifteen million acres were in the total wilderness system.
4. *Historical and Archeological resources* Regarding its history with growing respect, Congress has acted to preserve historical sites and archeological resources through the Antiquities Act of 1906, the Historic Sites Act of 1939, and the Historic Properties Preservation Act of 1966. The bicentennial celebrations of 1976 gave significant impetus to the designation and preservation of historical resources.

THE TENNESSEE VALLEY AUTHORITY

Created by act of Congress in 1933, the original purpose of the Tennessee Valley Authority (TVA) was to develop the Tennessee

River for navigation, flood control, and electric power. While recreation was not specified as a major purpose of TVA programs, it soon became apparent "that the construction of a water control system for the Tennessee River would create a whole new range of recreation opportunities unfamiliar to this inland region of great natural beauty."[13]

According to Don Hammer, Wetlands ecologist, "TVA has developed new policies to assure maximum enjoyment of the region's outdoor recreation potential for valley residents and visitors. One result of this effort has been a concerted program to improve selected areas of reservoir shorelines and to provide additional access to TVA lakes."[14]

Of equal importance to many recreation enthusiasts are the opportunities afforded by the valley's thirty-eight thousand miles of free-running streams. TVA has identified forty streams with major recreation potential and has begun development of thirty-five access points along some of these streams for those who enjoy canoeing or floating. While the TVA itself does not operate recreation facilities, it does make land available to other public agencies or private groups for development.

Land Between The Lakes, located between Kentucky Lake and Lake Barkley in western Kentucky and Tennessee, is mid-America's newest outdoor recreation and environmental education area. Camping, fishing, boating, hunting, hiking, and wild-

Figure 12-7 Land between the Lakes is a 170,000 acre peninsula being developed by the Tennessee Valley Authority as a public outdoor demonstration in recreation, environmental education, resource management, and energy conservation. Observe the specially designed trailer circle within Hillman Ferry Campground. (Courtesy Tennessee Valley Authority.)

life observation are favorite recreational activities in this area developed by the TVA.

Bruce Rowland, TVA landscape architect, said "Today, the system of dams and reservoirs built by TVA provides flood control for homes, farms, and factories. Hydroelectric power from the dams provides a clean and renewable source of low–cost energy. The great dam building era in the Tennessee Valley is over, though. Now TVA's major concern with the region's water resources is to manage them more efficiently and effectively."[15]

BUREAU OF INDIAN AFFAIRS

The primary responsibility of the bureau is to provide service to American Indian tribes in health, education, economic development, and land management. Created in 1824 within the control of the War Department, the bureau was transferred to civilian control with the creation of the Department of the Interior.

Indian–owned properties today include about fifty–eight million acres with more than fifty–five hundred lakes. Approximately six hundred thousand Indians reside on or near more than fifty million acres of reservation lands.

Increasing self–government is occurring in much of "Indian country." On most of the United States' 267 reservations, substantial power already has been handed over to the tribes from the federal government. The turnovers have given new heart to those seeking to raise social and economic levels of Indians. More and more tribal councils are running activities, including the schools, recreation programs, the police and work on roads.

The three leisure activities that draw the largest participation and spectators among Indian people are pow wows, rodeos, and ball games of various types. Rodeo is so popular among Indians that they have formed their own American Indian Rodeo Cowboys Association (AIRCA). Tribal fairs are popular events with Indian people who travel cross–country to attend the favorite fairs. The Navajo National Fair in 1978 drew a crowd of one hundred and five thousand.

OUTDOOR RECREATION RESOURCES REVIEW COMMISSION (ORRRC)

In the 1950s rapid growth in people's demand for recreation, combined with increasing development of rural and urban lands for housing, commercial, and industrial uses, put more pressure on public and private efforts to meet recreation needs and protect recreation resources. These problems led to the creation of the Outdoor Recreation Resources Review Commission (ORRRC) and to a resurgence of federal interest in parks and recreation. ORRRC reports in 1962 clearly indicated continuing rapid losses of metropolitan open space and the importance of close–to–home recreation activities for city residents.

The U.S. Department of Agriculture provides assistance to rural residents to establish private recreation enterprises. Its Federal Extension Service gives aid to community recreation planning in rural areas and advises states on outdoor recreation development, working through extension agents at land grant agricultural colleges.

OTHER FEDERAL AGENCIES

In addition to the resource–management agencies, a number of federal agencies have made a significant contribution to outdoor recreation by providing technical and financial assistance. Many programs of the federal government provide services to special groups or purposes.

The largest federal landowner in urban regions is the Department of Defense, but, except for the Corps of Engineers reservoir sites, its lands are not generally open to the public.

Programs for military personnel, veterans, and federal employees have been effective in meeting their needs and demands.

While there has been an increase in services for the disadvantaged, the recreation needs and living conditions for disadvantaged segments of the population are still alarmingly acute. From a positive standpoint, it should be noted that the Education for All Handicapped Children Act of 1975 (PL–94–142) upheld the federal government's recognition of recreation as a significant area of service for special populations.

Department of Health and Human Services

This department administers many federal programs related to recreation. The Office of Education provides recreation services to state and local school systems, colleges, universities, and professional organizations. Working through state and national agencies and organizations, the Children's Bureau has shown a continuing interest in providing recreation opportunities for all children and youth.

The Public Health Service assists other federal agencies in planning sanitary developments in parks, camps, bathing and boating areas, picnic areas, and trailer parks. Working chiefly through the states, it assists in planning standards and inspection programs for bathing sanitation, food handling, disposal of refuse and sewage, and various problems in camps and parks.

The Rehabilitation Services Administration administers the federal law authorizing vocational rehabilitation programs designed to help the physically and mentally disabled. A number of college programs training therapeutic recreation specialists are receiving grants for curriculum development and scholarships by the Vocational Services Administration.

The Administration on Aging is concerned with problems of older persons in society. In promoting programs for aging persons, the federal agency provides grants for training of professional personnel and demonstration projects intended to prepare professional staffs for work with older people. The largest number of local projects have involved recreation and leisure–time activities, with particular emphasis on senior centers.

Department of Housing and Urban Development

The federal government has been very active in promoting slum clearance and assisting housing programs in the United States' cities. Established in 1965, the Department of Housing and Urban Development (HUD) has been effective in encouraging the provision of recreation areas and facilities to meet the needs of the residents of housing projects. The department is responsible for a wide range of federally assisted programs, including public housing, mass transit, urban renewal and planning, community facilities, and open space.

The federal government has provided increasing support for parks and recreation in urban areas. The Open Space Program in HUD was established in 1961 and its function merged into Community Development Block Grants in 1974. During that time period, $683 million was obligated for acquisition of 349,361 acres of land.

During the 1960s the Demonstration Cities and Metropolitan Development Act and the Neighborhood Facilities Program made available substantial matching funds to help develop parks, playgrounds, youth centers, and other facilities. The Model Cities Program provided extensive planning and development grants in depressed urban areas.

Office of Water Research and Technology

The Water Research and Development Act of 1978 provides for innovative research, technology development, and technology transfer to meet expanding water needs of the nation. By combining and strengthening two previous federal water research laws— the Water Resources Act and the Saline Water Act—the new law provides a more efficient way for the Secretary of the Interior, acting through the Office of Water Research and Technology, to assure that water of sufficient quality and quantity will be available to meet the United States' urgent needs.

Environmental Protection Agency

Alarm and concern over the deteriorating environment led in 1970 to the establishment of the Environmental Protection Agency as an independent agency to control and abate air and water pollution and to reduce hazards from noxious wastes, pesticides, herbicides, noise, and radiation. As an advocate for a livable environment, it assists the efforts of other federal agencies to improve the environment.

The Council of Environmental Quality in the executive office of the president, established by the National Environmental Policy Act of 1969, recommends policies to improve the environment.

The Armed Forces

Recreation first became recognized as an important need of the U.S. military forces in World War I. At this time, a number of national agencies, including the YMCA, the Salvation Army, the American Red Cross, and others undertook to provide recreation and social services for uniformed personnel in state–side posts and overseas.

When it became apparent that organized social and recreation programs were helpful in maintaining morale, counteracting fatigue, and reducing other service problems, special services divisions were established to meet the need.

Today, the four branches of the Armed Forces provide recreation for service members and their dependents ranging from dependent youth activities to inter–service athletic programs. These programs are organized by the Morale, Welfare, and Recreation Division of the Armed Forces.

George Marchas and Frances B. O'Malley wrote: "Morale, Welfare, and Recreation provides leisure activity programs that encourage creative self–expression, cultural appreciations, self development and enjoyment."[16]

Figure 12–8 Dependent youth activities are among the numerous recreation programs provided by the Morale, Welfare, and Recreation Division of the Armed Forces (MWR). Here, children at the Mather Air Force Base Youth Center are greeted by supervisor John Spencer, left, and his assistant, Bruce Jolley.

On almost every base around the world, there is a special service division which provides recreation for the military member and his or her dependents. Marchas and O'Malley reported that "The staffing of these special service divisions is made up of approximately 55,000 full and part–time employees. Twenty percent of those employed represent military members, 50 percent appropriated fund employees (GS workers) and 30 percent non–appropriated fund employees."[17]

Military recreation personnel are employed in either of the following two categories:

Appropriated Funds Civil Service employees who are paid for by the taxpayer; funds are appropriated by Congress.

Non–Appropriated Funds The salaries come from funds that are generated locally, either by revenue–producing activities such as rentals of ski equipment, camping equipment, bowling alley fees, theater admissions, and returns from PX profits.

Veterans Administration

Being the federal government's largest independent agency, the Veterans Administration (V.A.) uses a multi–billion dollar budget to service more than twenty–eight million veterans and their dependents throughout the nation. Through its recreation section in the Physical Medicine and Rehabilitation Service, the Veterans Administration operates a program at each V.A. hospital and home. Its program has three aspects: medical care, insurance, and financial assistance for veterans.

Recreation now functions as an independent service or as a section of Voluntary Service in all V.A. medical centers having recreation programs. Recreation therapists are responsible for providing recreation activities for patients/members, both in the V.A. medical centers and in the communities.

Under professional leadership, the recreation program is considered part of the medical treatment and rehabilitation. Activities include sports, music, arts, crafts, entertainment, motion pictures, hospitality services, special events, and hobbies.

United Service Organizations, Inc.

Founded in 1941, the United Service Organizations, Inc. (USO) is a voluntary civilian agency, serving the many needs of the men and women in the Armed Forces.

In contrast to the "boy meets girl" atmosphere, the dances, and big entertainment programs of the past, today the emphasis is on helping GIs and their families cope with practical peacetime problems. The big effort is to give down–to–earth help to servicemen and women with their off–base problems in the United States and overseas. To do this, the organization uses about forty thousand

volunteers, plus four hundred salaried employees in centers at home and abroad.

The USO has forty–five regular centers in the United States, some in downtown locations, others in booths at airports. Overseas, there are eighteen permanent centers plus many mobile locations.

As in wartime, most of the entertainers used by the USO abroad come free. Performers in the traveling USO shows—some professionals and others collegians—get no salary. They normally receive a flat $40 a day for food and lodging and the Department of Defense picks up the tab for transportation.

National Foundation on the Arts and the Humanities

Created as an independent agency in 1965, the National Foundation on the Arts and the Humanities encourages national programs in the arts (dance, music, drama, folk art, creative writing, architecture, painting, sculpture, photography, design, motion pictures, and television) and humanities (the study of language, literature, history, and philosophy), through two major divisions: the National Endowment for the Arts and the National Endowment for the Humanities. A third division, the Federal Council on the Arts and Humanities, coordinates the activities of the two endowments.

The endowments have affected millions through activities ranging from scholarly studies of Shakespeare to television's "The Adams Chronicles." Ballet's rapid rise is attributed in large part to support by the arts endowment. The growth of opera, theater, and orchestras also is widely linked to endowment help. The two agencies have spent more than $1 billion to nurture culture since they were founded in 1965.

Office of Economic Opportunity

During the early 1960s under the Johnson administration, a number of antipoverty programs were initiated by the federal government which gave significant support to the

Figure 12–9 Wolf Trap Farm Park in Vienna, Virginia, near Washington, D.C., is the first national park for the performing arts. Opened in 1971, the Foundation serves as an inspiring example that parks might encourage singing, dancing, and acting. (Courtesy Wolf Trap Foundation.)

provisions of recreation services for economically disadvantaged urban populations. The Office of Economic Opportunity (OEO) was created to coordinate all antipoverty programs on the federal level.

Among the major programs sponsored by OEO were:

Job Corps This program provided training in vocational and basic academic subjects for out–of–work, out–of–school young men and women between the ages of sixteen and twenty–one. This residential program operated in both urban and rural settings, with recreation representing an important aspect.

Vista (Volunteers in Service to America) Viewed by some as a domestic Peace Corps, VISTA assigned several thousand workers, including many college graduates, to work in poverty areas including rural slums, impoverished villages, and Indian reservations. VISTA volunteers played an important role in providing local recreation programs and community beautification projects.

Neighborhood Youth Corps The Economic Opportunity Act established training programs for unemployed young people in cities, as well as some suburban or rural poverty areas. Subcontractors were largely governmental and voluntary nonprofit agencies, although many young people were assigned direct recreational leadership responsibilities with recreation and park agencies, schools, hospitals, and community centers.

Federal assistance programs provided $1.2 billion, or 35.4 percent of all funds used by cities and counties for parks and recreation in fiscal year 1976. The four federal assistance programs contributing most of the federal dollars for parks and recreation are, in order of importance, the Comprehensive Employment and Training Act programs (CETA), General Revenue Sharing (GRS), the Community Development Block Grants (CDBG), and the Land and Water Conservation Fund (LWFC).

During the 1960s, the OEO provided substantial grant money to community action programs, particularly in urban slums, to meet the summer recreation needs of poor people. Most of these programs, however, were either sharply reduced, terminated, or transferred to other agencies. The Neighborhood Youth Corps, though, continued to provide summer work programs for youth. In addition, the Department of Transportation provided fund programs to bus children from urban slums to recreation programs in outlying parks. The Recreation Support Program, sponsored by the Department of Labor, aided many urban recreation departments in providing summer youth programs. The Community Services Administration by 1976 had monitored more than $300 million in grants to almost nine hundred local community action agencies.

Two other specially funded federal programs which have had significant effect on recreation are CETA and LEAA. CETA has provided important job training and employment opportunities for the poor and unemployed. Thousands of CETA workers have been assigned by cities and other agencies to recreation and park jobs. In 1981, however, severe cutbacks were made which resulted in thousands of lay offs and the future of CETA is seriously in jeopardy. LEAA (Law Enforcement–Assistance Act) has been concerned with the overall spectrum of crime prevention. With recreation as an important component, this program has funded anti–delinquency programs and assisted in the improvement of correctional agencies. The Department of Recreation of the Virginia Council on Criminal Justice developed training manuals and a course to help implement recreation programs in correctional institutions.

President's Council on Physical Fitness and Sports

Created in 1956 to stimulate the physical fitness of the nation's youth, the President's Council has played a key role in improving the fitness level of both youth and adults. After steady progress and reorganization in 1968 when it broadened its activities to include sports participation, the council today serves as a potent force in continuing to upgrade the physical fitness status of the United States.

The President's Council has been very successful in promoting a school–centered program for physical fitness. It has also been effective in developing special working relationships with colleges and universities, community groups, voluntary agencies, and other organizations.

The council has been able to mobilize mass media to communicate the need to be fit to the general public. In conducting a nationwide promotional campaign, it has effectively utilized radio, television, newspapers, movies, and articles in prominent national magazines.

Many regional physical fitness clinics have been conducted by the President's Council featuring some of the nation's physical fitness leaders and the council staff. Several fitness films have been produced, and publications have been printed and made available both to the communication media and to all segments of the population.

One of the most successful programs to be developed and conducted by the council is the Presidential Sports Award Program. The program was designed to encourage regular involvement in a wide variety of popular lifetime sports. Any individual fifteen years of

Figure 12–10 Qualifying for the Presidential Sports Award are these two backpackers en route to the Mt. Whitney area in California's Inyo National Forest. (Courtesy U.S. Forest Service.)

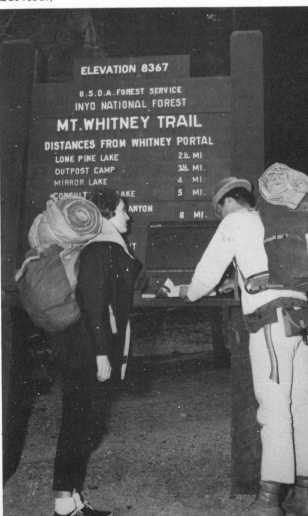

age or older is eligible to receive the Presidential Sports Award, including a Presidential Certificate of Achievement, a blazer patch, lapel pin, decal, and membership card reflecting participation in the program.

The object of the new program is to encourage more adults to become active participants in sports, rather than being content with a spectator's role. The council believes that the physical and mental benefits resulting from vigorous exercise contribute significantly to personal health, appearance, and performance.

Standards for the Presidential Sports Award program were developed by the council in cooperation with forty–five major sports governing bodies and coaches' asso-

ciations. The award is being offered in thirty–eight sports, ranging from archery to water skiing. Bowling has been the most popular award sport, followed by jogging, swimming, tennis, bicycling, karate, riding, softball, golf, and skiing. The basic principle governing qualification for the new award is a minimum of fifty hours of participation, spread over at least fifty activity sessions, within a four–month period.

The candidate obtains a log, selects a sport (or several), keeps a record of his or her activity in the log and, upon fulfilling the qualifying standards, sends the completed log, together with a $4.00 fee to: Presidential Sports Award, P.O. Box 5214, FDR Post Office, New York, New York 10022.

QUESTIONS FOR DISCUSSION

1. What functions do the various federal agencies have in regard to recreation?
2. Identify five federal agencies directly involved in resource management.
3. What forces and interest led to the establishment of the National Park Service?
4. Are the original criteria for selecting a national park site still valid today?
5. What is your concept of the National Park System? How does it differ from the present operation of the National Park Service?
6. What is the chief difference between national and state parks?
7. Discuss briefly the preservation–use concept as practiced by the National Park Service.
8. The National Park Service, increasingly, has been following the policy of bringing national parks and recreation areas closer to where people live and work. Do you support this recent emphasis on meeting urban recreation needs?
9. What is the function and role of the U.S. Forest Service?
10. Why was the Land and Water Conservation Fund established?
11. What were the responsibilities of the Heritage Conservation and Recreation Service?
12. Discuss the purposes of the Tennessee Valley Authority. What function does it have in regard to outdoor recreation?
13. What are the two categories in which military recreation personnel are employed?
14. What is the primary object of the President's Sports Award Program?

REFERENCES

1. Organization and Functions, Document No. 0–274–118 (Washington, D.C.: United States Department of the Interior, 1967), p. 16.

2. Brochure, "Yosemite Park . . . Fall, Winter, Spring" (Yosemite Park, California: Yosemite Park and Curry Company, 1977), p. 2.

3. Elvin R. Johnson, *Park Resources for Recreation* (Columbus: Charles E. Merrill Co., 1972), p. 118.

4. Clayne R. Jensen, *Outdoor Recreation in America* (Minneapolis: Burgess Publishing Company, 1970), p. 62.

5. "The Urban Park Dilemma," *Parks and Recreation Magazine*, July 1975, p. 17.

6. Richard Kraus, *Recreation and Leisure in Modern Society*, 2nd ed. (Santa Monica: Goodyear Publishing Company, 1978), p. 215.

7. Clayne R. Jensen, *Outdoor Recreation*, p. 68.

8. Douglas M. Knudson, *Outdoor Recreation* (New York: Macmillan Publishing Company, 1980), p. 306.

9. Elvin Johnson, *Park Resources for Recreation*, p. 114.

10. Knudson, p. 306.

11. "Washington Scene," *Parks and Recreation Magazine*, April 1981, p. 14.

12. Ibid.

13. Jack H. Hendrix, "Recreation in the Tennessee Valley," *Parks and Recreation Magazine*, April 1973, p. 41.

14. Tennessee Valley Authority Annual Report, 1978, Knoxville, Tennessee, p. 37.

15. Ibid., p. 35.

16. "Recreation Career Opportunities with the Armed Forces," *EMPLOY*, A Service of the National Recreation and Park Association, Vol. VI, No. 8, April 1980, p. 2.

17. Ibid., p. 15.

Figure 13–1 People in Scandinavian countries enjoy vigorous outdoor sports. Here, two Norwegian women enjoy a leisurely journey on a cross–country ski track. (Courtesy of Norges Idrettsforbund.)

13
International Recreation

The park and recreation movement is making a strong impact throughout the world. Indeed, play speaks a universal language. Whatever the differences in their languages and customs may be, people of all nations have responded to the multitude of opportunities for recreation and leisure.

Increasingly, recreation, parks, and leisure–time experiences are holding an important place on the international scene. This is already evident in the increased volume in travel, the similarity of recreation habits of the people of different countries, and the growth and impact of such international organizations as the World Leisure and Recreation Association.

Leisure–time activities have existed in some form and to some degree in every culture that we know about. "All cultural groups are essentially alike in their basic psychological equipment and mechanisms, regardless of their differences in time, geography and physique," wrote Clayne Jensen. "Cultural differences among them reflect only the responses of essentially similar organisms to unlike conditions."[1]

In a growing number of countries, dedicated leaders are discovering how beneficial a well–rounded program in parks and recreation can be toward life enrichment. They have found that people who play together are relaxed and understanding. Even though they speak different languages and have different customs, people from different nations can communicate effectively through recreation. Still, the people of the world have yet to create the type of effective international exchange capable of achieving more positive understanding among each other. It is hoped that future cultural and recreational

Recreation is an international language.

contacts and changes among nations will contribute significantly toward a better world. Representing a "power for peace," they have the potential to help bring people together in mutual understanding and respect.

In many areas of the world, consumer spending in leisure pursuits is on the increase. The growing interest and awareness in the leisure services industry is particularly strong in North America, Western Europe, Japan, Australia, and Eastern Europe. Furthermore, an editorial bulletin of the World Leisure and Recreation Association stated "There is a probability that the less affluent countries will follow this trend in the years ahead, as their economic and social situations progress. This evolution appears to be the product of shorter working hours and the growing ability of many people to take advantage of recreational opportunities that require spending, as well as the essentially no–cost activities."[2]

Throughout the world, leisure and recreation are recognized as contributing substantially and significantly to advancing one's growth as a human being. Once subsistence needs are met for individuals, families, or settlements, then the range of human cultural, intellectual, and spiritual capacities become possible.

Many forms of recreation in the United States were transferred to this country from various parts of the world, particularly western Europe. The first colonists, for example, brought with them their native songs, games, folk dances, sports, and hobbies. Through the years, the continued migration of people has kept alive many of the folkways of the old countries, even though the language and many of the customs have been forgotten by the new generations.

"The influence of the European cultural arts upon the American way of life has certainly been significant," wrote Clayne Jensen. "Further, our city parks have been influenced strongly by the French, German, English and Danish, and most of the early

Figure 13–2 The arts provide an unparalleled opportunity for people of all ages to better know themselves and find greater meaning in life. Here, a young man in Paris finds his painting to be a satisfying and rewarding leisure–time experience.

park designers and architects in America were from those countries."[3]

Likewise, influences from the Orient, Africa, the Middle East, and South America have influenced American customs, leisure interests, and the overall way of life.

LEISURE: A WORLDWIDE CONCERN

The fact that leisure is a worldwide concern and the social problems surrounding it universal was perhaps the most revealing fact that emerged from the first meeting of international experts on leisure. Hosted by the World Leisure and Recreation Association, delegates from twenty–one countries and eleven international organizations met on the campus of Michigan State University in September 1977.

Cor Westland, professor of leisure studies at the University of Ottawa, Canada and chairman of one of the the five working groups, pointed out that "It became clear to all that we will have to study leisure from a world perspective, that we will have to pay more attention to world leisure patterns and that there is indeed a world movement towards ethnic identity."[4]

Some delegates suggested that leisure behavior is highly influenced by the varying value structures, and problems are primarily of a sociopsychological nature. So many regions of the world lack financial, educational, physical, and human resources. Furthermore, many people are insufficiently aware, informed, or motivated.

"It is therefore little wonder that a high level of consensus existed on the need to train leaders," said Westland. "We must train leaders with the required knowledge and skills, to indeed enhance the quality of people's lives, to provide guidance and counseling and to equalize leisure and recreation opportunities."[5]

Westland stated that "Although the leader who can teach, who can transmit new skills and techniques was considered important, the central place in the provision of recrea-

Figure 13–3 Leisure is a worldwide concern. Kenya, like other rapidly developing countries, is facing for the first time the problems that come with urbanization. The volleyball action scene above took place at a youth center. (Courtesy World Leisure and Recreation Association.)

Figure 13–4 Leisure should be studied from a world perspective. Here, Professor Cor Westland of Canada chairs one of the INTER-CALL Conference working groups at the First World Conference of Experts on Leadership for Leisure. (Courtesy World Leisure and Recreation Association.)

tion services was awarded to the 'animateur,' the leader who manages to create interests, to raise curiosities, and who thus enables people to develop their talents and to live a full life as a complete human being."[6]

One of the strongest views at the conference was that education for leisure and recreation must be a component of all education.[7] There is an urgent need for a philosophical base, for clearly articulated principles, concepts, and ideals. Leaders need theory and skills as well as practical experience.

THE LEISURE ENVIRONMENT IN EUROPE

The patterns of leisure in different European countries are determined by the geographical, social, and economic conditions in each country. Sandra Mason and W. H. Martin of Leisure Consultants, a research agency based in London, England, did extensive survey work on leisure in fourteen European countries.[8] The study provided facts and figures on the patterns of leisure time, leisure activities and leisure spending in each country, and an analysis of background factors that influence the way leisure is used.

The survey suggests a bright future for companies and agencies offering leisure goods and services. According to Mason and Martin, "The evolution appears to be the product of shorter working hours and the growing ability of many people to take advantage of recreational opportunities. This trend means higher standards of social behavior and better life quality through the constructive use of leisure."[9]

Personal and social conditions influence what people would like to do with their leisure, while geographical, economic, and institutional conditions act as constraints on what activities and spending are practically possible. Age and family status are particularly important factors determining how people use their leisure time.

According to Mason and Martin, three

groups of activities dominate the use of leisure time in Europe. These are watching television and listening to the radio, social
contacts with friends and family, and reading. Together they probably take up an average between two–thirds and three–quarters
of all leisure time in normal working weeks.
Well over half of all normal leisure time is
spent at home and casual social contacts,
and eating and drinking out take up a large
part of the leisure time in the week that is
spent outside the home.[10]

European governments are heavily involved with the leisure industry though none
has laid down a policy towards leisure as
such. They are extensively involved in the
support of sport and recreation, cultural
forms of entertainment and tourism, and in
the control of the sale of alcoholic drink and
gambling.

IMPORTANCE OF LEISURE
IN CANADIAN SOCIETY

An interesting indication of the importance
of leisure in Canadian society is the fact that
the provincial ministers at a conference in
1974 unanimously decided to consider recreation as a social utility, of equal importance
to education, health, and public works.

Cor Westland believes there has been a
shift in national policy in Canada away from
the traditional economic growth orientation
towards a more human centered society.
"Issues surrounding human growth and fulfillment are getting a higher priority in
Canada," said Westland, "which inevitably
will be reflected in the importance of leisure
as a value."[11]

Currently, all levels of government in Canada play a role in the provision of recreation
services. The emphasis is at the municipal
level, and Westland said there are few cities
which have not included into their structures
separate departments for recreation.

The private sector is a major element of the
Canadian recreation delivery system. "Canadians are firmly convinced that private
enterprise must play a dominant role in

Figure 13–5   The beauty of Canadian Parks.
As parks in Canada continue to enjoy unparalleled growth and popularity all levels
of government are placing greater emphasis
on recreation and leisure–time services. This
magnificent scene is Maligne Lake in Jasper
National Park, Alberta. (Courtesy Canadian
Parks and Recreation Association.)

day–to–day life," said Westland. "The majority is still convinced that private, non-
tax–supported organizations are vital elements in the development of a society aimed
at maintaining the diversity which has become a trade mark of Canadian culture."[12]

"Every Canadian should have the opportunity to pursue the recreation experiences of
his choice," said Westland. "Obviously, there
are barriers that are in part economic, social,
psychological, but primarily educational.
The higher the level of education, the higher
the level of understanding and motivation,
and the greater the diversity in activity
patterns."[13]

LEISURE AND RECREATIONAL
ACTIVITIES IN JAPAN

Interest in leisure–time activities is steadily
increasing in Japan, although it has yet to

reach the level in other highly industrialized countries. According to a Japan Economic Research Center tabulation of indicators of economic and industrial activities, "Working days, which shrank from 255 days in 1970 to 236 days in 1975, will be reduced to 211 days by 1985. The reduction of working hours results in an increase in free time."[14]

In his study titled, "Leisure and Recreational Activities," Kinji Kawamura listed the following general trends of leisure activities in Japan:

1. Recreation activities are becoming increasingly diversified and more brisk, particularly among the younger generations.
2. The Japanese are showing increasingly more interest in the types of light, social sports in which any person can easily participate at any time.
3. Recreational activities that have a higher degree of participation are becoming increasingly appealing to the Japanese.
4. The Japanese ability to differentiate among varying kinds of recreational activities is steadily increasing.
5. Gambling–type activities such as pachinko (pinball), horse racing, and bicycle racing, have diminished in popularity.
6. The Japanese attitude toward travel is undergoing significant changes, with an inclination toward long, leisurely trips.[15]

Interest in Japan is rapidly growing in such "light sports" as walking, jogging, running, catch–ball playing, cycling, swimming, table tennis, baseball, ice–skating, and volleyball. The Japanese, particularly those in their teens and twenties, are showing increasing interest in such social sports activities as golf, skiing, and tennis.

More leisure hours are being spent with one's own family members and in the community of residence. As a result, there appears to be increasing interest in such near–at–hand leisure activities as dining out, shopping, walking, and visiting amusement parks, museums, zoos, and aquariums.

LATIN AMERICAN COUNTRIES EXPAND RECREATION AND LEISURE

Technological progress in Latin American countries has resulted in more free time and less working time. As these countries become more industrialized, people not only have more time to spare, but have the economic conditions to enjoy the values of leisure.

Latin America has 370 million inhabitants, ranking it fifth in population among the eight world regions. However, Latin America has the second fastest rate of population growth in the world. Interestingly, 42 percent of its population is under 14 years of age, its urban dwellers comprise 65 percent of the total population, and illiteracy is well over the 50 percent level.[16]

Nelson Melendez, Executive Director of the World Leisure and Recreation Association, stated that: "One of the major goals of Latin American leisure service organizations is to enable individuals to freely participate, with no ulterior motive, in activities to creatively express their identity and to develop solid values, habits, and attitudes."[17]

To achieve this objective, several programs have been instituted. People in Brazil are being educated to use their leisure more creatively. Renato Requixa wrote: "Leisure is increasingly recognized as a relevant and important educational tool, with emphasis on its use in psychosomatic rehabilitation, above all for city–dwellers."[18] Colombia is exploring solutions to urban recreational problems. In Mexico, recreational programs are being developed for industrialized populations. Peru is providing activities for diverse needs. Venezuela's program starts with children and young adults and filters from there into the family and community.

"Regardless of the method, the emphasis is on permitting freedom of choice in activities," wrote Melendez, "developing habits that strengthen personality, making recreation an end in itself, and expressing individual identity."[19]

On September 26, 1980, fourteen Latin American countries convened in Santiago,

Figure 13–6 The beauty and splendor of Grand Canyon National Park. This great scenic attraction was set aside in 1916 to be preserved in its natural condition and is among the select natural sites to be on the World Heritage List. (Courtesy National Park Service.) Above, the symbol selected for World Heritage Sites.

Chile to create the Latin American Leisure and Recreation Association (ALATIR). Among its activities are the formation of national recreation associations in the member countries and the development of professional and voluntary leadership through educational seminars. Leadership development is also being boosted with three regional training institutes in 1981 and numerous leadership exchange programs between different countries.

WORLD HERITAGE SITES

Twelve cultural and natural sites in seven countries have become the first locations to be included on a World Heritage List, setting

them aside for preservation. The World Heritage Sites are a group of natural and cultural properties judged to be of such outstanding universal value that they are a part of the heritage of all people. In placing sites on the list, the first of its kind ever drawn up, the World Heritage Committee ensures that special steps will be taken to preserve them from deterioration or neglect so that they may be enjoyed by people for centuries to come.[20]

The World Heritage Committee is the working body of the World Heritage Convention, which was negotiated in 1972 under the auspices of the United Nations Educational Scientific and Cultural Organization (UNESCO).

The first World Heritage sites as selected in 1978 are:

NATURAL

Country	Site	Description
Canada	Nahanni	A national park in the Northwest Territories containing abundant wildlife and magnificent natural scenery.
Ecuador	Galapagos Islands	These nineteen islands in the Pacific Ocean were made famous by Charles Darwin's expedition that inspired his theory of evolution.

Ethiopia	Simien	This national park includes a massive mountain area known as the Roof of Africa and is the habitat of several rare species of animals.
United States	Yellowstone	The first national park in the world, established in 1872.

CULTURAL

Country	Site	Description
Canada	L'Anse Aux Meadows	Site of the oldest known European settlement in the New World, and the only Norse site found in North America.
Ecuador	Old City of Quito	Largest and best preserved historic center in South America. Originated in the Spanish settlement in 1534.
Ethiopia	Rock Hewn Churches of Lalibela	Monumental architectural achievements associated with the Queen of Sheba and King Solomon.
West Germany	Aachen Cathedral	One of the finest examples of early artistic architecture in Europe. Dates from the late 8th century when Charlemagne built the Palace Chapel.
Poland	Wieliczka Salt Mines	In operation since the end of the 15th century.
Poland	Historic Center of Cracow	Includes the site of medieval Cracow, with beginnings in the 13th century, and the royal castle of Wawel, dating from the 16th century.
Senegal	Island of Goree	Location for hundreds of years that served as a central transit point in the African slave trade. Island contains many buildings of considerable architectural interest.
United States	Mesa Verde	Preserves the cliff dwellings and other ruins of the Pueblo culture which flourished during the 9th and 13th centuries.[21]

Since the original list in 1978, additional heritage sites have been announced. Those in the United States are:

Grand Canyon National Park (Arizona)

Everglades National Park (Florida)
Independence National Historical Park (Pennsylvania)
Wrangell–St. Elias National Monument (Alaska)

SIGNIFICANT CONCEPTS AND PROGRAMS IN THE WORLD

As the recreation and park movement continues to experience worldwide growth and awareness, many concepts and programs have provided significant impact on the leisure lifestyles of people. While the list is never ending, several have taken on special importance because of their potential to enhance the quality of people's lives.

ADVENTURE PLAYGROUNDS

Popular in Europe for more than a quarter of a century, and later in Australia and New

Zealand, adventure playgrounds have gained increasing prominence in the United States. While adventure playgrounds have influenced playground design throughout the world, they have not enjoyed the popularity in North America that they have in Europe. In England and Wales, for example, there are an estimated three hundred adventure playgrounds and more than seven hundred full–time play workers.

In 1943 in Copenhagen, professor C. T. Sorenson, a Danish landscape designer, established the first adventure playground . . .

Figure 13–7 An adventure playground gives children the opportunity to create their own play environment. Using scrap lumber and other junk materials, they can build houses, forts, slides, rope swings, and many other facilities. Drummond Abernethy, right, is a leading authority of the Adventure Playground idea. (Courtesy *Play Times: Journal of the National Playing Fields Association*, London, England and Drummond Abernethy.)

the "Emdrup Junk Playground." According to Alfred Ledermann and Alfred Trachsel, "Sorenson had observed, while walking through the city, how children were more fascinated in handling boards and demolition material on building sites than in playing with the ready–made equipment of his fine playgrounds."[22]

What is an Adventure Playground?

Drummond Abernethy of London, one of the originators of the adventure playground idea, said: "An adventure playground is a place where children of all ages can do many things they can no longer easily do in our crowded urban society—create his or her own play environment."[23] At adventure playgrounds, children have the opportunity to build shacks, forts, and treehouses out of donated scrap lumber, stringing up rope swings, constructing mud slides, tunnels, shallow lakes, and rafts.

Philosophy

The importance of an adventure playground as a natural play environment was clearly stated by Tom Hungerford who conducted a fieldwork study at the Huntington Beach Adventure Playground. More than seven thousand children frequent the playground each year. Hungerford discovered at the playground the basis for the development of a well–rounded adult: "Before construction of a fort the child must first use his *imagination* to think up a design. He then must *organize* his thoughts and gather the correct materials for the job. While constructing the fort he develops hand–eye *coordination*, while hammering and sawing, *creativity* when making unplanned additions, and *leadership skills* if he is working with others. He may learn that working within a group is the most successful way to accomplish a goal. When completion occurs, there is concrete evidence of *accomplishment*, which brings *recognition* from peers. This leads to *personal satisfaction* and a feeling of *self–assurance*."[24]

Area and Facilities

In general, any piece of land that offers trees, undulating terrain, shrubbery, or water and steep bluffs, may be developed as an adventure playground. According to Bill Vance of the Huntington Beach Adventure Playground, "Such an area, preferably, will be located far enough from residential neighborhoods so that the noise and unsightliness of the area will not be a factor."[25] Precaution should be taken not to overdevelop an adventure playground. In a natural area, a portion of land should be graded off nearly flat to accommodate building but caution should be taken against ruining the natural environment.

"The key to a successful adventure playground is to keep bringing in fresh junk," said Steve Simms, who has served as play leader at two adventure playgrounds. "When I pull up with a load of 'new' scrap, the kids swarm over the truck immediately. The rest is up to the kids—to do what they want, to play, to develop, to build, to do all the things that relate to natural play."[26]

Leadership

The leader of an adventure playground is someone who animates, enables, and helps. The leader wanders about, from place to place, always looking on what is happening. She or he never gets involved for too long with any one group. This is to insure that any kid who wants to talk to the leader, who needs help of any kind, can go up to her or him at any time. The leader should be someone who obviously loves kids, who knows how to understand the behavior patterns of children.

Programming the Area

The whole idea of the adventure playground is freedom of play. Children are allowed to do virtually anything within reason, including building either at the bottom or up on the sides of the hills, rafting, fishing, sliding on the hills, swinging on the rope swing, building fires, outdoor cooking, and numerous other activities.

"Generally, with the exception of overnight campouts," said Vance, "you should program nothing. If you will leave the children to develop their own ideas, the number of suggestions you will hear will be overwhelming."[27]

The Huntington Beach Adventure Playground *"How-To" Manual* can be obtained for $2.00 per copy by writing: Community Services Department, P.O. Box 190, Huntington Beach, California 92648.

NEW ZEALAND'S "COME ALIVE CAMPAIGN"

In 1975, New Zealand launched a national program designed to put more zeal into the people and make their "time off" more fittingly, "time in." Referred to as the "Come Alive Campaign," the program is sponsored by the national government. Through national advertising they try to encourage people to make "worthy use" of their free-time.

"Come Alive," similar to "Participation" in Canada, uses the following objectives as a guide:

1. Help people become aware of a wide variety of activities available to them.
2. Directly encourage people to participate in activities of their choice.
3. Endeavor to reach the handicapped, the disabled, and the aged or those who have "dropped out."
4. Make special effort to communicate with those who seemingly do not participate in anything except their regular jobs.[28]

Originally the idea of "Come Alive" was to stimulate interest in four major cities, but the program grew so rapidly that it soon involved more than fifty local town committees. According to Professor Richard L. Ramsey of the University of British Columbia (Canada), "Six area coordinators employed on a full-time basis organized the groundwork for the establishment of these committees. As a result, a large number of area and local committees with thousands of volunteers helped to organize and promote interest and involvement."[29]

GERMANY'S FAMOUS "GOLDEN PLAN"

As far back as the late 1950s, the Federal Republic of Germany saw leisure use as a matter of national concern. An intensive national survey was conducted to assess the recreation needs of the population for space, facilities and leadership. The survey represented the basis for Germany's famous "Golden Plan," which placed considerable stress on people's most precious possession, physical and mental health.

In 1960, the late Dr. George von Opel, was most instrumental in implementing the "Golden Plan" which called for expanded play opportunities for German citizens. According to von Opel, the movement would use recreation as therapy and develop the art of living through the wise use of leisure.

The "Golden Plan" emphasized the need to arouse the public to the conditions. Government, communities, and political parties could no longer escape responsibility. The success of the "Golden Plan" has drawn the envy of many nations. While the financial cost for the programs has surpassed the original estimate of 6.3 million Deutsche marks, the overall impact on the German people has been far-reaching.

The basic theme of the campaign was "More fun in your leisure time." Press ads, posters, television and radio spots, two cinema films, and an intensive public relations campaign were all used in an effort to get the message over to the people.

Three special booklets were written including an attractively designed booklet in full color, titled "One–hundred Tips for Enjoying Your Leisure." In conjunction with this campaign was a fitness promotion featuring the cartoon "Trimmy." Today, advertising and promotion to advance recreation and leisure time sports have reached the annual cost of 12 million Deutsche marks.

Figure 13–8 A great "riverpark" in the Ruhr Valley. Germany's "Golden Plan" is to provide excellent recreational facilities and programs accessible to all. The government spent considerable money in the mass media urging people to take advantage of them. (Courtesy World Leisure and Recreation Association.)

THE VOLKSMARCH

The volksmarch, a longtime tradition in Europe, is spreading to other areas of the world. Commonly known as the "people's march" or "A walk through the woods," the event first began in Switzerland and then moved up to Bavaria and Southern Germany and other European countries.

Hiking events in Europe have become more and more popular because participation is open to every age-group, and the number of participants is almost unlimited. The biggest walk reportedly was organized by a United States military command in Germany, in which an estimated twelve thousand people participated. The American's enthusiastic exposure and positive response to hiking and walking events in Europe has resulted in their growing popularity in the United States.

Distances for volksmarches vary from ten to twenty kilometers, sometimes thirty to forty.

While the woods and fields typify a picturesque route for a walk, organizers try to take participants to places of interest, that is, parks and zoos, castles, old parts of town, walking through forests, along rivers, lakes, and waterfalls—the more scenic the route the better.

Schedule

Walks generally start around 7:00 or 8:00 A.M., depending on the time of the year, and they finish around four or five o'clock in the afternoon. Participants may walk anytime during that time. Many walks offer two distances, usually ten and twenty kilometers.

Awards

An effective awards system should be developed, one which will make people anxious to participate. Medals and awards are paid for by the participants themselves. Peo-

Figure 13–9 The traditional European volksmarch enables people, the young and old alike, to enjoy the pleasure and rewards of hiking over the countryside, through scenic woods, and along the seaside, a beautiful lake or river. (Courtesy German National Tourist Office.)

ple need goals to walk for, such as the number of marches, the total distance of a series of walks, or the medal of the individual walk itself. An annual award for the number of walks and total distance walked has proven effective to stimulate interest in volksmarches.

Future of the Volksmarch

With the growth of leisure time, emphasis on physical fitness, and the need for relaxation and escape, the popularity of hiking and walking could reach unprecedented proportions in the future. Whereas jogging was the craze of the 1970s, hiking could well be the favorite leisure pastime of the 1980s.

The key to the success of volksmarches will be organization, and the formation of volksmarch associations across the country. If volksmarches can be successfully conducted in a few key areas, the concept could spread nationally.

WORLD LEISURE AND RECREATION ASSOCIATION

A nonprofit, international service agency, this organization is dedicated to improving individual and community life through the constructive use of leisure and recreation. Its main purpose has been to: (1) provide a central clearing house for the exchange of information and experiences among recreation officials throughout the world; (2) assist countries in establishing central recreation service agencies, programs, facilities, and leadership training; and (3) promote a world recreation movement designed to enrich the human spirit through the wholesome use of leisure.

WLRA conducts service programs in education, research, information exchange, and contract consultation. It performs its services globally through cooperation with other international associations, specialized agencies of the United Nations, affiliated regional associations and with national organizations in more than one hundred countries.

The WLRA is governed by an international Board of Directors and is a totally independent organization. It has rendered world services continuously since its founding in 1956 as the International Recreation Association. The present name was adopted in 1973.

For further information, write to: World Leisure and Recreation Association, United Nations Plaza, 345 East 46 Street, New York, N.Y. 10017, U.S.A.

QUESTIONS FOR DISCUSSION

1. Why is recreation regarded as "an international language?"
2. In what areas and hemispheres in the world has the leisure services industry enjoyed the greatest growth, interest, and awareness?
3. Generally speaking, what countries of the world have been most influential on American customs, leisure interests, and our overall way of life?
4. Discuss: The social problems surrounding leisure are universal. Do you agree?
5. How are the patterns of leisure in different countries determined?
6. What three groups of activities dominate the use of leisure time in Europe?
7. Identify some of the most prominent World Heritage Sites.
8. Describe an adventure playground.
9. What opportunities does an adventure playground provide children?

10. Essentially, what is the primary objective of Germany's famous "Golden Plan?"
11. Discuss some of the benefits of New Zealand's "Come Alive Campaign."
12. What is a volksmarch and why do people go on them?
13. Describe an ideal route for a volksmarch.
14. What is the main purpose of the World Leisure and Recreation Association?

REFERENCES

1. Clayne R. Jensen, *Leisure and Recreation* (Philadelphia: Lea & Febiger, 1977), p. 169.
2. Editorial, *WLRA Bulletin*, Vol. XXII, No. 2, 1979.
3. Jensen, *Leisure and Recreation*, p. 174.
4. Allen V. Sapora, Editor, *Proceedings and Papers, The First World Conference of Experts on Leadership for Leisure* (New York: World Leisure and Recreation Asociation, 1978), p. 4.
5. Ibid., p. 5.
6. Ibid.
7. Ibid., p. vi.
8. Sandra Mason and W. H. Martin, "Leisure in Western Europe, An Overview of Practices, Trends and Economics," *WLRA Bulletin*, Vol. XXII, No. 2, 1979, p. 1.
9. Ibid.
10. Ibid., pp. 1–2.
11. Cor Westland, "Recreation Leadership in Canada," *Proceedings and Papers, The First World Conference of Experts on Leadership for Leisure* (World Leisure and Recreation Association, New York, N.Y., 1978), p. 199.
12. Ibid., p. 200.
13. Ibid., p. 202.
14. Kinji Kawamura, "Leisure and Recreational Activities," *About Japan Series #4* (Foreign Press Center, Tokyo, Japan: 1977), p. 2.
15. Ibid.
16. Nelson Melendez, WLRA Commentary, *WLRA Journal*, May/June 1981, p. 2.
17. "Countries Expand Recreation and Leisure Programs," *WLRA Journal*, May/June 1981, p. 3.
18. Renato Requixa, "Brazil Expands Leisure through Education," *WLRA Journal*, May/June, p. 6.
19. "Countries Expand Recreation and Leisure Programs," *WLRA Journal*, p. 3.
20. "Sites Selected for World Heritage List," *WLRA Bulletin*, Volume XXI, No. 5, November/December 1978, p. 2.
21. Ibid.
22. Alfred Ledermann and Alfred Trachsel, *Creative Playground and Recreation Centers* (New York: Frederick A. Praeger, 1959), p. 14.
23. Drummond Abernethy, Taken from a recorded address, "Adventure Playgrounds." American River College, Sacramento, California, March 7, 1980.
24. *"How-To" Manual*, Adventure Playground, City of Huntington Beach, California, p. 2.
25. Ibid., p. 5.
26. Richard Louv, "Playgrounds; Kids Build 'Em Better," *Family Weekly*, December 2, 1979, p. 5.
27. *"How To" Manual*, p. 8.
28. Richard L. Ramsey, "New Zealand—1975", *WLRA Bulletin*, September/October 1978, p. 3.
29. Ibid.

IV
Organized Recreation in Other Sectors

Figure 14-1 Resort recreation traditionally has had a major impact on the leisure life-styles of Americans. With higher gasoline prices and energy conservation, however, the resort industry is undergoing some changes. Resort enterprises closer to urban areas, of course, will benefit and more distant resorts will be tied in closely with charter bus and airline services. Here, skiers riding a chairlift at Terry Peak Ski Resort in South Dakota's Black Hills enjoy a mile–high view of the surrounding area. (Courtesy South Dakota Division of Tourism.)

14
PRIVATE AND COMMERCIAL RECREATION

As an evergrowing sector in the leisure services field, private and commercial recreation has made a major contribution in meeting the mass leisure needs of modern society. Commercial recreation is a multi–billion dollar industry which supplies a significantly higher percentage of the recreation and leisure opportunities than does the public sector. Indeed, commercial and private recreation has enjoyed remarkable growth and should continue to grow due to the new awareness of the necessity for quality leisure.

Private and commercial recreation enterprises are essentially businesses employing millions of people. Those who operate them are interested primarily in the bottom line net profit figure. Richard Talbot, marketing representative for Marine World/Africa USA in Redwood City, wrote: "Commercial recreation is any profit–making or nonprofit enterprise, whose business is leisure service, and which is not funded by public monies. Obviously, this encompasses a broad range of enterprises, including profit–making corporations, independent businesses, non-profit employee recreation organizations, and non-profit community recreation programs whose support comes from private donations."[1]

Like other products and services in business, commercial recreation depends upon public demand. "If there is no demand, if there is no market, if there are no sales, there will be no profit and hence, eventually, no commercial recreation," explained Meyer, Brightbill, and Sessoms. "When the profit disappears, so does the commercial recreation enterprise."[2]

The range of services and opportunities provided by the commercial sector is extensive and diverse. Companies from many different areas of business are diversifying into the leisure field. The recent growth of the theme park business, the racquetball boom, travel and tourism, and resorts are all major reasons why commercial recreation represents the fastest growing job sector in the leisure–time industry today. The huge spectrum of enterprises includes movie theaters, amusement parks, ski lodges, vacation travel, private clubs, resorts and beaches, theme parks, sightseeing boats, and similar activities.

Commercial enterprises of wide variety have been responsible for stimulating unprecedented interest in many forms of sports and entertainment. They have had a tremendous influence on such sports as golf, bowling, skiing, football, baseball, and basketball. The cultural arts area has also benefited greatly by the favorable influence of commercial recreation.

The largest item in the leisure budget is recreational equipment, such as boats, camping vehicles, motor bikes, color television sets, snowmobiles, and surfboards. The purchase of products used in the pursuit of pleasure or relaxation has had a spectacular effect on the nation's economy. The sporting goods business has been a lucrative one, offering many opportunities, from manufacturing to sales management. Supplying recreation businesses and recreationists is possibly a bigger source of profit than the actual fees for the sports and entertainment.

Private enterprise is often able to offer a service at less cost to the taxpayer. Furthermore, it may be able to do the job on a more professional and efficient basis. "As public demand for certain kinds of recreation increases, so does the commercialization of the activity, for the people of the United States have demonstrated both their willingness and their ability to pay for their recreation."[3]

Many authorities believe the trend is toward more "pay as you go" services and facilities in the public sector as governments struggle to keep expenditures subordinate to revenues and because of the reluctance of the public to increase taxes to support such facilities. "To maintain their desirability, the commercial recreation organization must be adaptable, dynamic, sensitive to its client's needs, and willing to accept some risks," said Talbot. "Perhaps the element of financial risk is the key factor that distinguishes commercial operations from their municipal counterparts."[4]

CATEGORIES OF COMMERCIAL RECREATION ENTERPRISES

Arlin Epperson suggested the following five categories of facilities or enterprises:

1. *Spectator activities:* college and professional sports, racing, movies, exhibitions, concerts, cultural/historical/educational attractions, eating, entertainment.
2. *Outdoor attractions and amusements:* county and state fairs, amusement theme parks, tourist attractions.
3. *Participative activities:* golf, tennis, bicycling, bowling, skating (ice and roller), skiing, camping.
4. *Mechanized sports:* supported strongly by manufacturing industries, boating, bicycling, snowmobiling, motorcycling, off–road–vehicles, recreation vehicles.
5. *Clubs, resorts, housing developments, home associations, second homes:* multiactivity enterprises with either geographical or membership requirements, or those that provide lodging or both; health or sports clubs.[5]

SPECTATOR ACTIVITIES

Americans, indeed, are on a leisure living binge, both as participants and as spectators. While the biggest boom is in personal participation, there is also one in spectator events and activities as well. More people than ever are paying to watch organized sports events, despite constantly rising ad-

Figure 14–2   Commercial Recreation Enterprise. This marina at Folsom Lake State Park in California is privately leased by a concessionaire who provides slip rentals for boats, fuel, and numerous other concession services. Commercial recreation, a major sector in the leisure services industry, involves a system of private enterprise in which the participant or customer pays and the purveyor makes a profit.

mission prices in economically hard times. Watching sports events in person or through television is a major leisure–time pursuit. Watching television continues to be the most popular indoor activity, with over 95 percent of the population watching the tube for an average of nineteen hours per week.

Interest in the arts, literature, and in museums of art, history, and science is so popular that cultural activities have surpassed sports in some areas of the country in the numbers of participants and spectators. Festivals of music, art, dance, and drama continue to attract huge crowds.

The entertainment industry, from nightclubs to Broadway stage and theater productions and touring shows, not only provide employment for millions of people but involve billions of dollars. Broadway theaters are breaking their attendance records, and opera and ballet are thriving across the United States.

Professional sports leagues, once confined to baseball and football, now operate nationwide in hockey, basketball, soccer, and tennis. Touring golf, bowling, and tennis professionals move throughout the country to year–round competing in weekly tournaments.

Dollars and vast prestige rides on the success of big time collegiate football and basketball. The *U.S. News & World Report* wrote that "Today's (televised sports) programs are widely viewed as having as much in common with the entertainment industry (a $29 million network–television contract for football) as with education."[6]

Professional and collegiate sports provide opportunities in stadium operation and management, concessions management, souvenir program direction and advertising, ticket management and sales, publicity and sports information.

Motion Pictures

After a period of audience decline and the conversion of large theaters into smaller houses, the public continues to stream back to the movies. While the development of videodiscs in television sets poses a serious long range challenge to theaters, present signs point to continuing prosperity for theaters showing the type of films that audiences want to see. Movies are by far the most important away from home spectator activity. More than 64 percent of the population, twelve and under, goes to movies an average of more than one time per month.

Although the great popularity of television has cut sharply into attendance at motion picture theaters, box office receipts still totaled more than $2.3 billion in 1977. However, television movies constitute another dimension to the income enjoyed by the motion picture industry. "Still, the wide picture and better technical projection of the big screen provide an experience that even the new large–screen televisions cannot reproduce."[7]

Television and Radio

No single industry has had such a powerful impact on public tastes, desires, and leisure pursuits than television. In the average household, the TV set is on for more than six hours a day. Television has contributed greatly to the popularity of various sports. "In addition to occupying a vast amount of people's free time," said Joseph Curtis, "television programs have taught golf, tennis, swimming, fishing, and an infinite number and variety of diversions."[8]

Radio and television as media of news and communication continue to increase in appeal and overall market. Millions of people have an opportunity to be entertained, informed, and enriched by a wide variety of programs. Portable transistor radios are owned by millions of people in the U.S. as well as in countries of low income. Recent milestones in the enormous growth of television include the development of channels using UHF and VHF frequencies, cable television, ESPN sports network, and Home Box Office.

Automobile Racing

One of the most popular forms of spectator sport in terms of paid attendance is automobile racing. While those attending horse racing events come primarily to bet, auto racing fans, in contrast, attend because of the spectator appeal of the sport. Richard Kraus remarked that "Because automobile racing must necessarily cover large areas, the crowd is spread out, and huge numbers may watch at once."[9] The Indianapolis 500, for example, attracts over two hundred and fifty thousand spectators, and auto racing abroad is even more popular.

Horse Racing

While horse racing is considered a spectator sport, those attending come primarily to bet at parimutual windows. Indeed, they do come to the tracks, as indicated by the huge numbers who watch and bet on the horses. Approximately 100 million spectators attend horse and greyhound racing events annually in the United States.

CULTURAL/EDUCATIONAL/ HISTORICAL ATTRACTIONS

The growth of cultural activities in the United States and Canada has been phenomenal. Indeed, a "cultural" explosion has been evidenced by the building of cultural centers and museums, growth in spectator events, and participation in these events. Much of this growth in participation and attendance has centered around amateur music, theater, dance, and art.

Since 1960, more than one–hundred performing arts complexes have been developed in the United States at a cost of $1 billion. Washington's John F. Kennedy Center for the Performing Arts opened in 1971. The Lincoln Center for the Performing Arts in New York is a private, nonprofit institution that opened in 1962 at a cost of $190 million. This magnificent facility contains six major buildings with thirteen auditoriums offering music, drama, opera, and ballet.[10]

Museums have proven to be top entertainment spots. A Louis Harris study reported that the United States has some six thousand museums that total more than 300 million admissions each year. Major league sports games attract only 70 million annual admissions.[11]

Classical music appears to play a larger part in United States cultural life than ever before. The resurgence of jazz characterized the 1970s, as attendance at jazz festivals and concerts broke all past records.

EATING/DINING

Americans now eat one of every three meals outside the home. The restaurant industry accounted for 4.5 percent of the United States gross national product, or $64 billion, in 1974. There are more restaurants than any other business, with more than five hundred thousand serving units across the United States.

In recent years, one segment of the industry, the quick food chains, has exceeded all others in growth. Hamburger places are the most popular, with more than twenty-five thousand units; chickens are second, with nearly six thousand units; followed by pizza and taco establishments.

In a 1975 consumer attitude survey conducted by the National Restaurant Association, Americans were asked to reveal their reasons for dining out. "Nobody has to cook or clean up," and "a change of pace," were frequent answers to the question.

ENTERTAINMENT COMPLEXES

The entertainment business is a lucrative element of commercial recreation. There are hundreds of thousands of people who actively patronize night clubs, cabarets, dance halls, cocktail lounges, pubs, and casinos. Amusement and entertainment occupations include jobs to entertain clientele, providing commercial amusements; live or filmed performances; presentation of shows and professional athletic contests; and personal services in entertainment establishments.

Types of Entertainment Complexes

Perry Jones, who conducted a study on nightclubs and entertainment complexes, categorized them in the following manner:[12]

Local Facility The local club is one generally found in residential areas or in the midst of an industrial area. Often referred to as the "corner pub," this type of club can also be found near college campuses or in a shopping center.

Moderate Facility The most common type of entertainment social complex is the moderate facility. Equipment may include a small stage/bandstand, weekend entertainment, jukebox, large TV screen, pool table, shuffleboard table, pinball machines, computer games, dance floor, stage lighting, and cocktail seating.

Figure 14–3 Night clubs and entertainment complexes provide music, dancing, and social fun for millions of Americans. As more people stay closer to home, look for local entertainment to broaden in scope and popularity. Here, Perry Jones and his country and western band provide musical accompaniment for vocalist Faith O'Hara.

Full Entertainment Complex Many full entertainment complexes operate around the restaurant idea. Food is the main product of service and entertainment is secondary. Whether private, commercial, or public, the primary output of a full complex focuses on leisure–time social recreational programs, services, and activities on a full–time basis.

Maximum Facility While a maximum facility has many of the properties of the previous categories, this facility will most often offer plush decor combined with headliner entertainment and hotel facilities. Many examples of the maximum facility can be found in Las Vegas and other casino cities, such as casino gambling, nightly entertainment, hotel accommodations, convention rooms, swimming pools, tennis and racquetball courts, health spas, and fitness centers.

Specialized Clubs These clubs are centered around an environment or theme. Examples are golf clubs, tennis/racquetball clubs, ski resorts, yacht clubs, and country clubs. Creative ideas may center around current fads and attitudes, such as the latest craze, disco roller skating.

OUTDOOR ATTRACTIONS AND AMUSEMENTS

The outdoor amusement industry is the fastest growing and most popular segment of the entire entertainment and recreation industries. According to Arlin Epperson, "More and more people are finding out that a visit to an amusement park is one of the most enjoyable ways of spending money to have fun."[13]

The outdoor amusement industry is serviced by its own trade association, the International Association of Amusement Parks and Attractions. Its membership is comprised of 350 leading amusement parks, theme parks, and tourist attractions.

When Walt Disney started the revolution in the amusement park industry in the 1950s, he established a set of basic rules to be followed, which included: 1) emphasize extreme cleanliness; 2) offer something for all ages; 3) employ as many personable and friendly students as possible; 4) insist that the park's personnel wear clean and neat uniforms; and 5) eliminate the cheap souvenir shop. These rules have been observed by all successful theme park operators and administrators since.[14]

State and County Fairs

State and county fairs are among America's best loved institutions. Through the decades, they have been able to retain their strong popularity in America. "A blend of nostalgic lure and modern entertainment, they appeal to people of all ages," wrote Lila Perl, author of "America Goes to the Fair."[15]

After a leveling off in attendance during the mid–1970s, huge numbers of men, women, and children are attracted to major

fairs in the United States and Canada. According to the International Association of Fairs and Expositions, more than 150 million Americans today spend in excess of $250 million at 2,150 state and county fairs.[16]

Amusement/Theme Parks

A theme park is "an amusement park whose total character and mood is derived from a definite theme." In July 1955, Disneyland, the world's first modern theme park, opened in Anaheim, California. Today, theme parks produce revenue estimated at more than $1 billion annually.[17]

The theme park area of commercial recreation represents one of the fastest growing segments in the leisure services industry. The most spectacular growth was recorded by the forty major theme parks, such as Walt Disney's Disneyland in Southern California. The combined revenues of Disneyland and

Figure 14–4 Theme parks are in the business of entertaining people. Services provided by the park contribute to the portrayal of the theme. Here, Rivers of America carry Disneyland's three–masted sailing ship "Columbia" to Tom Sawyer's Island. In the distance is the famed Matterhorn Mountain and other exciting attractions of the "Magic Kingdom." (Courtesy Walt Disney's Disneyland at Anaheim, California.)

Disney World (Florida) earned $68 million in revenue in 1975. The Disney parks account for almost one–third of the theme park business, with Six Flags (Georgia) in second place, followed by Busch Gardens.

Theme parks are in the business of entertaining people. The services provided by a theme park should contribute to the portrayal of that theme. In the *EMPLOY* publication, John M. Carter grouped them into the following categories:[19]

- General Services
- Operations
- Merchandise
- Food and Beverage
- Grounds and Facilities
- Public Relations
- Animal Areas
- Entertainment and Live Shows
- Marketing
- Hotel and Motels

The *Annual Report of World Travel Trends and Markets* indicated that "Theme parks outdraw professional sports by better than 40 percent. In 1974 the sixty–eight teams in major league baseball, football, and basketball drew an audience of 46.9 million. In the same year thirty–eight theme parks drew 76.5 million visitors."[18]

PARTICIPATIVE ACTIVITIES/ INDIVIDUAL SPORTS

Participation in leisure–time activities, particularly sports, represents a major interest for the great mass of youth and adults today. As Richard Kraus pointed out, "Sports have become big business; they are moneymakers, sponsored by powerful commercial interests and promoted by advertising, public relations, television, radio, magazines, and newspapers."[20] Gambling is one of the fastest growing pastimes in the commercial recreation field, with turnover estimated at $80 billion a year.

Similar to their European counterparts, Americans increasingly are participating in a wide variety of sports. There are nearly twenty million golfers in the United States, playing regularly on about eleven thousand courses. More people than ever before, approximately forty million, are playing tennis. The millions of fishermen, hunters, archers, mountain climbers, and joggers contribute to the burgeoning numbers of Americans involved in leisure participation.

Bicycling

As the price of gasoline continues to increase, one form of transportation and recreation remains relatively inexpensive: the bicycle. In addition to being one of the oldest forms of human–powered transportation, biking is also excellent exercise, and its cardiovascular benefits are well documented. The comeback of the bicycle continues to delight bike manufacturers. Cycling ranks as the fourth most popular sport among Americans, trailing behind walking, swimming, and bowling. In 1979, some ten million bicycles were sold.

Bowling

Bowling is a family game now, and bowling centers are large, brightly lit buildings that cater to players of all ages. Women's leagues flourish, and children and senior citizens enjoy special rates. Many bowling centers even offer free babysitting.

Today, there are about nine thousand bowling centers in the United States operating a total of one hundred and forty thousand lanes. There are an estimated thirty million bowlers in the United States, about a third of which are women and another three million are children.

There are approximately eight hundred and fifty thousand junior bowlers nationwide, ranging in age from four to twenty, and all bowl at least once a week, mainly on Saturday mornings from September through May. Their leagues are divided according to age, and the handicap system is employed to allow the least talented bowlers to compete with the best.

Camping

The multitude of campsites throughout the United States provides the opportunity for individuals and families to enjoy the refreshing experience of living with nature. Private resident and day camps provide the majority of organized camping to youth in the United States and Canada. Fees range from $150.00 to $200.00 per week and include all camp services while the child is at camp. Private camps, although more expensive than YMCA, Boy Scouts, or public camps, are usually able to provide more comprehensive programs and facilities.

Private fishing camps offer wilderness fishing to those willing to pay the fee. There are numerous camps in Canada, with the weekly fee averaging between $1,500 to $2,000. This price includes air fares, lodging, food, and guide service.

The current trend is toward the more specialized camps, such as camps for people with handicaps. People with handicaps, in evergrowing numbers, are responding to the significant increase in the number of special camps.

Dance

The United States is in the midst of a new cultural development, the dance explosion. "At no other time in the country's history has dance—notably ballet and modern dance—been so popular," wrote Anna Kisselgoff. "Nor has an art form flourished in such concentrated creativity and diversity of styles."[21]

Statistics from the National Endowment for the Arts are indicative of the great popularity of the dance today. In 1966, the allocation for the Endowment's Dance Program was $605,250. In 1978, it was $6,938,270.[22]

Social dancing is more popular than ever. Indeed, touch dancing and good grooming are back in style. Discos became one of the biggest entertainment phenomena of the 1970s. Discos opened in everything from Holiday Inns and Hilton hotels to rural potato barns. The chance to boogie again is appealing to all social classes.

Hunting

Hunting is an extremely popular activity throughout the United States and Canada.

While hunting has a high danger potential, strong emphasis on safety has resulted in a very good safety record. This can be attributed to the fact that many states require that novice hunters take courses in the use of firearms and qualifying tests before being given licenses.

Shooting preserves are privately owned and rely on pen–raised birds for the majority of their game. Preserves in the United States offer a variety of game such as pheasants, quail, ducks, geese, rabbits, and large game (deer, etc.). Special services make the private gun club or preserve attractive. Services include guide and dogs, game cleaning and picking, food and beverage service, and lodging.

Photography

As more fast films emerge to permit photographic shooting under virtually any lighting conditions, Americans produced more than eight billion still images in 1978. Photography has taken its place on walls, in magazines, and in the streets. Manufacturers of single–lens reflex (SLR) 35 mm cameras are largely responsible for the huge international popularity of this leisure pastime.

Racquet Sports

Sports played with a racquet, especially racquetball, paddleball, and platform tennis, have enjoyed a tremendous rise in popularity. According to author Philip E. Allsen, "The relative inexpensiveness of the equipment, the ease with which one can learn the games, and the excellent physical activity offered are basic reasons for the popularity."[23]

Racquetball is the fastest growing participant sport in the country, according to a survey of United States households conducted by the A.C. Nielson Company. Participation in racquetball is up 283 percent over the three-year period from 1976 to 1979 and currently boasts an estimated 10,654,000 individual participants.

Why the strong interest in racquetball? "Unlike in tennis, it is a snap to hit the ball," wrote Frank Satterthwaite. "The hollow rubber ball is about the size of a tennisball, but it bounces higher, and it just sort of hangs there and says, 'Hit me,' which is easy enough to do with that short–handled racquet."[24]

Skating

Skating is now regarded as more than fun. Both ice and roller skating are an excellent form of exercise. In fact, research conducted at UCLA concluded that skating seems to be a better form of exercise than jogging. Those who desire competition, physical contact, and team play find ice hockey a challenging sport.

Skating is an excellent lifetime sport which, ideally, should be learned early in life. Many high schools have introduced skating and other lifetime sports that students may participate in as adults. Although commercial facilities close to the school are often used, many schools have outdoor space for ice skating.

Snow Skiing

The two types of skiing that are most popular in the United States are Alpine (downhill) and Nordic, also known as cross–country or ski touring. Facilities range from a simple rope tow to a lift with elaborate cable cars. An Alpine skiing area requires a snow-covered, north–facing slope with a minimum grade of 20 percent, and additional level ground sufficient for a horizontal run and a parking lot.

The cross-country skiing movement continues to flourish. Not only do skiers seek the solitude of the countryside but look for more challenges: marathons, NASTAR racing, and week–long wilderness expeditions.

There are more than five hundred touring centers in the United States and Canada. Skiers have a wide choice of centers with a network of marked and groomed trails as well as luxurious inns or basic warming huts nearby. Centers offer instruction, rentals, guided wilderness and moonlight tours, overnight camping, and orientation.

Of the thousands of areas in the United States, more than 90 percent are privately owned. Ski resorts, rather than ski areas, are rapidly becoming the rule. Many are located on Forest Service lands, particularly those in the West.

Swimming

Swimming, with approximately 110 million participants (nearly one out of every two Americans), continues to be the nation's favorite sporting activity. Swimming expenditures total $4 billion annually. Carlson, MacLean, Deppe, and Peterson explained that "The construction and maintenance of the 890,000 swimming pools, of which over two–thirds are residential, explain much of the cost. Other swimming expenses include suits and water–related gear, such as surfboards, and equipment for skin and scuba diving."[25]

Swimming is enjoyed with other recreation activities, such as boating, picnicking, and scuba diving. Water–related activities like water skiing, wind–surfing, and underwater exploration are some of the most popular recreational and leisure pursuits in the United States.

Tennis

Tennis has become a big business. In 1973 there were twenty million tennis players in the United States. In 1980 there were nearly forty million. The popularity of the sport can be attributed to a number of factors. The game can provide a brisk physical workout in a short time. It can be played into middle age and beyond, and basic equipment and playing fees are inexpensive. Most authorities believe the boom has started to level off, due largely to the fact that there are so many more sports people can play today.

An outdoor tennis center should include four or more tennis courts, ideally six to ten. Fewer units make it uneconomical to staff or manage, according to Joseph Curtis.[26] A small utility building should contain locker rooms, rest rooms, tennis supply shop, showers, lounge, and simple food service.

Wilderness Outfitters

Offering a variety of experiences, wilderness outfitting has become a lucrative business. Arlin Epperson categorized wilderness outfitting businesses into five main types: 1) hiking or backpacking trips, 2) river running, 3) mountain climbing, 4) instructional, and 5) ski touring.

The Colorado River Grand Canyon rafting outfitters gross $4.5 million per season. "Exotic, exciting, educational, and expensive are the adjectives that best describe most of the trips offered by these outfitters," wrote Epperson.[27]

MECHANIZED SPORTS

The great popularity of mechanized sports is a major reason why outdoor recreation has a powerful economic impact on today's leisure world. Boating, snowmobiling, motorcycles and bikes, off-road vehicles, and recreation vehicles represent the huge specter of mechanized sports enterprises. Yet, it should be noted that as gasoline supplies grow tighter and prices for fuel climb higher, mechanized sports may be adversely affected.

Boating

More reservoirs and marinas are being built each year to accommodate boaters. The majority of boating marinas and boat launching facilities are privately owned or developed. Some of the boating services provided are launching, mooring, rental boats, dry storage, fuel, and overnight accommodations.

"Boating is a particularly important form of recreational activity," noted Kraus, "because it provides the basis for many other pastimes: fishing, scuba diving, water-skiing, and especially camping."[28] A recent trend in boating is the growing interest in rafting, canoeing, and kayaking.

Motorcycling

Generally, this sport can be divided into two major categories—road motorcycling and off-road motorcycling. Off-road, or "trail riding" on public land occurs on "trails" that are not public streets or highways, such as fire roads, logging trails, and power line right-of-ways.

According to the American Motorcyclist Association, "Trail riding, like other outdoor recreational activity, should be correctly managed so as to fulfill the needs of the American public for outdoor recreation while minimizing the adverse effects upon the environment."[29]

Off-road Vehicles

Until the early 1970s, no special facilities were planned for those who drove dune buggies, four-wheel jeeps and motorcycles. Joseph and Virginia McCall noted that "For many years, off-road vehicles (ORVs) were free to roam over publicly owned lands with few limitations. The nearness of the California desert to Los Angeles brought about a crisis of overuse and forced the Bureau of Land Management (BLM) to begin the development of formal recreation areas, with patrols and restrictions, on the desert."[30]

The BLM proceeded to zone the public lands as open, restricted use, non-use, or closed areas. They constructed way stations—facilities where fresh water, rest rooms, and developed campgrounds for tent and trailer are available for ORV owners.

"Because sand can withstand heavy usage," said McCall and McCall, "the problems arising from the popularity of dune buggies come mostly from their using the shoulders of existing highways for parking and congregating, which causes traffic hazards."[31]

Recreation Vehicles

The leisure boom has given rise to many types of recreation vehicles, such as snowmobiles, four–wheel drive vehicles, dune buggies, and minibikes.

A recreational vehicle is a moving unit, either powered by itself or pulled by another vehicle. The Recreation Vehicle Industry Association established the term "recreation vehicle" to encompass all vehicles primarily designed as temporary living quarters for recreation, camping, and travel—whether they include their own motor power, are mounted on a powered chassis, or are towed by another vehicle. On the other hand, all–terrain, off–road vehicles, motorcycles, and snowmobiles usually are not classed as recreation vehicles.

There are six basic recreation vehicle categories: 1) camping trailers; 2) truck campers; 3) travel trailers; 4) motor–homes; 5) five wheelers; and 6) van conversions.

More than twenty-five million Americans are currently enjoying the lifestyle offered by recreation vehicles. For many, an RV offers a "home away from home." For others, it is a means of taking their home with them, in miniature form, plus the benefit of enjoying the great outdoors.

Snowmobiling

Snowmobiling has risen to one of the fastest growing recreation activities in the country. In the western states, snowmobiles operate mostly on Forest Service lands and are generally restricted to designated routes. In the East, which has a scarcity of usable land, private snowmobile runs have been opened on golf courses and farm lands.

The most popular activity of snowmobile clubs is snow cruising. A variety of activities occur on these cruises such as campouts and cookouts.

Numerous problems continue to surround the snowmobile, affecting those who sell, rent, and provide snowmobiles, or places for them to operate. The high accident rate, the noise, and damage to the land are some of the problems. The ski–tracked vehicle can carry two persons at speeds up to fifty miles an hour. Average cost for a snowmobile is $1,000.

CLUBS, RESORTS, HOUSING DEVELOPMENTS, AND HOMES

The desire for an enjoyable atmosphere for leisure–time fun, social interests, and sports participation is largely responsible for the popularity of clubs, resorts, housing developments, and vacation homes. In turn, this segment of the leisure industry is providing an increasing number of job opportunities for professional recreators.

The urge to get away for long weekends has created a boom in vacationland and condominium ownership sales. Interest in vacation and holiday homes has resulted in a flourishing market for land.

Private Clubs

Private clubs are no longer the privilege of just the very wealthy or socially prominent. With today's emphasis on recreation and leisure–time activities, there is a club for almost everyone. According to the Club Managers Association of America, "Clubs may vary in size and purpose, but they all have one thing in common: They are composed of people who are interested in joining together for companionship, recreation and entertainment."[32]

The objective of clubs is to provide a pleasant atmosphere for social interests and for participation in sports activities. Club participation is usually by annual membership.

Many private organizations and companies provide facilities or instruction related to tennis, racquetball, swimming, golf, skiing, boating, and hunting or fishing. Richard Kraus wrote that "Such clubs frequently exist as independent, incorporated bodies, owning their own facilities, with policy set by elected officers and boards, and with the actual work of maintenance, instruction, and supervision carried out by paid employees."[33]

The growth of health spas, fitness centers, and workout gymnasiums has increased dramatically in recent years. Each has its own methods, its own type of exercise equipment, and its own goals.

Facilities for a sports club or fitness center may include the following:

- Workout gymnasium
- Sauna
- Locker room
- Ice skating
- Tennis
- Racquetball
- Handball
- Weightlifting
- Restaurant or snack bar
- Bar or lounge
- Social activity area

Racquetball Clubs

Racquetball has been called the fastest growing sport in the country. Indeed, indoor racquet clubs are attracting a new breed of sports–minded Americans possessing an intense appetite for activity. The growing number of schools and colleges offering instruction in racquetball is a significant indication of recent enthusiasm and support. Richard B. Flynn wrote: "The most popular facility construction in recent years is the indoor tennis and racquetball club—providing a variety of leisure activities for people of varied ages and levels of ability."[34]

Application of the indoor racquet club concept ranges from a small single–purpose venture (racquetball/handball courts or tennis courts only) to more elaborate multipurpose facilities (including courts, swimming pool, health club, restaurant, pro shop, etc.).

Linda Fjeldsted wrote: "Racquetball has become the fashionable sport for the society set, the latest avenue to physical fitness, rapidly taking over the sporting spotlight held by tennis just a couple of years ago."[35]

Country Clubs

There are probably more country clubs in existence than any other type of private recreation enterprise. Most of them are private and operate on a nonprofit basis. Many country clubs, however, are struggling for financial existence as maintenance and upkeep take a large part of their revenue.

Country clubs are usually located in a suburban or rural area. However, due to urban sprawl and the expansion of communities, some of the older country clubs have become more urban. They are recreational in nature, catering to the social and athletic interests of their membership. Generally, their facilities include a club house, swimming pools, tennis courts, and a golf course. Hosting a golf tournament, organizing a formal dinner–dance, and supervising the many departments are some of the responsibilities of the management staff.

The manager should be familiar with many responsibilities of a very broad scope, such as the following: the construction and development of new tennis courts, repair and maintenance of swimming pools, supervision of numerous employees; the purchasing and upkeep of equipment, and the management of land and other property.

Of the 11,800 clubs in operation in the United States, 8,500 are "total facility" clubs. These feature a club house, facilities for food and beverage, and in the case of country clubs, golf courses and other recreational facilities as well as many planned programs.

There are approximately 1.2 million full and part–time employees at these clubs, which comprises a total payroll of $3.8 billion annually. The total membership is well over seven million, and when wives and children are included, more than fourteen million people are involved in the use of their club's facilities each year.[36]

CLUB MANAGEMENT

A career in private club management can be a rewarding future for those who care about people. A well run club has the appearance of a dynamic organization with well defined lines of authority and responsibility to achieve its goals.

Types Private clubs today include country, town and luncheon, athletic, women's,

OLD CROW CANYON RACQUETBALL CLUB—
A Racquetball Club with a Country Club Atmosphere

This popular club in San Ramon, California has put into practice the concept of a big recreation center. Lou Quint, Jr., club manager, believes that "The name of the game is programming. What we are doing at Old Crow is taking a recreation philosophy and incorporating it into a racquetball setting. We provide many of the services usually offered by a community recreation center. In addition to the racquetball play on ten fully air-conditioned courts, programs for men and women include exercise classes, a Nautilus Fitness Center, whirlpool baths and saunas, a varied social schedule from fashion shows to fun runs, trips and excursions, and in-house racquetball tournaments and leagues."

Quint pointed out, however, that the underlying factor, for any racquetball or private club is that it is a business, that it is there for one reason—to make money. Quint said: "We never forget that the three most important things in the operation of a racquetball club are: (1) cleanliness, (2) service, and (3) program. The program also helps the profit–center area such as pro–shop and food–service areas."

To effectively manage a club, an individual first has to be organized. The manager must not be afraid to delegate. Quint meets every other Wednesday with his division heads. He hears their input and then he provides input of his own.

Second, a manager should have high ethical standards and be willing to keep everything on a high professional level. The manager must be willing to put in the hours. To be a successful manager, a person has to do a good job of communication. A club manager has to be able to speak to groups, talk to people one on one. From the financial standpoint, he or she has to keep a close watch on the overhead, the utilities, and the payroll.

Figure 14–5 Racquetball is not only a lot of fun, but it is easy to play. Players can compete in singles, doubles, or mixed competition.

Figure 14–6 Serving the membership is the primary concern of both management and ownership. Here, Lou Quint, Jr., manager, and Scott Stringer, president of the Old Crow Canyon Racquetball Club, discuss the day's program.

tennis, yacht, swimming, and others of similar character. Many large corporations also have built club facilities for their employees.

Staff   The managerial skills required for each type of club are quite basic, but specific requirements often vary. Although education is essential, the experience and on–the–job learning experience is a major factor in executive development. A good background in business administration is very important.

To qualify for a top management position, an individual must be willing to begin at a lower position and work his or her way to the top. There are many assistant and mid–management positions which are available that will lead to a higher–level job.

The average salary of a club manager is $20,000-$62,000, depending on the size, type, and location of the club, as well as the manager's experience and education. Many clubs offer bonuses, fringe benefits, housing, and vacation allowances. Annual salaries for assistant managers vary between $20,000-$30,000.

Job Description   There are more than two hundred possible job descriptions for people employed at a private club. The manager of a small club must be a "jack of all trades," while a large club operation with five hundred to two thousand members may employ as many as one-hundred paid personnel.

Personal Characteristics   A sense of humor, ability to get along with others, a sense of personal pride, the ability to accept supervision and supervise others are among the talents and special abilities of those who make successful club managers. A good attitude in dealing with people, as well as an open mind are among the qualities which can lead to a successful career.

Areas of Knowledge   Club managers today must be familiar with all aspects of a club's operation. Basically, the manager's responsibility may be divided into five management areas: facilities, program or services, personnel, finances, and sales. They should be knowledgeable in administration, public relations and operational procedures, food and beverage preparation, service and purchasing, maintenance, housekeeping, recreation, and personnel supervision.

Program Ideas   Program ideas will come from the theme and local interest of the club. The key to successful programming is to listen to and follow the interests of your community and clientele.

The following is a brief list of some popular special events that can be conducted by a club:

- Pool tournaments
- Talent shows
- Hootenanny sing alongs
- Bingo nights
- Large television screen
- Shuffleboard tournaments
- Dance contests
- Singles mixer night
- Parties for professional and civic groups
- Gong show contest

RESORT RECREATION

The phenomenal growth and popularity of the resort industry has created a vast array of recreation services and multimillion dollar hotel facilities and marinas. Ranging from the very simple to vast clubs, resorts experienced rapid growth in the 1970s due to increased expendable income and population mobility. Fifty percent of all resorts are owned by large corporations, while 40 percent are owned by individuals. Governmental agencies run approximately 10 percent of all resorts.

A resort may promote primarily one or two specific activities such as tennis or golf, while another may promote water sports such as skiing, fishing, canoeing, or swimming.

A resort is a full service hostelry which provides leisure services and facilities. Full service hostelry means a property which has convention facilities, lodging, room services, and food. The types of positions available for park and recreation graduates include recreation director, operations manager, and operations staff.

Resort recreation management covers a broad sector of the total commercial recreation industry, such as leisure services, amusement parks, food services, lodging, conventions, sporting events, professional entertainment, and management of athletic facilities.

According to Roger Childers, Recreation Director, Callaway Gardens (Pine Mountain, Georgia), "The basic objective of recreation management in the resort business is to provide quality leisure services to a predetermined market to achieve an established occupancy rate which will yield the desired profit goal to the corporation."[37] To achieve this basic objective, the professional is responsible for the following:

● Marketing
● Programming
● Administration

Figure 14–7 Tahoe Donner, a resort community for all seasons. Tahoe Donner, a $40–million, four–season family resort community in the High Sierras of California offers resort living in a country–club setting. Property owners can enjoy an eighteen–hole golf course; swim, and play tennis as members of the Racquet and Swim Club; saddle up at the equestrian center; go sailing, water ski, or just relax on the beach at Donner Lake; or park a camper or RV in a private campground. The winter season offers skiing at Donner's magnificent ski facilities. (Courtesy Dart Resorts.)

MGM GRAND HOTEL, RENO

The MGM Grand is a huge recreation complex, featuring a twenty–six story hotel and casino houses. The MGM Grand Hotel in Reno, Nevada probably has a greater variety of sports facilities than any other casino–hotel in the world. As for gambling, MGM-Reno has 2000 slot machines, 102 blackjack tables, sixteen poker tables, ten crap tables, and much more.

The fifty-lane bowling alley has the latest AMF lanes and pin–setting equipment. Nearby are eight tennis courts (three all-weather surfaced), lighted outdoor and five indoor. An outdoor swimming pool has a spacious patio area at pool side. Separate health club facilities for men and women are completely out-fitted with exercise equipment, weights, saunas, and steam rooms.

On the casino level in the recreation area is jai alai, the world's fastest sport, with pari–mutual betting. The pelota, or ball, is rock hard and often exceeds speeds of 175 miles per hour. A field of thirty–two professional jai alai players rack up prize money based on their own wins. The fronton seats 2,115 in upholstered theater–type seats for the card of twelve games, nightly except Mondays.

A 292–hookup Camperland is also located on the MGM Property. Complete with a market, laundry facilities, and a self–service gas station, the recreational vehicle park overlooks the Truckee River.

HOUSING DEVELOPMENTS AND HOME ASSOCIATIONS

An increasing number of people are purchasing homes in subdivisions, condominiums, or housing developments because of the location of the recreation and leisure services associated with the development. Recreation facilities such as a golf course, lake, swimming pool, or other leisure attraction help sell homes.

One of the strongest selling points in home development projects is attractive recreational facilities. Swimming pools, tennis courts, health spas, golf courses and other recreational facilities are provided for the residents of apartment buildings, condominiums, or one–family home developments.

Increasingly, second homes are being developed in clusters and groups, which take advantage of beaches, golf courses, ski lodges, harbors, mountain retreats, and numerous other facilities.

Vacation Homes

The desire to get away for long weekends has created a boom in vacationland sales. Interest in vacation and holiday homes has resulted in a flourishing market for land.

Retirement or adult communities have been established, which place strong emphasis on the provision of extensive leisure opportunities for residents. Sun City, Arizona, a leading retirement community, for example, has golf courses, recreation centers, lawn bowling green, an amphitheater, a stadium, two lakes, and many other special recreation facilities and programs.

More and more land developers are offering special amenities for community use, such as clubhouses, riding stables, tennis courts, marinas, swimming pools, private beaches, and ski slopes.

Shopping Centers

The development of shopping centers of this type is a most promising concept in the leisure services industry. A rural tourist–recreation shopping center is an area outside the boundaries of a standard metropolitan statistical area, where the diversity in recreation activities and facilities dominate the region's landscape and economy. Outdoor activities include flower and music festivals, horseshows, fairs, drama, athletic events, and art displays.

Among the characteristics of these centers are: 1) relative location to large population concentrations; 2) undulating topography; 3) aesthetics; 4) spaciousness; 5) blocks of land in public ownerships.

APARTMENT COMPLEX RECREATION

Although the various settings often resemble that of municipal recreation, apartment complex recreation is a part of the private/commercial employment sector. Apartment complex recreation involves planning and implementing a complete recreation program for the residents of a given development. Social, athletic, cultural, and educational activities typify programs at apartment complexes. These may include tennis courts, swimming pools, golf courses, gymnasiums, health centers, weightrooms, saunas, as well as playgrounds, clubhouses, and other facilities for organized play.[38]

In residential developments, professional activity directors are employed to organize leagues, supervise day camps, hire part–time staff to provide instruction, and plan special events with community groups.

The apartment complex recreation program must satisfy the owner, the community manager, and the residents. According to Lynn Mikels and Elaine Potts, the purpose of the program is twofold:

1. It should help with marketing by making the complex more appealing to potential residents.
2. It should increase the renewal rate by creating a friendly atmosphere where people can meet one another and by providing enriching and enjoyable activities.[39]

Figure 14–8 Barbeque socials are among many special events and activities offered residents of The Meadows apartment complex in Citrus Heights, California. Above, Patti Berglund, activity director (right), and George Mendoza, manager of the complex, team up to conduct a pool–side social.

To achieve the goals of the program, the director must involve the residents in the program as volunteers and actual participants. He or she must get to know the residents personally and understand their needs.

Types Of Service

A wide variety of different adult activities are sponsored by apartment complexes. Traditional luaus, Las Vegas Nights, and cocktail hours are among the many activities which enable residents to meet one another in a relaxed atmosphere. Special interest clubs in bridge, skiing, and outdoor pursuits have proven very popular to the residents of apartment complexes. Sports and physical fitness activities are also popular. Many complexes sponsor their own leagues and tournaments.

TRAVEL AND TOURISM

Domestic pleasure travel is the second largest component of the leisure budget and includes vacation trips and overnight journeys. The travel and tourism industry encompasses a wide variety of businesses and enterprises amounting to more than $61 billion a year in sales, and is second only to grocery store sales, reported Discover America Travel Organizations, Inc. "Tourism and travel sustains the employment of more than four million Americans," said Arlin Epperson. "In forty–six of the fifty states, tourism ranks as one of the top three leading industries."[40]

According to Robert S. Milne, "Travel is the movement of people, and tourism concerns the entire business of leisure travel and related supporting activities."[41]

Travel

Travel leads as one of the most popular leisure activities in the world. As leisure time increases and incomes rise, so does the travel and tourism business. Most travel agencies do not organize tours themselves, rather, they are in the business of selling trips and tours offered by travel wholesalers and carriers. There are approximately fifteen thousand travel agencies in the United States. Some of these are operated by the owner alone. The average agency, however, has five or six full–time and two part–time employees.

Management and administration skills are most essential for a travel agent, but a desire to work with people is even more important. The travel agent gives out a considerable amount of advice and information to prospective travelers, but he or she makes no money unless tickets and hotel reservations are sold. Working for a travel agency, therefore, means selling.

The largest travel trade association in the nation is the American Society of Travel Agents, Inc. (ASTA), which requires members to have at least three years experience plus appointment by a minimum of two major transportation conferences.

Tourism

Tourism is the business of attracting tourists and supplying them with what they want. A tourist is a person traveling for pleasure, and one of the main things he or she wants is recreation. Tourism is the third largest retail industry in the United States, exceeded only by the food and automobile industries. More than four–and–one–half million people are employed by the industry in the United States.

Clayne Jensen listed five major components within the tourism group: 1) attracting a market for tourism; 2) providing transportation to places of interest; 3) providing attractions for tourist participation; 4) housing, feeding, and serving tourists; and 5) informing people about attractions, services, facilities, and transportation, then making specific arrangements for them.[42]

The tourism industry is of a very wide scope, with many different types of jobs available. States, cities, and other areas are recognizing the importance of bringing tourism to their areas. Tourists mean revenue and jobs. As a result, convention and visitor bureaus work hard to bring visitors to their cities, as do state departments of tourism to bring more people to their states. Visitors spend money on food, lodging, entertainment, and recreation. This generates increased revenue and increased employment.

Those employed in the tourist industry are involved in arranging transportation, food and lodging, and entertainment. Job responsibilities include promotional work, business management, personnel management, and public relations.

QUESTIONS FOR DISCUSSION

1. Basically, what is a commercial recreation enterprise?
2. Describe the tremendous scope and popularity of commercial recreation.
3. List the five categories of commercial recreation facilities or enterprises.
4. Discuss some of the most popular recreation opportunities provided by the private and commercial sector.
5. What are the most common types of entertainment complexes as categorized by Perry Jones?
6. How would you describe a theme park?
7. What basic rules did Walt Disney establish when he started the revolution in amusement parks back in the 1950s?
8. List the six basic recreation vehicle categories and discuss their future in relation to the growing energy crisis, particularly the price of fuel.
9. What is your definition of a private club? The purpose?
10. To what do you attribute the success of the Old Crow Canyon Racquetball Club in San Ramon?
11. Review the personal characteristics of a successful club manager.
12. Discuss the need for conducting a feasibility study when starting a commercial recreation business.
13. What impact have the economy and energy crises had on the resort industry? What changes or new approaches to these problems do you look for?
14. List Clayne Jensen's five major components within the tourism group.

REFERENCES

1. Richard Talbot, "Commercial Recreation: An Emerging Giant," *California Parks and Recreation*, August/September, 1978, p. 14.
2. Harold D. Meyer, Charles K. Brightbill, and H. Douglas Sessoms, *Community Recreation* (Englewood Cliffs, N.J.: Prentice–Hall, Inc., 1969), p. 282.
3. Ibid., p. 284.

4. Richard Talbot, "Commercial Recreation," p. 14.

5. Arlin Epperson, *Private and Commercial Recreation* (New York: John Wiley & Sons, 1977), p. 110.

6. "Behind Scandals in Big-Time College Sports," *U.S. News & World Report*, February 11, 1980, p. 61.

7. Reynold Carlson, Janet MacLean, Theodore Deppe, and James Peterson, *Recreation and Leisure—The Changing Scene* 3rd ed. (Belmont, California: Wadsworth Publishing Company, Inc., 1979), p. 66.

8. Joseph Curtis, *Recreation, Theory and Practice* (St. Louis: the C. V. Mosby Company, 1979), p. 13.

9. Richard Kraus, *Recreation and Leisure in Modern Society*, 2nd ed. (Santa Monica, Calif.: Goodyear Publishing Company, 1978), p. 112.

10. Carlson, MacLean, Deppe, and Peterson, *Recreation and Leisure*, p. 64.

11. Brie Quinby, "What in the World," *Family Weekly*, May 25, 1980, p. 23.

12. Perry Jones, "Entertainment Complexes," unpublished manuscript, American River College, January, 1980, pp. 5–8.

13. Epperson, *Private and Commercial Recreation*, p. 117.

14. Robert S. Milne, "Theme Amusement Parks," *The Americana Annual* 1975, Grolier Incorporated, p. 48.

15. Lila Perl, "America Goes to the Fair," *Family Weekly*.

16. Ibid.

17. "Commercial Travel Attractions—Theme Parks," *The Big Picture—Travel '76*, Annual Report, World Travel Trends and Markets, Vol. 21, p. 33.

18. Ibid.

19. John M. Carter, *EMPLOY, A Service of the National Recreation and Park Association*, Arlington, Virginia, Vol. V, No. 3, November 1978, pp. 3–4.

20. Kraus, *Recreation and Leisure*, p. 102.

21. Anna Kisselgoff, "The Dance Explosion," *The Americana Annual* 1979, Grolier Incorporated, pp. 178 and 180.

22. Ibid.

23. Philip E. Allsen, "The Racquet Sports," *Americana Annual* 1979, Grolier Incorporated, p. 33.

24. Frank Satterthwaite, "Racquetball: It's Easy, Fun and Cheap to Play," *Family Weekly*, March 27, 1977, p. 14.

25. Carlson, et al., *Recreation and Leisure—The Changing Scene*, p. 63.

26. Curtis, *Recreation, Theory and Practice*, p. 208.

27. Epperson, *Private and Commercial Recreation*, p. 134.

28. Kraus, *Recreation and Leisure*, 2nd ed. pp. 105–106.

29. AMA Position, "Motorcycling on Public Land," American Motorcyclist Association, Westerville, Ohio, December, 1978.

30. Joseph McCall and Virginia McCall, *Outdoor Recreation* (Beverly Hills, Calif.: Bruce, Division of Benziger Bruce & Glencoe, 1977), pp. 217–18.

31. Ibid.

32. "Club Management," Club Managers Association of America, Washington, D.C., 1978, p. 7.

33. Kraus, *Recreation and Leisure*, 2nd ed. p. 272.

34. Richard B. Flynn, "Indoor Racquet Clubs," *JOPER*, November–December 1977, p. 45.

35. Linda Fjeldsted, "Racquetball: A 'Smashing' New Sport." *Sacramento Union*, November 2, 1978, p. C3.

36. "Club Management," pp. 7–8.

37. Roger Childers, "Resort Recreation," *EMPLOY*, National Recreation and Park Association, May 1977, p. 1.

38. "Apartment Complex Recreation," *EMPLOY*, National Recreation and Park Association, Vol. IV, No. 5, January 1978, p. 1.

39. Ibid., p. 2.

40. Epperson, *Private and Commercial Recreation*, p. 3.

41. Robert S. Milne, *Opportunities in Travel Careers* (Louisville: Vocational Guidance Manuals, Inc., 1976), p. 13.

42. Clayne Jensen, *Recreation and Leisure Time Careers* (Louisville: Vocational Guidance Manuals, 1976), p. 19.

Figure 15–1 Jogging before work, during the lunch hour, or after work is one of the most popular forms of exercise among employee groups today. Here, students at the Xerox International Center for Training and Management Development join Brent Arnold (right), Manager of Physical Fitness and Recreation, for a refreshing morning jog on one of the roads at the Center. (Courtesy of Xerox Corporation, Leesburg, Virginia.)

15
Industrial Recreation

Industrial recreation and employee services are the terms used to describe the leisure activities enjoyed by employees, managers, and executives of business and industrial firms. These activities, programs, events, and services may be provided by the company, the employees themselves through employee recreation associations, or more commonly today by a combination of the two.

Industrial recreation has developed into a multi–billion dollar leisure delivery system, estimated by some experts as a $6 billion annual commitment. It has expanded both in the nature of services and in the total number of companies developing employee recreation programs.

Industrial recreation is on the upswing as the trend toward employer provided recreation and services grows. Yet, the potential of employee recreation has not been fully recognized, and in many companies, the role of employee recreation is still underrated.

According to Eric Ovlen, Executive Director, Lockheed Employees Recreation Association, "The industrial sector is a sleeping giant. The *Wall Street Journal* says there are 50,000 major corporations in the United States, but only a small percentage of those have formal recreation programs. It seems to me that there are a multitude of potential jobs in our sector, particularly in light of the developing area of employee benefits."[1]

Actually, industrial recreation is one of the oldest specialized areas of recreation. Steven C. Malmquist pointed out that its development even precedes that of municipal recreation. "Only recently, however, has it been recognized for the valuable contribution it makes to individuals and businesses in this country."[2]

Why industrial recreation? The question can best be answered through the outlined objectives which industrial recreation administrators have developed. "There is a bottom line profit expected in return for the services offered," said Melvin C. Byers. "Corporations are in a business venture and anytime there is expense or effort given, they must relate to the profit–ability of the company in one way or another."[3]

From the company point of view, the basic principle of industrial recreation is that wholesome recreation makes workers brighter, more enthusiastic, and more productive members of the labor team.

Most companies want their employees to be alive, if not robust, and recognize the economic importance of keeping people productive and on the job. Norman Sklarewitz wrote that "In cold dollars–and–sense terms, it's extremely expensive for a company to lose the services of both seasoned and promising executives to incapacitating illnesses."[4]

Recreation becomes a key factor in productivity by giving the individual status and recognition, as well as improving his or her morale. C. J. Pilliod, chairman of the board for Goodyear Tire and Rubber Company suggests that "A diversified selection of activities for employees, members of their families and retirees is the fiber that joins our people into a well–knit, friendly group—on and off the job."[5]

There is no question that employees benefit from recreational facilities, but management finds them advantageous as well. They make recruiting easier and reduce turnover because happy employees are less likely to quit or be lured away, are absent less, and are more productive.

Figure 15–2 The Oktoberfest, a favorite German tradition, is among the dances held throughout the year by the Lockheed Employees' Recreation Association. Above, employees and the management staff enthusiastically participate in the Polonaise. Increasingly, management is realizing the benefits to be derived from healthy employees who work and enjoy their leisure time together. (Courtesy Lockheed Employees' Recreation Association.)

Fitness has become a major area of employee activity programs, as corporations, increasingly, are providing incentives for employees to become physically fit. Hundreds of American corporations now encourage their employees to participate in physical fitness activities.

BACKGROUND/HISTORY

The field of industrial recreation was first recognized in 1854 when the Peacedale Manufacturing Company in Peacedale, Rhode Island, provided a library for employees and their families. This eventually led to the construction of a recreation–library facility.

In 1868 the YMCA became the first private agency to work with industry in serving the needs of workers. Its cooperation with the Union Pacific Railroad Company was the first of a series of YMCA projects to help industrial workers during off–the–job hours. The first employee recreation association on record was the Metropolitan Life Insurance Company formed in 1894.

In the decades that followed, a number of manufacturing concerns began to sponsor trips and annual excursions or picnics for their workers. Kraus reported that "Some, like the National Cash Register Company in Dayton, Ohio, or the Joliet Steel Company in Joliet, Illinois, built clubhouses or auditoriums for their employees. Others, like the

Pullman Company of Chicago and the Conant Thread Company of Massachusetts, provided activities ranging from athletic programs and facilities to outings and social events."[6]

A 1913 survey conducted by the U.S. Bureau of Labor Statistics indicated that more than half of the fifty–one firms polled offered some form of employee recreation.

During World War I, industrial recreation programs grew rapidly as a means of recruiting and holding employees in war industries. Some cities formed industrial recreation associations, like New Haven, Connecticut which established the Industrial Recreation Federation in 1919.

Industrial recreation programs and services continued to spread during the "Golden Twenties." The number of companies offering recreation to their employees increased slowly and steadily as a means of improving employee–employer relations.

To sell the recreation concept to business, it had to be shown to be of some value, in terms of dollars and cents, to management. Soon, executives of many companies became convinced that recreation would benefit not only the employee but the company as well.

The problem of funding industrial recreation programs generally went unsolved since management was not yet convinced of their effectiveness in terms of dollars and cents. "An extremely novel approach to funding them was developed," reported Malmquist. "The vending machine was beginning to be commonplace in our factories and office buildings. Since it was the employee's money that went into these machines, it stood to reason that the employees should reap the benefits of any profit from them."[7]

In a 1957 survey of 900 large companies, it was found that approximately 50 percent of them relied on profits from their vending machines to help finance their activities. Since that time several alternative ways of financing these programs have evolved, but as Malmquist wrote, vending machines still play an important part in the funding of employee recreation programs.[8]

Gradually, businesses and industrial firms began to share the burden of financing the programs with the employees. In some cases the company has assumed the entire bill. In 1960, two-hundred-and-forty of the country's leading companies spent about $50 million for recreation services, facilities, and staff operations. In 1977, the number of companies involved numbered well over fifty thousand and they spent close to $3 billion to exercise, entertain, and educate their employees.[9]

However, the shortcomings of untrained leaders became increasingly obvious. The great majority of the leaders lacked specific training in recreation management. Purdue University, under the direction of Floyd R. Eastwood, set up the first program for a degree for professional industrial recreation workers. The creation of full–time professional positions increased steadily.

The National Industrial Recreation Association (NIRA) was incorporated in 1941 as a nonprofit association to represent and foster business, industry, and governmental employee recreation programs. NIRA has steadily grown in membership, service, and recognition to become today the only organization of its type in this sector of recreation and leisure services. Since the industrial sector offers a variety of services which are not limited to the leisure field, the organization will soon be known as the National Employees Services Association.

By 1963 the National Industrial Recreation Association had grown in total membership to more than eight–hundred large corporations. The *New York Times* in 1975 reported that, "Despite a severe economic slump, 500,000 private concerns throughout the United States were spending $2 billion a year on recreation–related programs."[10]

Industrial recreation which started as a questionable venture in employee relations was now firmly established as an important management function in American industry. Carlson, MacLean, Deppe, and Peterson wrote that "Employee unions and management alike began developing facilities which not only housed ongoing athletic programs but also served a broader range of leisure pursuits, including cultural, social and educational activities."[11]

VALUES AND BENEFITS

There are numerous values and benefits of a well–organized employee recreation program, including the following:

1. Promoting employee efficiency.
2. Improving employer–employee relations.
3. Helping employees consume surplus energy and relieve pressure and emotions.
4. Boosting morale of both labor and management.
5. Providing incentive for employment and recruitment appeal.
6. Promoting greater employee stability and motivation.
7. Establishing good community relations and cooperation.
8. Promoting low absenteeism.

ADMINISTRATIVE PATTERNS

There is no single administrative pattern prevalent among companies, simply because companies vary so greatly in structure and working forces. Kraus listed a number of typical arrangements:

1. The company takes complete responsibility for an organized recreation program, providing facilities and leadership, and maintaining control of the operation.
2. Facilities or a capital outlay for developing areas and facilities are provided by the employer. Management and employees, however, share responsibility for operating the program.
3. The employees are in total charge of the program, but the employer may provide the facilities.
4. An independent employees' association has complete responsibility for the recreation program and uses facilities that it has developed away from the plant.

Figure 15–3 Today an executive's lunchtime is just as likely to consist of two sets of tennis as a couple of cocktails. Tennis lessons for Xerox employees are another popular part of the company's recreation program. (Courtesy Xerox International Center for Training and Management Development.)

5. A union operates a program of employee recreation, by using union–owned buildings, campsites, or other facilities.
6. Under a contractual agreement, a cooperative program between the company and the surrounding community may be established in which the industrial recreation program may make use of public facilities.[12]

FINANCES

Operating costs for recreation programs vary almost as widely as the programs themselves. "While some programs have annual budgets of more than $750,000, others manage on less than $5,000," wrote Mary Tuthill. "The average is about $11,000, according to a recent study."[13]

Most employee recreation programs are

financed through a combination of the following methods:

1. Company financing.
2. Employee recreation association dues.
3. Admissions, charges, and fees.
4. Profits from vending machines, snack bars, canteens, etc.
5. Activity dues or assessments.

More and more, companies are participating in the organizing, staffing, and financing of recreation programs. However, the new fitness center at Lockheed–Sunnyvale is being totally paid for by the employees themselves, via a no–interest $200,000 loan from the company. Annual memberships and program fees will repay the company in about four years or less. The same funds used to pay for the fitness center will continue to be available after the loan is paid off. The same loan process can then be used for future development.

How much of the cost a company picks up varies. Many directors of industrial programs feel that employees should be required to pay something so they value the benefit more.

PROGRAMS AND FACILITIES

Industrial recreation programs use the same major categories as municipal recreation. Some companies promote sports and physical fitness, while others emphasize clubs, classes, social events, crafts, or special interest groups. Additional employees services include tickets and hotel reservations, discounts, merchandise, RV parking, and corporate child care.

Sports leagues were the principal reason most early industrial recreation councils were founded. Today, sports leagues are more popular than ever. The Oakland Industrial Recreation Association, for example, sponsors employee leagues in basketball, volleyball, and softball. It also sponsors instruction programs for tennis and badminton. In Phoenix, the Industrial Recreation Association sponsors leagues in basketball, slow–pitch softball, and golf.

Industrial recreation programs must emphasize variety, not only physical activities but mental as well. Developing the mental and physical well–being of the employee should be the prime purpose of the program.

"There must be an ever on–going program of services, that not only are beneficial to the employee, but are enjoyed by his or her family as well," said Melvin C. Byers. "These benefits can be classified as beneficial from economic, convenience, educational or healthful aspects."[14]

Syncrude Corporation in Alberta, Canada provides a wide range of facilities for twenty–three hundred workers. These include a gymnasium with a full size basketball court, a weight room, a pool hall, ping–pong tables, a card room for table games, a women's recreation hall, an outdoor arena, and a softball and soccer field.

A noon hour fitness break has been added to the Syncrude recreation program, following a successful pilot program. Vince Alit, recreation director at Syncrude's North Camp, explained: "Essentially, the program involves a stimulating ten–minute period of exercises which can be done in an office or conference room without special clothing or equipment. Participants felt they were physically and mentally better and have requested continuation of the program."

An increasing number of city and county recreation departments are co–sponsoring special programs with industrial and business groups. Many companies are assisting in the sponsorship of sports programs and tournaments, summer shows and concerts, portable programming, and similar events. Substantial subsidies are being provided by companies.

TYPES OF SERVICES

A diversified program of activities, events, and services is the key to the success of an industrial recreation program. This is because each employee possesses various de-

EXAMPLES OF SUCCESSFUL PROGRAMS

Several examples of diversified industrial recreation programs are:

Lockheed Employees' Recreation Association, Sunnyvale, California

LERA, as it is more commonly called, became incorporated in 1963 as a non–profit tax exempt organization. It has the unique distinction of not only being an industrial community recreation program, but a world–wide program as well.

According to Eric Ovlen, Executive Director, "The purpose of LERA is to foster, conduct, and coordinate the social, educational, recreational, and athletic activities of the employees of Lockheed Missiles & Space Company, Inc." LERA is managed by a professional staff which is guided by an employee elected Board of Directors.

All company employees are members of LERA as long as they remain employed at LMSC. Spouses, children, and dependents of employees living in the same household may also share in the activities of LERA as associate members. Honorary memberships are given to retired employees of Lockheed Aircraft Corporation and LMSC.

A nine–person staff directs a wide range of activities, including forty–two special interest clubs (e.g., archery, bowling), golf and tennis tournaments, picnics, trips, tours and cruises. LERA also provides a central ticket office which sells tickets to many cultural events, commercial amusements and entertainment, sporting events, and hotel accommodations.

Building 160 contains the main offices of LERA, and from here the professional staff administers a complete world–wide program. Other facilities within the building include offices for the staff, a ticket office, 300 seat auditorium, complete photography laboratory, fully equipped amateur radio station, martial arts room, lounge, small kitchen, and conference room.

The newest facility is the new 3,000 square foot LERA Family Fitness Center which includes locker and shower facilities for men and women, as well as an exercise room. Health and fitness classes include relaxation and stress reduction, yoga, aerobics, dance–exercise, fitness assessment, exercise, and weight control programs.

Building 162 contains the meeting rooms for the various clubs that are a part of LERA. There is a complete indoor, ten–lane, small bore rifle and pistol range equipped with automatic targets, a fully equipped lapidary shop, a ceramic lab complete with kilns, a model railroad layout, and meeting rooms. In addition, LERA owns seven airplanes for the use of the flying club which are kept at the San Jose Airport.

LERA also provides for noon–hour recreation. Equipment that may be requested and issued without charge includes playing cards (both bridge and pinochle), chess, checkers, cribbage, and table tennis.

The majority of the clubs meet in the LERA building complex once a month with a few meetings every week. They are classified according to interests— cultural, hobby, outdoors, sports, aquatics, and aviation.

Sports and physical fitness play an important role in the activities at LERA. With the cooperation of the Fremont School District and the Sunnyvale Parks and Recreation Department facilities, LERA has been able to provide a well–rounded athletic program. Softball competition for men and women begins in April and runs through October. Bas-

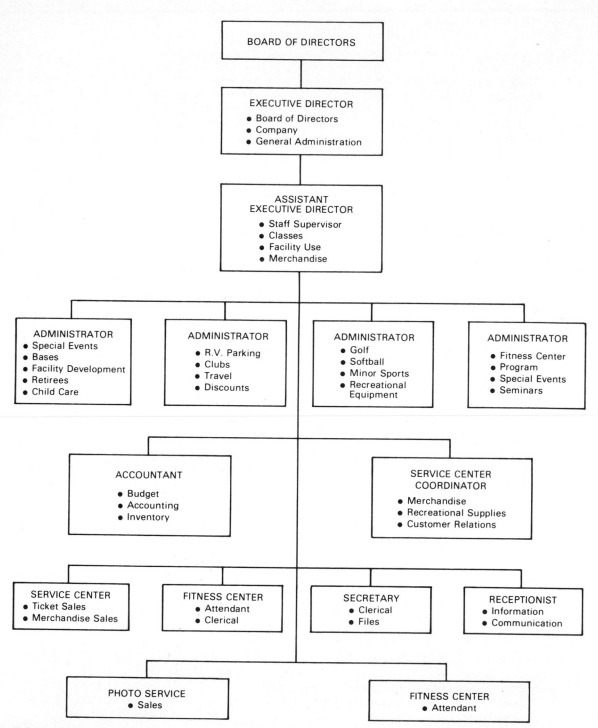

Figure 15–4   Organizational chart of the Lockheed Employees' Recreation Association, Sunnyvale, NIRA's award-winning program in 1980.

competition for men and women begins in April and runs through October. Basketball and volleyball is offered during the winter months of November through March. The LERA golf program runs year–round averaging twenty–three tournaments per year. The bowling program involves four leagues from September through May. There are also programs in tennis, judo, table tennis, soccer, and badminton that are held on a weekly basis throughout the year.

Texas Instruments, Inc. (Dallas, Texas)

A nonprofit corporation for employees of Texas Instruments, Inc., the Texins Association is owned by the employees and managed by a thirteen–member board of directors. However, the company gives a large annual contribution. All employees and their families are eligible on a fee membership basis.

The Texins Association employs a full–time staff of ten and various part–time people. The staff is headed by Richard M. Brown, general manager, who reports to the board.

Activities, services, and even facilities offered by the Texins Association are dictated by the interests and needs of the employees. Activities range from general sports, athletics, and hobbies to social and cultural functions and mental skill development. Indeed, the Texins program is what the employee wants and is willing to support.

Figure 15–5 Employees of Texas Instruments have available to them one of the finest employee recreation programs in industry. They call it Texins Association. (Courtesy Texas Instruments, Inc.)

All Texins clubs are managed by an executive committee and officers elected by their members. These people are all volunteers. There are currently seventeen different clubs within the Texins Association, ranging from the archery club to the engineer's wives club. The bass, divers, gem and mineral, Texoma, and rod & gun clubs are very popular at Texas Instruments.

The Texins intramural athletics program include major sports such as bowling, softball, flag football, volleyball, and basketball, and are offered on a men's, women's, or mixed league basis.

The Texins Texoma Club occupies sixty–six acres at the tip of Preston Peninsula on Lake Texoma. This family recreation park offers facilities for boating, swimming, fishing, camping, picnicking, and sports activities such as softball, volleyball, croquet, and horseshoes. Class and instruction offerings include painting, investments, speed reading, tennis, crafts, and belly dancing.

Xerox, Leesburg

The impressive Xerox–Leesburg, Virginia recreation facilities reflect the company's belief that a physically fit employee is a mentally fit, productive employee. Situated on 2,265 beautifully wooded acres on the Potomac River, the unique facility is called the Xerox International Center for Training and Management Development. The function of the center is to educate Xerox men and women in sales, service, and management development programs. They reside at the center for periods of one to four weeks.

To meet the need for outlets for releasing stress and tension, the training center includes a carefully planned Physical Fitness and Recreation Center which is open seven days a week. Sports and leisure activities are numerous at the center, including racquetball, basketball, swimming, volleyball, tennis, table games, and many more. Both indoor and outdoor jogging tracks, as well as an outdoor swimming pool are provided. Indoor facilities include an exercise room with mechanical treadmills, ergometers, and a sixteen–station circuit trainer.

According to Brent Arnold, manager of the elaborate center, "Our program is committed to providing meaningful experiences to participants at all levels: instructional skills classes, tournaments, or activities for the nonathletic individual."

Figure 15–6 Sponsorship of sports teams is a popular type of company recreation. This industrial volleyball program at Xerox provides numerous benefits to the employees and trainees who participate. (Courtesy Xerox Corporation.)

grees of ability, skill level, related past experiences and preferred interests.

EMPLOY, in its September 1978 issue on industrial recreation, categorized services into the following four types:[15]

Instructional The majority of instructional classes are designed to educate the beginner in a particular activity. Programs include: 1) physical fitness; 2) sports activity; 3) arts, drama, and music; and 4) adult education.

Social/Cultural Cultural programs are prepared to develop creativity. Social activities include travel, dances, picnics, theater outings, sports events, and the Christmas party. Noon–hour or lunchtime recreation can be another important responsibility, unless employees elect a thirty–minute lunch period. Table games, cards, table tennis, pool, dart boards, and television are often provided in employee lounges and cafeterias.

Physical Fitness Through fitness programs, employees are able to lose weight, obtain a lower heartbeat, and lower their blood pressure.

Sports and Athletics These activities provide employees with competitive outlets or low–key team or individual competition. Programs range from intramural and industrial league teams, contests, and tournaments, to special sports clubs, activities, and experiences. Noon–hour recreation activities offer volleyball, swimming, shuffleboard, handball, jogging, and tennis.

Corporate childcare is expected to become a viable component within the program of employee services. A growing trend, child care will impact a whole lifestyle.

FITNESS BOOM

The fitness boom has invaded business and industry. For thousands of employees across the nation in offices, board rooms, and factories, the coffee break has turned into an exercise session. The facilities range from access to the nearby YMCA to the building of elaborate company gymnasiums. M. G. Sholtis wrote that "Executives who used to linger over lunch are collaborating these days on the jogging path. And companies that once provided no more than an annual office picnic are installing gymnasiums and other physical fitness facilities on their premises."[16]

"At offices and plants across the country, a growing number of workers are jogging, swimming, playing handball and tennis and doing calisthenics—all with the support and encouragement of their employers."[17]

The spread of company–sponsored physical fitness programs is rapidly becoming a big fringe benefit at hundreds of firms. Rolm Corporation in Santa Clara, California, has opened an elaborate facility for its 2,000 workers. Inside are two racquetball–handball courts, an exercise room, a game room, a sauna, a steam bath, and a hot tub. Outside are two pools, a volleyball court, two lighted

Figure 15–7 A well–equipped physical fitness center is one of the most popular facilities a company recreation program can offer. Hundreds of corporations now have employee fitness programs and facilities. Here, Xerox Corporation employees and trainees at the Fitness and Recreation Center are shown exercising on the circuit weight trainer. (Courtesy Xerox Corporation.)

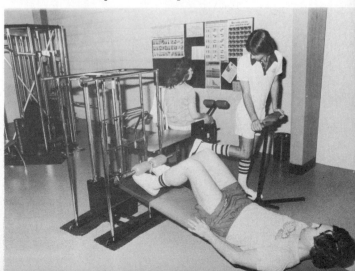

tennis courts, a basketball half-court, an 880-yard track, and an exercise course.

Getting employees to adopt healthy lifestyles is the primary aim of such programs—not just to exercise. Company executives are finding that it is good business to keep their employees feeling good and on the job, so they can do a more effective job. In Canada, the federal government has provided major support to the drive to increase cardiovascular and aerobic fitness programs in business settings.

The benefits of exercise are being recognized by private industry, which loses an estimated fifty-two million workdays to heart disease and $1 billion to common backaches in lost output each year. As Mary L. Tuthill explained: "Studies produced in several countries indicate that workers who took part in regular exercise were in better general health, were absent less, and produced more."[18]

CLUBS

Employee clubs have been one the most popular areas of programming, with the variety as diverse as the leisure industry itself. Noon-hour recreation programs in the past have taken full advantage of a somewhat captive audience, offering a variety of activity and entertainment. However, since an increasing number of employees are preferring thirty-minute lunch periods, the noon-hour may soon be receiving less emphasis by industrial recreators.[19]

Among the clubs sponsored by the Convair Recreation Association of General Dynamics are:

Ceramics	Hi Fi	Camera
Sculpture	Square Dance	Science
Table Tennis	Toastmaster	Wives
Fishing	Chess	Bridge
Ballroom	Model Railroad	Sports Car

Figure 15–8 Special interest classes such as this karate activity are offered throughout the year by the Lockheed Employees' Recreation Association in Sunnyvale. The Kung Fu Club is one of the many clubs organized by LERA. (Courtesy Lockheed Employees' Recreation Association.)

SERVING RETIRED EMPLOYEES

Unions are becoming increasingly aware of the need to serve their retired members. Unions, increasingly, are offering their older members courses in preparing for retirement, with emphasis on developing leisure skills and resources, along with other units on retirement finances, housing, and health problems. "Recognizing the trauma associated with retirement," Frank Guadagnolo pointed out that, "industry is now attempting to provide the retiree or alumnus with various opportunities in company involvement, thus reducing the degree of disengagement."[20]

An excellent example of a company's concern for their employees who have retired is the program offered by Raytheon Company of Andover, Massachusetts. All retiring employees are involved in a series of pre–retirement counseling programs.

CLUSTER–JOINT EFFORT PROGRAMS

A potential development area for new positions is in the large number of small business and industrial plants in the U.S. and Canada that employ one hundred workers or less. According to Curtis, "at least 25,000 of these plants exist, but it is quite unlikely that they will ever employ full–time recreation persons to work with their 35, 55, or 75 employees. Instead, they are beginning to realize the advantage of pooling their recreation and physical fitness needs in clusters of four or five companies."[21]

Curtis advised a young unemployed recreation person in the Chicago area to create her own job by using the cluster/pooling technique. In describing her success, she reported that: "I visited fifteen industrial plants, all near each other in a large industrial park, and all employing from 50 to 250 people each. None had any recreation personnel, and very few had more than a semblance of a recreation program. After a month's effort, I convinced six firms to contract with me for $2,000 each for one year. I promised them, not a full–time program, but approximately one–third time program, plus training of their own volunteers. I utilized my $12,000 budget as follows: salary for me, $8,000; second–hand van, $800; movie projector, sound system and player, other hardware, $1,000. The balance, $2,200, I am using for part–time leadership to help me, plus stationery, printing, postage, etc."[22]

Through a joint effort, employees of several companies can be combined into various programs and activities. The same "clustering" technique can be applied to sport leagues, drama club, dances, hobby groups, arts and crafts, and numerous other activities.

QUESTIONS FOR DISCUSSION

1. Why is employee recreation such a growing trend among business and industrial firms across the nation?
2. Who benefits from a well organized employee recreation program?
3. Develop a brief rationale which would justify making recreation an important component in industrial personnel services.
4. Identify the primary values and benefits of a well organized employee recreation program.
5. List the four major types of services conducted by industrial recreation programs.
6. What methods are generally used to finance employee recreation programs?
7. Discuss the rapidly growing nationwide interest in company–sponsored physical fitness programs.

8. What is the primary aim of such programs?
9. Describe briefly the increasing awareness by unions and industrial firms of the need to serve their retired members.
10. Basically, what is the new "cluster/pooling" technique that appears to be growing in practice on behalf of small businesses and industrial plants?

REFERENCES

1. Eric Ovlen, "Summary Reports of Four SPRE Community College Workshops," National Recreation and Park Association, July 17, 1978, p. 16.
2. Steven C. Malmquist, "Industrial Recreation in America Today: Its Purpose, Applications and Benefits," prepared for HPER 270 course, St. Mary's College, Moraga, Calif., July 24, 1977, p. 1.
3. Melvin C. Byers, "Why Industrial Recreation?" *Proceedings and Papers, the First World Conference*, World Leisure and Recreation Association, New York, 1978, p. 275.
4. Norman Sklarewitz, "Business Trends," *California Magazine*, November 1978, p. 122.
5. Mary Tuthill, "All Work and Enough Play Keep Employees Fit," *Nation's Business*, November 1979, p. 82.
6. Richard Kraus, *Recreation Today—Program Planning and Leadership*, 2nd ed. (Santa Monica, Ca.: Goodyear Publishing Company, 1977), p. 263.
7. Malmquist, "Industrial Recreation in America," p. 4.
8. Ibid.
9. Ibid.
10. Nadine Brozan, "Company Recreation, Now It's More Than Softball," The *New York Times*, November 25, 1975, p. 34.
11. Reynold Carlson, Janet MacLean, Theodore Deppe, and James Peterson, *Recreation and Leisure, The Changing Scene*, 3rd ed. (Belmont, Ca.: Wadsworth Publishing Company, Inc., 1979), p. 177.
12. Kraus, *Recreation Today—Program Planning and Leadership*, 2nd ed., pp. 265–66.
13. Tuthill, "All Work and Enough Play," p. 87.
14. Byers, "Why Industrial Recreation?", p. 276.
15. "Industrial Recreation," *EMPLOY*, A Service of the National Recreation and Park Association, September 1978, p. 3.
16. M. G. Sholtis, "Fitness Boom." *Leisure Today*, JOPER, April 1979, p. 14.
17. "As Companies Jump on Fitness Bandwagon," *U.S. News & World Report*, January 28, 1980, p. 36.
18. Tuthill, "All Work and Enough Play," p. 84.
19. Geoffrey Godbey, *Recreation, Park and Leisure Services* (Philadelphia: W. B. Saunders Company, 1978), pp. 180–81.
20. Godbey, *Recreation, Park and Leisure Services*, p. 181.
21. Joseph E. Curtis, *Recreation—Theory and Practice*, (St. Louis: C. V. Mosby Company, 1979), p. 75.
22. Ibid., p. 76.

Figure 16–1 Participatory recreation still receives major program emphasis with youth–serving organizations such as the YMCA. Four–year–old Julie Acres receives expert help from Barbara Godfrey, an experienced gymnastics instructor. (Courtesy H. A. Schaden.)

16
Voluntary/Youth Serving Agencies

Voluntary agencies in America, both national and local, have traditionally played an important role in serving the recreation needs of the community. Increasingly, this sector in the recreation and leisure services field is being referred to as nonprofit leisure agencies. These include youth–serving organizations, special interest organizations, religious affiliated agencies, settlement houses, community centers, antipoverty organizations, and similar other groups.

Voluntary agencies are nongovernmental, nonprofit organizations which have been established to meet important social needs, including recreation and leisure services. Operating costs are usually derived from contributions, fees, charges, and membership dues. Many voluntary agencies also have a share in the United Fund, Community Chest, or other charitable fund raising efforts. In addition, many receive strong support from public funds for special programs.

"Tax–exempt, yet not tax–supported, independent, yet in varying degrees related to government, these organizations evolved to meet needs that were not met by government," wrote Carlson, Deppe, MacLean and Peterson. "Those that have continued over the years have responded to the changing demands of society, experimenting, offering new approaches, and revising their goals."[1]

Recreation, informal education and group services continue to be a major concern of the voluntary sector. Youth and young adults continue to be the central concern of private nonprofit agencies. Services to preschool children and elderly people are increasing.

New programs aimed at social adjustment are beginning to receive more attention. These programs are aimed specifically at troubled youths, youthful offenders, service groups, and special health problems.

Voluntary agencies operating in urban areas, however, are finding it increasingly difficult to upgrade, maintain, and operate their building–centered facilities. Due to rising costs and the loss of middle–class support, some of these agencies have had to close their inner city facilities.

CHARACTERISTICS OF VOLUNTARY AGENCIES

Organizations in the community considered as voluntary generally have the following characteristics:

1. Membership and administrative control are voluntary.
2. Funding relies heavily on public contributions.
3. Community organizations are designed to meet the expressed social needs of neighborhood residents.
4. Leadership is typically nonprofessional, under the direction of professionally trained administrators and a lay board.

TYPES OF VOLUNTARY AGENCIES

Richard Kraus categorized voluntary agencies into the following types:

1. Youth–serving organizations.
2. Religious social agencies.
3. Settlement houses and community centers.
4. Antipoverty organizations.
5. Special interest organizations.

6. Agencies serving special populations.
7. Professional organizations serving the recreation and park field.[2]

YOUTH–SERVING ORGANIZATIONS

Recreation has played an important role in the programs of most voluntary youth–serving organizations. In most cases, they have been very active in the provision of recreational services. Thousands of young people throughout the world are served daily by the various nonprofit youth organizations whose total membership totals more than thirty million people.

The values of recreation in enriching life, improving physical and mental health, and promoting good fellowship are so apparent that its place in youth–serving organizations seems secure. Helping young boys and girls realize their full growth potential continues to be a major goal of youth–serving agencies.

Youth–serving agencies organized at the local community level are usually designated as local voluntary organizations. Primarily oriented toward children and youth, their services are generally classified as facility, outreach, outdoor, or religious.

The professional leaders, supervisors, and administrators who are employed in this field need to have special training and a special preparation for employment. Nearly eighteen hundred new professionals are needed each year by national youth agencies to continue meeting the needs of young people.

Functioning directly through local branches or chapters, youth–serving groups, through the years, have placed prime emphasis in such goals as social development and good citizenship. Generally, they have provided a diversity of programs in recreation activity.

Most youth organizations have become more responsive to community needs. For example, Camp Fire Girls opened their membership in its Horizon Clubs to boys. Conversely, Boys' Clubs started enrolling girls, and Boy Scouts has admitted girls to

Figure 16–2 The many values of recreation, such as promoting good fellowship, social development, and physical and mental health have had a positive influence on the lives of millions of youth served by youth–serving agencies. The Big and Little Brother, Big and Little Sister relationships, as shown here, have worked remarkable changes in children involved in the program. (Courtesy Big Brothers/Big Sisters, Inc.)

its Explorer Posts. Many agencies are providing vocational guidance for older youth.

Increasingly, youth agencies are helping to solve social problems through work with the poor, people with handicaps, juvenile delinquents, and racial minorities.

BACKGROUND OF YOUTH–SERVING AGENCIES

The mid–nineteenth century is generally regarded as the era in which youth–serving agencies first began. The first agency organized to serve youth was the Young Men's Christian Association (YMCA), founded in England in the 1840s, and established in America in 1851 in Boston. The Young Women's Christian Association (YWCA) started in Boston in 1866.

Strong religious organizations for youth followed under the sponsorship of the National Jewish Welfare Board. Patterned on the Christian Associations, young men's and women's Hebrew associations were formed in the 1850s–1870s. Many of the Ys became a part of the strong Jewish community center movement which followed World War I and includes B'nai B'rith youth organizations, established in the mid–1920s.

Other important organized movements also developed during the closing years of the nineteenth century. As early as 1887, settlement houses were established as a social and recreation service agency. Hull House which opened in 1889 in Chicago under the direction of Jane Addams, "provided not only supervised playground types of activities but became a center for both social pleasure and talent development."[3]

After the Amateur Athletic Union was established in the late 1880s small ethnic group communities stabilized and began to foster all types of club organizations, usually focused on sports. The most popular were the Turnverein societies, the New York Knickerbocker clubs (baseball), and the Westchester Polo Club.

The Boys' Clubs united in 1906, while Girls' Clubs did not formally unite until 1945. The organization of Woodcraft Indians (Rangers) was founded in 1902, and was one of the forerunners to Lord Baden–Powell's Boy Scouts of America, established in 1910. Juliette Gordon Low founded the Girl Scouts of America in 1912, modeled after Lady Baden–Powell's English Girl Guides. The incorporation of early rural youth into the 4–H program, established in 1916, was the result of the Smith–Lever Congressional Act. The Camp Fire Girls organization was established by the Luther Gulicks in 1910, followed by the younger Blue Birds group in 1913.

Other youth–serving agencies established in the early 1900s were the American Youth Hostels, Inc., Salvation Army youth programs, the Pioneer Girls, the Christian Service Brigade, and the Young Life and American Youth Foundations.

The age groups for which most recreation youth–serving agencies were organized ranged between six and eighteen. While the scope of the program activities varied among the organizations, major emphasis has been on the development of good citizenship and character building.

ORGANIZATIONAL STRUCTURE

The typical organizational pattern for youth–serving agencies involves a central national office with a specialized professional staff. The regional offices usually cover more than one state, often as many as eight or ten. Each regional office has a number of distinct units under its jurisdiction.

Typically, a national office is guided by a board of directors, all of whom are lay personnel. The board appoints an executive director who employs a professional staff at the central office. Such functions as fund raising, public relations, and finance are the responsibilities of those at the central office.

Financial support of such organizations as the YMCA is generally as follows:

30% United Way
30% Fees and Charges
30% Memberships
10% Miscellaneous (foundation proposals, grants, governmental funding, special projects, etc.)

The organizational structure of the Girl Scouts, for example, includes six regional offices that are staffed professionally with directors and accompanying staff. Each regional office is responsible to the national office and serves as a liaison to its councils. The two major functions of the regional offices are training, for both professional staff and volunteers, and the development of program materials.

SCOUTING USA

In the United States, more than four million scouts and more than one million adults participate regularly in 430 local councils, while the worldwide scouting movement involves more than one hundred other countries. The Boy Scouts were organized in England in 1908 by Sir Robert Baden–Powell. Two years later, the Boy Scouts of America was founded in 1910. Its national council operates through an extensive system of regional councils and local units. Although programs of community service are promoted, the scouting program is based chiefly on the appeal of the outdoors and organized camping.

Typically, Scout programs stress mental and physical fitness, vocational and social development, and the enrichment of youth hobbies and prevocational interests. They have relied heavily on outdoor adventure and scouting skills and on community service activities. The original Scouting program emphasis on outdoor adventure and skills has been broadened to include urban activities.

With a new name, Scouting USA is attempting to meet the needs of contemporary youth. Requirements have been modified for mentally and physically retarded youngsters. Twelve skill award areas are now provided to members. Scouting is an outdoor program for boys 11–17. A boy progresses from Scout to Tenderfoot to Second Class to First Class and can earn merit badges to advance through Star, Life, and Eagle awards.

Figure 16–3 Map and compass is taught by Eagle Scout Mark Leinmiller of Marietta, Georgia (center) at Philmont Scout Ranch and Explorer Base, Cimarron, New Mexico. The rangers at Philmont, one of Scouting's "High Adventure" bases, are a specially trained cadre of young men and women whose job it is to assist the crews as they arrive, get oriented, and set out on the trail. (Courtesy Scouting/USA.)

More than three thousand professional scout executives and regional staff members are employed in the Scout organization, but the bulk of actual Scout leadership is provided by parents and other interested adult volunteers. Sponsored by committees of influential citizens, each troop is led by a volunteer adult scout master.

The Scouting program operates through three main divisions:

Cub Scouts   A home–centered program, mothers and fathers help boys from seven through eleven years of age progress from Bobcat to Wolf and Bear. They can become Webelos at age ten.

Scouting   An outdoor program for boys eleven to eighteen years of age.

Exploring   A contemporary program for boys and girls and young men and women ages fifteen through twenty in vocational explorations, outdoor adventures, service, social activities, personal fitness, and citizenship, with attention given to special–interest groups.

Financial Support

The national organization is supported largely through the annual registration fee paid by each boy and adult plus income from the sale of Scouting equipment, bequests, and special gifts. Local councils are supported by communities through the United Way, sustaining membership enrollment, bequests, and special contributions.

The national office of Scouting USA has been moved from New Jersey to Texas. The new address is: P.O. Box 61030, Dallas/Fort Worth Airport, Texas 75261.

GIRL SCOUTS USA

As the largest girls' youth–membership organization, the Girl Scouts program is dedicated to the purpose of helping girls between seven and seventeen prepare for responsibilities both in the home and in the community. The Girl Scouts today have approximately 3.5 million members in 355 councils. They remain an all–girl organization as a result of a 1975 decision not to admit boys as members.

The Girl Scouts provides a sequential program of activities centered around the home, the arts, and the outdoors, with emphasis on character and citizenship development, community service, international understanding, health, and safety.

Like the Boy Scouts, Girl Scouts today conduct many special programs for the poor, the physically handicapped, mentally retarded, and emotionally disturbed.

The Girl Scouts program is adapted to the needs and interests of four age groupings:

Brownie Scouts   For girls of ages six and eight, Brownies meet weekly with their leaders, usually at school, homes, or churches for parties, games, crafts, trips, and camping. They accomplish the Brownie "Bs" (Be Discoverers, Be Ready Helpers, and Be Friendmakers).

Junior Girl Scouts   A program for girls of ages nine, ten, and eleven, Junior Scouts are organized into groups of from twenty to thirty–two girls. Troops are divided into patrols of six to eight members each, with a patrol leader in charge.

Cadette Girl Scouts   For girls of ages twelve to fourteen, Cadettes face four challenges that test their performances in real–life situations: 1) social dependability; 2) emergency preparedness; 3) active citizenship; and 4) Girl Scout promise.

Senior Girl Scouts   Senior Scouts, for high school girls between fourteen and seventeen, concentrate on special interests and name their troops accordingly, such as the Mariners, Trail Blazers, and Explorers. Service to others and vocational exploration are two of the primary purposes of the Senior Scouts program.

Another area of Girl Scouting is the Campus Girl Scouts program through which college students serve the community.

The national office of Girl Scouts is located at 830 Third Avenue, New York, New York, 10022.

CAMP FIRE

The Camp Fire program helps young people to develop their uniqueness as individuals, to share and plan with others, and to take responsibility for their actions. The purpose of Camp Fire, Inc. is to provide, through a program of informal education, opportunities for youth to realize their potential and to function effectively as caring, self–directed individuals responsible to themselves and to others.

The national organization was founded in 1910 by Dr. and Mrs. Luther Halsey Gulick along with other educators who saw a need to provide leisure–time, recreational, and informal educational activities for girls. Camp Fire has continually made changes and adaptations to update its own programs. The most recent change was made in 1975 when the national structure was changed to allow each community the flexibility of meeting each council's particular needs, including the recruitment of boys into the program. The traditional program was expanded by providing more variety and flexibility, such as drop–in and daycare programs, coed activities, adult enrichment and career development seminars, and special programs for people with handicaps.

Camp Fire which serves girls and boys, ages 6 to 18, is divided into four club levels:

Blue Bird clubs For girls or boys in the first through third grades, members have fun learning to make things, learning about nature and the outdoors, going to interesting places, and making friends.

Adventure clubs For girls or boys in the fourth through sixth grades, adventurers develop new skills in creative arts, sports, citizenship, outdoor living, science home arts, and business.

Discovery clubs For girls or boys in junior high school, members learn problem solving and decision–making, focusing on current social and personal issues.

Horizon clubs Club members of high school age are encouraged to explore opportunities for career directions and hobbies, home and family life, working with others by giving service and sharing expertise. The national office of Camp Fire, Inc. is located at 4601 Madison Avenue, Kansas City, Missouri 64112.

Figure 16–4 The use of voluntary leadership is perhaps the most distinguishing characteristic of youth–serving agencies. While paid leaders handle the administrative responsibilities, the face–to–face leadership has been performed by volunteers, such as this Camp Fire adult leader.

BOYS' CLUBS OF AMERICA

Founded in 1906 and serving today nearly one million boys aged seven to fifteen, this organization is concerned with youth from low–income families and poor neighborhoods. The Boys' Clubs of America is one of the fastest–growing youth movements in the United States, with more than eleven hundred clubs in more than seven hundred cities and towns.

The national goals and objectives of the Boys' Clubs include the following: citizenship education and leadership development; fitness, health, and preparation for leisure time; educational–vocational motivation, intergroup understanding and value development; and enrichment of family and community life.

The recreation oriented programs offer sports and games, arts and crafts, camping, and social activities, in addition to services in work training, job placement, remedial education, and guidance. Boys' Clubs often extend services to older and younger boys, girls, and even the elderly.

Boys' Clubs of America is located at 771 First Avenue, New York, New York 10017.

GIRLS CLUBS OF AMERICA

Founded in 1945, the Girls Clubs of America is a nationwide federation of centers that provides girls with opportunities to recognize their worth as human beings, develop their talents and abilities, and prepare for adulthood. A Girls Club is unique in that it is open every day—after school, in the evening, on Saturday, and during the summer.

There are more than 258 affiliated clubs in 128 cities, serving more than 215,000 girls from six to eighteen. Statistics in 1977 show that 92 percent of the members are from families with an annual income of under $10,000; 49 percent represent minority groups.

Girls Clubs in 34 states offer programs in tutoring and specialized learning, physical fitness and team sports, career development, performing and fine arts, health and sexuality education, parenting and homemaking skills, and individual and group counseling.

Affiliated clubs are independent incorporated units funded by local community funds, dues from member clubs, as well as by individual, corporation, and foundation contributions. Government and private foundation grants are secured by the Girls Clubs of America for national programs as well as training, seminars, and workshops for member Girls Club staff and board members.

Girls Clubs provide daily programs of varied activities, including homecraft, music, art, games, good grooming, health, community service, camping, and outdoor summer programs.

The national office of Girls Clubs of America is located at: 133 East 62nd Street, New York, New York 10021.

YMCA (YOUNG MEN'S CHRISTIAN ASSOCIATION)

Established in 1851, the Young Men's Christian Association (YMCA) is the oldest youth–serving agency of a national scope. Dedicated to Christian ideals, it is concerned with citizenship training, promotion of physical fitness and health, world peace, community welfare, wholesome social life, and recreation.

There are approximately fifteen hundred associations serving communities, institutions, and colleges, with a total membership of more than two million members and associates. Each local YMCA is a self–governing unit affiliated with other YMCAs throughout the nation through the National Council.

Physical education and recreation are deeply rooted in the YMCA program. However, the image and program emphasis of the YMCA has changed significantly in recent years. Kenneth Briggs wrote that "Without discarding its physical education program, the Y has over the last decade adopted new goals, shifting from its old role as a 'service station' for Christian youth to one as an active advocate of such social causes as racial tolerance, improved health care and better juvenile justice."[4]

The YMCA program stresses social activities, informal education programs such as crafts and dramatics, forums, public affairs groups, occupational guidance services, and seminars on preparation for marriage and adult life. Featuring Hi–Y Clubs for boys through high school age, YMCA programs include numerous banquets, sports, and craft events for appropriate age groups.

With strong emphasis in outdoor living, the YMCA operates more than four hundred residence camps and twelve hundred day camps for all age groups. Increasingly, the YMCA and YWCA both are working closely with other organizations in joint programs. YMCA programs and services are reaching out beyond the scope of Y facilities and into schools, churches, and community centers.

Much of the YMCAs youth work involves the following groups and clubs: Y–Indian Guides (six to nine–year–old boys and their fathers); Y–Indian Princesses (six to nine–year–old girls and their fathers); Y–Indian Maidens (six to nine–year–old girls and their mothers); and Y–Trailblazers (boys older than nine years of age and their fathers).

Gra–Y (boys) and Tri–Gra–Y (girls) include youngsters from nine through twelve years of age. Junior Hi–Y and Junior Tri–Y are clubs for boys and girls in seventh through ninth grades. Hi–Y, Tri–Hi–Y, and Co–Ed–Hi–Y are for high school youth who engage in a wide range of activities.

Adult Clubs

In addition to the men's service clubs, the YMCA sponsors international management clubs for supervisors and managers in business, clubs for older adults and young married couples, and clubs for single parents.

For more information about the YMCA, write to the Young Men's Christian Association, 291 Broadway, New York, New York 10007.

YWCA (YOUNG WOMEN'S CHRISTIAN ASSOCIATION)

Although not affiliated with the YMCA, the Young Women's Christian Association (YWCA) provides similar programs and services. The YWCA was established in 1885 in London to meet the needs of young women going to work in the cities. The YWCA's informal groupwork with girls and women has involved a variety of educational, religious, and social activities.

Most YWCAs offer a wide range of instructional classes in all sorts of physical activities, sports and dance skills, aquatics, fine and performing arts, crafts, hobbies, personal enrichment, business skills, and club activity at various age levels.

Primarily, the program serves high school girls in Y–Teens, women in industry clubs, and groups for women in various businesses and professions. Membership in the YWCA is open to any female older than twelve years of age. Today, there are more than nine million members, in nearly two thousand local associations in the United States. Most members are between fifteen and thirty–five years old. More than three hundred and ten thousand boys and men are associates of the YWCA.

Y–Teens are twelve to seventeen–year–old members who participate through interest groups, clubs, classes, co–ed recreation centers, health activities, and camping.

Various social, cultural, and recreation programs are carried on by community associations. The wide range of YWCA classes feature homemaking, shorthand, typing, and Bible study. Recreation activities include arts and crafts, swimming, volleyball, bowling, dramatics, and music. Outdoor activities such as camping are very popular.

The national office of the YWCA is located at 600 Lexington Avenue, New York, New York 10027.

BIG BROTHERS/BIG SISTERS

Big Brothers/Big Sisters, Inc. is a volunteer organization whose purpose is to match a man with a fatherless boy or a woman with a motherless girl so that the adult can be a companion, friend, and guide.

Philadelphia is the national headquarters of Big Brother/Big Sisters of America (BB/BSA). The organization was created in June 1977 through the merger of two formerly separate agencies—Big Brothers of America, founded in Cincinnati in 1903, and Big Sisters International, founded in New York in 1908.

The Problem

There are more than seven million children in this country between the ages of six and eighteen who live in single–parent homes. Twenty percent of all children in this country currently live with only one parent, and their numbers are increasing each year. What these children have in common is that they are lonely and in need of a warm dependable friendship of a Big Brother or Big Sister.

The Concept

The Big Brother/Big Sister concept is simple—match the young girl or boy with a mature, stable adult who can provide regular guidance, understanding, and acceptance. The aim is not to find a parent substitute in the child's life, but rather, a very special, long–term friend in whom the child can confide and whose behavior he or she can emulate.

Men and women who volunteer as Big Brothers or Big Sisters are screened carefully to assure their qualifications and suitability. The goal of their relationships is friendship, companionship, and social interaction.

The national office of Big Brothers/Big Sisters, Inc. is located at: 117 South 17th Street, Suite 1200, Philadelphia, Pennsylvania 19103.

4–H CLUBS

Though subsidized by public funds, 4–H is a voluntary membership organization composed of nearly one hundred and thirty thousand clubs and guided by five hundred and fifty thousand adult and teenage leaders trained by professional, county expansion agents. Today, 4–H has more than 5.5 million members who come from farms and rural areas, as well as from the suburbs and the inner city. A survey in 1975 showed that only 23 percent of its members lived on farms, while 40 percent lived in towns with less than ten thousand population and in open country.

Today about two–thirds of 4–H funds come from taxes and the remainder from private sources. A nongovernment agency, the National 4–H Council derives private support at the national level.

The 4–H idea, with adaptations, has spread to more than eighty countries. Through the International 4–H Youth Exchange, young Americans may visit other countries and young foreigners may live and work with American farm families.

The primary purpose of the 4–H Club organization is to promote better living in primarily agricultural and rural areas and cities. Under volunteer adult leaders, each local club develops activities such as demonstrations, judging events, exhibits, and recreational events. The members of each club plan their own program, elect officers, conduct meetings, and carry out their projects under the guidance of adult and teen leaders. In agricultural activities, a 4–H member may raise a calf or grow an acre of crops. In homemaking, a club member may learn to sew a dress or make a family meal.

For further information, write: 4–H Clubs, Extension Service, Department of Agriculture, Washington, D.C. 20250.

JUNIOR ACHIEVEMENT

Founded in 1919, this organization serves more than three hundred thousand youth who learn about free enterprise. The success of 4–H Clubs prompted Horace Moses, president of the Strathmore Paper Company in Springfield, Massachusetts, to ask: "Why not apply the same principles of 'learning by doing' to the business world?"[5]

The basic unit of Junior Achievement is the company. A company is usually made up of about fifteen members and is advised by three adults. These adult advisors are volunteers from business or industry in the community. The young people of the company make up their board of directors, labor force, sales staff, and any other positions which are needed.

Members of Junior Achievement develop a realistic understanding of the organization and operation of a business enterprise. They build self–confidence and develop leadership ability.

Junior Achievement is supported financially by more than seventy thousand subscribers, mainly corporations and business people. More than nine hundred field staff, aided by twenty–seven thousand volunteers, administer programs in one thousand communities.

The national office of Junior Achievement is located at 909 Third Avenue, New York, New York 10022.

CATHOLIC YOUTH ORGANIZATION

Providing spiritual, social, and recreational services, the Catholic Youth Organization (CYO) is the leading Catholic agency for young people in the United States.

CYO originated as early as the 1930s when a number of dioceses under the leadership of Bishop Sheil of Chicago experimented with various forms of youth organizations, but it was not officially established as a national organization until 1951.

Through participation in CYO activities, Catholic youth are involved in retreats, religious education, and other activities to strengthen and enrich their faith. Leisure and the creative recreational involvement of young people is recognized by CYO leaders as having strong potential for both social and spiritual growth.

The social programs have proven valuable in attracting and involving young people in center activities, which helps the priest and his staff maintain meaningful contact with the young people.

Sports have a strong priority in CYO programs, not only as a means of attracting young people but as a way to impart desirable spiritual values. "Sports, well understood and practiced . . . contributes to the development of the whole person because it demands generous effort, careful self–control, mastery of self and respect for others, complete commitment and team spirit."[6]

Many of the recreational programs are sponsored directly by the CYO at various centers or administered and financed by diocesan headquarters. Other activities take place at specific parishes under the direction of parish priests.

POLICE ATHLETIC LEAGUE

Established originally in New York City to serve disadvantaged youth in urban slums, Police Athletic Leagues today are sponsored in more than one hundred cities.

Police Athletic Leagues provide extensive recreation programming, indoor centers, and summer play–streets, with a strong emphasis on sports and games.

Operating chiefly in poverty areas, they also maintain placement and counseling services which provide job training and assist school dropouts. Much of their funding assistance comes from voluntary contributions, although technical assistance and cooperation is rendered by various municipal police departments.

AMERICAN RED CROSS

In peace as well as in war, the American Red Cross has provided recreation to the United States armed forces and has conducted extensive hospital recreation programs. The nation's outstanding disaster relief agency has worked very closely with the federal government.

Red Cross lifesaving, water safety, and first aid courses have made water sports safer and more satisfying, particularly to those who receive certification by meeting requirements.

Red Cross youth programs for children from elementary grades through high school encourage international friendships, community service, and health and safety programs. Children become members by participating in programs or contributing to the Red Cross Youth Service Programs Fund.

The national headquarters of the American Red Cross is: 17th and D Streets, N.W., Washington, D.C. 20006.

USO (UNITED SERVICE ORGANIZATIONS)

The USO was organized in 1941 as a cooperative venture of six national agencies: Jewish Welfare Board, Salvation Army, Catholic Community Service, YMCA, YWCA, and the National Traveler's Aid. The USO operates clubs for men and women in the armed forces. During World War II, as well as in Korea and Vietnam, the USO provided outstanding entertainment for the fighting forces overseas, with the strong support of Hollywood stars, headed by Bob Hope.

Programs today include not only recreation and entertainment at USO Centers but also aid in housing and counseling, family programs, and various other services.

YMHA AND YWHA (YOUNG MEN'S AND YOUNG WOMEN'S HEBREW ASSOCIATION)

Like the YMCA and YWCA, the Jewish Ys are not regarded primarily as recreation agencies, but rather as community organizations devoted to social service.

Characterized by a strong Jewish cultural component, the purpose of the YMHA and YWHA revolve around the following basic functions:

1. Meeting the leisure–time social, cultural, and recreational needs of its membership.
2. Teaching leadership responsibility and democratic process through group participation.
3. Stimulating individual growth and personality development through group and community participation.

4. Encouraging citizenship education and responsibility.
5. Providing guidance services, including individual counseling.

This national organization identifies social group work as its major professional discipline. Typical program activities include a nursery school, an after–school and summer camp program for children, and a varied assortment of social, athletic, and cultural activities for all age groups.

The program emphasis of the Jewish Ys perhaps has been the two broad areas of sports and physical fitness and cultural arts. The cultural activities at many of their centers include extensive programs in the performing arts, graphic arts, poetry, and other creative endeavors.

SPECIAL–INTEREST ORGANIZATIONS

These organizations comprise another major type of voluntary agency which promotes activities and public support for a particular type of recreation. Many special–interest organizations are developed on a national basis with full–time staff members who handle promotional efforts and press for favorable legislation and public action. Organizations of this type are often found in athletics, the arts, music, drama, and theater.

Sports, Fitness, and Play

An increasing number of special–interest organizations are promoting specific types of recreational interests, fitness and play on a nationwide basis.

National Jogging Association The National Jogging Association (NJA) was founded in 1968 on the basic premise that "Jogging is the most practical and economical way for the greatest number of people to achieve and maintain physical fitness." A nonprofit, tax–exempt educational organization, the association receives no government funding and depends upon membership dues for its basic support. NJA's challenge programs, free distribution of jogging information packets, and sponsorship of National Jogging Day are part of the association's expanding public service program.

The New Games Foundation A nonprofit, educational organization, the foundation communicates a style of play encouraging participation, trust, and creativity. It serves a seed function by teaching the skills and concepts of New Games refereeing in cities across the country.

Created in 1974, the foundation has offered New Games trainings and presentations in more than ninety cities, thirty–nine

states, and five foreign countries. The foundation also provides New Games literature, equipment, and materials. The New Games Foundation Training Program is offered in cooperation with the National Recreation and Park Association and made possible, in part, by a grant from The Charles Stewart Mott Foundation.

New Games is a new approach to play combining elements of traditional games and sports with new understandings about human relations. "When we play New Games," said Pat Harrington, "we seek joy as well as challenge. We care about the fun of playing, rather than the outcome. Because everyone, regardless of ability, can have fun, anyone can play New Games."[7]

Further information can be obtained by

Figure 16–5 New games stress participation, not competition. People try to get to the other side before the parachute is brought down around them. Popular among all age groups, it is one of many new games where emphasis is on participation. (Courtesy Oakland County Parks and Recreation Commission, Michigan.)

writing: The New Games Foundation, P.O. Box 7901, San Francisco, California 94120; Telephone (415) 664–6900.

Hershey Track and Field for Youth Across the country, youngsters, aged nine to fifteen, take part each year in Hershey's National Track and Field Youth Program set up by local parks and recreation departments. Approximately 2.5 million boys and girls participate in the local events, with the winners going on to compete in district and state meets. State winners are then selected, based on their scores, to be members of the regional teams. The regional winners each receive an expense–paid trip to the national finals held in August in Charleston, West Virginia.

Youth Sports Organizations The following is a list of additional organizations which serve the sports needs of youth:

- Amateur Athletic Union
- American Bowling Congress
- American Youth Soccer Organization
- National Junior Tennis League, Inc.
- National Youth baseball programs which include: Little League, Inc., Babe Ruth, Legion, Pony–Colt
- Pop Warner Football
- United States Soccer Federation
- United States Tennis Association
- Youth Basketball Association

Outdoor Recreation and Conservation

There are numerous examples of special interest organizations with a special concern for outdoor recreation and conservation.

American Youth Hostels The American Youth Hostels (AYH) is a nonprofit organization which gained much of its impetus from the European hostel movement. The primary purpose of the youth hostels is to help all, especially young people, gain a greater understanding of the world and its people, through outdoor activities, educational and recreational travel, and related programs.

The youth hostels maintain centers that provide simple overnight accommodations in scenic, historical, and cultural areas.

Hosteling offers young people a way to experience the world for themselves—on two feet, two wheels, or via public transportation—while taking advantage of lodging provided by hostels. Traditionally, bicycling has been the primary means of travel for hostel dwellers, although in getting to the starting point of a trip, other forms of transportation are used.

There are thirty–one local AYH councils in the United States which sponsor varied adventure trips and excursions for young people, and give leadership training in ski–touring, camping, snowshoeing, sailing, canoeing and rafting, and similar activities.

American Youth Hostels, Inc., is located at: 20 West 17th Street, New York, New York 10011.

Appalachian Mountain Club Founded on a regional basis in the East in 1876, this organization's purpose was initially to "explore the mountains of New England and adjacent regions . . . for scientific and artistic purposes, and . . . to cultivate an interest in geographical studies."[8] Although practical conservation is still a primary concern, the club has also acquired numerous camp properties, published maps and guides, and maintained hundreds of miles of trails and a network of shelters and huts throughout the White Mountains for use by its members.

The club has promoted many outdoor sports such as skiing, mountain climbing, snowshoeing, smooth and white–water canoeing, and rock climbing. Their programs of instruction and leadership training have set high standards of expertise.

Keep America Beautiful, Inc. A national, nonprofit, public service organization, Keep America Beautiful, Inc. (KAB) was founded in 1953 to prevent littering and to encourage the individual to accept personal responsibility for a sound environment. Today, KAB is meeting these objectives through the CLEAN COMMUNITY SYSTEM (CCS).

KAB is funded by citizen members and more than one–hundred companies, trade associations, and labor unions. As KABs major program, CCS has been responsible for changing community attitudes about loose trash and improving waste–handling practices, resulting in sustained litter reductions of up to 70 percent.

For further information contact: Keep America Beautiful, Inc., 99 Park Avenue, New York, New York 10016.

National Audubon Society The National Audubon Society was established in the United States in 1905. It strives to advance public understanding of the values and wise use of natural resources. The society sponsors four nature camps in the United States which are dedicated to developing in adults (particularly teachers) an appreciation for nature and a sense of responsibility for the protection of natural resources.

The society owns and operates a number of land and water bird sanctuaries. These sanctuaries are visited by millions of people each year. It also does wildlife research, operates model nature centers, and publishes educational materials, such as the Audubon bimonthly magazine.

The national office of the society is: 1130 Fifth Avenue, New York, New York 10028.

National Campers and Hikers Association The National Campers and Hikers Association is recognized as the largest international family camping organization in North America. The association was established in 1954 for the purpose of educating the public about the conservation of natural resources and especially about the use and values of the outdoors. Among its functions is the promotion of varied forms of camping and hiking, as well as offering services in trip planning and campsite locations. Its monthly magazine is entitled *Camping Guide*.

The national office of the association is: 7172 Transit Road, Buffalo, New York 14221.

National Wildlife Federation The National Wildlife Federation, the nation's larg-
est conservation organization, was organized in 1936 for the purpose of encouraging the intelligent management of the life–sustaining resources of the earth—its soil, water, forest, plant life, and wildlife—and to promote and encourage the pursuit of knowledge, appreciation, and wise use of these resources.

The federation has eight hundred thousand national members and it classifies an additional 3.7 million people as members of state affiliates and other subsidiaries, or as contributors.

It sponsors an extensive educational program and provides, free of charge, much educational material, including the *National Wildlife Magazine*, a bimonthly publication.

The national office is located at: 1412 16th Street, N.W., Washington, D.C. 20036.

Sierra Club Founded in 1892 and headed by the famous naturalist John Muir

Figure 16–6 Appreciation for nature. This nature talk was given to children on the shore of the Chattanooga River in Sumter National Forest in South Carolina. Many special interest organizations are dedicated to developing in youth and adults a sense of responsibility for the protection of natural resources. (Courtesy U.S. Forest Service.)

during its first two decades, the Sierra Club, in the words of Lawrence E. Davies, has sought to make Americans aware "of what we have lost and can lose during 200 years of continuing exploitation of our resources."[9]

The Sierra Club had its first outing in 1901 when 200 people were taken to Yosemite in the Sierra Nevada. Four years later, Yosemite Valley became protected and was added to the National Park as a direct result of Muir and the Sierra Club.

The Sierra Club is one of the largest and oldest environmental organizations in the world. Originally, its main activity was the outing program, but over the years, its scope has been broadened to include publishing books on the environment, lobbying for improved conservation legislation, and conducting litigation when the environment is threatened.

For more than three–quarters of a century, the Sierra Club has made the connection that "if you introduce people into the wilderness, you will have a better chance of preserving the wilderness and other natural resources."[10]

The Club is a private organization and is totally self–supporting. It raises $7,500,000 annually from membership dues, private donations, and from its publishing and outing programs. It now has more than one hundred seventy–five thousand members and a paid professional staff of 125, headquartered in San Francisco, with offices in New York, Washington, D.C., and eight other cities in the United States.

ADULT ORGANIZATIONS INTERESTED IN YOUTH

Many community and national civic organizations have provided noteworthy services and active support of youth agencies and organizations. Some of the typical groups are as follows: Kiwanis, Rotary, Lions, and Optimist clubs; the Junior Chamber of Commerce, National Congress of Parents and Teachers, American Legion, American Farm Bureau Federation, Federation of Women's Clubs, Police Athletic Leagues, Na-

tional Grange, and Business and Professional Women's Clubs.

The service club, fraternal order, or lodge has been one of the most influential types of voluntary organizations. Fraternal orders and lodges have increased steadily in numbers in recent years.

ORGANIZATIONS SERVING SPECIAL POPULATIONS

Meeting the needs of individuals with special limitations is another important category of voluntary organizations in American and Canadian communities today. Organizations such as the American Cerebral Palsy Association or the National Association for Retarded Children have been effective in providing special services for the disabled.

There has been a large expansion of Golden Age Clubs and social centers for the aging, many of them established by churches, local service organizations, and other voluntary agencies.

Voluntary organizations have been responsible for the establishment of numerous after–care centers, such as social clubs of halfway houses, to provide counseling, vocational, and social programs for discharged mental patients. Other organizations serve the interests and needs of the blind, deaf, and other people with disabilities.

ORGANIZATIONS SERVING THE DISADVANTAGED

Many voluntary agencies concentrate on meeting the needs of the poor, particularly urban children and youth in slum areas. Although their purpose is similar to that of settlement houses, their functions are somewhat more restricted, with less emphasis on social work leadership and projects.

The Children's Aid Society, founded in 1853 as a nonsectarian agency to provide care for orphaned and destitute children, is a good example of voluntary agencies which serve disadvantaged children and youth. Today, the diverse number of services include childcare, free hot lunches, foster home placement, an adoption service, nurse services, and a free day nursery. Extensive camping opportunities are provided by the society in seven large centers in deprived areas of New York City.

SETTLEMENT HOUSES AND COMMUNITY CENTERS

Operating primarily in disadvantaged areas of major cities, the settlement house has provided a diverse array of recreational services. Founded in the United States in the late nineteenth and early twentieth century, they are generally regarded as social work agencies. In addition to recreation and cultural enrichment goals, approximately two hundred and fifty settlement houses nationwide provide educational, counseling, and health services to those they serve. Funding is now derived from both private and government sources.

LOOKING TO THE FUTURE

Most Americans have a high regard for voluntary youth–serving agencies. The large numbers of men and women who serve as volunteers is indicative of the strong public support for the youth agency movement. As Robert Hanson and Reynold Carlson wrote:

"Parents may not always encourage their own children to be members, but they nevertheless regard membership in youth organizations as important for young people in general."[11]

As society continues to change at a rapid pace, youth agencies, if they are to survive, must continually study social trends, their own functions, and the suitability of their programs to new needs and interests. School and city taxes are setting priorities which are unfavorable to recreation services by governmental agencies. As a result, the donation–supported agencies are experiencing renewed interest in membership and program participation.

"The times are right for agency services," said Patricia Farrell. "What appears to be on the horizon is a return to less expensive ways of providing recreational activity, with an emphasis on people–to–people relationships rather than on sophisticated facilities. Perhaps the young progressive, in the model of Jane Addams and President Kennedy's Peace Corps volunteer, will seek experiences in youth work, volunteering his or her talents to helping young boys and girls realize their full growth potential."[12]

Hanson and Carlson added that: "The problems of our uncertain age gravely challenge the strength of youth agencies. How they meet these challenges will determine the future influence of these organizations on individuals and on the character of American society."[13]

QUESTIONS FOR DISCUSSION

1. Define a voluntary agency or organization.
2. List the primary characteristics of voluntary agencies.
3. Basically, what values of recreation have proven most beneficial to the membership of youth–serving agencies?
4. Discuss several of the most prominent voluntary agencies.
5. Describe briefly the organizational pattern for youth-serving agencies.

6. Discuss the most significant change in the image and program emphasis of the YWCA.
7. Explain briefly the concept of the Big Brother/Big Sister organization.
8. What special–interest organizations have been most prominent in your community?
9. Identify some examples of special–interest organizations which have a special concern for outdoor recreation and conservation.
10. Discuss the future of voluntary/youth–serving agencies. What appears to be on the horizon?

REFERENCES

1. Reynold Carlson, Theodore Deppe, Janet MacLean, and James Peterson, *Recreation and Leisure* (Belmont, Calif.: Wadsworth Publishing Company, 1979), p. 163.
2. Richard Kraus, *Recreation and Leisure in Modern Society*, 2nd ed. (Santa Monica, Calif.: Goodyear Pubishing Company, 1978), pp. 259–60.
3. Geoffrey Godbey, *Recreation and Park and Leisure Services* (Philadelphia: W. B. Saunders Company, 1978), p. 188.
4. Kenneth A. Briggs, "YMCA Branches Stress Social Activism," The *New York Times*, 23 November 1976, p. 1.
5. *Junior Achievement Company Manual*, advisor edition, 5th printing (New York: Junior Achievement, Inc., 1970).
6. *Guidelines for Diocesan/National CYO Coach's Federation* (Washington, D.C.: National CYO Federation, 1976), pp. 1–2.
7. "New Games Training Program" (San Francisco: New Games Foundation, Spring 1979), p. 1.
8. Kraus, *Recreation and Leisure*, 2nd ed., p. 270.
9. Lawrence E. Davies, "Sierra Club Maps Expansion," The *New York Times*, 9 December 1967, p. 52.
10. Gaynor Franklin, "The Sierra Club and Its Outing Program," The First World Conference, World Leisure and Recreation Association, New York, 1978, p. 279.
11. Robert F. Hanson and Reynold E. Carlson, *Organizations for Children and Youth* (Englewood Cliffs, N.J.: Prentice-Hall, Inc., 1972), p. 208.
12. Godbey, *Recreation and Park and Leisure Services*, p. 198.
13. Hanson and Carlson, *Organizations for Children and Youth*, p. 218.

V
Serving the Community

Figure 17–1 A bicycle trip through the park can be an emotionally relaxing and physically stimulating experience. The use of leisure should be an important part of an individual's daily living throughout one's lifetime. (Courtesy Bicycle Manufacturers' Association of America, Inc.)

17
Recreation and the Community

As American life becomes more and more leisure–oriented, the number of settings that provide recreation opportunities and services continue to increase. While each setting or surrounding is involved with its own unique contribution, all exist primarily to meet the needs of the public at large. As the use of leisure time becomes more diverse, society cannot expect governmental and tax–supported agencies to provide all the recreational needs of a community.

Although government is involved with functions that are of broad concern to the entire population, there are many other groups and agencies that are meeting the needs of a particular segment of the population. The home, church, and school, our major social institutions, are assuming a greater role in a rapidly growing society.

Indeed, these and various agencies and organizations are making valuable contributions to the organized recreation movement—contributions that have resulted in higher goals and standards in our use of leisure time.

A variety of other types of sponsors provide recreation programs in the community. These include Boys Clubs, settlement houses, industrial recreation agencies, religiously affiliated agencies, antipoverty groups, and many local and national organizations serving people with handicaps.

In the years ahead, the resources of all kinds of recreation agencies and settings will be needed to serve the increasing leisure–time needs and the growing demand for challenging recreation activities and programs.

Recreation programs and activities take place in many different settings. In addition to parks, playgrounds, and recreation centers, leisure–time activities and experiences are enjoyed in the home, the school, or at work and the church. There are, for example, numerous recreation and leisure activities which can be accomplished in or around the home.

"Churches, municipal agencies, youth–serving organizations, clubs, schools, and even commercial ventures are realizing that each has a responsibility toward uniting the family in recreation," wrote Carlson, MacLean, Deppe, and Peterson. "At the same time, clubs, centers, and other programs for people with special needs are increasing in number."[1]

THE FAMILY

Although modern living has tended to take people away from their homes, the home is still the chief recreation center of millions of American families. Traditionally, the home has been the center of entertainment for the family.

Today's family is still the primary source of developing leisure attitudes of its young members. "Whether children are reared by their parents, relatives, or baby–sitters, it is usually in the home that they receive their first and most lasting set of values and first learn how to play," wrote Carlson, Deppe, MacLean, and Peterson. "Mom and Dad as recreation leaders still outnumber any other category of recreation leadership."[2]

A great variety of relatively new leisure activities has been added to the experience of most families. In fact, Clark Vincent remarked that "It is quite possible that today's family produces more of its own recreation than did the family of fifty or hundred years ago."[3] Millions of dollars are spent each year on sports equipment, cameras, barbecue equipment, camping, and many other family pursuits.

Despite various outside influences such as commercialized leisure, there are still many forms of recreation activity that family members can enjoy together. Geoffrey Godbey and Stanley Parker pointed out that "The home is the place where family members do most of their television viewing, reading, hobby puttering, and general relaxing. Most social contact with relatives and friends occur in the context of the home."[4]

Additional forces having an impact on the quality and pattern of American family life are given by Joseph Curtis: "Early social sophistication of children; women's liberation; heavy television viewing; wide mobility through cars, cycles, and vans; and a highly charged advertising atmosphere are just a few. The result is a fragmented family life and a tendency toward erratic choices of leisure places and things."[5]

The changes occurring in the traditional family group continue to have strong impact on the future of recreation and leisure services. According to Curtis, "There will be an increasing need for family recreation that is cheaper, more exciting, and more convenient to urban neighborhoods."[6]

Figure 17–2 Family fun. Opportunities should be provided in the community for the family to play together. The Daddy–Daughter Date Nite is an annual special event sponsored by the Naperville Park District, Illinois.

THE CHANGING HOUSEHOLD

Today's complex and mobile society definitely has weakened the stability of the family. In doing so, the traditional extended family of parents, grandparents, and grandchildren has been supplemented or replaced by a number of alternative lifestyles. Many children are being reared by one parent. The proportion of children in one–parent households has climbed sharply. There are nearly half as many divorces as marriages today, and the rise in the numbers of unmarried mothers is alarming.

Millions of unmarried Americans have adopted a lifestyle that is affecting every part of the country. The number of people living alone or with unmarried roommates increased more than 40 percent over the past decade. The effects of the "Singles Phenomenon" on housing, business and social life have been extensive.[7]

After retirement, more older people are choosing to keep their homes, travel, or enter retirement communities rather than live with their children. If their health fails, they are more likely to seek care in nursing homes than in their children's homes.

More and more mothers have chosen to work outside the home. As a result, more small children will be reared by close relatives, baby–sitters, and nurseries.

NEED FOR FAMILY UNITY

Recreation can serve to strengthen a family and keep it together. Godbey and Parker wrote that "It is possible to maintain family solidarity and unity of purpose through leisure–time pursuits."[8]

Through a program called "Take a Family Break," the San Marcos Park and Recreation Department has encouraged family unity in recreational activities. "Take a Family Break" is a chart of recreational activities offered as suggestions of things to do together.[9] They include a walk around the neighborhood, climbing hills, planting trees, singing, and going to a movie. The course takes a family a year to complete since it includes seasonal activities such as camping, swimming, going to the beach, and building snowmen. According to Pam Scholl, who developed the program, "Take a Family Break" is an incentive for families to get out together for the purpose of having fun together."[10]

Married couples and families should strive to integrate their leisure and social lifestyles. Of course, the greatest problem in integrating leisure and family styles exists when fam-

ily members differ in their expectations. One cannot assume that all families are alike in their need for leisure or a particular leisure activity. Dennis Orthner wrote that "Failure to establish a leisure pattern appropriate to lifestyle expectations threatens the stability of the family."[11]

Parents who seldom or never play with their children rarely know them completely. Joy and happiness are basic needs that should be satisfied in childhood if the child is to grow normally and become a well–adjusted adult. Consequently, new ways are urgently needed to re–establish the authority and importance of the family. There should be a strong emphasis on services that will strengthen parents and aid the family as a whole. Giving families a chance to perform as families, to mingle with other families, and to learn from them should be one of the major goals of organizations and agencies in the community. "One of the greatest potentials for involving adults with children lies in play and recreation," stated Ruth Tefferteller. "Arousing parental interest in the children's activities through mutual participation in dances, outings, and parties helped a child

Figure 17–3   Play and recreation involving children and their parents can contribute immeasurably to better family relationships and happiness. Here, a mother and her daughters enjoy a "Game of Life."

to build a community of parents and families around these children."[12]

ACTIVITIES AT HOME

Many activities can be conducted at home, in a game room, or in the yard. Table tennis, badminton, and shuffleboard are popular sports suitable for the backyard or driveway. Basketball hoops can be attached easily to a garage. Children can learn to catch and throw baseballs and footballs in the yard or at a nearby playground. A multiple sports area in an ordinary backyard can include a basketball hoop, a solid wall for throwing or hitting against, an open area for croquet, a portable ping–pong table, and badminton posts.

Family recreation does not mean that the entire family must participate in each activity. However, there should be a proper balance of activity and participation in the family recreation program.

"Joint activities, such as game playing, casual conversation, or hiking, require each person to recognize the needs of the others and dialogue becomes necessary for successful participation," wrote Godbey and Parker. "This increases the level of understanding between the participants and reinforces the ability of the family members to adjust to one another in other situations as well."[13]

Many families maintain second homes for summer recreation and vacation use, while for many people, motor homes, campers, and trailers serve as second homes. In addition, family camping clubs and camping facilities are enjoying continued popularity.

Family fun nights at community centers, church family dinners and workshops, and PTA potluck dinners and picnics are all geared to family recreation and enjoyment.

THE SCHOOL

The importance and value of school recreation are becoming more apparent as the need for well organized and diversified recreational programs becomes greater. For years, schools have been involved in outdoor recreation, conservation, and environmental education. Both the public and private schools in the community have provided a great number of leisure experiences for their students. In doing so, they have used their facilities to sponsor and conduct a wide variety of leisure programs and activities.

Schools today are faced with how to prepare people to live in a society in which their leisure hours may surpass their work hours. As Charles Brightbill and Tony Mobley wrote: "The real test of our future school will be its capacity to help the student prepare not only for a work–centered existence but also for a leisure–centered life."[14]

EDUCATION FOR LEISURE

The ability of every citizen to make wise leisure choices is most essential in a society becoming steadily leisure–oriented. The school joins with the home, church, and other agencies in assuming this very important role.

At the present time, we have in our society almost no concept of preparing people for a life of meaningful, significant leisure. We have been culturally conditioned to getting personal satisfaction from "a job well done." We do not even know whether people can accept leisure as a resource for a satisfying way of life. Most people do not know how to use leisure in a creative, positive way without apologies.

To make leisure an asset for a society, we must begin to chip away at the antiquated work ethic and come up with a system in which leisure, not work, is a desirable and socially acceptable goal. If we can teach people to use their leisure without feeling guilty, we will be contributing to positive, mentally healthy attitudes.

According to Carlson, MacLean, Deppe, and Peterson: "Leisure education is a process through which individuals acquire the appropriate attitudes, skills, knowledge, and

Figure 17–4 Educating for leisure. The development of such skills and interests as swimming can lead to the enjoyment of leisure activities. This swimming class was sponsored by the Community School program in Flint, Michigan. (Courtesy of Flint Community Schools, Flint, Michigan.)

behaviors that will allow them to benefit from their leisure choices."[15]

The education for leisure process should include:

1. The development of a sound philosophy of leisure.
2. The development of skills and knowledges that lead to the enjoyment of leisure activities.
3. The creation of desirable attitudes, interests, and habits toward recreation activities and enjoyment.
4. The development of wholesome personalized traits through recreation experiences.
5. Counseling in the wise use of leisure time.

Increasingly, leisure counseling will prove to be a valuable part of leisure education. In the future, the efforts of counselors will be focused on leisure opportunities and choices as well as on occupation or career decisions.

THE SCHOOL'S RESPONSIBILITIES

The major responsibility of the school in the area of recreation is to educate students toward the best use of their leisure time. Indeed, the schools have enormous potential to educate for satisfying use of leisure. Yet, as Carlson, MacLean, Deppe, and Peterson noted, "Educating for leisure is not solely the responsibility of public education. The church, the home, and the park and recreation agencies must accept their responsibilities and obligations."[16] Still, the schools are in a position and have the resources to do much in developing wholesome interests and attitudes toward leisure time.

The school has the important task of helping students acquire lifelong interests, appreciations, and skills in a broad range of recreational activities. Opportunities should then be provided for them to use these acquired recreation skills.

The school has the additional responsibility to provide opportunities in which the various recreation activities taught can be practiced, interests deepened, and skills perfected. Participation in intramural sports, club organization, and the provision of recreational equipment and facilities can provide further enjoyment of these interests.

Education must first become aware of the deep meanings of leisure and recreation. "The most fundamental objective of education is the development of individual human dignity," wrote William R. McKinney. "Education for worthy use of leisure, one of the seven cardinal principles, has the potential to add greatly to man's dignity. Educators must begin to realize that leisure intelligently spent contributes significantly to positive personality development, dynamic physical and mental health, and perhaps most importantly, it is the greatest avenue of learning."[17]

School recreation involves a great many teachers who teach subjects in the areas of the recreation program. With all of its resources, therefore, the school can play and should play an ever increasing role in providing recreation services and opportunities.

Figure 17–5 Various Chicano artists worked on this mural wall, giving students at a New Mexico high school a different sort of learning experience.

In carrying out this function, however, the school should not attempt to duplicate the efforts of other established recreation agencies. Instead, they should seek to coordinate the school's programs with those of other agencies in the community.

Schools can make available their valuable areas and facilities to the total community. School personnel represent some of the strongest sources of community leadership. Teachers can provide valuable resources of skills and leadership that can be utilized in community recreation programs.

A new sense of responsibility relative to education for understanding, protecting,

and using the environment appears to be growing. Educators increasingly are becoming more responsible in helping young people in understanding environmental problems and to seek their solutions.

HISTORY OF THE COMMUNITY SCHOOL

Known as the father of the community school concept, Frank J. Manley planted the seeds for many programs of community and human betterment in the areas of adult education, health, recreation, and job training.

His theory that school facilities should be used on a twenty–four–hour basis for the benefit of the entire community inspired philanthropist Charles Stewart Mott in 1935 to sponsor a summer recreation project which has grown into a concept of community education copied throughout the world.

"Those who knew him best say Manley's greatest talent was leadership, an almost indefinable combination of conviction and personality which inspired his staff and often the rest of the community to try things never tried before."[18]

For many years, the Mott Foundation has allotted funds to educational, health, and charitable projects. Before his death in 1973, Mr. Mott had given away more than $230 million, not counting his allocation of funds to the Mott Foundation.

Through workshops and a large intern program, Flint, Michigan, was made a laboratory for training educators to establish and operate community school programs throughout the nation. Many universities in Michigan and other parts of the country are involved in training community school leaders and setting up community education programs in their areas.

COMMUNITY EDUCATION

Community Education, the growth of which has been spurred by the driving commitment of the Mott Foundation, is a new force in American life. It all started back in 1926 when C. S. Mott established the Mott Foundation, "to maintain a fund and make grants from the fund for educational, health, welfare, cultural, civic and similar purposes which improve individual growth and development and strengthen society."[19]

An increasing number of communities have developed community–school programs, seeking to make the schools the center of neighborhood life by providing educational, recreational, cultural, and social programs and services to meet the needs and interests of all residents. Today, some 464 different school districts with several thousand school buildings are operating community school programs throughout the United States.

What is community education? According to Dr. V. M. "Bill" Kerensky, C. S. Mott Professor of Community Education at Florida Atlantic University, "Community Education is a process. When the people get involved, it is a democracy working at the grass roots level—the final step in what Mr. Mott visualized, building a better community, inventing your own future."[20]

Other educators in the movement think of community education as a philosophy, a conceptual basis for changing the role of the public schools by trying to help communities make maximum use of facilities.

Community education has expanded from the early community school ideal to a broad umbrella for diverse services, including health, recreation, and social welfare programs. The Community School director assigned to each school promotes and coordinates use of the school for adult and youth afterschool educational, recreational, and social enrichment activities.

Programs such as family, education, civic affairs meetings and recreation, counseling, YMCA, Boy Scouts, Girl Scouts, senior citizen activities, and school volunteerism are promoted. The community school concept thus involves the entire community and its resources in a system of cooperation and referral.

Passage of the first federal legislation, "The Community Schools Act," has given additional impetus to the development of community education programs. The emphasis placed upon broad citizen and community service agency involvement augurs well for interagency cooperative action.

The Southfield, Michigan Community Education Program joins the facilities of the Southfield Public Schools System with the organization and resources of the city of Southfield, giving the tax–paying public more efficient use of its school facilities. The program cooperates closely with the Southfield Parks and Recreation Department and the Human Resources Department.

Figure 17–6 The community education concept centers around the idea of keeping school facilities open after hours for use by the community. Through the generous financial support and inspiration of Charles Stewart Mott (pictured here) and the leadership of Frank Manley, the Mott Foundation has been a major force in improving the quality of life in the community. This outdoor ice rink is an example of how school facilities can serve the total community. (Courtesy Flint Community Schools, Flint, Michigan.)

Yet the establishment of community recreation services in community school settings has been hindered since the beginning by some serious problems. Many of the problems have centered around open competition and duplication of services, rather than close cooperative efforts.

Robert Artz pointed out that "A number of community school programs began by immediately establishing recreation programs not in cooperation with local park and recreation agencies, but in competition with

them. Instead of multiplying the possible services to a community, the program has immediately duplicated activities, reproduced facilities already available."[21]

CONCEPTS OF PARK–SCHOOL PLANNING

The park–school concept involves cooperation between school and municipal authorities in the acquisition, development, and operation of properties designated for both school and municipal recreation use.

The public schools, parks, and other public recreation properties belong to the people. Therefore, it is in the best interest of the residents of each district to coordinate, integrate, and consolidate public facilities when basic functions are compatible. Wheaton, Illinois, provides an excellent example of joint development of a long–range educational and recreational program for the residents of the Wheaton Park District and Wheaton–Warrenville Community Unit School District #200. Obtaining the maximum use of facilities is the major aim of the agreement.

Where cities have committed themselves to the park–school concept, development is usually done by one of the following methods:

1. Establishing a park area adjacent to an existing school and developing it for use by either agency.
2. Constructing a school near or even adjacent to an existing park to take advantage of the existing park land.
3. Making adjustments in building design.
4. Eliminating fences that divide parks and adjacent schools.
5. Master–planning school development and park development together, so that when a school is built, adjacent parkland is also purchased.

THE CHURCH

Recreation is assuming an increasingly important role in the programs of the American churches and religious institutions. Many are currently conducting well–rounded recreation programs for their members, and indications are that many more will be placing more emphasis on recreation services in the future.

Geoffrey Godbey and Stanley Parker wrote that "Despite the general decline of religious belief and observance, the various churches and other religious bodies play a substantial part in providing organized lei-

sure facilities for large numbers of people."[22]

Indeed, recreation under religious sponsorship has undergone dramatic changes during the last three decades. As a result, progressive religious leaders are recognizing that one's spiritual life cannot be separated from one's physical, mental, and social life. Play and recreation can be a social force of great potential value for community life.

While the church is no longer the center of leisure activity that it once was in many American communities, churches and synagogues continue to sponsor a wide assortment of leisure activities. Surveying the attitudes of church leaders toward the role of the church in the use of leisure, Tony Mobley and Richard Raus found that these leaders believed that the church should provide for the recreation and leisure needs of its members because wholesome fellowship strengthens the church.[23]

In addition to having its own recreation program, the religious institution has responsibility to further the community recreation program. In doing so, it should cooperate with other community agencies in providing meaningful recreation opportunities of the quality and variety to meet community needs. Whenever possible, church facilities and equipment should be made available for community recreation activities.

An increasing number of religious leaders feel the church recreation and leisure program should take its place along with other church programs, that is, religious education, service, mission work, music, and stewardship. The church hierarchy, to achieve this goal, should employ experienced recreation leaders, recruit trained volunteers, and seek the counsel and guidance of the professional and lay organizations that are the spearheads of the leisure revolution.

Benefits

The provision of meaningful leisure opportunities for church members and their families can be extremely beneficial to their well–being. Brightbill and Mobley wrote: "The new leisure creates a whole new fron-

Figure 17–7 Recreation activities such as this volleyball game have traditionally been a part of church youth fellowship programs. A growing number of religious leaders are now advocating increased emphasis on recreational experiences in the church setting.

tier for religious education, much of it directed toward the potentials of the spiritual life as a means for abundant and satisfying living."[24]

Some of the specific benefits derived include:

1. Creating a stronger church fellowship.
2. Enlistment of new members.
3. Revitalizing church members not previously active.
4. Building character in the areas of cooperation, good sportsmanship, acceptance of responsibility.

Staff

Large churches may be able to afford the services of a professionally qualified recreation director, but small churches may have to use part–time leadership and/or services of volunteers. In some communities, the municipal recreation department might employ a qualified leader to work with religious institutions.

The key to church recreation is the program and not the facility.

Ideally, each church should have a recreation committee to coordinate the recreation activities with the overall church program. The chairperson of this committee could join with chairpeople from other church recreation committees to create a central church recreation committee. This larger committee would represent the various churches in community recreation affairs.

Whenever necessary, the church might employ recreation leaders of its own, or join other churches in securing someone to organize and coordinate recreation activities for those churches represented on the committee. In providing a well–rounded program to the church groups involved, the leader should also train and use the services of volunteers.

Program

The church program should be varied enough to meet the needs and interests of the entire congregation. Essentially, the number and types of activities offered in various faiths and denominations vary with the philosophy of the church, the leadership and facilities available, and the culture and mores of the community.

Churches that wish to operate more effectively in providing recreation services to their congregations should take the following steps:

1. Organize a recreation committee.
2. Carefully survey and estimate recreational needs.
3. Review available facilities and resources.
4. Develop a separate recreation budget.
5. Obtain capable leadership to conduct the recreation activities.
6. Coordinate services and activities with other agencies within the community.[25]

Activities

The following is a list of activities sponsored by religious groups:

1. Social recreation such as picnics, family nights, potluck suppers, game nights, banquets, bazaars, and dances.
2. Vacation Bible schools.
3. Fellowship groups, youth clubs, Scout programs, and adult interest clubs.
4. Sports activities such as softball, basketball, bowling, and volleyball.
5. Arts, crafts, and hobby workshops.
6. Camping, nature study, and other outdoor activities.
7. Study and discussion groups.
8. Volunteer community services.
9. Coffee houses for youth.
10. Cultural activities such as literature, music, and travel.

Churches generally depend upon commercial facilities such as pools, skating rinks, bowling alleys, and campsites. Others reciprocate with recreation agencies by permitting uses of temples and meeting halls for leisure activities.

Many churches operate camp sites. An excellent example of one of California's finest church camps is Calvin Crest, a Presbyterian Conference Center managed jointly by the Presbyteries of San Joaquin and Stockton. Combining Christian education with an attractive outdoor setting and imaginative programming, Calvin Crest offers children from grades four through eight such popular activities as horseback riding, log rafts, log rolling, swimming, nature crafts, fishing, climbing trees, archery, barbecues, and moonlight hikes.

Finance

The financial support for the recreation program usually comes from the church budget. Ideally, it should be the practice of the church to set aside funds and plan a budget for recreation.

The cost of church recreation activities in terms of personal effort and financial support, however, is more than repaid in terms of the spiritual values for which the church stands.

Financing might be done through the following methods:

1. The church budget.
2. Contributions through drives, campaigns, and pledges.
3. Collections, donations, and admission for special events.
4. Sponsorship by the men's club or a church society.

QUESTIONS FOR DISCUSSION

1. In a leisure–oriented society, what should be the role and responsibilities of the family? The school? The church?
2. Describe some of the numerous recreation activities and experiences which occur in these settings.
3. Traditionally, the home has been the center of entertainment for most families in the United States. Will the home remain the chief recreation center for millions of American families?
4. What are some of the values of play and recreation involving children and their parents that contribute to better family relationships and happiness?
5. How can leisure–time pursuits strengthen a family and help keep it together?
6. What is the role of the school in regard to the leisure time of its students and families and residents in the community?
7. What is a community–school? What is the community–school concept?
8. Discuss the community education movement, its goals and objectives.
9. Who has the responsibility for leisure education? What should be included in the education for leisure process?
10. Explain briefly the park–school concept. Why is it in the best interest of the people and the tax dollar?
11. Discuss the role of recreation in the programs of American churches and religious institutions.
12. List three benefits of meaningful leisure opportunities for church members and their families.

REFERENCES

1. Reynold Carlson, Janet MacLean, Theodore Deppe and James Peterson, *Recreation and Leisure—The Changing Scene*, 3rd ed. (Belmont, Calif.: Wadsworth Company, 1979), p. 187.
2. Ibid., pp. 184–85.
3. Clark Vincent, "Mental Health and the Family," *Marriage and the Family*, February 1967.
4. Geoffrey Godbey and Stanley Parker, *Leisure Studies and Services: An Overview* (Philadelphia: W. B. Saunders Company, 1976), p. 80.
5. Joseph E. Curtis, *Recreation—Theory and Practice* (St. Louis: The C. V. Mosby Company, 1979), p. 300.
6. Ibid.
7. "The Singles Phenomenon," *U.S. News & World Report*, April 21, 1977, pp. 57–58.
8. Godbey and Parker, *Leisure Studies and Services*, p. 80.
9. "Take a Family Break," *California Parks & Recreation*, June 1975, p. 29.
10. Ibid.
11. Godbey and Parker, *Leisure Studies and Services*, pp. 85–86.
12. Ruth S. Tellerteller, "Recreation and Family Needs," *Recreation*, November 1963, p. 423.
13. Godbey and Parker, *Leisure Studies and Services*, pp. 80–81.
14. Charles K. Brightbill and Tony A. Mobley, *Educating for Leisure–Centered Living*, 2nd ed. (New York: John Wiley and Sons, 1977), p. 113.
15. Carlson, et al., *Recreation and Leisure*, p. 143.
16. Ibid., p. 158.
17. William R. McKinney, "The Role of Community Education," *Management Strategy*, Vol. 3, No. 3, 1979, pp. 1 and 4.
18. *The Flint Journal*, Booth Newspapers, Inc., Flint, Michigan, June 8, 1972, p. 1.
19. B. Robert Anderson, "Community Education—A Force Whose Time Has Come," Reprinted from *Consumers Power World*, 1975.

20. Ibid.

21. Robert M. Artz, "Cooperation—What the Community School Movement Can't Do Without," *Parks and Recreation Magazine*, October, 1974, pp. 76–78.

22. Godbey and Parker, *Leisure Studies and Services*, p. 52.

23. Tony Mobley and Richard Raus, *A Survey of the Attitudes of Church Leaders* (Field Problem: Indiana University, 1964), p. 45.

24. Brightbill and Mobley, *Educating for Leisure*, p. 110.

25. Richard Kraus, *Recreation Today: Program Planning and Leadership*, 2nd ed. (Santa Monica, Calif.: Goodyear Company, 1977), p. 166.

Figure 18–1 The Special Olympics program has given millions of retarded children and youth a feeling of worth and a measure of fulfillment to their lives. The Special Olympics teaches the mentally retarded to believe in themselves . . . "I can do it!" This scene took place at the First Winter Special Olympics in Michigan. (Courtesy Michigan Special Olympics Committee, Mount Pleasant.)

18
Recreation for Special Groups

There is a growing sensitivity and concern among professional recreators for people who are disadvantaged because of physical or mental limitations or are socially, culturally, or economically deprived. Only within the past decade have those in the recreation and leisure services field taken a serious approach to meeting the needs and interests of these special segments of our society.

There are many reasons why efforts on behalf of our special populations have often been sporadic and ineffective. Thomas Stein and Douglas Sessoms explained that "Lack of funds, shortage of trained leaders, and inappropriate design and/or location of areas and facilities are some of the reasons given by administrators for not providing viable services to many special populations. However, it is suspected that one overriding factor affecting our general lack of service to these groups is that of misunderstanding or lack of knowledge about the psychological, social, and physiological condition of disadvantaged individuals."[1]

Progressively, however, organized recreation is beginning to provide more comprehensive programs, involving stronger leadership and financial support, for such disadvantaged groups as the physically ill and people with handicaps, the mentally ill and retarded, the aged, the economically deprived, and youthful and adult offenders.

Gerald S. O'Morrow wrote: "The term special populations (or groups) describes those individuals who, because of a variety of circumstances, differ from the average in their physical, emotional, social, and intellectual behavior."[2]

Community recreators, in growing numbers, are beginning to recognize both their responsibility to provide services to special populations and the fundamental right of handicapped individuals to receive the services. Indeed, a major challenge of professional recreators during the next quarter of this century will be dealing with the leisure behavior of special populations. If leisure agencies, public as well as private, are to provide recreation for everyone, then they must concern themselves with the needs of *all* special populations.

THERAPEUTIC RECREATION

One of the most rapidly expanding specialized fields within the recreation profession is therapeutic recreation, "generally referring to those recreation services that are provided in relation to recovery or adjustment to illness, disability, or a specific social problem."[3]

The therapeutic recreation movement has expanded its scope considerably. Initially, the field was geared primarily to the needs of psychiatric or other long-term patients in federal, or large, state hospitals. Today, however, the movement provides rehabilitation-oriented services in treatment centers to the physically disabled, the mentally retarded, psychiatric patients, the socially disabled, and dependent aging persons. From the institutionally based program, the trend has been toward a community based one.

According to Elliott M. Avedon, "The phrase 'therapeutic recreation' was first coined to distinguish experiences and services offered to persons in special residential settings who are ill, impaired, or had some degree of disability that prevented them from using recreation resources, services, and experiences offered to the public at large. Later, the phrase referred to services to persons who had special needs, regardless of their place of residence or limitations."[4]

In defining the meaning of therapeutic recreation, Edith L. Ball, wrote: "In most dictionary definitions of the word recreation, the idea of refreshment or re–vitalization is predominant. A secondary consideration is that it is 'pleasing.' The adjective therapeutic is defined as 'the art of healing, remedial.' Putting the two together one could define therapeutic recreation as 'pleasing refreshment that is remedial.' "[5]

The greatest growth in therapeutic recreation services occurred during World War II and in the decade that followed. The successful efforts of the American Red Cross in conducting programs in military hospitals brought attention to the value of therapeutic recreation to both the morale and the treatment of hospitalized servicemen. Immediately following World War II (1945), another landmark in the growth of therapeutic recreation was the establishment of the Recreation Service of the Hospital Services Division within Veteran's Administration (VA) hospitals. In 1960, recreation services were structured within the Recreation Section of the Physical Medicine and Rehabilitation Service of the VA hospitals. Geoffrey Godbey noted that "The programs and professional staffing patterns that were developed in VA hospitals were outstanding, and this national showcase for therapeutic recreation had much to do with the subsequent development of recreation programs in state psychiatric hospitals, state schools for the retarded, physical rehabilitation centers and other types of treatment centers throughout the country."[6]

The National Therapeutic Recreation Society (NTRS) has made significant strides in developing therapeutic recreation into a profession. In particular, it has moved toward improved standards for practitioners by continually upgrading the NTRS registration program. Over the years NTRS has made strong progress in three areas: (1) registration standards, (2) program standards, and (3) university accreditation standards.

Significantly, the Georgia General Assembly in 1980 passed Senate Bill 454 requiring all therapeutic recreators working in medically based settings to hold a license granted by the State Board of Recreation Examiners. The bill makes Georgia the second state to pass such legislation, preceded only by Utah in 1975.

The ill or handicapped present new challenges for society as their numbers continue to grow at an alarming rate. Although there has been a tremendous growth in the numbers of recreation professionals and services in this field, great numbers of disabled individuals are still unserved. Statistics compiled by the National Center for Health Statistics indicate that there are approximately sixty–eight million persons in the United States with limiting or disabling conditions.

Figure 18–2 Therapeutic recreation services. Through their involvement in recreation activities, patients can receive a big emotional and social lift. Here, hospitalized children participate in a special party conducted by the recreation therapist and activity leaders.

SCOPE OF THERAPEUTIC RECREATION SERVICE

There are several major settings in which therapeutic recreation service is provided:

Hospitals of varied sponsorship—Veterans Administration, military, voluntary, state, county, municipal, public health, and others.

Nursing Homes—generally regarded as extended–care facilities for ill or disabled aging persons.

Schools or Residential Centers for Specific Disabilities—offer services to the physically disabled, mentally retarded, or emotionally disturbed.

Special Schools or Treatment Centers for the Socially Deviant—include adult penal institutions and reformatories and special schools for youth.

Homes for Aged Persons—residential centers provide therapeutic services to aged persons.

Centers for Physical Medicine and Rehabilitation—treat those with serious physical disabilities.

Public Recreation and Park Department Programs—have initiated a number of new programs to serve the disabled.

After–Care Centers and Sheltered Workshops—geared particularly to the problems of mental illness, mental retardation, and drug addiction.

Programs of Voluntary Agencies—a number of national organizations promote services for specific groups of people with handicaps.

PHASES IN THE THERAPEUTIC RECREATION PROCESS

While the basic concept of the process suggests it is a unified whole, O'Morrow divided the therapeutic recreation process into four specific steps:

1. An assessment of the special population member's therapeutic recreation needs.

2. The development (planning) of goals for therapeutic recreation action.
3. The implementation of therapeutic recreation action to meet the goals.
4. An evaluation of the effectiveness of therapeutic recreation action.[7]

ROLE OF THE THERAPEUTIC RECREATION SPECIALIST

The primary role of the recreational therapist is to plan, organize, and direct the therapeutic recreational activities in the hospital or community, in accordance with the treatment goals for the individual patients. The therapist works in a medically approved program of varied activities that assist the patients in their personal adjustment and progress. The therapeutic recreation specialist serves as a counselor to patients or clients, an educator in the community, an organizer, researcher, or as a consultant.

MODELS OF THERAPEUTIC RECREATION SERVICE

Gerald S. O'Morrow has outlined five basic models of therapeutic recreation service:

1. *Custodial* Refers to maintaining or acting as guardian for special populations in such institutions as nursing homes, homes for the aged, mental hospitals, special schools for the mentally retarded, and correctional centers.
2. *Medical–Clinical Model* Regarded as the most familiar model for institutionally based recreation service, it is characterized, in O'Morrow's words, by a "doctor–centered, illness–oriented approach to patient care and treatment."
3. *Therapeutic Milieu Model* Using recreation as a significant therapeutic tool in treatment programs, the patient is reeducated in terms of attitudes or modes of behavior that will equip him or her to return to the community, family, job, and other environments.

4. *Education and Training Model* Various forms of activity therapy are used to overcome physical, psychological, or social disability and to equip the patient or client for independent community living.
5. *Community Model* This model implies that a critical aspect of recreation service for the disabled lies in the provision of a wide range of leisure opportunities geared to meeting their needs. Essentially, recreation services are provided by three types of sponsors: (a) public recreation and park departments, (b) voluntary agencies with a specific concern for the disabled, and (c) therapeutic agencies or institutions which serve outpatients or other disabled persons living in the community.[8]

PROGRAM

Well planned recreation programs have proven highly effective in bolstering a patient's morale. Making the patient happier and more cooperative will support the other treatment measures and lead toward a speedier recovery.

Recreation activities for the ill and disabled must be planned in terms of the patient's interests, needs, and capabilities. His or her leisure experiences should be related to the treatment aims, which vary with the illness, disability, and patient.

Activity programs are the backbone of the provision of therapeutic recreation service. Equally as important as activities is leadership.

The following are some of the typical categories of activities in therapeutic recreation:

1. Social activities
2. Entertainment
3. Sports and active games
4. Hobbies
5. Arts and crafts
6. Performing arts
7. Service activities
8. Outdoor recreation
9. Motor activities
10. Special events

LEISURE COUNSELING

In addition to therapeutic recreation services, the need for leisure counseling has been receiving growing attention. Experience has shown that such counseling has contributed to the rehabilitation process by helping individuals deal more effectively with their free time.

Scout Lee Gunn wrote: "Leisure counseling is a helping relationship intended to assist an individual in gathering information, solving problems, and making personal decisions regarding meaningful leisure and play behaviors, values, and pursuits."[9]

With professional guidance and counseling, withdrawn patients in the hospital environment can begin to participate in social–recreational activities. Many rehospitalized patients tend to lapse into solitary ways on discharge; this behavior can reactivate old patterns of pathological behavior. This observation suggests the need for individual guidance through a leisure counseling service.

RECREATION FOR PEOPLE WITH HANDICAPS

One of the most significant social trends of the past two decades has been the changing attitude of the public toward handicapped or disabled persons. While indifference and rejection once characterized the public's attitude, today it is giving way to a genuine concern and positive action by a more responsive society.

In the past, the needs of handicapped people were often overlooked by recreation programs in the community. In far too many communities in the United States, there has been a serious lack of year–round social, cultural, and educational opportunities for children whose physical and mental disabilities have prevented them from taking part in various activities with others of like interests.

As to why municipal parks and recreation agencies have, generally, been slow in starting programs for the handicapped, several basic reasons can be mentioned. First, these

Figure 18–3 By using his mouth to paint, Jimmy Rodolfos, with firm determination, conquered his handicap. An accident suffered while swimming caused a paralysis from his neck down. With diligence and great energy, Rodolfos learned to paint with his mouth. Despite their handicap, he and other artists of the Association support themselves with their paintings. (Courtesy Association of Handicapped Artists, Inc.)

types of services are very costly due to the number of staff required to operate and supervise the program. Additional reasons are the shortage of trained recreation therapists in municipal agencies, lack of transportation to enable people with handicaps to travel to the program, the higher degree of difficulty in preparing and organizing programs for handicapped people, and the general lack of awareness on the part of the agency as to the scope of the needs of people with handicaps.

Increasingly, however, recreational professionals and others concerned with the needs of the disabled have worked tirelessly to improve the opportunities available to them, in both institutional and community settings. Since the White Conference for the Handicapped in 1960, there has been considerable legislation that has compelled the schools and governmental agencies to provide increased services for people with disabilities. As a result, programs of "mainstreaming," "normalization," and deinstitutionalization have been increasing steadily.

States and local districts nationwide are striving to meet the requirements of Public Law 94–142, which requires an individualized educational plan for each child with a handicap so that he or she would only go to a special class as needed. People with handicaps must get equal opportunity to participate in all federally financed programs and activities, under new Department of Health, Education and Welfare guidelines.

The signing into law on October 14, 1978 of the Rehabilitation Services Amendments marked the continuation of the national commitment to equality of opportunity for America's thirty–six million adults, youths, and children with handicaps. The new law, P.L. 95–602, extends and revises the Rehabilitation Act of 1973 and authorizes $4.9 billion over four years for activities to mainstream and enrich the lives of the severely disabled.

The Rehabilitation Act provides individuals with handicaps with the opportunity to obtain independent living services and vocational, rehabilitation, and employment opportunities geared to individual needs and interests. Most importantly, the law emphasizes the critical role of recreation in rehabilitating the ill and disabled.

Definition

In 1960 at the White House Conference on Children and Youth, a child with a handicap was defined as "one who cannot play, learn, work, or do the things other children of his age can do; or is hindered in achieving his full physical, mental, and social potentialities, whether by disability which is initially mild but potentially handicapping or by a serious disability involving several areas of functions with the probability of life–long impairment."[10]

While "handicapped" still refers to people with disabilities, its meaning has changed to describe individuals with degrees of difference physically, mentally, psychologically, and socially. "It no longer refers to the extent of the disability except as that disability limits that person competitively or in reaching a particular objective."[11]

Types of Handicaps

There are many types of handicaps or disabilities for which an increasing number of recreation programs are providing services. They include the blind or partially sighted; the deaf; the cardiac, the diabetic, and the tubercular; the orthopedically and neurologically handicapped; the physically disabled, including amputees, paraplegics, and post–polio patients; people with mental handicaps, and those with physical illnesses of short– or long–term duration who may be home–bound or hospitalized. Other conditions that involve a degree of disability include arthritis, cerebral palsy, multiple sclerosis, and muscular dystrophy.

Needs of the Handicapped

Individuals with handicaps have the same needs as normal persons in our society. In addition, they have special needs stemming from their particular handicap. The ill and the disabled have the same need to belong, to create, to feel secure, to love and be loved, to feel significant, and to experience new adventure.

The following principles were suggested by Janet Pomeroy:

1. People with handicaps have the same basic needs, desires, and rights as all other people.
2. People with physical handicaps should have the opportunity to participate in recreation activities with the people without handicaps whenever this is possible.
3. Activities should be as nearly like those for people without handicaps as possible.[12]

Benefits

Satisfying recreation activities can help relieve tensions, create substitute experiences for meeting basic needs, and serve as a therapeutic aid to mental health. Wholesome recreation opportunities can help make the patient more receptive to treatment through a happier environment. For the physically ill or disabled, recreation activities can provide the needed stimulus to do physical exercise that will improve their health. The patient may gain confidence and self–respect and develop an ability to inter-relate with people again.

Children with physical or mental handicaps who are too severely handicapped to be included in special schools benefit greatly by attending daily programs where they learn to play together. For the first time they experience companionship, self–expression, and achievement. Timid and withdrawn children have responded favorably to group play by laughing and singing.

Adaptation

With imagination and creativity, recreational activities and facilities can be effectively adapted to the needs of people with handicaps. In providing increasing services to the disabled, recreation programs have had to provide transportation for participants, including buses with lifts, buildings with stairs, ramps, and various other adaptations.

Adaptation is a most important factor in program development due to the physical, mental, emotional, and social status of the participant. There are many ways in which recreational activities can be adapted for participation by those with disabilities. One of the most basic is substituting a different body position than is normally used, such as sitting or semi–reclining rather than standing. Substitution of slower movements for faster movements, decreasing distances, reducing the size of the court, and simplifying the activity are other means of adapting activities for the disabled. In addition, players may have the use of oral, visual, and kinesthetic cues.

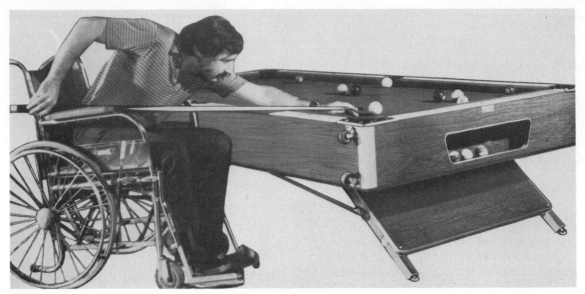

Figure 18–4 Recreational activities and facilities, such as this pocket billiard table which provides an adjustable height from 24 to 30 inches, can be effectively adapted to the needs of handicapped persons. (Courtesy North American Recreation Equipment Company.)

Mainstreaming

Representing a major trend in modern society, mainstreaming is generally regarded as the effort to enable disabled persons to become integrated members of society. Scout Lee Gunn, in describing mainstreaming does not mean that people with handicaps will be "normal" but that they will have every opportunity to fit into society and that society will accept them. People with disabilities need to be moved as close as possible to the "norm" and those people who make up the norm must be educated about the needs of people with handicaps.[13]

However, disabled persons themselves do not always wish to be integrated into community recreation programs. They may not be psychologically ready. True, mainstreaming is a very desirable goal, but it cannot be achieved by administrative decisions or parental pressure alone. Instead, as Kraus observed, it requires a process of careful education, preparation and skilled leadership in order to succeed.[14]

In his study on "Normalization and Recreation Service Delivery Systems," Bernard E. Thorn wrote: "The principle of normalization holds that the most desired placement or service is one that provides the least restrictive and least segregated environment for the handicapped individual while ensuring sufficient support to protect the dignity and rights and meet the special needs of each participant."[15]

"Achieving the principle of normalization cannot be viewed as the simple mainstreaming of the handicapped individual into regular recreation agencies," explained Thorn. "Rather, it is predicated on a continuum of support services that allows for varying degrees of intensities of recreation programs."[16]

Sheltered Programs

Sheltered activities are those with other children having disabilities and will probably always be required for some children and adults with severe degrees of disability. They provide the least restrictive environ-

CENTERS FOR PEOPLE WITH HANDICAPS

An increasing number of recreation centers for people with handicaps are being patterned after the original center, the famed Recreation Center for the Handicapped in San Francisco.

SAN FRANCISCO CENTER FOR THE HANDICAPPED

The idea for establishing the Recreation Center for the Handicapped grew out of the experience Janet Pomeroy gained while a sophomore in junior college and as a volunteer worker at a school for children with severe handicaps in San Mateo County from 1950 to 1952. It was there that she first saw the need for social and cultural opportunities for these children who were excluded from recreational activities provided for children without handicaps. The center was founded in 1952 with six teens with severe handicaps, and today, after three decades of service, it has served more than ten thousand children and adults with severe physical and mental handicaps. Many of them have been mainstreamed into community life.

Under Pomeroy's direction, the center is recognized nationally and internationally as a pioneer and a model in developing community recreation, education, and socialization programs for people with multi-handicaps of all races and creeds. The center is a nonprofit corporation which provides recreation and camping programs for all ages and all types of handicaps, ranging from mildly or profoundly retarded to people with physical handicaps who are not retarded.

Thirty-two different disabling conditions are represented in the current enrollment of more than sixteen hundred. No one is considered too young, too old

Figure 18–5 The recreation center for the handicapped in San Francisco is recognized internationally as a pioneer and a model in developing community recreation programs for the multi–handicapped. Under the direction of its founder, Janet Pomeroy, the Center serves children and adults of all ages and every level and type of disability. (Courtesy Recreation Center for the Handicapped, San Francisco.)

or to have too many handicaps. They come to the center on crutches, in wheelchairs, and even portable gurneys.

Purpose The center provides recreation, socialization, education, and rehabilitation programs for individuals with special needs in the least restrictive environment. The philosophy of the center is based on the principle that the people with handicaps are people first; secondly, they are handicapped.

Staff personnel Headed by a director and coordinator of programs, the professional recreation staff at the center includes five program supervisors; a coordinator of volunteer services; a social worker; a recreation counselor; recreation leaders; specialists in physical fitness, arts and crafts, drama, and music; assistants; aides; and program helpers.

The business staff consists of the business manager, secretaries and clerical workers, coordinator of transportation, drivers, facilities manager, housekeeper, and chief cook. More than two hundred volunteers supplement the regular staff at the center in San Francisco.

"Creating a proper atmosphere sets the stage for successful programming," said Pomeroy. "The attitude an approach of the staff is extremely important in creating a warm and friendly atmosphere."

Lack of adequately trained staff is often mentioned as a barrier to municipal recreation programs for people with handicaps. Yet, according to Pomeroy, it is often a mistake to overemphasize the need for highly trained professionals to administer all recreation programs for people with handicaps. She emphasized that "Experiences of the center have indicated that the amount of special knowledge about the handicapped is nowhere near as important as the ability to adapt and lead activities."[17]

Program Programs at the center are conducted six days each week from 8:00 A.M. to 10:00 P.M. for six major divisions. They include the children's division, day care division, adult division, outreach division, aquatics and physical education.

Outdoor activities are also provided on a day campsite adjacent to the center and at Lake Merced—a nearby zoo, playground, and a beach. Resident camping is provided at La Honda, approximately sixty miles from San Francisco.

Three large buildings consist of the main recreation center facility, a swimming pool complex, and a gymnasium with adapted equipment and a weight lifting room designed for muscle building and stamina training.

The center's broad spectrum of services include:

- Arts and crafts in its well–equipped room with abundant materials and kiln for ceramics.
- Games and physical fitness activities inside and out.
- Social gatherings around the fireplace in the large activity Main Hall.
- Rehearsals and productions of drama and music from the stage.
- Pre–school and day care–readiness for school programs.
- Infant stimulation and early childhood development.
- Picnics and barbecues right outside any door on the patio.
- Meals served from the kitchen—not only nutritious, but also another means of teaching self–help and independent skills for all ages.

Physical fitness activities include recreational and instructional swimming in 86 degree water, tumbling, relays, rope skipping, running, ball and tire games. Field trips are taken to such places of interest as art fairs and festivals, movie theaters, ice and roller skating rinks, and museums.

Outreach Recreation is a mobile satellite program. Inaugerated in 1970 under a grant from the San Francisco Foundation, the outreach program serves individuals, many of whom are bedfast, from infancy to adulthood. Program activities encompass the broad areas of arts and crafts, games, hobbies, adapted physical fitness, music, cooking, drama, trips and excursions, and community service projects.

Transportation Children in wheelchairs, on crutches, and even portable cots are transported from their homes to the center and returned. The recreation center owns and operates 20 buses, which are in operation six days each week from 8:00 A.M. to 11:30 P.M. All buses are equipped with lifts and straps and harnesses for holding bedfast persons.

Finances Twenty–seven percent of the operating budget at the center is raised by staff and the board of directors through personal solicitation of individuals, service clubs and groups, by letter solicitation, and by working with groups who conduct benefits for the center. Fund raising events such as horse shows, luncheons, bazaars, and rummage sales are conducted annually by these groups.

Some funds are received through contractual services from the San Francisco Recreation and Park Department, Golden Gate Regional Center State Department Office of Child Development and the San Francisco Social Services Department. The center is also financed through some federal and state grants received for previously institutionalized persons with mental handicaps and illness.

Figure 18–6   A ramp into the swimming pool at the San Francisco Center for the Handicapped allows wheelchairs and gurneys to deliver the swimmer into the warm therapeutic water. Swimming provides a handicapped person with the type of exercise and a freedom of movement he or she cannot enjoy out of water. The warm water helps strengthen the muscles and improves the circulation and coordination. (Courtesy Recreation Center for the Handicapped, San Francisco.)

ment to develop social and activity skills. Many individuals with disabilities enjoy the opportunity to continue friendships that may have developed in sheltered settings.

Facilities

In recent years, there have been increasing efforts to provide effective access to recreation facilities for individuals with limited mobility such as those with wheelchairs, crutches, and braces. Many federal, state, and local authorities have made significant efforts to make recreation and park facilities accessible to people with physical disabilities.

Federal and state standards are being established that must be observed by municipalities wishing to qualify for assistance in the development of park and recreation facilities. Under these standards, facilities of various types are becoming more accessible, safe, and convenient for the disabled.

RECREATION FOR PEOPLE WITH MENTAL HANDICAPS

Only within the past ten years have organized recreation services for the people with mental handicaps emerged as a major contributing factor to the well–being of this long neglected special group. The recreational and social needs of people with mental handicaps had received very little attention until the early 1960s. In 1962, the President's Panel on Mental Retardation, instituted by President John F. Kennedy, recommended that local communities, in cooperation with federal and state agencies, provide expanded services for children and youth with mental handicaps. This was the first large–scale effort to cope with the problem of mental retardation nationally.

A growing number of communities and counties have since successfully initiated recreation programs and services for people with mental handicaps. Many programs have become a reality through financial aid from the Joseph P. Kennedy Foundation; the National Association for Retarded Children;

the American Association for Health, Physical Education, and Recreation; and the Federal Department of Health, Education, and Welfare.

State and municipal organizations have promoted a variety of services and programs, including vocational rehabilitation, sheltered workshops, education, recreation, and, very important, legislation to serve the needs of people with mental handicaps.

Still, in many communities, there is a definite lack of agencies and programs. While there are signs of increasing activity on the part of public and private recreation agencies, there has been inadequate implementation. Many of the organizations and agencies responsible for developing such programs have demonstrated an unsure approach as to how to implement them.

Hope and love give people with mental handicaps a chance.

What Is Mental Retardation?

As defined by the president's panel on mental retardation, "The mentally retarded are children and adults who, as a result of inadequately developed intelligence, are significantly impaired in their ability to learn and to adapt to the demands of society."[18]

The American Association on Mental Deficiency defined mental retardation as: ". . . subaverage intellectual functioning which originates during the developmental period, and is associated with impairment or inadaptive behavior."[19]

Gerald O'Morrow noted that under this definition, "all three conditions must ensue before a person is labeled mentally retarded."[20] Unfortunately, mental retardation has an organic cause which is incurable. However, mild forms of retardation are curable, in the sense that such individuals can participate in community life, hold jobs, and live as responsible citizens.

From early childhood, the person with a

mental handicap has experienced marked delay and a difficulty in learning and has been relatively ineffective in applying whatever he or she has learned to the problems of ordinary living. He or she needs special training and guidance to make the most of his or her capacities.

Play, which should be a normal aspect of development, is often lacking in the lives of children with mental handicaps. According to Julian U. Stein, "Mentally retarded boys and girls do not play spontaneously or innovate as normal children. They have to be taught to play whether the play be individual, parallel, or group. Many of the motor skills and abilities basic to play and recreation that most normal children learn from association and play with the gang on the block must be taught to the retarded."[21] As the child with a mental handicap experiences success through play, he or she will gain confidence in himself or herself and in his or her ability.

Characteristics of people with mental handicaps vary with the level of retardation. No single individual has all of the same characteristics. Some of the characteristics of the person with a mental handicap are short attention span, immature interests, lack of imagination, deficiencies in the higher mental powers, inadequate learning, and disruptive group behavior. Others may express their insecurity and fear of failure and reproof by withdrawing. They may refuse to be drawn into group activities or participate in any way.

Extent of Retardation

Gene A. Hayes estimated that 3 percent of the population of the United States are mentally retarded and that approximately one hundred and twenty-six thousand children born each year are retarded at birth.[22] Various estimates indicate that half of the people with mental handicaps are children and youth younger than the age of twenty.

According to Fred J. Krause, executive director of the President's Committee on Mental Retardation, "There are approximately six million Americans who, as a result of inad-

equately developed intelligence, are significantly impaired in their ability to learn and to adapt to the demands of society. At least 85 percent of these represent a moderate form of retardation, and a good portion of these children could be taught to function effectively if acted on early."[23]

Classification

The American Association on Mental Deficiency (AAMD) has developed a system of classifying people with mental handicaps in five different groups or categories.[24] Yet, the intelligence quotient by itself can be misleading in determining the capability of a person. It must be used with other measurements of the individual's abilities and potentials.

There are two common classifications of measured intelligence used in the United States. One, the AAMD classification, is divided into five levels of retardation: borderline, mild, moderate, severe, and profound.

A second classification, associated more with education, divides mental retardation into three broad educational subgroups: the educable mentally retarded (EMR), who are pupils approximately in the IQ range of 50 to 80; the trainable mentally retarded (TMR), who obtain IQ scores of from 20 to 49; and the custodial or dependent mentally retarded (CMR or DMR), whose IQ scores are below 20.

"When these two classifications are compared," said O'Morrow, "it would appear that the AAMD classification carries less stigma and has significance not only for differential educational treatment but also for self-sufficiency, use of leisure, and vocational potential. An IQ score is of minimal value in telling us something about the child's physical, emotional, social, and vocational potentialities for total adaptation to his environment."[25]

Causes of Mental Retardation

There are more than two hundred causes related to mental retardation. The causes include the following: problems incurred during pregnancy or in childbirth; genetic or hereditary factors; illness; disease or accident; and social or environmental deprivation.

Gene Hayes said "A great many professional people now believe that the cause of retardation does not have to be either heredity or environment but can be both heredity and environment. A retarded child may become emotionally disturbed as a result of repeated rejection on the part of his parents, other adults, and/or his peer group."[26]

Mothers with a history of chronic alcoholism, extremely heavy smoking or serious drug problems run more risk of premature delivery, low birth weight, and similar problems that often result in mental retardation and other developmental disabilities.

Needs

Those who have served people with mental handicaps have discovered that their needs and aspirations are no different from the normal population. And they have a strong need for love, affection, and understanding. They must have food, shelter, and, if possible, a job.

The person with a mental handicap is unique, however, in that some of his or her needs appear exaggerated. Most people with mental handicaps are slow in learning new skills simply because they do not have the mental ability to do them. Quite often, they must be taught activities by different methods than those used with normal individuals.

Achievement and acceptance stimulate the child with a mental handicap in learning to do things for himself or herself. As he or she experiences success through play, he or she will gain confidence in himself or herself and in his or her ability. He or she will feel more desire, drive, and motivation to take part in a variety of activities.

The majority of children and youth with mental handicaps live with their families. Only the children with more severe handicaps are institutionalized. "The retarded child living at home has little recreation opportunity," wrote Joan Ramm. "He may make friends with the children in his special class at school, but unlike the normal children who can play with their school chums in the neighborhood after school hours, retarded children are transported from their homes in different parts of town and have few friends in their own neighborhoods. Many just sit and watch television."[27]

Objectives

The following are some of the desirable objectives in meeting the psychosocial needs of people with mental handicaps that can be attained through recreation activity programs:

Physical Development

1. Physical health and appearance
2. Balanced growth
3. Improved posture body mechanics, and control of movement

Social Development

1. Better self–care skills
2. Participation with the family
3. Respect for the rights of others
4. Become more sociable, outgoing and friendly

Emotional Development

1. Improved self–confidence and courage
2. Self–image and self–respect
3. Fun and enjoyment
4. Become more independent
5. Greater security in different situations

Staff

Ideally, the recreation program should be directed by a recreation leader who has had direct experience with people with mental handicaps and professional training in the field of therapeutic services. If the leader has not had specialized training, the program may be directed by a qualified recreation leader, assisted by consultants or representatives of community organizations who have sufficient expertise in the field of mental retardation.

The use of a sufficient number of volunteers is highly important to the success of the program. In working with people with mental handicaps, the ratio of staff to participants must be high. Therefore, volunteers should be recruited from colleges and high schools, civic groups, women's auxiliaries, religious groups, fraternal orders, or service clubs. In particular, recreation students from colleges and universities are an excellent source of leaders and aides for programs involving people with mental handicaps.

Parents can be involved in planning the program and providing a limited amount of leadership and services. In-service training, orientation, and on-the-job supervision should be provided for all workers, professional and volunteer alike.

Program Development

Programs for people with mental handicaps should include a wide variety of activities, as well as counseling and personal guidance for participants. Activities should involve ones that need only casual and unstructured participation as well as those that demand careful leadership and instruction. Whenever possible, activities should be integrated, giving people with mental handicaps an opportunity to mix with the non-disabled. Educable people with mental handicaps, particularly, can function quite effectively socially on a higher level.

Programs for people with mental handicaps should help the individual gain confidence in what he or she can accomplish. Activities should be meaningful and geared to the person's needs and capabilities.

In Milwaukee, the disabled are helped to develop skills and to make recreational choices. The goal of many is to leave these sheltered recreation programs behind and join in regular activities. "We don't concentrate on the disabilities," explained Gloria Hoeft, supervisor of the Developmental Activity Program of the Recreation Division.

Developmental activity programs not only provide structural activities for those who need direction in developing recreational

Figure 18–7 This Saturday morning softball program at American River College in Sacramento gives retarded boys and girls the opportunity to play on a team under trained leadership. Since retarded persons are slow in learning new skills, the leader must be patient, helpful, and understanding, as demonstrated here.

skills, such as art, dance, music, sports, and games, but also encourage adults and teens to make their own recreational choices whenever possible.

"An ultimate goal of the institution's recreation program should be to prepare the retarded person so that he may leave the institution and immediately begin to function in the community in his avocational as well as his vocational activities," said Gene Hayes.[28]

Leadership Guidelines

The following guidelines are suggested for leaders working with the people with mental handicaps:

1. Repetition is most essential. People with mental handicaps learn more slowly than people without mental handicaps.

Additional time must be allowed in teaching a skill.

2. Progression is important, beginning with more simple routines.
3. Simplify the rules and regulations and introduce new ones gradually.
4. Demonstrate as much as possible, since the person with a mental handicap learns by imitation.
5. Give instructions clearly, using vivid gestures.
6. Warmth, understanding, and a genuine expression of sincerity and care will do much to establish a positive relationship.
7. Use considerable praise and encouragement. Enable the person with a mental handicap to derive success in his or her participation.
8. Emphasize group activities involving team work and cooperation.
9. Allow for smooth transition from one activity to another.
10. Make it possible for the individual to gain self–satisfaction by accomplishing a task by himself or herself.

Activities for People with Mental Handicaps

Typically, recreation programs for people with mental handicaps have emphasized the following areas of activity:

1. Sports and physical fitness activities
2. Low organized games and contests
3. Creative arts (arts, crafts, music, drama, and dance)
4. Special events and trips
5. Training in living skills
6. Camping and outdoor activities
7. Excursions into the community
8. Entertainment

Bowling Bowling has been one of the most successful sports activities for the person with mental handicaps. Bowling provides much needed physical activity in a desirable social setting. Participants are taught to keep score, as well as keep track of bowling order.

Special Olympics This sports program involves national competition for retarded children and youth throughout U.S. cities. They compete in track and field, swimming, and other events; and ultimately national champions are selected. Funded by the Kennedy Foundation and other public and private sources, the Special Olympics have been sponsored by major cities and have involved thousands of participants.

Diners Club Dining outside the home in a restaurant provides important opportunities to learn and to practice social skills. On his or her visit to a restaurant with a leader, the person with a mental handicap can practice ordering, conversing, and conducting himself or herself in a socially acceptable manner. In acquiring the necessary skills and security, he or she will be able to dine out on his or her own and with his or her family.

Trips Trips for people with mental handicaps can provide many new and satisfying experiences. They can be escorted to baseball and football games and wrestling matches. Visits to zoos, museums, department stores, recreation facilities, and food stores are typical excursions for the person with a mental handicap.

Music Singing and other musical activities are usually included in programs for mentally handicapped children to provide relaxing, entertaining, and enjoyable activities for the participants.

Scouting The objectives of scouting are character building, citizenship training, and physical fitness. To the handicapped child scouting can provide a sense of belonging, accomplishment, and association with others.

THE DEVELOPMENTALLY DISABLED CHILD

Developmentally disabled children were once thought to be mentally retarded. The following sensorimotor disorders can affect any one of the child's main areas of development: motor, symbolic, social, and numerical. As knowledge of learning disabilities increase, a "slower child" is often the victim of a disability (such as dyslexia) that conceals his or her otherwise normal I.Q.

Curtis explained that "Since such disorders can seriously hamper the child's potential for both academic and physical progress and will probably not be evident until the child is compared with others of the same age, recreation leaders must be constantly alert for any signs of developmental disabilities."[29]

THE EMOTIONALLY DISTURBED CHILD

The problems of the emotionally disturbed child can stem from any traumatic experience and often result in depression, aggression, crippling shyness, or other compulsive behaviors. The emotionally disturbed child needs acceptance and encouragement, since many have lost confidence, self–esteem, and a sense of security.

Emotionally disturbed children may demonstrate these emotional problems in various ways. Extremely aggressive behavior, for example, is considerably more of a problem with boys than with girls. Curtis wrote that "Psychiatrists tend to think of aggression as a learned reaction brought on by parental and/or societal rewards and punishments."[30]

RECREATION FOR LATER MATURITY

Recreation for the aging is one of the most vital areas of concern in the American society today and represents a major challenge for the organized recreation field. During the past two decades, major changes have taken place in the family structure that have caused the isolation of the aged.

Today, the smaller, two–generation family unit provides the aged person little room and little sense of personal contribution. As a re-

sult, an increasing number of older persons are living alone in small apartments or single–room units. Often, they are unable to take care of themselves properly. Consequently, more and more older people are experiencing difficulty adjusting to their new status in life. An increasing number are choosing withdrawal or disengagement from society.

Kraus reported that there are approximately twenty–three million persons sixty–five years old or older, about twice the number from twenty years ago. They constitute more than 10 percent of the entire population. About 70 percent of older Americans live in their homes or with relatives, while about 25 percent live alone or with a nonrelative and about 5 percent live in institutions.[31]

As millions of people join the aging society, the concerns of this group must become the interest and concern of the community. The elderly person must be given a fairer share of the recreation tax dollar if his or her increasing needs are to be served. If older people are to be physically and emotionally healthy, they must continue to have a full range of social and recreational opportunities which can help fulfill their need for friendship, social involvement, and creative activity.

Following retirement, many older persons tend to decline both physically and emotionally if they do not have social and recreation opportunities. The result is loneliness, alcoholism, mental illness, and even suicide. Social isolation is even more prevalent among aging persons with special disabilities, and is perhaps the most serious problem confronting the older person with a visual handicap.

While federal programs directed by the Office of Aging in the Department of Health and Human Services are viewed as effective in stimulating local response to meeting senior citizens' needs, available funds are generally insufficient to meet recreation needs. The recreation and park profession must also develop a stronger sense of responsibility by greatly expanding its programs in this area. Many millions of aged persons are still unserved, providing the field with a challenge it cannot ignore.

Definitions

Gerontology—The study of the aging process and of aged persons in society.
Geriatrics—The branch of medicine dealing with medical problems of the aged.

> **We do not cease playing because we are old; we grow old because we cease playing.**
>
> Joseph Lee

Needs of the Aging

The basic needs of aged persons are the same as for anyone at any age: new experiences, security, recognition, response, participation, self–expression, and creativity.

The elderly person's psychological needs are affection, understanding, appreciation, and a sense of worth and usefulness. The aging person's feelings of inferiority and inadequacy stem primarily from loss of status and the various disabilities of old age.

Upon retirement, the working person is faced with a big increase of free time and a decrease in income. "The satisfying and constructive use of leisure is a key factor in the morale and self–image of aging persons," said Peter Verhoven. "After having dropped or at least substantially reduced the work role, it becomes exceedingly difficult for them to find interesting and rewarding uses of their leisure."[32]

Helping middle age adults prepare for retirement should be a prime concern to society. Mid–career clinics can examine the goals of their working life, consider possible changes, and suggest added interests and involvements outside of work.

In helping the aging adjust to social, psychological, economic, or physiological changes, the following programs and assistance should be provided by governmental and community agencies and organizations:

1. Health assistance and hospital medical care
2. Economic security
3. Housing and maintenance assistance
4. Opportunity for meaningful social relationships
5. A sense of importance and contribution to society
6. Challenging physical and mental activities
7. A position of respect and dignity
8. Helping those who are unable to live independently

The Contribution of Recreation

Increasingly, recreation is playing a greater role in the lives of aging persons. To fill their leisure hours and meet some of their personal needs, interesting and challenging recreation opportunities can make a major contribution in the following areas:

Figure 18–8 Shuffleboard tournament for senior citizens. Paul Robertson of Carmichael shows his winning form in the tournament finals at the Garden West Mobile Estates in West Sacramento. (Courtesy Mission Oaks Recreation and Park District.)

1. Improve physical health
2. Re–awaken creative impulses
3. Encourage social involvement
4. Play meaningful roles in society
5. Have a positive outlook on life
6. Other social services

Programs for the Aging

Studies on how aging persons use their leisure indicate that the most often mentioned activities are very similar to the types of leisure activities participated in by people of other age groups. The majority of activities sponsored by recreation agencies is carried on in meetings of clubs, commonly called "Golden Age" clubs. Members enjoy the responsibility of planning their meetings and preparing for their special events and activities, assisted by recreation leaders.

Other recreation services provided for aging persons in institutional or community settings include senior citizens' centers and clubs, special residential centers, hospitals or nursing homes, and homebound programs.

> **If you have not had an interest or hobby during your life, you are lost when you are old and have nothing to do.**

Developing the program The development and implementation of an activities program for the aged depends primarily on what the individuals themselves want to do. Learning an individual's interests is the basis for planning the start of the program, and it is the key to keeping the program continually effective. Any organizational plan, however, should take into consideration existing facilities and programs in the community. Before initiating the program, a survey should be made to determine the leisure needs of the group to be served.

If given the opportunity to share in the program's organization themselves, the elderly who participate will display considerably more interest and spirit. Some activities

should be provided that will extend over a considerable period of time and challenge the continued interest and dedication of the participants. Activities with long–term appeal may serve psychologically as work substitutes.

Program activities The most popular recreation activities for the aging are those of a social nature in which such qualities as fun, sociability, companionship, and belonging are given prime emphasis. Increasingly, physical exercise and active games are becoming an integral part of programs for the aging. A growing number of senior citizens are exercising regularly, many on vigorous, stimulating programs.

Generally, activities for the aging are broken down into the following areas:

1. Arts and crafts
2. Music
3. Exercise programs
4. Games and contests
5. Dramatics
6. Dance
7. Religious services
8. Films
9. Hobbies
10. Social programs
11. Trips and outings
12. Community service

A typical summer program at Sacramento, California's Senior Citizen Center offers equipment and space for such card games as bridge, canasta, and pinochle. There are chess and checkers. Outside are shuffleboard and croquet grounds. Dances are scheduled regularly. Instruction is offered in oil painting, mosaic, and ceramics.

Many senior citizen programs offer chartered air flights to Europe, Hawaii, and Alaska at greatly reduced prices. Regular bus tours are scheduled to scenic and appealing locations.

Programs in nursing homes Recreation in nursing homes is a significant part of the total concept of patient care and treatment program that includes medicine, nursing, physical therapy, religion, occupational therapy, social work services, and recreation.

Recreation activities for the aging should be scheduled at hours of greatest leisure and should avoid conflict with nursing care or medical treatment. While some activities can be offered in the morning, the afternoons usually provide the largest segment of free time. Most group activities are scheduled after lunch. Individual activities or special events can be planned for the early evening hours. Programs should be geared to serve the needs of patients who are bedridden or limited in mobility as well as those who are able to move around easily.

> **Many exercises are done to music, lightening the atmosphere and making participants less self-conscious.**

Leadership Guidelines

Effective supervision and leadership are essential to a successful recreation program for the aged. It has been said that working with this age group requires more skill and ability than with any other. Perhaps the most challenging part of a leader's job is to encourage people to get involved. Therefore, the job is to provide activities that present a challenge and make people want to participate and to achieve.

The following are some important leadership guidelines for supervision of the aged:

1. Provide a broad and varied program for all.
2. Encourage participants to take an active role in planning. The professional leader should not attempt to dominate the group.
3. Create a friendly environment in which everyone will feel secure, accepted, and liked.
4. Consider the unique limitations of old age.
5. Consider individual education, eco-

nomic status, recreational experience, and skills.
6. Do not allow the more aggressive members to dominate the others.
7. Provide the type of facilities appropriate to the particular group.
8. Emphasize enjoyment, fun, and companionship.
9. Provide instruction whenever desirable.
10. Do not make sudden changes in the program or procedures unless approved by the group.
11. Encourage members to participate but don't pressure them.
12. Play no favorites and avoid controversy.

Research on Aging

Gerontologists are convinced that "the lack of social integration is a vital causative factor in mental disorders of the aging."[33] A number of recent studies support their belief that the types of social relations experienced by the aged are a crucial factor in their mental health.

Much of the research on the aging has dealt with the problems of geriatric patients in institutional settings. Such research has substantiated the views of earlier studies that much of the deterioration of older persons results from the circumstances under which they live and is not organic in nature. Dr. William C. Menninger stated that: "People who stay young despite their years, do so because of an active interest that provides satisfaction through participation."[34]

Many experimental projects have suggested that confused, deteriorated, and withdrawn geriatric patients have made significant improvements as a result of recreation activities designed to promote social interaction.

National Organization

The National Council on the Aging (NCOA) is a private, nonprofit, voluntary agency that provides leadership and assistance to organizations and individuals concerned with the field of aging. The programs

Figure 18–9 The Panhandlers Kitchen Band is comprised of an enthusiastic group of senior citizens who perform regularly at social functions in the Sacramento area. Many of their engagements are at retirement home complexes and nursing home facilities.

and activities of NCOA are centered on research and information, advocacy of a better quality of life or the elderly, training, technical assistance, and consultation. Further information can be obtained by writing to the National Council on the Aging, 1828 L Street, N.W., Washington, D.C. 20036.

Public and Private Assistance

For several decades, the federal government and various state programs have provided varied forms of assistance for aging Americans. Social Security has provided retirement income, and the Medicare program has relieved the burden of medical costs for the aged by helping to pay for hospital bills, stays in extended–care facilities, and medical bills for those who live at home. Many research programs and demonstration projects have been funded. Yet, governmental assistance, at best, has been insufficient to meet the growing needs of the aging.

Many programs have been made available to the aging by public and private agencies, such as Foster Grandparents, Home Health Aides, VISTA (Volunteers in Service to America), Operation Green Thumb, Head Start, community action programs, sheltered workshops, volunteer service, home care, and adult education programs.

Retirement Communities

Large numbers of elderly persons have chosen in recent years to live in retirement villages or communities established specifically for older people. Among the most outstanding retirement communities in the country are Heritage Village in Connecticut, Walnut Creek in California, and Sun City in Arizona. Regarded as the largest of its kind in America with more than forty thousand residents, Sun City has nine golf courses, six shopping centers, five recreation centers, an amphitheater, stadium, two lakes, and a lawn bowling green.

Retirement communities place considerable emphasis on offering a wide variety of recreational facilities, hobbies, clubs, and programs. Their prime concern is to attract new residents and meet the needs of all interest groups and levels of capability. A members council usually serves in making policy and helping to carry out scheduled activities.

Housing Units and Residential Facilities

A different form of residential development for the elderly is found in apartment buildings or other special housing units. These may involve a single high–rise apartment building or converted hotel or garden apartments. There is also the large complex providing three or four different kinds of living arrangements such as nursing home facilities for the ill and dependent aged, along with separate housing for the semi–dependent and relatively independent units for those in good health.

Outreach services have also been developed to assist elderly persons who have serious impairments and cannot leave their homes. Recreation may be provided on a one–to–one basis, with leaders bringing in hobby activities, teaching skills, or helping the homebound persons use their leisure.

Institutional Programs for the Aging

There are approximately twenty–three thousand nursing homes in the United States today, in addition to thousands of chronic care and special geriatric units in hospitals. Nursing homes are of all types, operated by public authorities, voluntary organizations, and proprietary owners. Many nursing homes were established when the federal government began to pay for nursing home care through Medicaid. By the mid–1970s, $4.4 billion of Medicaid's overall $12.7 billion budget was spent on the elderly, although many unscrupulous operators provided substandard services and facilities.[35]

RECREATION FOR THE DISADVANTAGED

Although millions of affluent Americans have accumulated both wealth and leisure–time opportunities, the disadvantaged have been deprived of sufficient facilities and services to lead a normal life. There are today well over thirty million people in the United States who are considered economically deprived. In addition to the economic type of deprivation there are three other types of disadvantage: education, cultural, and social.

The disadvantaged were defined by Carlson, Deppe, and MacLean as "Those who have been denied the ability to meet their potential because of social or environmental circumstances, rather than personal actions."[36] The terms disadvantaged and minority are not synonymous, they wrote, although the chances of being disadvantaged often seem to increase if an individual is a member of a minority group.

The economically, as well as the culturally and educationally disadvantaged are often the same people who are recreationally disadvantaged, although there are many exceptions to this.

The Nature and Extent of Poverty

The poor or economically deprived were defined by James Murphy ". . . as people who are not now maintaining a decent standard of living and whose basic needs exceed their means to satisfy them."[37]

Poor people and various disadvantaged groups are the most in need of recreation services in the community. This is particularly true because they have the least financial resources available.

According to the Office of Economic Opportunity, the number of poor Americans is approximately 30 million people, many of whom are members of racial minority groups. This figure is based on a flexible "poverty line" of about $3,500 per family per annum. "Living chiefly in cities, the poor suffer from poor municipal services, deteriorated housing, inferior schools, higher prices, and inadequate food," declared Richard Kraus.[38]

Although poverty in America has decreased somewhat, there is still an ever–widening gap between the rich and the poor.

Needs of the Disadvantaged

While recreation opportunities for most inner city residents are insufficient, city agencies and community leaders usually identify the needs of disadvantaged youth as their most pressing concern. The needs of inner city youth are intensified, not only by residence in recreation deficient neighborhoods, but by other social and economic disadvantages.

Efforts to meet the special needs of disadvantaged people have increased, but there are still great numbers of poor Americans without organized recreational opportunities. Since many commercial recreation opportunities are unavailable to the poor, greater services should be offered by government recreation agencies, as well as by voluntary social organizations.

The Role of Recreation

Recreation and leisure service has a vital role to play in efforts to improve the lives of the disadvantaged. Sociologists are convinced that a lack of recreation and leisure is a major feature of disadvantagement and a major source of discontent.

The recreation profession did not begin to take an active interest in meeting the leisure needs of the poor—particularly the nonwhite poor—until the 1960s.

According to Richard Kraus:

> This came about as a consequence of the federal antipoverty program, which provided special funding to serve the disadvantaged; it did not gain full impetus until urban rioting erupted throughout the nation in 1964 and 1965 and brought the needs of inner-city residents forcefully to the attention of the public. In city after city where serious riots had occurred in recent summers, one of the angry complaints of ghetto residents had been about the lack of adequate parks, swimming pools, recreation programs, and leadership.[39]

Program Guidelines

In approaching the leisure problems of the disadvantaged, recreation agencies should implement the following program guidelines:

1. Recognizing ethnic and cultural differences in program offerings.
2. Providing services in public housing developments.
3. Creating much-needed jobs in the economically depressed areas.
4. Coping with social ills in community life with positive action programs.
5. Instilling a sense of purpose in the lives of disadvantaged people.
6. Establishing mutual trust between the department staff and the public being served.
7. Establishing a compensatory recreation program, in which disadvantaged areas are often given more funds than the city as a whole.
8. Providing a decentralized recreation program that can serve various geographic areas.
9. Recruiting, training, and employing indigenous leaders and encouraging them to broaden their education.
10. Personalizing recreation and bringing it down to the neighborhood level.

New Programs

Houston's special recreation program, "The Fun Company," provides enjoyment to economically disadvantaged youth, ages six through twenty, through recreation and employment. During the summer of 1977, thirty thousand youth participated in drama, dance, athletics, competitive sports, beautification projects, and field trips. "Fun Company" was funded through Community Development Block Grant monies, and most of its 1,640 staff were hired through the CETA program.

The Youth Conservation Corps (YCC) provides a work-education experience for young people between fifteen and eighteen. The departments of Interior and Agriculture operate the program. The work is conservation-related and is done on public lands. Environmental education programs are an integral part of all work projects.

Trained Leadership Needed

In providing recreation and leisure services for the economically disadvantaged, recreation workers are needed who have a deep concern for people. In addition to being skilled in recreation leadership and program development, leaders must accept the underprivileged as they are and deal honestly with them.

In recruiting, the recreation profession must offer opportunities to potential leaders to provide meaningful and satisfying service. Competitive salaries and benefits will provide the incentive necessary to attract high–level leadership. Greater effort should be made by the profession to recruit and hire disadvantaged and minority group members.

SERVING SOCIALLY DEVIANT YOUTH

An increasing number of children and youth are experiencing various degrees of personal disturbance that make it difficult for them to function adequately in the community or in regular schools. The concept of social deviance includes such special problems as juvenile delinquency, drug addiction, alcoholism, aggressive and hostile behavior, and other problems. The socially maladjusted who are unable or unwilling to conform to the demands of society require special care or rehabilitation.

The causes of delinquency have been widely debated. Kraus suggested that "There are basically two schools of thought—one that sees it as a psychological or psychogenic problem and another that sees it primarily from a sociological or cultural viewpoint."[41]

The psychological view, as described by Kraus, sees habitual antisocial or criminal activity as an outcome of defective personality structure, resulting from feelings of inferiority, poorly developed control mechanisms, or inadequate or disturbed family relationships. A typical delinquent is highly insecure and has a strong tendency toward aggressive and hostile behavior.[42]

The sociological view of delinquency views it primarily as the result of cultural and environmental factors. According to Kraus, "This view is supported by evidence that there is a much higher percentage of delinquent behavior in low–income areas—marked by slum housing, poor schools, broken or unstable families and the lack of desirable adult models—than in middle or upper–class neighborhoods.[43]

There appears to be a meaningful relationship between the leisure and recreational patterns of many youth gang members and their criminal activities. Supported by considerable evidence, the relationship takes two forms:

1. Play itself frequently is used in antisocial ways. Leisure becomes the time in which early delinquent patterns are established.
2. Youthful offenders typically have not learned to use their leisure in constructive and creative ways.

Skill and sensitivity of recreation leaders is the main component of successful programs for troubled youth. Dedicated and imaginative leadership can help overcome deficiencies in physical facilities and equipment.

The Roving Leader Approach

A number of cities in the United States have assigned special youth workers the job of making contact with unaffiliated youth. According to this approach, roving leaders go out into the street or neighborhood hangouts where problem youth may be located.

Roving leaders have the following tasks:

1. To help gang youth make use of available community resources.
2. To encourage drop–outs to return to school.
3. To intervene on their behalf with school authorities.
4. To make court appearances in support of the youth, and provide assistance in hearing or correctional procedures.
5. To help boys and girls develop a more favorable understanding of adults and the total society.
6. To help them understand the consequences of their antisocial acts.[40]

RECREATION IN CORRECTIONAL INSTITUTIONS

Despite a growing awareness of the value of recreation, the provision of recreation services in correctional institutions is quite limited. "Prison recreation services are still seen in an administrative context rather than in a strict rehabilitative context," according to Larry Neal, "as a privilege with deprivation used as punishment, or as a means of reducing riots, or as an aid in inmate adjustment to prison life."[44]

While recreation services are endorsed highly by many prison administrators, others feel the role of recreation is primarily to relieve custodial pressures. "Unfortunately, recreation is seldom viewed as a treatment tool by correctional personnel," said Garland Wollard, Director of Education for the U.S. Bureau of Prisons. "This has resulted in a potentially significant treatment program being relegated to a minor treatment position."[45]

In the past, recreation in prisons has experienced a low priority because of other needs considered more important. In many institutions, appropriations for recreation amount to what's left after everything else has been taken care of. With minimal facilities and equipment, correctional institutions often are so understaffed and overcrowded, that they are unable to provide the type of recreation activities needed.

The fact that recreation has had a low priority status in correctional institutions can be attributed to a number of reasons. Many people still regard recreation as "fun and games," a privilege or luxury given prison inmates only when they are good or deserving.

The reasons for the lack of progress in the area of correctional recreation are many. In his report on "Correctional Recreation: A Stalemate on Progress," James L. Krug pointed out that "Recreation has been viewed by prison officials and the general public as a diversionary activity and not as a treatment tool. The recreation field, too, has had little to offer the correctional administrator. Few universities offer training in the area, and the scarcity of research is clearly evident.[46]

"Fortunately, attitudes have improved in recent years," reports Kraus, "and many prisons have adopted more innovative approaches to rehabilitation, including more meaningful vocational programs and counseling services, furloughs so that inmates may visit their families, and others. Some innovative state and federal prisons have even experimented with minimum–security, coeducational programs, in an effort to help prisoners adjust to the outside world when they are released."[47]

According to Morris W. Stewart of the University of Maryland and chairperson of the National Therapeutic Recreation Society (NTRS) Committee on Corrections: "Professional recreators have a very weak foothold within correctional systems. Because an individual has athletic skills or interests, he or she becomes the logical choice to assume responsibilities for recreation services. The civil service system has relieved some of this favoritism, but it will take several years before untrained individuals are replaced by professional recreators."[48]

A Need for Reform

Turmoil in penal institutions is neither new nor unique, but the increasing number of disturbances and violence have alarmed the American public. In addition to the general discontent with the methods and facilities used in treating inmates, penal institutions have failed to rehabilitate and assist them in their readjustment to society.

According to Marion and Carroll Hormachea, "Corrections is the means whereby society punishes those who violate its laws. In addition, the system of corrections has as its charge the preparation of the offender to return to society as a productive member."[49]

What is needed is a widespread revolution in public attitudes and the infusion of large sums of money to replace vengeance with rehabilitation in the correctional system, according to Kraus.[50] There is an urgent need to interpret to the public the significance and long-term effects of a well-planned and well-executed recreation program in a correctional institution. Recreation can be one of the most important rehabilitative tools.

Enforcement of Standards

Standards on recreation and inmate activities for adult correctional facilities are available from the American Correctional Association. Significantly, these standards have been used as a guideline on litigation proceedings. Krug wrote that "Various court cases have identified the absence of exercise and recreation as cruel and unusual punishment and a violation of the Eighth Amendment. In 1977 and 1978, nine decisions have been handed down ordering prisoner access to outdoor recreation."[51]

Numerous other suits are taking place dealing with the prisoners' right to recreation, the volume of time allotted for recreation pursuits, and the prisoners' access to recreation while segregated.

The Role of Recreation

Recreation can play an important role in the total treatment and rehabilitation process of those institutionalized. Skills, interests, and knowledge learned in professionally planned recreation programs can have a strong carry-over value when inmates return to society.

"Recreation is really the only neutral ground that you can meet a ward on," according to Bill Scanlon. "Any other time, you are the man, and he's locked up."

"Within the prison environment, leisure time weighs heavily on the hands of the inmate," wrote Krug. "Forty-four percent of the inmates' waking time is available for leisure activity. Through proper construction of this time, the inmate can develop new and unfound talents."[52]

A comprehensive recreation program should be developed to offer the inmate a choice of leisure-time activities. The program should offer a variety of activities to serve his or her needs and interests as well

as lessen the frustrations and tensions of prison life. "When the inmate leads a more balanced life combining work and recreation," wrote Marion and Carroll Hormachea, "treatment personnel as well as custodial personnel are able to work more effectively with the individual and his problems and thus prepare him for eventual release"[53]

Skills, interests, and knowledge learned in recreation programs and activities can have a strong carry-over value when they return to society. Among the inmates of correctional institutions there are many who have no knowledge or skills which will enable them to make acceptable use of their leisure.

The need to recruit young professionals into the corrections field is most apparent. Furthermore, recreation curricula must better prepare students for placement in correctional settings. Students need to be encouraged to enter the corrections area. Through fieldwork and internship programs, students can be provided with much needed practical experience.

Krug concluded that "it is time for action and progress. For too long the recreation profession has set aside or ignored the possibilities represented by the corrections process."[54]

Staff

To derive the greatest impact, recreation programs must be professionally planned and conducted. Qualified leadership in recreation activities will provide the necessary continuity and program progression.

There should be one full-time leader in each correctional institution, assisted by part-time and volunteer workers. "The full-time leader, or director, should be a professionally trained, skilled recreation worker with understanding of the application of the leisure-time program of inmates to their morale, social, mental, and physical rehabilitation, their adjustment to the institution and their preparation for release."[55]

In addition to planning and organization, the recreation director should handle such items as funds and physical facilities. Included in the institution's recreation budget should be funds for equipment facilities, supplies, and personnel. The director should be assisted by various recreation leaders who will actually conduct the program. Leaders should be trained in music, physical education, and arts and crafts.

In correctional recreation facilities, it is difficult to classify or standardize positions and titles. However, the following are the titles found in institutional and community positions:

Institutional: Recreation Director, Recreation Coordinator, Activity Supervisor, Group Life Coordinator, and Youth Counselor.

Community: Roving Leader, Detached Worker, Street Leader/Counselor.

Program

Good recreation programming should be a part of the daily life of any institution. Actually, recreation in a correctional institution does not vary a great deal from the types found in other settings of society.

In satisfying the various needs of inmates, the recreation director should provide as much program variety as conditions and resources will allow. Among the activities that have proven popular are:

1. Team sports
2. Individual sports
3. Combative sports
4. Attending outside sports events
5. Movies
6. Musical performances
7. Cultural activities (art, crafts, drama, music)
8. Literary events (reading and writing)
9. Discussion groups
10. Radio and television
11. Photography

Since many inmates are not interested in team sports and competitive games, a more diversified range of quiet, individual or small–group, creative interests and hobbies should be made available. The many forms of leisure activities allow wards and inmates to express their feelings in a socially acceptable manner.

RECREATION IN YOUTH INSTITUTIONS

Increasingly, recreation is playing a significant role in serving socially deviant children and youth in correctional institutions. Among the many different types of institutions are both public and private residential treatment centers. Known in the past as reform schools, they are now called training schools or residential treatment centers. In addition, many special homes are operated by voluntary and religious organizations.

Generally, the provision of recreation services in youth institutions has been very limited. However, there are a number of outstanding programs of recreation in youth institutions throughout the United States.

CHEROKEE LODGE

This housing unit for drug abusers at the Northern Reception Center Clinic of the California Youth Authority (CYA) in Sacramento conducted a well–rounded innovative recreation program. The program gave its wards a sense of individual accomplishment, achievement, and has helped establish rapport between them and their counselors.

"We run one or two big evening functions each week, like Casino Night, Co–ed parties, and movies," said William Scanlon, Senior Counselor, "but we offer our fellows many low organized games such as ping–pong, pool, cards, checkers, and chess." Aggression–reducing activities are given major emphasis in CYA dorms. This "controlled–violence" provides for the frustrations to be relieved through aggressive action.

"Wards have a definite willingness to participate in group activities," said Scanlon, "They like games of bluffing, conning, and chance. Many wards like to compete alone, not on a large basis, but on a one–on–one basis. We use a lot of arts and crafts to give them a sense of accomplishment and to help build their self–image.

The people who helped Scanlon's program the most were the volunteers from the colleges. "We found that their support not only increased the effectiveness of full–time staff members but our clients reduced considerably their "hostile acting–out." They displayed much greater motivation."

WINTU LODGE

Perhaps the most innovative recreation and leisure programming in the CYA today is at Wintu Lodge, a psychiatric unit at the Northern Reception Center/Clinic in Sacramento. Developed by Len Ralston, a veteran senior counselor with a strong background in recreation and leisure services, Wintu Lodge offers a well balanced program of highly active physical team and individual sports, as well as less active, mentally stimulating games and hobbies.

Wintu's leisure program under Ralston's direction features such progressive innovations as:

Figure 18–10 Wards at Wintu Lodge, a unit of the California Youth Authority, are given mentally stimulating board games, like this chess session, as well as much needed aggression–reducing activities. Here, Len Ralston, a veteran counselor, and his recreation intern provide both instruction and leisure counseling services.

1. The *Leisure Interest Assessment/Testing program* provides for each ward to be interviewed as to his leisure interests and skills. Ralston uses the Mirenda Leisure Interest finder, devised by Joseph J. Mirenda, and the "Comprehensive Evaluation In Recreational Therapy Scale: A Tool for Patient Evaluation."[56] The "Ralston Social Pastimes Skills Inventory" covers the resident's working knowledge of traditional pastimes.
2. *Leisure counseling services* provides a better understanding of the leisure patterns of clients and helps guide them in appropriate directions.
3. *An organizational structure* similar to a typical city department of leisure services, i.e. staff, budget, maintenance, etc., with emphasis on recreation therapy services traditionally offered in a medical center.
4. *Board game olympics competition*, involving individual or teams comprised of Wintu wards and recreation students from nearby colleges are held.
5. *A frame of fame* was created to recognize outstanding achievement in the area of leisure. Candidates are selected based on achievement, conduct, attitude, and skill.
6. *Wintu Leisure News* is a weekly publication which features sports and recreation highlights, as well as individual and team scores and results.

Wintu's professional staff is headed by a leisure management specialist (four-year degree), an activity coordinator leader (two-year degree), and a recreation therapist specialist. It is supported by many recreation students from local colleges.

QUESTIONS FOR DISCUSSION

1. While there are many reasons why efforts on behalf of special populations have often been ineffective, what factor did Stein and Sessoms cite as perhaps the most overriding?
2. What is meant by the term *therapeutic recreation*?
3. Identify several of the most active settings in the community where therapeutic recreation services are offered.
4. How can we gain a greater sensitivity to the presence, needs, and aspirations of persons with a physical disability?
5. How should the local recreation agency attempt to provide for the needs of people with physical handicaps?
6. Why is "adaptation" the key word in planning and conducting recreation programs and activities for people with handicaps?
7. Define: *leisure counseling*. Discuss the role it serves in facilitating leisure development.
8. Discuss the growing practice of mainstreaming or integrating disabled persons into community recreation programs in contrast to the sheltered activities they have been accustomed to in the past.
9. What is mental retardation?
10. Review the type of recreation and leisure programs that have met the needs and interests of the mentally retarded and developmentally disabled.

11. Discuss the problem of loneliness, one of the most persistent and universal afflictions of the aging.
12. Discuss the growing popularity of physical exercise and active games for the aging.
13. Essentially, what are the needs of the disadvantaged?
14. Discuss the role of recreation services in correctional institutions.
15. Set up a program of recreation activities and events which would be designed for a correctional institution for young people.

REFERENCES

1. Thomas A. Stein and H. Douglas Sessoms, *Recreation and Special Populations*, 2nd ed. (Boston: Holbrook Press, Inc., 1973), p. 11.
2. Gerald S. O'Morrow, *Therapeutic Recreation* (Reston: Va.: Reston Publishing Company, 1976), p. 9.
3. *EMPLOY*, National Recreation and Park Association, Vol. VI, Number 5, January 1980, p. 1.
4. Elliott M. Avedon, *Therapeutic Recreation Service* (Englewood, N.J.: Prentice Hall, Inc., 1974).
5. Edith Ball, writing in Marion and Carroll Hormachea, *Recreation in Modern Society* (Boston: Holbrook Press, Inc., 1972), p. 144.
6. Geoffrey Godbey, *Recreation, Park and Leisure Services* (Philadelphia: W. B. Saunders Company, 1978), pp. 118–19.
7. O'Morrow, *Therapeutic Recreation*, pp. 178–79.
8. Ibid., pp. 161–172.
9. Scout Lee Gunn, "Leisure Counseling," *EMPLOY*, National Recreation and Park Association, Arlington, Virginia, October 1978, p. 2.
10. Janet Pomeroy, *Recreation for the Physically Handicapped* (New York: The Macmillan Company, 1964), p. 20.
11. Stein and Sessoms, *Recreation and Special Populations*, pp. 201–202.
12. Pomeroy, *Recreation for the Physically Handicapped*, p. 20.
13. Scout Lee Gunn, "Mainstreaming is a Two-Way Street," *Journal of Physical Education and Recreation*, September, 1976, p. 48.
14. Richard Kraus, *Therapeutic Recreation Service: Principles and Practices* 2nd ed. (Philadelphia: W. B. Saunders Company, 1978), p. 48.
15. Anne L. Binkley, "Research Update." *Parks and Recreation Magazine*, June 1981, p. 18.
16. Ibid.
17. Janet Pomeroy, "State of the Art in Community Recreation for the Handicapped," American Alliance for Health, Physical Education, and Recreation, 1976.
18. Rick F. Heber, "A Manual on Terminology and Classification in Mental Retardation," *American Journal of Mental Deficiency*, 1959, p. 3.
19. Ibid.
20. O'Morrow, *Therapeutic Recreation*, p. 25.
21. Julian U. Stein, "The Mentally Retarded Need Recreation," *Parks and Recreation Magazine*, July 1966, p. 574.
22. Gene Hayes, writing in Stein and Sessoms, *Recreation and Special Populations*, pp. 67–68.
23. Fred J. Krause, "New Roles, New Hope for Mentally Retarded, *U.S. News & World Report*, August 28, 1978, p. 45.
24. Hayes, in *Recreation and Special Populations*, pp. 67–68.
25. O'Morrow, *Therapeutic Recreation*, p. 27.
26. Hayes, in *Recreation and Special Populations*, p. 68.
27. Joan Ramm, "Challenge: Recreation and Fitness for the Mentally Retarded," *Journal for American Association for Health, Physical Education and Recreation*, September 1966, p. 1.
28. Hayes, in *Recreation and Special Populations*, p. 100.
29. Joseph E. Curtis, *Recreation—Theory and Practice* (St. Louis: C. V. Mosby Company, 1979), p. 163.
30. Ibid., p. 162.
31. Kraus, *Therapeutic Recreation Service*, 2nd ed., p. 142.
32. Peter Verhoven, writing in Stein and Sessoms, *Recreation and Special Populations*, p. 394.
33. Howard G. Danford and Max Shirley, *Crea-*

tive Leadership in Recreation, 2nd ed. (Boston: Allyn and Bacon, Inc., 1970), p. 323.

34. Carol Lucas, *Recreational Activity Development for the Aging* (Springfield, Illinois: Charles C. Thomas, Publisher, 1962), p. 3.

35. Kraus, *Therapeutic Recreation Service*, 2nd ed., p. 243.

36. Carlson, Deppe, and MacLean, *Recreation and Leisure*, p. 282.

37. James Murphy, writing in Stein and Sessoms, *Recreation and Special Populations*, p. 285.

38. Kraus, *Therapeutic Recreation Service*, 2nd ed., p. 7.

39. Richard Kraus, *Recreation and Leisure in Modern Society*, 1st ed. (New York: Meredith Corporation/Appleton–Century–Crofts, 1971), pp. 388–89.

40. *Roving Leader Program*, Manual of Washington, D.C. Recreation Department, 1970, pp. 4–5.

41. Kraus, *Therapeutic Recreation Service*, 2nd ed., pp. 261–62.

42. Ibid., p. 261.

43. Ibid.

44. Larry L. Neal, "Prison Reform—A Historical Glimpse at Recreation's Role, *Therapeutic Recreation Journal*, 6, No. 3, 1972, p. 113.

45. Garland Wolland, "Recreation in a Prison Environment," *Therapeutic Recreation Journal*, 6, No. 3, 1972, p. 115.

46. James L. Krug, "Correctional Recreation: A Stalemate on Progress," *Parks & Recreation Magazine*, November 1979, p. 36.

47. Richard Kraus, *Recreation and Leisure in Modern Society*, 2nd ed. (Santa Monica: Goodyear Company, 1978), p. 350.

48. Morris W. Stewart, "Employment in Correctional Recreation," *EMPLOY*, National Recreation and Park Association, April 1978, p. 4.

49. Marion and Carroll Hormachea, writing in Stein and Sessoms, *Recreation and Special Populations*, p. 105.

50. Kraus, *Therapeutic Recreation Service*, 2nd ed., pp. 275–58.

51. Krug, "Correctional Recreation," p. 38.

52. Ibid., p. 82.

53. Marion and Carroll Hormachea, in *Recreation and Special Populations*, p. 113.

54. Krug, *Correctional Recreation*, p. 82.

55. Larry Neal, "Manpower Needs in the Correctional Field," *Therapeutic Recreation Journal*, 6, No. 3, 1972, p. 125.

56. Robert Parker, Curtis Ellison, Thomas Kirby, and M. J. Short, "The Comprehensive Evaluation in Recreational Therapy Scale: A Tool for Patient Evaluation." *Therapeutic Recreation Journal*, Arlington, National Recreation and Park Association, Vol. IX, No. 4, Fourth Quarter, 1975, pp. 143–152.

VI
Leadership, Program Planning, and Organization

Figure 19–1 Effective leadership. The leaders, the most important element of the program, set the pace and spirit and influence the quality of involvement of the participants. Here, a young leader directs the action at one of the many neighborhood playgrounds operated by the Sacramento Parks and Recreation Department.

19
The Art of Leadership

Leadership is the most important single factor in the successful operation of a recreation program. Without leadership, no group or organization can produce worthwhile action in the direction of its goals. A program plan is only as good as the quality of leadership responsible for executing it.

In the field of recreation and leisure services, the term, "leader," in a technical sense, usually applies to the face–to–face group leader or program specialist, who provides direct leadership to individuals or groups of participants. "Direct program leadership is the firing line of any recreation department or agency," wrote Richard Kraus. "Whether full– or part–time, generalist or specialist, the program leader is directly concerned with groups that are involved in carrying on recreational activities."[1]

Research indicates that leadership has a highly positive correlation with the eventual success or failure of a recreation program. The activity leaders should have the ability to motivate participants to continue in the recreation program. To achieve a successful program, the activity leader must be well organized and be able to communicate organization to the activity participants.

More than ever, there is a critical need today for inspired leadership to stimulate and motivate people in satisfying use of their leisure time.

> **There are three kinds of people in the world. Those who watch things happen, those who make things happen, and those who say "What happened?"**
> **Ann Landers**

LEADERSHIP—DEFINED

A leader is typically defined as one who leads or guides others, or one who presides, conducts, or directs a group or program. The emphasis in these phases is on guiding and directing. According to Ordway Tead: "Leadership is the activity of influencing people to cooperate towards some goal which they come to find desirable."[2]

An effective leader knows how to make things happen, encouraging and stimulating participants to reach their highest level of capacity in a given experience. A self–starter, he or she can create plans and set them in motion. Many authorities, however, consider the leader's role more as one who persuades others, who binds a group together and motivates it toward goals. In making things happen, the good leader is creating experiences, not anticipating them.

Leadership is something more than mere instruction. It means guidance in the selection of recreation activities, stimulating people to become interested in those forms of leisure pursuits which are most beneficial. The leader is one who exerts influence on people's use of leisure time by persuading them and providing opportunities for them. Indeed, an individual is a leader when his or her ideas or actions influence others. The description of leadership by J. N. Pfiffner and R. Presthus was similar—"the art of coordinating and motivating the individuals and groups to achieve desired ends."[3]

In describing the type of leadership needed, Cor Westland wrote that "As educational levels rise and incomes increase, the need for activity leaders seems to decrease, to be replaced by the 'animateur,' the 'motivator,' the leader who can help people discover their talents, and facilitates the finding of solutions."[4]

Clayne Jensen pointed out that "Leadership can be both direct and indirect, with direct leadership resulting from direct contact between the leader and those being led, and indirect leadership resulting from the leader purposely influencing people without having contact with them."[5]

> **When you are first and others follow, that is called LEADERSHIP.**

TYPES OF LEADERSHIP

The leader in the recreation and leisure services field performs many roles. Essentially, there are five major types of leadership:

1. *Activity and group leadership.* This type of face–to–face leadership works directly with people as they participate in recreation activities.
2. *Supervision of face–to–face leaders.* The supervisor may be responsible for one or more program areas, with such functions as planning, promotion, development, and supervision.
3. *Administrative* or *executive leadership,* with emphasis on policy making, planning, developing, controlling, and evaluating services.
4. *Civic* or *community leadership.* These are lay leaders who may serve as members of boards, commissions, councils, committees, or other citizen groups that support the local recreation department.
5. *Educational leadership.* Recreation educators in the colleges and universities among whose chief responsibilities is the professional education of recreation and park personnel.

Figure 19–2 Recreation leadership is stimulating people to become interested in various forms of leisure activity. A child's self–confidence can be greatly bolstered by the encouragement of and praise of leaders. This ring–throwing activity took place at a Hallowe'en costume party.

LEADERSHIP STYLES

Of the various styles of leadership behavior, three are most frequently practiced: the authoritarian, the democratic, and the participative. "In a sense, these describe a complete range of behavior, from the dominating autocrat to the retiring nonleader," said Sidney Lutzin and Edward Storey.[6] Leadership styles depend on such factors as the leader's personality and the goals of the group.

The four most common styles of leadership are:

1. *The autocratic or authoritarian leader* assumes full responsibility and dictates the action of the group. He or she insists upon exercising personally all the decision–making power. This type of leader often shows little concern for the needs and problems of subordinates.
2. *The democratic leader* involves the group in the planning, the establishment of goals, assignment of tasks necessary to accomplish the goals, and evaluation of the program. In this style, the leader either delegates responsibilities to his or her subordinates or gives them equal voice in policy determination.

    Democratic leadership style is used frequently in leisure services. According to Edith Ball and Robert Cipriano, "The leader works with the group to determine the program to be conducted. For example, a group of young people may wish to participate in social activities. The leader responds by helping the group to plan and organize those activities."[7]
3. *Laissez faire leadership* grows out of the situation, letting leadership emerge as the situation and needs of the group develop. "As a meeting progresses," wrote Ball, "a person emerges as an individual who has certain abilities to form the group and organize it to achieve its purposes."[8]
4. *The participative leadership* style represents an intermediate position between these extremes. The leader shares some decision–making authority with his or her

subordinates, but clearly retains ultimate responsibility for the decisions that are made. In their listing of leadership styles, Ball and Cipriano referred to laissez faire leadership as a style that grows out of the group activity.[9]

Depending on the situation, all of these styles may be used effectively. While autocratic leadership is often condemned, there are occasions when it is an effective leadership style. "A group of elderly people, for example, have come to a center for some type of activity," explained Ball and Cipriano. "For most of their lives these people have been told what to do—as children by parents and teachers and as adults by their boss or some other authority. They have had little or no opportunity to express their wishes. This kind of group is not ready for a democratic approach, for they would not know how to use it. An autocratic style can be effective in the beginning with a gradual shifting of responsibility from the leader to the group as the group becomes ready for these responsibilities."[10]

Beal, Bohlen, and Raudabaugh suggested that "The democratic leader has the ability to perceive the direction in which the group is moving and to move in that direction more rapidly than the group as a whole. Democracy moves slowly. One of the reasons for this is that a democratic leader is seldom one who is far superior to his group."[11]

Although no one leadership style is best for all situations, more and more administrators are following a participative or humanistic style. Executives and employees are both responding favorably to this type of leadership.

THEORIES OF GROUP LEADERSHIP

Several basic theories of group leadership have emerged during recent years, including the following:

Trait theory This theory suggested that there were certain specific traits or qualities shared by all successful leaders. Individual characteristics were seen as the major determinants of leadership. In his famous essay on heroes, Thomas Carlyle saw the leader as a person endowed with unique qualities that captured the imagination of the masses. The trait theory suggests that there is a certain combination of traits that underlies leadership, such as intelligence, courage, warmth and enthusiasm, sensitivity, energy, professional drive, and responsibility.

Situational theory   This theory suggests that teachers arise or emerge in situations where their personal qualities or capabilities will best serve group members. Kraus stated that "It is apparent that a person does not become a leader simply by possessing some combination of traits. Instead, the personal characteristics of the leader must be relevant to the characteristics, activities, interests, and needs of the group he seeks to serve."[1]

In some situations, a group may require that a leader be a morale builder, negotiator, or an expert in human relations. Thus, leadership selection is most likely to be affected by the demands and needs of a given situation rather than by possession of a particular leadership trait or a set of traits.

Functional theory   This view suggests that leadership arises from the complex needs of the group for specific kinds of tasks to be performed. Different members of the group may assume that leadership is a shared process in which the functions to be performed determine who the leaders will be. According to this theory, leadership is neither a single skill nor the responsibility of a single individual. Instead, it is a process in which all group members share in varying degrees.

Contingency theory   An increasing amount of research has been conducted by social psychologists suggesting that emergent leadership is heavily dependent on the interaction of a number of variables. The variables in this theory include the make–up of the group and its values or felt needs regard-

ing leadership styles; the actual demands of the situation and what the leader must accomplish and bring to the task; and the qualities, capabilities, and personal needs of the leader.

The contingency model of leadership is significant in that it demonstrates that the type of leadership behavior that is most likely to be effective depends on the situation and the task to be performed. In addition, it specifies ways of examining tasks to determine what leadership behaviors are likely to be most successful in carrying them out.

Composite theory   A composite theory of recreation leadership suggests that in different assignments or situations, different kinds of leadership skills or approaches may be required. The interaction–oriented approach to leadership may be appropriate in some cases, while in others the work–oriented approach is required.

CHARACTERISTICS OF THE SUCCESSFUL LEADER

Cecil E. Goode listed the following characteristics of the effective leader in working organizations:

Mental ability. Studies indicate that there is a positive relationship between mental ability and leadership.

Breadth of interest and aptitudes. The leader must be a well–rounded individual. He or she must have a wide general knowledge, a wide range of aptitudes, and be broadly interested.

Language facilities. The leader is able to speak and write fluently. Language facility is important to the leader.

Maturity. The effective leader is mentally and emotionally mature. He or she has grown up and shows a minimum of antisocial attitudes.

Motivation. The personal motivation of leaders is a very significant factor. Inner drive or motive power is the important element which propels a leader. He or she has a strong will to achieve, likes his or her work, has a strong urge to excel.

Social Orientation. The leader relies heavily on social skills. He or she realizes that the success of an undertaking often depends upon the extent to which he or she can get others to work together.

Leadership skills. The success of the executive or supervisor is determined more by his or her ability to plan and organize the work of others and to inspire and instruct them, than his or her technical knowledge of the work at hand.

Integrity. A leader has integrity or character. Integrity is defined as moral soundness, honesty, uprightness. He or she can be trusted and relied upon.[13]

FUNCTIONS OF A RECREATION LEADER

Playground and recreation center leaders in Stockton, California, are expected to function in the following ways, as described in the Stockton Recreation and Park Department Leader's Manual:

An Organizer Make survey of your playground and neighborhood to find out what it has and what it needs.

A Leader Teach games, both old and new. Direct club organizations and promote indoor and outdoor activities as outlined by the supervisors.

A Host Encourage all persons attending the playground or center to enter into the various activites.

A Coach Develop teams and competitive events of all kinds, giving instructions when necessary.

A Teacher Promote literature and study clubs, dramatics, hand work, and nature lore.

An Advertiser Provide a bulletin board. Plan a program at least one day ahead; attractively display all announcements.

A Clerk See that all reports are submitted on time to the main office.

A First-Aider Apply first aid only in emergency. Know the accident procedure completely and thoroughly.

An Authority Supervise carefully lavatories and out-of-the-way places. Eliminate all smoking, swearing, rowdyism and gambling.

A Friend One of your most important jobs as a leader is to be a friend to all who participate on your playground or in your center.[14]

QUALIFICATIONS FOR SUCCESSFUL LEADERSHIP

A good, qualified leader is essential to a successful community recreation program. The following are qualities expected of all professional recreation leaders:

1. A sincere liking for people as human beings; understanding their needs and interests.
2. A pleasing friendly person who is liked by his or her followers.
3. Genuinely dependable, punctual, responsible, fair, and impartial.
4. Straightforward, forthright, patient, and courteous in dealing with others.
5. Productive, willing to help, gets things done with an abundance of energy and contagious enthusiasm.
6. Warmth, compassionate, a cheerful disposition, a good sense of humor.
7. Capable of arousing acceptance of people and motivating others into action.
8. As a "spark plug", he or she initiates action, makes things happen.
9. A team player rather than an individual effort, taking pride in program and organization.
10. A wide range of skills, interests, and professional knowledge as well as a broad repertoire of activity ideas.
11. Good character, behaves in an ethically consistent manner, with high personal standards and morals.
12. Good judgment and discretion, able to grasp the heart of important problems and situations, knows when to act.

13. Intelligent with the capacity to conceptualize (formulate ideas) and organize, but also to be practical.
14. Tolerance for ambiguous situations until things become clear.
15. The ability to be flexible, to adapt and adjust activities when needed with creativity and ingenuity.
16. The ability to remain calm and cool during moments of excitement and occasional difficulty.
17. Working effectively with others, a cooperative attitude, and the ability to create congenial relationships among individuals and groups.
18. Articulate, communicating effectively with people.
19. The quality of being a self–starter—the ability to clearly identify goals and move vigorously toward them.
20. A good organizer and planner with the ability to delegate responsibility and the authority to make decisions.
21. Perseverance, able to stick to a task and see it through regardless of the difficulties.
22. The desire and determination to give 100 percent on the job.

> **To avoid criticism:**
> **Do nothing**
> **Say nothing**
> **Be nothing**

DUTIES OF THE RECREATION LEADER

The following are duties and responsibilities which face–to–face leaders employed with public agencies are expected to perform:

1. Plan, organize and conduct a well–balanced recreation program in line with the needs and interests of participants.

2. Lead, teach, and direct in a variety of program activity areas.
3. Be responsible for the safety, maintenance, and cleanliness of the recreation area.
4. Keep records of attendance, supplies, accidents, and special events.
5. Hold periodic special events.
6. Inspect daily the recreational area and equipment as a safeguard to accidents.
7. Conduct a comprehensive program of public and community relations through announcements, fliers, bulletin boards, releases to the news media, and similar methods.
8. Administer first aid efficiently to the injured.
9. Become familiar with the neighborhood surrounding the area.
10. Get to know the members of the group, and show an interest in each individual.
11. Be attired in clothing appropriate to the work involved.
12. Communicate ideas to the group and arouse enthusiasm for action to be taken.

Figure 19–3 The ability to teach and demonstrate is an important qualification for the recreation leader. An experienced, well rounded leader, like Bill Smithies, has developed leadership proficiency in many activity skills, such as the popular frisbee.

13. Help the group examine and clarify its goals and purposes.
14. Challenge the group with new or different ways to achieve their goals.
15. Develop secondary or assistant leaders, supervise volunteers, and assign them with various responsibilities.
16. Maintain control and discipline and deal with problems of discipline or antisocial behavior.
17. Help group members evaluate their progress, with constant improvement being the goal.
18. Adhere carefully to department personnel practices and regulations.
19. Take part in in–service training programs sponsored by the department, as well as play a significant overall role in the affairs of the department.

> **People helping people:**
> . . . **You touch one child,**
> . . . **You make one old person smile,**
> . . . **You save one tree.**
> Leo Buscaglia

MAJOR QUALITIES OF THE DYNAMIC LEADER

While there are numerous qualities and characteristics of an outstanding recreation leader, the following are major assets to leaders providing recreation and leisure services:

Communication Communication is perhaps the greatest tool of the group leader.

Figure 19–4 Communicating effectively with groups of people in one–to–one situations is very important for leadership work. Here, Randy Riblet, as emcee, handles the microphone at the annual Easter Egg Party for the Sacramento Children's Receiving Home.

The success or failure of most leaders can be determined by how well they communicate with their followers.

Cecil Gibbs, a noted authority on leadership in the field of business, explained that "Communication is the process by which one person influences another and is therefore basic to leadership."[15]

Four basic factors of communication are:

1. Gain attention.
2. Retain attention.
3. State ideas precisely.
4. Be a good listener.

Concentration   Another key to effective leadership is concentration. The leader should develop the habit of pinpointing what he or she is going to do and get rid of all extraneous thoughts. When leading or conducting an activity, the people, and only the people, should be his or her single thought.

The Power of Praise   A simple "Thank you" or "Well done!" is an absolutely essential tool for many leaders or managers. Yet, the practice of letting people know their work is recognized and appreciated occurs too seldom in most offices and departments.

"If you do not give your staff credit for the work they do, you will not get the best performance from them," said Niki Scott. "It's called positive reinforcement, reward conditioning involving manipulation and motivational psychology."[16]

Commitment   The person who is capable of making an aggressive effort to achieve results, regardless of obstacles, has the kind of commitment capability that makes a good leader.

Do they only have work experience or have they also given of themselves as a volunteer? Have they worked productively in difficult work environments? Can the person persevere under pressure situations?

Personality   A dynamic and wholesome personality is an essential requisite of a rec-

reation leader. "By personality is meant the sum and organization of all traits that go to make up the person and that condition or determine his role in the group," wrote Martin and Esther Neumeyer.[17]

Character   Character is so essential for recreation leadership because of the intimate relationship between the leader and the group. "Back of every contact between them is the silent influence of the leader's life," wrote Martin and Esther Neumeyer. "Children are prone to imitate those who direct their play life."[18]

By character is meant the integration and organization of attitudes and habits, also interests and sentiments, as they are oriented with reference to moral values and standards.

Faith   "Faith is an anchorage which enables one to hold steady, and to maintain poise and a mental balance in time of crisis," said Martin and Esther Neumeyer. "It creates confidence in self and human nature, and strengthens courage to uphold principles and to maintain convictions."[19] If a person has confidence in himself or herself and in the ability to carry on, he or she is not likely to succumb to an inferiority complex.

> **"If I had my life to live over again,
> I'd smell more flowers.
> I'd hug more children.
> I'd tell more people that I love them."**
> **Leo Buscaglia**

Making decisions   "The ability to make decisions is a tremendous attribute," said Kirk Breed, general manager of the Cal Expo State Fair. "One thing you can give to your students is to teach them to make decisions— clear and crisp and solid decisions."

Proper work habits   Create successful work habits, and a person will create a successful future. About 80 percent of what we

> **Rather than luck, making things happen and working hard is what it's all about!**

> **There is no limit to what people can do or where they can go if they don't mind who gets the credit.**

do every day is habit. To succeed as an individual, he or she must have successful habits.

MOTIVATING PEOPLE

Industrial psychologists have identified five important principles of motivation, which, if mastered, can help an individual be a more effective people–handler:

1. *Build people's self–esteem.* The more confident people feel, the better they perform.
2. *Focus on the problem, not personality.* Talk only about the problem or performance, not attitude or personality.
3. *Use reinforcement to shape behavior.* The technique of reinforcement encourages desirable behavior and discourages undesirable behavior.
4. *Actively listen.* Active listening assures the other party that you understand. Listening is especially valuable in emotional exhanges.
5. *Set solid goals.* Keep communicating, keep in touch, and keep reviewing the problem.[20]

Additional Suggestions in Motivating People:

- Emphasize the positive, not the negative.
- Be at ease, optimistic, and positive in manner.
- Speak clearly and distinctly in a pleasing but firm voice. Project your voice.
- Allow your interest and enthusiasm to be contagious.

- Try to have every individual participate.
- Emphasize team spirit and loyalty.
- Keep active throughout the activity.

SELF–CONCEPT AND THE RECREATION LEADER

Recreation is an excellent vehicle for people to gain self–respect and self–esteem. Everyone has a basic need for them. Recreation leaders are in a unique position to improve the self–concept of those they deal with.

Hints on Improving Self–Concept

1. Praise the strengths of a person and what he or she is doing.
2. Set realistic goals for people.
3. Don't subject people, especially children, to failure situations.
4. Provide opportunities for success and mastery of tasks.

Figure 19–5 Building people's self–esteem is most important in motivating people. Supported by encouragement and praise from her leader, this senior citizen feels much more positive and confident about the craft project.

5. Allow self–evaluation of tasks and projects emphasizing strengths.
6. People with a low self–concept look to others for reassurance—build that confidence up!
7. Help people identify problem areas and indicators of success or failure.
8. Be a warm and understanding leader.

UNDERSTANDING HUMAN BEHAVIOR

As a leader understands why people behave as they do and the forces that drive them on, he or she is able to influence their behavior more effectively. Recreation people are continually involved in the conduct of activities whose outcomes are more than fun, enjoyment, and relaxation.

A boy or girl playing softball on a playground team is having fun, but since the "whole person" is involved many other things are also happening to that person. He or she is active, therefore physiological outcomes, either good or bad, are certain to result, and skills, either properly or improperly executed, are engaged in. His or her intellectual operations may involve the learning of rules and the making of intelligent decisions during play. These intellectual operations interlock with the development of social behavior as he or she responds to teammates, opponents, the officials, spectators, and to the coach or leader. The emotions may be aroused in many of these responses. Moral and ethical choices may have to be made.[21]

The recreation leader, therefore, must directly be concerned with all of the outcomes of the activity. "If he shuts his eyes to moral and ethical values," suggests Howard Danford, "he may develop a skillful player who is also a bully, a liar, a cheat, and a thief. If he ignores social behavior, he may contribute to the development of non–cooperative, selfish individualists whose sole concern is themselves."[22]

Human beings constantly are searching for goals. People behave the way they do in order to satisfy their need for self–esteem, personal adequacy, or self–enhancement. "This is why they join groups," said Danford.[23]

EFFECTIVE GAME LEADERSHIP

Successful leadership of a low organized game does not occur just by chance. A well–conducted game is the result of the correct execution of a list of leadership guidelines and principles. Used by outstanding recreation leaders, the process of successful game leadership is comprised of the following helpful hints:

1. Pick the activity that is appropriate for the occasion.
2. Understand the rules and procedures of the game.
3. Get the players into the basic formation or group needed to start the game.
4. Use some signal to secure the players' attention and to start activities.
5. Make sure you have the "complete attention" of the group.
6. Introduce yourself and tell the group the name of the game.

Figure 19–6 When leading games that involve parallel lines, the leader (Ron Degler) stands between the lines at the end. This exciting balloon–tossing game is highly popular with both participants and spectators.

7. Have them take the appropriate formation or divide into teams, lines, or other arrangements.
8. Explain the game in as lively and enthusiastic a manner as possible.
9. State simply and clearly the directions for playing the game.
10. Make sure everyone in the group can hear you. Sound off!
11. Demonstrate the game briefly if necessary.
12. Give a brief explanation of the game.
13. Ask the group if they have any questions.
14. Have a good starting cue to begin the game, such as "Get ready, set, go!"
15. Cut the game off while interest in it is still fairly high.

PSYCHOLOGICAL EFFECTS OF GAME FORMATIONS

Game formations have definite psychological effects on the players. In their book *Social Games for Recreation*, Evelyne Borst and Elmer Mitchell listed some of these effects:

- Standing or sitting in a circle has a unifying effect on the players by giving them a feeling of belonging and being a part of the group.
- The action of assembling, scattering, and reassembling has a defrosting effect, minimizing self–consciousness by keeping everyone busy.
- Standing in a line creates in individuals a feeling of "action," for the line frequently is the springboard for activity.
- Standing in files, one player behind the other, symbolizes relays–group competition.[24]

Starting, guiding, and stopping are three important techniques of game leadership in capturing the interest of the participant and keeping the tempo moving. The leader must be able to start and accelerate the opening activity and maintain a spirit of fun and co-

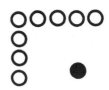

Figure 19–7 Group formations. Formations of groups have important psychological effects on the players and should be employed to the best advantage. These diagrams are group formations often used by recreation leaders.

operation. Then, with good continuity, the leader can guide the players from one activity to the next.

BUILDING RAPPORT WITH CHILDREN

The following are ways to build a positive playground atmosphere:

- Learn names.
- Be a good listener.
- Use a non–challenging way to correct children.
- Talk at their level.
- Show a genuine interest in each child and their projects.
- Make the child feel important.
- Be firm, fair, impartial, and consistent.

DISCIPLINE

The most desirable relationship between a leader and playground patrons is one of mutual respect and cooperation. The word *discipline* is not synonymous with punishment. Good discipline is control and direction of behavior—listening, informing, structuring, and responding. The goal of discipline is self–control. A good leader is firm but friendly, not harsh or punishing, not lax or hesitant. Repeated warning without action weakens the leader's position in the eyes of the children.

The need for enforcing discipline is least evident when there is a great amount of interesting activity. The best way to secure good discipline on the playground is to start the first day in a businesslike manner. Everyone should be kept busy. Rules must be followed and obeyed, though, and the leader must insist that they be obeyed. They must be clear, concise, and practical. The wise leader will first try every means of correction before resorting to suspension—a warning on the first offense, a penalty on the second. He or she is aware that when the child leaves the playground, he or she can no longer try

to help the youngster, and the child may get into more serious difficulty

To be of value, discipline must be positive and constructive and in direct relation to the offense committed. First, the leader must be certain that he or she has the facts of the case and be sure who committed the offense. Second, the offender must understand why he or she is being punished and that it is done as a means of correction, not revenge. Punishment should be used as little as possible, and the objective should be educational.

Discipline problems should be solved by the leader in charge. A leader should not allow the problem to continue without making a concerted effort to solve it. The best discipline is the preventative discipline of an active, interesting program conducted by a courteous, sympathetic, enthusiastic leader. Peer pressure is often an effective means of discipline and control. Children and youth who are disruptive are confronted by other children.

The following methods of disciplining can be employed:

- Talk to the child and explain "rule" infringement.
- Keep the child out of the activity for 15–30 minutes.
- Exclude the child from the playground for one or two days.
- Exclusion for a longer period of time must first be discussed with the district supervisor.
- If possible, anticipate serious problems and discuss them with your supervisor.

In building a positive playground atmosphere for more effective control, leaders should:

- Learn the names of participants.
- Encourage children to talk with leaders.
- Make the child feel important.
- Be a good listener.
- Use a nonchallenging way of correcting the children.
- Be firm as well as fair and impartial.
- Be consistent in your application of rules and regulations.

Figure 19-8 Discipline and control. Rules must be followed and obeyed. With children who attend the playground regularly, however, it is seldom necessary to do more than call attention to their misconduct or disregard for rules.

- Identify and work with "natural leaders."
- Show a genuine interest in individuals.

EVALUATING THE LEADER

The primary tool for leadership evaluation is the attainment of the defined production goals. "Whatever method is used," said Edith Ball and Robert Cipriano, "the goal of every evaluation program is to improve the quality of services given to people. What happens to people as they participate, becomes the important consideration."[25]

"Evaluation is a process of determining the extent to which leadership has accomplished what it set out to accomplish," said Danford. "Evaluation begins with a statement of the goals to be sought and ends with an appraisal of the degree to which these goals have been realized."[26]

There are several methods for evaluation of leadership and the program:

1. Day–by–day evaluation of program by the leader and the group.
2. Periodic evaluation to determine the extent of goal achievement.
3. Observation and evaluation of program by outside experts.
4. Self–evaluation of programs by representatives of the staff and various groups.[27]

QUESTIONS FOR DISCUSSION

1. What is leadership?
2. List the five major types of leadership within a recreation and leisure services agency or organization.
3. Why is the effectiveness or abilities of the front line leader so crucial to the program success?
4. Discuss and compare the four most common styles of leadership.

5. Discuss some of the most important guidelines in leadership.
6. Discuss how the recreation leader can build good rapport with children.
7. Discuss the process of successful game leadership.
8. Why is it important for the activity leader to be aware of agency values and philosophy?
9. Review and analyze the basic theories of group leadership.
10. Explain the evaluation process.
11. What methods of evaluating leadership are commonly used?
12. Discuss and analyze the entire area of discipline and control. What is often the best discipline or approach by the leadership staff?

REFERENCES

1. Richard Kraus, *Recreation Today: Program Planning and Leadership*, 2nd ed. (Santa Monica, Calif.: Goodyear Publishing Company, 1977), pp. 281–82.
2. Ordway Tead, *The Art of Leadership* (New York: McGraw–Hill Company, 1931), p. 20.
3. Clayne Jensen, *Leisure and Recreation: Introduction and Overview* (Philadelphia: Lea & Febiger, 1977), p. 208.
4. Cor Westland, "Recreation Leadership in Canada," *Proceedings and Papers:* The First World Conference of Experts on Leadership for Leisure; World Leisure and Recreation Association, 1978, p. 202.
5. Jensen, *Leisure and Recreation*, p. 208.
6. Sidney Lutzin and Edward Storey, *Managing Municipal Leisure Services* (Washington, D.C.: International City Management Association, 1973), p. 52.
7. Edith L. Ball and Robert E. Cipriano, *Leisure Services Preparation* (Englewood Cliffs, N.J.: Prentice–Hall, Inc., 1978), p. 176.
8. Ibid.
9. Ibid.
10. Ibid.
11. George Beal, Joe Bohlen, and Neil Raudabaugh, *Leadership and Dynamic Group Action* (Ames, Iowa: The Iowa State University Press, 1962), p. 34.
12. Richard Kraus and Barbara Bates, *Recreation Leadership and Supervision* (Philadelphia: W. B. Saunders Company, 1975), pp. 54–55.
13. Cecil E. Goode, "Significant Research on Leadership," *Personnel Magazine*, American Management Association, March 1951.
14. *Leader's Manual*, Stockton Recreation and Park Department, Stockton, California.
15. Cecil Gibbs, "Communicating Effectively in Business," printed brochure, Chicago, Illinois, 1978, p. 3.
16. Bernard L. Rosenbaum, "How Good People–Handlers Motivate Others," *Nation's Business*, March 1978, pp. 78–80.
17. Martin H. and Esther S. Neumeyer, *Leisure and Recreation* (New York: A. S. Barnes and Company, 1936), p. 370.
18. Ibid., p. 372.
19. Ibid., p. 373.
20. Bernard L. Rosenbaum, "How Good People–Handlers Motivate Others," p. 78–80.
21. Howard G. Danford and Max Shirley, *Creative Leadership in Recreation*, 2nd ed. (Boston: Allyn and Bacon, Inc., 1970), p. 31.
22. Ibid.
23. Ibid., p. 61.
24. Evelyne Borst and Elmer Mitchell, *Social Games for Recreation* (New York: The Ronald Press, 1959), pp. 5–6.
25. Ball and Cipriano, *Leisure Services Preparation*, p. 179.
26. Danford and Shirley, *Creative Leadership*, p. 103.
27. Ball and Cipriano, *Leisure Services Preparation*, p. 179.

Figure 20–1 Good program organization requires effective scheduling of time. The scene here is immediately following a football skills contest of a Pigskin Jamboree. Those at the scorer's table are quickly totaling up the scores to determine the winners, while a juggler entertains the large crowd of participants. The result: a smooth, pleasant ending to a successful event.

20
Program Planning and Organization

The recreation program of a department or organization consists of the activities or experiences available to the participant. Recreation agencies serve people through program activities and services. In the public sector the term *program*, generally, refers to the broad range of recreation activities and services for all ages and groups. In some situations, though, the terms "program" and "activity" are used interchangeably. According to Jesse Reynolds and Marion Hormachea, "Program usually refers to the total, while activity pertains to a specified unit or a single item of the program."[1]

Activities may be regularly scheduled for specific times, organized or informal. They may be supervised, self–sustaining, special, occasional, or drop in. Ideally, activities are selected and conducted by leaders for the specific purpose of achieving certain values. As a result, the leaders should be careful in their selection of activities.

Essentially, programs differ according to the breadth of services offered and the concentration of interests of the participants. Programs vary with financial support, facilities available, leadership qualifications, and administrative policies. Hence, the program emphasis in one city may be on sports, in another, on the performing arts.

Increasingly, park and recreation professionals are being challenged to offer comprehensive recreation programs for all ages and income levels.

THE PLANNING PROCESS

Planning is the process of arranging the various elements of a program in a manner designed to obtain constructive and worthwhile results. Effective planning and organization can help attain immediate goals and determine long–range objectives. Participants at the first National Workshop on Recreation agreed that "The objective of program planning is to provide those experiences that will bring to the participant the most satisfying values and that in addition will have desirable social effects."[2]

Recreation leaders must organize and conduct activities in a manner that will accomplish this major objective. In planning a successful program, the agency or individ-

Figure 20–2 Satisfying recreation experiences. Providing experiences that bring participants the most satisfaction is a major objective in program planning. Here, children at the playground enjoy a snow cone treat on a hot summer day.

ual must understand the essential elements in providing wholesome and satisfying recreation experiences. Many factors that can determine the success or failure of the program must be considered and thoroughly analyzed.

Programming is a process of planning that takes hours of time before the first participant ever steps into a facility. Good programming does not just happen—it is made to happen. Planners should have a course of action, a plan to follow. A well-trained professional staff which is creative, enthusiastic, and sensitive to user needs is the key ingredient in a successful recreation program.

MEETING NEEDS AND INTERESTS

A program of recreation activities should be determined by the needs, interests, and desires of the people to be served. However, what people need and want can vary considerably. As a rule, people prefer activities that they are knowledgeable about or are familiar with.

Although the needs of the participants are foremost in determining program objectives, the aims of any program should be in line with a sound and wholesome educational and cultural philosophy. In addition, the overall objectives of the agency should have a direct bearing on program offerings and priorities.

In planning recreation programs, it is essential to determine the specific needs of each neighborhood or area within a community. In conducting such a comprehensive inventory, a detailed study of all facilities and services should be carried out by the recreation and park department.

The study should involve a systematic survey of the expressed wishes of the residents of the neighborhood to be served. This can be done through public meetings or hearings of such community groups as Parent-Teacher Associations, advisory groups, councils, or civic committees. Interest checklists or surveys have proven effective in securing a representative sampling of all age groups.

Since recreation needs vary greatly and change from time to time, it is very important that planners and administrators stay up-to-date on needs and make necessary changes and adjustments.

STRIVING FOR GOALS AND OBJECTIVES

The goals and objectives of programs vary considerably as to different situations and community needs and interests. In general, all programs relate to the purpose and objectives of the agency or organization. In essence, program becomes the method through which goals and objectives are accomplished. Program goals involve long range actions, while program objectives are of short range duration.

THE QUEST FOR VALUES

Activities should be selected and conducted by leaders for the specific purpose of achieving certain goals and values. Howard Danford wrote that "This implies that leadership should be clear in the identification of its goals, careful in its selection of activities through which these goals are to be reached, and effective in the methods by which the activities are conducted."[3]

"If every leisure activity had equal value, the problem of program planning would be a relatively simple one," explained Danford. "But activities are no more equal in value than men are equal in wealth or intelligence."[4]

Virginia Musselman presented a strong challenge in stirring words when she declared that "Behind the skills we can teach, beyond the programs we can provide, must come a deliberate strong emphasis on the basic values of life. If we place more emphasis on strength, fleetness of foot, quickness of eye and of wit than we place on respect for human dignity, appreciation of goodness and beauty, and responsibility for the rights and privileges of all, then we are slated for oblivion."[5]

MAJOR AGE GROUPS

The age of the participants is generally regarded as the single most significant basis of recreation program planning. Richard Kraus emphasized that "Programming for each age group must be related to the total process of development."[6]

Grouping people by age has been a common way to play recreation programs and activities. When working with children, age grouping is a familiar pattern. "The key is to use age groups for program activity only when it makes sense to do so," said Patricia Farrell. "Some activities easily accommodate a broad range of ages, particularly programs in art, music, dance, and the theater." Farrell recommended that with people younger than 18, an age span greater than two or three years should be avoided.[7]

Children—Preschool, 6 to 8–year–olds, and 9 to 12–year–olds.
Teenagers—Younger adolescents, 13 to 15–year–olds, and older, 16 to 19.
Adults–Young, single, younger married couples, and middle–aged group in 40s and 50s.
Aging—Minimum age of 55 or 60, those who are retired, also called senior citizens, the elderly.

MAJOR ELEMENTS IN PROGRAM PLANNING

The following elements can influence significantly the process of planning recreation programs:

The people. The basic recreation needs and interests of the people to be served must be thoroughly understood. Variations in recreation interests must be considered in relation to "different age groups, both sexes, and of people with varying racial and cultural backgrounds and in different environments."[8]

Leadership. The leader is the most important element in the recreation program. Through the leader's expertise and guidance, the participants can gain experiences that are both growth–oriented and satisfying. Without leadership, the best facility will lie idle while program offerings fail to meet their potential.

Areas and facilities. The next important element, perhaps, is the provision of properly developed recreation areas to meet the leisure needs of citizens. "Areas" refer to park and recreation play spaces of varying types, while "facilities" refer to buildings, fields, pools, special structures, and equipment that are a part of these areas. Knowledge of the facility and equipment requirements of activities is required in effective program planning.

Finance. Sufficient funds are needed to provide adequate recreation opportunities for all the people. Many activities cannot be conducted successfully unless money is available to pay for the cost of leadership, equipment, supplies, and other items of expense. The cost of providing an activity must be carefully considered before it is implemented.

Activities. The component parts of any program are the activities or events which provide the appeal and interest of the program. Only through activity can people satisfy their leisure–time interests and desires. In planning programs, the leader must consider the suitability of various activities for people of different age, sex, and skill, as well as groups of different sizes.

Publicity/Promotion. Publicity seeks to inform, to impart information. To be effective, it must have some news value. Promotion, too, seeks to inform, but also seeks to "promote" activity on behalf of a specific program or project.

Publicity stimulates interest in the program by making potential participants aware that the program exists and reminding them of it in new and interesting ways throughout the year.

Public relations is a combination of the terms, publicity and promotion, plus day–to–day activities designed to build sound and productive relations in a community that will enhance a group's reputation and its ability to serve.

Figure 20–3 Publicity stimulates interest. This program sign which lights up at night is an excellent method of publicizing coming events. It has stimulated attendance at special events sponsored by the Youth Activities Center at Mather Air Force Base.

Safety. No program should be initiated without observing essential rules to ensure the safety of all participants and spectators. Therefore, safety is not only essential but should be a major element in planning and organizing programs. Strict observance of all safety rules in activities and equipment use is the leader's chief responsibility. "Safety First" should be the deciding factor in the selection of all activities.

APPROACHES TO PROGRAM PLANNING

Through the years, there have been numerous approaches and practices used in planning and organizing recreation programs. While most of them have proven to be of significant value, individually, each approach is considered vulnerable to weaknesses and ineffectiveness. Recreation leaders who have organized successful programs have employed a combination of approaches and theories in planning their activities. They have not limited their planning to a single approach.

1. *Traditional Approach* Program is built chiefly on the basis of what has been done in the past. Learn what programs have proven successful in the past and present the same activities.
2. *Current Practices Approach* Rely strongly on what other recreators and program directors are doing in the community and take advantage of their successful methods and ideas.
3. *Expressed Desires Approach* Determine what the people are interested in and give them what they want, relying on surveys and interest checklists.
4. *Authoritarian Approach* The administrative staff simply make all decisions with respect to activities, based on their personal judgment. Participants do not actively share in the planning.
5. *Sociopolitical* This new approach, suggested by Richard Kraus, sees community recreation programming as influenced by sociopolitical factors, such as the demands of pressure groups and the varying social needs of different neighborhoods in the community.
6. *Community Leadership Approach* Based on strong input from neighborhood boards and committees.[9]

Used individually, these approaches could result in unsound planning, but combined with good judgment, they are highly effective. Most department recreation program planning is a mix of all these approaches.

Nothing can spark a program more than a varied, rich, creative, and challenging approach to planning and leadership. Conversely, programs that show lack of imagination and initiative, and offer a narrow range of recreation interests, will attract few participants.

Figure 20–4 Traditional events which have been successful in the past should be given strong consideration for the future. This Hallowe'en Costume Contest has had the benefit of a favorable reputation and a strong publicity campaign.

BASIC PRINCIPLES IN PROGRAM PLANNING

The following are just a few of the principles which can serve as a guide to program planning.

1. Effective leadership is the backbone of any successful recreation program.
2. The program should consist of many and varied activities related to the needs, interests, and abilities of people of both sexes and of all ages.
3. The worth of an activity should be assessed in terms of its effects upon people. The program should be people centered.
4. The program should consist of activities that develop values sought by leadership.
5. Programs should be developed that are acceptable to the culture, customs, and tradition of the community.
6. An effective program must provide activities in which people are interested and strive for more satisfying and rewarding experiences.
7. The program should provide lifetime activities in which interest will continue over many years.
8. Equal opportunities should be extended to everyone, regardless of race, sex, creed, social or economic status.
9. The program should emphasize activities that relate to one another.
10. Leaders should invite participants to share responsibility for program planning. Involve the participants.

11. The leadership staff should operate on a sound philosophical basis of recreation and leisure, a good working knowledge of the basic theories of play.
12. The program should be sufficiently flexible to permit adaptation to varying situations.
13. Grouping is a significant factor in programming.
14. Program development should be positive in direction but gradual in pace.
15. Adequate financial support is necessary for success of any activity or program.
16. Safe and healthful conditions should be provided for all recreational activities.
17. Continuous evaluation is a major factor in program improvement.
18. Opportunities should be provided for a family to play together.
19. Programs should offer relaxing activities as well as active forms of recreation.
20. The need of the ill and people with handicaps should be served with a well–rounded program of activities.
21. Overplan rather than underplan.
22. Have a keen eye for details. Use a check list in most areas of planning and organization.
23. All recreators should have a sound knowledge and understanding of the policies, rules, and regulations stated in the department's policy manual.
24. Program planners should survey needs and interests, existing services, and potential resources.
25. Programs should involve the cooperation and assistance of other agencies in the community.
26. Through effective public relations and communication, the program should be effectively interpreted to the public.
27. Programs should make the most efficient and imaginative use of available resources and facilities.
28. Activities should be scheduled at appropriate times to insure maximum participation.
29. Programs should involve challenge, adventure, and anticipation.
30. The progressive leader seeks constantly to innovate, develop the program, and to provide more meaningful services.

Specific Elements in Planning

- Basic needs and interests
- Goals and objectives
- Available resources (staff, facilities, equipment, etc.)
- Amount of supervision needed
- Relative importance of activity
- Age groups
- Sexes
- Size of groups
- Time period
- Time allotment
- Types of groups
- Schedule making
- Setting atmosphere
- Weather
- Indoor or outdoor
- Supplies and equipment
- Attendance
- Skills/level
- Flexibility/adaptation
- Discipline and control
- In–service training
- Agency guidelines
- Self–directed or supervised

SPECIAL FACTORS IN PROGRAM SUCCESS

In addition to arranging the major and specific elements and the correct execution of guidelines and principles, there are a number of special factors or ingredients that are essential to a dynamic program. Combined with "a little bit of style and class," they typify outstanding programs . . . those that *ring the bell!*

Creativity

Creative thinking can be a great asset to any recreation staff. William Penn Mott, Jr. believes that the best recreation program is one that fosters ". . . the type of climate that encourages imaginative, positive thinking, new ideas and a desire to excel." According to Mott, "We must dare to try new ideas to meet the great social changes of our time. If he is timid and afraid to accept and try new ideas, even the most imaginative person soon becomes frustrated and discouraged."[10]

The following are some of Mott's guidelines that can start any department along the path of creative programming:

- Permit free and open discussion of all problems.
- Give department heads equal opportunity to review all plans.
- Encourage the flow of magazines, periodicals, and books through all departments. Read!
- Encourage employees and provide incentives and opportunities for them to receive continuing education. Think!
- Hold regular staff meetings and general meetings of all employees. Communicate!
- Encourage ideas and act upon them giving due credit; or, if rejected, give reason.
- Encourage inquisitiveness.
- Create an atmosphere of urgency and action. Make things happen!
- Allow employees the freedom of judgment and permit "calculated risk" decisions.
- Review your operations. Are they up-to-date? Or are you just satisfied? Plan ahead!
- Seek out other creative people. They will tend to stimulate your thinking.
- Look for new ways to do old chores. In making your routine more exciting, ask yourself, "How else might I do it?"

Imagination

There is just one ingredient for a successful program that no formula can provide—imagination. The creative leader has the imagination, vision, and ingenuity to think or dream up all types of imaginative happenings and fun situations. The leader sees things through the eyes of his or her followers. He or she puts himself or herself in their shoes and helps them make their dreams come through. Keeping in mind what the needs and desires of the participants are, he or she strives to inject into the program spontaneous, fresh activities and even an occasional crazy stunt.

The imaginative and creative leader is particularly popular on the playground where a child's ability to dream and imagine knows no bounds. The leader simply has to draw it out. Bringing to the playground "Captain Bloodybones" or some fictitious character will excite every child's interest and fancy.

Communication

Success or failure in leadership is often determined by how well leaders communicate with their followers. Basically, communication is the process by which one person influences another.

The following are some important steps to better communication:

1. Think clearly before you speak.
2. Listen intently to your group.
3. Make sure your group can see and hear you.
4. Speak persuasively, with feeling and assurance.
5. Know your subject, what you are talking about.
6. Be brief, concise, and to the point.
7. Choose your words wisely.
8. Use your voice to the best advantage, loud and clear when necessary.
9. Have good diction, enunciate, and emphasize key words.
10. Use a proper pace, rather than rapid chatter.
11. Speak with confidence and a postive frame of mind.
12. Have an idea what you want to say, then go ahead and say it.

Flexibility

Program plans should be flexible enough so they may be revised to cope with changing conditions and unexpected needs. The alert leader anticipates difficulties and prepares for them.

Flexibility calls for some important foresight and anticipation on the part of both the planning staff and the leaders. The necessary alternatives and resources for flexibility must be available. For example, a picnic group, in the event of rain or inclement weather, should have adequate indoor facilities with which to change from an outdoor setting to an indoor one. The leader who has a wide assortment of games, program materials, and offerings will have the flexibility to make appropriate changes and adjustments when necessary.

Praise and Encouragement

No other tactic can achieve the result that praise and pleasure in an individual's accomplishment can provide. Desire can be greatly diminished or destroyed completely by lack of response or by discouragement by the leader.

Leaders should give praise when their participants do something good. People respond quickly and affirmatively to praise. The leader must never let the learner get frustrated and give up. "Keep working," and "You can do it!" should be steadily repeated by the leader.

Learning from mistakes should take place in a friendly and relaxed atmosphere. Participants should not be unduly embarrassed, ridiculed, or humiliated because of errors they make while learning. Therefore, by praising what they do correctly, the leader can encourage pupils to keep trying until they master the skill.

> **A child's self-confidence, the feeling he can do whatever he sets out to do, is built on praise and encouragement.**
> **Elizabeth Post**

Motivation

The ability to persuade people to participate is one of the most important qualities of leadership. Leadership involves the ability to motivate and persuade people to take some kind of action. The leader's ability to motivate the group is often determined by skills of communication.

Dedication and Courage

The dedicated leader has great pride in himself or herself, as well as his or her organization and profession. He or she is never satisfied with "an adequate performance," merely getting the job done. He or she is continuously striving for excellence, giving 100 per cent. He or she is ready to give extra effort at all times.

Courageous and devoted to a high level of service, the dedicated leader will never give up, but always strive for progress and a better program. The leader who will "hang in there" even under difficult circumstances can set a great example for both the followers and fellow staff members.

SCHEDULING PROGRAMS

Program scheduling is a very important aspect of program planning. Programs offered at the wrong time, too often, or with insufficient time can be jeopardized right from the beginning. Effective scheduling, on the other hand, implies that an activity is offered at the right time of the year, week, and day, and in combination with other appealing program elements. Essentially, scheduling involves coordination of location, time, dates, leadership, and activities.

In making up schedules for public recreation programs, the following factors should be considered:

Nature of the activity: quiet, active, educational, regular or special, informally or formally organized, competitive or non-competitive.

Facilities available: indoor or outdoor, regular or specialized, supervised or self-directing, participant or spectator oriented, seasonal or year-round, lighted or unlighted.

Staff available: supervised or self–directed, professional or volunteer, routine or highly skilled.

Funds available: free or fee, self–sustaining or supervised, adequate funding available.

Time requirement: length of period required, how often, and what time period (morning, afternoon, evening).

Characteristics of participants: age, sex, skill level, normal or handicapped, condition of health.

Time Scheduling

Generally, programs are broken down according to the following time units: yearly, seasonal, weekly, and daily.

Yearly schedule Serving as a master calendar, this unit takes into consideration community events which may affect various recreation activities such as holidays, opening and closing of schools, summer school, church activities, community celebrations, and major special events.

Seasonal schedule Planning for seasonal programs reflects such factors as the climate, school year, and the traditional seasons. A seasonal program might highlight the activities for the season and provide for different skill levels in each activity, possibly culminating with a special event.

Weekly schedule In addition to regular daily schedules, most recreation agencies and organizations schedule a number of special events or classes at various points during the week. For example, playground and community center programs are scheduled on a weekly basis. The weekly schedule might be a series of daily schedules plus a staff meeting at the beginning of the week and one or more special features. Sports tournaments are often conducted during the week at neighborhood playgrounds. Special program themes are based on a weekly schedule.

Daily schedule Planning daily schedules involves dividing the available time into time blocks during the morning, afternoon, and evening. Various types of activities can be offered concurrently or in sequence to each other. Daily schedules will vary with the needs of the participants and skills of staff. Different levels of skills may be scheduled on alternate days. The number of time blocks, of course, depends on the number of staff in an area. A specific program can be developed for each age group within a particular time block. Periodically, all of the age groups can join together in a special activity, such as a carnival, trip, or some other event.

SELECTION OF ACTIVITIES

A major concern of agencies and organizations providing recreation and leisure services is to determine what activities to offer and on what basis. The following factors should be considered:

Needs and interests of groups The expressed interests, past experiences, level of skills, age level, physical and mental capability, sex make–up, social maturity, and numbers to be served should be given close attention.

Goals and objectives of department Activities should meet specific goals and objectives and the underlying philosophy of the agency or organization.

Administrative feasibility The overall input into the program, such as organizational time, expenses, and staffing, should be administratively feasible.

Organizational sponsor Programs are sponsored by different organizations and units of a department. Therefore, within a departmental structure, scheduling decisions must be made to determine which division or unit will be responsible for a program or activity.

Physical location Based on need and demand, the location of the program or activities has to be determined. Adequacy of facilities should be of prime concern.

Figure 20–5 The greatest good for the greatest number is a good rule to follow in selecting program activities on a community–wide basis. The Wollman Ice Skating Rink in Central Park has a high priority, drawing participants from all over New York City's five boroughs. Open from late fall through April, it features recreational and instructional skating as well as competitive events. (Courtesy New York City Parks and Recreation Department.)

In the selection process, activities which have been strongly requested by individuals and groups in interest surveys should be given priority. Based on various factors, the recreation director and his or her staff then determines which activities should have: (a) the highest priority; (b) medium priority; (c) lowest priority.

CLASSIFICATION OF ACTIVITIES

Classification of activities is used by the program planner as a frame of reference in selecting a balanced program of activities and in meeting the diverse needs of participants.

Recreation activities can be classified in the following ways: indoor and outdoor; age or sex of participants; individual or group; mental or physical; active or passive; participant or spectator.

The most common classification of recreation activities is by the following ten types:

1. Arts and Crafts
2. Dance
3. Drama
4. Music and Rhythm
5. Nature and Outings
6. Sports and Games
7. Educational
8. Services performed
9. Special Events
10. Miscellaneous activities.

PROGRAM AREAS AND ACTIVITIES

The great variety of activities and events that occupy the leisure time of people is called recreation. Indeed, the evergrowing field of recreation and leisure services is limitless, ranging from the low organized type to those requiring highly organized planning, from individual to group enjoyments. Some activities can be physical, others are characterized by mental or social skills and interests.

Recreation activities can be grouped in a number of ways. The traditional approach, however, is to classify activities according to several broad areas and types of recreation interests. All types of recreation have one characteristic in common—they provide an important outlet for some basic urge or need.

ARTS AND CRAFTS

With the exception of games and sports, arts and crafts are one of the oldest forms of recreation activities provided by public recreation and park agencies. They are almost unlimited in scope, and may range from painting a paper bag mask for a holiday affair to the intricate three–dimensional design of stage sets; from sand modeling to wood and soap carving; from jewelry to ceramics; from random finger painting to the painting of landscapes; or from simple whittling to building boats.

An individual's experiences in arts and crafts should be of a progressive nature. Beginning with projects involving elementary skills, one should be provided with opportunities that demand more advanced instruction and skills.

Although activities in arts and crafts can involve expensive projects, some of the most satisfying are the most inexpensive ones. Scrap or discarded materials such as old tires, bottles, tin cans, and box crates can be obtained for nothing and used to create interesting works of art.

Values

People have always had the need to express their creativity and communicate it to one another. In no other area of the recreation program does an individual come as close to the job of creation as in arts and crafts activities. From primitive etchings to contemporary art, various media have been used to express the artist's feelings. By utilizing their abilities and expressing themselves through art, people can reduce some of the tensions of modern living, and as a result develop a sense of fulfillment.

Figure 20–6 The joy of creation. Experiences in arts and crafts should be of a progressive nature. As skills increase, participants may seek more specialized training. This playground scene is a registered fee program conducted by the St. Louis County Department of Parks and Recreation. (Courtesy St. Louis County Recreation Division.)

Role of the Leader

A successful leader need not be a highly skilled artist or craftsman. A leader, however, should know how to do many of the crafts. More important than being a skilled performer is the ability to teach. The key to good leadership is effective communication—the ability to transmit ideas both directly and indirectly.

The arts and crafts leader must understand that the values received by the participant through the activity itself are more important than the object being made. The quality of the experience is most essential to the success of the program.

DANCING

During the last two decades, there has been a spectacular increase in the number of persons and groups participating in various kinds of dancing. Increased leisure has been a contributing factor to the growth of dancing, but perhaps more significant has been the establishment of public recreation and school programs employing leadership skilled in the dance arts.

Throughout the nation, large numbers of children, teenagers, and adults have enrolled in classes in ballroom, social, folk and square dancing, tap, ballet, and modern dance. People are asking for country, ballroom, and touch dancing. There is a wide range of dance music, like rock and roll, new wave, and country.

Values of Dance

The many types of dance offer numerous values and rewards to those who participate regularly. Many people like to dance simply for fun and enjoyment; others feel dancing provides a release of tensions. Certainly, the values in dancing involve a significant contribution to both mental and physical well–being. The development of poise, self–confidence, and personal adequacy are additional values to be gained through social dancing. For many, it offers an opportunity for dating and getting to know members of the opposite sex.

Leadership in Dance

For instructional classes in dance, the trained leader or instructor is most desirable. He or she must have the ability and background to plan and conduct a well–rounded program of activities. Generally, the dance teacher has the responsibility to teach effectively the basic skills and to provide wholesome social experiences.

Hiring a regular recreation leader to serve as a dance instructor rather than a dance specialist can be a serious mistake. A more sensible solution would be to increase fees and use the additional funds to employ a more qualified person. However, playground leaders should be qualified to provide limited instruction in rhythms and folk

dances for children, or the more simple square and social dances which are a regular part of the playground or center program. Still, when the public is charged a fee, they deserve a qualified leader who can meet a near professional level of proficiency.

DRAMA

Drama is a very old form of recreative expression. Contributing to the release of tensions, drama gives temporary escape from reality and is a powerful source for development of creative interests not always found in other forms of human activity. The tools necessary for its expression are for the most part voice and body.

Drama activities may be the simple and unpretentious children's story hours, the unsophisticated development of dramatic play of the young child, the organizing of play reading clubs, the construction of puppets or marionettes, the elaborate presentation of an annual pageant or festival involving all of the performing arts and hundreds of skilled players, or bringing into the community professional dramatic or musical comedy productions of national reputation.

In meeting the growing demands of the public for "the performing arts," many public recreation and park agencies have improved existing drama and theater activities, and have initiated new programs under various auspices. There has been closer cooperation among public recreation agencies and various community groups and people concerned with the drama field.

Values of Drama

Drama in the recreation program offers participants opportunities to express themselves through imaginative and dramatic play.

Children can develop poise and self–control from training and experience on a stage. Qualities such as tolerance and empathy can also be stimulated and enriched through participation in a drama activity. A new sympathy and respect for one another is developed. Being a part of a group where everyone is working together toward a common goal can give a child a feeling of belonging he or she may never have had before.

Preschool children are surprisingly creative when they are given a familiar story to act out in their own words. Every exercise in creative thought and self–expression is an excellent opportunity to release the pent–up feelings children often have no way to express.

Drama activities can provide a framework for channeling the creative drives of young people. Experience and participation in drama can stimulate, inspire, and direct the talents of young people so they may achieve the realization of their own abilities.

Drama also provides entertainment for the passive participant. Through the various drama presentations, the viewer often finds escape and leisure entertainment in the unfolding drama or lively, musical comedy productions.

Drama also has an important place in numerous social recreation activities. The element of drama can make a game highly enjoyable to all ages. Dramatic games include guessing games, charades, and singing games. The action and dialogue of skits can be very exciting.

Leadership

The leader of a children's drama program should have a working knowledge of creative dramatics and of children's literature and plays.

A specialist trained in the drama area is, of course, ideal; however, the well–rounded and experienced recreation leader can become a good drama leader, provided he or she has in–service or supplementary training, with emphasis on the philosophy and techniques of creative dramatics, as well as the technique of acting and play production.

For the community theater, though, trained professional leadership is absolutely essential. Drama specialists are recruited

from several sources, but the main source is from local colleges. Students majoring in drama find this type of work an excellent opportunity to gain experience in an atmosphere where creativeness is given freedom for expression.

MUSIC

In every culture and nation of the world, music has been an integral part of life. Indeed, music is universal in its appeal, providing emotional responses which have given people great pleasure and rewards.

Music in recreation occurs in a wide assortment of settings and activities. It can satisfy any age, sex, taste, mood, or level of ability. On the playground, music may consist of informal sings in the late summer morning or afternoon. The construction of instruments and the creation of a playground orchestra can be challenging and satisfying to children. Teenage choral and orchestral groups can be organized in community cen-

Figure 20–7 The sound of music can liven up the spirit and atmosphere of any program event, which can motivate people to participate. This senior citizens summer picnic took place in a well–shaded park in Flint, Michigan. (Courtesy Flint Municipal Parks and Recreation Department.)

ters. Music is often used with other activities, accompanying civic celebrations, pageants, sports events, and ceremonials.

Indeed, unlimited opportunities for listening to good music are available to the American people. In addition to radio and television, the majority of American citizens have stereo record players, band concerts, and various other musical presentations at their disposal.

Values

The unique appeal and interest of music has provided people with many values. "No other activity in the recreation program can weld a group together as does music in a community sing," said John H. Jenny. "The mood of music is able to change the mood of man."[11]

The pleasure of hearing or participating in music provides considerable enjoyment. Even more appealing is the ongoing, pulsating rhythm of music, which invariably causes a humming, singing, or whistling response on the part of the listener.

The Role of Leadership

Effective use of music by the entire recreation staff can offer a recreation program much needed spirit and enthusiasm. Through group singing, rhythmic movement, and the playing of many types of musical instruments, leadership can create the type of atmosphere that no other area of recreation can match. Easy–to–remember songs can be highly pleasing for both children and adults to sing. Playing one's own musical instrument can be a challenging and exhilarating experience.

On the playground, the use of rhythm instruments can be one of the most delightful and pleasing experiences children can have. The typical playground orchestra includes drums, tom–toms, and shaking instruments such as tambourines, clappers, and rattles.

SOCIAL RECREATION

The wide range of opportunities for social life among people of all ages indicates the importance of social recreation experience in daily living. Essentially, the primary value of social recreation in a recreation program is its contribution to the social life of the participant.

Social recreation includes activities that help create a spirit of fun, fellowship, and sociability. A child's birthday party; teen centers and dances; trips by the family to the lake; watching sports, music, and drama events; adult square dances; and Golden Age Club activities are prime examples of the tremendous interest in social recreation opportunities.

People of all ages have a need for social recreation. Children and adolescents find social activities exciting and satisfying. Young men and women need opportunities to meet and become acquainted with persons of the opposite sex.

Social recreation is practiced through an informal approach, which is adapted to the interest and ability of the participants. The imagination and ingenuity of the leader are important elements, but the needs and interest of the group should dictate the type of activities offered.

No one needs advance preparation to participate in social recreation activity. They should be able to use whatever skills they have. Emphasis on skill and winning should be minimized.

Values in Game Play

Many important personal and social values and outcomes can be achieved from participation in games. The outstanding leader has definite goals in mind in organizing and conducting games for every occasion. Players can learn to:

Music is the universal language of humanity.

Play according to the rules
Accept boundaries
Develop new skills and interests
Take turns
Accept defeats as well as victories in good
    spirit
Develop good sportsmanship
Cooperate with others
Be decisive

Objectives

The personal objectives of social recreation are to provide opportunities for the development of:

Worthy use of leisure time
Emotional releases and relaxation
A sense of personal worth
New friendships
Identification with others
A sense of belonging
Experiences in democratic living
Self–expression
Creative experiences
Leadership qualities

Planning Parties

Successful party leadership depends upon careful planning. Activities, wisely selected, must be balanced with both active and passive games, and with good continuity and progression effectively presented to reach a fitting climax.

Committees can be appointed to plan the program, refreshments, and decorations. Under the direction and guidance of the party chairman, the group should determine the theme and object of the party, setting the time and place of the event. Invitations, decorations, and refreshments can be built around a theme.

Evaluation

In evaluating a social event, the following questions should be used to determine its success, with emphasis on suggestions and recommendations for future planning.

Figure 20–8 Sociability and fun in social recreation games are far more important than who wins or who loses. These young people find the grapefruit relay a most hilarious experience.

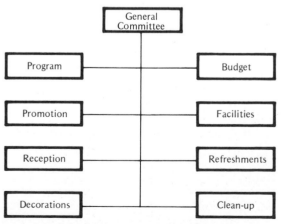

Figure 20–9 Organization chart for conducting a party or social event.

- Was there evidence of careful planning?
- Was the event organized?
- Was there variety and continuity?
- Did the event show unity and interest?
- Was it started on time?
- Were the activities suited to the group?
- Did the leaders share responsibilities?
- Did the activities follow the central theme?
- Did the activities move smoothly from one to another?
- Were the leaders friendly and enthusiastic?
- Did they have good rapport with participants?
- Were they aware of group reactions?
- Were they flexible and tactful in handling mistakes or emergencies?
- Did everyone have a good time?
- Did the event finish with a climax or a pleasing ending?

SPORTS AND ACTIVE GAMES

The growth of sports has been one of the most remarkable trends in the recreation and leisure field during the past two decades. In participation, the sharpest increases have been in swimming, bowling, tennis, baseball, and softball.

Although millions of people enjoy spectator sports, participant sports have an even greater appeal. The sharp growth in sports participation can be attributed to such significant factors as increased leisure time, growing affluence, emphasis on the importance of physical fitness, and television coverage of sports events. Jogging has increased considerably among both men and women.

Many traditional sports have had significant adaptations which have made them suitable for those previously considered too young, too old, or handicapped. Slow–pitch softball, for example, has been a tremendously popular activity among people too old to play fast pitch softball or baseball.

People with physical handicaps have found wheelchair bowling and basketball very much to their liking, while those with mental handicaps enjoy swimming, softball, and roller skating.

Recreation agencies are being confronted with greatly increased demands for ball fields, tennis courts, golf courses, marinas, swimming pools, skating rinks, and other sports facilities.

Sports for girls and women have grown tremendously during the past decade, and indications are that the sharp rise will continue in the future.

Values

People participate in sports and games primarily for fun; they also participate for the enjoyment that comes from participation and athletic achievement. Indeed, the urge to play for enjoyment, satisfaction, accomplishment, and fellowship accounts for the majority of participants. Sports participation provides much needed physical exercise to keep our bodies strong and healthy. Muscles strengthen, reactions quicken, and breathing eases, as exercise and sports develop and improve the human body. As a person's physical being improves, so does his or her mental state and general well–being.

On the playground level, boys and girls have the opportunity to experience competitive sports activity and to develop beneficial behavior skills such as sportsmanship, fair play, and team play. The chance to be a member of a team can be a most rewarding social experience particularly when one considers the lack of belonging and commitment on the part of so many of our youth today.

Psychologically, sports provide participants an opportunity to "let off steam." By entering into vigorous, competitive play, individuals are able to express their aggressive or combative instincts. More than any other area, it is in athletics that people's competitive instincts come into play.

While "playing to win" is normal, competition and the winning element must not dominate a sports program. In too many sports programs, the goal is to win at all costs, resulting in an overemphasis on winning. As a result of this overemphasis, the more important goals and ideals of sports are almost completely ignored.

Types of Sports Activities

Sports activities are classified under the following major groups:

- *Team Sports* Team activities provide participants with the opportunity to "play on a team."
- *Individual Sports* Activities that can be played on an individual basis.
- *Dual Sports* Sports that involve two or more participants.
- *Low Organized Games and Contests* Game activities which require few rules and little organization.
- *Aquatics* Water–related sports and activities.
- *Combative Sports* Activities and sports which involve direct combat—one person against another.
- *Co–recreational sports* Sports and games in which boys and girls or men and women play together on the same team.

Types of Sports and Game Tournaments

In organizing competition, one of the first steps is selecting the tournament best suited to the sport. Several different types of tournaments exist, and they require a close examination before making a selection.

Among the factors that will determine the type of tournament to be used are the number of entries, the time allotted for playing the tourney, the available facilities, and the advantages and disadvantages of each tournament structure.

Seeding The method of seeding can play an important role in elimination tournaments. A "seeded" team or player is considered to be highly rated in skill. The purpose of seeding is to prevent the highly skilled entries from eliminating each other in the early rounds. This is accomplished by placing the seeded teams, or players, in separate brackets. Generally, two out of every four entries are seeded.

Byes A bye is a dummy team, or player, that is placed in the tournament and matched against an opponent, but does not compete. If the original number of contestants is an exact power of two (2, 4, 8, 16, 32, etc.), the use of a bye or byes is not required. But, when the total number of contestants does not balance out to an even power of two, the system of byes is used to make up the difference. If there were only 13 teams, which is not a perfect power of two, the number of byes to be used would be 16 minus 13, or 3. Seeded teams are usually awarded the byes. A team that is awarded a bye automatically advances to the second round.

Preliminary qualifying rounds Where there are a great number of contestants, it may be necessary to conduct preliminary qualifying rounds to cut down the field. The teams that play in this "pre–tournament" are drawn by lot or chosen because of poor or unknown ability. After the necessary number of rounds are completed to reduce the field to the desired number, the regular elimination tournament can be charted and scheduled.

Single elimination tournament This is a quick and simple method of determining a champion. Because losers are eliminated, half of the contestants in each round are immediately removed from further play. The single elimination tourney is valuable when the number of entries is large, the tourney period is short, and the facilities are limited.

Consolation tournament The consolation tournament is set up to give the losers of first matches in the single elimination tournament an opportunity for further competition by placing them in consolation rounds. Weaker teams who may have drawn (and been defeated by) a seeded team in the first round and teams who have traveled long distances are given a second chance to compete.

Double elimination tournament This tournament requires a much longer period of play than the single elimination. Each team must be defeated twice before being

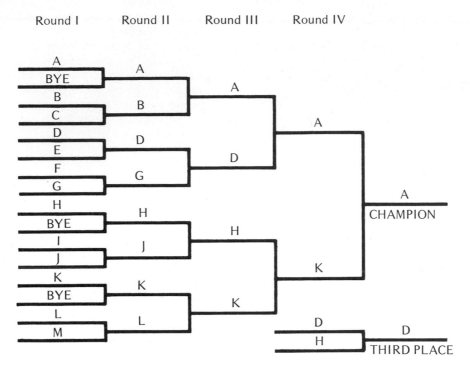

Figure 20–10 Single elimination tournament.

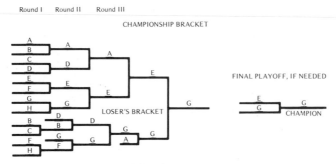

Figure 20–11 Double elimination tournament.

eliminated from further competition. As shown in Figure 20–11, the championship bracket is carried on in the usual manner, with the defeated teams dropping into the losers' bracket. The teams that win out in both brackets are matched for the championship.

Considering all types of tournaments, double elimination is probably the best to use in determining a regional, area, or national championship. Since it guarantees each entry two matches before being eliminated, this tournament is readily accepted.

Round Robin tournaments Requiring a longer period of time for completion, the Round Robin tournament provides more participation for every contestant than any other type of tourney. Every player, or team, com-

1-8	1-7	1-6	1-5	1-4	1-3	1-2
2-7	8-6	7-5	6-4	5-3	4-2	3-8
3-6	2-5	8-4	7-3	6-2	5-8	4-7
4-5	3-4	2-3	8-2	7-8	6-7	5-6

1-8	2-5	7-5	6-4	7-8	1-3	5-6
2-7	8-6	1-6	7-3	5-3	4-2	1-2
3-6	1-7	8-4	1-5	6-2	5-8	4-7
4-5	3-4	2-3	8-2	1-4	6-7	3-8

Figure 20–12   Round robin tournament before field adjustments (above) and after field adjustments (below).

petes against every other player, or team, which stimulates interest throughout the playing season. The Round Robin tournament is best suited to league play, since it is important for each team participating to play every other team at least once.

Perhaps the easiest method for arranging a Round Robin is the rotation method. In arranging a draw for an even number of teams—six as an example—number one remains stationary and the others rotate around it counterclockwise until the original combination is reached.

When teams do not have "home" fields or courts, a Round Robin schedule should be adjusted so that each team plays approximately the same number of games on each field or court.

The final outcome of such a tournament is decided on a percentage basis. The winner is determined according to the percentage of victories, which is obtained by dividing the number of victories by the number of games played.

Ladder tournament   One of the best known of the extended type of tournaments, the ladder tournament can be used very effectively at playgrounds, camps, or clubs to develop and sustain interest in tennis, handball, table tennis, horseshoes, and similar activities. Usually this type of tournament continues for several months, since the object is for each entry to reach his or her highest level on the ladder. Contestants are permitted to challenge one and two positions above their own.

SPECIAL EVENTS

Special events are often referred to by recreation professionals as "frosting on the cake." Special events are perhaps the most enjoyable and appealing phase of the entire recreation program. They are considered "the spice" and the highlight of the year's program.

A special event is one that departs from the normal routine and requires special planning and assistance. It should be related to the program being conducted; however, it should not dominate or interfere with the other important phases of the program. Ideally, an event should be built around a special occasion, celebration, or holiday, thus giving it added meaning.

The variety of special events is almost unlimited. The only limiting factor is the imagination and creativity of the leaders. The cost of the event and the interests of the public, though, are factors to be considered in the choice of special events.

Values

Special events can generate a unique interest and enjoyment among both participants and the leaders. Playground–sponsored events have proven highly effective in promoting the overall program, encouraging greater numbers of participants and spectators. In many instances, a special event is the culmination of a much larger program. As a result, the public spotlight is focused on events that can capture the interest and imagination of the public. Often, an event is designed to provide a demonstration and appropriate display of what the program has accomplished.

Special events can provide a strong incentive for those on the playground or organization to become more involved in the program, in addition to motivating others who have been unaware of the activities.

Leadership Needed

Leaders for special activities should be dependable, friendly, and like to work with people. Important responsibilities should be delegated to selected leaders by the chairman. However, the specific individual in charge, such as the chairman, must "call the shots" and be responsible for keeping the momentum going, for "trouble shooting," and for coping with possible "emergency situations."

Publicity and Promotion

To attract people to an event, an effective publicity campaign should be organized and conducted. Starting two or three weeks before the event, the campaign should include flyers, posters, news releases to the news media, banners, a telephone committee, and group visitations "to get the word out and beat the drums."

PROGRAM ORGANIZATION CHECK LIST

A successful special event is the direct result of good planning. The following is a list

Figure 20–13 The bicycle rodeo, an annual event in most communities, is a challenging test of riding skills and safety practices that has been solidly supported by law enforcement agencies and service clubs. School assemblies and classroom study should precede the rodeo event.

of suggestions that should be considered in planning and conducting a special event:

Pre–Preparation and Planning

1. Attention to details.
2. Follow a check list.
3. Day before review of check lists.

Conducting a Special Event

1. Take sufficient time to set–up.
2. Extend a warm welcome.
3. Start on time.
4. Select a good emcee.
5. Communicate with the group.
6. Good variety and diversity.
7. Establish good continuity and strive for momentum.
8. Smooth transition from one activity to the next.
9. Be safety conscious; anticipate problem situations.
10. Cope effectively with problems.
11. Continual evaluation; make some adjustments if necessary.
12. Strive for an enjoyable wind–up/climax. Have your participants leave on a happy note!

Post–Event Details

1. Follow–up publicity.
2. Evaluation of event.
3. Send out thank you letters and calls.

Musical Accompaniment

A must for any special event, background music will provide the atmosphere so necessary in developing the proper spirit and tempo.

Safety

A careful check for potential dangers or hazards should be conducted prior to the event. The condition of chairs and bleachers, the play areas, and equipment and apparatus should be closely inspected.

Finances

A budget of anticipated income and expenditures should be prepared, item by item. Essentially, the resources that can be utilized must be in relationship to the finances available. Of course, a low budget often motivates recreators to get out and get some donations and contributions. A low budget can also spur a leader to do some creative "mooching" and to make things that cost nothing.

The supervisor or leader in charge of a program should take into consideration the following expenditures: leadership needs, maintenance of facilities, purchase of supplies and equipment, and transportation. Should a fee be charged? If so, how much?

Equipment and Supplies

Detailed checklists should be prepared for both equipment and supplies needed for the event. Never forget that "little things mean a lot." Items should be boxed up and ready for use the day before the event so that the chairman may check them off.

Facilities

Facilities for the event should be reserved well in advance, and reservation papers should be filled out. To provide flexibility in the event of adverse weather, indoor accommodations should also be available if outdoor activity is impossible. Is the facility large enough for the anticipated number of participants?

Evaluation

In addition to continual evaluation throughout the event, the chairman, assisted by committee chairmen, should prepare an evaluation report. The final typed report, including a summary of highlights, strong points, weak points, and recommendations, should follow the evaluation meeting, which should be held immediately after the event. This report can then be filed until the following year when it can be carefully studied.

ORGANIZING AND CONDUCTING ACTIVITIES AND EVENTS

Since recreation activities are so diverse in nature, their organization and conduct require the use of many different methods and procedures of implementing and conducting the various activities. In addition to a general knowledge of the major activities and areas in recreation, the leader should possess a thorough understanding of principles in program planning. The leader must then apply these principles of organizational planning and conduct the program accordingly.

The art of staging a successful event is similar to that of successful party–giving: whatever is planned moves so smoothly that the guests remark how effortlessly the leader or host entertains. One key to the impression of effortlessness is the amount of constructive, effective effort put into the event. Any good event is the direct result of good planning, regardless of the effort.

PLANNING A PLAYGROUND PROGRAM

Imagination, planning, and organizational ingenuity combined with enthusiastic leadership can produce an exciting and stimulating program that will keep children returning to the program day after day. Children go where they have the most fun, and if the leaders can develop the playground into the "fun capital of the neighborhood," that is where children will be found. However, should the playground bring the same routine activities day after day, the leaders will find themselves in a "quiet village." Dull, routine, unimaginative, and uninspiring activities will drive attendance down more than anything else. The program should produce something new and different every day, along with lots of surprises.

Generally, the unsuccessful, poorly attended playground program is one that lacks variety and diversity. Instead, a well–balanced program of activities should be sprinkled with special features that will capture the interest and imagination of the children and keep them coming back.

A summer playground program is usually planned on a weekly basis with the following factors in mind:

1. *Selecting activities for schedule.* Playground activities are selected on the basis of type, age level, and group size. They are then fitted into the weekly schedule in appropriate time blocks. Activities such as softball or track and field, which require at least an hour to play, should be placed into a major time block; story telling might require a shorter time period.

2. *Use of areas.* In scheduling activities, the leader must plan effectively in setting aside appropriate areas for participation. A typical playground scene might include the following: tables for arts and crafts; playfield and blacktop areas for group games, softball, volleyball, or tetherball; a wading pool; an area for game equipment; and a shady tree area for story telling and quiet games.

3. *Dividing day into major time periods.* The daily playground program is scheduled according to specific major time blocks. Typically, the schedule should include at least one time block of an hour during the morning and possibly two during the afternoon. Shorter time periods should be worked in to allow for activities that require less time, for setting up and collecting equipment, for free play, and for various other responsibilities.

4. *Scheduling simultaneous activities.* Generally, most playground programs involve more than one group scheduled at the same time. This is particularly true when there are enough children on the playground to justify dividing them into groups.

Some activities require direct supervision; others can be carried on under general supervision. Having learned the activity, a group involved in a quiet game need not be given close leadership, but an activity such as folk dancing would require direct supervision.

5. *Younger children must not be overlooked.* Playground leaders will often give much of their attention to the older boys and girls because they are easier to organize and stronger in expressing their desires. It should be remembered, however, that the younger children need leadership as much as the older boys and girls.

6. *Time for routine responsibilities.* Playground leaders must set aside time to handle staff responsibilities and routine functions. These include the inspection of equipment and facilities before opening the playground, clean–up, staff meetings, filling out forms, and similar details.

7. *Assigning activities to appropriate time periods.* Active games and strenuous activities should be scheduled during morning hours; quiet activities are usually offered in the afternoon periods. Generally, two physical activities should not be held one after another. Instead, a less strenuous activity could separate the two. For example, an arts and crafts period could be fitted in between a gymnastics activity and a softball team practice.

Activities that have proven more popular could be offered daily, whereas some programs could be presented just once or twice a week. Special events and trips are usually scheduled during afternoon hours, but there are some exceptions in which an event is held in the morning.

8. *Special weekly themes.* Designating a special theme each week to the summer playground program has been a popular practice of recreation departments. The theme system has been effective in giving a purpose to activities and events. Not only is the special event or trip based upon this theme but other activities such as arts and crafts, music, and dancing may carry out the theme.

SUMMER PLAYGROUND PROGRAM
Overall Theme—"Blast Off to Summer Fun"

Week	Theme	Special Event
1	Hawaiian Aloha	Hawaiian Night Luau
2	Pirate Week	Treasure Hunt
3	Hobo Week	Hobo Cookout
4	Safari Week	Pet Show
5	Sportsman Week	Fishing Derby, Trip to Big League Game
6	Camp Week	Overnight Campout
7	Western Week	Frontier Day
8	Astronaut Week	Outer Space Circus
9	Olympic Week	Junior Olympics Meet
10	Cultural Arts Week	Art Exhibit, Aquacade, Dance and Drama Festival

Financing Recreation

Finance and budget are essentially the responsibilities of the administrative staff; however, all department personnel should have an understanding of budget procedures, policies of finance, and the control of expenditures and incoming revenue. Since many agencies follow a program budgeting ap-

Figure 20–14 The neighborhood playground. A city–wide system of playgrounds is perhaps the heart of any community recreation program. This creatively laid out playground in Roseville, California, stimulated the interest and imagination of the children.

Time	Sun.	Mon.	Tues.	Wed.	Thur.	Fri.	Sat.
9–10 A.M.		Low organized games (Practice) Team games	Gymnastics–Tumbling Broom hockey	Low organized contests (Tournament action) Team games	Gymnastics–Tumbling Broom hockey	Low organized contests (Tournament action) Preparation for next weeks event	
10–11 A.M.		Arts and crafts Sport clinic (featuring guest coaches and athletes)	Puppetry Musical games	Arts and crafts Surprise feature (activity or visitor)	Puppetry Musical games	Softball game	
11–12 A.M.		Softball practice Storytelling	Track & field practice Nature hike	Softball practice Play activities	Track & field practice Group games	Singing games	
12–1 P.M.		Free play Quiet hour	Free play	Free play Preparation for pet show	Free play	Free play	
1–2 P.M.		Folk dancing Rhythm band practice	Swimming Visit to the local pool	Rhythm band practice	Pet show	Folk dancing Club meetings	
2–3 P.M.		Drama activity (skits)		Drama activity (one-act play rehearsal)		Dept. staff meeting	

Figure 20–15   Typical weekly schedule of a summer playground program.

proach, all staff members should be prepared to carry out the procedures of accounting and control as directed by the administrator.

The term "budget" is used to denote a plan prepared by an administrator or board for financing the work of a department or organization for a given period of time.

Many organizations and government departments use the "program budgeting" system of fiscal management. Budgets are designed in such a manner that large units of work, or special programs, are identified, isolated, and clearly presented. The boys' basketball program, for example, can be identified and described, thus enabling the administrative staff to determine what the unit cost of this program is.

Some of the financial areas of concern that supervisory and face–to–face leaders are involved with are:

- Keeping accurate financial records in the collection of fees and charges.
- Following department policies in requesting the purchase of supplies and equipment; using authorized requisition or purchase order forms.
- Channeling all financial matters through the business office.
- Assisting the administrator in making financial and budgetary estimates for the fiscal year ahead.

Volunteers

Volunteers can make the difference between a good program and an outstanding one. Volunteers can be found everywhere; the task is to recruit and train them. They can function in three general areas: administrative, program–related, and service–oriented.

The selecting, orienting, and training of volunteers are vital to any volunteer program. Edginton, Compton, and Hanson wrote that: "Volunteers should be selected in much the same way that staff persons are selected—on the basis of application, interview, and demonstration of skills and knowledge. Orienting the volunteer to organize philosophy, purpose, objectives, and policies should be followed with specific training as to the nature of the volunteer's tasks and how they are to be carried out."[12]

Volunteers should be made to feel a part of the organization. They need to feel that what they are doing is important. When they do a good job, they should be recognized for it. Perhaps the best strategy for managing a successful volunteer program is to treat volunteers as much like paid staff as possible. On a day–to–day basis, the regular leaders should thank them personally. Later, a thank you note, certificate of service, or recognition should be extended them.

Publicity and Promotion

The best playground program in the world can be wasted unless the children and their parents know about it. The following are some methods and materials for promoting activities and events:

1. *Bulletin boards.* Announcements of activities and coming events should be attractively displayed. Material should be kept up–to–date with fresh features added regularly. Daily and weekly schedules should be posted along with colorful illustrations which will attract the attention. Records and accomplishments of individuals and teams can be posted.
2. *Monthly bulletin.* A monthly bulletin with a name such as the "Recreation Reporter" can prove a highly popular publication for any recreation department. Many agencies distribute as many as several thousand copies monthly.
3. *Flyers.* The flyer can help sell the playground program. It is a handbill and can be given directly to participants. It can also be sent home with the children as a program of coming events that may be of interest to others in the neighborhood.
4. *Posters.* Posters can be placed in buildings, on fences, or outside of buildings. They can be made of tagboard, butcher paper, or construction paper. Make them big (3' by 6') and use a letterspray kit.

The children can help paint posters the leader sketches out.

5. *Photos of playground.* Photographs of activities and the children can be valuable to the interest and morale on the playground. Pictures can be placed in a scrapbook or displayed on the bulletin board. Later, pictures can appear in reports to the administrator. Colored slides can be very effective for group talks and at board meetings.

6. *Playground newspaper.* This newsy little publication can provide considerable interest and appeal to children and their parents. In addition to publicizing playground activities, the newspaper can develop much needed morale and spirit.

7. *News media.* Newspaper, radio, and television releases featuring articles and pictures will help build sound public attitudes and inform the public. All news releases and pictures must be sent through the supervisor, never directly to the newspaper.

8. *Announcements.* Posters or flyers publicizing a particular activity or event should be placed in prime locations such as recreation centers, schools, and store windows. Verbal and written announcements, direct mail, the telephone, bulletin boards, and banners are other methods.

9. *Personal contacts.* Contact with the public should be made by talks before community groups and organizations and through informal chats with people who visit the recreation agency.

10. *Exhibitions, demonstrations, and clinics.* These are ways to acquaint the public with the various program offerings and instill an interest to participate. Motion pictures and filmstrips can create interest in the program.

Awards

The granting of trophies or other awards tends to emphasize winning rather than participation. Therefore, there are many professionals who feel trophies should be kept to a minimum. In no case should awards or prizes be offered as the main inducement to participate in playground activities. Group awards of plaques or cups are recommended since they emphasize group cooperation. The general feeling among professional recreators is that inexpensive awards are justified because they serve as an incentive to participation and improvement. In fact, in city sports leagues income from fees paid by participants is used to purchase trophies and other awards. Most recreation departments have a variety of playground award certificates, ribbons, and participation cards that can be given to winners in contests, tournaments, and so forth.

Forms

The object of a form is to provide information. If it is incorrect, it is of no value. Only a well–developed form will be of value to the department. Accurate playground attendance must be taken daily at the peak of attendance during both the morning and afternoon sessions.

The following forms should be used by the leader in conducting a playground program:

- Registration card (for each child)
- Attendance report
- Accident report
- Employee time sheet
- Requisition order
- Property damage
- Parent's permission release

Safety

Safety on the playground is essential. At no time should the program be initiated without observing essential rules to ensure the safety of all participants and spectators. Instruction should be given by leaders in the correct methods of play. Enforcement of simple rules will eliminate many potential hazards. "Safety First" should be the deciding factor in the selection of all activities.

Accidents

One of the best ways to prevent accidents is for the leader to be on the job and alert at all times. In situations involving injury, a judgment must be made by the leader as to the seriousness of the overall situation. First aid assistance should be given immediately. If it appears the accident is serious, the patient should not be moved and should be made as comfortable as possible. Emergency care or ambulance service then should be called for according to procedures authorized by the administrator.

The family should be notified of the circumstances surrounding the accident and what has been done. An accurate accident report should then be made out by the leaders, including testimony by witnesses, and delivered to the district office within twenty–four hours.

Generally, playground staff are directed never to call for or send an injured person to a local doctor or a private hospital, unless directed to do so by the parents. Since registration cards are available on every child, including their parents' telephone numbers, the leader can contact the parents soon after first aid and a careful diagnosis has been rendered.

Liability in Public Recreation

Recreation personnel, both in the public and private sectors, may be subject to personal damage suits "if an injury to a person or property occurs while under their supervision, if negligence, error, or failure to carry out the responsibilities of their job is claimed against them."[13]

While there have been few instances where claims against individual employees have been upheld in court, every individual should understand the factors involving problems of liability. Many claims result from individual neglect or a failure of equipment. Accidents, breakage, and misuse of equipment by participants may also be responsible.

Liability is a state, condition, or obligation for which an agency or individual is legally responsible. An area of major concern to recreation personnel is that of tort liability. Tort is a wrongful act, injury, or damage for which a civil action may be brought. Most tort liability suits involve negligence and/or nuisance.

Negligence is the violation of an absolute duty or failure to take into consideration the interests of others and resulting in injury. According to Robert Sternloff and Roger Warren, "Negligence is failure to act as a reasonable and prudent person would have acted under the circumstances; and unintentional breach of legal duty, causing damage reasonably foreseeable without which breach damage would not have occurred."[14]

Generally a recreation leader or employee is liable only if negligence can be proven. An example of negligence is a department or person's failure to repair a broken playground swing, on which a child later breaks an arm or leg.

No longer can recreation personnel assume that they are free from liability merely because they are fulfilling their governmental function. Many states have successfully repealed statutes giving governmental employees protection from legal redress for their torts. Because of the changing climate relative to tort liability, the professional recreator must be knowledgeable about insurance laws and liability coverage. He or she should exercise caution in supervision and be able to anticipate problems that could lead to legal action.

Evaluation of a Program

The aim of evaluation is to determine the extent of progress toward specific goals. It is used to measure objectively what a program is trying to accomplish. Evaluation of programs and services is an ongoing process. At the conclusion of a recreation program, participants can be given a special evaluation form to complete. Program leaders should take the effort to explain and discuss the evaluation with participants. Following each program period, the staff meets as a group to review and evaluate the programs. Program evaluations are generally made once a year, usually at the end of a completed program. They are used in planning next year's programs.

Evaluation is necessary to critically examine a program's effectiveness. As they cope with the fiscal demands of today's tight economy, recreators need to account for and justify the worth of their programs. Basically, there are five major areas for evaluation: (1) areas and facilities; (2) program, including activities and services; (3) staff, including full–time, part–time/seasonal, and volunteers; (4) administration; and (5) the effect of services and activities on the participants.

Evaluation can be quantitative or qualitative. Traditionally, park and recreation standards have largely been concerned with quantitative values, such as counting procedures. However, as the leisure services industry becomes more concerned with the quality of life, more effective forms of measurement which involve many variables will need to be qualitatively applied.

The following items can be included in an evaluation report, either in a form or questionnaire:

1. Name of event, date, time, and location
2. Number of participants, spectators, and staff
3. Location effectiveness
4. Program cost
5. Adequacy of supplies and equipment
6. Safety hazards
7. Recommendations and suggestions on improvement
8. Participant reaction
9. Comments on having program again
10. Signature of supervisor or leader in charge

Questions such as the following might appear on the evaluation report:

- Did you schedule activities for all ages?
- Did you arouse and maintain interest?

- Were you cheerful and friendly to everyone?
- Did you listen to people and hear what they had to say?
- Were you flexible enough to make the necessary adjustments when emergency situations arose?
- Were you creative in introducing new program features?
- Did the activities contribute to the best interests of the participants?
- Was the program well–balanced and varied?
- Did you cooperate effectively with other employees on the staff?
- Did participants develop wholesome skills and attitudes?
- Did you publicize your programs sufficiently and keep everyone informed?
- Were you prompt in submitting reports, requisitions, weekly schedules, etc. to the district office?
- Did you consider the needs and interests of everyone?
- Were you flexible and open minded to suggestions and ideas to improve the program?
- Did you involve participants in planning and the organization of the program?
- Did you use all the available community resources, such as places to visit, voluntary help, and available supplies, equipment, and facilities?

After a program has ended, a file of materials describing the program should be assembled including the following:[15]

1. Copy of flier, instruction sheets, etc.
2. Photographs of the event
3. Copies of all news releases written and clippings
4. Evaluation sheet

A manila folder can be used for each program and placed in a file. A master program file can be of great value in the evaluation process and in planning future programs.

QUESTIONS FOR DISCUSSION

1. In the public sector, what does the word "program" refer to?
2. Explain briefly the "planning process", as given in the text.
3. Discuss the major steps in developing or implementing a recreation program.
4. How can a recreation department survey the needs and interests of the people to be served?
5. What are the major elements of planning programs?
6. Discuss three special factors in program success.
7. What are the ingredients of a successful special event?
8. What are the respective roles of the leader and the supervisor in the implementation of programs?
9. Develop a program of activities within a major area of activity (sports, arts and crafts, etc.) for a playground or recreation center.
10. Set up a Round Robin tournament for an eight–entry league.
11. Using a chart form, prepare a typical weekly playground schedule from Monday through Friday and indicate the hours of the day.
12. Outline an effective publicity/promotion campaign for a special event.
13. Why is it important to evaluate programs?
14. Discuss some criteria which can be used in evaluating a program.

REFERENCES

1. Jesse Reynolds and Marion Hormachea, *Public Recreation Administration* (Reston, Virginia: Reston Publishing Company, 1976), p. 221.
2. Committee at National Workshop on Recreation: Recreation for Community Living (Chicago: The Athletic Institute, 1952), p. 139.
3. Howard G. Danford and Max Shirley, *Creative Leadership in Recreation*, 2nd ed. (Boston: Allyn and Bacon, Inc., 1970), p. 109.
4. Ibid.
5. Virginia Musselman, "Ten Challenges to Program," *Recreation*, LIII, No. 10, 1960, p. 467.
6. Richard G. Kraus, *Recreation Today—Program Planning and Leadership* (Santa Monica: Goodyear Company, 1977), pp. 103–104.
7. Patricia Farrell, the Process of Recreation Programming (New York: John Wiley & Sons, 1978), p. 13.
8. Second National Workshop in Recreation: The Recreation Program (Chicago: The Athletic Institute, 1963), p. 6.
9. Kraus, *Recreation Today*, p. 83.
10. William Penn Mott, Jr., "The Creative Approach to Parks and Recreation," *Recreation Magazine*, September 1965, p. 340.
11. John H. Jenny, *Recreation Education* (Philadelphia: W. B. Saunders Company, 1955), p. 76.
12. Christopher Edginton, David Compton, and Carole Hanson, *Recreation and Leisure Programming* (Philadelphia: Saunders College, 1980), p. 158.
13. Reynolds and Hormachea, *Public Recreation Administration*, p. 49.
14. Robert E. Sternloff and Roger Warren, *Park and Recreation Maintenance Management* (Boston: Holbrook Press, Inc., 1977), p. 345.
15. Joseph E. Curtis, *Recreation, Theory and Practice* (St. Louis: C. V. Mosby Company, 1979), p. 177.

VII
Challenges of the Recreation and Park Movement

Figure 21-1 Protection of the environment must continue to be a high priority with park systems on all levels. Forests, wildlife, and scenic and historical resources must be protected, such as this magnificent setting, the Sawtooth National Forest in Idaho. (Courtesy U.S. Forest Service and Bluford W. Muir.)

21
Issues and Problems Facing Recreation and Parks

While the United States' total leisure–time expenditures exceed $240 billion annually, the rapid development of the recreation and leisure movement has not been without problems and major issues. Inflation, the high cost of living, taxes, crime, vandalism, drug abuse, the energy crisis, and environmental quality are some of the most serious problems which have affected our way of life and the leisure industry itself. Yet, Americans have not lost their enthusiasm for a good time, as indicated quite convincingly by the total annual expenditures on recreation and leisure. In record numbers, people of all ages are turning to some form of leisure–time activity, with unprecedented interest in fitness and sports.

Despite the phenomenal growth of the parks and recreation movement and greater awareness toward leisure living, there are numerous problems and issues related to the role of the leisure services industry which continue to have a significant impact on society. Perhaps the most challenging problem of the 1980s will be how to finance public parks and recreation programs, particularly those provided by local municipalities. The tax revolt has caused many agencies to seek alternate means of financing parks and recreation programs, such as those discussed later in this chapter.

Clayne Jensen defined an issue as "an identified problem which must be confronted and which has arguments both pro and con, but which is not immediately solvable." Jensen explained that "Some issues are resolvable, but many issues are continuous in the sense that they are never completely resolved, but are only debated, struggled with, and sometimes partially solved."[1]

Since recreators deal largely with the same issues and problems, they need to get together and talk about about their mutual concerns. Conferences, institutes, and seminars provide the opportunity to discuss issues and compose statements to clarify and validate their concerns, and to express commitment and hope.

The park and recreation movement has faced and will continue to face a crisis, but it is not alone in the struggle for local, state, and national priorities. Business, industry, agriculture, and education have also been affected.

If it faces up to the many challenges and problem areas, the recreation and leisure movement has great promise as an emerging profession. Students who have chosen recreation and leisure services as a career can either accept these challenges with a firm commitment to meet them, or they can sit on the sidelines and allow their chosen field to fail to live up to its tremendous potential.

ARSON—FORESTS ABLAZE

Arson cost more than $9 billion and seven hundred lives in 1979, including fires which destroyed some of the most beautiful forest areas in America. A suspected arsonist is arrested for setting forty-nine fires in the Lake Tahoe Basin. At Lake Elsinore in Southern California a deliberately set fire chars 2,500 acres of brush and for a time threatens 200 homes. Arsonists like these are responsible each year for thousands of fires throughout the nation. In 1979, arsonists were responsible for 675 of the fires on land protected by the California Department of Forestry alone.

Why do they do it? According to Walt

Bolster of the California Department of Forestry law enforcement division, "Everyone we catch has a different reason. You'd need a psychiatrist to talk to every one of them to classify the reasons. Roughly, however, there are the young persons who set fires maliciously, the beer drinkers and drug takers, who do it just to turn on. Some arsonists set fires to defraud insurance companies, some set fires for spite or because of grudges against someone."[2]

"The surge in intentionally set fires goes on," wrote *U.S. World & News Report*. "Insurance fraud is partly to blame, but vandalism and revenge are even more common motives. The chief motives behind arson in the U.S. are psychological rather than economic, as in arson–for–profit insurance ripoffs."[3]

Some blazes are set by terrorists and some are set because a man wants a job fighting fires for money or for the excitement of firefighting. Often when an arsonist finally is caught, the person has been responsible for fifty to one hundred fires that season.

The population of known fire setters is dominated by youngsters, who are often motivated by youth–gang peer pressure. In the decade of the 70s, 54.6 percent of all arrested arsonists were under 18 years of age.[4]

Solutions

Arson is far too complex and difficult to control for one to devise a simple solution. Tossing a lighted match or a burning cigarette into a hot, dry area of brush or grassland is easy to do and not be seen and apprehended. As was mentioned earlier, arsonists who are caught have different reasons for setting fires. Education obviously has a responsibility to do a more effective job in teaching environmental protection and a greater concern for our natural resources. Yet, in today's society, the number of people suffering in varying degrees from psychological and emotional disorders or behavior patterns leaves one to wonder if the arson problem can be reduced to a large degree.

Perhaps a stronger and more diligent ef-fort could be made in seeking out the sick, neurotic individual who has already caused numerous fires. Stiffer penalties upon conviction, even a more convincing threat of criminal incarceration, should be considered by law enforcement authorities. If society and education can reduce the far too numerous acts of carelessness which lead to many fires, it will be a significant accomplishment.

BIKE BANDITS

Most bike thieves strike in recreational areas, school yards, parks, and the like. Shopping areas are also popular. Bicyclers can take certain preventive measures by taking heed of the following:

- Register the bike.
- Keep a bill of sale and a color photo of the bike.
- Get an electric pencil and engrave your driver's license number or social security number.
- Get a good padlock.
- Lock the bike in the right place.

BOREDOM—COPING WITH IT

Boredom has become the disease of our time, yet there are some very effective ways to cope with boredom. Young people are particularly subject to boredom. As many as 20 percent of American adolescents are handicapped by significant boredom and depression, according to psychiatrist Dr. M. Robert Wilson of Baribault, Minnesota. "This handicap often leads to loss of self–esteem and, in extreme cases, to suicide," said Dr. Wilson.[5]

Solutions

An effective prescription for avoiding boredom is for the individual to diversify interests and involvements into areas and activities that are beyond the normal routine. "Making a commitment to some idea or objective outside one's familiar world—finding a new challenge—can end boredom almost immediately," wrote Judson Gooding.[6]

Vigorous physical activity is highly recommended, too, especially for those who work in office jobs. "Go and do it" is the positive attitude to take.

CRIME AND VIOLENCE

Crime or fear of crime is a deterrent to park use in almost all of the core cities of America, as well as in many suburban jurisdictions. Crime, violence, and vandalism severely restrict recreation opportunities. The protection of users and the prevention of crime and vandalism are pressing management problems in nearly all cities, particularly in core cities. These problems reduce the quantity of available recreation resources and diminish the quality of recreation opportunities.

Violence in many cities reflects a trend that has alarmed authorities across the nation— a sharp rise in wanton behavior by youngsters. A recent study indicates that nearly half the violent street crimes in the nation's one thousand cities with populations greater than twenty–five thousand are committed by youth groups.

"Municipal parks should provide their own armed security guards to combat park violence and crime," said Larry Olson, chief of public safety for the East Bay Regional Park District, Hayward, California. "Officers in the East Bay District patrol in well–equipped police cars, helicopters and motorcycles. Park ordinances limit areas where alcoholic beverages can be consumed and how loud music may be played. The old adage that parks are for everybody is no longer true. We don't create them for gambling, drinking, and fighting. We've decided that these people are not welcome and when we see these elements, we move in and let them know they're not welcome."[7]

Law officers say gangs can be prevented if they are resisted from the start. Demonstration of unity is very important, such as the presence of neighbors in court to show sup-

port for friends victimized by hoodlums. "Show the gang it's not one person they are fighting but the whole community."

Cities that have a relatively high sense of security in their park and recreation areas cite three ingredients for the absence of a crime problem:

1. Strong neighborhood ties.
2. Widespread pride in the areas.
3. A constant neighborhood vigil.

Solutions

Greater emphasis in schools on standards of good behavior, ethics, morals, and citizenship.

Citizens action programs involving meetings and activities.

A major effort should be made to build a wholesome climate in the community.

Recreation programs should make a stronger contribution to the strengthening of citizenship and moral fiber.

Tighter and more effective law enforcement.

The threat of longer prison sentences as a deterrent to crime.

Aggressive investigation and successful prosecution of offenders are essential in controlling youth–gang activity.

ENERGY CRISIS

Recreation and park providers are heavily dependent upon the use of energy to perform their services. Many agencies and organizations have had to curtail services due to the rising cost of energy.

Although the energy squeeze has a profound effect on the entire leisure economy, the resort and tourist travel industries have experienced the most serious decrease in business. As gasoline supplies grow tighter and prices climb higher, travelers in many metropolitan areas are changing their vacation plans and looking for recreation close to home. Some are leaving their cars at home in favor of other means of transportation. Motels, roadside restaurants, and remote vacation areas across the nation are being affected.

The greatest impact of reduced energy consumption on recreation and leisure–time patterns will be that people will spend more time at home. Reduced gasoline supplies and higher prices will mean that better bus systems will need to be designed for people to get to recreation areas.

"The automobile has shaped not only our economic system, but our way of life as well," wrote Lester R. Brown. "Now there are signs that this age is coming to an end. Automobile use by Americans has shown a sharp decline. While gasoline usage has been falling, the use of public transportation has been rising. Mass transit ridership has been increasing since 1973."[8]

Americans, however, will adjust their budgets to meet the rising cost of energy in order to escape from the overcrowded cities to be in the out–of–doors. Rather than trav-

eling on long vacations, Americans will be using their RV's for shorter, "one–tank–full" trips. Both government and private developers must seek to provide more and better recreation facilities closer to population centers to meet this demand.

Energy consumption will be curtailed, as the United States enters a period of unprecedented conservationism. Artificial ice rinks will be built with proper roofing and insulation to protect against the elements. Increasingly, recreation planning for individuals and groups will include car pooling, as well as bus and train transportation.

The 1980s will bring important new developments in energy production, including greater use of solar energy in both homes and industry, and the first United States plants for making synthetic fuels. Within the next two to three decades, alternative fuel sources now under development will become readily available to supplement the diminishing fossil–fuel sources.

Figure 21–2 Reduced reliance on the automobile, particularly for commuting, is reflected in mass transit ridership. Americans are showing new interest in bicycles and mopeds, the other economically attractive alternatives to the private passenger car.

Solutions

More participation and emphasis in programs and activities closer to home, particularly in the urban setting.

More day–use recreation areas should be developed near or within population centers.

Conservation of power and natural resources by individuals and agencies, such as reduced driving speeds and greater use of the smaller, economy automobile.

Greater research, experimentation, and use of new sources of energy.

Less dependence on the automobile and greater emphasis on mass transportation.

Continued popularity in bicycling which has prompted more bicycle programs and bike trails.

Car pools to and from various classes and activities.

More emphasis on day camps and campgrounds closer to urban centers.

Significant increase in the number of weekend programs at local parks and recreation areas.

ENVIRONMENTAL CRISIS

The quality of the environment will continue to be a major issue. People must be made to realize the need to protect their environment. The cause of land, air, water, and noise pollution and the ugliness of our cities is people.

At the same time that people have built up a high standard of living, they have permitted the standard of environment to deteriorate. As Aldo Leopold, eloquent spokesman for environmental quality, states in *Sand County Almanac*, "We abuse land because we regard it as a commodity belonging to us. When we see land as a community to which we belong, we may begin to use it with love and respect."[9]

Some of the most satisfying and rewarding pleasures in life are to experience the sight of natural beauty, to sit in silence free from all noise and hear the sound of birds and to breathe clean and fresh air. Yet, the environment of many Americans has become ugly and polluted.

Today unclean air threatens the health of most Americans. We have polluted almost every large river, lake, and bay in the country. Within our communities, ugliness is much too frequent—unclean streets, unattractive billboards, poorly planned cluttered business areas, residential areas lacking care and maintenance, and litter everywhere.

The Lake Tahoe basin's environmental quality, for example, is being strained to the "breaking point" because of largely uncontrolled urbanization during the past decade. A recent environmental assessment has revealed dramatic declines in the High Sierra lakes' air, water, and visual quality since 1970. The study also details increases in algae growth, destruction of sensitive stream and meadow lands, loss of wildlife habitats, and overcrowding in housing and transportation systems. The report warns these trends must be arrested and reversed if Tahoe is to be protected for future generations.

Litter is ugly and destroys the appearance of our parks. "The frustrations of the endless round of litter cleanup and the senseless degradation of nature's beauty are compounded by the unproductive use of staff time for this cleanup task," wrote Kristina Goodrich. "But perhaps the most worrisome cost of all in this day of inflation is the cost to the taxpayer."[10]

The establishment of policies and controls at the local level are needed to clean our cities, towns, and natural environment. Their acceptance and enforcement will require the cooperation and efforts of each and every responsible citizen and agency.

Jensen wrote: "In dealing with the environment we must learn not how to master nature but how to master ourselves, our institutions, and our technology. There is no question that just as man, through technology and through carelessness, has polluted his environment, he can also depollute it. The real question is whether enough citizens want action in the correction of pollution."[11]

Solutions

Develop individual concepts of the importance of beauty and an attractive environment.

Protect our precious resources of air, water, and land against pollution.

Preserve for future generations the wildlife and scenic beauty.

Encourage unified action by community groups and organizations in controlling pollution and the ugliness of our environment.

Develop political awareness and support that involve the passage and enforcement of laws at various levels. Without political action, little can be accomplished.

Discover what federal grants–in–aid and technical assistance from state agencies are available to help local governments.

A responsible citizen can take the following action:

Write to congressional leaders informing them of the dangers of pollution and environmental destruction.

When questionable actions by agencies occur, write to the department head.

Figure 21–3   The revitalization movement in urban areas continues to grow, as cities struggle to move from their old role as dense manufacturing centers toward a new image as meccas for services, trade, and leisure. The downtown skyline of San Antonio, Texas (shown here) has changed considerably in recent years with the addition of several hotels and the Tower of the Americas. (Courtesy San Antonio Convention and Visitors Bureau.)

Organize citizen protest meetings.

Join local conservation organizations and citizen advisory planning committees.

Seek injunctions against agencies which attempt to use park areas for nonrecreational purposes.

FINANCING PARKS AND RECREATION

Financing park operations and maintenance may be the most challenging problem of the next decade. While many agencies still have funds available for capital improvements, increasingly these cannot be used due to the scarcity of funds for maintaining existing facilities.

Costs have risen so sharply that local public recreation budgets can no longer provide the level of services for land acquisition, capital development, and operations and maintenance that it has provided in the past. Park agencies are developing new approaches for financing parks and recreation services which include charging fees and relying less on property tax revenues.

The tax revolt which was initiated by Proposition 13 in California, and later in other states, has had the greatest impact on recreation management. Proposition 2½, a referendum passed by 60 percent of the electorate in Massachusetts went into effect July 1, 1981. Basically, it states that local property taxes will be limited to no more than 2½ percent of assessed value, compared to the

6 to 8 percent level previously prevailing in many communities. As a result, cities largely dependent on property taxes have had to severely cut costs. The first programs reduced have been capital improvements and land acquisition funded by tax dollars.

With the "tax revolt" intensifying across the country, many public officials realize that their state could be the next to pass a drastic measure affecting state support of municipal services, including schools.

In Massachusetts, there was a wide range of reaction to Proposition 2½ among administrators of municipal recreation programs. Feelings ranged from predictions of gloom and doom, resignation and "if that's what the taxpayers want, that is what they'll get" to "roll–up–the–sleeves–and–let's–get–to–work" attitude.[12]

Hardest hit, of course, are the large cities. The Boston Park and Recreation Department, for example, faces a similarly bleak outlook. With a budget slashed from $9.6 million to $3.1 million, there is literally not enough money to open up gyms, light ball fields, or pay officials.

There are park departments that are planning on providing nearly all of the programs they have offered in the past. Finding new means of funding will hold the key for park departments elsewhere in the country, where the budget crunch is closing in.

Solutions

In essence, it is an attitude problem. While some predict a gloomy picture, there are those who believe it will take time for agencies to recover and adjust. The worst alternative is abrupt eliminations of programs, especially if there is no alternate funding. If, indeed, the public wants parks and recreation programs, somebody has got to pay for them—if not through taxes, then in some other form.

"We're not fearful of Proposition 2½," said Richard Foot, Park and Recreation Director of Needham (population 35,000), a city outside of Boston. "We're excited to deal with the issue and have developed a multi–faceted strategy to compensate for a loss of $26,000 in operating funds, a 15 percent budget reduction."[13]

Here are the highlights of Needham's strategy:

1. *User fees and charges*. The department has increased or instituted new fees to lower the net cost of services to the taxpayer.
2. *Volunteerism*. Considered the backbone of the municipal recreation department for years, volunteerism has been expanded since the referendum passed, with more than five hundred volunteers giving active leadership.
3. *Private sector management*. The department has "spun off" a number of programs, including the Needham Swim Team Parents Association, Needham Track Club, etc., all of which have their own insurance, bank accounts and leadership, and will conduct their own fund–raisers to operate the programs.
4. *Permanent donation fund*. A trust fund has been created by the department into which memorial gifts and other philanthropic donations may be made.
5. *Creative fund raising*. The department has actively sought private sector funds for community recreation, from the Lions Club, a local bank, Jaycees, and Polaroid Corporation.
6. *Public relations*. The department has aggressively stepped up its media relations program, constantly keeping the department in the public eye.
7. *Advisory and advocacy groups*. The commission has formed a number of special interest advisory groups, such as a sailing committee, a bikeways planning committee and a program evaluation and user fee study committee.[14]

"We should not rely too heavily upon fees and charges as a primary source of revenue," H. Douglas Sessoms pointed out. "A more diversified pattern of funding must develop—taxes, grants, user fees—all of these will be required to sustain our effort."[15] The biggest criticism of fees and charges, however, is that they tend to discourage recreational participation by economically disadvantaged groups.

Proposition 2½ in Massachusetts and 13 in California can serve as an example to the rest of the nation—that the era of the tax revolt is upon us, and the traditional sources of funding for municipal recreation programs simply can no longer be relied upon. Park systems must recognize this fact and begin actively seeking alternate means of financing and operating their programs.

INFLATION

With such pressures on every facet of society, it is easy to see why people name inflation as the nation's biggest problem and demand a new campaign to curb it. Indeed, coping with inflation is a major administrative challenge for today's recreation professionals.

In countless ways, inflation is playing havoc with the way Americans live. The cost of necessities—food, shelter, clothing, and health care—is taking a bigger bite of the family budget, leaving less for luxuries that enhance life.

John Cunniff described the plight of many: "Smaller, less elaborate houses. Two or more households sharing one house. Smaller automobiles. Smaller families. Shorter and less expensive vacations. Wives working to bring in a second income."[16]

Although the world economy still faces "severe" problems, there are signs that inflationary pressures are abating. "The process of adjustment to recent pressures caused by inflation, recession, and high oil prices will be slow and entail sacrifices," said Jacques de Larosiere, managing director of the International Monetary Fund.[17]

Solutions

People have made many adjustments to cope with the impact of inflation, willingly in some instances and forced to in others, such as higher taxes, high interest rates and, in general, economic deterioration.

Wage and price controls are favored by the majority of Americans, according to a 1981 Gallup Poll. In contrast to the public as a whole, though, business and labor leaders have traditionally opposed controls. Significant progress has been made in controlling inflation in three European nations, the Netherlands, Switzerland and West Germany. Management and labor in each nation meet regularly to review the economic scene and jointly set the level of wage increases.[18]

INTEGRATION: A WHOLE COMMUNITY APPROACH

Integration, the process of bringing people with differences together to promote more dignified, respected, and equitable lifestyles for all, has always been a volatile issue in the United States. In recent years, society has increasingly become more greatly aware of the need to integrate the individual with a disability or handicap into the "normal" society. However, Carol Stensrud, Assistant Professor at California State University at Chico, points out that "There has been relatively little progress toward the day when people with a disability or a handicapping condition will be able to participate fully in normal community life. A whole community approach is needed. In other words, there must be true access for the disabled and handicapped to all services and all aspects of community life including school, home, work, leisure, health, welfare, transportation, civic involvement, and religion. If we don't consider all aspects of community life, we will not obtain true integration."[19]

Legislation has taken steps to promote integration efforts. Federal Legislation P.L. 94–142 (Education for the Handicapped Children) and Section 504 of the Rehabilitation Act mandate that individuals previously labeled and left aside will be afforded public education and public service that are as nondiscriminatory and highly integrated as is possible.

Integrated programs require accessible transportation to and from community services. To be truly accessible, transportation for individuals with handicaps and disabilities should operate on a regular schedule—days, evenings, and weekends.

Stensrud suggests, "It is time for communities to educate themselves, and then to coordinate, cooperate, plan together toward the day when social and physical barriers to the handicapped will be gone."[20]

LEISURE—HOW TO USE IT?

The majority of the American people are experiencing greater amounts of leisure time. Many of these people actually do not know what to do with their increased leisure. They need guidance in determining how to make their lives more enjoyable and rewarding, to learn how to relax.

Whether leisure will be a blessing or a curse will in all likelihood be determined by the knowledge and ability to use leisure constructively and creatively. Much will depend on our educational system, which has always been geared to preparing our young people to "make a living." In a leisure–oriented society, education's job will be to prepare people for meaningful leisure, in addition to a career job.

Educating people to accept and use leisure will continue to be recreation's major challenge. The goal of every recreator should be to change people's attitudes toward a higher value for leisure. The use of leisure should be made important in an individual's daily living and throughout one's lifetime.

Solutions

Education for leisure should be part of every curriculum—elementary, junior and senior high, community college, and college–university.

The park and recreation profession, in a community–wide effort with all levels of education, must provide leisure skills, knowledge, and opportunities for all people.

The mass news media should be used to spread "the good word," to create a greater public awareness for the need for constructive, enjoyable leisure–time activity and experience.

Each Individual Should Know:

- His or her basic needs.
- The importance of leisure in daily living pattern.
- Factors that motivate choice of activities.
- An inventory of present leisure skills and activities.
- Available outlets for leisure in the community.
- Changes to make in his or her living pattern.
- How to develop a more enjoyable leisure living plan.

LEISURE COUNSELING—WHOSE ROLE IS IT?

Professionally, leisure counseling continues to be a hot issue, as recreators speak of it as an emerging role. An increasing number of individuals in the profession are currently providing their services as leisure counselors on a fee basis. H. Douglas Sessoms wrote: "The development of leisure counseling as a professional role in parks and recreation suggests that those who are involved in leisure counseling as their primary responsibility may end up as the true professionals."[21]

Is leisure counseling a profession in its own right, or is it a job function, a set of tasks performed by most recreation professionals regardless of title? Sessoms advocates an intermediate position which holds leisure counseling as a specialty within the park and recreation profession. He explained that "in order to become a leisure counselor, he or she must first be educated as a generalist. Leisure counseling would require the layering of specialized education and training on top of the general preparation given all recreators."[22]

Leisure counseling specialists advise people on alternative ways and places to use their time budgets in the same manner as investment counselors advise people on how to spend their discretionary income.

They assist people in reviewing the various leisure time alternatives in relationship to their particular skills, interests, finances, and leisure outlets.

Edwin Kiester, Jr. wrote: "Like marriage and sex counselors, leisure counselors use checklists, questionnaires, interviews, seminars and 'guided fantasies' to direct clients into sports, games, hobbies, adult education, charity work, arts and crafts—or just plain loafing, if that seems suitable."[23]

In the years ahead, computers will be used extensively in determining the leisure needs of people. Background and aptitude data on an individual will be fed into a computer, and from it will come a program or schedule of suggested activities that might satisfy the leisure needs of the person.

Leisure counseling involves in-depth analysis of a person's total being. It deals with one's mental, emotional, physical, and social nature. According to Kiester, "It is not something to just dabble in or to know a little about. Leisure counseling is an important area that requires sophisticated professional preparation."[24]

NATIONAL PARKS

Despite its growth, the national park system faces serious problems. The park service's budget has failed to increase in proportion to its expanded responsibilities. In 1916, the national park system consisted mostly of large western national parks, remote national monuments, and unique geologic or scenic marvels. Today, in contrast, the park service manages a nation wide network of parks and other facilities in urban as well as rural areas. Through various acts of Congress, the agency has been made responsible for national seashores, lakeshores

and recreational areas, many more historic areas, a few more large national parks, and even a cultural park—Wolf Trap Farm Park for the Performing Arts near Washington, D.C.

The park service's limited personnel is barely able to handle the most essential functions. "The multi–disciplined park ranger able to manage the natural resources and take care of visitors . . . has long since vanished," said Robert Kahn. "Park rangers today spend almost all of their time on visitor services and law enforcement, although many rangers perform limited resource management duties."[25]

After considerable controversy and debate throughout the 1970s, results of various studies indicate that the trend toward commercial services and entertainment within the national parks have gone too far and suggest a return to more natural values.

William Davis of the *Boston Globe*, wrote: "The basic disagreement was between those who wanted to add facilities and attractions to the parks, ranging from golf courses to rock music concerts, and those who thought such "improvements" were destroying the natural values the parks were established to preserve."[26]

Conservationists have been continually concerned over plans to expand the operations of private concessionaires in national parks. Under the proposal, many duties presently performed by the park staff, such as conducting tours and managing campgrounds, would be handed over to private firms. "Environmentalists argue that the record of concessionaires in some areas is bad. When given too free a hand, conservation groups say, private firms have allowed rampant commercialization of parks, which has led to overcrowding, overbuilding and destruction of fragile lands."[27]

Solutions

Several solutions have been proposed, among them a five–year moratorium on acquiring new parks, the possible return of some urban parks to the cities, and switching funds intended to buy new parks to maintaining the old ones.

Trailer camping has been restricted, road building curtailed, and private vehicles barred from areas where they formerly were allowed. The National Park Service has moved carefully to reverse the trend toward commercial services and entertainment.

OFF–ROAD VEHICLES

Misuse of off–road recreation vehicles (ORV) has done considerable damage to forest lands. More and more tracks from four–wheel–drive vehicles are reaching off the main roads and onto the public lands, many times illegally. Already, the telltale tracks and the erosion are proving to be a problem in the forest.

According to Steve Beck, a resources officer in the Sierra National Forest in California, "Many of the offenders are unaware of the damage they cause with the vehicles. They don't see the erosion and siltification that comes months after and the compaction of areas that will no longer support grass."

Many of the organized off–road and four–wheel–drive clubs generally are aware of the damage their vehicles can do and are taking preventative measures.

Solutions

- Establish policies and procedures to ensure that ORV use on public lands is controlled.
- Zoning will separate activities and assign space for ORV use other than that reserved for quiet uses.
- Build tracks away from campgrounds and require all riding be done only there.
- Allow ORV use on roads and designated trails but not in wilderness areas.

OPEN SPACE

The overcrowding and congestion experienced by the cities must be prevented in the suburban areas, where there is an urgent need to preserve open space and create parks.

Land use legislation is vitally needed to meet the increasing pressure of industrialization, technological advances, population growth, and rapid urbanization.

Meeting the recreational needs of an increasingly urbanized society will continue to receive major emphasis. Local, county, and state agencies should unify their efforts in a new "Parks to People" concept, providing new recreation areas near large cities.

Solutions

Reliable annual funding is vital to the development.

State legislation of an Open Space acquisition fund, based on a 1 percent real estate transfer tax, would provide regular monies to cities and counties for parks and open space purchase.

Another bill would authorize cities and counties to condemn land for open space uses.

Planning operations should be coordinated jointly among the various governmental units, particularly those that overlap and conflict with each other.

PHYSICAL FITNESS LAG

Many college students, even teenagers and adolescents, are in poor physical condition. Apparently some teenage girls cannot run a city block without stopping to rest. Many high school boys cannot chin themselves even once. One out of every six children ages ten to seventeen is weak or uncoordinated enough to be classed as physically underdeveloped. By the time they enter college, a large percentage of young men and women are already in alarmingly poor cardiovascular–pulmonary condition.

Older people, particularly the aging, have failed to exercise properly, and until only recently, society had a rather negative attitude toward exercise for the aged. People grew up believing that exercise for the aged was something to be avoided, inappropriate, and perhaps harmful.

Growing numbers of people, young and old alike, are finding new youth and vigor and satisfying social life in regular exercise programs. The concensus of medical research is that people who continue to exercise late into adult life live longer and are less likely to die from heart attacks. The amount of exercise one gets when he or she is older is more important to good health than how much they received earlier in life.

Solutions

- Maintain regular physical exercise and activity throughout the year.
- Engage in a variety of physical activities, i.e. running, walking, swimming, recreational sports (individual, team, social or competitive), exercises or stretching routines, etc., but do them regularly so they will become a habit.
- Combine exercises for flexibility, muscle toning, and for cardiovascular fitness.
- Be sure to stretch out and warm up before engaging in strenuous activity.

POPULATION

As America adds twenty–one million people in the coming decade, the new mix of ages, races, and regional spread will affect significantly the leisure industry, as it will business, crime, even taxes. Four–fifths of the population growth will be in persons in their 30s and 40s, most of the rest in the age sixty–and–older group. People older than sixty–five, most of them retired, will account for one out of every eight Americans by the end of the decade. Increased longevity, because of better health care, will raise the number of people in this age group by five million. A dramatic increase is expected in the oldest age bracket, people seventy–five or older.

There are more than 4.3 billion people in the world, and the figure is growing at a rate of 172 persons a minute. Most experts agree

Figure 21–4 Stimulating exercise for the aging is crucial to good health and a longer life. This drop–in exercise class for senior citizens offers a combination of stretching exercises for muscular fitness and aerobic exercises for cardiovascular fitness. (Courtesy City of Kettering, Ohio, Parks and Recreation Division.)

that there is nothing that can be done to prevent the world population from reaching 6 billion by the year 2000.

Solution

There is much that can and should be done in terms of motivating people to have smaller families and providing them with the means and education to limit their family size. Contraception in some developing nations is rapidly approaching the levels found in the United States. The two most popular methods are oral contraceptives and voluntary sterilization.

POVERTY AND UNEMPLOYMENT

While America is at its highest level of wealth, extensive poverty still exists and the unemployment rate is continuing to be a major problem. Those who lack equal opportunity to share in the nation's wealth are bitter and unhappy.

The nation's elderly, increasingly, have had to cope with poverty conditions. Even though Social Security payments have risen by 52 percent since 1969, more than 3 million elderly Americans still live below the government–defined "poverty line."

Despite a rising unemployment rate, employers, in city after city, claim they just cannot find enough workers to fill all the available jobs. The U.S. Employment Service regularly lists more than one hundred and fifty thousand openings that remain unfilled at the end of every month.

Why do so many jobs remain vacant while millions of people are hunting for work? Experts cite these reasons: skills, unattractive jobs, unemployment benefits, and location. Of all these reasons, the biggest obstacle facing unemployed workers is a lack of skills.

There is no easy solution to the intolerable living conditions experienced by those in poverty; the following measures, however, would help alleviate their plight.

Solutions

Find meaningful employment for those who can work.

For the ill, disabled, and the elderly, provide the necessary financial assistance to allow them to live above the "poverty line."

A larger portion of the budget should be made available to areas in low–income neighborhoods.

Increased recreation and leisure services should be made available without fees and charges.

Provide equal opportunities for education and employment for those in need.

RACIAL UNREST

Racial unrest and antagonism is still a serious problem in many large cities. "Many black people have 'made it', but rioting in Chattanooga, Miami, and elsewhere, ex-

perts say, reflects despair among the huge numbers still mired in poverty."[28]

After a quarter century of marches, protests, and legal battles, blacks insist that their drive for civil rights has failed to lift huge portions of their race out of poverty and hopelessness. They point to poor ghetto schools, aimless youth, unemployed adults, shabby housing, lagging incomes and stubborn vestiges of discrimination.

In regard to their needs and interests in parks and recreation, programs emphasizing cultural pride among racial or ethnic groups have alleviated pressure in this tense area. Arts and music programs designed especially for Afro– or Mexican–Americans, for example, have proven quite successful, while ethnic history and ethnic crafts programs have also been effective in developing cultural pride. The programs should be co–planned by the ethnic leaders as well as those on the recreation department staff.

Solutions

New forms of programs and activities should reflect racial demands for ethnically oriented activities, such as Afro–American arts, black history, and Mexican–American cultural programs.

Special teams of older neighborhood youth should be hired to maintain control of youth gangs and problem youth.

New personnel adaptations and innovations should be used to cope with the problem.

RVs—THEIR FUTURE

The recreational vehicle is an American phenomenon. It evolved during a period of cheap and plentiful energy that coincided with rapidly expanding personal incomes and growing amounts of leisure time. A sharp rise in gasoline prices and high interest rates, however, devastated the RV industry and resulted in a 66 percent dropoff in total sales in 1980. Membership in the Recreation Vehicle Industry Association declined from around 500 to just under 300 manufacturers.[29]

The recreation vehicle industry is now beginning to see solid evidence of a sales recovery. Shipments of RVs in 1981 were about 29 percent higher than the year before. According to David J. Humphreys, president of the Recreation Vehicle Industry Association, "Consumers who put off buying an RV until interest rates or gasoline prices decline just can't wait any longer. In addition, they've learned to adjust their strained budgets for purchases they consider important. And most of the 6 million RV families in this country consider RVing a very important part of their lifestyle."[30]

The industry also is optimistic that energy worries will not be as severe a drag on sales as in the past. Fuel supplies appear to be good, prices have stabilized, and the attitude governmental agencies have about energy use for recreational purposes has become more positive. The industry, furthermore, continues to make solid improvements in the fuel efficiency of RV vehicles.

Uncertainty about this nation's fuel supply has cast doubts about the future of the American RV, at least in its present oversized, overweight, and gas–hungry form. Quite likely, recreation vehicles will be forced to cut down on size to gain better gas mileage. Some of the RVs get as little as six miles per gallon, which is highly unsatisfactory in these fuel crisis times.

SAFER PLAY EQUIPMENT

Concerned about more than forty thousand injured children per year, government regulators are striving to make backyard swings, slides, and other playground equipment safer. The Consumer Product Safety Commission is working closely with equipment manufacturers to tighten existing voluntary standards for construction of home playground equipment.[31]

"Playgrounds will always be a place for skinned knees and elbows," said Rep. Newton I. Steers, Jr. (R., Md.), father of three active boys, "but many of the dangers of serious injury can be minimized."[32]

Solutions

- Better design should be constantly emphasized because some modern equipment has been found unsafe.
- Safer play areas should be designed for both bicycles and skateboards.
- Government should issue stronger federal safety standards and guidelines.

SNOWMOBILING

The snowmobile has refused to go away. The industry reports more people are trying snowmobiling each year. "The transformation of the snowmobile from outlaw vehicle to family sport machine is the result of an industry drive to improve both its product and its tarnished image," wrote Ron Koehler.[33]

Funds invested in research and development made the machines safer and quieter. The industry lobbied for favorable legislation and public trails for riders. Clubs have been successful in combining fellowship with discipline. Indeed, a key to the turnaround has been the snowmobile club. The International Snowmobile Industry Association estimates there are ten thousand clubs in the United States and Canada. One is VAST, the Vermont Association of Snow Travelers. When landowners began seeking legislation to ban snowmobiles from the state, snowmobilers organized and worked out a compromise. Their group negotiates for permission to cross a person's property. In return, it promises to maintain a snowmobile trail and stay off unmarked areas.

Close–unit snowmobile clubs and well–defined trails also cut down the number of injuries. In Wisconsin, more than 1,000 persons were injured on snowmobiles in the winter of 1974–75. That number was reduced to 388 in 1978–79.

Most observers agree the second most im-

Figure 21–5 Snowmobiling—a mechanized winter sport. While the popularity of snowmobiles as an exciting outdoor activity increases, new controls have been placed on their use. Serious problems have resulted in tighter rules. (Courtesy Artic Enterprises, Inc.)

portant step the industry and users took was creation of snowmobile trails. In all, some 190,000 miles of public and private trails are now open to the snowmobiler. Some of the national parks allow snowmobiling, while others have banned their use.

Snowmobiling still has its detractors though. The Sierra Club and many private landowners still seek to curb snowmobile use. "Although the industry has changed the minds of many lawmakers, a large portion of

the public still perceives the snowmobile as an expensive toy for Polar Bear Club types," said Koehler.[34]

STRESS—COPING WITH IT

One of the most common maladies facing American society today is that of stress and its physiological and psychological effects. Evidence indicates rather convincingly that there is a definite link between stress and physical illness.

Solutions

- Try to learn to develop coping strategies.
- Get outdoors and blow off steam physically, maybe by gardening, hitting a tennis ball or just taking a walk.
- Talking out your worries with people you respect and trust can sometimes help too.
- Learn to stop worrying and make your life more enjoyable.

Additional suggestions which can be helpful in breaking the worry habit:

- Keep busy.
- Recognize the things you cannot change, accept them, and don't fret over them.
- Get interested in others, thus diverting attention from your problems.
- Avoid becoming overtired. Adequate rest will help you cope with the stresses that will face you.

TECHNOLOGY AND AUTOMATION

The trend in America is to measure progress in terms of technological advances. However, advances in technology do not automatically bring with them equal benefits in advancing the quality of life. Sociologists maintain that there is a "culture lag" in society—the gap between technology and the way people live. A *Parks & Recreation* editorial stated that "Technology has taught us how to save time, but it has not taught us how to use time. This is the challenge to the recreator!"[35]

Mass production of goods and services has had a major effect on the American economy, making life easier and providing increased leisure time. Due to technological and automation advances, however, there has been a great reduction in the number of hours of work. The boredom and monotony of automated work has caused much dissatisfaction with large numbers of workers; for

others, automation has caused unemployment.

During the next decade, the average American will rely far more on computers and other electronic marvels to provide a wealth of information—and to improve the quality of life. Small home computers, plugged into standard television sets, will create still color pictures and graphic displays.

Computers, however, are causing many technological changes, including putting people out of work. Wider use of computers means more displacement of workers and the accompanying social problems. Labor unions have generally accepted new machines and methods as long as jobs of workers were guaranteed or workers were compensated for lost work or retrained for other jobs.

Solutions

Create new jobs for those unemployed because of automation.

Provide some means of achievement and satisfaction in boring and monotonous work.

Use the increased leisure time wisely and constructively.

Provide a more comprehensive recreation program for industrial workers, such as enjoyable activities during breaks and lunch hour, and challenging and creative leisure experiences during weekends, off-hours, and vacation time.

TELEVISION VIOLENCE

Watching television seems to be the great American pastime. There are now some 145.7 million television sets in use in this country, and almost 50 percent of the nation's seventy-five million households have 2 or more sets. The average family watches television 6.4 hours a day, or almost 45 hours a week.

The steady diet of violence on television, however, is a danger to society and is abusing children. According to William Glasser, "Television desensitizes children into viewing violence as a natural reaction, rather than a rare occurrence. A child's overuse of television interferes with the growth of his brain's capacity to handle the simple problems of everyday living. It also may cripple his creativity, his curiosity, and most of all his follow-through. Television does keep the child's mind occupied and stimulated, but in the passive way."[36]

Solutions

Plan to have one night each week with the television off.

Avoid using the television set as a baby-sitter.

Seek out programs made for children.

Help children distinguish between make-believe and real life on television.

Find other leisure activities besides television watching.

Figure 21–6 Trail bikes and other off–road vehicles have built up large numbers of users. Where use has been intensive, though, trails erode rapidly and there are evident impacts. In the national forests of California major damage has been done to meadows and stream banks. (Courtesy *American Motorcyclist Magazine.*)

TRAIL RIDING

Trail riders represent one of the largest and most committed segments of the motorcycle fraternity. In many cases, an individual will combine enthusiasm for trail riding with another form of recreation, such as camping, rock hounding, hunting, fishing, just exploring, or using the vehicle as a means of transportation.

Rapid increase in the motorcycle population and a corresponding increase in off–road motorcycling have parallels in other forms of outdoor recreation. The rapid expansion of the motorcycle market in the mid–1960s compares to a similar expansion in the popularity of hiking, backpacking, camping and most other types of outdoor recreation. The majority of trail biking, as hiking or horseback riding, is done on established trails such as fire roads, logging trails, or trails that were established by previous use.

Solutions

- Representing a legitimate form of outdoor recreation, the trailbike should be managed and provided for like any other form of recreation.
- Land managers, increasingly, are turning to positive, constructive techniques, rather than closure and prohibition.
- There are areas where trail bike use should be prohibited, and even areas where any type of recreational use should not be allowed.

TRANSPORTATION ACCESS TO PARKS

Accessibility is one of the keys to the effective use of park and recreation resources. People want park and recreation facilities within safe walking distance from home. They also want access to regional parks which have more varied natural environments.

Access to neighborhood parks is often restricted by physical barriers such as highways, railroad tracks, or industrial development. According to the 1978 National Urban Recreation Study, nearly all low–income neighborhoods studied report physical barriers to some local recreation facilities.

Recreation opportunities are often severely limited for people without cars. The Recreation Access Study (Department of Transportation, 1975) reported that an estimated 90–95 percent of all personal trips to significant recreational resources are made in private automobiles or recreational vehicles.

Solutions

- Transportation access by pedestrians or those using public transit systems should be given stronger consideration by park and recreation planners in the design and construction of new park and recreation facilities.
- City transportation and recreation systems should be more sensitive to the needs of cyclists.
- Bikeways which link together existing park and recreational areas are particularly needed in cities.

URBAN ELDERLY—HOW TO SERVE THEM

Programming is not meeting the special recreational needs of the growing urban senior citizen population, even though many cities are providing very good programs for the aging. The major obstacle to providing improved transportation to senior citizens is lack of coordination between the myriad of federal, state, and local programs affecting transportation for the elderly.

Solutions

- Innovative transportation programs are urgently needed to serve senior citizens.
- Sufficient transportation should be pro-

vided for the elderly to take advantage of recreation services.
- More outreach programs and special transportation to existing programs are especially needed.

VANDALISM

Increasing at an alarming rate, vandalism has grown from a nuisance–level problem to a major–loss factor. Shameful acts of vandalism, deliberate arson, and littering are making it necessary to close or severely restrict the use of many parks. The problem has become so serious that agencies have been forced to take major corrective action.

Vandalism is a major problem that costs United States taxpayers millions of dollars every year. The most common problems include "lawn jobs," defacing of trees and picnic tables and bleachers, spray painting and other decorating, broken glass (mostly beer bottles), and destruction of rest rooms. Culprits not only run over soft grass, but run down fledgling trees and decapitate drinking fountains.

Fear of park crime and vandalized facilities reduce park use. When users and park personnel are absent, vandalism increases, deterioration of facilities accelerates, and park use continues to drop, creating a vicious circle of nonuse and decay.

When vandalized facilities such as restrooms go unrepaired or are removed, potential park use is reduced. Repair of vandalized recreation facilities is costly, both in time and money, and these costs divert funds from essential recreation programs. The Chicago Park District, for example, estimates that 50 percent of maintenance time is spent on making repairs made necessary by vandalism.

More policing of parks and emphasis on design of vandal–proof facilities may reduce crime and vandalism, but excessive emphasis on physical security may detract from the enjoyment of recreation opportunities, discourage use, and often challenge vandals to greater violence.

Increasingly, when vandals get caught,

cities and districts are presenting them—or their parents—with a bill for the damages. Cities are now asking the courts to levy fines for replacement of the grass, trees, and whatever damages that range from $250 to $900 and sometimes more. Citizens, angry with the behavior of vandals, have become much more willing to make a commitment, to report vandalism when they see it, and follow through with the complaint against the vandals.

The theft and defacement of valuable works of art continues to be a disturbing and rapidly growing problem. Generally unknown before the 1970s, art vandalism is a form of violence which seems to represent a disturbed retaliation against society and its aesthetic heritage.

Art theft and vandalism can be attributed to several causes: 1) a sharp increase in the market value of paintings, sculptures, and other works of art; 2) art is becoming increasingly popular, as the public appreciation of art continues to rise.

Solutions

- Public involvement is essential to develop solutions that are adapted to the particular area.
- Each community has to examine its own problems and users.
- Prevention, through user involvement, should be the first aim.
- Law enforcement, the "cop" approach, is the least desirable alternative.
- Educating teenagers in the use of leisure time can be an important means of prevention.
- Programs should be developed which truly meet the needs and interests of teenagers.

Additional solutions are:

- Security inspections of department facilities.
- Tighter control on the issuance of keys to facilities.
- Night lighting and intrusion alarm devices.

- Park security officer approach.
- Street counselor and special problems programs.
- Making the community aware of the seriousness of the problem.
- Strengthen procedures for collecting restitution from parents.

WILDERNESS CONTROVERSY

Environmentalists and operators of recreation vehicles continue to clash over access to federal lands. Because of their great popularity, off–road vehicles have placed increasing pressures on federal land managers in recent years. Proponents of the RV industry would like to unlock vast sections of national parks and other federal lands to users of recreational vehicles.

America's last untouched forests are also the object of an intensifying battle that is raging between conservationists and lumber and business groups. While most conservationists support the preservation effort, commercial interests and others are angered at the prospect of having so much acreage put off limits to timber harvesting, road and building construction, oil and mineral exploration, off–road vehicles, motorboats, and airplanes.

Conservation groups have resisted opening up more federal lands to off–road vehicles on the ground that they pose a serious threat to land, wildlife and general public enjoyment of national parks. Presidential directives on off–road vehicle operations issued by Richard Nixon (1972) and Jimmy Carter (1977) were designed to prevent environmental damage to federal lands from use of such vehicles. In issuing his directive, Nixon said there often is a legitimate purpose in allowing recreation vehicles to use public lands. But he also recognized that they are "in frequent conflict with wise land and resource management practices, environmental values and other types of recreational activity."[37]

The Nixon executive order instructed federal land managers to designate trails and areas for off–road vehicles under tight controls assigned to protect land resources and the safety of "all" land users. Under its provisions, vehicles may be allowed in national parks and wildlife refuges, but only in areas where they won't adversely affect "natural, esthetic, or scenic values."[38] Carter strengthened the Nixon executive order in 1977 by giving federal land managers authority to close off areas immediately to recreational vehicles if other values are endangered.

When he took over as Interior Secretary, James Watt made no apologies for his commitment to economic development of "locked–up" public lands. He contended that environmentalists have had their way too long and have shielded too much of the public domain from economic development. Yet, he stunned traditional environmentalists by the speed with which he changed the course of policy–making at the Interior Department. One of his first acts was to reopen the question of oil drilling near four of Northern California's most beautiful beaches. Then he proposed that millions of acres of federal lands in the west be opened to unrestricted use by owners of dune buggies, motorcycles, and off–road vehicles.

According to Watt, the traditional conservationist and environmental groups, such as the Sierra Club, Wilderness Society, and Audubon, are extremists that do not reflect the public's desire for a reduced federal role in land–use policy. This reduced federal role would allow private developers greater access to public lands while eliminating further funds for acquisition of private land to enhance the public domain.[39]

Solution

Wilderness as a recreational resource will continue to be a highly controversial issue. Undoubtedly, the wilderness concept in the future will be challenged repeatedly by those who consider it impractical because of a growing population. Jensen stated "There is no question that the concept will need to be modified from time to time and in connection with certain areas as the increased number of people demand more multiple uses of the available land areas."[40]

Watt prides himself in being a man of decisive action—of avoiding the bureaucratic trap of "paralysis by analysis." But analysis, say his critics, is just what many environmental questions call for. *Newsweek* wrote: "Watt's impatience to exploit the West's vast reserves of energy and minerals is understandable. But while laws change, and Cabinet secretaries come and go, the land endures—bearing the marks forever of the decisions Watt is now taking."[41]

WORK DISSATISFACTION

A number of industrial psychologists have been saying for several years that one big cause of declining productivity in American industry is workers' frustration over the lack of opportunity for advancement and lack of satisfaction in their jobs.

Millions of Americans do repetitive, boring work with too little freedom and too much supervision. True, companies pay them well but often forget they are human.

Solutions

Industry should try harder to enrich jobs and make work more interesting or satisfying. Away from the job, the worker should:

Diversify interests and involvements into areas and activities that are beyond the normal routine.
Find a new challenge.
Look forward to something highly desirable.
Engage in vigorous physical activity especially those who work in office jobs.
"Go and do it"—there's the real key!

DRUG ABUSE AND ALCOHOLISM

Drug addiction and alcoholism continue to pose very serious problems to the users and to society. The use of alcohol and drugs is directly related to the leisure behavior of millions of Americans. The moderate use of stimulants and depressants, like drinking coffee, drinking beer at sporting events, or having a drink at a cocktail party is considered normal. However, there are an estimated ten million alcoholics in the United States today who cannot control their drinking and, as a result, have serious personal, social, and vocational problems. For years, drug abuse has also been a major problem.

Solutions

Although prevention is far more effective than cure, the following are some of the roles recreators may assume in the treatment of the addict or alcoholic:

- Assist them to develop skills and attitudes necessary to cope effectively with their free time.
- Provide leisure opportunities for the purpose of developing a new lifestyle.
- Suggest more constructive leisure outlets and activities to support behavior modification and an improved self–image and status in the community.
- Alcoholics Anonymous and Synanon have proven quite convincingly that peer pressure to refrain from addiction and the pride that comes from having succeeded and from being helpful to others can reinforce significantly the rehabilitation process.

YOUTH ALIENATION

Due to the high level peer group use of alcohol and drugs, many young people find themselves in total disregard for authority. Youth rebellion, delinquency, school dropouts, and the widespread use of drugs and alcohol are the major forms of social upheaval among our youth today.

While there are other factors that can affect the behavior and attitudes of our young people, studies have indicated that active recreational participation can contribute sig-

nificantly to maintaining emotional stability and well–being. In addition to offering pleasure and satisfaction, recreation can provide a sense of creative and personal accomplishment. Social and professional group experiences can give an individual a sense of belonging, so often lacking in today's society of broken homes or working parents too busy to properly take care of their children.

Solutions

- Maximize the planning effort and keep recreation programs as interesting as possible.
- Give problem people moral guidance and special attention.
- Make sure the individual feels wanted and develops a sense of belonging.
- Personal attention and some responsibilities should be given to the problem person.
- Provide youth with more exciting and challenging recreation and leisure experiences.
- Give them something constructive to do— get them interested in a job, a hobby, a leisure pastime.
- Parents can help considerably by establishing a closer relationship with their children, by developing warmth, understanding, and mutual respect for each other.
- Teenagers need an outlet for their expressions. They need a feeling of self worth.
- Provide youth with the sense of belonging that results from friendship and sociability.
- Membership in clubs and organizations is essential to the growth of young people, providing opportunities to learn to cooperate with others, accept group rules, and abide by the expressed desires of the group.

YOUTH SPORTS AND COMPETITION

Increasingly, recreation professionals, physical educators, coaches, parents, and concerned citizens are questioning the overemphasis on competition in organized programs. Competitive sports for many youngsters in Little League Baseball, Pop Warner football, and Biddy basketball can be rewarding, both socially and physically. However, sports can also be emotionally damaging to some children. Some of the most damaging effects do not originate from games but from the "win–or–else" attitudes of some coaches and parents. Too many coaches become so obsessed with the idea of winning that they completely lose sight of the purpose of the program.

Too many American parents think they are Vince Lombardis and wind up abusing their children—physically and psychologically—through sports, according to Dr. Thomas Tutko, a noted San Jose State professor of psychology. "What is happening is that many kids get burned out and are turned off to sports," said Tutko. "Many parents live their lives through their children. When a child wins, the parent thinks he is a winner. When a child fails, he interprets it as meaning he is not a success."[42]

According to Jonathan Brower, a sociologist at California State University at Fullerton, "A Little League ball game is a tough place for a vulnerable child, and it is made tougher by some coaches, who wanting victory above all else, rate players as athletes rather than persons and offer physical drills rather than emotional support."[43]

Solutions

By emphasizing and encouraging other worthy goals in recreation sports, along with controlled competition, the recreation professional can remove the "cancerous" idea that winning is the one and only goal. Play, properly organized and supervised, is essential to children. The prime objective of competitive sports, though, should be FUN and EXERCISE, not fierce competition. There is nothing more ego–building to a youngster than to say, "You really hit the ball good!" or "You rode your bike very well." That is what children want to hear.

Competition, though, is a very real part of society in the United States. Whether one re-

Figure 21–7 Low pressure youth baseball. An error by this eight–year–old third baseman did not place his self–esteem on the line because the program's emphasis is on enjoyment rather than winning. Children in the Carmichael Pee Wee Baseball program learn in a friendly and constructive atmosphere, under trained leadership who have a basic understanding of children's growth and development needs.

alizes it or not, an individual competes, in some degree, every day of his or her life. According to Dr. Rainer Martens, a nationally recognized sports psychologist at the University of Illinois, "A proper perspective of winning is not at all achieved by eliminating competition. Whether or not competition is healthy depends upon how we compete and what significance we put on the outcome."[44]

Those who advocate the elimination of competition, to be replaced with cooperative games, neglect the fact that sports demand just as much cooperation as they do competition. In team sports, good play requires cooperation with teammates.

DISRESPECT FOR AUTHORITY IN SPORTS

Respect for authority in sports has been degrading for years, particularly among the young. This, of course, is an unfortunate trend. Lines of authority are necessary to keep sports from becoming chaotic. The *Sporting News* wrote: "In this regard, sports figures are in a unique position to set an example. They are highly visible and much admired. Like it or not, they serve as role models for the youth of America—probably much more than they realize."[45]

Sports figures performing in the public eye have the responsibility of behaving within the rules and accepted customs of the sport. Run-ins with umpires by managers and coaches often go far beyond sport's behavioral boundaries. Many sports accept vigorous disagreements, but physical contact with an umpire or referee cannot be tolerated. The childish action of scooping up dirt and throwing it at an umpire, for example, is demeaning to the umpire and the officiating profession as a whole.

"Such degradation of authority should be dealt with harshly in all sports," continued the *Sporting News*. "So, too, should the schoolyard battles that sometimes erupt."[46]

QUESTIONS FOR DISCUSSION

1. Identify two major problems or issues in the recreation and leisure services field and attempt to give a solution.
2. While authorities for years have tried to deal more effectively with the arson problem, there is still no easy solution. What suggestions do you have?
3. Can you provide some practical solutions to the growing crime and violence problem in our parks and recreation areas?
4. In coping with the energy crisis, what are some practical solutions or remedies which the individual, as well as government and society, must work towards?
5. What are some steps that each citizen can take to provide for a better environment?
6. Financing parks and recreation continues to be one of the most challenging problems for recreation and park agencies. As property tax revenue and budget cuts continue, what alternative sources of revenue can agencies turn to?
7. Educating people to accept and use leisure will continue to be a major challenge for every educator and practitioner. What approach or methods in leisure education do you suggest?
8. As to the current controversy concerning the use of our national parks, what suggestions do you have as to their use and preservation?
9. Off-road vehicles continue to be a very controversial issue. What suggestions can you provide which would lessen the problem to forest land and the environment?
10. The snowmobile continues to be a controversial winter-time vehicle. What approach to their use can you give?
11. Discuss the increasing problems of youth sports, competition, and the over-emphasis on winning. What approach to competition and winning do you suggest for youth programs?
12. A growing number of medical authorities and experts on child growth and development are convinced that the steady diet of violence on television is abusing children. What do you suggest to remedy this serious national problem?
13. Vandalism continues to cost United States taxpayers millions of dollars each year. Do you agree with the solutions presented by the author? Or can you suggest other approaches?
14. Discuss the pros and cons of the "wilderness controversy" issue which is raging between conservationists and environmentalists on one side, as opposed to business, lumber, and oil interests, and the RV industry.

REFERENCES

1. Clayne R. Jensen, *Leisure and Recreation: Introduction and Overview* (Philadelphia: Lea & Febiger, 1977), p. 237.
2. Ken Payton, "Forests Ablaze," *Sacramento Bee*, September 1, 1978, p. B3.
3. "Arson in U.S. Reaches a Crisis Stage," *U.S. News & World Report*, June 8, 1981, p. 39.
4. Ibid.
5. Judson Gooding, "How to Cope with Boredom," *Reader's Digest*, p. 54.
6. Ibid.
7. Larry Olson, "Crime Prevention in Parks," Seminar, American River College, May 13, 1981.
8. Lester R. Brown, "Is the Car a Twentieth Century Dinosaur?" *Sacramento Bee*, April 27, 1980, Forum 1.
9. Aldo Leopold, *Sand County Almanac* (New York: Oxford University Press, 1966), p. 269.
10. Kristina Goodrich, "Litter, En Garde!" *Parks and Recreation Magazine*, March 1980, p. 39.
11. Clayne R. Jensen, *Outdoor Recreation in America*, (Minneapolis: Burgess Publishing Company, 1973), p. 233.
12. "What Happens When the Money Runs Out?" *Athletic Purchasing & Facilities*, July 1981, p. 44.
13. Ibid.
14. Ibid., p. 45.
15. Linda Thorsby Bynum, "The Future of Recreation and Parks," *Parks and Recreation Magazine*, August 1979, p. 24.
16. John Cunniff, "Retiring at 65 . . . Just Another Dream Delayed," *Sacramento Bee*, August 8, 1980, p. F10.
17. "IMF Director Says Inflation Subsiding", *San Francisco Chronicle*, July 6, 1981, p. 49.
18. George Gallup, "U.S. Public Favors Economic Controls," *The Sacramento Union*, July 2, 1981, p. A14.
19. Carol Stensrud, "Integration: A Whole Community Approach," *California Parks & Recreation*, April/May 1980, p. 9.
20. Ibid., p. 10.
21. H. Douglas Sessoms, "Leisure Counseling: A Frank Analysis of the Issues," *Parks and Recreation Magazine*, January 1981, p. 69.
22. Ibid., pp. 69 and 107.
23. Edwin Kiester, Jr., "They'll Help Organize Your Leisure Time," *Parade Magazine*, February 25, 1979, p. 24.
24. Ibid.
25. Richard L. Worsnop, "Parks Under Siege," *Sacramento Bee*, August 4, 1980, p. B8.
26. William Davis, "Travel—National Parks", *The Americana Annual*, 1976, Grolier Incorporated, p. 557.
27. "The 'Shameful' State of America's National Parks," *U.S. News & World Report*, May 25, 1981, p. 52.
28. "Black Anger On the Rise Again," *U.S. News & World Report*, August 4, 1980, p. 50.
29. James V. Higgins, "RV Industry Sees Solid Evidence of Recovery," United Press International, *Sacramento Bee*, July 10, 1981, p. C1.
30. Ibid.
31. Susan M. Gately, "Is Your Child's Playground Safe?" *Parade Magazine*, March 19, 1978, p. 16.
32. Ibid.
33. Ron Koehler, "Snowmobiles Refuse to Disappear", *Sacramento Bee*, January 1, 1981, p. E8.
34. Ibid.
35. Editorial, "Trends in Parks and Recreation," *Parks and Recreation Magazine*, May 1976, p. 19.
36. William Glasser, "Interview on Recreation", *U.S. News & World Report*, May 23, 1977, p. 75.
37. Leo Rennert, "State Resources Secretary, Watt to Tangle Over Off–Road Vehicles," *Sacramento Bee*, July 9, 1981, p. A22.
38. Ibid.
39. Ibid.
40. Clayne Jensen, *Outdoor Recreation in America*, p. 207.
41. "James Watt's Land Rush," *Newsweek*, June 29, 1981, p. 32.
42. Thomas Fortune, "Little League . . . Too Tough for Some Youngsters?" *Los Angeles Times*, July 8, 1979, p. 3.
43. Ibid.
44. Rainer Martens, "Youth Sports and Competition," Address, American River College, May 8, 1980.
45. "Our Opinion," *St. Louis Sporting News*, June 20, 1980, p. 6.
46. Ibid.

Figure 22–1 Seattle's freeway park complex. A park over the freeway meets the need for downtown passive open space. For residents of nearby apartments, it is a neighborhood park; for office workers, a pleasant place to lunch and converse. Nature's power balances people's as a cascading waterfall subdues the sounds of the freeway below. (Courtesy Seattle Department of Parks and Recreation.)

22

Trends and Challenges in Leisure and Recreation

Many changes in the leisure habits of Americans are occurring as more and more people in the nation are choosing to spend their free time in a more leisurely fashion. The shift in where the leisure time is spent is being accompanied by an overall increase in the leisure available to the average American.

Indeed, the public is becoming more aware of both the opportunities and the problems of increasing leisure time. This leisure awareness has contributed to the leisure boom and the evergrowing pursuit of the good life. Americans have indicated that they have no intention of giving up their R & R—rest and recreation—whatever it costs. The Economic Unit estimated that spending for leisure in 1981 would amount to $244 billion, an increase of 26 billion in a year.[1]

People continue to seek a more healthful and satisfying balance between work and recreation. They are also striving for a higher level of physical and mental health in which there is a more wholesome balance between activity and passivity.

The trend is no longer toward the massive growth of leisure many people had envisioned. Leisure is now growing at a very gradual rate. "The production worker is opting for more overtime work and a second 'moonlight' job in the 'free time' he has achieved. He prefers the increased income he can earn to buy the conveniences produced by technology (and cope with the rising prices of inflation). His image of a higher quality of life may be related more closely to possession of more hardware rather than more leisure."[2]

The trend to close–to–home leisure is becoming more pronounced as people seek to curb the rising costs of fuel and lodging. A strong shift has occurred toward the use of local parks, hobbies, movies, and community theater. Replacing spending on recreation vehicles are elaborate home–entertainment systems, such as computers, big–screen television, and video recorders.

Americans are becoming less dependent on the automobile. Instead of long car trips, more family vacations now are focusing on regional attractions. Major hotel chains are designing more of their new facilities as one–stop resorts that offer a wide variety of entertainment choices. Many of these are located close to major metropolitan areas. More people also are using buses and other public transportation on vacations.

Solar energy, park and playground design, new games and innovative programming are just a few of the areas in which new and exciting trends are occurring in our rapidly changing society. Developments in transportation, communication, education, economy, and population will continue to shape people's future choice of recreation and where they will seek it. William Penn Mott wrote: "The need to be prepared for these changes is a challenge the leisure services field must meet."[3]

Trends can be very perplexing, an editorial in *Parks and Recreation Magazine* stated. "Yet, we cannot serve our purpose effectively unless we can fathom them and provide some solutions."[4] Separating trends from wishes, however, can be a difficult task. A trend is defined as having a general direction or tendency; a course or drift. Conditions and changes are controlled by long–run social trends, not often by the actions of a single individual. Robert Theobald suggested that "If you want to bring about significant changes, you must work with others to create new trends."[5]

There has never been a better time for new innovative practices and creative demonstrations which will lead to trends in the leisure services field. "Recreation programmers need to be alert to changes in attitudes and lifestyles," said Kim Sprague. "Find out what is happening across the nation by exchanging programs with other professionals and departments."[6]

THE ARTS CONTINUE TO EXPLODE

Citizens in almost every community in the United States are promoting, participating in, or watching the arts. In fact, in many areas arts events now draw more people than do sports.

In New York state alone, attendance at nonprofit professional arts events exceeds seventy–five million. Outdoor summer festivals are being conducted all over the country. The grass–roots movement in the arts is spreading throughout the urban East. One of the most all–embracing community arts councils in the United States is the Council for the Arts in Westchester, serving an area with 265 cultural organizations and a population of 850,000.

Artists and arts organizations are turning increasingly to parks and recreation facilities for the presentation of their work. Indeed, parks are an ideal setting for the sharing of the many benefits the arts hold for everyone.

Figure 22–2 Cross-country skiing, the fastest growing winter sport, is a sport for everyone. Safer, easier, and more convenient than downhill, the popular Nordic sport appeals to many because of the freedom it provides. Here, a young couple receives some helpful tips from an experienced ski instructor at Sugar House West near Lake Tahoe, California.

Livingston L. Biddle, Jr., chairman of the National Endowment for the Arts, wrote: "The traditions of sidewalk art shows, Sunday afternoon outdoor concerts, craft fairs, and folk festivals have always found homes in the parks. But there is a renewed interest in the potential of these activities to revitalize urban areas and galvanize a sense of community identity and spirit."[7]

BACK TO THE BICYCLE

Of the nearly ten million bicycles sold in 1979, two–thirds went to adults and teenagers looking for gasoline–free transportation. Most of these bikes were used mainly for recreation, but many were put to work for commuting, shopping, and running errands. A wholesale return to bicycles could mean an enormous reduction in gasoline usage.

Side effects of the latest bicycle boom have been the construction of thousands of miles of bicycle paths where motorized vehicles are banned, demands by bicycle riders for better treatment, and a sharply rising rate of collisions between bicycles and automobiles.

The number of American bicyclists has passed one hundred million—up from thirty–five million riders as recently as 1960. This indicates that nearly half of the United States population are bicyclists.

CAMPS FOR ADULTS

Camp, once almost exclusively the preserve of the young, is becoming an adult adventure. The variety of experiences camps now offer to men and women increases each year.

At camps across the country, adults can spend their leisure time learning skiing or water skiing, mountain climbing or bicycling. They can become better golfers, equestrians, or tennis players. In the last few years more than two hundred and fifty tennis camps have been established.

"Camping is too valuable a commodity to be wasted on only the young," said Bernard Schiffman, deputy administrator of New York City's Human Resources Administration. "It is a rare privilege or opportunity for an individual at any age."[8]

Age appears to be no limit. Experts say the fastest–growing segment of adult camping has become camps for senior citizens. For younger adults, psychologists say, camp offers a chance to unwind, to refresh, to learn a skill with immediate tangible rewards. Camp can offer a sense of relevance and fellowship missing from everyday life.

COMPUTER GAME CRAZE

A growing number of electronic games are entertaining for adult and child alike, as they match wits with an opponent or with the game's computer. Indeed, technology has taken over the toy industry.

"Combining the play action of the once highly popular video games with the compactness and portability of the pocket calculator," wrote Bob Sylva, "the battery–operated electronic games are programmed to play a mind–boggling array of games, from sports, like baseball, football, etc., to educational, target and games of skill. Moreover, with varying levels of difficulty, most of the ingenious gadgets are diabolically programmed not to be beaten easily. Prices range from $9 to $70."[9]

Increasingly, Christmas shoppers are clamoring for electronic games, such as baseball, head to head electronic football, basketball, soccer, "Battlestar Galactica," "Comp IV," "Quiz Wiz," and scores of other beeping, blinking, mind–bending mechanisms.

CULTURE BOOM

An unprecedented explosion of culture has swept the United States in the past ten years. For the first time in history, a majority of Americans now take part in cultural pursuits, from attending museums to performing chamber music.

Despite the pace–setting growth of ballet

and opera, the theater is still the most popular form of the performing arts by far. The *U.S. News & World Report* indicated that "Sixty–two million seats a year are sold to dramatic productions from Key West to Fairbanks, and the number is growing every season."[10]

Growth has also been steady in another long–established field of the performing arts—symphony orchestras. Since 1971, attendance at concerts by the nation's fifteen–hundred symphonic groups has risen from twenty million to twenty–five million.

Expansion in the field of dance has also been astounding, with more than three hundred and fifty dance companies in the United States. Museums and galleries also are increasingly popular as Americans have become more interested in painting and sculpture. The greatest attraction of museums appears to be temporary exhibitions, particularly shows based on a theme. Many cultural experts attribute the arts boom to three main factors in the lives of individual Americans: increasing wealth, better education, and more leisure time.

Rising popularity of ballet is attributed in part to support from the National Endowment for the Arts. In addition, federal spending on culture is rising rapidly, bringing top music, dance, and literature to millions.

CYBERNATION

Cybernation is a word which refers to the combination of the computer and automation. "If the computer takes some joy out of life," said Charles K. Brightbill and Tony Mobley, "it also provides more time for people to do what they want to do."[11]

Cybernation will continue to cause many changes in our lifestyles, as well as the social systems we live in. Park systems must learn to cope with the many changes new technology and automation are bringing to leisure tastes. To meet the future's challenge in parks, agencies will need to know how to deal with the effects of transportation changes, better interpret the urban environment, and use communications advances to advantage. Indeed, satellites, the computer, and modern technology will revolutionize the present communications systems.

DECENTRALIZATION

A number of large public recreation and leisure service agencies have undergone administrative decentralization by dividing their constituencies into service areas or districts corresponding to geographical areas of the city and then assigning district supervisors to each of these districts. "The purpose of these local or district offices or committees," said Richard Kraus, and Joseph Curtis, "has been to bring municipal government closer to the people, to facilitate local control, or to achieve 'maximum participation' by neighborhood residents in the process of government."[12]

The degree to which government should be centralized or decentralized has long been the subject of political debate. Geoffrey Godbey wrote that "Decentralization reduces organizational scale and makes government more responsible to neighborhood needs; the citizen is more active in relation to neighborhood institutions, receives better services, and somehow becomes less alienated."[13]

In decentralization, district supervisors or directors are given more authority to distribute recreation resources and services within their district and to determine policy. Godbey wrote: "The advantage the district supervisor would have under decentralization would be the ability to perceive a need and act upon it with a minimum of delay, interference or consideration of the 'macro' political consequences. In effect, a large recreation agency would be made into a number of small ones, corresponding, perhaps, to neighborhoods and socio–economic boundaries."[14]

"In dealing with the community, we found that decentralization of services is the answer," said Solon Wisham. "The way you discover the community is the way you look at it, and you don't look at it from a centralized operation. One looks at the community from rubbing elbows with people on a day by day basis. He or she finds out what unique things there are about a neighborhood or community."

EMPLOYEE RECREATION GROWS

Industrial recreation is on the upswing as the trend toward employer–provided recreation grows. There is a definite growth in the employee recreation field as evidenced by the fact that the National Industrial Recreation Association has more than doubled its membership in the last few years (approximately two thousand).

Employee recreation will grow significantly, due largely to further urbanization which will be accompanied by increased employment by large companies and industrial plants.

There will be continued emphasis on improved fringe benefits, one of which is employee recreation. Clayne Jensen reported

that "Some large companies have found that the provision of attractive recreation opportunities often means more to employees than a higher salary, particularly if these benefits are available to members of the whole family."[15]

EXERCISING TO MUSIC

Whatever name it is called—DancErgetics, Aerobic Dance, or Dancercise, the basic concept is the same—exercising to music. Aerobic dancing is a patented program of total exercise using dance routines choreographed to popular music.

DancErgetics is a new exercise program which combines music and movement. It is a new way to discover body awareness, increase vitality, achieve emotional release, and enjoy some good music all at the same time. An estimated six million people in the United States are involved in some form of dance exercise.

Figure 22–3 Dance, physical exercise, and active games for the aging are growing in popularity. This senior enrichment class for people fifty and over is led by dance specialist Jason Beck. (Courtesy *Sacramento Bee* and City of Sacramento Department of Community Services.)

Rather than just concentrate on strengthening the heart and lungs or trimming the waistline, dance covers everything. Some of the dances are designed to slim the hips and buttocks, while others strengthen the arms and legs. Some make the individual loose and limber, and others are designed for more specific purposes.

Dancing is an excellent way of exercising and one that many people, particularly those older than forty, get much more fun out of than jogging. In addition to being very good for the back, dancing contributes to good poise and posture.

QUEST FOR FITNESS

During the last two decades, one of the most obvious changes on the American scene has been the steady increase in the number of people who exercise regularly. Never before have so many Americans spent so much time, energy, and money to get into shape and stay there.

Tens of millions of men and women have made physical fitness a part of their lives, regularly setting aside time for tennis, swimming, bicycling, jogging and the like. The sharp increase in women sports participants is one of the most important trends in the fitness boom. Senior citizens are active in sports and exercise activities that only a few years ago were thought to be the exclusive domain of the young.

Nearly half of all Americans—47 percent—participate in some form of daily physical exercise. Many are turning to exercise for reasons other than physical conditioning. Jogging continues to be a favorite body conditioner. Long–distance runners say that running brings them tranquility, enabling them to forget everyday troubles.

Jogging may be a popular American pastime, but walking ranks as the favorite form of exercise among Americans aged twenty and older. The President's Council on Physical Fitness and Sports reported that approximately forty–six million people walk regularly to keep in shape, which is nearly two out of every three Americans who exercise at all. Like running, walking will strengthen flabby muscles, tighten the stomach and make a person look and feel better.

The growing interest in active sports stems from a desire to keep in shape. An increasing number of people want to improve their bodies and physique. One of the country's fastest–growing sports, racquetball, is part of a trend toward more athletic, active recreation.

Aerobic dancing combines exercises with vigorous dance routines set to music. The routines consist of sit–ups, disco steps, ballet movements, skipping, jumping and jogging. They are designed to condition the heart and lungs, trim and firm the body, and promote flexibility.

Exercise circuits is one of the many kinds of facilities park and recreation departments are providing fitness enthusiasts. Parcourse, Ltd., a San Francisco–based firm, introduced the exercise circuit concept to the United States in 1973, calling its product the Parcourse Fitness Circuit. The Parcourse Fitness Circuit is a step beyond running. Participants walk, jog, or run the course, stopping at each of the eighteen exercise stations that stretch over a one to two–and–a–half–mile area. Parcourse, Ltd. has satisfied an essential need by developing the Parcourse Circuit for the disabled.

NEW KINDS OF PLAYGROUNDS

Park and recreation planners are becoming more innovative and they are coming up with new and imaginative kinds of play. By studying the behavior patterns of children at play, researchers are developing new insights on what type of play environment is more appealing and beneficial to them.

"Most youngsters tire of the conventional uses of slides, swings, and monkey bars in about six months," said Michael G. Wade, director of the University of Illinois Leisure Behavior Research Laboratory. "Then they try walking on seesaws, wrapping swings around their upper bars and pretending jungle gyms are forts."[16]

Instead of that expensive equipment, researchers advocate the use of an "adventure playground" full of boxes, ladders, cylinders and tires that can be stacked up, climbed on and swung in different ways. "Tomorrow's playgrounds might be regarded by some adults as piles of junk," said Wade, "but they provide children with an immense number of alternatives in how to play."[17] Researchers believe that "adventure playgrounds" of this type are especially helpful in countering the passivity often engendered in children who watch television for too many hours over too many years.

NEW RESPECT FOR OLD NEIGHBORHOODS

Large cities throughout America are taking a new look at their old–fashioned neighborhoods to see whether their close–knit, self–reliant ways offer a solution to urban decay. Park and recreation planners and other local officials are seeking to rekindle the neighborhood spirit, cooperation, and working together to provide recreation and leisure services to its residents. In many community neighborhoods, the planners are learning that human relationships are reinforced daily at social events and festivals, corner taverns, street encounters, PTA meetings, church suppers, etc.

Indeed, the survival of American cities depends to a major extent on the rejuvenation of the neighborhoods. If the decline of the neighborhoods can be arrested, or if neighborhood quality can be improved, the cities will inevitably benefit.

PARKS WHERE THE PEOPLE ARE

Ever since the Yosemite Valley became protected territory in 1864, federal funds for parks and recreation have been channeled overwhelmingly toward the great open spaces, far away from the centers of population where most of the nation's people live. Many city officials now believe it is time to reverse the priorities, to put parks and recreation areas where they are accessible to the 70 percent of the American people who live in urban areas. However, there are those who contend that urban parks are the responsibility of local municipalities, not the federal government. Interior Secretary James Watt, for example, does not believe the National Park System should run urban parks. Watt, in fact, has proposed that the federal government turn over national recreation areas, such as Gateway, to state and local governments.

Yet, more than forty–five million Americans live in households without cars, according to the National Urban Recreation Study released in 1978 by the Department of the Interior. The study deemphasized the acquisition of open space and recreation development in wide–open rural areas in favor of federally supported facilities in densely populated urban centers.

New urban facilities, while being costly, are proving extremely popular. The Gateway National Recreation, for instance, drew 9.6 million visitors in 1976, costing $6.6 million to operate. In the same year, Yellowstone National Park drew only 2.5 million visitors, with an operating cost of $7.6 million.

The creation of more urban parks will provide multiple benefits, save energy by bringing parks to where people live, and serve needy populations. But without the assistance of the federal government, either through funds or additional national recreation areas, the task of providing sufficient park and recreation areas for the burgeoning urban population will be most difficult.

HOUSING IN CLUSTERS

Cluster housing consists of houses grouped close together on a sizable tract in order to preserve open spaces larger than the individual yard for common recreation. Urban planners see it as a general concept to provide open space and to protect the surrounding environment.

The cluster plan at the Kingwood Lakes

Village Patio Homes in Houston, Texas, increased the number of units with frontage on or access to Lake Kingwood. Five of the six clusters have a lake view, and each cluster has its own private cul–de–sac for access.

The greenbelt system of wooded bike paths connects the patio homes to other residential areas, shopping centers, schools, and public recreational facilities. These recreational facilities include village greens, parks, picnic grounds, horseback riding areas, ball fields, boating lakes, camping grounds, and village pools.

NEW GAMES—AN ATTITUDE TOWARD PLAY

New Games offers a new direction to traditional sports—a way of playing that is exciting and enjoyable but requires no exceptional athletic ability. It is an attitude toward play, that people can and should play together for the fun of it.

"The New Games experience is both challenging and joyous," said a staff member of New Games, Inc. "We combine competition and cooperation to make it possible for players to compete as partners who give each other the chance to play well."

New Games are based on participation, not spectatorship. When people play New Games, how they play the game really is more important than whether they win or lose. When a game is fun for everyone, they all win together.

New Games Foundation is a nonprofit educational organization communicating a style of play encouraging participation, trust, and creativity. The foundation serves a seed function by teaching the skills and concepts of New Games refereeing in workshops across the country.

OUTDOOR ADVENTURE

Interest in outdoor adventure programs continues to soar. Increasingly, leisure service departments, as well as social, edu-

cational, and correctional agencies, are developing programs that include such activities as backpacking or canoe trips, white–water rafting, orienteering, rock climbing, winter camping, and cross–country skiing.

According to Jim Storms, two goals of adventure programming are:

To adapt or expand existing outdoor education programs to meet the needs of diverse age groups.
To provide experiences that increase self–confidence, self–esteem, group cooperation, and develop outdoor leisure skills.[18]

Many of the ideas for outdoor adventure or stress–challenge programs came from the activities and the educational philosophy of Outward Bound and its founder Kurt Hahn.

"Outdoor adventure programs have the potential to provide education experiences, positive personal experiences, and creative use of leisure time," said Storms. "Teenagers, an age group difficult to program for, especially may benefit from adventure programming."[19]

CHALLENGING AND EXCITING PLAY AREAS

New kinds of play equipment are challenging the imagination and creativity of children and inspiring their interest and curiosity. Designers are developing innovations in play equipment that provide great appeal to children. There has been growing criticism of traditional play equipment and designs at many playgrounds. Critics have declared that most of the older playgrounds fail to appeal to children, contending that the equipment and designs are fixed, static, and provide little opportunity for creative and imaginative exploration.

Theme Playgrounds

The entire playground is developed around a theme of interest to children. An example of such a facility includes a 65–foot–long Chinese junk, a Chinese wall maze, and play areas built to provide a stimulating environment reflecting Chinese culture. Other such facilities include a prehistoric park; a Mississippi River park complete with riverboat; a southwestern playground featuring a Spanish style fort; and a space age playground complete with space ships, rockets, and satellites.

"Heritage Village," a settlement comparable to the 1820–1860 era, has been created within the city limits of Kansas City, Missouri. The thirty–seven–unit village includes log cabins, barns, stables, and stores.

Steep Grades and Slopes

New approaches have been developed by designers in the use of levels in playgrounds. Increasingly, play areas have steep grades and contrasts in levels, which provide opportunities for children to coast down the hill,

hide, use rope swings or pulley rides, and climb along monkey bridges. Children can also pretend they are defending or attacking a fort.

Greater Use of Water

Increasingly, the key factor in outdoor recreation facilities and activities will be water. Participation in all kinds of activities involving water—boating, canoeing, sailing, surfing, swimming, water skiing, and underwater exploration—will continue to soar. More parks and play areas will be featured by scenic water falls, jetting fountains, and reflecting pools and streams.

PLAY FOR FUN AND PARTICIPATION

The trend toward greater participation in leisure sports and activities continues to rise in the United States. Advocates of the "par-

Figure 22–4 Automated surfing pool. This remarkable wave pool facility built in Decatur, Alabama, involves the wave generation process similar to ocean surfing. The wave equipment can create three–foot–high waves and whitecaps. (Courtesy Charles M. Graves Organization.)

ticipation for all" philosophy believe that emphasis during early childhood should be on fun and participation. Every boy or girl should feel good just for having taken part. They should be offered many new experiences in games and sports and the opportunity to specialize as they show an interest.

Children should be taught how to run, jump, skip, and throw, to learn muscle coordination and body control. In the past, children have been forced to play games in school before they even had mastered a basic skill, like catching a ball, needed to play the game.

Increasingly, recreation professionals, educators, coaches, parents, and concerned citizens are questioning the overemphasis on competition in organized programs. Many believe tax–supported leisure services fail to meet basic needs of the majority of participants.

What's wrong with the games people currently play? "Too many spectators and not enough participants," claims George Leonard, author of *The Ultimate Athlete*. "Why shouldn't we forget about winning and play games for the fun of it, games in which winning doesn't matter?"[20]

> **There is really no reason, but it is great FUN!**

PROFESSIONAL ACTIVISM

In recent years, the attitudes of park and recreation professionals appear to be changing. They are developing a willingness and enthusiasm to enter the fray and to argue persuasively for the programs they believe in. Professionals in the leisure services industry, in particular, have not always been effective in developing or presenting the case for improving the quality of life in our communities.

According to Larry Naake, "We have not always been forceful in articulating the relationship between the quality–of–life and the satisfaction of certain basic needs, especially security and health. We have sometimes been passive, rather than 'political,' in advocating our needs and their worth before the city councils, boards of supervisors, and the state legislature."[21]

Very few of the state affiliates of National Recreation and Park Association (NRPA) are seriously involved in state level advocacy efforts and political involvement. For instance, the Heritage Conservation and Recreation Service revealed that in 1979, 2,079 bills dealing directly and indirectly with recreation, natural or cultural resources were introduced in the state legislatures. Of these, 510, or 24 percent, were enacted into law. Another major area of concern is that the state affiliates are only rarely involved in advocacy activities to protect threatened or degraded recreation and park resources within the states.[22]

Sparked by a strong proposal by the Illinois State Association at the 1980 congress in Phoenix, a nationwide legislative advocacy movement is growing rapidly. John H. Davis, Executive Director of NRPA, stated that "We are seeking a longterm commitment by our affiliates to strong state level advocacy efforts."[23]

More than ever, the recreation and park movement needs leaders who can motivate people to do things, and goal setters who create a sense of going somewhere. Jack Foley and Frank Benest wrote that "At the professional as well as local levels, the field needs leaders who can influence public policy and generate common cause with human services providers, community volunteers, and citizen advocates. We must spawn a new activism."[24]

"We need leaders who can reform and revise recreation activities, to promote human development, physical and mental health, social action, and racial harmony," continued Foley and Benest. "Activities must become more in tune with people's basic needs. We need leaders who understand the concept of service delivery which involves maximizing citizen involvement."[25]

Foley and Benest concluded by stating that "Professionally, for too long we have meekly moved to the back of the bus, accepting our meager share of resources and our lack of status. Unless we soon adopt an assertive leadership posture, we may not even find ourselves on the bus."[26]

REACHING TOWARD PROFESSIONAL STATUS

The park and recreation field continues to reach for professionalism. In doing so, it is vital that recreators reexamine the most essential elements of their field. "Quality leadership that enhances human potential and spirit seems basic," a *Parks and Recreation* editorial stated. "We need a system that, to the greatest extent possible, assures quality park and recreation leadership responsibility attuned to change on a continuing basis. We need vehicles that provide initial and ongoing high quality education and professional development, and that restrict practice to those so qualified."[27]

The ingredients for attaining this goal include:

- viable accreditation and registration programs
- linkage of accreditation and registration
- inclusion of registration in job specifications that require park and recreation expertise[28]

RACQUETBALL CRAZE

The most popular facility construction in recent years is the indoor tennis and racquetball club—providing a variety of leisure activities for people of varied ages and levels of ability.

Racquetball has been called the fastest growing sport in the country. It is a young sport, tracing its beginnings to paddleball, a game popular in some circles in the 1920s and 1930s, played much like handball, only with short wooden paddles. Sometime during the late 1940s or early 1950s, the wood paddle was replaced with a strung racquet.

Figure 22–5 Legislative Action for park development. State Senator David Roberti (D–Hollywood) presents SB174 to colleagues on the Senate floor. SB174 called for the appropriation of $35 million each year for grants to cities, counties, and park and recreation districts for the acquisition and development of park and recreation areas. (Courtesy California Park and Recreation Society.)

According to Richard B. Flynn: "The indoor racquet clubs are attracting a new breed of sports–minded Americans possessing an intense appetite for activity. Attempts to satisfy that appetite have resulted in a profitable business for many while at the same time, forced municipal recreational programs to reexamine their facilities and program offerings."[29]

RESORT TIME–SHARING

As the cost of resort properties soars, the concept of time–sharing is catching on. Time–sharing involves purchase of a given block of time in resort accommodations. The owner shares the same unit with others who buy different blocks of time. The idea began in Europe and now is gaining a foothold in the United States as inflation pushes vacation property out of the reach of more and more families. The number of time–share owners has risen from seventeen thousand in 1975 to an estimated half–million in 1980.

Time–sharing's main attraction is that it offers people the chance to buy exclusive rights to vacation property—from apartments, luxury beach cottages, and mountain chalets to campgrounds—for a set period of time each year, usually one of four weeks. This frees owners from the expense and responsibility of managing a property year–round.

One of the most popular aspects of time–sharing is the opportunity for owners to trade with time–share owners elsewhere, thus enabling them to vacation in other places.

THE SINGLES PHENOMENON

An emerging lifestyle centered around the activities of millions of unmarried men and women has added a new dimension to American cities and towns. The "singles phenomenon" is affecting housing, social contacts, and recreation on a scale the United States has never seen before. The number of Americans living alone or with unmarried roommates has risen more than 40 percent over the last six years.

One of the most popular centers for singles on the west coast is Marina del Rey in Los Angeles, where ninety–five hundred apartment dwellers live on four hundred acres of the Pacific waterfront. Among the recreation amenities are 341 private boat slips, swimming pools, courts for tennis, paddle tennis and handball, and indoor golf.

THE BOOM IN YOUTH SOCCER

The "old world sport" of soccer is enjoying a popularity explosion among American

Figure 22–6 More youth are playing soccer as the popular international sport continues to grow in North America. Here, two girls teams in Orangevale, California, compete in league play.

youngsters and their parents because it is inexpensive, fun, and anyone can play. United States Soccer Federation officials report that there are more than one million players registered in youth soccer programs.

Aware that popularity can bring on the problems of overzealous coaches, fanatical parents and a win–at–any–cost attitude, soccer leaders are attempting to develop safeguards to keep the organized leagues focused on recreation with the stress on playing the game, not on winning.

SOFTBALL FEVER

Softball has swept the country, with an estimated twenty–two million players nationwide. The necessary ingredients for success are few: the basic equipment and refreshments, the camaraderie of the players, and the competitive urge.

"A major factor in the growth of interest," wrote Pat Sullivan, "could well be the discovery by many people that they didn't have to be world–class or even high school varsity level athletes to enjoy one type of softball—slow pitch. "The game of slow–pitch bears little resemblance to the windmilling, fast pitch version, which often boils down to a game of catch between pitcher and catcher."[30]

During the 1979 season in San Francisco there were 390 men's and women's softball teams—and 20 on the waiting list—vying for Recreation and Park Department facilities.

"There is nothing like hitting a home run," said Joan Tamplin, a graduate student at Stanford. One player, a transplanted New Yorker who says he plays the game fifty out of fifty–two weeks a year, said, 'Softball is in my blood. If a week goes by, if we're rained out, I start feeling very frustrated.' "[31]

A restaurant–bar in Santa Barbara has come up with a very successful promotional idea—nightly instant replay films of the men's softball league action. Films are taken of each game and later in the evening are shown on a large screen at the restaurant, usually before a packed house. Business has never been better!

SOLAR ENERGY

Considering the short time solar technology has been available, park involvement with solar power is considerable. The pressing need for park agencies to conserve energy and finances is leading more departments to consider the installation of solar energy in their facilities. Consequently, solar energy installation is increasingly a part of every park's building and improvement plans.

There are few settings as well suited to the use of solar energy as park and recreation facilities. Solar pool heating, for example, is an ideal application of solar energy, one which will receive major application as the cost of conventional energy increases.

While solar energy interpretation is exciting, Kristina Goodrich noted that other considerations enter into a decision to install it. According to Goodrich, "The key factor and

Figure 22–7 The Shenandoah Solar Recreation Center near Atlanta, Georgia, is one of the largest buildings in the world to be heated and cooled by the sun. Powered by a $726,000 solar system, the Recreation Center is now in operation with an ice skating rink, gymnasium, game room, meeting rooms, and office space. (Courtesy Shenandoah Development, Inc.)

bottom line to solar design incorporation is economics."[32]

Richmond Hill, Ontario, Canada, has the first public pool in Canada heated by solar energy. As a result of its own initiative and help from Ontario's Ministry of Energy, the town pool saves $800 in gas per year. Oregon state parks have also used solar power, retro-fitting/modifying a shower station to use solar energy, and constructing another to use solar power. The retrofitted shower in Washburne State Park saves 300 gallons of propane per season.

"How extensively solar power is used in America's parks is beyond reckoning," said Goodrich. "But growth of solar use in parks is assured by the character of the energy source, expected increases in energy needs and costs, and the evidence of interest found at every level of park management."[33]

THEME PARKS

Commercial theme parks represent one of the fastest growing segments in the lei-sure–time industry. Attendance at theme parks has grown almost 400 percent during the last decade, with the most spectacular growth recorded by forty major theme parks. The combined revenues of Disneyland and Disney World in 1975 set a new record of $68 million in revenue.

"Theme parks are in the business of enter-taining people," said John Certer, "all serv-ices which are provided by the theme park cooperatively contribute to the portrayal of that theme."[34]

The Disney parks now account for almost one–third of the theme park business, fol-lowed by Six Flags in second place, and Busch Gardens in third.

VOLUNTEERISM GROWS

The spirit of helping others is thriving na-tionwide. More than thirty–seven million people in this country now are engaged in volunteer work. The new ranks of volunteers are, by and large, more diverse in back-ground than in the past. Volunteers now in-clude teenagers, college students, retirees, and even corporate and union executives.

Why do they do it? Kenn Allen, executive director of the National Center for Voluntary Action, said: "There's a large pool of people out there who truly want to help someone else."

After Proposition 13 brought big cuts in the library budget of San Marino, California, 47 people volunteered to run the public library and now keep it open twenty hours a week.

Greensboro, N.C. conducts an excellent volunteer program. The Jaycee Sports Com-plex received the help of 4,000 volunteers for labor, valued at $750,000 to complete the project. Annually, 4,700 volunteers give 400,000 hours of free time to the athletic program.

THE EXPANDING ROLE OF THE YMCAs

Like never before, YMCA programs and services are reaching out beyond the scope of Y facilities and into schools, churches and community centers, where they meet the needs of many groups, including school–age children, older citizens and business and industry.

Whether it be an aerobic exercise class for kids, a stress management seminar at a local business or aquatic exercise for a senior cit-izens group, more likely than ever that YMCA program will be conducted at a neighborhood school, church, community center, or business.

"The Y has become a community resource center," said Dr. William Zuti, the YMCAs National Health Enhancement Director. "We knew we had the potential—the technical knowledge, the established programs, the personnel—that was needed to reach out and affect more people. The Y was chartered to serve the needs of the community to deal with family needs. Our major thrust is to serve this overwhelming demand for total health enhancement—from nutrition to fitness to smoking cessation to stress management—for as many people as possible."[35]

"Feelin' Good," combining exercise with educational activities, is a YMCA program aimed at children in kindergarten through ninth grade. Designed to be interesting and fun, the program deals more with the lifetime sport concept, placing greater emphasis on activities such as tennis and racquetball than football. "How many adults do you see staying fit through organized football?" said Zuti.[36]

Nationally, YMCAs are increasing their efforts to provide meaningful programs for older adults. Aquatic exercise classes for people with arthritis, for example, are definitely needed.

LIST OF TRENDS IN LEISURE AND RECREATION

The leisure and recreation movement has been characterized by a wide range of trends that have had a significant effect on its growth.

Areas and Facilities

- Using space over public and private urban development for leisure opportunities, e.g., decking over freeways, railroad yards, and parking lots for recreational use.
- Developing underground malls, plazas, and pathways that have multi–use recreational potentials.
- Making intensive use of rooftops for public and private recreational opportunities.
- Converting abandoned or obsolete buildings to public or private recreational uses, e.g., theaters, or supermarkets.
- The facilities of colleges increasingly will be integrated with park and recreation facilities to serve the entire community.
- Day care centers providing supervised play for children will continue to increase in number and importance.
- More and more recreation facilities and programs are being provided at apart-

ment complexes, condominiums, and mobile home parks.
- There will be a big increase in facilities for walking, jogging, and bicycling.
- Building or redeveloping high–rise structures for recreational use, e.g., tennis clubs, hostels, or play areas.
- Designers are beginning to include play areas in their plans for shopping centers, realizing that shoppers will linger if their children have somewhere to play.
- Public modes of transportation will increase as an alternative to the automobile, and will focus leisure activities and the development of leisure facilities closer to home and work.
- There will be a sharp increase in new multifaceted recreation facilities within the confines of local and public transportation networks, or within the confines of the work place.
- More effective safety and design standards are being established for playground equipment.
- Federal funding programs for recreation services will focus on inner city programs and facilities, rather than the rural and outlying area policies of the past.

Cultural Arts

- Cultural attractions such as symphony orchestras, ballet companies, opera, and theater are being supported by more cities.
- Making the arts available to more Americans will continue to be the goal of the leisure services field.
- Local colleges will play a major role in providing arts, cultural, and human development programs for adults.

Education

- Schools are placing greater emphasis on education for leisure.
- Leisure studies, involving the study of leisure in contemporary society, increasingly, will complement professional prep-

aration for recreation and parks at the undergraduate level.

- There is growing use of school facilities for recreation purposes.
- There is more emphasis on research needs in the park and recreation field.
- Computers are being used to help determine an individual's proficiency and suitability for a particular field of study.
- School districts have been forced through recent federal legislation to program activities equally for boys and girls.
- Community education is gaining acceptance.
- Community colleges will assume a dominant role in providing arts, cultural and human development programs for adults.

Energy

- The cost of energy will continue to soar, taking a substantial proportion of everybody's spending money.
- Gas shortages will force people to rediscover urban parks.
- Fuel economy will be the key to the vehicles of tomorrow.
- Cars will be smaller, sleeker and more fuel efficient—many of them powered by diesel fuel or electricity.
- Innovative forms of mass transport will eventually be established to substitute for the private automobile.
- The energy squeeze is curtailing travel plans and causing more people to stay closer to home.
- The energy problem is a long-te. n one that will mean a continuation of conservation attitudes and actions.

Environment

- There will be increased emphasis on "saving our environment," restoring and preventing further destruction.
- People will make gradual progress in restoring and maintaining a wholesome environment on earth.
- An environmental awareness and understanding among people is developing.

Fitness and Health

- The desire to keep fit is a recreation and health trend which continues to grow.
- The physical fitness revolution has taken over the nation.
- Millions of people are jogging, walking, and cycling, playing tennis and golf, joining health clubs.
- Large numbers are finding a special athletic niche—racquetball, swimming, soccer, basketball, softball, dancercise, karate, calisthenics, and weightlifting.
- Regular physical activity is contributing to longer life spans.
- Advanced medical and surgical care has contributed to a longer life.
- A normal and healthy life to the age of 90 or 95 is within the foreseeable future.

Housing

- Emphasis on multihousing (condos and apartments) will emerge steadily in the next few years, even a return to boarding homes, the construction of duplexes and mother-in-law suites.
- More houses will be factory built and engineered for saving energy, with computers to monitor heating and cooling.
- Joint living arrangements will become increasingly popular with older people, not just the traditional situation of an aging parent moving back in with children.

Leisure

- Leisure is expanding rapidly and occupying a greater portion of our lives.
- Continued technological and automated advancement is resulting in increased leisure time.
- More people are viewing leisure as an opportunity for a fuller life.
- People of all ages are demonstrating a greater variety of interests.
- People are becoming more selective in their choice of leisure-time experiences.
- Participants are deriving greater significance from leisure-time activities.

- The energy squeeze is curtailing travel plans and causing more people to stay closer to home.
- Computers are programming the leisure needs of people.
- There is greater affluence, more discretionary income, and more available time among the American people.
- Off–the–job lives tend to be overscheduled.
- There are continuing changes in lifestyles and social values, many oriented to leisure.

Leisure in the Home

- People will no longer just sleep in their homes—they will live in them, as indicated by the rapid rise in cable television, big–screen television, home movies, video cassette recorders, video disc players, video games, hot tubs, and spas.
- Exciting developments in the home will feature elaborate entertainment centers, computers, recreation equipment, and new types of furniture and appliances.
- The Mini–Sport Court provides the convenience of a year–round sports complex in the privacy of the backyard. Built by Sport Court of America, Inc., it has a smooth, concrete court for games such as paddle tennis, basketball, volleyball, badminton, shuffleboard and more.

Outdoor Recreation

- Organized camping, particularly day camping, has expanded.
- A great surge of popularity is occurring in camping, backpacking, hiking, and mountain climbing.
- The energy shortage is forcing more people to have their outdoor recreation experiences closer to home.
- Sharp increases have occurred in the number of bicycle paths, jogging and walking trails, river runs, and camping facilities.
- People will seek camp sites closer to home.
- Growing environmental concern is reflected in new outdoor programs that combine recreation and education.

- More people are opting for adventures— from mountain climbing to deep sea diving.
- Recreation vehicles will be significantly affected by the energy squeeze and some changes are in store for the industry.
- Off–road vehicles will face tighter restrictions by state and federal agencies.

Parks

- There will be new, more innovative designs in parks and playground facilities and equipment, such as:

  A floating marina, providing a safe harbor in the face of extreme weather.

  New, exciting amusement rides, such as the flume log ride which uses a constantly recirculating water system to carry riders down a sensational 2,100–foot waterway flume in a hollowed–out log.

  Cloverleaf softball complexes, four diamonds in a cloverleaf shape with a huge ultra–modern clubhouse in the center.

  Inland surfing facilities, the new inventions that involve the wave generation process similar to ocean surfing.
- More parks and play areas will be made available closer to people's homes.
- Space will be used to a better advantage, transforming roof tops and parking lots into neighborhood playgrounds.
- Existing parks that no longer meet the needs of users should be recycled to include such facilities as adventure playgrounds, community gardens, and energy–conserving landscapes.
- Mobile units and mini–park/areas, in greater numbers, are serving congested or remote areas.
- Greater creativity and originality is needed in children's play equipment and the design of outdoor areas.
- Adventure playgrounds which enable children to create their own play environment and do "their own thing" will grow in concept and popularity.

Park and Recreation Departments

- More park and recreation programs are being established on a county or regional basis, cutting across political boundaries.
- Future leisure services will become more decentralized, as efforts will be concentrated in areas controlled by the users—their homes and neighborhoods.
- The role of women in the job market and in leisure activities will continue to increase.
- The leisure services delivery system will become more complex, emphasizing service and assistance, not management and maintenance.
- Public recreation departments are now faced with the choice of organizing either separate teams for boys and girls or sex-integrated activities.
- There is a continuing trend in combining parks and recreation departments.
- There is a need for more effective urban planning.
- The professional status of those in the field is gaining wider recognition.

Private and Commercial Recreation

- There has been a spectacular rise in expenditures for commercial recreation.
- Private recreation centers, such as racquetball clubs, health spas, and sports clubs, have increased sharply.
- New theme parks, amusement complexes, and experimental villages have enjoyed great success.
- Amusement complexes, theme parks, and experimental villages will grow in popularity.
- The development of theme amusement parks will continue to exploit the yearnings for nostalgia.
- Restaurants will continue to lure more customers because of the growing number of working women and the additional income generated by two-income families.
- More people will invest in "time-sharing" of condominiums, a concept that gives families the use of a resort home for a cou- ple of weeks each year for a one-time payment.
- Gambling is likely to be a major growth area in the leisure industry.
- There will be a focus on multiple attractions management.
- Resorts and hotels are catering more to the elderly.
- Tax and development incentives for commercial recreation facilities will accelerate as communities turn closer to home.
- Private corporations will provide special park and recreational opportunities for their employees in or near cities.
- Private contractors will plan, design, manage, and maintain many services now provided by the public sector.
- Private concessionaires will provide more community and regional theme or amusement parks on public land.
- Amusement parks increasingly will be combined with shopping centers.

Professional Preparation

- Recreation as a field and as an area of study is moving toward professional status on a level with medicine, law, and education.
- Standards of the recreation profession will rise substantially, and services will be vastly improved.
- A general upgrading in the effectiveness of leadership will occur.
- New occupations will evolve in the field of leisure services.
- Recreation majors will be prepared to better understand and serve disadvantaged groups.
- Instilling in students an awareness, sensitivity, and a commitment to social issues will be a major aim of recreation education.
- Minority and low income students in greater numbers will be recruited and prepared for recreation service.

Programs

- Professionals are beginning to redefine recreation in terms of human develop-

Figure 22-8 Private recreation clubs and centers, for such sports as tennis, racquetball, and swimming, have increased sharply. These indoor tennis courts are located at the Northbrook Tennis Club in suburban Chicago. (Courtesy Appleton Electric Company, Chicago.)

ment. Rather than activities, facilities, or programs, more important is what happens to people.

- Roller skating continues to be very popular with all age groups.
- Cross–country skiing is rapidly overtaking the popularity of downhill skiing.
- Increased citizen involvement in the planning and execution of recreation programs is being encouraged by local agencies.
- The shift from the traditional rest–and–relaxation recreation to active–participation sports will continue.
- Shopping centers, in cooperation with community groups, are offering festivals, musical events, hobby shows, and benefits.
- Racquetball and soccer are enjoying increasing growth and development.
- Physical fitness, exercise, and sports continue to increase in popularity.
- Activities, encouraging physical and mental challenge or self–confidence, commonly called "risk" recreation, are increasing.
- More people are participating in more ac-

tivities which have the elements of danger, daring, and adventure.

- Increasing emphasis is being placed on the needs of minority and ethnic groups.
- Increased pride in ethnic background has resulted in ethnic festivals and cultural celebrations.
- A number of youth–serving agencies have made concerted efforts to keep abreast of the times.
- New and challenging leisure experiences are being provided people of all age groups.
- An increasing number of private firms are being hired by local and county governmental agencies, commercial, and resort companies to provide recreation services.
- There are greater opportunities for family recreation.
- There has been a sharp increase in more expensive activities.
- Aquatic or water–related activities are expanding rapidly.
- The number of activities requiring a fee or charge is increasing.
- Greater participation by women and girls in sports is occurring.

- There is growing equality between the sexes.
- Due to the energy crisis, municipal departments are offering more comprehensive weekend programs and activities.
- Popularity of lifetime sports such as tennis, golf, and bowling is greater than ever.
- YMCA programs and services continue to reach out beyond the scope of Y facilities and into schools, churches and community centers.
- The computer is being used increasingly as an aid both in financial management and in program activity analysis.
- Leisure co–operatives, involving individuals, organizations, or social groups are providing specialized leisure opportunities or equipment for their members.
- People are enjoying dancing to all forms of music, whether it be pop, rock, rhythm and blues, or country.

Special Populations

- Recreation programs and services to the disadvantaged, disabled, and aging are being expanded.
- Recreation services to the disabled are becoming more widespread, both in therapeutic institutions and in the community.
- Leisure counseling is becoming an important tool in helping the ill and disabled to choose among desirable recreation alternatives.
- The direction in programming is toward integration, rather than separation of those who differ from the "norm."
- Increased emphasis is on the use of recreation to re–engage handicapped individuals in the mainstream of community activity to the extent of their capabilities.
- Certification of therapeutic recreation personnel by state certification units is increasing.
- Stronger efforts are being made to remove architectural barriers that prevent participation in recreation choices.
- More effective recreation activities are gradually being established in many of our nation's jails and prisons.

State and National Parks

- There will be greater emphasis on ways to separate visitors from their cars once they reach parks.
- Alternative transportation will include tramways, monorails, and railways.
- Expanded recreation services on public lands will be made through efforts of federal and state governments.
- Wiser use of flood plains has contributed to the decrease of environmental disasters.
- State park systems, even national recreation areas, are expected to play a greater role in the larger metropolitan centers and participate more in joint ventures with other agencies in "threshold urban parks."

Travel

- Vacationers will travel to leisure spots by rail or air, as so many Europeans now do.
- The stream of tourists heading toward the United States is growing steadily larger.
- Rising fuel prices will curtail leisure travel patterns and redirect leisure participation closer to home and work.

Vandalism and Crime

- While crime generally will continue rising, crime associated with youth—vandalism, general mischief—probably will decline, due partly to the declining number of potential miscreants.
- Neighborhood "watch teams" are increasing in every region of the country. Faced with reduced police protection in many areas, more and more residents are prowling for troublemakers. Growth of the home–alarm industry typifies Americans' craving for safety.

Work

- The four–day workweek is spreading.
- There is a trend toward the shortened workday and workweek, with longer vacations and sabbaticals.

- There are increases in fringe benefits such as improved working conditions, pensions, and longer vacations.
- People's attitudes toward their work are changing, as the work ethic continues to decrease.

CHALLENGES OF THE FUTURE

The decade of the 1980s holds many challenges for those in the recreation and leisure services industry. Perhaps, the most important challenge of all is the job of educating people to accept and use leisure. Changing people's attitudes toward a higher value for leisure should be a never ending concern of all professional recreators and educators.

People in the future will need to be better informed about the values that can result from the proper use of leisure time. Practitioners in the field, on all levels, will need to be encouraged to develop more rewarding leisure pursuits for a higher quality of life.

The need for quality recreation services, parks and resources will increase as the effects of stress reach most segments of the American people. Practitioners and educators alike must demonstrate more convincingly that formal preparation in parks and recreation does make a difference in the quality of services delivered. "If that cannot be verified," said H. Douglas Sessoms, "then we will continue to see nonrecreators employed as "professionals."[37]

An Editorial in *Parks & Recreation Magazine* emphasized that "this decade of challenge must include the seeking of personal, professional, and organizational excellence. And it must be a response of commitment."[38]

One of the biggest challenges for recreation and park agencies is to recognize that the traditional sources of financial support can no longer be relied upon. With the era of the tax revolt spreading nationwide, governmental agencies, particularly those on the local level, must seek alternate means of financing and operating their programs. A

Figure 22–9 The challenge to re–vitalize inner cities and meet the urban recreation needs of America. Golden Gate Park, the green belt shown at right, and beautiful San Francisco were in clear view as this photograph was taken from over the Pacific Ocean. This magnificent park provides just about every form of relaxation and recreation a city–dweller, young or old, could ask for. Yet, many trees in the park are well past their time, and the park department, in cooperation with the U.S. Forest Service, has implemented tree planting programs to re–forest areas in need. (Courtesy *San Francisco Chronicle*.)

> **The goal of all professionals: Good, creative, and wholesome recreation, parks, and leisure services.**

wave of conservatism continues to sweep the country, the effects being felt both on the national and local levels. Cutbacks in services have become evident in education and municipal services, including parks and recreation, museums, libraries, performing arts, and many other programs and services. At the federal level, the Heritage Conservation and Recreation Service was abolished, and funding for the Land and Water Conservation Fund was sharply cut back.

Revitalizing the inner cities of America is a challenge a growing number of urban communities have already accepted. Making cities attractive places to live and work will help attract private investment and provide a strong incentive for citywide and neighborhood economic redevelopment. Tree planting programs need to be implemented for the purpose of reforesting areas that have trees past their time.

Another challenge for the recreation and leisure services industry is to improve the programming. Present programs much too often consist of activities designed to consume time, to fill idle hours. Instead, creative, positive leisure activities and experiences are needed to challenge people to change, to learn and to grow. "Enlightened, bold leaders are needed to plan and guide people's development, rather than organize activities based entirely on popular demand," wrote Dan Corbin and William Tait.[39]

Recreation leaders must begin to think of recreation experiences in terms of human development. The primary concern of recreation is not programs, facilities, or activities—it is what happens to people that counts. The challenge for leaders to be aware of human growth and development has never been greater. As Sy Gold wrote: "This awareness is causing us to re-examine the purpose of life and to ask what fulfillment really means."[40]

Meeting the leisure needs of special groups is another important challenge for those in the leisure services profession. We must respond to the challenge to make people recognize their leisure needs before they reach retirement.

The decade ahead will offer a variety of challenges to those in the leisure services field, but as H. Douglas Sessoms pointed out: "The degree to which we meet those opportunities will depend largely upon the actions we take now in conceptualizing who we are, what we can and should do, and how we go about meeting our task."[41]

QUESTIONS FOR DISCUSSION

1. Discuss some of the new and exciting trends in recreation and leisure.
2. Physical fitness, with emphasis on exercise and stimulating activity, continues to grow in popularity. What programs or services in your community are contributing to the "fitness boom"?
3. Why are people today seeking the help of leisure counselors in deciding among leisure–time alternatives?
4. What are some of the new trends in playground design and equipment?
5. Identify some of the challenging and exciting play equipment or areas in your community.
6. What is the basic concept of cluster housing? Is it a practical approach to housing development?
7. More recreation and park professionals are becoming more politically astute and willing to argue more persuasively for important legislation and vital issues, and

a greater share of the budget. Why is it essential for recreation professionals to be more active in the political arena?

8. Racquetball continues to enjoy great popularity. Do you believe its growth will continue or are there other leisure pastimes moving into the spotlight?
9. As solar energy continues to grow in use, what recreation and park facilities appear to be appropriate for conversion to solar energy?
10. Review and discuss some of the many trends and developments occuring in the private and commercial sector.
11. With the energy squeeze and the higher cost of fuel, more people will take advantage of the exciting new developments for leisure fun and entertainment in the home. Identify some of these.
12. New innovative and creative programs are being offered in all sectors of the leisure services industry. Can you identify some of the most popular?
13. Services for special groups continue to grow nationwide. Discuss some of the trends listed in this chapter.
14. Improving program quality and making leisure activities and experiences more meaningful and rewarding is one of the biggest challenges for the profession. Suggest the quality and level of excellence needed to challenge people to learn and grow, and to develop a more leisurely lifestyle.

REFERENCES

1. "A Look Ahead from the Nation's Capital", *U.S. News & World Report*, July 13, 1981.
2. Editorial, *Parks and Recreation Magazine*, May 1976, p. 19.
3. William Penn Mott, "Meeting the Future's Challenge in Parks," *Parks and Recreation Magazine*, May 1979, p. 36.
4. Editorial, *Parks & Recreation Magazine*, May 1976, p. 19.
5. Robert Theobald, in *Technology, Human Values and Leisure*, Max Kaplan and Phillip Busserman, eds. (Nashville, Tennessee: Abingdon Press, 1971), p. 29.
6. Kim Sprague, "How to Avoid the Programming Rut," *Parks and Recreation Magazine*, June 1980, p. 25.
7. Livingston L. Biddle, Jr., "Arts and Parks Combine to Revitalize Community Spirit", *Parks and Recreation Magazine*, July 1979, p. 21.
8. John J. Goldman, "Adults Attracted to Summer Camp," *Sacramento Bee*, March 27, 1977, p. A14.
9. Bob Sylva, "Are You Programmed to Cope with the Computer Game Craze?" *Sacramento Bee*, November 18, 1979, p. 1.
10. "The Culture Boom," *U.S. News & World Report*, August 8, 1977, p. 50.
11. Charles K. Brightbill and Tony Mobley, *Educating for Leisure-Centered Living*, 2nd ed. (New York: John Wiley and Sons, 1977), pp. 11–12.
12. Richard G. Kraus and Joseph E. Curtis, *Creative Administration in Recreation and Parks* (St. Louis: The C. V. Mosby Company, 1973), p. 80.
13. Geoffrey Godbey, *Recreation, Park and Leisure Services: Foundations, Organization, Administration* (Philadelphia: W. B. Saunders Company, 1978), p. 340.
14. Ibid., pp. 341–42.
15. Clayne R. Jensen, *Leisure and Recreation: Introduction and Overview* (Philadelphia: Lea & Febiger, 1977), p. 275.
16. "Playground of the Future", *U.S. News & World Report*, May 23, 1977, p. 73.
17. Ibid.
18. Jim Storms, "Guidelines on Adventure Programming," *Parks and Recreation Magazine*, April 1979, p. 24.
19. Ibid.

20. Edward R. Walsh, "New Games—In Pursuit of Creative Play," *Parks and Recreation Magazine*, May 1979, p. 49.
21. Larry E. Naake, "Promoting Leisure Services During Hard Times," *California Parks & Recreation*, August/September 1977, p. 6.
22. "An Agenda for the 1980s," *Parks and Recreation Magazine*, August 1980, p. 21.
23. Ibid.
24. Jack Foley and Frank Benest, "Proposition 13: The Aftermath," *Management Strategy*, Vol. 3, No. 2, 1979, page 4.
25. Ibid.
26. Ibid.
27. "A Legacy for the Future." *Parks and Recreation Magazine*, June 1981, p. 20.
28. Ibid.
29. Richard B. Flynn, "Indoor Racquet Clubs," *Journal of Physical Education and Recreation*, November–December, 1977, p. 45.
30. Pat Sullivan, "Softball Fever Hits the City," *San Francisco Chronicle*, May 11, 1979, p. 67.
31. Ibid.
32. Kristina Goodrich, "Trends '79 . . . A Bright Future in Parks," *Parks and Recreation Magazine*, May 1979, pp. 27–29.
33. Ibid., p. 70.
34. "Commercial Theme Parks," *EMPLOY.* A Service of the National Recreation and Park Association, Volume V. No. 3, November 1978, pp. 2–3.
35. "The Expanding Role of the YMCA's," *Athletic Purchasing and Facilities*, July 1981, p. 36.
36. Ibid.
37. Linda Thorsby Bynum, "The Future of Recreation and Parks," *Parks and Recreation Magazine*, August 1979, p. 25.
38. "The Challenging Decade," *Parks and Recreation Magazine*, January 1980, p. 41.
39. H. Dan Corbin and William J. Tait, *Education for Leisure* (Englewood Cliffs, N.J.: Prentice–Hall, Inc., 1973), pp. 153–54.
40. Seymour M. Gold, "Municipal Parks and Recreation—Rethinking the Future," *Recreation Canada*, No. 35/4/1977, p. 15.
41. H. Douglas Sessoms, "Programs and Professional Preparation in the 1980's", Presented at the SPRE Educational Institute, Congress of Parks and Recreation, New Orleans, October, 1979.

Index